BROTHER-SOULS

John Clellon Holmes,
Jack Kerouac,
and the Beat Generation

ANN CHARTERS AND SAMUEL CHARTERS

UNIVERSITY PRESS OF MISSISSIPPI / JACKSON

www.upress.state.ms.us

Designed by Peter D. Halverson

Photo on page ii of John Clellon Holmes and Jack Kerouac by
Shirley Holmes (1967).

The University Press of Mississippi is a member of the
Association of American University Presses.

First printing 2010

∞

Library of Congress Cataloging-in-Publication Data

Charters, Ann.
  Brother-souls : John Clellon Holmes, Jack Kerouac, and the
Beat generation / Ann Charters and Samuel Charters.
       p. cm.
  Includes bibliographical references and index.
  ISBN 978-1-60473-579-6 (cloth : alk. paper) —
ISBN 978-1-60473-580-2 (eBook) 1. Holmes, John Clellon,
1926—1988—Friends and associates. 2. Kerouac, Jack,
1922—1969—Friends and associates. 3. Authors, American—
20th century—Biography. 4. Beat generation. I. Charters,
Samuel Barclay. II. Title.
  PS3558.O3594Z6 2010
  813'.54—dc22
  [B]   2010010192

British Library Cataloging-in-Publication Data available

To John and Shirley,
and to Liz and Carl,
who also loved them

ALSO BY ANN CHARTERS

Bibliography of Works by Jack Kerouac
Beats & Company: Portrait of a Literary
* Generation*

BIOGRAPHY
Nobody: The Life of Bert Williams
Kerouac: A Biography

CRITICISM
Olson/Melville: A Study in Affinity

EDITOR
The Special View of History by Charles Olson
Scattered Poems by Jack Kerouac
Scenes Along the Road: Photographs of the
* Desolation Angels*
The Beats: Literary Bohemians in Post-War
* America*
The Portable Beat Reader
The Portable Sixties Reader
Beat Down to Your Soul: What Was the Beat
* Generation?*
The Portable Jack Kerouac Reader
Selected Letters of Jack Kerouac
The Story and Its Writer
The American Story and Its Writer
Major Writers of Short Fiction

ALSO BY ANN CHARTERS AND SAMUEL CHARTERS
I Love: The Story of Vladimir Mayakovsky
* and Lili Brik*
Blues Faces: A Portrait of the Blues
Literature and Its Writers: An Introduction
* to Fiction, Poetry and Drama*

ALSO BY SAMUEL CHARTERS

MUSIC
Jazz: New Orleans 1885–1957
The Country Blues
Jazz: A History of the New York Scene
The Poetry of the Blues
The Bluesmen: The Story and the Music of the
* Men Who Made the Blues*
Robert Johnson
The Legacy of the Blues: Art and Lives of
* Twelve Great Bluesmen*
Sweet as the Showers of Rain

Spelmännen (The Swedish Fiddlers)
The Roots of the Blues: An African Search
The Blues Makers
The Day Is So Long and the Wages So Small:
* Music on a Summer Island*
Walking a Blues Road: A Blues Reader,
* 1956–2004*
New Orleans: Playing a Jazz Chorus

POETRY
The Children
The Landscape at Bolinas
Heroes of the Prize Ring
Days, or, Days as Thoughts in a Season's
* Uncertainties*
To This Place
From a London Notebook
From a Swedish Notebook
Of Those Who Died: A Poem of the Spring
* of 1945*

FICTION
Mr. Jabi and Mr. Smythe
Jelly Roll Morton's Last Night at the Jungle Inn
Louisiana Black
·Elvis Presley Calls His Mother After The Ed
* Sullivan Show*

CRITICISM
Some Poems/Poets: Studies in American
* Underground Poetry Since 1945*

BIOGRAPHY
Mambo Time: The Story of Bebo Valdés

MEMOIR
A Country Year: A Chronicle

TRANSLATIONS
Baltics (from the Swedish of Tomas
* Tranströmer)*
We Women (from the Swedish of Edith
* Södergran)*
The Courtyard (from the Swedish of Bo
* Carpelan)*

New England—oldest and most homely of American places—it's what's fleeting and elusive in you that demands words! The centuries-old redbrick towns and upland farms remain, but the scribbling boys are stabbed by a premonition of their own mortality. Time, as inevitable as December, drives them on, and all too often away.

I was one of those ruminative boys, Jack Kerouac was another.
—JOHN CLELLON HOLMES

CONTENTS

ACKNOWLEDGMENTS

First and foremost, we would like to thank Holmes' sister Elizabeth Von Vogt and her husband, Carl, whose wholehearted sympathy and patient responses to our queries have made the task of writing this book easier. Furthermore, without Liz's endorsement of our project, we would not have had unlimited access to the materials in the Shirley and John Clellon Holmes archive, which were indispensable. We are also grateful to Holmes' sister Lila Dizefalo for the comments and the photographs she sent to us that contributed to our understanding of the Holmes family's early years.

Second, we thank the resourceful staff of the Howard Gotlieb Archival Research Center at the Mugar Library, Boston University. During the three years we worked among the boxes of materials in the Holmes Archive, the staff—especially Ryan Hendrickson—provided invaluable research support. Isaac Gewirtz in the Berg Collection at the New York Public Library, who assembled the outstanding "Beatific Kerouac" exhibition at the library in 2007, was also of considerable help in locating Kerouac items. We are also grateful to the librarians at the Harry Ransom Center at the University of Texas at Austin who furnished tapes of Holmes' workshops in 1982 at the twenty-fifth anniversary celebration of *On the Road* in Boulder, Colorado.

Literary scholars with special interests in the Beats, including Rick Ardinger, Jaap Van Der Bent, Tim Hunt, Arthur Knight, and Ronna Johnson, as well as Allen Ginsberg biographers Bill Morgan and Michael Schumacher, contributed much useful information, including their photographs, correspondence, and interviews with Holmes. In England, Carolyn Cassady and Jay and Fran Landesman offered hospitality and helpful recollections of their close friendships with Kerouac and Holmes. All of these friends and colleagues who shared their various materials with us made our book possible, though none of them are responsible for our errors of fact or omissions.

Finally, we thank our family and friends in Stockholm, New York City, Storrs, and Boston, especially Linda Mar and Sy Danberg and our daughters, Nora Charters and Mallay Occhiogrosso, who listened patiently and at length to our soul-searching endeavors over the years to understand the relationship between Holmes and Kerouac and the emergence of the Beat Generation.

A PROLOGUE

Our new apartment was in one of those time-stained buildings on Manhattan's Lower East Side that had been newly renovated to bring young renters into an old New York neighborhood. It was on St. Mark's Place, close to First Avenue, and despite the noise and dirt, the prevalent discomfort over street crime, and the tensions with older Polish and Ukrainian neighbors, it was on the Lower East Side. In the 1960s what was left of New York City's spirit of restless cultural experimentation had left Greenwich Village and moved a few blocks east to streets that were even shabbier, but considerably cheaper. Ann and I had been living up near Columbia University on the Upper West Side, not far from the old Beat hang-out the West End Bar, and when she completed her Ph.D. in American Literature, we'd had enough of the crumbling five-flight walk-up railroad flat on 109th Street. An apartment with clean walls and a working kitchen and toilet! Even if the new walls were cardboard-thin and the bare concrete stairs were just as steep to climb and even noisier going up and down. The move downtown bought us into touch with everything we'd come to New York for. The poet W. H. Auden lived across the street, and some mornings we'd see him, rumpled and silent, going to the corner for a newspaper.

Around us, within a few blocks of our new address, were the new generation of New York artists and writers who had revived the spirit of the anarchic artistic and literary movements that had brought the old Greenwich Village bohemian spirit to life again. Living close by were young poets who had picked up the energies of the Beat writers, many of the painters who had broken through the old boundaries of what art was expected to show us, and new jazz and rock musicians from Theolonius Monk to the Velvet Underground, who were performing in cramped clubs on the Bowery around the corner, or in storefronts across Tompkins Square Park, two blocks away. The Gem Spa, gathering place for everyone out for cigarettes or the Sunday *New York Times*, was on the corner a block from us.

The photographer Robert Frank had an apartment over a store on Third Avenue near Tenth Street. Anne Waldman and Lewis Warsh lived up the street on St. Mark's Place, where they produced their *Angel Hair* chapbooks and poetry collections. The poet and translator Paul Blackburn and the quintessential Lower East Side poet Ted Berrigan were only a few blocks away. Ed Sanders had opened his Peace Eye Bookshop in a location that had once been a kosher Jewish butcher shop on East Tenth Street, where he was publishing his mimeographed magazine *Fuck You: A Magazine of the Arts.* The writer Diane di Prima was operating her Poets' Theater and running a print shop on the Lower East Side where somehow she managed to publish both the loosely informal *Floating Bear* poetry newsletter and the Poets Press books, producing twenty-nine books of Beat writing that included Herbert Huncke's *Journal* in 1965 and Timothy Leary's *Psychedelic Prayers* a year later.

The cheap rents in our new neighborhood were only part of the excitement. On Second Avenue at Tenth Street was the St. Mark's Church, where there seemed to be an unending stream of readings and events centered on the Beats and the Fluxus artists and their clamorous Happenings. The Fugs, our neighborhood rock band, gave concerts in a dark, cavernous building on St. Mark's Place at the other end of the block, and on weekends the crowds flocked to dance at the Dome, Andy Warhol's place a few doors away on the same block. Across the street was a new psychedelic rock club, Circus Maximus, and there were light-show concerts/dances by the Velvet Underground across the street from Tompkins Square Park.

The writer in the neighborhood we saw most often was Allen Ginsberg, who was living with Peter Orlovsky a few blocks east of us on the other side of Avenue A. Ann had already briefly met Allen in Berkeley ten years earlier, when Peter brought her as his blind date to the cottage on Milvia Street where there was a pre-poetry-reading spaghetti party before the crowd moved on to a small theater on Stuart Street. It was at that tumultuous 1956 reading where Allen for the first time would read the complete version of "Howl" in a restaging of the Gallery Six reading of the year before. I had noticed Ann with Peter in the crowd in the lobby of the theater, looking at the drawings pinned up on the walls.

While living on St. Mark's Place, Ann worked with many of the neighborhood Lower East Side poets after she brought a borrowed tape recorder to a reading at St. Mark's Church protesting the war in Vietnam in the early spring of 1966. Once she had sorted out the tapes, she climbed the stairs to their apartments to take photographs of them for the LP of the reading we would release on our small record label, Portents. When she walked over to Allen's place, he was talking on the phone with Bob Dylan, and she photographed him sitting cross-legged on a mattress on the floor of his littered apartment. A short time later she marched with Ginsberg and the Fugs down Fifth Avenue to protest America's escalating war in Vietnam. It was also during these months that Bob Wilson of the Phoenix Book Shop asked her if she would be interested in compiling a bibliography of Jack Kerouac's writings for the series of bibliographies of the new writers he was publishing. She wrote to Kerouac through his mother, and he responded with an invitation for her to visit him in Hyannis in the house where he and his mother were living. He included instructions on how to find his house and his letter ended, "Throw these instructions away, rather, that is, bring 'em with you—'Beatniks' look like Spooks in my mother's poor door at midnight—You understand."

It was from the apartment on St. Mark's Place that she drove off in August 1966 to spend two days on Cape Cod with Jack and his mother, working with him in his neatly kept literary archive. During their days together Jack insisted that she should also talk to his friend John Clellon Holmes, who was living in Connecticut and could tell her about the home recordings they'd made in John's New York apartment years before and even more about Kerouac's books. A few months later she took the train to Old Saybrook and met John and his wife, Shirley, for the first time. Ann had already begun to think of writing more about Kerouac and one Sunday afternoon, on a sudden impulse, she decided to walk over to East Tenth Street to talk to Allen Ginsberg. Our long association with Allen began with their conversation that afternoon, and when we moved across the river to Brooklyn Heights to have enough room for our new daughter, Allen came over to spend evenings listening to classic blues records. The record that he wanted to hear most often was "Rabbit" Brown's "James Alley Blues," with its opening line, "Times ain't now nothin' like they used to be."

Jack Kerouac, John Clellon Holmes, Allen Ginsberg—all three were part of our lives. Our association became even closer after Jack's death, when Ann began her work on his first biography, and then went on to edit the *Kerouac Reader*, two volumes of his letters, the *Portable Beat Reader*, and the two-volume literary encyclopedia, *The Beats: Literary Bohemians in Postwar America*, in which John contributed an article on his flamboyant friends from the early Beat years, Jay and Fran Landesman. Jack's death came at almost the same moment as the death of another close poet friend, Charles Olson, and in need of solace, Ann drove to Ginsberg's farm in Cherry Valley and for a few days stayed close to Allen and the people there to regain her balance. In the 1970s, after we had moved to Stockholm, Allen, Peter, and Steve Taylor, a singer and their guitarist, lived with us for two weeks in the middle of a loosely arranged European tour.

In 1980 Allen asked Ann to come to the new Jack Kerouac School of Disembodied Poetics at the Naropa Institute in Boulder, Colorado, to team-teach with him in a course he titled "Wild Mouths: Oral Poetry in the Twentieth Century." She introduced the poetry of Soviet poet Vladimir Mayakovsky, and Allen responded with the poems of Walt Whitman. They gave the class together in the Boulder Public Library. She returned to Naropa the next summer to teach a course in Beat writing, and Allen brought us both to Boulder for the historic gathering the next summer of 1982 to celebrate Jack Kerouac and the twenty-fifth anniversary of the publication of *On the Road.* John was also staying in the same venerable hillside frame dormitory, a few doors down the corridor from us.

We saw John and Shirley more often over the next years, since their home in Old Saybrook was only an hour's drive from our house in Storrs, Connecticut. Ann and I stayed with them in Old Saybrook, and when John was writing his introduction to *Beats & Company* (1986), the book of Ann's photographs of himself and the other writers she had known, he and Shirley stayed over with us in Storrs, Connecticut, drinking and listening to the old jazz classics that we all loved.

What this has meant is that although *Brother-Souls* is a biography of two writers and their long relationship, it is also a book about friends, about moments we've known together, and about the scenes in New York and Berkeley that we lived through at the same time. This has made the work more difficult, since we were close to John in the last years of his life, and we shared so many battles against the boundaries of censorship and the tragedy of the Vietnam War with Allen. Even more emotionally difficult for us has been writing about the new, and darker, areas of John's and Shirley's personal lives that emerged in the voluminous archive materials John left. His instructions, however, were that we should have access to whatever he had written, and he made it clear that he wanted this side of their marriage to be part of anything that we would write.

In occasional scenes in later chapters we make an appearance, but the book isn't a memoir. It is the story of two complicated, talented, unsure men—the story of their individual difficulties and their relentless efforts together to solve some of their creative problems. Writing about these friends has been our own salute to their struggles and their achievements. It was a unique creative moment that still sends its voice of assurance, occasional despair, and ultimate optimism to a world that continues to find its own ways to understand and to accept what they achieved.

SAMUEL CHARTERS

BROTHER-SOULS

Chapter 1

A USABLE PAST

Dear Jack:

*I am reading your Doctor Sax and I am impelled to write even be-
fore I have finished it. I don't know what will happen to this book, but
it will always be close to me. I truly believe it is a wondrous thing. . . .
While you scurried over the dump that sunny day in 1936 to watch the
flood unfold [in Lowell, Mass.], I stood on the banks of the Pemagawassett River, running usually thin, but now swollen and outraged,
through Plymouth, N.H. to the north. Yes, it was the same flood. The
town was marooned for four days, no electricity or school, and milk
swung in over the river on a rope. I walked just outside of town, pon-
dering this great event, and saw the highway slip into vale and disappear in muddy water. How strange! It was the same flood, only I was
younger. Across the river there were flats, with jerry-built cheap houses,
and beyond them a wooden baseball stadium rarely used, and I stood
by the inundated railroad tracks on the town side of the river, carrying
a paper bag of hot doughnuts made that morning, in a worn lumber
jacket, studying the current that had laved around the porches of those
cheap houses and knocked some over and made a lake of the baseball
diamond. And continually ate up those doughnuts. Only there was no
sun; it had rained steadily for three weeks. The sky was leaden and the
boats were out. It was the same flood.*

—JOHN CLELLON HOLMES, letter to Jack Kerouac, October 15, 1952

John Clellon Holmes was only ten when the flood of 1936 prodded the rivers in the northeastern United States over their banks and into the surrounding towns and cities in New England. Jack Kerouac had just turned
fourteen. Each of them vividly remembered the flood, and for Holmes it
became one more point where their lives had crossed, even if miles apart

3

and only on the banks of flooded rivers. In their temperaments they were more different than they were alike, but their boyhood in New England towns was a place from their past they would always share. It wasn't only the coincidence that Kerouac saw the flooding of the Merrimack River from the town of Lowell, Massachusetts. Lowell is almost eighty miles to the south of Plymouth, New Hampshire, where Holmes went to see the rising water carrying a bag of doughnuts "just tonged out of the grease by our half-Algonquin cook, Dorothy."[1] A dozen miles downstream from Plymouth, the Pemagawassett River, whose relentless, rising crest Holmes stood watching, flowed into the Merrimack River at Bristol, New Hampshire, and became the mingled waters and the same debris that a few days later raged past Kerouac in the flood. As Holmes wrote,

> We would discover this eerie correspondence in our lives only years later in New York, up way past midnight, the river of traffic in the clashing street below roaring as loud as the converging rivers of our boyhood, and bringing the memory back to both of us at the same instant.[2]

In 1948, when Holmes and Kerouac first met, they were still young—Holmes was twenty-two, Kerouac was twenty-six—but despite bursts of anger and disappointment, periods when they saw each other only sporadically, stinging resentments, monumental outbursts and jealousies, they remained friends for the rest of their lives. At the end, it was only Holmes with whom Kerouac still felt close. As he looked back at their relationship, Holmes recognized Kerouac as what he called a "brother-soul."[3] They had been born on the same day, March 12, four years apart, another "eerie correspondence" in their lives. Kerouac was the older of the two, old enough to be Holmes' big brother, but after the first few months of their friendship it was accepted that John was the steadier brother whom Jack could always turn to for contact and argument, or for a drink, a party, or a place to sleep for the night.

They met as young, would-be writers, solemnly committed to the self-appointed task they had set themselves of becoming the most important novelists of twentieth-century America. In the postwar years the writing of the "great American novel" was still the goal of every aspiring author. They continued to assure themselves, as they assured the women who patiently worked to support them—Kerouac's mother and his girlfriends, Holmes' two wives—that they could someday make a living with their writing. But in the beginning, as they talked and argued in New York City in the early years of their friendship, the dream of finishing their books and finding someone willing to publish them was as far as their hopes took them. After they first met they wrote their next novels together—reading each other's chapters and forcing each other to justify what had made its way on to the page. Their continual arguments clarified the differences between them and helped to define the writers they became.

Though Kerouac published a novel first in 1950, two years later it was Holmes, with his first novel, *Go*, who received the only large publisher's advance that either of them was given during their writing careers. Holmes was also the first who tried to describe their group and what they were attempting to achieve, setting down in print what he and Kerouac had argued out over a long night of beer and bebop in the fall of 1948 when Kerouac first proposed the term "Beat Generation." Kerouac's later fame came to completely eclipse his friend's, and in the wake of this fame the issues that Kerouac's books raised continue to be proclaimed, argued, dismissed, and defended, while the books themselves continue to be read in virtually all of the world's major languages. The books Holmes spent so much of his life writing never achieved this level of visibility, but they also never entirely were lost, and he continues to be read for his clear-eyed view of what they experienced. Without Holmes' story an important dimension of Kerouac's story is missing—a dimension that adds to our knowledge about his life and the writers who influenced him, his struggles to write *On the Road*, and his last, lost years of alcoholism. Holmes' story in the same way would have a missing dimension without the presence in it of his life-long friend Jack Kerouac and the leading roles they played as members of what they were the first to call the Beat Generation.

Like most men and women who spend their lives writing, Holmes was the most sensitive and insightful portrayer of his own life, but for anyone looking for his early years, the story of his childhood is scattered through his letters, his journals, and his occasional essay memoirs. Few writers have given more than a glancing aside at their earliest years, though James Joyce in the opening line of his *Portrait of the Artist as a Young Man*—"When you wet the bed first it is warm and then it gets cold"—took us about as far back into those beginnings as anyone could be expected to go. Throughout his life Holmes often looked back at his past, repeating some of the same memories but casting them in different scenarios, leaving a shifting picture that sometimes is difficult to interpret.

What Holmes shared with Kerouac was both a New England background and a family living in a kind of social vacuum through the anxious years of the Depression. Each of them was estranged from his father—in

Holmes' case, a father who was away from his wife and children for long periods and finally left them in a strained divorce. Kerouac's father died of cancer only two years before Jack and John met, but Leo Kerouac was a father with whom Jack had fought for many years, and they never managed to untangle their differences. Both Kerouac and Holmes remained close to their mothers, Kerouac to the virtual exclusion of anyone else who attempted to come close to him, even his only child. Kerouac's confusions and optimistic ambitions became a theme in the story of their chaotic lives Holmes described in *Go* in 1952. As novelists they were forced to compromise with their insistence to write only the "truth" by the lawyers working with their publishers. To protect the publishers from potential lawsuits over libel, everyone they wrote about in their autobiographical fiction was concealed behind a pseudonym.

In *Go* Kerouac's name became "Gene Pasternak." In *On the Road*, the book published five years later about this same period of their lives, Holmes became "Ian MacArthur."[4] There is an eerie stereopticon effect in the overlaid descriptions of the same figures at the same moment in two books written within months of each other by the two friends, both neophyte writers, competitors, and often inseparable drinkers, who met almost daily during the time they wrote these early novels. Entire scenes appear in both books, and obviously whatever was the "reality" of that moment, it lies somewhere in the blurred double portrait. Despite the success of *On the Road*, of all the books written later about their lifestyle, *Go* is still the most honest. It is also the darkest portrayal of the Beat scene.

Kerouac finally worked through his discomfort at the depiction of himself in *Go*, as well as his resentment at Holmes' munificent publisher's advance for the paperback sale of the novel, but he never forgave his friend for the somber, despairing picture he painted of the lives they were leading. What neither of them could have anticipated was that nearly everyone who crowds the pages of *Go* and *On the Road* was to become a familiar figure to the intensely curious audience who later discovered the books. Each "fictional" character, based on a real person in their lives, would emerge as a real name and individual—some like Allen Ginsberg for what they would write, others like Neal Cassady for their vivid presence in the story.

For many of the people drifting through their books' pages, their story was an unhappy one. Beneath the cultural ferment and political sympathies they shared in the late 1940s was the same postwar social anomie that had left Holmes and Kerouac, along with many other gifted New England writers who were their contemporaries, such as Elizabeth Bishop, Robert Creeley, Robert Lowell, Charles Olson, Sylvia Plath, and Anne Sexton, drifting in an emotional sea. The sea charts that should have guided them into a calmer harbor had been redrawn so many times during the catastrophic events of the Depression, the Second World War, and the early years of the Cold War that any useful directions had been jettisoned a long time ago.

Like many young writers, Holmes kept a journal where he attempted to create some pattern in the drift and chaos of his life. Also like most young writers of his and Kerouac's generation, he spent many of his daily hours at his typewriter writing letters that were voluminous, immediate, unblinkingly candid, and often startling in their incessant questioning and their just as decided answering. To fill out the record of his daily writing stints, Holmes usually made carbon copies of the letters he wrote, and the copies found their way into the voluminous archive of journals, letters, and manuscripts he would leave behind him.

Kerouac wrote almost as many letters, most of them preserved by his friends, and after he discovered his style of "sketching" in the fall of 1951, he never left his mother's apartment without a small cheap notebook jammed into a pocket. Unlike Holmes, however, he printed the jottings in his notebooks, usually with a pencil, filling the narrow lined pages with short word-sketches and comments. Holmes' typed journal entries, in contrast, often continued from one single-spaced page to the next, some as closely reasoned as an exposition of a theme for debate, others loosely humorous and raunchily uninhibited. For Kerouac, the immediacy of the glimpsed events jotted down in his notebooks became the seed of the emotional affects and vivid descriptions he later created in his picaresque memoirs. For Holmes, the reasoned discourse of his journals became the web of ideas that were at the core of all his writing.

In an essay published a few months before his death in 1988, Holmes described his childhood in an impressionistic sketch that provides the setting for much that happened later in his life, though like any other personal memoir, it is most revealing in what was chosen to be included and what has been left out. He began it with an epigraph that in itself was enigmatic and confusing. He is probably the only writer who ever introduced an autobiographical sketch with a quote that he confessed he didn't know the meaning of himself.

> *"To salvage from life something on which one can build more life." I know this is a truth, and I don't know what it means.*
> *Why?*
> *I was born in Holyoke, Massachusetts (to a revered New England name that has never brought me any ease) and had a female relative who*

wore a choker, and a distant male relation who could remember the date
of William the Conqueror's invasion of England but not always his own
name. My grandfather, the doctor, saved a genteel New Jersey town from
the great flu epidemic, then died of the effort; while my other grandfa-
ther, the engineer, wore puttees and celluloid collars all his life in mining
camps from San Luis Potosi to Butte to support a colonial household out-
side of Boston, only to lose it when he was flown out of Canada, dying of
exposure and still far from Home. My father was "high strung," impetuous,
a failure after the Crash, a sentimentalist who always sang while in the
movies; and my mother, "long suffering," a Christian martyr, took me to
séances where the dead gossiped from the other world. I dutifully learned
to sail catboats and dance the rumba, all that was left of our "gentility"
as the thirties passed, and no reasons. These weren't the reasons.

In the winters we lived in houses too big, too drafty, and too rundown
for other people to live in, and I was invited to dances in the houses
where these other people lived, wearing a borrowed suit, there being a
shortage of "acceptable" boys, and my manners good. But every sum-
mer there were Peconic's empty beaches beyond the potato fields, far
out on Long Island's unfashionable North Fork, where the sandy bluffs
were perfect for cave-building, and you measured nerve and skill and
recklessness by swimming underwater through the space between the
diving-rocks, and the family's house on its headland up the beach, a
huge, shingled "cottage," silvered to a soft patina by nor'-easters, was all
of certainty and civility to me—my uncles in close harmony around the
upright piano, Great-Aunt Marge's pseudo-impressionistic dunescapes
drying on window sills everywhere, Great-Uncle Canby presiding like
a Quaker FDR over the summer's bounteous tables, while the Germany
of his graduate school days darkened to a mad rant of Teutonic voices
over the shortwave. Those summers were the last seamless times I was to
know—white duck trousers board-stiff with starch, commodious rooms
of wicker furniture, BLT's with too much mayonnaise, the mudguards of
yellow roadsters, the last long twilights of peace laddering the tranquil
surface of the Sound in bars of burnished gold all the way to—But those
weren't the reasons either.[5]

If the picture Holmes drew of his early years could have been framed it
would have been suffused with the lustrous sunlight of these idyllic summers at the beach with his father's family before the outbreak of the Second
World War. The realities, though—as is so often true with memories—cast
darker shadows which he was no more able to leave behind than he could

forget his impressions of the golden waves and the starched white duck trousers of his boyhood summers on Long Island Sound. He was born in Holyoke, Massachusetts, on March 12, 1926, and named after his father, John McClellan Holmes Sr., whose full name echoed that of his illustrious Civil War ancestor, the Union Army general and later presidential candidate John McClellan. John was the middle child in his family, with two sisters, Lila born two years earlier on March 1, 1924, and Elizabeth six years later on December 10, 1932. The "revered New England name" he mentioned in his poetic evocation of his childhood was the nineteenth-century American poet and essayist Oliver Wendell Holmes, with whom as a modern twentieth century novelist he felt he shared nothing at all except an obdurate New England-ness.

Both sides of Holmes' family contained highly educated and accomplished men and women. He could trace his paternal ancestry back ten generations to the time of Shakespeare, beginning with George Holmes, born in 1594 in England, who died in Roxbury, Massachusetts, in 1645. After he came to America he and his wife, Deborah (d. 1662), had a son Nathaniel Holmes (1639–1711), whose son Jehoshaphat (1690–1745) married Sarah Waldorf from the family that produced Ralph Waldo Emerson. Jehosaphat and Sarah sired Jehosaphat Junior (1721–1789), whose son Jehosaphat III (1758–1825) sired Edwin Holmes (1797–1873), educated as a minister in Union College, who married Sarah Marian McClellan, related to the general. Their son John McClellan Holmes graduated Williams College in 1853 and earned his Doctorate in Divinity at the theological seminary in New Brunswick, New Jersey, in 1857. His son, Edwin Holmes, born in Hudson, New York, in 1869, became John's grandfather Doctor Edwin Holmes.[6]

Educated at Williams College and trained in medicine at Johns Hopkins University followed by a year of postgraduate study in Berlin, Doctor Holmes married Frieda Shreck Boise in 1899. Their son—John's father—was born on December 16, 1899, in New York City. Doctor Holmes became the pediatrician for the family of the famous aviator Charles Lindberg and worked so tirelessly in Englewood, New Jersey, during the flu epidemic of 1918–1919 that he developed angina and died shortly after Holmes' birth. After her husband's death, Holmes' paternal grandmother, Frieda Boise Holmes, moved to New York City. Her father had been a professor of music at the Peabody Institute in Baltimore and a composer whose work included the first piano concerto written in the United States. Frieda Holmes was John's favorite grandmother. She later settled in Greenport, Long Island, not far from Peconic's beaches, where Holmes visited her every year until her death.[7]

Holmes' mother, Elizabeth Franklin Emmons Holmes, called "Betty," and her four sisters were the daughters of a direct descendant of Benjamin Franklin, so on both sides of the family John and his sisters inherited an innate sense of belonging to what his parents called "gentility," a privileged class in the American social tradition. This couldn't have been more unlike Kerouac's background as the son of French-Canadian immigrants. For most of his life Kerouac's language at home was a dialect of North American French known as *joual*, and friends from his youth remembered that he had difficulties with English until he was eighteen.

Betty Holmes and her sisters were the daughters of the eminent American mining engineer S. F. Emmons (1841–1911), who was working in Mexico when she was born in 1900, employed as a consultant in the construction of the Mexican National Railway. Later Betty told her own children stories about riding as a little girl out to the end of the line of newly laid track on a flatcar, seated on top of the heavy bags of gold coins used to pay the workers. Her father spent the next several years managing mines in Arizona, Montana, and other distant places. After his death, she was sent away to boarding school with her sisters. Betty studied music and art, but she wasn't allowed by her family to take a job as a piano accompanist at the Boston School of Music in 1920, since it was work then considered unsuitable for a young woman of her social class. She joined her mother and sisters in Englewood, New Jersey, and waited for someone to marry her.

Holmes' father grew up in Englewood with his two younger brothers, and he briefly attended Williams College before he dropped out at seventeen to enlist in the army in the months before the United States entered the First World War. His family framed a diploma he was awarded certifying he had a "Good Character" after he completed basic training at Fort Terry on Plumb Island in Gardiner's Bay, east of Orient Point off the coast of Long Island, from July 10 to August 6, 1916. Before he enlisted he had been seeing Betty's younger sister Martha in Englewood. He wrote to her while he was stationed in England, but she was considered "fast," with many other boyfriends, and she never bothered to answer his letters. It was Betty he turned to after his discharge, and they were married in June 1923. He began a series of jobs as an advertising salesman, and their first daughter, Lila, was born ten months later.

At the time of Holmes' birth in 1926 the country was flush with prosperity, with a confidence in the American future that should have been some guarantee that his parents' marriage would be a happy one. Holmes remembered his father as "an amiable, egocentric, sentimental man, who loved to talk and sing, who had a strong sex drive and equally strong guilt-feelings about it, who was very close to his two younger brothers and his mother (who was to outlive them all)."[8] Betty Holmes never lost her love for the classical music she'd studied as a girl. Throughout his boyhood John remembered that his mother listened every Saturday to radio broadcasts of the Metropolitan Opera—"Milton Cross from the Met was a weekend ritual in our houses."[9] Opera music might have been a constant in Holmes' early memories, but when he grew up it was the only music that didn't really interest him. It's not surprising, since he had such unhappy memories of his early years. After the economic crash of 1929 his father's career began to falter, and his parents' quarrels over their insecure financial situation led to extended separations as his father struggled to support the family.

In 1930 Holmes' parents moved apart in a trial separation, and his mother took him and his older sister Lila to Altadena, California, a suburb of Pasadena, for a year to live with her sister Dorothy, who had a large house with room enough to spare for the three of them. There John celebrated his fifth birthday and began school. He remembered "walking cracked sidewalks through the smell of eucalyptus on the way to kindergarten, the ancient palm tree in our damp patio."[10] After his parents decided to try again with their marriage, Betty took Lila and John back to the East Coast onboard a ship that sailed through the Panama Canal and on through the Caribbean Islands.

John's father met them when their ship docked in Manhattan, and he drove them to a newly built home on a country road a few miles outside Stamford, Connecticut. He'd managed to find a job doing advertising and sales promotion for the A. G. Spaulding Sporting Goods Company. It was 1931, however, the cruelest year of the Depression, when unemployment reached over 30 percent and banks collapsed everywhere in the country, taking their depositors' savings with them. Some American cities in their desperation were reduced to producing their own paper currency to keep their economies from collapsing. It was an unexpected moment of grace for the family that his father had found any kind of job. For young Holmes there were some good memories, including "the potent smell of my father's Camel cigarettes in the car as we drove to a bootlegger to get liquor for a friend's weekend visit; fear and attraction at the end of our road where there was a dense tangle of vines and undergrowth and trees into which the sun never reached."[11] For a time they were able to live at an unexpected level of comfort. John and his sister Lila attended the Lucy Paxton Country Day School, and his mother employed a maid. Nothing could hold out against the country's inexorable economic slide, but Holmes later persisted in blaming his father for continually disrupting their family life. When the job in Stamford ended, they returned to Englewood.

There were enough aunts and other relations in New Jersey to help them through their difficulties, since Betty's family was still affluent. John remembered that as a child he was taken to the mansion of his maternal grandmother to celebrate Thanksgivings and Christmases. His parents were still trying to breathe life back into their marriage, despite the increasing tensions between them. Their "reconciliation" baby, his sister Elizabeth, nicknamed "Liz," was born in 1932 at New York Hospital. His older sister Lila remembered that her Aunt Sally, one of her mother's sisters, had the family chauffeur drive her mother to the hospital for the delivery.

Probably in every language there is some expression for the common observation that the person any adult becomes was already shaped by their childhood. A well-worn formulation in educational circles is something like "Give me the child to the age of seven, and I'll give you the grown-up." Kerouac and Holmes were shaped by their early years—though for them the formative years continued to their adolescence. They were both conscious of their New England roots, but each was also conscious of coming from opposite ends of the New England social strata. Kerouac, like Holmes, returned to his childhood again and again in his books, though what he wrote were as much loosely imagined memoirs as novels, and there was even more blurring of the realities. He suggested many spellings of his name and imagined meanings for the word "Kerouac" in either Celtic or Gaelic. His family's background became part of Kerouac's first published novel, *The Town and the City*, though many of the details were shaped by the style of the writing, and the name of the city in New Hampshire where his parents met was changed from Nashua to "Lacoshua."

The earliest of Kerouac's ancestors on record is Urbain-Francois Le Bihan de Kervoac, the youngest of three sons of a notary, who was taken to court in Brittany after being accused of theft in 1720.[12] Though the charges were dropped, he emigrated from France to Quebec. After his father's death he apparently changed his name to Maurice-Louis Alexandre Le Bris de Keroack and died in 1736, leaving two sons to carry on his name. Since at least seven different ways of spelling the Kerouac surname exist in France and North America, and many of the later descendents were illiterate farmers with large numbers of children, it is impossible to trace the direct line of Kerouac's ancestry. Later in *Visions of Gerard* he wrote about his paternal grandfather, Jean-Baptiste Kirouac (1848–1906), whom he never met, as the pioneer in the family. In 1890, along with scores of other impoverished

French Canadians, Jean-Baptiste Kirouac and his wife, Clementine, with their twelve small children, left their barren pig farm in Quebec to descend on the small industrial town of Nashua in hilly New Hampshire. Most of their children died of diseases such as cholera and dropsy, but in the book Kerouac sentimentalized their life in "early Americana New Hampshire" as a blend of "pink suspenders, strawberry blondes, barbershop quartets, popcorn stands," and fistfights between boys who learned about America by following the adventures of Frank Merriwell, the rags to riches hero featured in the stories in the dimestore magazine *Tiptop Weekly*.[13]

One of the surviving children born to Jean-Baptiste was Kerouac's father, Leo, born in 1889 in St. Hubert, Canada. He was baptized Joseph Alcide Leon Kirouack, but the name had alternative spellings by the time of Jack's birth in Lowell on March 12, 1922. Jack was christened Jean Louis Kirouac (Keroack), while on his birth certificate his name was given as Jean-Louis Lebris de Kerouac. In Nashua his grandfather Jean-Baptiste had prospered enough as a carpenter for Leo to be sent off to a private school in Long Island. On his return from the school, Kerouac's father took a job with a French-language newspaper in Nashua, writing some of the news and becoming the paper's typesetter.

Kerouac's mother, Gabrielle Ange Levesque, was born in 1895 in St. Pacome, Quebec, another small French village, but through intermarriage she was one-quarter Iroquois, which Kerouac always regarded as a proud talisman of his ancestry. Her mother, Josephine Jean Levesque, died when Gabrielle was only a year old. Her father, Louis Levesque, left the village and moved to Nashua where, after a period in the mills, he became a tavernkeeper. He died in 1911. Orphaned at sixteen, Gabrielle was employed in a shoe factory in Nashua and lived in a boardinghouse with other mill girls. She endured a seventy-two-hour workweek until her marriage at the age of twenty to Leo in 1915. The owner of the newspaper employing Leo had bought out a failed French-language newspaper in Lowell, a short distance south of Nashua in Massachusetts, and Leo was sent to take over the general responsibility for doing whatever it took to get the newspaper out on the street. After his marriage he brought Gabrielle to Lowell, where they would live for the next twenty-five years. Jack was the youngest of their three children, born in Lowell after his brother, Gerard (1916–1926), and his sister, Caroline (1918–1964), nicknamed "Nin."

Kerouac's and Holmes' childhoods reflect something of the family background that shaped them, but there was also a dimension they couldn't have seen at the time that had as decisive an effect on the writers they became. The turmoil of Holmes' childhood, the continual moves, his parent's separations and final divorce left him with a completely discontinuous childhood. Most crucially he was continually coming into new schools, often taunted because of his newness, so disconcerted by the experience that finally, as a teenager and facing still another new school, he rebelled and failed to complete high school. At the same time, however, Holmes' social background had given him an unshakable sense of the larger American culture he inherited. However alienated he felt moving from one new house or one new school to another, he was always certain of his place in the society itself.

Kerouac's childhood had a completely different effect in shaping his consciousness of himself and the society around him. His family moved often in Lowell, but they always remained in the distinctive French-Canadian neighborhood above the north bank of the Merrimac River named Pawtucketville. It is still an area of modest wooden frame houses set along quiet back streets, or three- or four-story frame tenements along the neighborhood's one main thoroughfare, Moody Street (now University Avenue). With all of the family's moves, Kerouac still could walk from one house to another, and more important, he stayed in the same schools—first a French-speaking Catholic school, then the nearby English-speaking public school—and he kept the same close friends throughout his adolescence. He spoke *joual* at home, and his mother became even more protective of him after the death of his older brother, Gerard.

The innumerable houses and apartments where Holmes' parents settled briefly were within a few hours drive of each other, but there was no continuity to their neighborhoods, and in all of his early writing about his childhood Holmes never mentions feeling close to his parents or having a close friend. Kerouac's diaries and reminiscences, and the three memoir-novels he wrote about these years in Lowell, *Visions of Gerard, Doctor Sax*, and *Maggie Cassidy*, are filled with the sounds of his family and his friends' voices.

In a larger social context, however, Kerouac's childhood in a sheltered immigrant enclave, however stable, left him with a restricted view of the larger society that was the other side of the coin from Holmes' experiences growing up into adulthood. Kerouac was always certain of the neighborhood he was writing about. He understood its ambitions and its attitudes and he never lost the unique consciousness that this life growing up in a small separate community had given him. On the other hand, he had no larger perception of the culture beyond it, aside from the few books and movies nearly everyone in his generation encountered growing up as children in the United States. Kerouac's writing remained consistently personal, parochial, always focused on a small group of friends or a brief relationship with someone in that group, while Holmes in his books continually attempted to draw parallels between his own world and the larger American traditions and literary culture that he considered his own.

Holmes never considered his childhood, which he remembered for its uncertainties and his loneliness, as lending him any kind of social status, despite sporadic prodding from both his friends Kerouac and Allen Ginsberg about what they considered his "patrician" background. In 1977, however, in a poem written at the death of the poet Robert Lowell,[14] Holmes wrote in the last lines,

> . . . *This Holmes salutes that Lowell*
> *on this day of his abrupt departure for Back Bay.*
> *"Out of a Fever: For Robert Lowell (Sept. 13, 1977)"*

In these lines Holmes acknowledged their shared New England background. In the golden period of Boston's—and America's—nineteenth-century literary life their two writer ancestors, poet and editor James Russell Lowell and essayist, poet, novelist, and editor Oliver Wendell Holmes, were close friends.

Chapter 2

THE MAGIC OF WORDS

The bed's a place for dreams, and rest, and love—a private place. But our beds were like New England's stony fields. You had to work hard before you could dream in them, much less hope. You piled the stones into fences, you dug and heaved and dragged at them in all weathers, raging, despairing, intent, all alone at the task, but always brooding on more than the task—because you knew the fences would outlast you. . . . Early on we both began to write away the psychological bruises of nights spent in those rocky beds. . . . We were religious men without a creed.

—JOHN CLELLON HOLMES, "Rocks in Our Beds"[1]

The Depression had a devastating effect on every level of American society, including Kerouac's family in Lowell, where he was a high school student during the worst years. Despite the economic collapse, however, and despite the dislocations of his childhood, Holmes lived in a social world that had a measure of shelter from the hard times most of the country was facing. The collapse had left many large homes in Englewood vacant, and for a few years his parents moved from one to another. Holmes later figured that he had moved twenty times before his eighteenth birthday. Despite the birth of a new baby, Holmes' father began to spend increasing amounts of time away from home, and whenever he rejoined his family the quarrels with his wife would resume. Living in various short-term rental apartments in the half-empty mansions where they found themselves, Lila and John became accustomed to lying in bed in the dark and listening to their parents' angry words that often ended in what the children took to be violent sex. There was a temporary respite when their mother came into an inheritance from an unmarried uncle, which gave her a brief sense of finally coming into her own.

Holmes remembered that before his mother decided on which one of the thirty-room empty mansions she would rent, she drove their car through the streets on "The Hill," then Englewood's most elegant neighborhood, looking at one after another of the great houses she had envied all of her adult life. After their move, she insisted on installing a special furnace, even though they were only renters. She ordered gold brocade drapes sewn for the double living room windows. She hired a cook, who was entrusted with the responsibility of feeding the family well, and for the first time John and Lila were allowed to sit at the large table in the formal dining room to eat dinner with their parents.

After two years of this affluent lifestyle, they left Englewood in the summer of 1935 and moved again, this time to Plymouth, New Hampshire. Once again Holmes' father, despite all the odds against him, had found a new job as sales manager of Draper and Maynard, a manufacturer of sporting goods. Betty Holmes resisted the move, but he promised that she could continue to hire a maid who would help with the cooking and the housework. Holmes recalled, "My memories of those years [were] always buried in the quilted blankets, excelsior, and china barrels of gangs of burly Polski moving men, who loaded us on their trucks sixteen times in as many autumns."[2]

In New Hampshire, living in a dirt-poor, isolated small town ringed with the scrabbling farms on the surrounding mountains, Holmes remembered "being beaten-up my first day in school because I 'talked funny' (that is, I had no ascertainable accent), and being taken out into the woods to learn to shoot, obliterating a squirrel when I pulled both triggers of a double-barreled shotgun."[3] He was myopic and wore thick glasses, and he didn't enjoy hunting or playing sports so he didn't fit in with the crowd of local boys. Plymouth was built around a village green with a five- and ten-cent store on one side and a church on the other. Holmes' favorite place in town was the movie theater a short walk from home. After his tenth birthday, he was allowed to see the double features that played there twice a week. Increasingly introspective, he spent hours fantasizing about directing his own movies when he grew up.

Holmes' most important memory of Plymouth, which he shared with Kerouac, was the flood of 1936, when the Pemagawassett River overflowed its banks and John stood in awe watching it plunging through its gigantic gorge above the town. In Lowell Kerouac walked along the banks of the Merrimack River on higher ground in his Pawtucketville neighborhood, but downtown the flood waters rose to thirteen feet above street level and damaged his father's basement printing shop. Since the shop was uninsured, its loss meant the end of his father's small business.

Holmes' only happy memory during his years in New Hampshire was his parents' habit of reading aloud in the evenings. "My father used to read to my sisters and me—mostly bad, sentimental poetry, but the magic of words obviously left an impression."[4] Dickens was his father's favorite novelist, especially during the Christmas holidays, but Holmes also recalled that both his parents took turns reading aloud the entire novel *Gone with the Wind*, a best-seller in 1936. His best childhood memories were the summers the family spent on Long Island in the small beach community of Peconic, near Greenport on the North Fork of the island's eastern tip.

For several seasons his parents rented a small cottage in a cluster of other cottages a half mile from the Holmes' family summer home, a commodious old Long Island–style shingle house weathered silver from the ocean winds. Their rented cottage was on the beach, but the big house where they gathered for meals sat squarely in the middle of acres of flat fields planted in potatoes. None of the houses had electricity or indoor plumbing, but the main house had a large kitchen with a spacious ice box. Large blocks of ice were delivered daily to keep the food from spoiling for Holmes' paternal grandmother, her three sons and their families, and the hordes of aunts, uncles, cousins, and their friends who vacationed there.

Part of Holmes' pleasure from his summers at the beach was that he had the opportunity to read comic books in Peconic, something he wasn't permitted to do at home. One of his cousins, Bim, brought piles of comics with him. John's sister Lila remembered that her brother became "happy as a lark because Mom would not let him buy comic books. In fact, she bought the *New York Herald Tribune* and the *Times* on Sundays because they had no comics."[5] Betty Holmes much preferred that her children read English children's classics such as the Doctor Doolittle books, which John also devoured during his childhood. At their summer cottage the children spent most of their time at the beach, reached by a steep flight of wooden stairs leading down to the eroding sand dunes. For John and his sisters the choppy waters of the Sound filled their days, and they swam and dove off two special rocks that were separated by a barnacled underwater opening. One rock was John's and the other was Lila's, and with their youthful enthusiasm they spent hours jumping off their rocks and diving underwater. At the beach John looked forward to the bacon, lettuce, and tomato sandwiches dripping with mayonnaise that were always brought down from the big house for their summer lunches.

Snapshots of the Holmes family at the beach—sometimes even with his father included, since he vacationed at Peconic—show John surrounded by other children who were his cousins. He was tow-headed, usually in baggy black woolen swimming trunks with a contrasting white belt that only emphasized his chubbiness. He had a confident grin and squared shoulders. He and Lila weren't close as children, and in all of the photos he was standing at a distance from her. Lila, already maturing physically, wore clinging bathing suits that made her look much older than her younger brother. In photos that include his baby sister Liz, his mother usually held her within the protective circle of her arms, while his father stood in the middle of the group, a tall, handsome, well-muscled figure in a tight white T-shirt, clearly a favorite of the ladies gathered in front of their cottage or on the beach. Later Holmes recalled his father warbling and crooning the classic American songs of Gershwin, Kern, and Berlin in his "pretentious tenor voice" and playing Bing Crosby records on the wind-up portable phonograph they always brought along to the cottage.

John's relationship with his father was alternately affectionate and antagonistic. As Holmes wrote later,

> I thought of him as handsome and quixotic, sometimes great fun to be with, sometimes mysteriously preoccupied with depressions and anxieties. By the time I reached puberty (in the late 30's and early 40's), the natural rivalry between fathers and sons began to assert itself. By then our family had become "shabby genteel," he was drifting from job to job, his marriage of twenty years was beginning to come apart, and I took my mother's side. He became increasingly critical of me—I wasn't much interested in athletics, I was into books and music, and perhaps it dawned on him that I wanted to become an artist. He had once wanted to be a musician, had been discouraged from it by his doctor-father and the responsibility of a too-early marriage, and he took out some of his disappointment on me, or so it seemed at the time.[6]

Holmes grew closer to his mother, a deeply spiritual person all her life, who had given up the Unitarianism of her family background and was drawn to books about the occult. She read Blavatsky and Ouspensky, and she began to take her son to séances while they were still living in Plymouth, raising him to believe in the existence of a God and an afterlife. She was also interested in radical politics, sympathizing with Socialist causes. During their Long Island summers Holmes also listened to the conversations of his older, more sophisticated cousins, who stimulated his awareness of a growing world crisis in the late 1930s.

As the years of Depression ground on, its grip on the country never loosening, Holmes' father lost his job in New Hampshire, and the family once again returned to Englewood. In Lowell, Kerouac's father struggled to find small jobs to keep the family going. He worked in a print shop and spent hours in the French-American social club, drinking heavily. It was Kerouac's mother who found employment in one of the factories across the river, working as a cutter in a shoe factory. They were now living on the fourth floor of a wooden tenement above a lunchroom, with his bedroom looking down on busy Moody Street, the main thoroughfare in the Pawtucketville section of town. At Lowell High School Kerouac did well enough in his classes, and he had already begun to play football, the key that would open the door for him to begin a different life.

In Englewood Holmes—now called Johnny by his family—found himself living in a room on the third floor of another large, ugly mansion. By this time he had lost weight and developed what he called "a nervous temperament, and the secret longing for a final house."[7] At Dwight Morrow High School he remembered "the usual things—popularity obsession, the mad, romantic letch for girls, dancing school in autumn twilights when the burning leaves smelled like hashish (as the last male Holmes, I was expected to know how to dance well and sail a catboat in deep water), bad dreams before algebra tests."[8] Despite his difficulty with mathematics, he was an outstanding student. He read the newspaper daily, following the growing political tensions in Europe, and he excelled in his English classes.

Sex also began for Holmes in Englewood. From his third-story window he could see "the rust-colored smudge of New York lights over the river," and he recalled that he "dreamed glamorous dreams, and woke up one morning at thirteen, to find a humbler smudge on my mattress ticking, and learned to masturbate in a wink."[9] Like many adolescents, he became increasingly introspective. At Dwight Morrow High School, his homeroom teacher, Miss Eleanor Harvey, told his mother, "After a certain point, something in him closes off, a wall goes up, and you can get no farther." This was an insight that was as shocking to him, in its deceptive accuracy, "as a mirror-image (a facsimile of reality, but reversed), can sometimes be."[10] Adding to his sense of being different from the rest of his class, in his second year of high school Holmes had to take a job to augment his father's income, delivering milk to the houses of his schoolmates just before dawn, while an all-night radio station from New York told him "how immense and tireless and baffling was the world beyond the Hudson."[11]

Holmes' life abruptly changed, as life changed for all Americans, on December 7, 1941, when the Japanese bombed Pearl Harbor and the United States entered the Second World War. His parents decided to end their marriage and his father found employment in Washington, D.C., as a lobbyist. He left Englewood and a short time later met the woman who would become his second wife. Once again Holmess felt uprooted, but he was older now and feeling more independent. In the summer of 1942, when he was sixteen, he too "started leaving home."[12]

"Leaving home" was to become a theme in the books that Holmes and Kerouac were to write later, though their emotional responses to the journeys they made were visceral in their differences. In a kind of premonition of the trips that Kerouac would make a few years later, Holmes again went across the country, back to Southern California, where he and his mother and sister had lived for a year when he turned five. Leaving New York City in the July heat, he rode a Continental Trailways bus to Los Angeles to stay with his aunt Dorothy in Altadena. That summer he worked as an usher in a newsreel theater on Main Street in Los Angeles, spending his days in the dark theater watching the same newsreels of the war several times a day. The war left him "solemn with fatality—the war, which I knew I would be part, edging my mood, my hunger, with the cheap chrome of brevity."[13]

It was as Holmes was returning on a bus back to New York, that he glimpsed a sight of the America that would excite Kerouac on his own later travels. Outside of Tulsa, Oklahoma, three young African American men appeared out of what seemed to be a barren prairie wearing fashionable zoot suits. They boarded the bus, rode as far as the outskirts of Tulsa, and then disappeared "through a doorway full of smoke and saxophones."[14] It was an unforgettable "vision of wartime America as a monstrous dance land, extending from coast to coast."[15] This image of social upheaval related to jazz would surface later in his endless conversations with Kerouac about what they each had experienced as they came of age.

With so much writing that both Holmes and Kerouac left behind them, so many doors and windows casting light on their pasts, it would seem that we know everything we need to know about each of them. If Kerouac didn't leave so many pages of memoir in his journals as his friend Holmes, it was only because Kerouac found another way to present everything he wanted to tell us about his childhood and adolescence. It was there in the pages of novels that were in reality thinly disguised memoirs. Despite their occasional attempts to explain their motives, we don't have the key that would open the door to what we find on the pages of their books. We have their sour-sweet memories of the neighborhoods where they grew up, the failures or successes of their years in school, their friends or lack of friends, their difficult or their tender relationships with their mother or father. We go on adding more and more details, but we don't know the most important thing: We don't know why they became writers.

It would be simple to say that Kerouac, an adolescent growing up on the French-Canadian streets of his tenement neighborhood in Lowell, was supported in his desire to be a writer by his association with a group calling themselves the Young Prometheans, and particularly with Sebastian Sampas, another adolescent who became his close friend. It was Sampas, however, living in another section of Lowell, who went to find *him*. Sampas had heard at Lowell High School that Kerouac was interested in literature, and that he was already doing writing of his own. Sitting upstairs in his family's apartment, Kerouac heard someone shouting his name from the street, and when he went down the stairs it was Sampas, eager to meet him. In an author's questionnaire for *Lonesome Traveler*, Kerouac boasted that he was already writing when he was three, that he was drawing illustrated comic books with his own stories when he was eight, that by the time he was eleven he was writing short stories and a novel. What he never says is *why*.

Kerouac grew up in a deeply religious Catholic community. His neighbors were largely French-Canadian immigrants and their church was one of the pillars in their need for some identity in their new society. His mother, Gabrielle—also called Mémère by her children—prayed in church every day. Although there were other nationalities in the jumble of small New England mill towns like Lowell, religion dominated all of their lives. The girl for whom Kerouac first felt a serious crush when he was in high school, Mary Carney, was Irish, and her Catholicism in their adolescence was as strong as his. Two of his closest friends, Sebastian Sampas and George J. Apostolos, were Greek and, like the other immigrant families, deeply religious. When Kerouac, as a teenager, became troubled by giggling comments he heard in high school about his dream of being a writer, the person he turned to for some reassurance was his priest, Father Armand Morissette, usually called "Spike." He told Father Morisette that he was being laughed at because he told his friends that he wanted to be a writer. Morisette's answer was, "I'm not laughing." When Kerouac was surprised, Morisette assured him, "No, I think it's wonderful." Encouraged, Kerouac told him that he was going to be a writer and he was going to write a lot of books. When the Father warned him, "Writers are people like us. But let me warn you, you're in for a lot of disappointments." Kerouac's answer was a stubborn adolescent insistence, "I don't mind."[16]

If any one event of Kerouac's childhood would become a traumatic part of his adult consciousness it was not the family's moves or his father's problems; it was the death of his older brother Gerard from rheumatic fever when Jack was four. Gerard's illness wasted his body and he was in continual pain, but at the same time he had spiritual visions that made him a sainted figure in both their family and their French-Canadian religious community. All of Kerouac's biographers noted it wasn't possible for a four-year-old not to be jealous of the attention the family paid to Gerard, and Kerouac was sure that his mother's love for his sainted older brother was stronger than her love for him.

> *On hearing of Gerard's death, Jack ran joyfully to inform his father, glad that Gerard would no longer suffer, thinking his father would share his feelings. He had probably overheard grown-ups say that death would put an end to his suffering, would be the most merciful course of events. He was severely reprimanded.*[17]

That moment of confused misunderstanding by the four-year-old boy was to have a somber effect on his relationship with his father. Later Kerouac described in *Visions of Gerard*, his book about his older brother's death, how "gleeful" he felt when he ran up to inform his father that Gerard was dead.[18] Irrationally, Kerouac believed that Leo never forgave him for feeling this way.

As Kerouac wrote in *Vanity of Duluoz*, it was not until his family moved from Lowell in the summer of 1941, after he had finished his freshman year at Columbia, that he first experienced the feeling of displacement that had been a constant presence in Holmes' life. Giving up the struggle to support the family with his part-time jobs in Lowell, Leo finally was forced to take employment as a linotype operator in New Haven. With the family's strained finances, the only livable place they could afford to rent was a shabby beach cottage on the city's outskirts for forty dollars a month. Ironically, living on the shore of West Haven at Bradley Point, they were almost directly across the Long Island Sound from Peconic, where Holmes had spent the happiest summers of his childhood. It was another "eerie coincidence" in their lives. On bright, clear days they could have made out each other's distant shore across the choppy waters.

For both Holmes and Kerouac their diaries were their first apprenticeship as aspiring writers. Holmes began writing stories when he was still in grade school, filling notebooks with them written in blue ink, lurid tales of adventure inspired by the movies he saw every week. From the long lists of film titles in his diaries it's hard to imagine that there could have been a movie he missed. On school vacations he usually spent his afternoons in a movie theater. Between August 1, 1939, when he returned from camp at thirteen,

and the first day of school on September 6, he crowded in forty-one movies, including the one he liked best, *The Wizard of Oz.*[19]

Holmes' diaries also were filled with sexual fantasies and heavy-breathing accounts of school parties where he glimpsed girls' underwear and
danced close and kissed anyone who would let him, remembering a classmate named Jane Tipping as "the dirtiest girl I've ever seen."[20] In a second
diary from 1942, when he was sixteen, he imagined a fantasy seduction in
an account of a trip he pretended he'd taken from New York to Mexico
City to visit his maternal grandmother two summers' earlier. Fantasizing
about this imaginary visit, he described how he met the beautiful, half-
French, half-Mexican daughter of one of his grandmother's wealthy friends
in Mexico City. Actually Holmes' account reads like a diary entry written
by a teenager to conceal the details of an event he didn't want to forget but
couldn't openly describe. His "romance" in Mexico City could have been
something that had actually happened to him as a teenager in New Jersey
on a summer night in July:

> It was hot tonight and after we'd walked for awhile we came to the pond in
> the middle of the park. There was no one about so she suggested that we go
> swimming. I like an innocent fool, said "No suit." We went in anyway. The
> water felt good after those hot clothes and I remember her swimming on
> her back with the moon on her breasts. . . . I stood in the dark and helped
> her out. My god, even I went nuts seeing her like that. Her body was white
> and wet, and her lips looked dark in the night. I turned to get dressed and
> she put her hand on my shoulder. I turned about and looked at her. She
> was right up against me. I could feel the tips of her bosom. . . Well, from
> then on it was easy. We lay on the moss and I had her.[21]

A dozen years later Holmes also was to write novelistic third-person
accounts of a "fictional" love affair in his journals, which he described as
scenes intended for his next book, but what he was concealing again was an
intensely personal narrative. Perhaps he had done this before in his diary
when he wrote as a teenager:

> It was easy and I think for her painless, for I never in all my days felt a
> feeling like that. It seers through you. I remember feeling the wetness of
> her stomach when we did it. That's funny, isn't it, that I should remem-
> ber such things. We went in swimming to wash afterwards and then got
> dressed.[22]

Both Kerouac and Holmes kept diaries and journals when they were young, but we will never know what it was that made them turn to empty pages and begin filling them with words. Later Holmes noted in an autobiographical sketch that when he was eleven, he suddenly wrote his first poem in Englewood in ten minutes, telling of a glimpse he'd had of "someone's maid—coming up the road behind the house on the way to work." He didn't say *why* he wrote the poem—if, at the age of eleven, he knew himself—though he remembered that at the moment "it seemed necessary to capture the feeling."[23] He did come close once to revealing what it was that he felt had driven him to begin thinking in the larger ideas that came to dominate his writing. It was the day of the flood in 1936, when he'd stood on the New Hampshire river bank as its torrents swept past him. "And I had no words to deal with the perception, and thereby discovered the reality, and the necessity, of words. I ached to build pilings that would withstand the flood in me."[24]

Neither Kerouac nor Holmes ever explained fully what drove them to their lifelong obsession with putting their thoughts and stories into words. Holmes, however, as he continued in his endless quest for reasons and explanations, thought he found a partial answer in the New England consciousness that he and Kerouac shared, and in an essay he allowed himself the poetic freedom to try to capture the essence of his feeling.

Elective affinities, correspondences, analogies. Oh, New England, how you curse your scribblers with a double-view! The autumn twilight haunted by burnt August in the wood smoke; skeletal tree-shadows on virgin snow in the piercing clarity of winter-sun; the loosening loam and early budlets of hesitant, pastel spring; the summers, languid and abuzz and brief, tinged with the fore-knowledge of the red and yellow withering to come—in such seasonal places the senses are poised, keen, made avaricious by the immanence of change. The imagination smolders, flares, dies, only to flare again. And boys in attic rooms in redbrick factory towns, or in the kerosene kitchens of upland farms, or in sight of deep water in the Bostons and New Bedfords of the region, sit up late, alone, and one night start to write.[25]

Chapter 3

WHATEVER WORLD THERE WOULD BE

Those big elms stirring in the summer wind; that little depot platform on Long Island where the rails glinted in the late-morning sun back toward New York; those other discharges waiting quietly there beside the gum machines, oddly self-absorbed, quits now with the immense, chaotic event that had held us together; the canvas bag containing everything I owned—the ludicrous Jack Tar duds that condemn a man to looking a boy, and a couple of books, You Can't Go Home Again *and* Mrs. Dalloway. . . . *The unsettling realization that I might be anywhere that night, just anywhere the hours took me; consciousness of a beginning. . . . I was nineteen, medicated-out for chronic migraine, and I didn't care. Whatever world there would be was down the rails.*
—JOHN CLELLON HOLMES, "Clearing the Field"[1]

Although Holmes and Kerouac never lost their sense of their New England roots, it was to be New York that was their scene for twenty years, despite occasional periods away from the city and the scattering of the group of friends who brought them together. They each came to New York as teenagers, but Kerouac was older, and he was the first to arrive. Of all the anomalies of Kerouac's life, one of the most unexpected was that he came to New York City as a football player on a scholarship.

Kerouac had entered Lowell High School as a sophomore in 1936, and the athletic coaches quickly realized that he had natural talent. He was fast enough for the track team and muscular enough to become a star high school running back. He had the quick speed and balance that compensated for his medium-tall size. In high school this usually will be enough for a sports letter and a picture in the year book. Kerouac's year book football photograph captures him in full flight, the ball under his arm, his eyes looking ahead as he turns downfield. He was the kind of runner that the coach Lou Little at Columbia College in New York City recruited for his flashy offense formations, so Kerouac was offered a football scholarship to Columbia. There was one condition; that he spend a year at a Columbia preparatory school, Horace Mann, in the Bronx, north of Manhattan, to be better prepared academically for Columbia's classes. Kerouac was from the familiar New England mill town immigrant background that the coaches had met before, and their expectations were high.

Kerouac graduated from Lowell High School on June 28, 1939, and at the end of the summer he went to live with his mother's stepmother, who had an apartment in Brooklyn. The year at Horace Mann School was stressful. In his first months he was intimidated by the wealthy students who were brought to the campus in the family car while he commuted on the subway. With his relatives in Brooklyn he continued to speak *joual*, his dialect of French, but he spent his hours on the subway immersed in his homework. He was soon more at ease with the school's atmosphere. He met another student named Seymour Wyse who brought him to Harlem to listen to jazz, he published his first piece of fiction in the school literary magazine, and he wrote articles about sports and jazz for the Horace Mann paper.

The contradictions that confused the people in Kerouac's classes—the distance between the two poles of literature and football—never seemed to trouble Kerouac himself. He went back to Lowell for some of his weekends, and outside the school he quickly adapted to New York City's moods and tempo. Another student, Henri Cru, a tall, good-looking, dark-haired boy with a French background who had spent his early high school years abroad at a boarding school near Paris, become Kerouac's guide to the different New York world. They stayed friends, but Cru never finished his year at Horace Mann. He came from a comfortable background—his father was head of the French Department at Columbia University—but he was the family's difficult child, and he was dismissed from Horace Mann for selling condoms and switchblade knives to other students.

In September 1940 Kerouac entered Columbia and was assigned to the freshman squad on the football team. His career was short. In his first game he showed flashes of the brilliance that had brought him to Columbia, but he broke his leg in a heavy tackle in the second game and for months he had to get to classes on crutches. His success in his classes was a mirror of his interests. He did well in French and literature but failed chemistry, and he had to spend the summer of 1941 in Lowell making up the credits.

The differences in their ages never was important in the long friendship between Holmes and Kerouac, but though it was something they couldn't have anticipated, their ages in the last months of 1941 would have a decisive effect on their lives. When Pearl Harbor was attacked, Holmes was fifteen and Kerouac was nineteen. Holmes was still too young for the army or navy, while Kerouac was an obvious candidate for one of the military services. By their own accounts of their role in the war, neither was a hero. Kerouac had no political opinions that would have led him to become involved in the war, unlike Holmes, who had already as a teenager become militantly anti-fascist and was dismayed by the success of the German armies in Europe. In his teens Holmes had been moved by the anti-war films he had seen, and though not considering himself a pacifist he was unsure what use wars were.

Kerouac had no feelings about pacifism. He was at that moment clearly right-wing. In his journal for the period November 26–December 15, 1940, he enthusiastically endorsed Anne Morrow Lindbergh's *The Wave of the Future: A Confession of Faith* (1940), in which she describes Nazism as one of the "Forces of the Future," not one of the "'Forces of Evil.'" What was important for Kerouac was that "Hitlerism" promised "Economic freedom— that is, all shall eat."[2] It was also a sign of the anti-Semitism he had taken from his family, and that he only half-heartedly attempted to conceal from his friends.

In the fall of 1941, following his parents' relocation to New Haven in the summer for his father's new job as a linotype operator, Kerouac began his sophomore year at Columbia. Perhaps emotionally disturbed by his family's move from his childhood neighborhoods, he quickly quarreled with the football coaches when he was placed on the junior varsity team instead of the varsity, left the team, and abandoned his scholarship to Columbia.

Kerouac was uncomfortably aware that his parents were disgusted with him and he didn't want to move back home. Instead he went to Hartford, where he found a room, took a job at a gasoline station, and began writing a collection of short stories. The improving economic situation as the United States began to prepare for what seemed to be an impending war in Europe eventually made it possible for his parents to return to Lowell, where they found a new apartment in their old French-Canadian neighborhood. Although they were still upset with him, Kerouac immediately moved back home to his mother's hovering attentions and her cooking and found a job working as a sports reporter for the Lowell *Sun*. His situation with his father, Leo, never comfortable, had become even more tense after Kerouac had left Columbia. Leo was convinced that his son was a failure and that without any kind of education he would never have a real future.

Only a few weeks later, on December 7, 1941, the attack on Pearl Harbor changed the situation for Kerouac. This was a different war. In a fever of patriotism he rushed to sign up for an examination for the Naval Air Force, but learned there would be a delay before he was notified he'd been accepted. To escape the continuing tensions with his father, Kerouac abandoned his newspaper job in the early spring of 1942 and traveled to Washington, where he took a brief construction job working on the new Pentagon building. He returned to Lowell later in the spring, abruptly enlisted in the U.S. Marines in June, and then only a few hours later impulsively joined the Merchant Marine. Between July and October of 1942 he sailed on the SS *Dorchester*, a merchant ship transporting a construction crew and supplies to support military bases in Greenland. Kerouac was fortunate; on its next voyage through the North Atlantic, the ship was sunk by German torpedoes and all its crew lost.

When Kerouac, now twenty years old, returned to New York in the fall of 1942, he immediately looked up his friend from Horace Mann, Henri Cru, who had also enlisted in the Merchant Marine in the fervor of the first war months. Cru was now romantically involved with a girl named Edie Parker from Grosse Pointe, Michigan. She had left her sheltered, middle-class suburban life and moved to New York City to study art, and she was living with her grandmother in the same Upper West Side apartment building as Cru's family. In early October Cru had recognized her one night at the West End bar, a few weeks before Kerouac returned to New York. Soon Henri and Edie began a tentative affair, with neither of them sure where their relationship was leading. Although in her photographs from these years Edie looks thin, her face often anxious, with a loose tangle of hair and a muscular body, Cru considered her one of the most exciting women he'd ever seen, with sexy legs and a body as firm as an Olympic gymnast.

Cru finally decided that their relationship meant more to Edie than to him, and when Kerouac met him again he was planning to leave New York on another merchant ship. Cru was conscious that Edie and Jack had been instantly drawn to each other. Later what Edie remembered was that she was struck by Kerouac's good looks.

> *[Jack's] face was black-browed and firm-nosed, with the expressive curve of lips and the dark, somehow tender eyes that move you so in a loyal, sensitive animal. But it was the purity in that face, scowl or smile, that struck you first. You realized that the emotions surfaced on it unimpeded. Mothers warmed to him immediately; they thought him nice, respectful, even shy. Girls inspected him, their gazes snagged by those bony, Breton good looks, that ingathered aura of dense, some how buried maleness.[3]*

As Cru was leaving for his new merchant ship after the Christmas holidays in January 1943, he impulsively asked Kerouac to take care of Edie while he was at sea. Kerouac's affair with her began almost immediately after Cru's departure. For a few weeks he and Edie were together day and night. She remembered that Kerouac was an enthusiastic if bashful lover.

> *We slept together for eight months before we saw each other naked. He wore boxer shorts and I kept a sheet wrapped around me. If he heard a sound in the apartment he would quickly jump into his pants, which were always beside the bed. His skin was salty, his body odorless. When we made love I'd get prickly heat from his wiry chest hair.*[4]

Kerouac finally took the exam for the Naval Air Force program in January 1943, but it was a difficult exam, and he failed to pass. Still desperate to be in the service in some capacity, he enlisted in the U.S. Navy and was sent to boot camp in Newport, Rhode Island. He spent only a few months in the navy. During his training, he was incapable of following orders. After several reprimands for insubordination he was transferred to Bethesda, Maryland, for a series of psychiatric tests and confined to his room as the doctors examined him. He was finally diagnosed as suffering from "schizoid tendencies" and released from the navy in June 1943 with a psychiatric discharge. In another sign of the antagonism between Kerouac and his father, Leo, congratulated him, since he hated Roosevelt and continued to support Hitler, while Gabrielle Kerouac was only sorry that her son was no longer in the navy.

Edie Parker's explanation of Kerouac's failure to accept navy discipline reflected her love for him and her easy-going optimism:

> *Jack's personality fit into many categories—that was the kind of man he was. The Navy discharged him, in fact, for being schizoid, for having a split personality. In other words, one side was all man, while the other side was all intellectual—a poet and a dreamer. Sometimes one side of Jack would take over the other side and he would become depressed and melancholy; his family called him moody. I always ignored all his moods, and he was far too interested in everything to stay long in any depression.*[5]

Earlier, alone in Manhattan with Cru at sea and Kerouac in boot camp, Edie found a job at Best & Company, a fashionable Fifth Avenue department store, modeling clothes and working as a salesperson. She soon realized there was a problem. "It wasn't long before I noticed that something was wrong. Things were happening to my body, and I realized I was pregnant."[6] With no one else for support she told her grandmother, who was able to arrange for an abortion through a friend. The doctor told Edie she was three months pregnant, and he could take care of her, but she should wait two more months until the fetus was more advanced.

Finally Edie's doctor induced premature labor, and after hours of pain she had a still-born black-haired son. She wrote later that it was her confusion as to which of the men might have been the baby's father that decided her to have the abortion, but it seems clear that finally she was certain it was Jack's. While she was recuperating at her grandmother's apartment, Cru returned and was stunned at what had happened. He immediately insisted that they get married, but Edie refused.

A short time later, when Kerouac was released from the navy, all three met at the West End Bar. When Kerouac was told about the abortion, he became furious. Edie wrote that she never saw him so angry. After threatening to hit Cru, he stormed out of the bar. Edie remembered that Cru calmed her down, insisting that it would be all right, and at two in the morning, as Cru had predicted, there was a knock on the door of her grandmother's apartment. Since the older woman was hard of hearing and always went to bed early, Edie and Jack frequently came in and out of the apartment at late hours. Edie remembered,

It was Jack. He was sweating and seemed a little drunk. He asked me, "Don't you know I love you?" "Well, yes . . . I guess so," I said. He came in and we talked for a while about what we were going to do about our feelings. In the end we decided to try to find an apartment and live together.[7]

With their slender financial resources there was no way they could find an apartment themselves, so they moved into the small apartment of one of Edie's friends from her art classes at Columbia, Joan Vollmer Adams. Finally Edie and Joan began looking for another apartment with an extra bedroom where she could stay with Kerouac, even though he was working again as a merchant seaman. Two months later Kerouac signed aboard the SS *George Weems* as an ordinary merchant seaman headed for Liverpool, returning to New York City in October 1943.

It was Edie Parker who was to be the center of Kerouac's life for the next two years, through all the confusions that beset each of them, and even through the complications of their brief and unsuccessful marriage. Another Columbia student, Lucien Carr, who met Kerouac through Edie, felt that Edie "really was the best woman Jack ever got involved with, bar none. They were *perfect*, really perfect. . . . Jack couldn't be led, he was recalcitrant, and he was a pig, but he was everything in a man she ever thought 'could' exist."[8]

The earliest loose confederation of what would be called "the Beat Generation" collected on the Upper West Side of Manhattan at 421 West 118th Street in the apartment that Edie and Joan rented together. The lease was signed in the name of Mr. and Mrs. John Adams and Mr. and Mrs. Jack Kerouac. Joan had an allowance from her family for her studies at Barnard, as well as a monthly military stipend for herself and her infant daughter with her husband, Paul Adams, an army officer stationed in Europe. Edie also had an allowance from a family trust, so there was enough money for them to sign their lease.

Jack and Edie began officially living together on December 31, 1943. They both took jobs to help with the rent. Kerouac found a part-time job at the Columbia University cafeteria, only a few blocks away, hoping that he might be able to steal food sometimes to help keep them going. There was such a shortage of workers that Edie found employment as a longshoreman on the docks. She turned up for work bundled in sweaters against the cold, and since she wasn't as strong as the others in the work crew, she spent most of her time operating a fork lift.

It was at this rundown apartment a few blocks north of the Columbia campus and the West End bar that the early Beat group slowly gathered. Edie had noticed Lucien Carr across the studio in an art class she was auditing at Columbia. Struck by his good looks, she introduced him to Kerouac. Carr and his undergraduate friends, including another Columbia student whose room was down the dormitory corridor from his, Allen Ginsberg, were soon climbing the stairs to Joan and Edie's apartment. Through Carr the crowd also was introduced to an older man from St. Louis, Carr's hometown. This was William Burroughs, who had a small income from his family and was already involved with drugs. Soon after meeting Joan Adams, Burroughs began an affair with her.

Of all of them in the group it was Kerouac who was most committed to the idea of being a writer, and if there wasn't a party going on he sat up all night writing. To Carr and Burroughs he was the "writer." Two novels and parts of novels came out of Kerouac's nights of writing in the West 118th Street apartment. The first, *The Sea Is My Brother*, drew on his experiences as a merchant seaman. It was written in a romantic style derived from Thomas Wolfe. The second, *Orpheus Emerged*, used the milieu of the

Columbia campus and their apartment. Clearly recognizable among the characters is a voluble, likeable undergraduate named "Leo" who is modeled on the very young Ginsberg. Through the strained overwriting it is also possible to glimpse Kerouac's view of himself as the character "Michael" in the role of Leo's teacher. As they walk together near campus, they see a bird perched on the top branch of a tree.

> Leo laughed, "Hail to thee, blithe spirit. . . ."
> "No," cried Michael, "quiet, Leo. Listen to him. Do you remember what I was telling you about the impulse of God? The sparrow there is expressing it. He knows. Listen!"⁹

As a not yet twenty-two-year-old would-be novelist, Kerouac was teaching himself how to be a writer. Later the poet Robert Creeley understood that: "No one's told him how to write other than what he's got from books as best he can. There's no defining tradition for such as he is, no social habit sustaining him."¹⁰ For the others in Kerouac's crowd, the fact that he was trying to become a novelist was enough to mark him as unique.

At some point Jack and Edie decided that they should get married, since that was the usual relationship for couples during those years, even with the turmoil of the war. They got as far as their blood tests, but she still hesitated, since she was conscious that she would lose her allowance from her family, and Kerouac had promised faithfully to send his seaman's pay to his mother. The marriage finally took place, but under the pressure of circumstances neither of them could have foreseen.

In a series of events that were later to become familiar to the readers of Kerouac's books,¹¹ Lucien Carr was dogged by an older admirer, David Kammerer, who at one time had been his scoutmaster. In August 1944 Kammerer attempted to force Carr into a physical relationship one drunken night when they were sitting alone in Riverside Drive Park close to the Hudson River. In his panic Carr took out his penknife and stabbed Kammerer to death. Frightened at what he'd done, he pushed the body in the Hudson River, and then in desperation, some hours later he turned to his friends, making them accessories to his crime. Kerouac helped him conceal the knife, and later Carr went to Burroughs to ask him what to do. Both Kerouac and Burroughs were convinced that Carr had to turn himself in to the police, but it was many more hours before he could finally bring himself to do it. The next morning Edie and Jack were wakened by police pounding on their door. Kerouac was arrested and taken to the a city jail as an accessory to Kammerer's murder. Burroughs was questioned by the police as a witness, but his parents arranged for him to retain an attorney, so he was free on bail.

The charges against Kerouac were finally reduced to material witness and the amount of bail was substantially lowered, but his father angrily refused to help get him out of jail. Edie was the only one Jack could turn to, but she could get no money from her trust fund unless they were married. The police agreed to release Kerouac long enough for the ceremony. Whatever the circumstances, it was Edie's wedding day, so she went to buy a wedding dress accompanied by Lucien's girlfriend, Celine Young. Edie had a cousin who was working at Best & Company, and later Edie remembered,

> She said she had just the outfit, "not too dressy and great for a jailhouse wedding." We all giggled at that. She brought a Paris creation out of the back room that was not even on display yet. I tried it on. It had a creamy white top, large dolman sleeves nipped in at the wrists with tiny buttons down the front. It fitted tight at the waist and then flared out to a peplum. The skirt was black and semi-full, stopping just below the knees. It had a low neckline but you could button it up as high as you wanted. I must say I've never looked as good in an outfit again. We picked out a pair of high-heeled shoes and an envelope-type purse to match.[12]

The cost of the wedding outfit was $125, which Edie charged to her grandmother. On the afternoon of August 22, 1944, Edie and Jack were rushed to City Hall where Kerouac—handcuffed to the detective who had brought him from jail—repeated his marriage vows before a bored judge. Once Edie was married, her family sent the money for Kerouac to be released on bail after he'd spent nine days in jail.

Whatever Edie had dreamed of her marriage, the dream quickly dissipated. Her family in Grosse Point was appalled at what had happened. Leo and Gabrielle, however, were pleased that their son was marrying someone whom they thought must be an heiress. Soon after Kerouac had enlisted in the navy, his parents had left Lowell and moved to Ozone Park in Queens to take jobs in defense plants. They welcomed their new daughter-in-law with an elaborate family dinner, hoping that the young couple would move into a room in the Kerouac apartment. The anticipation was that, like a woman from Leo and Gabrielle's own background, Edie would continue working, and she would turn over both her trust fund allowance and her paychecks to her mother-in-law. Kerouac, however, was so upset that Edie's family had paid his bail that he felt it was an obligation that he had to re-pay immediately. Instead of staying with his parents, they moved to Grosse Point and lived uncomfortably with her parents in their Grosse Point man-sion while Kerouac worked at a defense plant at a job Edie's father found for him. When Kerouac had earned enough to clear the debt, he left Edie there with her parents and he returned to sea.

In New York City Kerouac signed up for a merchant seaman's voyage to Italy on the SS *Robert Treat Paine*, but he stayed with the ship only as far as Norfolk, Virginia. He found himself so bullied by a sadistic bosun, who called him "Pretty Boy, Baby Face," that he hastily disembarked and caught a bus back to New York City. After this incident Kerouac was blacklisted by the Maritime Union for a year. He was so upset about his inability to make any kind of living that after he came back to New York he hid for a short time, surreptitiously living in a dormitory room Ginsberg found for him at Columbia. When Edie returned to Manhattan and reunited with Kerouac in the fall of 1944, they moved into a new, large six-room communal apart-ment Joan had rented at 419 West 115th Street near Amsterdam Avenue, adjoining the Columbia dormitories of Hartley Hall and Livingstone Hall, where Ginsberg lived as an undergraduate until his expulsion in March 1945.

Soon the new apartment became the center for the old crowd. Over the next year virtually everyone who was associated with the early Beat movement—Burroughs, Kerouac, Ginsberg, Herbert Huncke, Hal Chase, and many others—drifted in and out, some of them staying for extended periods. The crowd had now moved on from alcohol to drugs, including morphine and Benzedrine obtained from drugstore nasal inhalers after Burroughs began injecting morphine in December 1944. Edie would come back from her job to find everyone sprawled together on the bed or the couch, too comatose to communicate. She wrote later, "I was the only one working, and most of the time we were eating mayonnaise sandwiches. . . . Jack called it a year of 'low, evil decadence.'"[13]

The continual pressure of dealing with the drug scene, holding her job, and dealing with Kerouac's increasing unhappiness finally became too much for Edie. She remembered that "by May [1945] the situation with Jack and the wear of working to support everyone and the whole scene pushed me over the edge. I left and went to live with my grandmother at her house in Asbury Park for the summer."[14] In the fall of 1945 Leo was diagnosed with cancer of the spleen, and Kerouac agreed to stay home in Ozone Park to care for him while Gabrielle supported the family by working in a Brook-lyn factory. Edie had finally moved back to Michigan, and after months of indecision she gave in to her mother's insistence and filed for annulment of the marriage on September 18, 1946.

Holmes' life also went through many changes during the war years. Although at first he was too young to face military service, the early years of the war were emotionally turbulent for him as his mother and father went though the trauma of separation and divorce. In the fall of 1942, when Kerouac had returned to New York after his tour of duty on the SS *Dorchester*, Holmes came back to Englewood after his summer in Los Angeles. He was sixteen, expecting to begin his junior year at Dwight Morrow High School, where his sister Lila had just graduated. His mother greeted him with the news that she had decided to leave New Jersey. To economize on expenses during her separation from John's father, Betty Holmes was moving into her married sister Martha's large home in Chappaqua, New York, where John, Liz, and Lila would also be welcome.

Betty Holmes' decision to leave Englewood came as a painful surprise. There had already been a numbing succession of moves and Holmes had begun over again in so many new schools that this time he balked at the thought of entering an unfamiliar high school as a member of the junior class. He protested to his mother that he faced the military draft in eighteen months, so what was the point of starting in a new high school if he didn't even have time to graduate? With persistent badgering, he won over his mother's reluctance. On October 2, 1942, after less than a month in the junior class at Dwight Morrow, Holmes dropped out of school and moved with his mother and two sisters to 13 Bedford Road in Chappaqua.

The countryside around Chappaqua and its neighboring town, Mt. Kisco, is one of the most tranquil, luminously beautiful landscapes north of New York City, but for Holmes it was only a background for the torment of adolescence he felt after leaving Englewood. On November 2, 1942, his mother signed a work permit that enabled him to apply for a job at the *Reader's Digest* magazine, which had moved its national headquarters to the quiet countryside. His mother and his older sister, Lila, had already found employment there working alongside his aunt Martha. With the shortage of able-bodied help during wartime, Holmes was also put to work that winter stuffing envelopes and labeling addresses on circulars and magazines in the subscription department at the *Reader's Digest*. He also taught himself to type with his two index fingers. He found his job unspeakably boring, but he started to smoke a pipe in an attempt to make a more mature impression on the people he worked with. Six feet tall, rail-thin, and just getting over two years of bad acne, he let his dark blonde hair grow long and slicked it back in the then-popular pompadour style with a high front wave that he thought (along with his pipe and the thick horn-rimmed glasses he wore for reading and watching movies) would make him look—at least to his nine-year-old adoring sister Liz—"sort of intellectual."[15]

After a few months working at the magazine, Betty Holmes rented a small cottage with a thatched roof in the Tudor style for her family, and they moved out of her sister's house. Holmes soon found himself alone. After living only a short time in Chappaqua, Lila married her fiancé and moved south with him when he began his training as a fighter pilot in the air force. In June 1943, when Liz finished the fourth grade, she and her mother rode the train cross-country to Aunt Dorothy's house in Altadena, California. Shortly afterwards Betty spent six weeks in Reno to establish the necessary residence to file for a Nevada divorce so that her ex-husband could marry again.

On his own for the first time, Holmes spent his salary on a collection of twenty pipes and exotic tobaccos and quarts of beer and on the jazz records he listened to constantly. After he came home from work he took off the dingy suit and tie he wore to his office job and put on a large flannel button-down lounging jacket with commodious pockets. Later he looked back at this time and wondered, "I was born for the 30's and my time was over. Did I start thinking like an old man then?"[16]

With his new sense of independence, John left his job at the *Reader's Digest* and rode the commuter train to Grand Central Station in Manhattan to work a temporary summer clerical job at a Wall Street firm. After office hours he enrolled in an evening Composition Class in the School of General Studies at Columbia University, a non-degree summer program that didn't require a high school transcript. He and Kerouac could have crossed each other's paths at almost any point in these months, after Kerouac had left the navy and returned to live with Edie Parker on the Upper West Side of Manhattan, but their first meeting would have to wait.

Holmes, like Kerouac, spent most of his free time reading and writing, the determined apprenticeship that they shared and that was to be the basis of their friendship. On his mother's bookshelves Holmes found Somerset Maugham novels, which were considered minor potboilers, but at Columbia he read James T. Farrell's novel-trilogy *Studs Lonigan* and in his classes discussed Ernest Hemingway's importance as a modern stylist. With a nearly obsessive need to write, Holmes found that his college composition course bolstered his confidence. He had begun writing what he remembered as "a windy novel"[17] before giving it up in Los Angeles, but that summer in Chappaqua he filled several spiral notebooks, writing two or three short stories a week and a novel about jazz that he nearly completed in three weeks.

At the *Reader's Digest* he had become interested in a woman three years older than himself, but just as inexperienced. Her name was Marian Milliambro, an attractive Italian-American who lived in a tiny garden house in Chappaqua with her mother and three brothers. Marian was sensitive about her diminutive height and broad hips, but she had beautiful long brown hair, intense brown eyes, a dark complexion, and a thin mouth that smiled easily. As the daughter of an Italian immigrant who worked as a gardener and handyman on the town's wealthy estates, she had no expectation of going on to college after she graduated from high school, so she had begun working full time at the *Reader's Digest*. Intensely self-conscious that she came from a working-class home, she felt herself to be John and Betty Holmes' social inferior, but she was also spirited and combative.

They first met on a bus soon after Holmes started his own job at the magazine. Later in his memoir *Nothing More to Declare* he wrote,

> *She had a knee bandage on when I first saw her, she was wearing a short box-back coat, a strand of dime-store pearls glimmered in the hollow of her throat, sitting on a muddy country bus, going to work. . . . Daring anyone to notice that her feet did not quite touch the floor. I don't remember the first time I took her out, or kissed her; I only remember the feeling of irony, recent hurt, and a certain tough-mindedness that hung around her face. I thought I saw an ally there.*[18]

After his mother's emotional reserve and her preoccupation with the uncertainties of her own life, Holmes was drawn to Marian's warm affection and good nature as much as he was drawn to her interest in him. They met at a moment when she was particularly vulnerable. She had been emotionally closer to her father than to anyone else in her family, and she was devastated by his unexpected death from a heart attack a few months before she met Holmes. Soon he was so involved with her that it upset him to see that she was still deeply depressed over the loss of her father. What confused him at the same time was that they had no real interests in common. It was the lonely summer and their emotional needs that drew them together. She showed no interest in the books he was reading, and something that was an even more sensitive point for him, she didn't share his enthusiasm for jazz music, though he tried hard for months to convert her.

During the summer of 1943 they made the rounds of traditional jazz clubs in Manhattan together. Even with his horn-rimmed glasses, his fancy hair style, and his pipe, seventeen-year-old Holmes still looked too young and gawky in his business suit to be admitted into a bar, but Marian appeared poised and confident for her twenty years. As a couple they could walk into a club, order a couple of beers, and stand close at the bar while he earnestly attempted to explain the music to her between the band numbers.

In his novel *Go*, written six years later, Holmes made his relationship with Marian the book's emotional center. She was named "Kathryn Hobbes," while he called himself "Paul Hobbes," and in the novel he wrote with painful honesty (and with echoes of D. H. Lawrence's prose cadences) about how he had bullied her into having sex with him.

> *With spring, his mother left for Reno to get a divorce so that his father could re-marry, and during her absence he and Kathryn slept together. He had been roughly suggesting it for weeks, relying on the conflict of fear and desire that occupied her. Finally, with cold, adult resolve, they made arrangements for her to come to his empty house one day.*
>
> *He watched her through the windows as she came down the lane under fretful trees that were heavy with rain—an absorbed little figure, self-conscious even though alone, defiant when passing other houses, her head thrown back with lofty disdain but her steps hesitant. They sat in his untidy, darkened room, pledged to it. After a while, after awkward embraces, and excitements that were intensified because of this very stumbling, they shyly undressed, wishing they had not promised themselves; somehow unable, after they faced each other in that dim room, naked but without innocence, to draw back.*
>
> *When his mother returned, Hobbes vaguely mentioned marriage to her, feeling no less discomfort than she but throwing it at her as if it were the threat of an action he would institute only if she raised objections to it. On top of his imminent draft, the thought of his marriage at so young an age dismayed her, but sensing his indecision, she did not rebuke him and he let it ride.*[19]

In the fall of 1943, after his mother and sister Liz returned to Chappaqua, Holmes reluctantly went back to his job at the *Reader's Digest*. He was upset because he was determined to write a novel with "psychological overtones,"[20] and he was certain that he wouldn't be able to complete it if he were forced to work a day job. The success he'd had writing essays and sketches for his college instructor encouraged him, and he wrote in his journal on October 1, 1943, "I like to do character, and so far I have had some luck in the things that I have written in that line." He was filled with dreams about what he considered his budding career as a writer, already disappointed because he knew that he wouldn't see any of his work published before he was drafted. His mother assured him that he had the necessary talent to become a professional writer, but his father, who still was in contact with the family, insisted that he had to stay at his full-time job until he was drafted. Holmes confided to his journal, "I know I won't be able to do anything of any consequence. To be a craftsman one must work at it all the time. I know that. You've got to think, eat, sleep and live writing."[21] He comforted himself with the thought that "when and if I get back [from the war] I'll be old enough to do as I please and to try to eke out a living at what I want to."[22]

Holmes received his draft notice in the spring of 1944, soon after his eighteenth birthday. At his draft board interview he found that every tenth draftee went into the navy, and he was the tenth in line. He served in the navy from June 20, 1944, to June 18, 1945, two days short of a full year. His extreme myopia kept him stationed in the United States, but the fact that he'd done well in his summer class at Columbia indicated to his examiners that he was intelligent enough to handle responsibility. Unlike Kerouac, who had been unable to accept the discipline of navy boot camp, Holmes completed his training. He was sent off to San Diego to be trained as a medic and graduated with the rank of hospital apprentice, second class.

Holmes went home on a four-day leave before he was scheduled to board a train to Southern California to begin his hospital training. Marian Milliambro met him in Manhattan on his return from boot camp so they could wait together for the train back to Chappaqua. Sitting together on a bench, Holmes felt closer to her than he ever had before and was "suddenly struck wordless by her palpable presence there."

> *I felt the actual suspiration of her breath, the stubborn life animating her small limbs; I glimpsed her consciousness going on and on beyond my selfish desire, and opened toward it willingly, selfless, for once . . . for she seemed to be everything that is contained in that fragrant and unsettling word, girl. It was our closest moment, we were dumb with quiet awareness, something passed between us, something that stilled the words in my astonished mouth.*[23]

Impulsively John and Marian decided to get married. They rode the subway downtown to City Hall for a license, and on August 30, 1944, a minister performed the simple ceremony in a small Episcopal church on lower Fifth Avenue in Manhattan. The couple spent a honeymoon night in a nearby hotel before Holmes set off the next day for the U.S. Naval Hospital Corps Training School in San Diego. As another "eerie correspondence," their marriage took place only a week after Edie and Jack had been married by a New York judge at City Hall.

In San Diego, lonely and far from home, Holmes wrote despairing letters to his young wife, complaining, "Today has been long, exhausting, and lonely. I found myself thinking of you during the various and sundry trivia which they throw at us here."[24] A few weeks later, Holmes was so disturbed by the sight of the maimed bodies of the wounded sailors sent back to the hospital from battles in the Pacific—nearly five thousand sailors had been wounded on Guadalcanal and Okinawa, and many had been shipped back to the hospital in San Diego for treatment—that he went behind the mess hall to weep.[25] Lying on his bunk with the other sailors after a day in the wards, Holmes felt helpless against his visions of the war, "millions everywhere struggling in a kind of murky darkness against enemies that could see them plainly and aimed with precision."[26] As he listened to the men talking in their bunks, he came close to sobs, restraining himself from rising up and screaming to everyone in earshot, "Change this, change it, change it before you become dead as it is!"[27]

Worried about her young husband's emotional state, Marian wanted to join him in San Diego, but she had never left New York and was apprehensive about the move. In late September 1944, Betty and Liz, who had both become very fond of Marian, decided that Holmes sounded so unhappy in his letters that they should all move together to Southern California to be close to him. The two of them could stay with Aunt Dorothy in Altadena while Marian went on to join John in San Diego. Years later Holmes said that his only good memory from his time in San Diego was of the great sex he enjoyed with Marian in her room at a residence hotel when he could slip away from the naval hospital for an hour or two to join her.

Holmes' training as a hospital orderly included studying a large manual consisting of scores of mimeographed pages on anatomy and physiology, including sheets of instruction about such things as pressure points, field dressings, and slings for fractured parts of the body. The final words in the manual reminded him that "NO CASE IS HOPELESS." Holmes saved his quizzes, defining terms such as "wound," "laceration," and "severe burn," as well as his "special exam" on September 29, 1944, on the treatment of an appendicitis patient referred by the X-ray department. Marian's stay in San Diego lasted only a few months, since by the second week of December Holmes found himself on a troop train being sent back across the United States to assume his duties at St. Albans Naval Hospital on Long Island,

New York. Clinging to his identity as a writer, he began another spiral note-book in San Diego on October 5, 1944, that he filled with poetry and plot ideas for short stories, and later he kept a record of his progress on the train taking him back to New York by dating the poems he wrote in a spiral notebook previously used to jot down nursing notes for the treatment of pneumonia and the "care of delirious patients in restraints." These poems began on December 10, 1944, with "Resurrection" written "somewhere in Texas"; December 11, 1944, "Tone Poem" written "somewhere in Arkansas"; and December 12, 1944, "Anthem in Transit" written "somewhere in Ohio."[28]

After Holmes left San Diego, Betty and Liz remained in California while Marian returned to New York City. She took a secretarial job and rented a small furnished room with a kitchenette on 96th Street, close to Central Park. As a married man Holmes could spend time there with his wife when he was off-duty, resting and listening to his favorite jazz records when he wasn't suffering from the frequent headaches that began after he took up his punishing duties at the hospital. Often trails of memories take years to make their way to the surface, and Holmes' horrific experiences during the year he spent in the navy hospitals didn't make their way into his writing until many years had passed. It wasn't until 1981, answering a question from interviewers, that he could respond spontaneously that his experiences in these months had been "shaping, maturing, severing, valuable."[29] It is a general assumption that someone who has not been in combat has not been tested by war's worst terrors, but Holmes' experience was harrowing in its own way. A quarter of a century later he still awoke from disturbing dreams of things he'd seen and heard in the crowded wards in the navy hospitals in San Diego and Long Island.

Holmes' duties sometimes brought him into New York City from Long Island, riding as an ambulance orderly to pick up sailors who had become ill as they celebrated their shore leaves in Manhattan, many with meningitis contracted in their overseas' assignments. He had to help drag them out of bars along Third Avenue, often the same bars where a year later he would be drinking himself. In the wards he found himself forced to inflict pain on the bedridden, inserting a catheter into a man's penis as the man lay helpless, and experiencing the agonizing pain almost as though it were his own. He cleaned thigh wounds so deep that his fingers could touch the bare bone. Despite his distress about the scenes he was witnessing, he couldn't help becoming close to the men in his care, even though he saw them as patients for only a brief time. He counted fifty of the men he nursed who died during the six months he worked in the Long Island hospital. For a hundred more who were left crippled and for whom "no June night would promise them anything but bitterness,"[30] he felt the same unhappy rush of sympathy and helplessness. He was haunted by memories of what he had seen at St. Albans Hospital,

> the whole garish nightmare world, where there was no sense, no reason, no end . . .that horrible red and black world of splintered pieces, the terrible fragments, still vaguely stirring in the ruins, fragments of living things, senselessly striking at themselves and all reality over and over again. A spiritual carnage that made the blood run cold. Men, boys, beaten, twisted, broken, out of mind and heart and soul too cruelly ripped. When I worked there, and thought there, and lived there, something inside me grew cold with terror. It was as if in all that fantastic unreality I had come to know reality at last.[31]

At St. Albans, Holmes began to pray each morning for fifteen minutes in the three chapels located in the hospital, visiting the Protestant, Catholic, and Jewish chapels in turn. One morning he discovered "in a flash" that he was just indulging in a familiar ritual that his mother had taught him as a boy, and that he didn't really believe he was praying to anyone. It was the end of his belief in God and "the simple Unitarian faith my mother gave me."[32]

After Holmes finally reported his migraine headaches to the hospital doctors, he was assigned to a bed himself at St. Albans, scheduled for a series of clinical tests while the authorities began to process the paperwork necessary to obtain his medical discharge from the navy. Unexpectedly, Holmes' hours of free time gave him the opportunity to begin a friendship with an older man who became his first mentor. Standing in the pay line one Tuesday morning, Holmes met Jim Macguire, an editor of the hospital newspaper whose conversations were so intriguing that over the next few weeks Holmes became radicalized as a Marxist by the time he was mustered out of the navy.

It was in many ways a natural progression for him. As early as 1938, though Holmes was only twelve, he had already sensed the tensions of the approaching war after listening to conversations among his relatives at his grandmother's summer cottage, and he was certain that he was opposed to fascism. As he entered his adolescence he strongly supported the war, since one of its loudly proclaimed goals was to rid the world of fascists, even though the anti-war films he saw as a teenager made him lean toward pacifism. It was the suffering he saw in the navy hospitals as he tended the severely wounded that made him lose his faith in God and turned him into a fervent pacifist. After his conversations with Macguire, Holmes agreed that it was capitalism that led to war, and since he was opposed to war for any reasons, it was only logical that anti-capitalist Marxism might be the answer.

Ten years older than Holmes, Macguire was a persuasive teacher. He had graduated from Brown University in 1938, hitchhiked in Europe, and earned a doctorate in history from Trinity College in Dublin, Ireland, before being drafted into the navy. He was short, with graying hair, and married to an Irish girl who had returned to the United States with him after the birth of their child. Friendly and gregarious, he had overheard Holmes' futile attempt to strike up a conversation about T. S. Eliot's poetry with another sailor in the pay line. Eliot's poetry happened to be one of Macguire's favorite topics, along with Irish literature and mythology, modern art, and Marxism. Confined to St. Albans as a patient, with time heavy on his hands until his medical discharge, Holmes was thunderstruck—he could spend hours listening to Macguire, and he had never had the opportunity to exchange ideas with anyone so knowledgeable about literature and politics. After a week the two men were inseparable. On April 29, 1945, Holmes wrote in his journal, "I was more than willing to listen. So I trailed him about the halls, ate chow with him, talked to him in the library."

As a graduate student in Dublin, Macguire had fraternized with members of the IRA and been held by the police. He told Holmes that though he liked living in the United States, he was disappointed because "people aren't mad enough over here. The rule is normality. Sometimes I think that only idiosyncrasy is interesting."[33] Later Holmes' sister Liz met her brother's friend and remembered him as a "sharp, acerbic little man—thick glasses, small jolly eyes and quick little stabs of insight and prejudices."[34] Macguire was the first intellectual Holmes had ever met, and he admired his friend's belief that ideas were essential in order for people to feel themselves fully alive, that "there was something stimulating about people who thought."[35] Passionate about Marxist theory, Macguire had convinced himself that a new world order would arise after the war, bringing with it economic and political freedom for everyone on earth. Holmes listened intently and only argued when the topics shifted to the existence of God and the true worth of poetry, subjects on which Holmes felt on firmer ground. After several weeks of Macguire's tutorials, Holmes discarded all his earlier poetry: "I can no longer write sweet lyric poetry in the industrial age."[36]

In the end, Holmes' searing experiences as a medic in the hospital wards changed him more deeply than the new political consciousness he absorbed from Macguire. His stint in the navy caused a shift in the ground on which he had built his life. It was only years later that he was able to clarify it for himself.

Anti-fascist though I had been since twelve, the experience [of the Second World War] ended war for me. . . . I've never written about any of this, except glancingly. War-memories encourage romanticization, and my paltry-few would be demeaned by that approach, being mostly visceral, having to do with the simple frailty of the body, and the hard fact of the scarred future. It grew to seem a grotesque madness to me. Though ours was perhaps the last "just" war, a war in which my youth and ignorance "believed," I came into the conviction that though there are things worth dying for, there is nothing worth killing for. . . . What defenses does an 18-year-old have against a dark river of day-to-day horror? We had a nutward-maxim in those days: "If you go sponge, you get squeezed." Maybe, all these years later, the delayed-squeeze has come. I know, suddenly, the faces have come back. And I can't even remember the names.[37]

In June 1945 the navy doctors concluded that Holmes' chronic headaches made it impossible for him to continue his duties in the hospital, and he was granted an honorable discharge. When he later wrote about the physical details of the day of his discharge, the mood of his description took on a tone of elegy. For everyone who has been in any of the armed services, there are two intensely experienced days that are unforgettable in the familiar set of memories everyone bears with them: the first day spent as a bewildered and helpless inductee swallowed up by the service and the last day when it finally spits them out. As Holmes looked back later at the day when he left the discharge center, at last out of uniform, he could still feel the wind in the trees, the boredom of the other discharged sailors waiting in the Long Island railroad station for a train into Manhattan, and his own confusion over what was waiting for him when he came back to Marian and picked up their married life together. At nineteen years old, the only thing he knew about his future with any certainty was that he wanted to be a writer and that with his honorable discharge he would be qualified to continue his education under the GI Bill.

Immediately ahead was a room and a kitchenette on West 96th Street just off the Park, and a wife I had married impulsively on boot leave, and—I didn't know, except that I would never go back to the house in Westchester from which I had been inducted so many pulled-roots, so many self-discoveries ago. The house was broken up, my mother in

California, my father in Washington, my sisters, who knew where; everything dispersed, sold off, in storage. I had nothing but time and myself; it seemed enough.[38]

Chapter 4

THE STALE BREAD OF DEDICATION

Peace came with the telegraphed thud of an anticlimax. That night in the midst of Times Square's drunken revel, wandering bewilderedly among the carnival crowds as through a contemporary ruin, I think I only dimly realized that from then on all joys, like the odd peace itself, would be provisional, but not that Dr. Caligari had joined with Dr. Einstein in an unholy chorus that would call the dance for all our subsequent somnambulist charades. The world had let the wind out of our philosophical balloons, and by September no one was dying by violence anywhere on a globe that had become a graveyard of ideas.
—JOHN CLELLON HOLMES, "Clearing the Field"[1]

Later in the summer of 1945, as Holmes slowly fought his way back from the emotional trauma of his hospital experiences, whatever uncertainties he felt about his future were swept into insignificance by the destruction of Hiroshima by an atom bomb on August 6. His optimistic ideas about a world with new economic goals that he had absorbed from Macguire seemed suddenly meaningless measured against the power of the new weapon. He wrote of the attack later as

"a crime without a name" or "antimatter," even the language of Lear proving inadequate to the descriptions of the shadows of atomized human beings left printed on Hiroshima's leveled walls, the "war aims" of half-a-decade vaporized in the split second it took to turn everyone left alive into casualties.[2]

The tumultuous celebrations in Times Square at the end of the war two weeks after the bomb was dropped seemed of less meaning to him than the potential level of human destruction that the atomic bomb made possible. Conscious that he was only one among many others who shared this response to Hiroshima, in the coming decades he, like them, was tormented by the fear and uncertainty that left them aware of themselves as "casualties"—their dreams of the future forever darkened by the threat that hung over them.

When Holmes arrived at the Columbia University campus in the autumn of 1945, he found a chaotic scene at the Registrar's Office. With the financial support of the GI Bill, which paid tuition and guaranteed a small monthly stipend for books and living expenses, so many veterans had shown up to enroll in classes that they found themselves signing for any courses that were available. Holmes enrolled in a course in modern British literature taught by visiting faculty, the Irish writers Mary and Padraic Colum. He also managed to talk his way into a graduate seminar on the philosophy of art taught by the distinguished art historian Suzanne Langer. When the registrar insisted that he get permission to join the seminar, Holmes walked over to the Philosophy Department and chatted a few minutes with Irwin Edman, the harassed department chairman, who after a moment was persuaded that he recognized Holmes and signed his permission slip. Meanwhile Holmes continued to tell the Registrar's Office that his high school transcripts from Englewood were on their way, insisting, "In the chaos of everything I can't get them from New Jersey."³

Holmes never lost his uneasy awareness that he'd lied about his academic credentials to get into Columbia, and he never completed a degree. He was familiar with the tall buildings of the uptown campus from the summer extension course he'd taken before he was drafted, but he never lost his sense of being an interloper. During the first two weeks in his graduate course in the philosophy of art he didn't understand a word Professor Langer said, so he immersed himself in the first books she required as the challenging background reading for her lectures, all three volumes of Ruskin's *Stones of Venice*.

Though Holmes was a veteran, he was only nineteen, younger than most of the other students in his classes. What most conspicuously set the veterans apart on college campuses was that their experiences of war had shaken some of them free of the society's usual sexual inhibitions. Holmes was soon one of these men on the prowl, and his tall if gawky frame, his wavy blonde hair, his sensitive face, and his horn-rimmed glasses made him very attractive to the women students. After a few exchanges the women usually moved on, since they quickly learned that he was obsessed with his writing, that he was married, and that his wife was supporting him with a series of poorly paid secretarial jobs. His own memory of this time was his "solemn tireless wooing. I kept reaching out from my marriage during these first years, still greedy with the war, though the war was over."[4] Keeping up the pose of the war-weary, coolly detached intellectual college student, he spent many hours, when he wasn't in class or in front of his typewriter, searching for sympathetic women who would have sex with him.

Holmes characterized his situation in describing one of his unsuccessful attempts at seduction:

> *I weighed 140 [pounds] stripped, shaved only twice a week, read Engels on the subways, longed to move to the Village but . . . wanted only the tenderness of sex . . . the mirror of assent in which to glimpse myself ten pounds heavier, without need of horn-rims, as certain to myself as Alan Ladd, or as obsessed as Myshkin, odd perhaps but attractive.*[5]

Holmes' contrasting self-images of himself as Alan Ladd, the film star of unassuming masculine attractiveness and quiet confidence, or as Prince Myshkin, the ideal, sainted hero of Dostoevsky's *The Idiot*, were a mirror of his confusions, and it wasn't surprising that a discouraging number of his attempts to seduce the young women in his Columbia classes either were unsuccessful or were a failure on his part if one of them unexpectedly gave in. It was finally a shy, slender, married woman whose husband was still away in the service who responded most fully to his attentions. Her name was Mira Kent, and she had enrolled in the graduate class in the philosophy of art at Columbia after recovering from a nervous breakdown. It is unclear whether they ever became lovers, but Holmes' clandestine meetings with her continued for a year. It was obvious to both of them that their affair would never become the central event in their lives. He knew that when Mira's husband returned home, he'd have to stop meeting her, but she told him that he could write to her anytime he wished.

Holmes' correspondence with Mira Kent continued for the next two and a half years. They rarely met, though after her husband's return Holmes missed her so intensely that he continued to ring the doorbell of her apartment before he finally accepted that she wouldn't see him anymore. In the spring of 1949 Marian found the carbon copies of John's letters to Mira in his desk and read passages such as Holmes' harsh assessment of their marriage: "We came together stupidly, out of youth, not knowing, daring each other to break through the twin shields we had built. And we did, and that bound us to each other."[6] Marian was devastated. Holmes denied that he and Mira had ever been lovers, but Marian insisted that he stop writing her.

The carbons of these letters to Mira, along with the carbons of other letters Holmes wrote to the two friends he'd met at St. Albans Hospital, Jim Macguire and Howard Friedman, accumulated in Holmes' desk drawer as an on-going diary. Friedman was a small, dark, shy Jewish man from Brooklyn who loved to listen to jazz and went on after his navy discharge to study for a doctorate in biology at the University of Chicago. Marian had no interest in her husband's intellectual passions for literature, philosophy, and classic jazz, so Holmes' letters to his absent friends were often several pages long, always single-spaced, filled with thoughts about his writing and his politics, the books he was reading, and his response to jazz records. About the same time that he began to write these long letters he also started typing page-long entries in a personal journal on cheap yellow second sheets, both as a way to practice developing ideas into essays and as a record of his feelings about daily events.

One evening Marian bought tickets for a group of one-act Soviet plays put on by drama students at Vassar College who'd been given permission free of charge by the Moscow Art Theatre to produce the plays in New York City. In the intermission they met a painter, Alan Woods-Thomas, who invited them back to his apartment in a slum tenement on East 89th Street for a drink. Alan and his wife, Annabelle, became John and Marian's first friends in Manhattan. Alan told them about a vacant cold-water flat in a tenement building on 89th Street near the East River they could rent for twenty-one dollars a month. The apartment was a dark, cramped place with four small rooms running into each other. The hall door opened into the kitchen, and two of the small rooms had no windows. They had a faucet with cold running water in the kitchen sink, but their bathroom was a filthy toilet in the hall shared with the other families on their floor. John and Marian discovered the apartment was so cockroach infested that they had to strip it down to its bare wooden floors and plaster walls before they repainted. The neighborhood was inhabited by poor working families, and naively Holmes thought that this would be an opportunity for him to mingle with the proletariat.

They soon found that they had little in common with their neighbors in the building and preferred to spend their spare time across the street with the Wood-Thomases, talking about art and politics. Holmes remembered that he visited nearly every day since he "needed so badly to be close to anyone who was thinking and working constantly at what he felt he should do."[7] Holmes had a hunger for what he called "the sort of mad life which I imagined I would blossom in,"[8] though he had no specific idea what sort of life that could be.

In Holmes' journal for August 4, 1946, nearly a year after he and Marian moved to East 89th Street, he described hours with Wood-Thomas, drinking glasses of cheap red wine while making windy speeches about the Communist Party and trying out his latest theories about the art of Salvadore Dali. Wood-Thomas was four years older than Holmes, a veteran of the Normandy invasion who had studied art at the Sorbonne and was now a dedicated painter trying to support his wife and child by doing art restoration. While he tolerated his young friend's enthusiasms, he was completely uninterested in Holmes' newly hatched ideas about radical politics or trendy art at the midtown galleries. He continued to work steadily for hours at his easel, refusing to rise to the bait and engage in Holmes' arguments, "the old pipe sticking out of his mouth, his short blonde hair ruffled on the high forehead, listening and yet not listening,"[9] until Holmes realized that he was spouting hot air. The experience of living in a tenement on East 89th ended Holmes' idealization of the proletariat, and his friendship with Woods-Thomas showed him that he needed to read more widely in Marxist literature if he wanted to hold his own ground in political discussions.

In the early fall of 1946, John and Marian moved into a much better apartment at 681 Lexington Avenue, where they would live for the rest of their marriage. Apartment 4C was a fourth-floor walk-up with only one bedroom and a narrow living room facing the noisy, heavily trafficked street below, but even without a kitchen it offered a great location in midtown Manhattan between 56th and 57th Streets, as well as a bathroom with hot and cold running water. It was in an unpretentious but respectable five-story building of twenty small apartments without an elevator, located above a busy delicatessen, near many bus routes, and with the Third Avenue elevated train a block away. They had signed a lease on this apartment and lived there during the summer of 1945 but then moved to East 89th Street for a year to save a considerable amount on the rent. At first they thought that they "didn't miss the sharp, smart exterior which manifested itself on Lexington Avenue,"[10] but after freezing through the winter in their roach-infested, cold-water flat they could hardly wait to move back to Lexington Avenue.

While they waited out their lease, Betty and Liz Holmes returned from California and subleased their apartment at 681 Lexington for a few months. Betty found a clerical job in midtown Manhattan, and she and Liz enjoyed living close to John and Marian. When their lease on East 89th Street ended he and Marian moved back into the Lexington Avenue apartment. There they learned that another apartment above them on the fifth floor would soon become vacant. Betty and Liz moved back into the building in January 1947, in time to celebrate John's twenty-first birthday.

The rent at 681 Lexington was relatively expensive, sixty dollars a month, three times that of East 89th Street. Marian's salary as a typist averaged thirty-five or forty dollars a week, but they felt that the luxury of not having to take cold baths in the kitchen was worth the price. If Marian lost one of her series of office jobs or she and John ran out of money before she got her paycheck, Betty often helped them pay the rent. Since their kitchen was only a hot plate over a small refrigerator shoved against a wall of the living room, they had to wash dishes in the bathroom sink. Usually they ate dinner at a Greek family restaurant a few blocks away, again relying on Betty's generous support. With her financial help, John and Marian had pulled off a minor miracle: with very little money they were managing to live in a cramped but decent apartment in Manhattan. They quickly made Glennon's, a seedy Irish saloon around the corner on Third Avenue with scuffed leather booths, their usual hangout, with ten-cent glasses of watery draft beer.

The new apartment on Lexington Avenue gave John and Marian their first sense of home, especially after Betty and Liz moved upstairs. With Betty guaranteeing their credit, they got their first telephone. When Marian was sleeping, Holmes could listen to his beloved jazz records late at night without hearing the inevitable banging on the wall and threats to call the police from the elderly widow who had lived in the next door apartment on East 89th Street. Holmes liked to write at night to the sound of jazz blasting out of his phonograph, and he was also sexually excited by the music, and he entered into the most passionate period of his marriage to Marian during their first years on Lexington Avenue. On January 31, 1947, he wrote in his journal that each of them desperately needed something to believe in, and they believed in what he called the

> *thrill of sex, the unknown dark mystery of the flesh and the soul entwined. It had dragged me on against my will. Someone once said that I watched people as I would watch a squashed toad. There was a curiosity for the lurid, the disgusting, that held me always. Sex was like a lake in which one went down and down and down and never came up from. I could slide into that lake on a moment's notice.*

Settling into their new apartment, Holmes prepared himself to become a writer. Though the cramped living room was mostly taken up by two shabby couches, he put a large desk in front of the tall, narrow windows overlooking Lexington Avenue. For three dollars a week he rented a new office-model typewriter, and soon he was sending out a stream of poems and stories to magazines. There were also daily stints of typing single-spaced journal entries and long letters to his friends. He continued to read the *Daily Worker* every day, sharing his copy of the newspaper with Marian, but instead of riding the subway uptown to his Columbia classes, he took the subway downtown to Union Square, first to pick up revolutionary pamphlets and Marxist books at the Worker's Bookshop and then to spend hours browsing in the used bookshops along Fourth Avenue.

Holmes hadn't lost his self-consciousness over his lack of education and he was determined to educate himself. He wrote in his journal that he was always "aware that I was stupid, loutish, that I had no right to desire to put something of my own down on paper, when so much of the world's knowledge was still unknown to me."[11] From the dusty, crowded shelves of the Fourth Avenue bookshops he began furtively slipping used copies of literary classics into the pockets of his shabby overcoat. He slowly assembled a personal library on home-made bookshelves that eventually took over every wall of the apartment. Nearly every night he read himself to sleep over a classic work of literature, consuming Dostoevsky, Tolstoy, Shakespeare, Melville, and other major authors with undiminished appetite.

As Holmes applied himself to the routine of becoming a full-time writer, he discovered that his talent seemed more suited to creating poems and essays than fiction. He persevered in his struggles over his short stories and his outlines for novels, however, since he was aware that he would never be able to make any money as a poet. All of his literary heroes were novelists, but the problem was that when Holmes tried to write fiction, he found it impossible to develop a convincing narrative line. Doggedly he dissected the short stories in old copies of *Colliers* and the *Saturday Evening Post* magazines, trying to learn how to craft commercial short fiction, but he remembered, "I could find no plot, I could not set the wheels rolling."[12] Lacking a gift as a realistic storyteller, Holmes decided to use the events of his own life as the basis for his fiction. As a teenager he'd had no trouble filling his notebooks' pages with fantasy adventure stories, but now he composed a laboriously detailed journal entry describing a trip to Greenwich Village with Alan and Annabelle Woods-Thomas, turning it into a sketch mocking his adolescent idealization of bohemian life. He modeled it self-consciously on the style of Ernest Hemingway's early laconic prose in *In Our Time*. Holmes' sketch began,

> We lived in a flat on Lexington Avenue, and we spent most of our time in the Village. We had only a two-room flat, and the bedroom was crammed

with excess stuff, so we lived in the other one. It wasn't a bad flat, but it cost us sixty dollars a month. I had most of my books around, and there was a picture or two on the walls. It was comfortable and looked quite Bohemian in a dim light. We spent most of our time in the Village, however.

We liked the Village, also we knew a lot of crazy people down there. It was affectation mostly. I was particularly sold on the artistic life in those days, and that was the reason. I thought they were all genius's [sic]. It wasn't until later that I thought they were a lot of phonies.

We used to take the subway down or the Fifth Avenue bus. It wasn't a long ride, but it made all the difference in the world. We got in the habit of eating in some crazy joint for fifty-cents, or listening to some jazz music in a bar somewhere. Once in a while we went to a play in a small theater down there. None of them were much good, but we had a lot of fun.[13]

Holmes sent the sketch out to magazines under the title "Days of Our Youth," and though it was rejected he liked it enough to keep a carbon typescript in his desk. After months of rejections, he decided it was time to give up short fiction and try to expand one of his stories, "The Wounded Faun," into the first chapters of what he hoped would become a novel that would earn him some money. He titled it "Frankel" after its protagonist, a hired killer who shoots a wealthy man and then falls in love with the victim's secretary. Attempting to write popular fiction, Holmes abandoned Hemingway as his stylistic model and moved on to Graham Greene.

Throughout 1947 Holmes' novel progressed by fits and starts as he struggled to bring his characters to life. He was drawn to an incremental style of writing that gave him an opportunity to write and rewrite his pages, trying to expand the emotional and philosophical implications of the situations he created for his characters. Dissatisfied with his work, he finally abandoned Greene as his model and set himself the even more challenging task of re-writing "Frankel" in Dostoevsky's style, believing that he had to plumb the depth of the souls of his characters if he wanted to dramatize his tragic sense of life. Holmes' philosophical approach to writing a novel meant that his progress was slow and painful. Throughout his career he would mostly work in this critical, self-conscious way, and his novels were completed only after long periods of toil and struggle.

Far from midtown Manhattan, in the distant neighborhood of Ozone Park in Queens, Jack Kerouac continued to live with his widowed mother after his father's death in May 1946. He now felt a new determination to succeed as a writer, aware that he had disappointed his parents by dropping out of Columbia and getting involved on the Upper West Side with people they considered to be bums. To show Mémère that he was serious, Kerouac had begun a novel that was the most ambitious project he'd ever attempted. Like Holmes, Kerouac considered Dostoevsky his favorite novelist, but Kerouac decided to write his new novel in the narrative style of his other literary hero, Thomas Wolfe, because Wolfe's sprawling autobiographical novels celebrating American life were taken more seriously than the hard-boiled "noir" style Kerouac had imitated the previous year when he'd collaborated with Burroughs in writing *And the Hippos Were Boiled in Their Tanks*, their attempt to describe the Carr-Kammerer tragedy. By the summer of 1947, Kerouac's old group had disbanded: Edie had returned to Michigan, and Joan and William Burroughs and Herbert Huncke were trying to grow a marijuana crop on a ramshackle ranch in New Waverly, Texas, where Ginsberg was visiting after his spring semester at Columbia.

After a year of working on his new novel, which he titled *The Town and the City*, Kerouac had written hundreds of pages and he was halfway through his manuscript. In July of 1947, as a reward for his hard work, he broke off to take his first cross-country trip. He told Mémère that he was going to San Francisco to earn money for their household expenses by shipping out in the merchant marine with his Horace Mann School buddy, Henri Cru. He also planned to stop in Denver to catch up with Ginsberg and a new friend they'd met in New York City the previous year. Kerouac later idealized him in *On the Road* as "a sideburned hero of the snowy West." The friend was Neal Cassady, who was to play a major role in Kerouac's life over the next decade.

On July 17, 1947, Kerouac began his trip West by saying good-bye to his mother and pushing past the subway turnstile in Queens. His adventures riding buses and hitchhiking from Chicago to Denver, his chaotic attempts to spend time with Ginsberg and Cassady in Denver, his subsequent weeks in Marin County working with Cru (Kerouac sent 75 percent of his wages back to his mother), and his two-week love affair at the end of the summer with a young Mexican woman named Bea Franco, whom he picked up on a bus ride to Los Angeles before he caught another bus back home to Mémère in Ozone Park, would become the first part of *On the Road* nearly four years later.

Holmes spent the summer of 1947 in Manhattan, slowly beginning to make his way into a wider literary circle. The Wood-Thomases introduced him to another aspiring novelist named Alan Harrington, who also lived on East

89th Street. Eight years older than Holmes and a Harvard graduate (class of 1939), Harrington was extremely tall and had a dingy blond crewcut. One of his eyes was cocked, and stared off toward the wall, which made Harrington give a first impression of being defensive and introverted, but he was amusing and had a wide circle of friends. Like Holmes, Harrington's parents had divorced and he was partially supported by his mother. He worked occasional jobs as a commercial writer to support his pregnant wife. Holmes took him as a mentor after Macguire and Wood-Thomas, hoping that Harrington could show him how to break into publishing.

Harrington brought Holmes to book parties given by publishers and introduced him to his friends, among them his Harvard classmate Bill Cannastra, a hard-drinking lawyer in his mid-twenties, and another Harvard friend Edward Stringham, also an aspiring writer who loved classical music and was doing layouts for the *New Yorker.* Alan also introduced Holmes to Rae Everitt, a recent Vassar graduate who was married but loved to flirt. In 1947 she was having a brief fling as an actress, but a year later she set herself up with her wealthy husband's support as a literary agent, trying to help Harrington and Holmes place their writing.

The new crowd welcomed Holmes into their circle as another veteran who shared their political idealism and passion for literature, music, and art. Like the others, Holmes considered himself politically on the Left, though he had no connection with any Communist organization. As he wrote fifteen years later, it was a political argument with his friends that led to too many martinis and throwing up over the side of the bed after they had spent the night arguing about the "reactionary rot" of writer Arthur Koestler.[14] Koestler's powerfully written, corrosive novel titled *Darkness at Noon* was a controversial exposure of the moral corruption and megalomania of the Soviet political system.

At their parties Holmes found himself involved in unending political arguments with his friends, and the more they wrangled over their interpretations of the contents of the *Daily Worker*, the more disillusioned he became. He grew so exasperated by the political situation that he wrote a letter to *PM* magazine, a weekly that supported the Communist line. In the issue of September 28, 1947, his letter appeared under the headline "Ship Going Down" in the "Letters from the Readers" section of the periodical. It was the first time Holmes had seen his words in print. He began,

> *I would like to be a liberal, but I find it impossible. It's rather like "talking of navigation as the ship is going down" (to quote Auden). The liberal cares more for his "independence" than for the creation of the kind of*

world he cares about. . . . I'm not a Communist, but economics speak very
loud these days, and they seem to tell me that the kind of system which
we defend will never work.

Appearing just a few days after the September 23, 1947, crisis at the
United Nations over the split between East and West Germany, Holmes'
letter reflected the tense postwar political situation that culminated in the
state of Cold War between Communist and capitalist nations that would
continue throughout his life. Through the spring months of 1948 Holmes
continued to think of himself as a radical, but as the year progressed it was
increasingly difficult for him to defend his attitude. Like most people on
the Left in the United States, he was deeply shaken by the events of February 24, 1948, when local Communist groups, some of them working within
the labor unions, seized control of the government of Czechoslovakia. On
March 10, 1948, the new Communist authorities announced that the foreign minister in the deposed government, Jan Masyrk, had jumped to his
death from a building in Prague. Throughout the world, however, there was
an immediate assumption that he had been thrown from the window by
Communist functionaries.

Holmes and his friends were aware that they weren't alone in their increasing dissatisfaction with both the Communist Party and mainstream
politics. Throughout the postwar world many aspiring young writers believed that "words were actions" and that through their writing they could
influence history.[15] Holmes' crowd was closely allied in their convictions to
the group of French writers whose name would often be linked with the
Beats in the following decade, the Existentialists. When Holmes described
himself in 1948 as a "young radical," he added that he was "filled with choice
Existentialist texts."[16] He sometimes glanced back to his earlier self by quoting Albert Camus, one of the French Existentialist writers whose ideas influenced European and American intellectual life during the postwar years.
Most of the controversy about the relationship between Existentialism and
the new Beat Generation that blossomed in the late 1950s has been forgotten, but for some time the journalists in this period were concerned about
real or imagined ties between the two groups.

The most widely read Existentialist authors in the United States, among
them Camus and Jean-Paul Sartre, insisted that individuals lived within
a world of infinite possibilities, and it was this ability to choose—in absolute freedom—that was the vital determinant in human activity. There
was no way Holmes could have missed the attention paid to their work.
Sartre's influential novel, *Nausea*, was published in English in 1949, and

his philosophical treatise *Being and Nothingness*, first published in France in 1943, was widely read in its original French and published in English in 1956. The writer, however, who had the most effect on Holmes was Camus, whose novels included *The Stranger* in 1946, *The Fall* in 1948, and *The Plague* in 1948. In 1956 the English edition of *The Rebel* was published, in which Camus' influential philosophical and historical "Essay on Man in Revolt" argued that it was necessary for each individual to take moral action after the so-called logical crime by which seventy million human beings were killed or enslaved during the appallingly cruel wars of the first half of the twentieth century.[17]

In 1944, when Jack Kerouac, Allen Ginsberg, and Lucien Carr were becoming friends in Jack and Edie's apartment on Morningside Heights, they had been excited by the earlier French Decadent poetic tradition of Arthur Rimbaud. There William Burroughs had also introduced Kerouac to the autobiographical writing of Ferdinand Céline. Holmes, who was always more strongly political, was drawn instead to the relentless logic and philosophic insights of the Existentialists. In *The Rebel*, Camus had argued for a spiritual dimension to human experience that had nothing to do with orthodox religions of any kind. Reading Camus gave Holmes the insight that all acts of rebellion indicated the presence of a moral choice. This idea was to become his religion and his politics after his eventual disenchantment with the Communist line.

At the age of twenty-one, the distractions of his omnivorous reading and his new friendships still couldn't keep Holmes from the one thing that gave his life whatever structure it possessed—his writing. His attempt to rewrite "Frankel" progressed mainly in fits and starts, and he found himself spending time writing poetry instead. The poems came easily, perhaps because he wasn't intimidated by any larger dream of making a career as a poet. His obsessive reading had included the new poetry journals and he could produce a finished poem almost daily, drawing on the characteristic styles of the mainstream younger poets whose work filled their pages. It was a richly productive period for American poetry, and almost unconsciously Holmes found himself drawn into it.

On September 13, 1947, he told his old friend Macguire, who had taken a job teaching English and Irish literature at Brown University, that Harrington had encouraged him to send out unsolicited book reviews to newspapers and journals, including one to *Poetry* magazine, in the hope that editors would then become familiar with Holmes' name. This was ironic because Holmes had tagged along with Harrington to a literary cocktail party for Peter Viereck, a young poet publishing in *Horizon* and *Atlantic* magazines and teaching at Smith College. At the party Holmes had met Robert Lowell, Viereck's friend and classmate at Harvard. Viereck had mistaken John for the older, established poet John Holmes, "only to be slightly chagrinned at his ignorance when I reminded him that *the* John Holmes taught at Tufts and had been publishing poetry for close to thirty years without making any appreciable dent in the Body Literary."[18]

After this confusion over his name, John began to sign his work "Clellon Holmes" to distinguish himself from the older poet. The fact that there was already a poet named John Holmes was disconcerting, but John was beginning to feel he was part of his own younger group. As he wrote in mid-December 1947, his new friends were artists and writers "whose success is confined to the good will and praise of their editors and dealers. We lick our wounds in company."[19]

At *Poetry* magazine, the editor told Holmes that his unsolicited review of a book by W. H. Auden couldn't be used because another reviewer had been assigned the book. But the editor had liked John's review, and at the end of 1947 he sent John a volume edited by Charles Warton, *A Second Book of Danish Verse*. Holmes' review of this anthology appeared in the March 1948 issue of *Poetry* in the month he turned twenty-two. Thanks to Harrington's canny advice, Holmes felt himself launched on the literary scene. Next, his first poem, "Frau Von Stein, My Brother's Keeper," was accepted with lightning speed by the prestigious literary magazine *Partisan Review*. Holmes remembered,

> *The reference, of course, is to a woman with whom Goethe has a long and intimate correspondence. The poem is about a similar relationship of my own—the woman's initials were M.B.K. [Mira Kent], which accounts for the second phrase of the title—and it was written in half an hour, mailed off to Delmore Schwartz, who was poetry editor of* Partisan, *accepted in a week, and published the next month.*[20]

Holmes' poem appeared in the May 1948 issue of *Partisan Review* that included Delmore Schwartz's article "Does Existentialism Still Exist?" spoofing the philosophical movement that everyone at the New York parties was talking about. Schwartz joked that "Existentialism means that no one else can take a bath for you," rather than as the earlier philosopher Heidegger once pointed out, "No one else can die for you." The magazine also printed Philip Rahv's essay "Disillusionment and Partial Answers," discussing the radical writers "made homeless by their break with the Soviet cause." It featured a chapter of Sartre's long essay, "For Whom Does One Write?" which considered "what happens to literature when the writer is led to reject the ideology of the ruling classes." A few pages along in the same issue, Josephine Herbst compared the literary achievement of Katherine Anne Porter and Gertrude Stein.

The *Partisan Review* sandwiched Holmes' poem between poems by John Berryman ("The Long Home") and Richard Wilbur ("Pity"). Composed in elegant triplet stanzas that echoed the older writers' fashionably poised distillation of melancholy and irony, Holmes had written a poem that in the technical complexities of its rhyme and meter, as well as its complicated syntax, comfortably held its own in one of the nation's most prominent intellectual magazines:

Frau Von Stein, My Brother's Keeper

Some postman rings but never sees you either.
You pick up letters, then take coffee or a class.
Reading them on a step somewhere who keeps my brother

When you read. You carefully wade his nerve's morass,
Seeking an upland in the words, a solid stone,
But reaching no neural bog you cannot gracefully pass.

You chose your role as comrade, knew he needed one.
Concerned recipient of him as letter-lover
You water whimsy and digest the purgative pun,

Temper the outbursts, make his definition move,
Say only, with your tact, you actually seek yourself
In this, a monologue you do not seek to smother

When you write. . . .

Though Holmes was later diffident about the poem that Delmore Schwartz had accepted, he had written it with conscious echoes of Goethe's poetry. He used a complicated *tersa rima* rhyme scheme that he later dismissed as being too much in a "Yeats-Auden tensely-metrical, rhymed mode."[21] The early poems Holmes published, however, are as much an indication of his aesthetic interests as they are a sign of the directions he *didn't* take. He instinctively managed to avoid most of the conventional pitfalls.

With all of his seeming academism, the poems were clearly written in edgy moments of personal crises that reflected his sense of alienation from both radical politics and the mainstream culture. It wasn't surprising that Holmes had such quick success, and if he had chosen to continue he might perhaps have joined the group of poets associated with Robert Lowell and John Berryman in the period of their great popularity.

The editors who quickly accepted his poetry sensed his talent. Both Delmore Schwartz, the poetry editor at *Partisan Review*, and Richard Eberhart at *Poetry*, who accepted Holmes' second poem for the July 1948 issue of the magazine, were established poets themselves, and they recognized his promise. Without any of his struggles learning how to write fiction, Holmes began publishing poetry in a number of important literary journals and magazines when he was still in his early twenties. What he accomplished as a poet with so little seeming effort by the age of twenty-two was the kind of dream of success that haunts many writers who will never see their work appear in any major publications. Over a period of three years, beginning with his first poem in *Partisan Review*, Holmes had poems accepted by *Poetry*, the *New Mexico Quarterly*, *Voices*, *Western Review*, the *Chicago Review*, *Saturday Review of Literature*, *Epoch*, *Wake*, and *Harper's*. As the editors who accepted his work recognized, Holmes was still feeling his way toward his voice as a poet, but he was clearly someone to be watched.

By the spring of 1948, although Holmes might have been satisfied with his rapid success with his poetry, he was still completely inexperienced as a fiction writer and couldn't get "Frankel" off the ground. Instead he proposed to rewrite it again as the first volume in an ambitious trilogy of novels that would examine the theme of contemporary morality from different political, philosophical, and social perspectives. Now Sartre, Camus, and Faulkner became his models. On May 3, 1948, Holmes told Howard Friedman that his new project "will be the largest work of my life. I am already plotting and planning and reading up for it. I may not be ready to write it for at least ten or fifteen years. Even then I may not be able to bring it off as I envisage [*sic*] it now."

Holmes sent Friedman his reading list, which included Aristotle's "Poetics," Homer's "Odyssey," the plays of Sophocles and Shakespeare, Nietzsche's "The Birth of Tragedy," Milton's "Samson Agonistes," Faulkner's *As I Lay Dying* and *The Sound and the Fury*, W. H. Auden's "For the Time Being," "The Sea and the Mirror," and other poems, and T. S. Eliot's *A Family Reunion*. Since Holmes was still dependent upon his wife and his mother for his pocket money, he didn't have the luxury of reading for six months, so once more he turned back to "Frankel." He wrote Macguire, "It's the novel that counts, and I am placing all my hopes on that."[22] Holmes worked on it from February to June 1948, stubbornly trying to finish a first draft after his previous stillborn efforts.

On April 22, 1948, he confided his sense of self-doubt to his journal, feeling desperately isolated as he sat alone for hours at his typewriter, unsure of his ability to complete his daunting project:

> *I get slowly separated from everything day after day here alone. I get un-
> real and thoroughly lazy and dreamy. This is horrible. I need something
> to stir me into work. . . . Last year I would not have dreamed that it was
> possible for me to have the luck I have had, but now it is never enough.
> The few little things that have happened seem very small, a shaky posi-
> tion entirely. I wish more poems could be [sold], and of course, some
> stories. . . . And I feel somehow that I have a lot of work ahead of me on
> the novel. I don't know why. I feel with poetry that I am just reaching the
> conscious stage with it, the level where I have some judgment of what I
> am after in it. I somehow do not feel that with novels. . . . They have to be
> firmly grounded, not just the sketching, sketching away that I do so often,
> this daubing in and rubbing out. All too effereal [sic], too loose and too
> meaningless. One needs a base, one needs to know what one is after. I
> need to ground myself [with] a new view of things, a direction.*

While Holmes struggled with "Frankel," after months of unemployment Marian had found a job she liked at the Dramatic Workshop of the New School in April 1948. She typed up plays and ran the mimeograph machine, and what for her was best of all, she could wear slacks to work. Along with her salary she got free tickets to all the Dramatic Workshop productions, including Andre Gide's adaptation of Kafka's *The Trial* and Robert Penn Warren's adaptation of his novel *All the King's Men*. Once again she and John had money to go out in the evenings together, enjoying the opportunity to escape their cluttered apartment and try different bars around the city. Holmes recalled that in those years, there were "10,000 places on this island where I can go and get a beer for a dime."[23] In his journal for May 25, 1948, he listed the bars in Manhattan he frequented: Glennon's, the San Remo, Clarke's, Louis on Sheridan Square, Julius's, Minetta's, and Murphy's at 95th Street and Madison Avenue, "a hole."

After the birth of his son Steve, Harrington had moved with his wife from East 89th Street to an apartment on East 61st Street, closer to Holmes. To pay the rent, Harrington had taken a daytime job at an advertising agency as a commercial writer. Since Marian was insistent that her husband start earning some money, Holmes also got in touch with the agency and accepted an assignment writing about real estate for one hundred dollars an article. Holmes hated the work and found he wasn't much good at it, though he gave it a try for a few months. He wrote Friedman, "If I could do an article every two weeks or so I could be making enough cabbage to keep us going."[24]

Guiltily aware that he was taking advantage of his wife's financial support, Holmes sneaked away to have casual affairs, telling himself that "a brief, candid embrace would redeem everything."[25] Afterwards he would pick a series of "pointless arguments" with Marian, since he believed that she "knew [he] was cheating but dared not mention it." This began a period of "feeling guilty because I didn't feel guilty."[26] Together John and Marian continued going to parties with Harrington, and they became closer friends with Edward Stringham, who lived on West 113rd Street near the Hudson River. The first time Holmes visited there he was fascinated with Stringham's bachelor apartment, which was "scrupulously clean, with blue and white walls, sparsely furnished in good taste."[27]

Stringham had an impressive collection of classical recordings, and he played excerpts from Alban Berg's opera *Wozzeck* as well as a Bela Bartok composition for percussion and strings that he'd taped from the radio. He also played them records he'd bought in Europe before the war, including Kurt Weill's *Three Penny Opera* and songs sung by Marlene Dietrich and the Swedish opera tenor Jussi Björling, whom Marian particularly admired. Then, for a change of pace, he put on a few old swing band records, which caused her to ask tipsily, "What the hell are they good for?" Harrington told her that she was being too intellectual, but Stringham defended her. To conclude the evening they strolled over to the West End Bar nearby on Broadway, the old hangout for Kerouac and the crowd around Columbia. It was the first time Holmes had ever been there. His impression was of

a long, raucous, crowded hall, with a huge juke box, and filled with drunk or drinking Columbia students. It felt to me like the atmosphere must have been in Berlin during the 'twenties or Munich where the students drank all night and argued about Expressionism. Left Edward at the corner and took a taxi back.[28]

Though his work on "Frankel" limped along, Holmes completed a short prose sketch written in jazz slang he titled "Tea for Two" that he sent along with a cover letter describing his novel-in-progress to the address of a new magazine in St. Louis whose first issue he'd seen in a Manhattan bookshop. On March 19, 1948, Holmes got back an encouraging letter typed on yellow stationary with a flashy red letterhead announcing the name of the magazine, *Neurotica*. It read,

> *Dear Holmes,*
>
> *I like your story very much and will probably print it in the next issue of* Neurotica.
>
> *While I am familiar with the vocabulary, I feel some sort of explanation at the beginning or the end of the story is perhaps a wise move for some of our squarer readers. I leave this to you, though.*
>
> *We pay a dollar a page upon publication. I trust this is all right with you.*
>
> *Cordially, Jay Landesman*
>
> *[Over]—Your novel sounds good. I would like to see a chapter of it sometime. J.*

A few days later, in Holmes' journal, he wrote that he'd sold a story "to that rather unhealthy little hybrid 'Neurotica' out in St. Louis."[29] At the end of June, as the world drifted closer to an international crisis in Germany with the Soviet blockade of Berlin, he learned that Landesman had come to New York and wanted to meet him. Holmes wondered what his friends would think. "How the hell do I know? He might be a real jerk."[30]

On the last day of June, the United States and Great Britain initiated a massive airlift of food and supplies that continued for over a year and kept Berlin alive and still in the Western orbit. That same day Harrington told Holmes about a new young writer he'd just met who had just completed a novel and shared their fascination with Dostoevsky. Holmes remembered the name, which was so unusual he knew he couldn't spell it correctly. He made the attempt anyway, and so it was that on June 30, 1948, at the start of the Berlin airlift, the name "Karawak" first appeared in Holmes' journal:

> *Karawak (this is incorrect spelling) was speaking with Alan Harrington about this book [*The Brothers Karamazov*] the other night while they were out together. He can quote whole speeches with great accuracy, and seems to have studied the complete book thoroughly.*

Chapter 5

A WEEKEND IN JULY

The long, muggy July 4th weekend in 1948 must be reckoned as a crucial date in my personal education. I was twenty-two, and just beginning to publish, and I suppose I was indistinguishable from three hundred other young intellectuals in New York in those days. We all read the same "little magazines," we all had first novels underway, and the same secret confusion about the drift of the times lay behind our individual ambitions to be the first to strike the "dominant note." In one sense at least, the lessening of my own confusion began that weekend. For all in two days I met four men who profoundly altered my life and mind—vastly different men, one from the other, who were nevertheless as representative of my generation and some of its preoccupations as any four very dissimilar individuals can be. There was something special about each of them that was outrageous, idiosyncratic, and against the grain of the time; what I took to be a unique view of the world has proved not to be so special after all. In any case, each had a share in sharpening whatever pen I weld, defining in their works and personalities some of the questions, and a few of the answers, that have plagued my times.
—JOHN CLELLON HOLMES, "July 4th Weekend"[1]

It's often chance collisions that most effect our lives, rather than the carefully planned encounters we often discount beforehand, since we have some idea of what to expect. In 1948 Holmes had no idea of the people he would meet on the Fourth of July weekend. What he noted in his journal was that the first days of July were very hot. It was hot and muggy and oppressive, with the stale breathlessness that hangs in the narrow corridors of the New York City streets, hemmed in on both sides by the weight of building fronts that leave no room for air to stir. There was a threat of rain that would at least have cooled the wind for a moment, but if people had anyplace to get away to, they left the city. Marian had fled to her family's house in Chappaqua, in its cooler shadows in the wooded hills of Westchester County. The weekend began slowly, since Holmes couldn't have known what was waiting for him, but over the next three days he would meet the four men— like him and different from him in as many ways—who would open the doors for him to a new understanding of his life and what it offered him.

The first of the four he met was a rebellious, ambitious, neophyte magazine publisher named Jay Landesman, who had travelled to New York City by train from St. Louis, where he was a partner in his family's antique business. Holmes had stayed behind in Manhattan to meet him on July 1. Landesman was the editor and half owner of a new literary magazine, *Neurotica*, that had published Holmes' first short story, "Tea for Two," in the magazine's second issue. It had just appeared on the tables of the Gotham Book Mart close to Times Square and the Four Seasons Book Shop in the Village, the shops Holmes haunted. Landesman had written Holmes and asked if Holmes could meet him and help him find more writers for his magazine.

About 9:00 p.m. Holmes took the subway down to the Village, where Landesman was staying, certain that he was going to meet a "nervous, effete young man."[2] Holmes had very dampened expectations about the meeting. He was happy to see one of his stories in print, but he didn't think any of his friends were eager to write for a new magazine published in St. Louis by someone they'd never heard of. Landesman had taken a small, grimy room on the top floor of the shabby Marlton Hotel on Eighth Street, and when the door opened Holmes found himself looking at a lanky, welcoming figure who was wearing black slacks and a black shirt, set off with a yellow tie. Even in the New York heat he was wearing desert boots. In Holmes' memoir of the weekend written twenty years later, "July 4th Weekend, 1948," he remembered that his first impression was that Landesman looked like "an affable Marseilles hood."[3] Holmes embroidered his impressions for the purposes of his memoir, describing Landesman as "surrounded by bottles of gin, stacks of books and newspapers, and several pretty girls."

Holmes' initial journal entry, seven pages written on July 2 describing their meeting the previous night, was considerably less colorful.

> *Jay Irving Landesman, clad in black shirt and yellow tie, was alone in the shabby garish hotel room when I arrived. He is a direct handsome guy about 26 or so. . . . He is not brilliant by any means, but he is easy to get along with. He has been seeing people about* Neurotica *and was*

in the fluent mood that such an ordeal would leave one. He likes being the publisher of a little magazine and seems to have started it with little or no qualms about the success of it. He's making it go, I think. He works in an antique business (a family affair), got the six hundred odd dollars necessary for the first issue and has made all his money back on it, selling five thousand copies.[4]

Holmes' later memory was that the first thing they talked about was tattoo parlors. Landesman had spent some time looking into the tattooing establishments around Times Square, watching sailors have their arms decorated with their girls' names or "with flags and hula girls,"[5] and he thought there could be an article on the scene for his magazine. They also discussed an article Landesman wanted Holmes to write, which was published in the magazine's next issue as "All the Good Roles Have Been Taken—the Plight of the Talented Untalented." Landesman even suggested that Holmes might want to be the magazine's New York editor. Since Landesman's own memories of the weekend took on a typically flamboyant tone, he would probably have been disappointed by Holmes' final judgment of the man he'd just met: "He's a very normal, nicely sincere and direct fellow, aware of his position but in a lovely unsophisticated way."[6]

The "several pretty girls" Holmes recalled in his memoir came into the room a short time later, and he devoted pages in his journal recording his impression of each of them.[7] They weren't, as he seemed to imply, Landesman's women friends. One was his wife, Pat, whom Holmes found to be "a simple Jewish girl, but very pretty, quite happy about things. An open look on her face. She comes from money, has some now with Jay. . . . A nice girl, who doesn't warm up and come all the way out at all. She keeps inside herself, thinks only of Jay, perhaps is afraid of some of the people she is now in contact with."[8]

Another of the women, Joan Chapman, was distantly related to Landesman, who had brought her into the group. To Holmes she seemed to be a type, "the career girl. She is married to a guy who teaches sociology, [and] she is trying to get a Doctor of Law [degree]."[9] Holmes found her the most interesting of the women who joined them.

She is going around the country getting thrown in jail to take down notes on a paper on institutions. Has only been in one so far, will be committed for juvenile delinquency here in N. Y. in eight days. She is thin, her hair drawn hecticly [sic] back . . . [and] she surges into a room, starts talking immediately, her voice rather nasal, mid-western. She carries a large brief case. . . . When asked if she masturbated in jail, and given a long argument about if she didn't she couldn't be objective about conditions there because she would be emotionally upset, she replied nervously, "Well, you must see I was brought up a Roman Catholic and that would go against my conditioning. It would make it harder for me to see things, because subconsciously I would consider it a sin."[10]

She put Holmes off balance with a question about his poem "Fear in the Afternoon" that had just appeared in *Poetry*. "I said: 'It was just a simple love poem.' Answer: 'What's so simple about love?' This was a comment, not a judgement, however."[11]

A man had also come with them, an artist named Herb Benjamin, who was living on Sullivan Street and supporting himself by painting portraits. Holmes found they shared literary interests in Sartre and Camus. Benjamin, like Holmes, was a navy veteran. He'd brought the woman he was living with, named Thalia, who was in Holmes' judgment "the prettiest girl of the bunch."[12] The other two in the group were someone named Cynthia, whom Holmes thought was "the promoter type girl, smart and in touch with people and things, gurgly speech, directness but sold on the anecdote and the quip,"[13] and a woman he knew from the Seven Seas Bookshop named Tashka.

They had all met at Landesman's room because they were going to go up to the Bronx to meet a new author he'd found for his magazine, someone named Gershon Legman. Landesman been told about Legman by a St. Louis friend named Beka Dougherty, who worked for *Time* magazine and knew he was looking for material. *Time* had recently presented an article on America's new little magazines, where *Neurotica* had been prominently mentioned. Landesman wrote about his New York journey in his own memoir written in the 1980s,

"I think Neurotica *is terrific," she [Beka] said in her cool* Time *magazine manner. "I put them on to you for the feature on Little Mags. You owe me a dinner." When I told her what I was looking for in New York, she said she knew the perfect man to write for* Neurotica.

"He's absolutely unprintable, but exactly what you need."[14]

He was Gershon Legman, an overweight, obsessive, eruptive, deeply pained idealist whose scrutiny was directed at American sexual mores. He was the second of the "outrageous" men Holmes would meet that weekend. Landesman recalled that after he'd talked with his friend Beka from *Time* he made a call to Legman.

After I introduced myself as the editor of Neurotica, *he cut me short.*
"It's a piece of garbage."[15]

Before Holmes came by the hotel Landesman had already had a brief, dazzling meeting with Legman, and he was curious to see if his new acquaintance had the same effect on his other friends. Holmes' exhausting encounter with Legman and Landesman—the night ended at five thirty the next morning—was the beginning of the events of the long muggy nights over the Fourth of July weekend that were to change his life. Landesman had come to New York, he later wrote in his memoir *Rebel Without Applause*, because his friend Dorothy, who was working at the Four Seasons bookshop, had insisted that he meet the people running the shops where his magazine was sold. Landesman had arrived in Manhattan to find that these bookstores still had windows full of dusty copies of Saul Bellow's novel *Dangling Man* from 1944. He'd been put off by most of the New Yorkers he'd met, who had "looked like literary executioners—arrogant, snobbish, waiting for a kill."[16] What Landesman wanted was "to set the town on its ass." He thought *Neurotica* was "the only voice around screaming for an end to censorship and sexual repression in a savage society."[17] As Holmes was to learn on his first night following his new friend's lead, there was nothing for him to do except fall in step with Landesman's irreverent tramp through what he considered the current American morass.

Landesman was insatiably curious about what he perceived as the idiosyncrasies of the society around him, and he had used his own money to pay for the printing of the first issue of *Neurotica* that he and his friend Richard Rubinstein had started in St. Louis in the spring of 1948. Their magazine would later be considered the first Beat literary journal. Landesman was older—he was born in 1919, which made him seven years older than Holmes—and he was also plugged into a personal sense of hipness that Holmes often found as bewildering as it was stimulating. Landesman was tall, slim, dark haired, flamboyantly handsome, voluble, and confidently convinced of the importance of his own good causes.

Unlike Holmes, whose family had limped through his childhood and then left him beached after his parents' divorce, Landesman was a member of a busy, successful St. Louis family. He had three older siblings, and he was especially close to his brother Fred. His father was a German artist who had come to St. Louis as part of a wave of German immigration that for a time made the German language and German culture as central to the city's consciousness as its Anglo-American backgrounds. Landesman's father had been brought to the United States to paint the decorative murals in the German pavilion at the St. Louis Exposition in 1904, and his skills were to help the family through the economic collapse of the 1930s. The Depression years were as difficult for the Landesmans as they were for everyone else, but Jay's father was given work painting murals for the federal government's W.P.A. art program, the relief agency that saved the careers of an entire generation of American artists. The program turned hundred of young painters into muralists and sent them out to decorate the nation's post offices and high school auditoriums.

While his father was occupied with his civic murals, Landesman's energetic and shamelessly domineering mother persevered with a small antique shop. Despite the severe economic conditions Jay attended the University of Missouri for the spring semester of 1938, where he joined the boxing team and for a time showed some interest in the R.O.T.C. He dropped out the next semester. Although he faced the draft, he was classified 4F and spent the war years working in a St. Louis defense plant. When the war ended his mother continued to run the family's antique shop, so in a move to get out from under her relentless efforts to control their lives, Landesman and his brothers expanded the business into a more elegant establishment renamed the Landesman Galleries, where he worked as one of the family partners. In the fall of 1945 he was married in what began as a love match, and his wife soon became pregnant. After she miscarried in her seventh month, the marriage foundered on her severe depression.

It was on Landesman's business trips to New York City, buying antiques for the family gallery, that he discovered the casual lifestyle of Greenwich Village. With the Village as an inspiration, he and a group of partners established a literary bar in St. Louis called Little Bohemia for St. Louis's artists and writers. With *Neurotica*, he and his friend Rubinstein deliberately set out to upset anyone who might idly open the magazine's cover. In a statement of purpose they wrote:

> Neurotica *is a literary exposition, defense, and correlation of the problems and personalities that in our culture are defined as "neurotic."*
>
> *It is said that if you tie a piece of red cloth to a gull's leg its fellow-gulls will peck it to pieces: and* Neurotica *wishes to draw an analog to this observation and the plight of today's creative "anxious" man.*
>
> *We are interested in exploring the creativeness of this man who has been forced to live underground.*[18]

Neurotica's openness to what was considered the neurotic side of the American attitudes toward sex attracted most of the attention, and the magazine had a surprisingly large distribution, even though most of the contributors were unknown. Holmes, continually prowling the magazine racks to find anything new, had read the first issue and submitted his short story "Tea For Two" as an insider's joke, since the "tea" was marijuana. It was written in an experimental "jive" language which served to set it at odds with the current literary idiom. Holmes later insisted that he was working with the casual slang he picked up from the traditional jazz musicians he had heard when he and Marian listened to music in Manhattan, the dixieland artists working in clubs like Nick's and Eddie Condon's, rather than the later self-conscious hipsterism of many of the first bop musicians. In the summer of 1948 the bop revolution was still a newcomer in New York's jazz clubs. Holmes wrote his story before he understood what the new musical style and its new artists, such as Charlie Parker and Dizzy Gillespie, would come to mean to him.

Holmes' short story, though it shows more youthful enthusiasm than literary skill, is interesting as a foreshadowing of the use of jazz vernacular language as the basis for a prose style, as Holmes and Kerouac, among many others, were to do later with the language of bop. Nothing dates more quickly than writing in a current slang idiom, however, and today Holmes' piece has the feel of something jotted down on a cocktail napkin between sets. It caught some of the tone of a hip musician's imagery, but there was also a discernable overlay of Raymond Chandler and Damon Runyon. The protagonist of the story is a jazz trumpeter named Becker, and after a few introductory paragraphs he meets one of the women who drift into the jazz clubs.

Then she came in. She wasn't the jazz sort. She was too severe and a little broken up around the eyes. She wasn't one of those cradle-babies, eager as hell to sample your weed and grab some of your vocabulary. She wandered in on the end of some magazine people from uptown who were slumming. She was dressed in tight cuts, with lines like a destroyer just out of the yards, and the mop pulled back over her ears. She strode a strong figure, this dream, and Becker melted down like putty. The boy wasn't the physiological type, you understand. He was just a temperament walking around in a frame he abused, but this one got his ire. She was offhand, and smoked like she'd been living on the gage since milk. She grabbed herself a waft of whiskey that would have eaten through a table, and listened to the jazz like it was Bach. She didn't put it on, this one; but sat around, her profile cutting dentures in the smoke.[19]

Despite its clumsiness, "Tea for Two" had a good-natured sense of the absurd that fit into the pages of *Neurotica*. Landesman's memories of his first meeting with Holmes were still vivid when he looked back in his memoir forty years later, though he also gave the details of what he recalled of the Fourth of July weekend a considerable spin. In the beginning his expectations of what his writer would be like were as far from the mark as Holmes' expectations about *him*.

> *Holmes, I thought, would be some far-out looking cat, shifty, probably strung out on weed. Imagine my surprise to meet a quiet, almost shy, tall, thin professorial type, with a magnificent Bobby Darin wave of blond hair. His thick, horn rim glasses slipping off his Bob Hope nose added a casual touch that prevented my saying, "What's a nice kid like you doing hanging out with all those hipsters?" He laughed easily and once we got drinks in our hands we both relaxed.*[20]

Holmes explained that he didn't think any of his friends were doing the kind of writing that could fit into *Neurotica*. After Landesman ordered drinks and pastrami sandwiches, the others who had arrived at his hotel room changed the subject. Gradually Holmes began to feel at ease. Landesman was friendly and began to call him "Johnny," asking if he wanted to go along with them to the Bronx. Holmes immediately agreed.

It was late when they left the subway and walked to the corner of Bronx Park, where the man they were supposed to meet was waiting for them. Landesman wrote about the evening in *Rebel Without Applause*, blending his impressions of the first time he'd met Gershon Legman with the night he brought Holmes and the others up to the Bronx along with him.

> *In the shadows stood a lonely figure; I knew immediately who it was. "Are you Landesman? I'm Legman."*
> *As he stepped out of the shadows, I saw a heavily-moustached, portly figure with a wild shock of hair that made me think of a young Balzac. . . . By the light of the platform, I saw the lines of thwarted ambition around his mouth, making it seem in a permanent state of rage.*[21]

It was the beginning of Landesman's turbulent literary relationship with Gershon Legman, whose effect on *Neurotica* was only a faint intimation of the effect he would try to have on American culture and social attitudes over the next decade.

Since Landesman had come with a group, Legman gave them a mock tour of his Bronx neighborhood as they walked with him to his shabby house around the corner from the park. He waved toward the butcher shop where he could buy sheep lung, the cheapest kind of meat he could find. He showed them the market where the grocer would sell Legman's wife, Beverly, old vegetables, "the vegetables that he ordinarily throws out with the garbage. Amazing what my wife can do with rotten greens and bruised tomatoes."[22] Legman and his wife were living in a cramped three-room cottage surrounded with a picket fence in need of repair that enclosed the unkempt patch of earth that passed for a lawn. Inside, the cottage was filled with books. Landesman wrote, with a touch of facetiousness,

> *Books were everywhere; stacked in the halls, used as furniture, and what little furniture there was, was upholstered in books. Books were marching menacingly out of the closets, trickling out of the toilet. . . . Legman introduced his wife, Beverly, who was administering what looked like mouth-to-mouth resuscitation to one of a dozen cats loitering the kitchen, waiting, as far as I could figure, to be read to.[23]*

Holmes was stunned by the sheer quantity of the mounds of books, but he was as impressed by the depth and the scholarly weight of what Legman collected. In his journal Holmes tried to give an idea of the immensity of the collection.

> *You enter the bedroom and this has more than token symbolism to it. Books everywhere, one whole wall is books and another records. The kitchen, with "I vomit" written in French on the wall, is littered with more books; a little room off this one is filled with filing cabinets and wooden boxes overflowing with comic books and other things he is "studying." Some etchings on the wall, the bed large with a nice deep red coverlet and a similar drape on the wall. The books that I saw were predominately on two subjects and it was the most exhaustive collection of each that I have ever seen. They were on language, all the way from dictionaries on all languages, to lexicons of slang and argot, little used expressions and dirty words, dictionaries of law phrases, scientific phrases and foreign bound books on the argot of Paris, etc, all and environs. Freudian monographs on the sexual connotations of words . . . it is the book collection of a researcher.[24]*

It was, however, the other subject of Legman's collection—books about sex, not language—which was to be at the root of most of the controversy that came to plague him.

The other topic is sex. Sex in all its variations. Hundreds of books, very rare, sacred and profane, accepted and rejected, on every aspect of the subject. Thousands of them that I have never even heard of, whole files on this sort of thing.[25]

Holmes was also startled to find that what little literary material Legman had on his shelves was there because of its relationship to his studies of sexuality. "Had Strindberg because he was anti-feminist, read Hemingway because he was a sadist, *et al.*"[26] Legman's vast record collection—ranging from the symphonic classics to a broad range of jazz and folk music—was as carefully listed and cataloged, all of its content related to his obsessive interest in sexual attitudes. He bought his comic books from the children in the neighborhood, and he had gathered cartons bulging with them, indexing them under the sexual perversion he felt each presented. The corollary to his fascination with sexual expression was his anger at what he saw as the barrier of censorship that prevented human sexuality from assuming its normal place in everyday life and instead channeled its expression into physical violence.

As he had done with the others he'd met at Landesman's hotel room, Holmes used his journal for a "sketch" of Legman, describing his monolog as he barraged the silenced group with ideas from his unpublished manuscript *Love and Death, A Study in Censorship.*

Gershon's speech was racy, quick, like quick thinking peoples' it was not always accurate. It had a surface shine, he could make a "rough" joke quickly. He was in a hurry about everything, did not drink. Hides behind the glasses and the moustache. Talks like a steam-roller, crushes you. Introduces topics so fast you can't correct some of his inaccuracies and over-emphases. Has the jargon of someone in the know, does know a lot people, thinks his work is the best in the field. May very well be.[27]

Legman treated them as one of his lecture audiences and presented the thesis of a chapter from his book, which Landesman had already decided to publish as an article. Holmes found that Legman's analysis of his subject was completely convincing. The article on comic books included

statistics on the increase of them, intricate analyses of the masturbation, homosexual[ity], sadistic perverted aspects in them, with huge masses of figures, in regards to this we saw the panels of covers that he used for visual compliments to his lecture, each of them divided into categories.

Penis symbolism, women and animals (etc etc etc etc). He showed, and very convincingly, that the hero becomes more and more like the classic villain, or he is subjected to women and hates them etc. This article (and I read it) hits harder than the other pieces I have recently read in SRL [the Saturday Review of Literature] *and other places on this subject. He's done a more thorough job than anyone else, and sees it all more clearly.*[28]

In a later essay about Legman, Holmes portrayed his wife, Beverly, as sitting silently, shyly in a corner. The only thing he remembered her saying was to tell them in a low voice—when she saw the bottle of whiskey they'd brought with them—that she didn't have any ice in the house. Writing in his journal the next morning, however, he described her personal role in her husband's torrential monolog.

She is something of a filing cabinet for Gershon, who asks her the references on this and that or the other thing and she seems to immediately remember. I wouldn't be surprised if she has to read everything he does and to remember things like that. He has everything filed away and at his fingertips, even her.[29]

A friend of Legman's, someone named John, had also turned up, but he sat silently, clearly annoyed at finding Legman with a house full of strangers. There was continual music, and Holmes noted old 78s by the brilliant Mozart soprano Conchita Supervia, "bits of Sibelius, and wonderful first recording of 'Hastings Street Boogie' by piano and guitar made about 1926."[30]

As far as anyone could tell, Legman and his wife subsisted on the very meager earnings he made acting as an occasional middleman between the book dealers whose shops he haunted on Fourth Avenue and a circle of wealthy collectors, or with odd jobs in the bookshops as a handyman or a part-time carpenter. He had worked for a short period as a bibliographer for the Kinsey Institute, but he had left after an argument about their filing system.

Whatever he did earned him very little, and often he and Beverly had to share food with the cats that were everywhere in the house. His visitors soon realized that the couch they were sitting on was the Legmans' bed, and what had been intended as the bedroom was choked with the years of research Legman had been doing into the questions of censorship and sexuality in the United States. No one was permitted into the bedroom itself. If Legman wanted to show them a particularly offensive example of the kind of censorship or graphic violence he was describing—a comic book or a study in neuroses—he rushed into the room and returned to drop it on a table in front of them. None of the difficulties he and Beverly were facing had shaken his belief in the importance of his ideas. Though the others who had joined Landesman on his mission to the Bronx became more wide-eyed and withdrawn as the evening flowed on, Legman made as strong an impression on Holmes as he did on Landesman.

The evening ended with Legman rudely challenging Landesman over the future of *Neurotica*:

> *"Well, Landesman . . . what's it going to be? This is the kind of stuff you should be publishing. All that crap about 'look at me, I'm neurotic!' is over." He fastened me with one of looks that made it obvious that he was worried about the opportunity he was handing me on a silver platter. He threw the manuscript,* Love and Death, A Study in Censorship, *in front of me.*
>
> *"I've had this manuscript rejected by every publisher from Appleton-Century to Ziff-David; forty-two in all. I've had it stuffed down the toilet in front of me by irate editors. It's been misplaced by three big publishing houses. I've been abused, sworn at, humiliated in front of secretaries. WHAT ARE YOU GOING TO DO ABOUT IT?" he screamed at me. Then he calmed down. "You know, Landesman,* Neurotica *could be something if you got rid of all that poetry and fake psychiatric prose. You've got a good idea there, the best that's come along in some time. It shouldn't be trusted to a dilettante like you." He tried hard to smile when he said that, but the grin froze half-way through.*[31]

Legman was born in 1917, which meant he was two years older than Landesman, and as Landesman became more involved in *Neurotica* he found himself being forced to accept Legman as a self-appointed arbiter of the magazine's contents. To Landesman and the small party he'd led to the Bronx, it must have seemed as though they had stirred up a nest of wasps. Legman had many things on his mind, and he had been waiting a long time for a chance to say them. He had begun collecting dirty jokes when he was nine, and his work combined the roles of psychologist and sexual researcher. What was unique in what he had done was that he worked within the disciplines of what would usually be considered folklore, except that the bulk of his immense folklore collection consisted of obscene limerics and dirty jokes. Although the populist philosophies widely discussed in the Depression years and the activities of the new Folk Music Archive of the Library of Congress had led to an interest in collecting and preserving the

American folk heritage of music and story, Legman had what was probably the most widely exchanged subject of vernacular folk expression—sex—virtually to himself.

If Legman had been only a collector he would still have been important as an indefatigable gatherer of obscure material—he had managed to find more than seventeen hundred obscene limericks—but he had done the tireless work of gathering the limericks and the books and magazines in order to make larger social generalizations about what lay behind the society's sexual neuroses. In his writings about his collection of limericks he emphasized that one of their consistent themes was their persistent misogynist attitude. Women were the continual victims of their barely concealed malice. In his work with the dirty joke—which became a classic two-volume study, despite the difficulties he had in finding publishers for both volumes—he pointed out that women were consistently portrayed negatively. Also he recognized that embedded in the large body of joke material were veiled attacks on most of the basic American social attitudes. He insisted that the American obsession with violence in its popular arts was a direct corollary to its repression of any expression of healthy sexuality.

After Legman's name became associated with *Neurotica*, he published sections of *Love and Death, A Study in Censorship* in the magazine and then with money he borrowed he bound together printed pages from the magazine to make a book. Later he confided to Landesman that he had the cover printed with a special red ink that would leave stains on the "fingers sweating with guilt" of its readers.[32] His insistence on the negative social effects of sexual censorship impressed Holmes and his friends, and their responses to Legman's emphatic opinions often can be glimpsed in their own writing about the censorship in the United States of any literature that dealt openly with sex.

In his book Legman attacked the social forces behind censorship, the common belief "that sex can be replaced by physical and emotional exertions measurably less violent than itself, such as calisthenics, cold baths, and bingo. The sinister absurdity of this pious hope is everywhere obvious."[33] The theme he developed in much of his writing was that American society exalts violence while it attempts to keep sexual expression hidden. As he concluded,

> We are faced in our culture by the insurmountable, schizophrenic contradiction that sex, which is legal in fact, is a crime on paper, while murder—a crime in fact—is, on paper, the best seller of all time. Civilization is not yet ready to let love and death fight it out in the market place, with free speech and four-color printing on both sides.[34]

On the subway back to Manhattan, Landesman, Holmes, and Joan Chapman, the woman who was doing prison research, began reading the manuscript of *Love and Death* that Legman had insisted they take home with them. Landesman passed the pages on to the others when he finished. He felt that his new discovery was "a Jeremiah crying in the wilderness with a howl that I had waited to hear all my life."[35] Herb Benjamin, the additional member of the party who had come up to the Bronx, made it clear that he considered Legman a psychiatric case and left. The others went to an all-night Waldorf cafeteria in the Village and sat up with endless cups of coffee, reading the manuscript, laughing at its emotional outbursts, but stunned by its insights. Chapman finally became too tired to continue and she left them there, still reading. At 5:30 a.m. Holmes and Landesman went out into the street, bleary eyed and hoarse from the long night. Each of them later described their feelings at that moment, and there is such a consistency in their recollections that each of them deserves a chance to speak for himself. Holmes wrote in "July 4th Weekend, 1948,"

> At 5:30, limp over cups of coffee, we sat under the dismal fluorescents of the Waldorf Cafeteria on Sixth Avenue and 8th Street finishing up the last smudged pages—pages of such power that they struck me, even through my weariness and all the stale cigarette smoke, as the most fiercely beautiful polemic I had ever read since Marx on the working day. And all these years later I can still see Landesman looking up through his sprawl, hair rumpled by the excitement of his thoughts, that absurd tie askew, and hear him say with astonishment, "Good God, do you realize? I've met an honest man!"[36]

Landesman's account, perhaps as a courteous gesture, gives Holmes a final line.

> "What if Legman's right?" Johnny asked. We looked at each other in disbelief at what we had experienced that night.
> "My God, Johnny, do you realize we've found an honest man?"
> "And not a moment too soon," Johnny added.[37]

Landesman concluded that when he finally got back to his hotel room and climbed wearily into bed, his wife wasn't upset that he'd gotten back so late, but she was annoyed that he brought the manuscript of Legman's book to bed with him.

Two nights later, Holmes' memory of the next meeting on July 3, 1948, was that the night was even muggier than the time he'd taken the subway to the Bronx with Landesman. Holmes wrote,

> *The east side streets smelled like a closet that hadn't been opened in a year. The body under the clothes was coated with a thin, oily sweat no matter what you did; there was a hint of seige in the motionless air; and anyone who was left in town deserved to feel like a bona fide survivor.*[38]

There were, however, compensations as the city's survivors banded together to get through the heat: "There were a lot of sudden, reckless parties up and down town that night—those unplanned celebrations created in an hour out of a telephone and a foundation of beer that were typical of a century with nothing much to celebrate."[39]

His own phone rang with one of those unplanned party invitations. Alan Harrington was going up to a party in Spanish Harlem that was being given by someone he knew from Columbia. Did Holmes want to come along? Holmes still thought of the drinking crowds he knew as being loosely territorial, and the Columbia crowd, scattered through the neighborhood around the university on Manhattan's Upper West Side, had only chance encounters with his crowd, which was "warrened"[40] around midtown Third Avenue and the Village. Now as they walked together through the stifling night toward the address Harrington had on East 121st Street near First Avenue, Holmes found himself moving into a neighborhood that was a different world from what he knew on Lexington Avenue.

> *The midtown avenues, emptied by the holiday and the heat, gradually gave way to guitars, crowded stoops, damp undershirts, and quick angers of those thronging streets (under their haze of frying beans) that no one escapes simply because it is hot, and we threaded our way down the chalked pavements of a particularly active block, wondering if we were on the right block.*
>
> *"This must be it, all right," Harrington said, "There's Kerouac."*[41]

Holmes stood beside Harrington, scrutinizing the other people on the street. Though he had no idea of what Kerouac looked like, Holmes had heard about him from several of his friends. The Kerouac he met that night was restless, idealistic, confused, and, like Holmes, haunted by literary ambitions.

I knew about Kerouac. He had written a thousand-page novel that was being passed around our crowd just then in a battered doctor's bag. Everyone who had seen it, and him, was enthusiastic, and five very different people had expressed that enthusiasm to me in curiously similar terms. The book, they said, was unwieldy, overly lyrical, and needed structuring (we talked like that then, and felt very professional), but it was also compassionate, stunningly written, and bursting with life. . . . I surveyed the people moving in and out of the sleazy little grocery up ahead (dark, good-looking men in sport shirts, most of them, with bags full of beer), but saw no one I would have identified as the author of a novel, weighing twenty pounds in the hand, that was being seriously touted to publishers by people I respected.[42]

To Holmes' surprise he realized that Kerouac was one of the people coming out of the store, "the tee-shirted younger brother of the others."[43] Kerouac had come downstairs to buy more beer, and he and Holmes talked for the first time as they waited for Harrington to come out with his own brown bag holding quart bottles of beer for the party. Holmes' description of that first encounter was the beginning of what would be his long, often renewed efforts to describe Kerouac's effect on people he met.

I don't remember anything we said. It was probably no more than the gauging, neutral chat beneath which young men take each other's measure, but I do remember my first impression. Under the boyish forelock, his strangely tender eyes noted me as we spoke, but all the time I felt that he was more keenly attuned to the tangled life of that street than to anything we were saying. It seemed to distract and stir him; he was at once excited and somehow emptied by it. Though he was just as straightforward, personable, buoyant, and attractive as I had been led to expect, there was a curious shyness under his exuberance; there was the touch of a moody thought around his mouth (like the reveler's sudden foretaste of the ashen dawn to come), and, above all, there was that quietly impressive intensity of consciousness.[44]

Twenty years later, in *Nothing More to Declare*, Holmes wrote that his first impression of Kerouac was of his startling good looks, like a "young John Garfield back in the neighborhood after college,"[45] comparing Kerouac to the handsome, dark-haired actor who had recently starred in the film version of James M. Cain's best-selling noir novel *The Postman Always Rings Twice*. Kerouac's own notebook entry about the Fourth of July party included a revealing line about his impression of Holmes' intelligence and wariness as Holmes stood watching the others with what Kerouac considered a wild *shrewd* look.[46]

Holmes and Harrington followed Kerouac back to what Holmes described as the "dark, smelly stairways through a hub-bub of mambo and Spanish laughter toward the sounds of bop and English talk."[47] They found the halls already filled with drinking students, and when they went inside Holmes observed that it was a typical slum cold-water flat similar to the one he and Marian had lived in on East 89th Street. Four "ill-ventilated, cramped rooms" opened off a kitchen that featured "damp plaster, dripping taps, worn linoleum."[48] In the noise and confusion of the crowded rooms, Holmes had only glimpses of another Columbia undergraduate, Allen Ginsberg, the person who he thought was giving the party. It was Ginsberg who would be the fourth person he would meet that weekend who would spin Holmes' life off in new directions.

The party itself was no different from dozens of others. It rushed on through the night in a raw haze of cigarette smoke, steadily emptied quart bottles of beer, and the relentless background of bop records on the phonograph. One thing Holmes remembered that made the night different from many other parties was that someone went over to the window and threw the empty bottles down into the clotheslines below them. Then, in the early hours of the morning, Ginsberg, who was continually moving from guest to guest, asking frantic questions and moving on without waiting for the answers, decided to add a Fourth of July touch to the din. Now stripped down to his undershirt in the muggy, crowded room, he set off a firecracker in a flower pot, which had been stuffed with cigarette butts during the evening, laughing gleefully at the litter flying through the smoke-filled air. Ginsberg was Holmes' age, but he seemed somehow younger—insecure, engaging, determined to be a center of attention, and hungry for some kind of center in his life. He also was to become one of Holmes' lifelong friends, but Holmes' memory of him at the party was less effusive, emphasizing Ginsberg's nervous energy:

> *There were too many people (most of whom I came to know well in the next year) for me to recall any longer just who was there and who was not. I don't remember any of them, except for the slight, aquiline young man, looking like an inquisitive dormouse in his black-rimmed glasses, his nostrils all but quivering, squirrel-like, with an abundance of awareness and delight, everything about him somehow* charged, *who came out of the crowd, greeted Harrington with exaggerated formality, and said to*

me, "I'm Allen Ginsberg. Who are you?"—following this with a funny little whinny of a laugh just in case I took it as effrontery.[49]

When they did have a moment to talk in the hubbub Ginsberg insisted on telling him about Kerouac's novel

"Have you read The Town and the City *yet? . . . Oh, you must. . . . Get Stringham to give it to you when he's finished. Or I'll see if I can't locate another copy. . . . It's full of these crazy poems, it's really a big hymn, you see. . . . And I'm in it too. . . . You ought to read it immediately, it's very important."*

Though they were obviously close friends, influencing one another back and forth, catalyzing each other with their very differences, Ginsberg spoke of Kerouac rather as an agent must speak of a client with whom he is personally involved, but never fails to represent in the professional sense because of that. I realized, all at once, that he knew that I was a writer too (and so might have useable connections), and he didn't intend to pass up an opportunity to cultivate anyone who might be helpful.

Still, I didn't feel that he was conning me. His enthusiasm for the book was equal to his affection for the man. It was just that he made no separation between the two.[50]

Although Holmes didn't write in his journal the morning after Ginsberg's party, as he would after so many parties later, he clearly understood the effect of the night on him when he wove these figures into his writing. He had met the last of the group of men who were to give him a totally new perspective on his life.

There is the danger of hindsight, of course, but I knew that when I left that party sometime after three, I was aware that if I remembered it at all, it was because I had met these two men. I liked Kerouac instinctively. He knew something I didn't know, he was already himself whereas I was still forming, and I felt strongly that we would be friends. . . . All in all, they impressed me, they intrigued me. There was a vividness about them, in their different ways, that spoke to me. But certainly I had no suspicion that something had begun that night that is not yet over.[51]

Chapter 6

A KIND OF BEATNESS

Blue Monday and I was out drinking last night. Block that sneer! No hangover, no pain. Jack Kerouac and Edward Stringham phoned a quarter of nine from over in a bar on 8th Ave. Come over! There is music: lights: girls: hilarity—lots!—joy—lots!

They had been listening to bebop with Dave Diamond, who had finally bolted in confusion from that nerve-racking experience. Lennie Tristano of all people has been walked out on! I can't say that I blame Diamond, who since his analysis has reached pay-dirt has been brutal and honest with people, tolerating nothing, crushing everything about him subject to pretence, etc: but out of the affair, Kerouac had gotten a letter to Alfred Kazin, whom Diamond knows well enough to address his epistle "Alfred dear"! Kerouac has written this tome, "The Town and the City," and the comment seems to be good. Jack was getting drunk rapidly and happily. Stringham was along for the ride.... Jack started talking about his next three novels, titled in the order of their appearance "Doctor Sax and the Moonman," "The Imbecile's Christmas," and "On the Road." He is planning to write them simultaneously. This may have been a figment of an alcoholic imagination. Stringham finally bolted (we were, by this time, in a place on the other side of the street where the beer was only a dime.) He left his raincoat and we finally abandoned Jack with three beers yet to finish and a desolate expression on his face.

—JOHN CLELLON HOLMES, letter to Mira Kent, October 18, 1948

Holmes wrote later that he felt like a different person after the first weekend of July, but he also remembered that as it all was happening he had no idea how it would effect his life. A perspiring weekend of edgy encounters with four new individuals as complicated and challenging as Landesman,

Legman, Kerouac, and Ginsberg would have been a puzzle to sort out for anyone, and Holmes had only a casual brush with each of them.

For the moment everyone had scattered. Landesman and his wife returned to St. Louis a few days after their meeting at the hotel, and although Holmes occasionally encountered Legman, the Bronx and his shabby rooms stuffed with books were Legman's world. Holmes left the city himself for a break in Chappaqua with Marian's family, but on July 12, 1948, he and Alan Harrington walked back up to Ginsberg's apartment for another party. It was his first chance to come closer to the scene he'd only glimpsed on the holiday weekend.

This time he included his impressions in his journal and he noted that there were "contacts made and impressions corrected."[1] He learned that it wasn't really Ginsberg's apartment, even though he'd hosted the party where Holmes had met both Ginsberg and Kerouac. It was actually the apartment of another Columbia student named Russell Durgin, who was there this time when they arrived. Durgin didn't, however, make much of an impression. Unaware that Durgin was recuperating from tuberculosis, Holmes described him as a slight man their age whose edges somehow seemed worn away.

Always drawn to books, Holmes discovered that even though the apartment was a decrepit tenement flat in a barrio neighborhood there was a fine literature collection, carefully filed in orange crates. Durgin was a theology student and the collection was concentrated on his interest in sixteenth- and seventeenth-century religious writing and poetry. Holmes particularly noticed a handsome, early, complete edition of Dryden's work. He also found that with the confusion of the party behind them and with a chance to talk, he liked Ginsberg. Holmes responded to Ginsberg's voluble manner and his lack of pretence, as well as Ginsberg's sudden enthusiasms and willingness to listen to his side of their conversation.

I even liked the overly nervous, expectant and wondering smile that will flash across his face when he is inwardly appreciating something which he is not at all sure you will like as well. You catch him in the moment of ecstasy over one thing or another, and this smile is his way of telling you to come on in, the water's fine.[2]

A disappointment for Holmes was that he didn't see Kerouac at the apartment. He'd felt an instinctive response to Kerouac but he'd only seen him for a few minutes. He had no idea that Kerouac's life was even more disheveled than his own. Once Kerouac had finished the first draft of *The*

Town and the City, he was desperate to get out of his mother's apartment. He was sending a stream of excited letters to his Denver friend Neal Cassady, filling pages with unlikely plans for them all to live together with Cassady's second wife, Carolyn—hopefully on a ranch that they would own somehow. His windy schemes were wildly impractical, and in a self-conscious aside he admitted that they should think of his plans only as metaphors for what he was actually dreaming.

A few weeks before Kerouac and Holmes first met, Kerouac had been left alone in Ozone Park when his mother went to Rocky Mount, North Carolina, to stay with his married sister Caroline, who had just had her first baby. Kerouac dutifully wrote Mémère that he was doing very well taking care of himself, and he turned to his novel again, continuing to revise and polish what he'd done. At the same time he was composing letters to Cassady with his improbable schemes of all of them living together in some kind of large house with rooms for everyone. In his letters he also complained that he wasn't seeing much of Ginsberg after Ginsberg had left Durgin's apartment and gone back to stay with his father in Paterson, New Jersey.

In mid-September 1948 Kerouac departed for North Carolina himself, and for a month he lived with his sister and her husband, parking cars in his brother-in-law's parking lot. To his increasing concern, the manuscript of *The Town and the City*, the bulky weight of pages he had carried around in the black doctor's bag, wasn't making any impression on the publishers who quickly glanced at it in the hope that they'd found a new Thomas Wolfe. While Kerouac was living in his sister's house, he decided for a short period that he was in love with the young nurse his sister had hired to help with the baby, dreaming that he might be able to marry her if he had any money—and if he weren't such a rough-edged character.

At that point Holmes also had no idea that Kerouac was so inextricably tied to his mother. Jack and Gabrielle's relationship had only intensified when his father, on his death bed, had made Kerouac swear that he would always take care of Mémère. The truth, however, was that for most of these years it was his mother, with her grueling, low-paying factory jobs and later her social security checks, who took care of him. Kerouac's letters to Cassady continued from North Carolina; one, on October 3, included an angry attack on homosexuality, which Kerouac considered a vice, ending with an emotional denial that he could ever be thought of as "queer" himself. He was friends with Allen Ginsberg, but Ginsberg was going through an agonizing crisis over his own sexuality, and whatever hung in the air between them was expressed so vaguely that Kerouac ignored it.

In August 1948 Holmes had met Kerouac a second time at Alan Harrington's, with Edward Stringham included in the evening. As Holmes noted again in his journal, "I like Jack immensely,"[3] and he repeated what he had written before about his immediate pleasure at Kerouac's naïveté.

> *He is sincere, forthright, and I think it would be correct to say that he has a* naïveté *which is more than simply put on. It is not only a certain literary freshness. There is something really youthful and self-conscious about him. People think him brilliant or knowing only by default. I like him because of this. What Alan takes for tactics, I think is loneliness, trouble and the rest.*[4]

Kerouac's response to Holmes was also positive. According to biographer Paul Maher Jr., "Kerouac accepted Holmes as a close friend almost immediately.[5] Before Kerouac left for Rocky Mount, he let Holmes read the manuscript of *The Town and the City*, the thousand-page manuscript in its black doctor's bag. Harrington had also completed a draft of his first novel, and on September 13, 1948, Holmes wrote two separate journal entries discussing his responses to the manuscripts that the two neophyte writers had given so much effort to finish. He liked many things about Kerouac's massive draft, but it was Harrington's manuscript that impressed him more. Holmes' overall disappointment with *The Town and the* City was that Kerouac seemed uneasy with larger generalizations: "He does not comprehend fully intense ideas."[6]

> *His [Kerouac's] ideas are more mannerisms (family, father-and-son, separation of intellectuals from the people etc.). These are not ideas, they are fragments of observations. . . . I asked Alan if he [Jack] had another book in him. Alan said, surely. I hope that he is correct. This one is baldly autobiographical and, I think, rather weak in certain spots. He does not connect things well.*[7]

Despite his reservations Holmes' conclusions were still positive, and he was moved by the strain of sentimentality that was already evident in Kerouac's writing, a sentimentality that Holmes rigorously denied himself in his own pages.

> *On top of it, however, there is this very real, terribly beautifully felt writing, this true physical and (often) spiritual conception of America and the general ambition of the whole project. It is a book that he has felt and*

lived through and this gives it backbone. He will publish it I think. But it needs work.[8]

Holmes' reaction to Harrington's novel—written as a separate journal entry the same day—had fewer reservations. Holmes was impressed with the intellectual framing of Harrington's novel, which validated his concern in his own work with the structuring of a novel around ideas.

He has hit things very hard and he is never pretentious or overly intellectual. He can write philosophy and ideas as ad men write about shaving lotion. It is quick talk, the kind of thing we understand here, the sort of thing that has brought life and color and punch [to] American literature. He has got it, and I think we can be assured the rest of the book, properly pruned and held together, will be a great book of a new kind of writing here in America, the idea-writing of young, talented men like Alan who think and care about this country.[9]

There was prescience in Holmes' comment. Though Harrington would abandon this early novel, he would publish several novels of ideas—including *The Revelations of Dr. Modesto* (1955), *The Secret Swinger* (1966), and *Paradise I* (1977)—that influenced a later generation of authors such as Thomas Pynchon and Edward Abbey, who admired Harrington's writing.

By the fall of 1948 Holmes had begun to change out of the second-hand costume of the European intellectual he had squeezed himself into. With some trepidation he was trying on some of the new ideas he'd encountered during that first weekend in July. Perhaps as a sign of his unconscious drift, he again found himself in trouble with his novel. He had begun to rewrite it with considerable enthusiasm. The first chapters had gone so quickly that he had been able to complete a first draft a few days before he met Landesman and Legman. Now Holmes found himself becalmed as he faced the more difficult job of revising his book. On the surface his life went on unchanged—the nights drinking beer at Glennon's, the parties with Marian, the hours of wrangling talk and music with his friends—but with the novel stalled, the days drifted past.

Whatever doubts Holmes had about many of his earlier ideas, he still considered himself a Marxist, though, like most other American intellectuals, he now dismissed the Soviet Union's socialist experiment as a disastrous failure. He had drawn back from his earlier political postures, but the fall of 1948 was a complicated moment in American politics, and he found himself briefly working with Harrington at the fringes of the drama.

The Communist seizure of power in Czechoslovakia the year before had ended any sympathies Holmes had felt for the Soviet Union and its relentless efforts to expand further into Europe, but he still considered himself as somewhere on the Left, still certain that change was necessary in the United States. Like many others who had become disillusioned with Communism as a political system, he was sympathetic to the attempt of Henry Wallace and his Progressive Party to influence the approaching presidential election in the fall of 1948. Wallace had been vice president during Roosevelt's third term of office, when his background as a Midwest farmer was considered an asset for the Democrats to assure rural voters that Roosevelt hadn't forgotten the catastrophic conditions that had devastated the farmers' economy.

Wallace was an idealistic, committed supporter of the New Deal, but his liberal ideas were so far from the political center that the Democratic Party leaders were concerned enough to pass him over as vice presidential candidate for Roosevelt's controversial fourth-term candidacy in 1944. Instead the party chose another Midwesterner, Harry Truman, from Missouri, who became president after Roosevelt's death in the spring of 1945. It was Truman who made what the Republicans derided as compromising concessions to the Soviet Union as the war in Europe was ending. Truman had disturbed the country's liberals by authorizing the dropping of atomic bombs in Japan to hurry the end of the war in Asia. Truman's pragmatic approach to relations with the Soviet Union also upset much of the American military and the anti-Communist press. His campaign for reelection seemed hopeless.

In the midst of the rising tensions, a body of documentary evidence now seems to make it clear that the American Communist Party, which felt it had enough influence in the newly created industrial union, the C.I.O., to play a role in the coming election, decided to mount a challenge to the two established political parties. Without acknowledging its role in the campaign, in the fall of 1947 it secured enough signatures on voter's petitions in California to create a new political party with Wallace as its spokesman. The party was considerably to the Left of either the Republicans or the Democrats, and it was named "Progressive Citizens of America"—or the Progressive Party.

When the party duly nominated Wallace as its candidate for president there was no one, even the leaders of the Communist Party, who thought he had a chance to win. What seems to have been their strategy was that Wallace would capture enough Democratic voters to ensure Truman's defeat, and the winner would be the Republican candidate Thomas E. Dewey. They regarded him as so far to the political right that in the ensuing disruption he would alienate the country's voters and there would be a chance to present an acceptable candidate supporting the party's views in the election of 1952.

Despite a small army of informants embedded both within the leadership of the Communist Party and in the new party itself, the persistent efforts of the F.B.I. have never been successful in determining whether Wallace himself was conscious of what he was representing. At the time of his nomination he was in an influential position in New York as editor of the *New Republic* magazine, and he accepted the offer with a crusader's zeal.

Holmes was unaware of any of these implications of the Wallace campaign, but he was restless and dissatisfied and he was drawn to the Quixotic tone of Wallace's candidacy. Over the spring and the summer of 1948 Wallace led one of the most liberal political campaigns that the country had ever seen. He appeared on speaker's platforms with African American leaders, he refused to address segregated audiences, and he declined to make appearances in states that had enacted legislation creating the system of legal apartheid that denied the rights of black citizens. He aroused heated opposition from conservative groups by his spirited defense of the social legislation of the New Deal.

The immediate issue, however, for the American Communist Party, was the newly created Marshall Plan. The United States was proposing to offer substantial aid for the battered European governments bracing to fend off further Communist expansion. Czechoslovakia had already fallen, in the summer there was fighting on the Paris streets between the Communist workers and the police, and the Russians had blockaded Berlin to force it into the Soviet zone in East Germany. Despite this evidence filling the newspapers Wallace opposed the American plan, calling it the "Martial Plan." When he was accused of having Communist support, his response was "If they want to support me, I can't stop them."[10]

Betty Holmes was one of the hopeful idealists who believed in the Wallace campaign, and in May she had already asked her son to write a long letter to his older sister, Lila, and her husband, Jack, in California. In his letter to them on May 14, 1948, Holmes gravely assured them that Betty understood "the California papers are not notorious for their correct handling of some national issues."[11]

By the middle of the summer, as Holmes was struggling with his novel and Kerouac was fretting in his mother's apartment, dreaming of a home with the Cassadys in the West, the political situation changed. Wallace lost the support of the labor unions, which had been struggling against their own Communist supporters for many years and were uneasy at his sympathies for Communist goals. The unions' defections effectively doomed his campaign.

Holmes was sympathetic enough to Wallace's dilemma to let his mother persuade him to offer his own help. He and Harrington became familiar faces at the Progressive Party's office at 39 Park Avenue. On July 25 he wrote Mira Kent that they had been doing more work for Wallace's campaign.

> *Have been doing more publicity work for Henry, through 39 Park. Somebody in Iowa got an idea which needed good copy so they came to Harrington and me, I don't know why. We had to struggle for three evenings to bat out just a little. It makes you feel that you are helping. (Doesn't that sound liberal?) This idea was a switch on the Burma Shave angle. Signs strung along the road with a continuous jingle. We batted out about ten sets for them. Really syncophant stuff, but it may help. It's gratis in any case.*[12]

Despite his idealism, Holmes was resigned to the inevitability of Wallace's defeat, and—like the rest of country—he was assured by the press and the opinion polls that Truman had no chance for reelection. After working with Harrington on the campaign, he went back to his struggle to revise his novel.

On August 23, 1948, he wrote a seven-page, single-spaced letter to his friend Howard Friedman discussing his work-in-progress in minute detail. What the letter made clear was that Holmes regarded his novel as a moral dilemma dramatized as a "thriller-morality play."[13] It was also obvious that like many inexperienced writers he was trying to make a thin plot carry a caravan's weight of intellectual baggage. Over the next weeks he continued his efforts to rewrite his first chapters, but like the camel that has finally been loaded with one straw too many, the novel refused to get to its feet.

The second week of October 1948, after Kerouac returned from Rocky Mount, he and Holmes became closer friends. He soon was dropping in at John and Marian's apartment whenever he wanted to break away from the endless hours at his typewriter in Ozone Park, revising *The Town and the City* and working on new projects. Since Kerouac and Holmes were both broke, they usually spent their afternoons on long walks criss-crossing Manhattan, stopping in shabby neighborhood bars where they could buy beer for a dime a glass.

Betty and Liz Holmes were still living in their apartment upstairs on the fifth floor, and if it was quiet when Liz got home from high school she'd sometimes knock on her brother's door. Over the months she met most of

his friends. Of all of them, it was Kerouac who attracted her, just as he attracted almost every woman he met during these years in New York. In her
memoir, *681 Lexington Avenue*, Liz remembered her first encounter with
Kerouac and wrote a warm description of Holmes' cramped apartment.

> *I don't remember the first time I met Jack Kerouac. That is strange be-*
> *cause I loved him right off, even if I can't pinpoint when the "right off"*
> *was. I see him sitting in a straight chair in John's apartment—afternoon.*
> *The chair is between a low bookcase by the couch, which forms a right*
> *angle with more couch and the kitchen table. I am on another couch, all*
> *with bookcases filling the walls above them. Across from me is the kitchen*
> *area—apartment fridge with hot plate and shelves. The phonograph is*
> *across from the couch near Jack and of course, a loud record is on, this*
> *one a mambo. . . . Jack has a saucepan upside down between his legs with*
> *the handle in his crotch and he is bongo-ing. He bobs his head a bit and*
> *looks around—at the music, at John bouncing near the player, at me. A*
> *lick of black hair falls to his forehead, his wide, fragile lips pucker out and*
> *then break into a smile, the eyes light up.*[14]

On October 10, 1948, Holmes filled the pages of his journal with another
of his incisive and sympathetic sketches of the new friends he was meeting through Kerouac. This time he gave the sketch a title, "*Lucien Carr—*
immediate impressions." The previous night Kerouac had phoned about
ten thirty from the drugstore below his mother's apartment in Ozone Park
to say that he was going into Manhattan to meet Carr at Sellmann's bar on
42nd Street, and he wanted John and Marian to join them. They walked
downtown from their apartment at 56th Street in the crisp autumn darkness and arrived at Times Square before Kerouac did. Holmes introduced
himself to Carr, who bought them drinks while they waited for Kerouac.
Holmes' impression of Carr was immediately positive.

> *He is an attractive person, the slightly sallow skin that is so smooth, like a*
> *boy's, the thin blonde hair that is never quite arranged, the almond eyes,*
> *sloe-narrow, the almost morose sensitive mouth that occasionally breaks*
> *into the widest white smile I have ever seen. The hunched shoulders, the*
> *slight body. He looks like a young boy except that looking into his face*
> *tells you something other than that. It seems that what he does is "work*
> *and drink," and that is what he's interested in. He has a strange cultivated*
> *voice, that at first sounds almost effected, but which levels off as you talk*
> *with him.*[15]

Holmes found that Carr spoke easily about the stabbing of David Kammerer after he'd made unwanted homosexual advances. Carr had served
two years in the state reformatory, and he spoke just as casually about his
prison experiences. "Marian was as taken I think, though she found him
distant."[16] Kerouac rushed in a few minutes later, announcing with some
excitement that he was now enrolled in the New School for Social Research
on West Ninth Street. He was taking literature courses in which he'd read
Dostoevsky, Tolstoy, Melville, and others. Carr continued to pay for the
drinks after they crossed the street to enter an Eighth Avenue bar, staying
until he had to leave for the United Press International offices nearby where
he worked as an editor on the night desk.

Through the fall, if Holmes wasn't writing and no one else had dropped
by, he often went upstairs to his mother's apartment, though they usually
drifted into one of their interminable arguments. There was little contact
with his father, who was living in Washington, D.C., but a few days after
meeting Carr, there was a phone call from him. Holmes' father was in New
York City on business and wondered if John could meet him at the Pennsylvania Railroad Station.

Holmes had never forgiven him for the divorce, and their occasional
meetings had been stormy. They hadn't seen each other in over a year, and
their attempt to have dinner was as unsuccessful as their other meetings.
Holmes wrote to Mira Kent on October 18: "It was a painful, senseless experience, accomplishing nothing, giving neither of us any satisfaction, but he
was reluctant to let it go at that. Words were said (they always are between
us) that no one really means and it ended on a properly filial and thus false
note. It disturbed me."[17]

As Holmes struggled with his own novel's revisions he was also disturbed
with Kerouac's boast that he'd now begun working on three new books at
the same time that he was revising *The Town and the City*. Kerouac had
gotten as far as titling them, and it is clear that the process of germination
had already begun for books that later he would try to find a way to write—
Doctor Sax and the Moonman, a novel about the myth of America; *The Imbecile's Christmas*, about someone imbecilic enough to accept anything he is
told; and *On the Road*, a story of two hitchhikers on their way to California,
one looking for his girl, the other on the way to an illusionary Hollywood.

Holmes was still in contact with Landesman back in St. Louis, who was
trying to decide if he should move to New York. Landesman had assured
Holmes that he was interested in printing whatever Holmes wanted to write
for him, which for a young writer is the equivalent of a rainbow appearing in

the sky. The autumn 1948 issue of *Neurotica 3* included the first of many of Holmes' essays analyzing cultural phenomena. Later Holmes' cultural essays on a range of subjects would become his most highly regarded work.

In "All the Good Roles Have Been Taken—The Plight of the Talented Untalented," he divided the hangers-on in any artistic community into two groups he called "the spear carriers," or extras, and "the Perpetual Students," or explorers.[18] Holmes concluded his *Neurotica* essay by summarizing the difference between them: "The one apes the latest fashion; the other insists upon believing he will create the next one."[19] Landesman was delighted with the natural ease of Holmes' writing and sent one of his characteristic breezy letters on September 1, 1948, saying he was featuring the essay in an advertisement for his magazine in the October issue of *Partisan Review*.

Throughout the fall of 1948 Holmes doggedly persisted with the writing he was engaged in, his almost-finished novel and his poetry. The novel was his only justification for his life of dependency on his wife's tedious secretarial jobs. Whatever differences there were between him and Kerouac, they shared a complicated dependency on women who were effectively paying for the hours they each could spend at the typewriter.

Poetry continued to be a creative door that always stood open for Holmes, but he had already discovered that the money he might make from it wouldn't be enough to keep him in cigarettes. Whatever he felt about his own chances, he couldn't help but be conscious that someone like Norman Mailer, who had just published his first novel, *The Naked and the Dead*, based on his war experience, was making a great deal more money than Holmes could ever make as a poet. Holmes didn't stop sending off his poems, however, and they often found an immediate response from editors who recognized his potential. Another poem, "Love and Chemistry," was accepted by the *New Mexico Quarterly* for publication in the winter, and Holmes' poems would continue to appear regularly in magazines over the next two years.

Holmes' difficulties with his novel didn't stop the flow of writing in the pages of his journals and his long letters to friends. On October 8, 1948, he typed a long, single-spaced hymn to jazz and its meaning to him. It was, perhaps unconsciously, his elegy to the older generation of Dixieland musicians he'd first heard as a teenager listening to radio broadcasts in Englewood and then in the small clubs in the Village when he broke away to the city as a relief from life in Chappaqua. It was also his anguished protest at the sounds of the new jazz that was challenging the way of playing that he loved. Holmes' initial hostile reaction to bebop may seem to strike a discordant note, but it was a feeling that was almost universal among serious fans of classic jazz during that period. Holmes wrote,

> *Now we have be-bop, which is a sick, neurotic expression of the present post-war days, mechanized to a fault, atomized out of any discernible rhythm, obliterated under the shower of slick technical variations, ruined. But jazz is still played, the kind that I heard ten years ago. It is sadder now, the men are older, they have seen too many years pass without finding safety, but they play on. And there are kids learning their ropes with these men now, who will carry on in the traditions of genuine New Orleans and Chicago jazz. What it means to them, because they play, and to me and others like me, because we listen, can't be overwhelmed by all the escape-hatch mechanisms which even the music business must create to lull people away from the harsh realities of this country.*[20]

Holmes' emotional attachment to traditional jazz styles was so intense that it helps to explain the complex feelings he experienced when he gave in to Kerouac's badgering and began to listen seriously to the still new sounds of bebop only a few weeks later. For Marian it was all jazz, and as Holmes noted many times in his letters and journals, she didn't like any of it. He was just as relentlessly critical of her genuine love of Italian opera, and the issue of their music was never resolved between them.

At the end of the fall Alan Harrington left New York, giving up his apartment in an attempt to save money so he could return to his own novel. He and his wife, Virginia, and young son, Steve, went to live with his mother in Tucson, Arizona, where she had a large house in the desert. On November 4, 1948, Holmes wrote him a long and mostly jubilant letter. To everyone's complete surprise and disbelief, Truman had beaten Dewey for the presidency. Holmes had never had any hopes for the Wallace campaign, but Truman, despite what Holmes felt as his failure to address liberal issues, was at least a better choice than any Republican candidate might have been. Holmes responded that he recognized that the election had been decided on personal issues.

> *The election of Truman is one of those indeterminables that you often spoke of that rock the boat of the iron-clad system of things. It is certainly heartening and proves that the American people would still rather have a man for president than a machine, no matter who that man. It's a victory for the polemic over the platitude, human frailty over the faultless cipher.*[21]

In the general euphoria over the election, Legman threw a party to celebrate the appearance of his first article in *Neurotica 3*. Holmes described
the mood in a letter to Howard Friedman on November 8, 1948.

Last Tuesday, after being about the ONLY PEOPLE to vote for Wallace,
we went up to Gershon Legman's wonderful cottage in the Bronx. (He is
the fellow who wrote that marvelous piece on the comics in Neurotica 3,
now out. I have an article in it as well.) He was giving a a party celebrat-
ing publication and his birthday. We spent a rather eclectic evening up
there listening to records, milling about in mobs of people and chinning
with a Reichian analyst and a chronic lyer [sic]. . . . Once back [home] I
stayed awake all night listening to the concussion of the upset, alternating
my shock with cheers.

Almost as if the planets had come into conjunction for Holmes, he began to find his way through the thicket of his novel's revisions. Marian, at
the same time, was still enjoying her job at the New School as a typist in the
office of the Dramatic Workshop, even if they were as pressed for money as
ever.

Legman's volcanic utterances about sexuality in American society might
have been controversial for the American mainstream, but to the crowd
around Kerouac and Holmes he was only confirming what they had already
decided for themselves. One of the most insistent themes in the early Beat
group's polemics was the demand for greater sexual freedom, or at least
for a greater sexual honesty, and in Legman's pages they found a bristling
reinforcement of their own convictions. When Kerouac climbed the stairs
to the apartment at 681 Lexington, usually in the afternoons before Marian came home from her job, or later after she'd gone to bed, his sexual
adventures were one of his persistent themes. As he boasted on one of his
drunken nights when Holmes trailed after him as he looked for a girl, "I laid
Lucien Carr's girl, Celine, you know. He says I'm a slob."[22] Then as the night
went on and they "crept along the silent streets" of student apartments near
Columbia as he prowled for girls, he burst out, "I'm an animal. That's all I
am. But I can accept it."[23]
  Holmes was still attempting to placate his own conscience, nagged by
his uneasy sense that despite his commitment to Marian and his marriage
he was continually attracted to other women, even if many of his attempts
at seduction got him nowhere. For the others in the group their obsessive

interest in sex fueled the intensity of their incessant round of parties and drunken sessions in nearby barrooms and in each other's apartments.

In a journal entry on November 10, 1948, Holmes described a night talking with Kerouac after his friend had gone "stark raving mad with a new theory about the sexual regeneration of the world."[24] Kerouac had spent the previous weekend with a couple living in Poughkeepsie, north of New York City, who had what he thought was an open marriage. In a burst of male braggadocio, Kerouac described an afternoon of rampant sex with his friend's wife. He left Holmes with the impression that the couple

> *seem to live with no restrictions, she can sleep with whomsoever she takes a fancy to and so can he. They had a mad, old house filled with empty beer bottles and a baby of a few months. . . . Jack was entranced and the wife came up to him at one point and said, "I've always liked you, Jack," and they went to bed. He had her about six times and the husband was right in the next room. In fact a young high school girl came in and the husband took her upstairs for some fun.*[25]

Kerouac's new revelation was that everybody is like an apple, only waiting to be eaten, and they should just walk around without their clothes and have sex with anyone they chose. "This seemed to be the large thing that came to him this weekend and he built upon it endlessly with quotes from other friends."[26] Holmes' transcription of the conversation might have reflected his own thoughts, because in Kerouac's journal entry for November 3, 1948, when he described his visit to Poughkeepsie, he mentioned neither his friends' open marriage nor having sex with his friend's wife. Instead Kerouac noted that a seventeen-year-old girl came to visit and that he was the one she went upstairs to have sex with after she'd been in the house only thirty minutes.[27]

Then, for the first time in his journals, on November 10, 1948, Holmes noted that Kerouac began telling him about someone named Neal Cassady.

> *Take Neil Cassidy [sic] for instance, there's a real appley kind of guy. He wrote me all about this orgy they had out in Frisco, a white girl, a colored girl and a colored boy, all real gone on gage, doing everything. At one point the girl got up and stood on her head, spread her legs and screamed "eat me, eat me like I was food." I asked him sarcastically what Cassidy had done. "Oh, I guess he ate the girl, laid the colored one and blew the colored boy." I remarked that I thought Cassidy must have a remarkable capacity. "Oh, sure. He's everything. A vast semeny kind of guy, you know?"*

Kerouac went on to describe his first sexual experience with the girl he named "Maggie Cassidy" in one of the books he later wrote about his adolescence in Lowell, insisting that every man is only a penis.

> *He built on this, real concern mirrored in his face which I choose at this point to believe is the kind of objectivisation [sic] of nascent sexuality, a thing we all go through. At some point, particularly after some conspicuous sexual success like his weekend, we thirst for more and more and we seek somehow to make our experience not only universal but profound beyond all its obvious limitations. That's what Jack was trying to do with all this.*[28]

By the time Kerouac had finished with his theories about a new sexuality, they were listening to Symphony Sid, the all-night disc jockey who was their guide to the New York jazz scene, while Marian slept in the other room. Another friend, Tom Livornese, had come over to sleep on the sofa and he became entangled in the night's long arguments. Kerouac was now expanding on his other writing projects. "We had on Symphony Sid by this time and Jack was talking about *On the Road*, which he is writing, even though I think at this point he should stick to *Doctor Sax*. He went on and on talking about it madly, creating it in a way before our eyes."[29]

As the talk drifted on to the new music, bebop, Holmes became exasperated by his friends' lack of knowledge about jazz, despite their impetuous emotional responses to what they were hearing on the radio. He still regarded bebop as commercialized, over-technical frenzy. In his journal he launched into a long, impatient analysis about why they really didn't have the musical knowledge to understand what was happening in the new jazz. Holmes was beginning to be tired of all of the talk, none of it leading to anything, even if he was also drawn to the energy of their excited exchanges and to what he thought of as their sense of rebellion.

Holmes was aware that his new group of friends had already aroused antagonism from many people around them. He understood that Kerouac and Ginsberg "deny this society because it denies them."[30] For the first of what would become a long series of defenses over the course of his writing career, Holmes defended the group, even though—since this was his journal—the only one he was defending them against was himself. Trying to find historical figures to compare them with, he turned again to Dostoevsky.

> *Kerouac calls it a "kind of revolution." I see it only as a final sympton of our sickness. It is not confined to New York. He has traveled everywhere,*

hitch-hiking, stealing cars, walking, riding the rods and everywhere these people live. He accepts it, only because his experience has shown him that he cannot reject it. It is present and to more and more Americans (young people ruined by the war, dissatisfied, questing, yearning for things they have ceased to believe in, desiring to fulfill themselves even if this can be accomplished only at the expense of destroying themselves as well), more and more of them are turning to it. It is not bohemianism and there is little or no overtly intellectual character to it. It is an honest "what the hell" attitude, the result of the sexual sterility which has become America in the last forty years, the social vacuum and the psychological upheaval (still confined only to the underside). These people are questing. When among them you feel what Dostoevsky must have felt mixing with the dregs of Russia during his imprisonment in Siberia: you feel at once horrified and intriqued, because these people are living "reality" at the pressure-point, thinking (even the ignorant ones) upon pregnant questions the rest of us are too secure to know about. They are testing themselves (albeit unknowingly) in the crucible, trying to discover (equally unconsciously) what is right and what is wrong.[31]

It was just another one of these late autumn nights in 1948 when Holmes and Kerouac sat up until morning with quarts of beer, arguing, talking, rhapsodizing while Symphony Sid blared in the background, that Holmes cajoled Kerouac into finding some term that would define the vague unease they all were feeling—some term that would define their group.

Everyone I knew felt it in one way or another—that bottled eagerness for talk, for joy, for excitement, for sensation, for new truths. Whatever the reason, everyone of my age had a look of impatience, unreleased ecstasy and the presence of buried worlds within.

I kept goading Jack to characterise this new attitude, and one evening as he described the way the young hipsters of Times Square walked down the street—watchful, catlike, inquisitive, close to the buildings, in the street but not of it—I interrupted him to say that I thought we all walked like that, but what was the peculiar quality of mind behind it?

"It's a kind of furtiveness," he said. "Like we were a generation of furtives. You know—with an inner knowledge there's no use flaunting on that level, the level of the 'public,' a kind of beatness—I mean, right down to it, to ourselves, because we all really know where we are—and a weariness with all the forms, all the conventions of the world. . . . It's something like that. So I guess you might say we're a beat generation," and he laughed a

conspiratorial, the Shadow knows kind of laugh at his own words and at the look on my face.[32]

With Kerouac's half serious suggestion that they were a "Beat Generation," Holmes immediately realized that his friend had stumbled onto the essential element that distinguished them from the "Lost Generation" of the 1920s, that earlier generation of writers who had challenged the American mainstream. "That's It!" Kerouac remembered Holmes responding.[33] It was a moment of inspiration on Kerouac's part. In later years his attempts to explain what he meant became more and more blurred as he drifted further from the Times Square characters and the small group of friends he was attempting to describe in the fall of 1948.

In the beginning Kerouac was certainly implying that "beat," in the street sense, meant being a deadbeat like his Times Square friend Herbert Huncke, a misfit, someone beaten down by all the things happening around them, an oppressed class out of touch with society. "Beat" would also describe Lucien Carr after he'd been released from prison, who Kerouac believed "is on the bottom now and it can't get much worse."[34] Holmes and Kerouac had a few friends in common—including Ginsberg, Harrington, Stringham, and Bill Cannastra—and they all felt that America was locked into what they considered the country's sexual and drug hypocrisies, all the while denying the threat of atomic annihilation.

For Holmes there was a whiff of existential rebellion in the term, suggesting the quest for a spiritual dimension to life that would redeem the struggle. Like Camus he believed "that only one thing has ever been asked of our [postwar] generation—that it should be able to cope with despair."[35] During his early conversations with Kerouac he felt as though he and Jack "were on a spiritual journey, in search of our very souls."[36] Both shared an impatience with what Holmes considered "the 'little literary life,' with the quarterly-idiots drooling the latest about [Henry] James, with the truncated scholarly types in their corduroy jackets drinking beer as if it were sherry."[37] Instead, in the months to come Holmes felt himself "joining an underground that had no mission. . . . [A]ll along the lust for freedom, for some unbreakable certainty, for some grounded vision. . . . Jack and I stood on snowy street corner, flailing quarts of beer, and singing bop to the police cars."[38]

A few years earlier, Huncke, as a friend of William Burroughs, had introduced Kerouac and Ginsberg to the late night Times Square scene, with its risky drug dealing, prostitution, its glare of lights, its all night cafeterias, and its movie houses strung along 42nd Street that sometimes let people sleep all night through the films. Huncke was a junky who had turned his life into a series of thefts and robberies to support his habit, sometimes carrying a pistol if armed robbery seemed like a useful idea. To blur the picture, he was also gentle and intelligent, a small, diffident, soft-spoken gay man with pleasing manners and considerable charm. The kind of person Kerouac was describing in his characterization of the new "Beats" was as close to Huncke as to any of the other members of their group, and the characterization also extended to others such as Ginsberg and Carr, as well as Burroughs and Cassady, whom Holmes hadn't met.

Later the term "Beat" was vague enough to describe a literary movement that was conveniently expanded by media journalists to include any writer they felt would amplify and strengthen the "Beat" image they associated with their own definition of the term, but when Kerouac and Holmes first used the expression they were only referring their small group of close friends and to the attitudes they expounded over their endless nights of sexual boasting and alcohol-fueled argument. Kerouac's proposal for a name was probably only half-serious. The "Beat Generation" he was describing was a dozen or so of the men in their crowd, with the women who came and went in their lives only occasionally acknowledged as being there on the scene. At the moment when Kerouac used the term, the literary achievement of the Beat Generation—outside of contributions to school publications by Ginsberg and Kerouac—consisted of Holmes' two published poems, his review of a book of Danish poetry that had appeared in *Poetry* magazine, and one short story and an essay in *Neurotica*.

In his journals Holmes was still unconvinced that the new attitudes Kerouac was attempting to describe would actually lead to anything. He insisted that both Kerouac and Ginsberg spent too much of their time talking about their feelings when they both should be reading more seriously in philosophy and literature. Despite the tangles of his own personal life, Holmes was still only twenty-two, and he pestered the others with a twenty-two-year-old's certainties. Whatever Holmes thought of Kerouac's concept of a Beat Generation, in December 1948 its most conspicuous figure suddenly showed up below his window on Lexington Avenue in the person of Neal Cassady, who had driven a new gray and maroon Hudson automobile in a careening journey across the country with his teenage ex-wife, LuAnne, to visit his New York friends. After a few weeks trailing in Cassady's wake, Holmes finally understood what Kerouac had been trying to tell him.

Chapter 7

NEAL & CO.

*It is now eleven o'clock blue Monday morning and while I [sit writing?]
this thing for you, two "friends" lie on the couches where they have been
all night. I have been thundering about the apartment for an hour or
more, making feeble noises in the effort to wake them. Now they lie in
each other's arms, for all the world like little children, and they joke
playfully, early morning jokes, while outside their car is probably frozen. On its windshield, as I see it from here, there is a little oblong of
cardboard which tells them to appear at the magistrate's court sometime next week and pay a fine for leaving it there all night. The weekend is over and I have nothing to say, judge.*

*Surprisingly enough little drinking was done, except for the eve itself.
I was up most of the last three days and nights with an endless series of
people picked up from an even more endless and vague series of parties
that went on and on. We drove all over the city, through the driving
snow, rutting ourselves in drifts, singing, chanting, missing other cars,
etc. There was even an after-hours place in Harlem, where the music
was mad and the drinks a dollar and we all pooled what money there
was left and had four drinks for eight people. This was five o'clock some
morning that I seem to have forgotten. Now the weekend is over and
the residue of it lies on my couch and I can't get to work [and] I dash
this off to you. I am incapable of thinking coherently, though I feel quite
dry and peaceful inside. That is the feeling I suppose, beyond a certain
point to get pleasantly numb and little penetrates. It seems that these
last three days have been one endless conclave after another. I have
walked, lain, stumbled and fallen through dozens of apartments, over
the strew of bottles and bodies, listened to mad music, to driving saxes
and seering [sic] trumpets, pushed my way through crowds, fallen into
people, danced with them, never argued because that is for the week
not the weekend. . . . We smoked tea most of the weekend which was a
kick because it leaves you no after effect and you get coherently high*

without losing your grip. But consequently the sequence of things has become lost and I can remember everything that occurred but not in the surely exact order.
—JOHN CLELLON HOLMES, letter to Mira Kent, January 3, 1949

On January 4, 1949, the day after Holmes wrote to Mira Kent about the two "friends"—Neal Cassady and his ex-wife, LuAnne—sleeping on his couch while he made noises around them in an effort to wake them up, he wrote a letter to Alan Harrington in Arizona, describing the arrival of Neal Cassady in New York at the beginning of the week. Cassady's abrupt arrivals in New York have become so much the material of the Beat legend that Holmes' description, written the day after Cassady and LuAnne had left the apartment, helps to set what sometimes seem to be mythic events within a more realistic frame.

What Holmes didn't know was the recent background behind Cassady's appearance. He wasn't aware that Neal, newly married to Carolyn Robinson, had used all of their small savings on a sudden whim to put a down payment on a new maroon and gray Hudson automobile so he could drive to New York. It was some time before Holmes understood that after Cassady had left his wife with their four-month-old-baby girl so broke in San Francisco that Carolyn had to apply for welfare, he had set out for New York with a friend, Al Hinkle, and his newly married wife, Helen, and then just as casually decided to stop in Denver to pick up LuAnne, whom Cassady had married when she was fifteen.

Holmes was also unaware that the new baby with Carolyn was in reality Cassady's fifth child, the other four by teenagers he had been involved with briefly in his tumultuous career in Denver. When LuAnne arrived with him on his first trip to New York the year before, they were still married. Hinkle had the impression that Helen had enough money to pay for their trip, but she had said good-bye to them in Arizona. They picked up a hitchhiker and Helen was told she'd have to sit on her new husband's lap in the back seat for the next thousand miles. She rode a bus to New Orleans instead, and said they would find her waiting for them at William Burroughs' house across the river in the New Orleans' suburb of Algiers. The new plan was that they would pick her up on the way back to San Francisco.

Holmes' excited account of their appearance at his apartment, written in his journal the next morning, caught some of the impetuousness of the interminable party that was about to engulf him. He had already heard from

Ginsberg that Cassady was in New York. Ginsberg had been wildly trying to locate him while at the same time Cassady was just as nervously trying to reach Ginsberg, since Cassady and his entourage had arrived in Manhattan on December 28 without any money and without a place to stay. They'd left messages for each other with all of their mutual friends, and Holmes was one of the people whose telephone number Cassady had been given. Holmes wrote in his journal, "They had arrived, cold and hungry, called us and called Lucien and many others and found everyone out. They were mad for some tea and had to go down into the streets every 20 minutes to start the motor because they had no anti-freeze in the car."[1]

Cassady drove LuAnne and Al Hinkle down to Times Square, where they scored for marijuana, and then headed uptown to Edward Stringham's apartment.

These people had tea and were brought back to Edward's where they smoked the little tea there was in a water-pipe which gives a great kick to a very little tea. They stayed till five and then took off for Ozone to sleep. Edward said they were mad, mad, mad and played his records for hours, beating and dancing and going crazy.[2]

"Ozone" was Ozone Park in Queens, where Kerouac was living with his mother. The next night, December 29, Ginsberg, Kerouac, Cassady, and Hinkle, as Holmes wrote, "descended on us from nowhere." Mémère had cooked them dinner, and LuAnne stayed behind in Ozone Park to wash clothes. Holmes' first impression of Cassady was wary, still colored by the stories he heard from Kerouac about Cassady's chaotic sex life.

They came to us about ten and I saw what he meant. Neal is a slight, wiry, knowing little guy with an angular, sunken kind of face, a swirling nose, and scraggy reddish hair: first impression shrewd ugliness. Al Hinkle, the opposite, dressed in good suit, natty tie, tall guy of enormous build, with shiny blondish hair in a wave, masculine and yet a little boy's face.[3]

For the first few moments, all of the people who had just climbed Holmes' staircase tried to think of something to say. Ginsberg was "silent and mysterious." He was obsessed with Cassady and clearly overwhelmed with seeing him in New York again. After they had begun a sexual relationship the year before, Ginsberg had desperately followed Cassady when he returned to Denver. Once there Ginsberg pretended to sleep in Carolyn Robinson's room on the couch only a foot or two away when Cassady initiated his relationship with his new girlfriend by getting into her bed and abruptly climbing on top of her in an aggressive show of intimidation that was close to rape.

Arriving with Cassady and company at Holmes' apartment, Kerouac was also nervous, even though by now he and Holmes were friends and he'd been to the apartment many times. He filled the silence by going to the phonograph.

> Jack put on records immediately because I saw that Neal was itchy, nervous and filled with what Edward [Stringham] said was "tremendous nervous tension." This is the understatement of the year. He is frenetic, working himself constantly into a state of apoplexy with whatever may be around to assist him, in this case my bop records. He stood by the phonograph, in his striped sharpie suit and sport shirt, in a stooped, bent position, stamping his feet in little beats and then moving back and forth in the same spot in a queer little shuffling movement. His hands quivered before him, his head bobbed to the music, his shoulders accented the strange bop off-beats. It was a kind of induced disequilibrium. As the music went on, he got wilder, the feet accenting each beat more dogmatically, the head taking a definite pattern, the mouth agape and mumbling an occasional "go."[4]

Kerouac leaned close to Holmes to tell him that Cassady screamed "Go" at bop clubs, where people would begin to shout "Go" back at him. Kerouac concluded, "He's crazy," and Holmes continued in a laconic tone,

> To which I can attest, but he [Neal] is authentically furtive or beat, or whatever the parlance is this week. His mouth comes open and his prominent upper teeth, very white and even, come out at you and he gapes and his eyes laugh maniacally and he says in a rather high-pitched and definitive voice, "Yes! Yes!" this term of affirmation taking on all kinds of meaning when he uses it.[5]

Holmes was also now aware that Ginsberg was "madly in love" with Cassady and finally disappeared into the bathroom with him "for a long time, for whatever operation it was that Ginsberg was eager to perform on him."

A few days later Holmes' account in his letter to Harrington was less frenetic.

The holidays were endless and exhausting. Jack's friend, Neal Cassady
from Denver, was here with his ex-wife, LuAnne and a friend, Al. They
had a 1949 Hudson and no money, had driven across the country by way
of L.A., Tuscon, Denver, New Orleans, North Carolina, and Trenton. They
descended one night like manna from heaven or the plague. It is difficult
at this point to tell which epithet is more appropriate. . . . Jack plans to go
down to New Orleans with these people and find work. He is frankly down
*about his book [*The Town and the City*] and is impossible to straighten*
out at this point. The glamor attached to Neal and his friends is irresist-
ible to someone like Jack and he sees them as the apotheosis of everything
that "life should be." I will have to admit they are interesting and tremen-
dously easy to like. That they suffer from the same lack of center that Jack
does to a degree does not actually drain from their appeal; but they have
no social sense whatsoever, and I mean this in all ways. Jack's description
of the "beat" generation, whatever its excesses in the direction of rhapsody
and generalization, is quite accurate when it comes to Neal & Co. They
are possessed of the most phenomenal energy imaginable (and this is sad
only because it is rarely expended in a good cause); they are rootless, not
at all negative in their values (?) and they give of themselves without ei-
ther pretence or malice aforethought.[6]

Over the next few months Holmes was to return again and again in
his letters and journals to the complicated questions that Cassady raised.
He was conscious of Cassady's attraction for the rest of the group, and
aware that for Kerouac he was the dream figure of the kind of man Kerouac
wanted to be. Everyone who encountered Cassady during this period seems
to have written about him, but no one circled him so intently as Holmes.
His conclusion was that the basis of Cassady's appeal for the others was his
total lack of a moral sense. He was free of what the people around Holmes
considered were the social constraints that had been imposed upon them
since their childhood. For the people trailing after him, Cassady was the
ultimate Existentialist, acting out their own ideals of limitless free choice.

Occasionally in letters to some of the women whose lives he had casually disrupted Cassady acknowledged his irresponsibility and begged for
their understanding, but guilt didn't seem to be an emotion that Cassady
was familiar with. For Holmes' crowd, dealing with their own troubled con-
sciences at their nervous sexual infidelities and financial instabilities, Cassady's ability to live without looking back to question the chaos he left in
his wake was something they found admirable.

At the same time, Cassady appeared to be in many ways the embodiment of a Dostoyevskian hero, the crowd's other idol, since so far as the people he encountered in New York knew, he was without inhibitions or self-doubts as well. What surprised Holmes was that despite all of his self-focused careening through other people's lives, Cassady still was pleasant to be around. One of the less weighty conclusions for the New Yorkers who met him was that since Cassady was from the West and he was obviously different from anyone they'd ever met, he could be a kind of stereotypic "cowboy." Their concept of cowboys had been created by the movies they'd seen, and Cassady's swagger seemed to fit the stereotype. As Holmes described the morning with Neal and LuAnne in his letter to Harrington, he and Cassady sat talking in classic "cowboy" fashion while LuAnne did the housework.

> We [John and Marian] let them sleep here for two nights because they were without money or quarters and it was too cold to camp in the car, and they were marvelous guests, full of unsticky gratitude and eager to do anything about the apartment that had to be done. Neal sat back, talking to me about lots of things while LuAnne swept, made beds, washed dishes and dusted. The most surprising thing I noticed about them is the constant affirmative "yes!" Neal's three most distinctive expressions are: "go! go!" (while listening to bop), "that's right" (at almost any time and to almost any contribution to the conversation), and, with mouth wonderfully agape and his [head] wagging, "yes! yes!" . . . He sizes people up very quickly, although he has the same propensity to type certain kinds as Jack does. LuAnne, a rather pretty, lithe girl who is comrade to everyone, has elements of shyness in her, but when you have won her confidence, she opens up and talks a blue streak. . . .
>
> They drink very rarely, getting "hung up" on marijuana and music. They are terrifically healthy people, although they seem to do nothing but abuse their bodies (it would come under the heading of abuse for me at least).[7]

For the three weeks Cassady and his friends hung out in the city, nothing was quite the same for anyone in New York. Kerouac followed them everywhere, sometimes making it back to Ozone Park to sleep, other times sleeping wherever he happened to be when he was too exhausted or he'd had too much to drink to keep going. Some of the time they lived in Ginsberg's apartment at 1401 York Avenue. Since Ginsberg was working nights at the AP news bureau, Neal and LuAnne took over his bed, and Ginsberg slept on the sofa when he got in from work. The apartment was on the fourth floor of a dark stairway in a run-down building that Holmes described as roach-infested and smelling of dirt and garbage. Other times the gang slept wherever the night's parties had left them. LuAnne found a temporary job as a waitress in a Radio City coffee shop in midtown, and Cassady spent the hours she was working with Kerouac and Ginsberg, the three of them constantly trying to pick up girls for sex.

Hinkle moved in with a woman he met at the West End Bar, a tough ex-Marine named Rhoda. Hinkle also had occasional sex with Ginsberg's friend Alan Ansen, who dropped in and out of the scene. Holmes' journals give a more realistic view of what was happening in those chaotic weeks than the sentimental descriptions Kerouac wrote later as he began to romanticize his past. Holmes found himself turning into a kind of strained and often baffled Boswell in the shambling crowd, joining them as they flowed, without direction or any purpose he could discern, from one apartment to another, and from one bar to still another jazz club.

It was only by coincidence that when Cassady came to New York, Kerouac had finally convinced Holmes that he should begin listening to the bop styles that were the new musical language for the people in Cassady's crowd. Already as a teenager Holmes had been passionately immersed in New Orleans and Chicago small band jazz, and his lists of the records he loved and artists he responded to make it clear that he was knowledgeable and dedicated. For everyone who had identified with earlier jazz, the new bop seemed to be a frenetic technical display that was driving their music out of the clubs and off their radios. Only a few weeks before, Holmes was attacking bop in his letters and journals.

Bop, however, challenged more than musical tastes. In a way that is almost impossible to understand today, for young fans like Holmes who loved their music, the classic jazz artists represented the struggle of idealistic musicians against the commercial interests that had seized the music industry. In their eyes, to accept bop was to accept the cruel reality that money ran the world. The new and more knowing, musically sophisticated audience for bop found the faith of young fans such Holmes in the earlier jazz almost laughable. Their new heroes were musicians like Gillespie and Parker, Miles Davis, Charlie Mingus, Thelonius Monk, Stan Getz, Gerry Mulligan, and Chet Baker.

For Kerouac there was no problem, since he'd never paid any prolonged attention to the jazz that Holmes loved. What Kerouac finally began to listen to seriously was bop, which had only in recent months emerged from the obscurity of the Harlem clubs where it had first found its musical voice. In mid-November 1948, a month after he had come back to New York and enrolled in the New School, Kerouac insisted that Holmes had to listen to the new music, and finally the records he played, as Holmes wrote, "have broken a hole in my dike."[8] It was initially pianist Lennie Tristano whose artistry opened Holmes up to the new sounds. On November 8 Holmes wrote to Howard Friedman,

> *Have you heard any records by a blind piano man called Lennie Trista-no? I have been beseiged by them lately, because Kerouac knows and loves him. He is very good I think. The only bop-type stuff I have heard that is creative and authentic. . . . There is no bone crushing ensemble behind him, none of the histrionics that we come to associate with bop, no trills, no mad cascading runs, no sheer (but empty) technical futility. It is all muted, quite soft, very diminished and modern. Perhaps more truly classical music than jazz.*[9]

Holmes' letter continued, however, with an excited panegyric to classic Louis Armstrong recordings from 1928 to 1930 that he was listening to at the same time. Two weeks later, on November 22, 1948, he noted in his journal that while he was talking to Kerouac they were listening to Symphony Sid, "which is nothing but screaming bop."[10] Tristano's music, though, intent and cerebral, restlessly probing harmonic and rhythmic limits, continued to interest him, and finally he capitulated completely to the new sounds. The next day, on November 23, he wrote a mock "affadavit" to Kerouac,

> *Holmesdocument #1*
> *Madvast file #333*
> *Subject: Trist . . .*
> *Item one: I have purchased records by the above mentioned genius and unqualifiedly state at this point, "I give up. I am oversold. I surrender, dear." Having listened to each side an average of eighty times, I feel in about three months I will be qualified as an expert on Tristano, having graduated from my present state as abject admirer and disciple. The following signed affidavit has been registered with the County Clerk (opinion bureau, music division, modern department, Tristano section): "I, John Holmes, being of mad mind and vast body, do hereby swear that one L. Tristano has managed to do the impossible, namely create a new kind of modern music, so melodically compelling, so technically sharp, so emotionally exciting, and so complexly [sic] expressive that it has blown the top of my head off."*[11]

Holmes went on to admit ruefully, "From the above meandering, you may gather that I have come over to the 'enemy.'"[12] Tristano, for many older enthusiasts, was a bridge between their traditional jazz music and what they could hear of the new bebop. One of the elements of the older classic style that gave it its uniqueness was its level of collective improvisation between the lead instruments, and this was completely missing from the new style. Tristano, who had grown up in Chicago, played with a fuller style, some of his brilliance stemming from his own love for the music of blind Harlem pianist Art Tatum. Developing complex rhythmic structures with both hands, Tristano was a virtuoso who created the excitement of the collective ensemble style that John loved while at the same time he explored the complex new bop harmonies and rough-edged melodies.

Tristano had moved to New York in 1946, where he spent much of his time teaching. Many of his students, among them alto saxophonist Lee Konitz and guitarist Billy Bauer, added their own instrumental voice to the complex ensembles of many of Tristano's small group recordings. In 1947, the year before Kerouac introduced his music to Holmes, one of the country's leading music magazines, *Metronome*, named Tristano "Musician of the Year." By the time Cassady showed up a month after Holmes had begun listening to the new sounds, Holmes was a committed bop enthusiast, already a little jaded with some of the records he was hearing on Symphony Sid's radio program.

Holmes' pages of journals and letters from the weeks Cassady was in New York cast a clearer light on nearly everything that filled the lives of Kerouac and the group at that moment, not only their continually shifting relationships, but also their seemingly endless parties and the clubs they crowded into to listen to the new jazz that obsessed them. If they decided they wanted to hear music, Marian usually came with them, though she either avoided most of the parties or stayed only for a few drinks and a little dancing before she went back to the apartment to get some sleep so she could get up to go to her office job. She still intensely disliked the music that fascinated her husband, but she had accepted the reality that if she wanted to see much of him, she had to come along with him to the clubs.

A week after Neal and LuAnne spent the weekend at their apartment, Marian followed the crowd when Holmes joined Kerouac and Cassady, along with Edward Stringham and a friend, for a night at a new bop club called the Royal Roost. Holmes' journal was almost laconic in its appraisal of the scene they encountered. His entry on January 8, 1949, is one of the most literal descriptions of what actually happened when they went to listen to bebop.

We went to the Royal Roost on Saturday last with Neal & Co., and Ed-
ward and Les. An evening was spent with much complications about Lu-
Anne who was at work and getting in, etc. But we finally got there and by
a process of infiltration got up to the front of the bleacher seats they have
for the proletariat. It is a great low barn-like room, which fans out from
the doorway into wide proportions, where there are classy Hollywood-
night-club type tables and scurrying waiters with bop ties. It is dark as
the devil, with a real low feeling to it. . . . Marian characterized the clien-
tele of the place as a bunch of "low-foreheads" which is perhaps unkind,
but quite accurate physically. The predominance of sharpie suits, long
hair and heavy-rimmed glasses was also noticeable. . . . There were more
men than girls. There were very few couples. There was a big business gloss
to the waiters and bouncers that contrasted with the eager knowingness
of the habitues. I got the definite feeling that this was a successful cult,
it was making money for all concerned, but there was a kind of back-of-
the-hand contempt on the part of the managers of the club for the young
roughnecks who supported them.[13]

The Royal Roost was one of the jazz clubs that had opened in the center of Manhattan for the crowds who had suddenly discovered the new music. The club's first bop concert had been held there the previous April. Bird-land was the best known of the new music venues, but there were suddenly enough audiences to fill almost any space that was opened. The mood was still high after the Second World War, and the incessant bop rhythms and the abrupt, angular melodic lines seemed a mirror image of the inner questioning that someone like Holmes or Kerouac was feeling.

At the Roost the only seats they were able to get were behind an artificial tree that supported the ceiling, with branches that Holmes thought looked like "snakes or arms." The Roost also had one of the first electric light shows to enhance the effect of the music. It was a large room and the bandstand was some distance from their tree, but the pink and yellow lights that pointed out the soloists and highlighted the drummers and the staging were almost as exciting as the music. Holmes reluctantly acknowledged, "It was quite a nifty piece of showmanship and the effect of madness and goneness was played upon very consciously."[14]

Though Holmes didn't realize it at the time he jotted down his notes, he was one of the first writers to attempt to describe the stage manner of Charlie Parker's new trumpeter, the very young Miles Davis.

The music disappointed me, I liked the records that I have much better.
The music was as knowing and, if I may use the term, commercialized

as the place itself. The musicians watched the crowd and never really went off except in slow numbers. They watched the crowd slyly, waiting to see what notes and what phrases brought forth a reaction. These would then be repeated. There was individualism to some of it, oddness and mechanicalness to most of it. . . . Parker played a lovely solo on something I can't remember, a popular song and his was by far the most mannerly and accomplished group, although the trumpet [Miles] was only a kind of calypso echo of Charlie. He seemed to have a kind of stoic indifference to the crowd which pleased me, and yet his work, which is difficult anyway and so unrhythmical, gave me some trouble. I was aware always that he knew just what he was trying to do and I liked the damn-your-eyes quality of much that he played.[15]

As Holmes tried to pinpoint his feelings about the music, he began writing in a vivid, metaphoric language that would soon become the accepted verbal style of music criticism for a new generation of jazz writers.

Charlie Ventura was bop big band, complete with a blond girl singer with low-forehead boppist haircut and sleek dress. His band was iron clad, show-piece stuff and whatever take-offs they did were carefully planned and lacked all sort of spontaneity at all. He stood, limned in a spot-light, playing his sax bent backwards and watching everything with a quiet knowingness that I did not appreciate. Shelley Manne on drums with [Flip] Phillips gesticulated and brought kudos from the crowd, his lantern jaw swung far out to the right of his face and he looked something like a spastic trying to say hello. His crew-cut head was narrow like a beetle's in the spotlight that blinded him. I was not impressed by his work.[16]

At the Royal Roost none of the others noticed Holmes' reserved response to the music. Cassady never heard a group that failed to send him into his head-swinging ecstasy, and Kerouac was usually only a step behind. Whatever the music was like, the night always turned into a chaotic party. By the time they left, Cassady, perspiring heavily as he always did when the music excited him, had stripped down to his undershirt. Holmes wrote,

In the cheap seats there were no drinks, no tables to sip them from. Jack went out and bought a bottle and straws and we passed it around under the coats, taking long pulls on it. After a while the straw got a hole in it and one got air and raw whiskey at the same time and we all quickly got a nice one tied on. One had to pass this thing from row to row when the lights went down and dip one's head to take a pull on that straw. Neal was "going" to the music and Jack was feeling LuAnne nicely and things were building. Les, adaptable guy that he is, was getting along well and only Marian and Edward were unhappy and me a bit because it was not what I had thought it was going to be. . . . We beat our exit about eleven-thirty, had coffee and cake somewhere, talked the evening over and then Marian and I came home. My coat was left in Neal's car in the confusion, madness, glitter and paroxysmed hecticism [sic] of Times Square somewhere. He finally brought it back this morning.[17]

In the next decade, when the "Beats" had become a part of the trendy vocabulary, a stream of paperback novels huckstered the scene. The artists who created the book jackets attempted to imagine what an unsophisticated audience would have expected the new bohemians to look like in the midst of their wild parties. Usually the illustration on the book cover showed three or four couples, one couple dancing, a woman with her blouse partly unbuttoned staring into the eyes of a man sitting close to her on a couch, and in the background someone lighting up what the readers could interpret as a marijuana cigarette. Only the jacket of one of the few serious books about their scene managed to reflect some of the chaos that Holmes captured in his day-after journal entries. The jacket for the 1952 novel *Who Walk in Darkness* by Chandler Brossard showed a dense New York party crowd, the men in coats and ties, the women in party dresses, everyone presenting themselves to someone else, drinks in their hands, and the noise of what would have been their shrill talk almost lifting from artist's drawing.

Not even Brossard's book jacket, however, could have captured the total anarchy of the night of the final party with Cassady that Holmes described. In his hurriedly typed pages the next morning he immortalized the farewell party at 681 Lexington before Neal and LuAnne began the trip back to California. On January 19, 1949, Holmes wrote in his journal,

When I got home, a little tired, and expecting a quiet evening, there were countless people in attendance. Neal, LuAnne, Jack, Ginsberg, Russell Durgin and John Hollander. They were heading for California today and this was their last night in town. They had purportedly just stopped in. A party developed when Jean Barrows and her new friend dropped in with three quarts of beer and joined this polyglot throng. . . . Ginsberg was by this time talking about weed and LuAnne wanted to get fucked and everything was breaking up. Lucien blew in, just off the job and wanting liquor and feeling free because Barbara was at home in bed with a cold. Neal was depressed, although he went nicely to the music with Jean's friend who used to be a drummer down at Nick's and likes bop, I take it. LuAnne and Jack were "going" as well, and they gave us countless imitations of the evening that was spent at [Alan] Ansen's, where the boy-monster had read them Beaudelaire and Poe, played Verdi and talked about everything while walking around in a pair of pajamas with no seat to them. . . . Ansen came into town with them then, read the Bible at top voice all the way and embarrassed even these unembarrassable people. Jean and her friend finally left, perplexed, disliking it I think, but gone anyway.[18]

There was an unspoken agreement at the parties that whatever happened, it wasn't to be questioned—at least not until the day after. Holmes was conscious that as the night went on his wife often drifted over to Lucien Carr, whose haunted good looks stood out even in a group where most of the men were good looking. Marian still occasionally asserted her Italian upbringing, even though the crowd paid no attention to so slight a distinction, and she stood for a time by the phonograph with Russell Durgin listening to Italian opera records. Holmes noted with some contempt that they "mooned about Caruso."[19]

Holmes had been inhibited with Jean Perkins Barrows in the apartment, since she was the daughter of the famed editor Maxell Perkins, who had shepherded the books of Fitzgerald, Hemingway, and Thomas Wolfe into print, among many others. Once she'd left,

We could let down our hair, although there was little left to bring down. Everyone got "hung up" on writing obscenities on our bathroom wall and the whole place was scribbled with things like "John fucks Marian," "Neal fucks LuAnne," "Jack fucks God," "When anyone fucks they fuck themselves" and other tasty items of like nature. Durgin was going to sleep about this time and Lucien and Marian cleaned up the bathroom while LuAnne puked, her stomach giving her some trouble and the pressing [sic] doing no good. Then we all lay around talking madly and listening to Symphony Sid. I got close to Jack, who said he was going to be back in two weeks with LuAnne and we played child-like for an hour or so, beating LuAnne to the music [they softly patted her stomach in time to the rhythm of the records] and drinking more beer. Ginsberg was sitting in Neal's lap and I was lying on LuAnne and then Lucien and Marian came and lay on top of us. The couch has a bend in it as of this morning. Marian and Lucien then went out for drinks down at the Venetian and we went on, playing talking, beating, going. Lucien, the lazy dog, hadn't gotten up to piss in the bathroom but had it done it in a succession of beer bottles and these Jack proceeded to pour out the window while LuAnne urged him on. They sexually danced and she said to me while Marian was still there, "One day Jack's going to line us all up [the girls] and see who tastes 'better.'" I take it that they have had at each other and I also take it that Neal doesn't go for it too much. LuAnne was covered with discolorations from the beatings he has given her the last few days.[20]

Surprisingly, the one who was the least involved with the party's tumult was Cassady, who drifted from person to person, unsure of himself when he wasn't the center of the action. He produced a pistol, which he had borrowed from Al Hinkle in San Francisco to frighten LuAnne into annulling their marriage so he could marry Carolyn, but in the general drunkeness no one paid much attention to him.

Neal said a few enigmatical words to me, re LuAnne and Marian being after other men which I told him was highly trivial at this point, but he could not see it. He was playing with that gun all night, snapping it back and forth, shooting himself in the head and in gayer moments pointing it from the groin and "going." But he was not happy last night and that was the truth.[21]

As the night dwindled down there was only the small group of regulars left. Holmes was conscious that Carr, across the room "was still making love to my wife."[22] (In the late 1940s the word described something closer to today's term "making out," and Holmes never intimated in any of his journals or letters that Marian was actually unfaithful to him, though he probably would have welcomed it on her part, since it would help ease his conscience over his occasional extramarital affairs. When he wrote about the unfaithfulness of the character he called "Kathryn," as he named Marian in *Go*, he later insisted with some remorse that it was only a plot device.) Marian finally left the scene and went to bed, since she had to get up to go to her job, while Carr went back to his apartment and to Barbara Hale, the young woman he was currently living with. Cassady had already returned to Ginsberg's apartment, where he waited for LuAnne to come back with Kerouac.

Soon after that everything broke down. The place was in a shambles and Jack was bleary eyed and happy and finally went into the bathroom with LuAnne and lay in the bathtub with her. They had been playfully feeling

one another up all night and she turned to him once and said, at my be-
hest, "Jack, I want your soul, that's what I want."[23]

After the tumult of their stay in New York, Holmes found he was relieved
when Neal, LuAnne, Al, and his girlfriend Rhoda finally got back into the
battered Hudson for the return journey to the West Coast, but he was also
disappointed that Kerouac had left with them.

Last night we saw Jack Kerouac, Neal, LuAnne, Al and a girl named Rhoda
off for New Orleans, Tuscon, San Francisco and points there between. Their
decision to go was sudden, their departure itself chaotic. Stringham was
along and a girl-friend of his (?) named Lucia who is studying Italian at
the New School and is a painter. . . . The evening was pointless, except that
they got off for the West, with about thirty dollars, the car and some jewelry
[that Neal had stolen from Kerouac's New School instructor Elbert Lenrow]
that is hockable. I was glad, in a way, to see them finally off. They have all
been hovering on this decision for weeks, vacillating from one plan to the
next, and if Jack is ever to get back and set to work again, it is better that
they go immediately.[24]

The plan, at least at the moment when everyone got into the car, was that
LuAnne and Jack would return to New York "in a week or so," and LuAnne
would move into Ginsberg's apartment and take whatever jobs came along.
Holmes, perhaps without understanding how much he was revealing of his
jealousy of Cassady's attraction for Kerouac, went on to pontificate about the
effect Cassady was having on Kerouac's writing.

I got rather close to Jack again last night, after two or three weeks of see-
ing him rarely and having to watch his ridiculous infatuation with Neal.
Jack is in many ways one of the most talented people that I know. He has
a gift that is unusual because it is unrecognized. These people threatened
in many ways to tear him away from his responsibility to that gift. I think
that going on this trip with them was a bad idea, but it may cure him (for
a time) of the attraction their kind of rootless life holds for him. He is fas-
cinated by their sexual off-handedness, the share-and-share-alike quality
of everything they do, and the constant sense of experiencial improvisa-
tion which seems attached to even the smallest enterprise they embark
on. Neal, an electric and immediately attractive person, wins [over] Jack
whose sense of discrimination is not tremendous when the gloss is bright
enough.[25]

At the same time, however, Holmes was close enough to Kerouac to understand another motivation behind his friend's decision to leave with Cassady. Holmes was sympathetic to what he called the "enormous moral problems"[26] that Kerouac wrestled with in his relationship with his mother, especially with accepting her financial support from her job at a Brooklyn factory because he refused to find any kind of work that would help her pay their expenses. Leaving with Cassady was a temporary way for Kerouac to avoid dealing with a dependency on his mother that he couldn't bring himself to face.

With more of a balance than most twenty-two-year-olds manage to achieve, Holmes was also prescient in his discussion of Cassady. Of all the descriptions of the impression Cassady made on the people he met in New York, Holmes' comment was certainly the most balanced and shrewd.

Neal, a tower of unfathomable energy, does not destroy people's natural defenses against him: he leaps over them. He leaves your capacity to judge him intact, but he makes it useless. He moves so quickly that one can only concentrate on trying to keep up. Those that fall behind are forgotten. When he wants something, he displays a tremendous arsenal of weapons of all varieties by which to attain his end. Kindness, thoughtfulness, charm, malice, amoralism: it is all possible with Neal. And yet when one knows him, one can only sympathize because he is unhappy, slightly manic-depressive and decidedly lonely, for all the flies that swarm about him. . . . Neal I find extremely likeable, but to say that he needs other people's participation to make his life significant is putting it mildly.[2]

As Kerouac and Holmes said goodbye before the party in the Hudson started the trip back to San Francisco, Kerouac assured Holmes that he wasn't going to stay away long. Holmes remembered him saying, "Trust me. I'll be back in two weeks for a quiet life."[28]

Kerouac's life, as Holmes already realized, would always be a search for an imagined quiet life that he would find only for brief moments, moments that he never was able to sustain. What Holmes—or Kerouac—couldn't know was that the chaotic cross-country journey with Cassady at the wheel of the Hudson would become some of the most memorable pages of the book Kerouac would write two years later.

Chapter 8

THIS PARTICULAR KIND OF MADNESS

My life seems to be disorganized again and I look to the end of the novel with hope and expectation. Perhaps a kind of sanity again, an end of worry for the time being, the graceful, careless reading of anything that falls my way, the indolent days, the plans planned and abandoned, the indulgences, getting jobs perhaps, living again. But certainly an end to this particular kind of madness, like the "Sweet Georgia Bop" that screams near my ear now. That has got to stop, like a debilitating drug saps me. I don't make any sense out of it, but the pulse of the blood. I pick up a biography of Melville in the library, feeling compelled to read about him, and yet wary lest I get off the track. I veer to both sides of it now, eager to be done, to be done, to be done, at last to be done. I shall have to wait. Perhaps in a week it will be finished and then no matter what, something new. Poetry and short stories and a deliciously point-less intellectual life. Maybe . . .
—JOHN CLELLON HOLMES, journal, February 24, 1949

In his disappointment with Kerouac for being drawn into the excitement of driving off with Neal Cassady to New Orleans and San Francisco on January 19, 1949, Holmes noted, almost in a scolding tone, that for Kerouac it was a way to avoid facing his own dilemmas. However in the doubts that became a recurring theme in Holmes' journals and letters after the group finally left, it was clear that the weeks when Cassady was roaring around Manhattan—either "manna from heaven or the plague,"[1] as Holmes had written in a letter to Harrington in Tuscon—had also given Holmes the chance to put off facing some of his own demons.

In the stale silence of the months that followed, he had to return to his novel and face his growing uncertainty about the quality of the book he'd struggled with for so long. Even when Kerouac came back to New York

City a few weeks later, the spring months that lay ahead of Holmes were more difficult than he had ever imagined. At many despairing moments he was no longer certain he could deal with the self-doubt that was engulfing him.

Soon he had an intimation of the depth of his confusions. On January 21, 1949, two days after the others had left, Holmes found himself facing an empty evening with Marian away, and he invited the woman who was acting as his literary agent, Rae Everitt, out for drinks and dinner. It was a night that hinted at the turmoil he would go through over the next months. At the restaurant they talked casually, then since Rae had tickets for a showing of a new film, they went to the Museum of Modern Art to see a movie that had been produced, directed by, and starred Shankar, one of India's best known dancers. Holmes was bored by the film, though Shankar was present with his wife and small son, and he also didn't like the "mixed European yogi bunch"[2] that was in the audience. He slipped away with Rae and they found a small bar on 52nd Street where they sat drinking and talking. Holmes suddenly heard himself opening up to her, telling her everything that was eroding his confidence. In his journal the next day he wrote,

> I opened to her, for reasons I never know when I open to anyone. I told her things about what I feel and think, my work, my concern with politics and mankind, Neal and Jack and Alan. I opened much too wide, leaving myself in left field and feeling, when it was over, as though I had made a complete fool of myself.[3]

His agent's response was an effort to reassure him that he hadn't looked foolish. "She kissed me across the table when she saw I was thus constrained and it was something of a perfect moment, because whether she actually understood or not, she made me feel once more at ease, as though getting through to someone is not the absurd dream I often think it is."[4]

When they left the bar the night was cold and drizzling and the streets were empty. They walked slowly along Lexington Avenue, both of them nervously aware that with Marian away, he was going to take Rae back to his apartment. Once inside the door he began to kiss her and at first she held herself away from him. He told her, "Expect me to help you only up to a point and then I must help myself,"[5] and he felt her give way to him. But as he held her he realized that he was unable to do anything. When Rae tried to help him, Holmes' despair only intensified.

She gave herself up to me quite purely, and only once asked in a wonder-ing, small voice, "What's the matter, sweetheart?" I could not say to her because I did not know. She took off her clothes and I felt her all against me, her long tawny body, with straight white legs and full breasts. But I was dead inside me for some unknown reason. We gave it up and she was tight and wounded. I assured her, not knowing whether to believe myself, that it was my fault. . . . I was by this time tortured in the middle of things that pained me deeply, longing and sadness that I could not understand. I remembered that she had taken my mouth between her lips and bitten against me hard so great was her desire, which I could not, strangely, seem to rise to. I walked her part of the way home, took the subway with her, feeling it all different somehow, afraid of myself.[6]

When Rae came to the apartment again the next afternoon to talk with him, she told him she had decided that they shouldn't try to be togeth-er again, and with this uncertainty cleared away he suddenly felt himself aroused, but this time they stopped by mutual agreement. Holmes was so relieved that the helplessness of the night before had passed that he felt "a sudden and almost simultaneous sense of relief and joy. . . . It needed no particular satisfaction, the little thrusting and playing that was done was enough."[7]

Holmes was still spending his days in the apartment at his typewriter, even if now he was writing as much in his journals and in his letters as he was struggling to complete the revisions on his manuscript. He still, however, was hearing about Kerouac. At the beginning of February he received a long letter from Harrington, living on his mother's ranch in the desert out-side of Tucson. Harrington had just spent an afternoon with Jack, Neal, and LuAnne—as well as Holmes' mother, Betty, who was visiting one of her sisters in the city and considering the possibility of buying a house nearby. When Betty Holmes called Harrington about nine in the morning he invited her over for coffee.

A number of people were in the house, including Alan's wife, Virginia, and his mother's new husband, who had just stumbled in from a three-day drunk. As Harrington looked out the window he saw his mother and Betty Holmes slowly walking together across the courtyard, while Virginia, still in her bathrobe, ran out of the kitchen to get dressed. Then, as Harrington wrote, while everyone was exchanging breathless greetings, "I happened to look out of the window again, and there was Jack Kerouac."[8]

Kerouac had just arrived in another car with Cassady, LuAnne, and a hitchhiker named Leo. At that same moment Harrington's stepfather rushed out of the house, started his car, and roared off toward Tucson to do something about his hangover. Harrington and Kerouac began to talk while LuAnne used the bathroom and a happily smiling Cassady explained that Hinkle had stayed behind in New Orleans with his wife. The travelers were hungry, not having eaten since they left Burroughs' home in Algiers. They were also "utterly broke."[9]

Harrington and his wife had only fifteen dollars, but they lent five to Kerouac to fill the much battered Hudson's tank with gas. Cassady was certain that if they only had five more dollars they'd be all right, and finally they decided that they would pawn the hitchhiker's overcoat. Harrington called a friend to ask about the chances of selling some of the marijuana that Burroughs had given Cassady in New Orleans, but Harrington was warned that there had been a number of police raids in Tucson, and the town was shut down. So Cassady and his tired passengers brought out some of their merchandise and settled down for the afternoon. As Harrington remarked laconically, "We had the kind of afternoon at the ranch that must be famil-iar to you."[10] Cassady got high immediately, and his "entire motor apparatus became jerky."[11] Harrington chose to stay with whiskey and settled back to watch. "Cigarettes passed from mouth to mouth, and the music was punc-tuated by that frantic, hissing intake of breath, and everybody went around scientifically holding their noses, and at last expelling the mystical intoxi-cant with a gasp."[12]

Harrington's sarcasm about the group's behavior, however, didn't in-clude Kerouac, who had exclaimed excitedly when he first arrived that he had seen a horse at the ranch and he wanted to go riding.

> *Once again Jack showed me the "spiritual chastity" I respect so much in him of participating completely in the ceremonies, the disorganized yet highly ritualistic good time, and still being himself, awake, goodnatured, and full of joy not only in the music and whiskey and tea, but in all things— so much so that, as the sun was going down, he vanished, keeping his date with the horse and the sunset. Looking through the picture window we saw him riding gallantly among the cacti, a serene figure, lonely, smiling.[13]*

In his answering letter on January 31, Holmes wrote that he was im-pressed that Harrington had immediately understood the dynamic of Cassady's crowd, something that had taken Holmes two or three weeks. The aimlessness of the wanderings, he felt, was a mirror of Cassady's aim-lessness as he rushed from one new scheme to another and one place to another. Most of Cassady's impulses left nothing more tangible than the numbers on the Hudson's odometer, and they had gotten as far as Tucson only by stealing gas from out-of-the-way filling stations. Cassady's ragged passengers had no choice except to stay with the car, since they'd come so far it would have been harder to go back than to keep going.

Holmes was reassured that Kerouac had been more like himself, and that he hadn't been deflected from his plans to go on with his writing by his meeting with Burroughs, whom Holmes considered to be "the Wotan behind so much of this."[14] After his own experiences with Cassady, Holmes could also tell Harrington not to worry about whatever they'd done in their afternoon visit.

> *I was not worried that they would extract from you whatever cash you might have on hand, but I knew they would try. Giving five to Jack is a safe investment which you will get back I am sure. We lent them ten once (through Jack) and he was nervous and unhappy until he had paid it back. He realizes, as very often they do not, that everyone is in difficult straits, even though they have organized their resources with a little better eye to economy.[15]*

Kerouac returned to New York from San Francisco in mid-February 1949, only a week or two later than when he had said he would be back. He didn't have LuAnne with him. She had decided to stay in San Francisco after she and Kerouac had spent a night together in a cheap hotel room. She was ostensibly waiting for her fiance, who worked out of San Francisco as a merchant seaman. Cassady had a tense homecoming with his wife, Carolyn, and their baby, leaving Jack and LuAnne in the hotel until he was certain he'd been forgiven for the calamitous trip. Kerouac was finally welcomed into the apartment, and despite the awkwardness of the situation he and Carolyn quickly found themselves at ease with each other. LuAnne was still in the hotel, however, and Cassady continued to slip away to see her. One night she called him at home, only to have Carolyn answer the phone. Carolyn became so furious at learning that LuAnne had come back with them that Kerouac fled from the apartment and immediately took a bus back to New York with money wired him by his mother.

With Kerouac in New York City, some of the old antic confusions took over again. On his first day back he looked for his friends at the New School, and he ran into Betty Holmes, who had returned from her trip to Arizona. She told him that everyone was up at the docks on the Hudson River, saying goodbye to Cassady's Denver friend Ed White, who was sailing on the

Queen Mary for Europe. Since Kerouac didn't have any money, he had to walk the nearly fifty blocks from the Village to the docks. He appeared on the pier, coming out from behind a trunk, and, as Holmes noted in his journal, he looked "weary and beat."[16]

Shipboard departures were generally one of the classic moments of hectic confusion along the piers in Manhattan, since the passengers were allowed aboard early enough to have friends down to their staterooms for a last shipboard party. The ships were a maze of corridors and staterooms, people were continually getting lost, luggage turned up in the wrong staterooms, and in the alcoholic haze that followed the parties many of the visitors became even more thoroughly lost as they fumbled their way up to the decks and to the gangways as the ships prepared to depart.

John and Marian managed to get on board with Edward Stringham and Kerouac, and Ginsberg also found his way. "After threading our way down into the entrails of the monster,"[17] Holmes wrote in his journal on February 16, they found White with three friends, all of them drinking steadily. The ship's personnel had tried to maintain some sort of order by issuing visitor's passes to limit the number of people roaming the corridors. Three other friends who had come to see White off, Tom and Julia Livornese, and Hal Chase, were left somewhere in the noisy crowd on the dock, since all the passes had already been given out.

When the signal came for visitors to go ashore, Kerouac, by this time very drunk, decided he didn't want to leave the ship and tried to hide in one of the stateroom closets. Holmes decided it was easier to deal with Ginsberg, who was even drunker, so he took Ginsberg off the ship, put him in a taxi, and started back as the others were disembarking. As Holmes got to the ship, he wrote in his journal that "Marian, Edward and Jack came tottering down the long cavernous pier, just after Truman Capote, looking like a loaded little girl, had staggered by with a party of friends."[18]

The group stumbled across town, leaving a trail of tipped-over ash-cans behind them and singing loudly in their pleasure at being together again. They stopped somewhere for hamburgers, where Kerouac ate a dish of ketchup. At this point Marian had had enough, so they found her a cab, and they went on to a club called the Clique. Kerouac still was exhausted from his cross country bus trip, but he and Holmes hung on through the night at the Clique, which was a small room featuring more introspective jazz. The two groups alternating on the bandstand were the small bands led by Lenny Tristano and English pianist George Shearing, who like Tristano was also blind. For Holmes, hearing Tristano, who had first opened his ears to the new music only a few weeks before, it was, "a beautiful, lovely soft evening of American chamber music, thrills to the ear."[19] With Kerouac in the city again, Holmes felt that his life took on some of its old savour, and the two friends sat drinking until four in the morning. "The music was quiet and superb and I felt a very strange, sober delicacy slipping over me as the hours passed."[20]

Since it was so late Kerouac slept on a couch at 681 Lexington, and in the morning Ginsberg came up the stairs and stayed to read them poetry until he went downtown with Kerouac to the New School. John and Marian ended Kerouac's homecoming by going to a movie.

Marian still clung to the idea of their marriage, though it was increasingly obvious that her husband was more involved in everything else that was going on around him, whether or not he could admit it to himself. When she opened her apartment door after her long day working at the office she never knew who would be waiting for her, wondering if she was going to come up with something to eat or drink. It was Kerouac who was most often there, though he was upset when she flared-up at Holmes, as Kerouac later wrote in *Visions of Cody*.[21] Marian was continually exhausted from the struggle to keep up with the round of parties and drinking and still get to her job the next morning. For both John and Marian their mornings were a steady blur of hangovers. Holmes still continued to act as though his wife enjoyed being part of the crowd, and there were a handful of people, like Carr and Kerouac, whom she genuinely liked. Others whom Holmes introduced her to were more problematic.

One Sunday afternoon she went with him to Gershon Legman's decrepit house in the Bronx, where they listened to music—everything from Mozart to marches and calypso—and had what John felt was a good time. Beverly, Legman's wife, was also there, and they spent much of the afternoon looking through some of large collections of erotica Legman had gathered, "the volumes on homosexuality, and the collections of epigraphs in latrines and subway stations, the dictionaries he is compiling of lewd words and inscriptions. He showed us whole rafts of obscene photos all listed under subjects and actions."[22] Marian was shocked at the photographs, while Holmes became interested in the idea that some of the pornography Legman was showing them was also making an aesthetic statement. Holmes wrote in his journal,

> We saw one that he took of friends that was lovely, with soft burnished lighting and thrusting bodies, very graceful but not at all pornographic, couldn't excite anyone because it was too ethereally beautiful. The others,

professional and amateur, at least were dirty, which is a negative virtue.
Some of them were playfully nice, but most were the really lewd, obscene
and horrible variety that only brings forth disgust.[23]

However Marian regarded an afternoon spent reading collections of toilet wall jottings and looking at pornographic photos, for Holmes it was a stimulating few hours. He found, again, that he liked Legman and that he was impressed with his intelligence and integrity. On a domestic note the Legmans gave John and Marian a coffee table, which they planned to pick up in a few days.

Even with the thousands of words that filled Holmes' journals during these sorely stressed months, it is still a question why he wasn't more satisfied with the poetry he was writing that was being accepted and published, and why he continued to agonize over the novel that was going so badly. When Harington wrote that he was finishing "Hamtrack," the title he'd given his new novel later published as *The Revelations of Dr. Modesto* (1955), Holmes was surprised and unsettled. He answered Harrington with questions about the progress his friend had made with the book. "The news that 'Hamtrack' will be finished by June at once makes me joyful and somewhat confused. Will it all be done, or just the first draft, or just the final draft of the first section? You must have been making considerable progress, for which I am thankful."[24]

The poetry that was appearing regularly wasn't helping Holmes' unrelentingly precarious financial situation, but almost without any effort—there are no notes in his journals about any struggles with a poem—he was beginning to be regarded as an up-and-coming young poet. In an offhand paragraph in his journal entry on February 16, 1949, he added that he'd gotten a "nice note" from a man named Howard Griffin, who was editing an issue on postwar poets for *Voices* magazine. Two of his poems had been accepted for the issue. "They have taken 'Theorum' and 'Instructions,' two poems that I care about and this makes me happy." Griffin wanted Holmes to have lunch with him and show him more poetry. Holmes' response was "Will do first, reserve judgement on it to effect second."[25]

What was obvious in Holmes' laconic comment was that he had made the choice to place all of his writing capital in his novel, which he was now calling "The Transgressors." He was still uncertain of his identity as a writer either of poetry or fiction. Even if his poetry was already finding readers, it continued to be something that gave him only a small, very measured sense of satisfaction. A novel was the only thing that matched the size of his youthful ambitions.

This was the time when new American novels were taken very seriously. Norman Mailer's *The Naked and the Dead* had been a literary sensation, and the year before *Life* magazine ran a full-page photograph of Truman Capote to illustrate an article about him and other young novelists including Gore Vidal and Calder Willingham titled "Young U.S. Writers: A Refreshing Group of Newcomers on the Literary Scene Is Ready to Tackle Almost Anything." Vidal explained that "after the war everybody was waiting for the next Hemingway-Fitzgerald generation to appear."[26]

Holmes' problem was that "The Transgressors" still continued to elude him. He began his journal entry on February 24 with an emotional outburst, "How to explain this kind of creative fervor that I have now, that demands that I write something down I do not even recognize, and yet will not allow me to actually get into the chapter that has to be done?"[27] He continued in his journal—after declaring that he simply wanted "to be done, to be done, to be done, at last be done"—with a scathing dismissal of his work and where it had led him. At this point, however, he understood that despite his despair he had no other door to open.

I am sick of doubting this book, of dreaming for it, hoping for the best of it, testing everything that comes my way by the measuring stick it supplies. That too will be finished. I can now only work on rather mutely and hope that it is good, know that I have done all that is best for me at this period. It is not what I want entirely, and I hesitate to think too much on it for fear I will stumble on some hidden trap in it and see clearly for the first time what I COULD have done with it and then have to face a long, long period of changing it again. I know that after a certain time work should be taken away from artists because they polish it, only to maim it out of some crude, but loving symmetry it had originally. . . . I feel at this moment as though I had lost all the boundaries, all the markers of my life in writing this, in bringing it this far, faltering every step of the way, testing everything, doubting everything.[28]

Holmes still was able to find small crumbs of comfort in what he was doing, even if his occasional moments of optimism had often as little reality as his darker moments of self-doubt. As he went on with the same journal entry where he'd described his state as "this particular kind of madness," he began to find things in his prose that he liked.

It is a painful process, this piece by piece work, this stone by stone con-
struction. It pays off, however, because I can go back over the structure
now, and find whole sections that stand beautifully strong and durable.
They have depth to them, density and weight. Or that is how it looks to
me sometimes.[29]

Holmes' ability to find something that he considered good in his writing
was the strongest characteristic of his life during this time. Just as he was
able to conclude in his journal that he'd finally been pleased with the next
day's "thrusting and playing" with his agent after he had been devastated by
his impotence when he tried to make love to her, he could pull himself away
from his first despairing reaction to his novel by finding newer sections that
he decided were closer to what he had attempted to bring off. His resilience
was what was to pull him through the crisis that came with his book a few
weeks later.

Kerouac had been going through some of the same doubts and uncertainties over *The Town and the City*. The manuscript he'd finally finished was
rejected by Scribner's and Little, Brown, but it had been recommended
to editor Robert Giroux at Harcourt, Brace by Mark Van Doren, one of
Ginsberg's professors at Columbia. Holmes had left the manuscript of "The
Transgressors" with an editor named Glauber at Knopf, and they met for
lunch on Tuesday, March 29, to discuss the book. Despite Holmes' own
dissatisfaction with the novel, he wasn't prepared for the casual dismissal
of the work he'd given his life to for the past two years. As Holmes wrote
to Harrington the next day, "it was a painful experience for both, I think."
Holmes continued:

I asked him to tell me what he thought, to spare no horses, to tear into it
if that had been his reaction. He lectured me for a long while on struc-
ture . . . but in a vague way, calling on such diverse authorities for his
expansive ideas as Gilbert and Sullivan, Joyce, the questing scientist etc.
I was perplexed by what he said and asked him, in what I am sure was
good faith, to show me where, specifically all this applied to my book. He
would only answer with another elusive query on applicability itself.[30]

Holmes became more and more confused when his efforts to find
something specific in Glauber's comments only led to further allusions he
couldn't follow. When he asked if Glauber had found the characters believable, the editor asked in return, "What do you mean by believable?" Holmes floundered: "Acceptable! Credible! Consistent!" In the end it was the

imprecise expression of the editor's rejection of the novel that left Holmes helpless.

> *But the only impression that I received was this: that he had not liked it, but that he would not tell me, in specific terms, why he didn't. I tried desperately to get him to do so, even though I was in a state of turmoil during the whole interview due to the fact that everything he said was not at all what I had been expecting. . . . He was kind in everything he said, that I must allow. He was friendly and not all patronizing. I felt he was in an embarrassing position, almost as though he had to get a novice off the hook. But his evasiveness did not impress me as being honest or helpful. My salient, specific questions all resulted in nothing more than another question hurled at me.[31]*

Holmes was devastated by the interview, but his long day of purgatory had only begun. He stumbled back to the apartment, "limping like a whipped dog," convinced that it was his own "secrecy" about the novel and his own hesitations and suspicions about the quality of his writing that had led to his failure.[32] He locked himself in the apartment, close to hysteria, and he was trying to struggle back to some measure of calm when Kerouac called him from a cafeteria at Lexington and 58th Street, only two blocks away.

Without stopping to think, Holmes rushed out of the apartment to join his friend for coffee. When Holmes got to the cafeteria he found Kerouac with the sports page of a newspaper open in front of him while he jotted words down in a writing pad. Kerouac said he was writing lyrics to a song for their friend Tom Livornese, and he went on talking casually. Too upset to stay silent, "shaking like a leaf," Holmes poured out his story of his unsuccessful meeting with Glauber and his novel's rejection. Holmes went on with the story of the afternoon in his letter to Harrington:

> *I saw a shadow flit across his face. I passed it off. I asked him what he had been doing since Saturday night when we saw him last. He laughed slightly, a sort of gleeful, uncertain giggle and would not answer. I thought that perhaps he had met the "great love of his life" or something and pressed him. The same shadow of concern glinted in his eyes, and then he said, "Harcourt Brace is going to take my novel, and they're going to give me a thousand dollars advance next week."[33]*

Holmes sat stunned, at first unable to believe what his friend had told him, but despite his confusion, conscious that he was overjoyed for Kerouac. He realized with a wrench of irony that Kerouac's interview with the editor at Harcourt Brace, only an hour before Kerouac had called him, had taken place at the same moment that "The Transgressors" was being rejected. Kerouac had been as overwhelmed by the acceptance of *The Town and the City* as Holmes had been with his own rejection, and Kerouac had simply wandered for an hour before he went to the cafeteria and called his friend. As they walked back to 681 Lexington, Holmes noted that Kerouac seemed dazed by the afternoon's events. He wasn't depressed, but "newly aware."

> He suddenly said, "I want to sit down and write letters, I feel that I want to lay every woman I see, as if I could." He laughed at that, as though trying to keep his composure. "You know, John, I wish Alan were here, and Edward and Diamond and everyone. This never would have happened without all of you."[34]

What Holmes grasped in his confused response to Kerouac's laughing outburst was that in Kerouac's rush of gratitude he was finding himself almost unable to talk about what had happened. Suddenly Holmes realized that Kerouac hadn't told his mother the good news. "She knew, when he left the house that morning, that he was going to see Harcourt and she would be dying of curiousity. "When does she get out of work, Jack?" He glanced at the clock absently: "Oh, it's late, isn't it? She got out at five." It was now twenty after."[35]

Kerouac still couldn't bring himself to go home, and they sat listening to records until Holmes finally sent him back to Ozone Park to tell his mother what had happened. Holmes wrote in his journal, "I knew it would mean everything in the world to her. He went, quite contritely because he seemed to have forgotten everything, and said, on the stairs, 'You know, it's funny. You can actually make a living as a writer!'"[36] For Holmes the evening somehow dragged past. After Kerouac left he found himself facing the enormity of his own dilemma, but at that moment some friends knocked on his door and soon afterward Marian came back from work. They sat down for a quiet dinner and talked until midnight, drinking a little before they finally went to bed. The day was over.

Whatever emotions Holmes was feeling after the turmoil and elation of the previous day, he woke up the next morning realizing that he had to consider his situation seriously. The vagueness of the Knopf editor's comments about his novel at the interview still upset him, but he couldn't shrug them off. He couldn't look at his face in the morning mirror and tell himself that he disagreed with what Glauber had told him. He couldn't insist to himself that his book was really better than the editor's opinion, since he was no longer certain about anything.

His first thought was that he would give the manuscript to Edward Stringham, who was further along in his career as a professional writer, and then he'd probably ask Kerouac to read it, since his friend had said the day before that he wanted to give it to his editor Robert Giroux at Harcourt Brace. In a moment of painful self-criticism, Holmes was aware that he had to be realistic about what was possible for him. In his long letter to Harrington he took a long glance at his situation with a flat mood of acceptance.

> My next steps are still unclear, although giving it to Edward will be the first move I think. I have always told myself that I would give myself this one book to prove that I can write, and I think to a certain extent I shall try to live up to that. It is too early to tell anything on a long-range basis and one publisher's opinion is not awfully conclusive, particularly when the opinion itself was so vague and general, but nevertheless I must stop pampering myself in every way.[37]

Holmes eventually decided that if Stringham and Kerouac felt there was any reason to go back to the manuscript, he would try to rework the novel's central character, but he also had to come to terms with his situation. He admitted in some dismay, "I certainly should apply myself to the pressing problems of security and the future, no matter how unprepared I am to shoulder them."[38]

Holmes might have found it less upsetting if he hadn't had the news of Kerouac's succcessful sale on the same day as "The Transgressors" was rejected. Like any writer struggling with a long manuscript, Holmes was uncomfortably aware that most first novels don't find their way into print. What is published as the writer's "first" novel is usually at least the third or fourth, and the apprentice work only appears later if there is a serious interest in following the path of the writer's development.

Holmes had begun an early novel before he went into the service, but it doesn't seem to have been finished. Kerouac, on the other hand, had began *The Town and the City* after he had already completed at least three apprentice novels. What Holmes had to accept was that Kerouac's novel had sold, while his hadn't. He stiffly reminded himself that the one thing he needed now was to be honest with himself.

Both Stringham and Kerouac read "The Transgressors" in the next few weeks. Stringham, as a professional writer, approached the manuscript concerned with finding what had gone wrong. At some point he had already told Holmes that he didn't think this was "the book."[39] He was certain that Holmes would go on to write something much stronger. Nevertheless, when he and Holmes met he had a sheaf of notes and he had made a sketch of the book's structure to demonstrate its weaknesses. He still felt the book was publishable since it was better than a lot of books that did make it to print. "It is far better than many that are," as Holmes quoted him in another letter to Harrington a month later, on April 28, 1949. Holmes added, "It was the sort of conversation that makes one feel better, even though one's props are knocked away."[40] Stringham made it clear that he did think Holmes could write, which at this point was the most important thing Holmes could hear.

Kerouac's response was more personal and more direct. As Holmes wrote Harrington,

> *Jack had entirely different reactions. He also made close notes as he read along. He took it with him one evening and read it at home that night. "I wanted to phone you at eight o'clock," he said, when he arrived in a rain storm the next evening, "But I was afraid you would still be sound asleep and you can't talk these things over on the phone."*[41]

Surprisingly, Kerouac's concerns centered on the question of literary technique, citing T. S. Eliot as the source of his judgment. Holmes told Harrington that Kerouac had said, "It's all a question of technique, John. Everything else is great! You know, I was thinking while I read your book that everything in life is a matter of technique. What Eliot says is right: Art is the same, only techniques change."[42]

At one point—in response to Holmes' uncertainties about whether he should go back to the manuscript—Kerouac insisted that to abandon this book "would be a sin."[43] In his letter to Harrington, Holmes concluded that both of his friends had come to the manuscript from their own very divergent points of view. Stringham's professional advice had been "more neutral, more thoughtful," but Kerouac's had been direct and spontaneous.

> *Jack's smacked of that intensely personal creative immersal in things which is his greatest virtue. When I left him at the subway he said, "I meant everything I said, John. Edward's read a lot more stuff than I have, and he may know a lot better. But then he may be a little jaded." That last was to make me feel better and was, I assure you, quite unnecessary at that moment. I was feeling quite humble and thankful to one and all.*[44]

Now the question for Holmes was what he would do next.

Chapter 9

ANGELIC VISIONS

Energy, a manic verbal energy pouring out of the mouth, a feverish energy of mind with which words cannot keep pace, that inexhaustible flux of a consciousness in the act of exploding outward: when I think of Ginsberg, it is this raw, psychic energy that flickers behind my personal images.

I remember him roving up and down the rugless, creaking floor of my apartment at 681 Lexington Avenue, a spare, hunched, tireless shape driving back and forth between me and the soot-smudged windows of a bleak autumn afternoon in 1948, the long, high-ceilinged room an undersea blur of cigarette smoke, his fluent and absorbed voice droning on and on in what I think of now as a single long sentence that trailed behind him in a undulating wraith of words, his mind erupting out of his parched lips with such involuntary convulsions that he kept moving up and down, as if combating nausea.

His small, quick lucid eyes glowed yellow behind the glasses; a sudden nasal laugh, at once macabre and frightened, would break into the words now and then, as if he had heard them as I was hearing them, and wanted me to know he knew. Then he would stare expressionlessly out the window, still talking, but all the while watching the traffic that gnashed and roared so witlessly down in the dark cavern of the street, seeing (though I didn't know it then)

> *"the motionless buildings*
> *of New York rotting*
> *under the tides of Heaven,"*

against which his mind struggled, like King Canute, to prevent an inundation of his consciousness.
—JOHN CLELLON HOLMES, "The Consciousness Widener"[1]

In the spring of 1949, as Holmes struggled to deal with the disappointment of his novel's rejection, he began to realize that he was closer to an answer to his dilemma than he understood. What he had learned from his opportunities to read portions of the manuscript of *The Town and the City*, with its final chapters describing Ginsberg and others in their crowd, was that their everyday lives—their friends and their lifestyle—could be a subject that would free him to introduce the themes of rebellion and moral defeat that continued to tantalize him. Kerouac's autobiographical approach to fiction had its origins in his admiration for the novels of Thomas Wolfe. Since Holmes had taken Hemingway, Graham Greene, Dostoevsky, and Camus as his models, he had never considered this way of writing a novel, and he approached it by cautious steps.

What Holmes called sketching in his journals had already brought him closer to Kerouac's subject material, their friends and their turbulent world. Creating his informal prose portraits—as though Holmes had been conscious himself of his inexperience as he clumsily attempted to breathe life into the central characters in "The Transgressors"—he was using his journal's pages to sharpen his writing skills. Whatever difficulties John had developing his novel's fictional characters, his long, perceptive analyses of some of the people he'd met during the past months had taken him on to a more assured level of writing. Even in his early sketches, as he worked to develop an idea of the personality and the motivations of new acquaintances such as Landesman and Legman, his observations were perceptive and shrewd.

On February 23, 1949, when Holmes met Herbert Huncke for the first time, Holmes caught a glimpse of the gritty reality that would become the material for his new novel. Huncke was an indigent thief, hustler, and drug addict who had been an early guide for Burroughs, Kerouac, and Ginsberg in their prowls on the night scene in Times Square. The descriptive portrait that Holmes wrote in the pages of his journal comes so close to the real person that his description of Huncke would be immediately recognizable to anyone who knew him.

Huncke had been one of the names Holmes had heard from Ginsberg and Kerouac. Holmes understood that Huncke had moved into Ginsberg's sublet apartment on East 121st Street during the summer before. Ginsberg had endured Huncke's interminable drug-fueled talk; then while Ginsberg was out, Huncke ate all the food in the apartment, took the little money he could find, and disappeared, along with Ginsberg's last suits, his jacket, the winter clothes that Russell Durgin had left in the apartment, and—what was the most upsetting for Ginsberg—between twenty and thirty of the most important books from Durgin's collection. They were not only of considerable value,but they also contained Durgin's notes on his reading. Ginsberg despaired of undoing the damage, but he insisted that he would pay Durgin for everything he'd lost.

Huncke stayed hidden, then was arrested again for possession of marijuana and sentenced to sixty days confinement on Riker's Island. Ginsberg, who didn't seem to have learned anything from his previous experience, wrote to Huncke and told him he could stay in the new apartment Ginsberg had found at 1401 York Avenue until he was able to find some kind of job. Huncke, however, never received the letter, and following his release he wandered New York's winter streets, certain that Ginsberg would never take him in again. He lived on the streets, stealing luggage from travelers in the 50th Street Greyhound Bus terminal, then selling what he found in the luggage for the Benzedrine, doughnuts, and coffee that kept him going. When he finally dragged himself to the door of Ginsberg's apartment in the middle of February 1949, he was destitute, ragged, filthy, his feet swollen and bleeding from the icy streets. He spent most of the next two weeks sleeping in Ginsberg's bed, while Ginsberg, who had finally graduated from Columbia and was working nights as a copy boy at the Associated Press, slept in the daytime on the sofa.

On February 23, when Holmes went over to York Avenue to meet Huncke for the first time, he knew only the more edgy outlines of Huncke's story, and Holmes seems to have decided not to believe most of it. As always in these weeks, Kerouac was with him when they went to Ginsberg's apartment with two other friends. The shrewd sketch of Huncke in Holmes' journal has the effect of a snapshot—this was Huncke at just that moment when they all crowded into the room where he was waiting for them.

After dinner with Edward [Stringham] and George [Wickstrom] at the Czechoslovakian National Hall, [and] a quick flying taxi ride down to the New School to pick up Jack, we went up to Ginsberg's to see the legendary Huncke, who has been sleeping for the past week or so there, but I mean sleeping all the time. I found him a very slight, little man, about 33, with a thin, slightly emaciated body, a round sunken face, and a clear lucid voice. I met him in the darkness, not knowing quite what to expect because he had been sleeping. He has dark, large eyes, with imposing eyebrows and a rather effeminate manner in some inoffensive respects. He seemed calculating yet sincere and obviously Ginsberg had told him of our conversation last Monday morning in which I had inquired about Huncke's future plans, his life, etc. He singled me out . . . as the skeptic in the crowd, and we got along almost immediately. George, who was a little off the ground with Benzedrine, talked incessantly about things and Huncke listened politely, with some interest and a kind of formality and tolerance that was strange to me. He was not at all what I had expected, not at all derelict or miserable, but more like a nervous host receiving guests late at night and shyly eager to have everyone like one another. He talked lucidly, without any of the expressions that Ginsberg and Jack have described him as using. He had a nice command of words although he used them somewhat hesitantly. He has a wide mouth and straight black hair brushed straight back, and he looks like a little French drummer in the provinces or a tired esthete who has had too many years of the semi-mad life in or around New York. He has a kind of little boy's figure, slight legs and thin arms, and he sat back, borrowing cigarettes and telling us about the life of a narcotic addict and passer. . . . Once, when every one else was out of the room, he turned to me, somewhat shamefacedly but with conviction, and asked me what I knew about him.[2]

Ginsberg had admitted to Holmes that Huncke had stolen books from their friend Durgin, and Holmes wondered for a moment if this was what was on Huncke's mind. Huncke went on, however, without referring to anything specific. "He said, quite like some down-at-the-heels English reprobate in a Maughm story, 'I've always thought it was unfortunate for people to get preconceptions before they meet other people.' I concurred, trying to put him on his ease."[3]

Holmes was immediately conscious of the personal charm that made Huncke fascinating to the others in the group. He was dependant on drugs and supported his habits with break-ins, petty theft, and armed robbery, but a word that often came to mind to someone meeting Huncke was that he was "courtly," and Holmes fastened on to this unexpected quality of his "courtliness."

He might have been the editor of a little magazine, receiving out of town artists at twelve o'clock in the evening, calling upon his knowledge of what they had written, bringing everything off with aplomb and winning their respect and interest. . . . He was open about jail and stealing and things like that and I found his manner here fascinating. The only thing which I did not like was the way in which we sat around him, more or less like eager and wide-eyed freshmen who have at last been invited into the sanctum-sanctorum of some brilliant upperclassman who talked with an edge of

*tolerance in his voice, but who really enjoyed his position and our interest
as much as we did. I found him on the whole, almost urbane, and Edward
later described him as a "man of the world," which was quite accurate. His
world was odd, terrifying and strange, but he occupied it like someone on
the* New Yorker *occupies the third stool at the Algonquin bar.*[4]

In the weeks that followed, Ginsberg watched passively as Huncke slowly
took over his derelict apartment, his clothes, and any food or cigarettes
that Ginsberg brought back with him. Huncke slept in the bed that had
been a present from Kerouac, the bed Leo Kerouac had died in. When
Ginsberg woke up in the afternoon from sleeping on the sofa, he'd find
Huncke smoking a cigarette, wearing his clothes, and expecting with some
impatience something to eat and somebody to listen to him.

In March Ginsberg came home and discovered that a woman he knew,
a tall, thin, attractive woman named Vickie Russell, had dropped by to
visit Huncke. She was a Benzedrine addict and erratic dealer in narcotics
who had been part of the shifting crowd around William Burroughs and
Joan Adams, the woman who had become Burroughs' common law wife,
years before. With Russell was her current boyfriend, a small-time criminal
named "Little Jack" Melody, who was on parole from prison, where he'd
served six months for stealing a safe. Within a few days the pair had also
moved in with Ginsberg, and many mornings when he came back from his
job he found Russell and Melody asleep in the bed and Huncke on the sofa,
so he had to stretch out on the floor. The Benzedrine and marijuana—which
they all shared—were the only things that kept Ginsberg functioning.

Holmes stayed in touch with Ginsberg, but he had no idea of what was
happening in the York Avenue apartment. By the middle of April 1949, as
Ginsberg's situation was becoming increasingly surreal, Holmes decided
that he would abandon "The Transgressors," though Rae Everitt still insisted on sending the manuscript around to publishers. Almost with a relieved
shrug Holmes turned his still restless ambitions to something else.

He was also feeling considerable pressure from Marian, whose patience
was growing thin. There was never any money. Some nights they wouldn't
have been able to eat if Betty Holmes hadn't paid for their dinner. Betty also
continued to help with their rent, since the nights of steady drinking, even
ten-cent beers, and the movies and the jazz clubs they frequented drained
away the dollars from Marian's slender paychecks. She kept insisting that
Holmes find some paying work that would help to support them.

With his near paranoid sensitivity to his lack of a high school diploma
and a college degree, Holmes didn't feel that he could apply for any kind of

office job. It was this stubborn, inborn refusal to give in to the bare realities of their lives—which Holmes shared with Kerouac—that defined both their failure and their ultimate success. Even if Marian tried to understand why Holmes could never consider any role for himself except that of a writer, she had increasing difficulties accepting what it was doing to their lives. After she found the copies of Holmes' letters to Mira Kent, she began having trouble sleeping through the night, waking up frequently with bad dreams. Yet Holmes, even if he understood what was happening to their marriage, was unwilling to change.

Though Kerouac's situation in many ways was similar to Holmes', there was also a crucial difference. Kerouac was being supported by his mother, not by his wife or one of the women he sometimes lived with. Gabrielle Kerouac's job at a shoe factory was more arduous than Marian's office job, since it was physically more demanding. But for Gabrielle, a lonely French Canadian widow, with poor English and no friends in her isolated neighborhood, her son's dependency gave her emotional satisfaction. So long as he was virtually incapable of dealing with adult responsibility, she would still have him close by her. Marian had married with the conventional expectation that she and John would have a life together that would include at least some economic security, and she wanted to have children. As she came closer to thirty she felt her life draining away in a stream of endless parties, continual drunkenness, and shrilly excited conversations that usually didn't include her.

Although Holmes was floundering in his dreams of becoming a novelist, in the spring of 1949 he suddenly became visible as a rising young poet. *Poetry* published two poems in January, "Doctor Trustus" and "Les Italiennes," and a review in April. *Voices*, an important new journal, included two consciously literary poetic exercises, "Two Poems after the Elizabethans," in the spring issue. Over the next months there were also "Poseidon" and "The Mansions in the House," two more poems in *Western Review* and the *Chicago Review*. The *Saturday Review of Literature* followed with another poem, "The Critical New Ism," in September. Confident in the wide acceptance for his work, Holmes' poetry took on a new assurance and technical facility, with a level of skill he seemed almost to take for granted.

After the wrenching meeting with the Knopf editor who had rejected "The Transgressors," Holmes reminded himself that he had only started this one novel to see if he could write, and he thought briefly of keeping himself to his promise. Within a few weeks, however, he was already presenting his ideas for a new novel to his friends. Unlike many young, would-be writers who despite their lack of success persist in repeating their early mistakes, he was learning from his failure. After he shook off the pain of his disappointment, he began to consider a new approach to what he was doing, seeking a fresh language and a new subject. Most of the other writers Holmes knew gave up their struggle after a series of rejections, but for Holmes and Kerouac, their initial failure, however they defined it, was the goad that turned them into the writers they finally became.

Although Holmes felt that now he was moving onto new ground, he still was using Dostoevsky as a literary model. He described his grandiose new ideas about "The Transgressors" in a letter to his friend Howard Friedman on May 4, 1949. As if to justify his persistent refusal to stop writing and take some kind of job, Holmes proposed again that he would revise this novel into the opening volume of a large Dostoevskian trilogy. He explained loftily that he intended "an investigation, by no means wholly intellectual or conscious, of the avenues of rebellion in the 20th Century."[5] He envisioned the still unwritten second novel of the trilogy, which he planned to title "The Visionary," would follow "The Transgressors" in the way that Dostoevsky's *The Idiot* followed *Crime and Punishment*. What was different about his new concept was that he was not going to follow the old literary models—instead he was going to use the crowd he was part of as the setting, and the "visionary" he wanted to take as his protagonist was Allen Ginsberg.

What followed in his letter was a long and serious attempt to describe Ginsberg in much the way Holmes had written about his meeting with Huncke in his journal. As he'd done in that profile, he probed what he saw of Ginsberg's personality in the kind of sketching exercise that would be the basis for his characterization of Ginsberg in the novel. Holmes' description was more nuanced and more fully developed than the shorter sketch he'd made of Huncke, but Holmes also was conscious that Ginsberg's story was considerably more complicated than that of their Times Square renegade. Holmes told Friedman:

About a year ago I met a young man named Allen Ginsberg, who is 22 and writes intense, Blakean poetry that is very bad, most of it, but supercharged with a flaring mysticism which is real even though it is neurotic. He is the reference figure for this book, from him I will depart. I met him before he had his "visions," and found him an earnest, intelligent person, difficult to be with for very long because of a kind of malignant intensity that was combined with something close to manic-hysteria at times. I went to a party he gave and found him shirtless, shoeless, running about a crazy cold-water flat up in Harlem, playing be bop and hustling frantically for a disparate group of guests. He sat on the floor and I talked to him about Céline, and his servile eagerness at once impressed and repulsed me. . . . I noticed a strangely formal civility to him then, tinged with a feeling of inferiority. I learned later from people who knew him better that he was convinced of his own ugliness and courted the company of others who were distorted and malformed. He expressed this idea: "Everyone has a monster, the thing they could not bear to be faced with. I want to confront them with their monster."

I saw him infrequently until Harrington left town. Then I spent several days in drugging and exhausting conversation with him. By this time he had had his visions, and I heard stories of him lying on the floor among dozens of people after long days of drinking, crying about the clouds, and beyond them the gates that he could see. I, of course, wrote most of this stuff off, and as it turns out, it was mostly fabricated, undoubtedly by Allen himself.[6]

As he came closer to a decision to use Ginsberg as the subject of his next novel, Holmes became more interested in the "visions" and what their meaning was for his friend. In his biography of Ginsberg, Barry Miles described the moment in the previous summer of 1948 when Ginsberg experienced his "Blake" visions, a moment that was to have a profound effect on his life and was to be echoed in the writing of many other people about him.

The summer heat was on. Allen lay on his bed by the open window, reading William Blake. The book was open to the poem "Ah! Sunflower," from Songs of Innocence and Songs of Experience. *Allen had his pants open and he was absentmindedly masturbating while he read; he had just come when he heard a deep, ancient voice reading the poem out loud. He immediately knew, without thinking, that it was the voice of Blake himself, coming to him across the vault of time. The voice was prophetic, tender. It didn't seem to be coming from his head; it seemed to be in the room, but no one was there. He described it: "The peculiar quality of the voice was something unforgettable because it was like God had a human voice, with all the infinite tenderness and mortal gravity of a living Creator speaking to his son."*[7]

Ginsberg immediately understood that he *was* the sunflower himself. "My body suddenly felt light . . . [and] it was a sudden awakening into a totally deeper real universe than I'd been existing in."[8] Two further poems of Blake's took him again into his visionary world, and in his need to share what he experienced "he crawled out onto the fire escape and tapped on the next-door window. 'I've seen God,' Ginsberg cried, startling the two young women inside. They slammed the window shut in his face."[9]

In his excitement Ginsberg told everyone he knew about his visionary moment hearing William Blake, but at first Holmes failed to question Ginsberg closely about the experience. When Holmes wrote Friedman, however, Ginsberg was very much on his mind. Ginsberg's helplessness in dealing with the situations he stumbled into had led to his disastrous involvement with the criminal shadows of Huncke's life. On April 22, 1949, Ginsberg had been arrested, and though his father had succeeded in having him released after three days in jail, he was facing a possible long sentence as a receiver of stolen goods. Continuing his letter to Friedman on May 4, Holmes described how Huncke, Vickie Russell, and Little Jack Melody had exploited Ginsberg:

> *They moved into his apartment, moved him to the couch and he was powerless to get rid of them. He was fascinated and thrilled at first, feeling, one supposes, that he was "in on something," that he was with "real people" who were not intellectuals. . . . He was, by this time, working for Associated Press as a copy boy at night and trying to pay off some debts which these very people had incurred with friends of his.*[10]

As the days passed, Ginsberg's apartment had slowly filled with the spoils of the robberies that his three friends had carried out—usually break-ins late at night when he was at his job. Most of what they were accumulating was stolen clothing, but they brought back anything they'd found in their break-ins or in their quick snatches of travelers' luggage. Ginsberg seems to have thought of himself as acting a role from one of the books of Genet or Céline that he admired. On one of the trio's night excursions he acted as their lookout, and on three or four occasions he helped them carry what they'd stolen up to his apartment.

Ginsberg's mood of prurient curiosity changed abruptly when he learned that Burroughs had been arrested for possession of heroin and an illegal firearm in New Orleans after his house had been ransacked by the police. Both Ginsberg and Kerouac were aware that they had written many letters to Burroughs, and their letters had thoughtlessly mentioned drugs. Kerouac had been trying to interest his mother in using the money he'd been advanced for *The Town and the City* to move with him to Denver and begin a new life, and the upsetting news from New Orleans acted as a further spur. Kerouac had already been jailed for assisting Lucien Carr conceal the death of David Kammerer in 1944, and he was frightened at the possibility his letters would be found and he would be arrested again.

On April 21, 1949, when Ginsberg went to Carr to tell him about what had happened, Carr's response was similar to Kerouac's. He was on parole for manslaughter, and any hint of criminal activity could return him to the penitentiary with his sentence reinstated. Carr had begged his friends not to mention him in their letters, but neither Kerouac nor Ginsberg had taken him seriously, and Carr was angry about the situation. He insisted that Ginsberg force the others to remove the stolen goods from the apartment and find someplace else to live.

Ginsberg found his three intruders sleeping when he returned from Carr's apartment. He spent the day anxiously trying to assemble any writing—poetry, letters or journals—that could be incriminating, including his personal confessions that he knew would be considered pornographic. He put everything in an envelope in his desk drawer and went to sleep while the others went back on the streets for another robbery. They woke him about 9:00 p.m. to help carry what they'd taken upstairs and when he looked at the things they'd stolen—jewelry, furs, and clothing worth thousands of dollars—Ginsberg was forced to accept the fact that he was in a difficult situation. He went to work as usual, with a foreboding that this time something disastrous hung on the horizon.

When Ginsberg returned from his job on the morning of April 22, 1949, he realized that he had to make some move, and he insisted that everything had to be taken out of the apartment. Melody agreed and told him he'd already been planning to bring it all to Long Island that morning. Huncke stayed behind, but Ginsberg decided to ride with Melody and Vickie Russell, clutching his envelope of letters and manuscripts. He was nervously telling them about his travels in the Merchant Marine when Melody made an illegal turn in Queens in front of two policemen in a cruiser. After one of the officers signaled for the sedan to stop, Melody panicked. Ginsberg hadn't understood that he was driving a stolen car and that under the terms of his parole he was forbidden to drive.

Melody kept his foot on the gas, attempting to flee while Ginsberg huddled in the back seat, terrified at the seriousness of his situation. After a brief, careening chase, Melody slammed into a curb, hit a telephone pole, and overturned the car. He cried out to the others to get away if they could. The doors had flown open, and in the confusion Russell and Ginsberg managed to escape into the crowd that quickly gathered. Ginsberg realized in dismay, however, that he'd left his papers in the back seat of the car. Envelopes of recent letters from his father included the address of his apartment, and the police would find them and trace him to York Avenue. Huncke was still in the apartment when Ginsberg and Russell returned. In a short time police detectives showed up to arrest all three of them.

Ginsberg's confused legal situation dragged in all of his friends over the next several weeks. While he waited for trial there was hectic bargaining between his lawyer—whose expenses were paid by his father and his brother—and the police about possible ways to separate him from the other three with whom he'd been arrested. It was clear that Ginsberg had only been on the sidelines of the actual crimes the group had committed, even if for some weeks he had been a fascinated witness and a gullible accomplice. A number of people at Columbia University who knew him, among them his professors Lionel Trilling and Mark Van Doren, insisted that he was not a criminal, and Ginsberg's father, newly remarried, brought him home to live in Paterson until the grand jury convened to consider the case.

On May 10, 1949, Holmes wrote to Kerouac, who was now in Denver, where he had brought his mother, sister, and her husband, hoping to begin an idyllic new life. Ginsberg had phoned Holmes and told him that he'd gone with his lawyer to Van Doren's office and that Van Doren had assured the lawyer that he was willing to help, while continuing to talk about the disturbing things Ginsberg had done as a student. In his letter, Holmes described the scene with derision:

The lawyer nods his head disconsolately. "Will you help this young man?" he says, remembering his thousand dollars [his fee for taking the case]. Van Doren thinks effectively for a moment. "I'll see. First get him in here so that I can ask him a question." Allen comes in sheepishly and Van Doren levels a serious eye in his direction. "Now, Allen, I want you to answer one question." Allen smiles nervously, fidgeting with his fingers. Van Doren glances meaningfully at the lawyer and then says, "Do you believe in this society?" Allen feels a laugh trembling in his stomach, but is aware that it isn't appropriate to the situation. "Of course," he replied, knowing they know there is no other answer he can give. "And I do," he told me later, "think I do. Well, I guess I HAVE to, don't I?" With this matter out of the way, Van Doren says he will help in any manner that he can.[11]

At the beginning of June 1949, the grand jury freed Ginsberg from criminal charges, with the stipulation that he seek psychiatric help. He spent most of the next eight months as a patient at the New York State Psychiatric Institute on West 168th Street in Manhattan. He was free to leave every afternoon from 4:00 to 7:00 p.m., and if he had someone who would be responsible for him, he could spend his weekends away from the hospital. The bedroom in his father's house was acceptable as an alternate residence. For his friends it was difficult to take what had happened to him seriously, since they continued to see him almost as often as they had before.

At the hospital Ginsberg looked forward to free psychiatric treatment, but he was never fortunate enough to talk to a sympathetic doctor. He had better luck communicating with a fellow patient, a man who was about his own age just gaining consciousness after an insulin shock treatment. The man studied him, smiled pleasantly, and asked, "Who are you?" Ginsberg answered, "I'm Myshkin," naming the saintly central character in the Dostoevsky novel *The Idiot*. The man responded, "I'm Kirilov," naming the evil personage from Dostoevsky's *The Possessed*. Ginsberg had just met Carl Solomon, the friend Ginsberg referred to six years later in the title of his ground-breaking poem "Howl for Carl Solomon."

Solomon, two years younger than Ginsberg, had been born in the Bronx. When he was eleven, his father died, and later Solomon said that he drifted into a deep depression that turned into "indiscipline and intellectual adventure that eventually became complete confusion."[12] He graduated high school at fifteen and enrolled at City College of New York, but he dropped out in 1943 to work as a merchant seaman. Self-taught, he read Dada and Surrealist poetry and traveled to France to attend the first play of Jean Genet and hear Antonin Artaud read poetry. After identifying with Kafka's hero K, Solomon decided he was insane. In 1949, when he turned twenty-one, he voluntarily committed himself to shock treatment at the New York State Psychiatric Institute, where he met Ginsberg.

It was necessary, as part of his treatment, for Ginsberg to accept the hospital's diagnosis that he was mentally ill, so he hid much of what he was feeling from his doctors, conforming with their analysis of his condition. He admitted to Kerouac in a letter that though he had attached so much importance to his visions of William Blake, "The people here see more visions in a day than I do in a year."[13] Holmes, however, sensed that Ginsberg's psychological state was more complicated than anything he was admitting to his doctors at the hospital. On May 10, 1949, Holmes continued in his letter to Kerouac,

> *Though he is desperately seeking "self desecration," this sort of thing usually tapers off when it comes to destroying one's self. Whether it will with Allen is another matter. He will go to incredible lengths to conform to his ideas on himself. Remember that he has always savored as well as*

detested the feeling of rejection. Hasn't he courted rejection, wishing that everyone should be confronted with their "monster" in him? What is this but the desire that he achieve stature by the depths to which he is willing to push himself in the eyes of others?[14]

It was certainly Holmes' view of Ginsberg as this complicated figure—like a fictional character invented by Dostoevsky—that decided him to make Ginsberg the central figure in his next book.

The form of Holmes' new novel took a more definitive shape as he made notes at 681 Lexington before he and Marian left for a vacation in Provincetown on Cape Cod. They were both impatiently waiting for their first break from the continual pressures of his writing and her job that had hung over them since they'd come to New York. By spending the summer in a lonely cottage on the dunes four miles from Provincetown, Holmes hoped to gain some perspective on his creative problems as well as strengthen his marriage, which had begun to unravel after his wife had found his letters to Mira Kent. Already by mid-May he had made a detailed sketch of the literary materials and sources he intended to use in what he was thinking of as the Ginsberg novel. On May 31, he and Marian went to Chappaqua to spend a few days with her family, then traveled by train to Providence, where they spent the night with his navy friend Jim Macguire, who had just finished teaching his classes at Brown University and was looking forward to a summer in Europe.

Another Harvard friend of Edward Stringham's, Roger Lyndon, who was teaching mathematics at Princeton, had found the cottage for John and Marian on an isolated stretch of the coast outside of Provincetown. They would share it with Stringham and his companion George Wickstrom. Russell and his wife, Susan, were spending the weeks at a nearby cottage at the same time. Holmes began hinting to his friends that he was thinking of writing something new and that it might be a novel about a Ginsberg-like figure. His diffident hint to Harrington was that he might "give it a whirl."[15] Most of the pages of Holmes' first letters from Provincetown, however, were filled with the excitement of his discovery of the empty beach, which stirred his memories of his summers with his parents and his sisters at Peconic on Long Island during his childhood. On June 21, 1949, he wrote to Kerouac,

The weather has been invariably good, the days long, slow burners without the insistent wind we had at first. Sometimes in the morning we will

awake in the middle of a thick fog bank that rolls in from the ocean si-lently, but it burns off toward noon. To walk on the beach in the center of a thick fog is an odd experience. Shapes present themselves to the eye in-distinctly, form and re-form as one gets closer to them and finally solidify into actuality. A cluster of sitting gulls, fooled by the fog, will suddenly erupt before one's face and swirl off into the mist, clacking like crows, to settle again after one has passed. The planes, seeking to land at the local airport up the beach from us, buzz blindly above you, circling again and again waiting for an open patch. Last evening we had the first whispers of a storm, but it blew around us in the night and today was blearily humid and sunny. I hoped the storm would strike us here, because the greasy clouds last night, the growing brackishness of the sea, and the rising of a sharp wind, reminded me of storm-weather in Peconic and I was eager for a break in the nearly monotonous golden evenings and blue days.[16]

Their small cottage was on the dunes facing the ocean side of Cape Cod close to the road to the airport. It had a sleeping loft where John and Mar-ian looked out a large window at night under a ceiling decorated by fishing nets, with "a whole string of bobbing fishing lights" visible on the horizon.[17] At the cottage Holmes had available a stockpile of Benzedrine in drugstore inhalers, and he spent days in what he later remembered as "benny-lugubri-ousness, erections that would never go down because of the sweet-tasting strips from the inhaler, fucking fucking up and down the dunes, lying back at last exhausted, but still unexpended."[18] Writing to his mother and sister back in New York City, Holmes told them that within a few days he and Marian became "brown as dune turkeys and briny and hard from our walks to town."[19]

Marian couldn't swim and she spent her afternoons trying to read the novels John had brought along for her so they could talk about books. Among Holmes' selections were Austen's *Northanger Abbey*, Zola's *Germi-nal*, and Flaubert's *A Sentimental Education*. They discovered that Bill Can-nastra, the hard-drinking New York lawyer they'd met through Harrington, was also summering in Provincetown, working on a scallop boat while liv-ing with a young woman in a ramshackle shack near the road to the dunes surrounding their rented cottage. After a storm, Holmes continued in his letter to Betty and Liz, "The surf was bigger, driven by the wind closer to shore, and we all bathed nude in it, shivering in the cold wind, while Marian cackled taunts at us from the beach."[20]

On their occasional trips to Provincetown, Holmes and his friends set-tled into one of the few bars they'd found where beer still cost a dime and they could play the juke box until they ran out of nickels.[21] Holmes cast a wary eye on the affluent tourists from Boston and New York City beginning to flood Commercial Street, the narrow main street of town, since he and Marian were trying to live as cheaply as possible on their meager funds.

> *Already the entire San Remo crowd is filling the bars, picking one called the Mayflower as their favorite, and one would not like to get into the habit of frequenting such places very often. . . .[Conrad] Aiken, Mary McCarthy and others will be featured in the annual lecture series to be given in conjunction with the "art movies" which are run every year. The painting schools are opening, Hans Hoffman has arrived, and a neat little avant garde book store serves the needs of the blistering, sun-lotioned intellectuals who parade in slow, even streams down the main streets, eddying out onto piers or into bars. . . . I often wonder why some of these people bother to come up here if they must bring with them all the city pleasures and habits. Do any of them ever swim or hike or sweat? No answer.[22]*

Nine days after their arrival, on June 9, Holmes wrote a friendly letter to Ginsberg, giving him an idyllic view of their vacation life.

> *Postmark Provincetown. We are here, surrounded by endless sand dunes and the flanks of the ocean on three sides. We are four miles from town, inaccessible in every way, and being devoured by nature on all sides. For comfort and a connection with the ruder pleasures, we have brought Rimbaud, Baudelaire, Stevens, Thomas, Dante, Donne, and Blake. When the sun, sea and burnished bodies become too much for us, we retreat to the darkest corner we can find and submerge, leering privately. I expect to work but the horizon is rife with diversions.*
>
> *I am also reading the elegies of Rilke for another time, finding them sweeping and sincere. I thought of you when I read: "Every angel is terrible," not with a bang but with a whimper. I saw Jack in "continuance does not concern him" and then, looking over the rolling dunes, a Sahara for the imagination or the wink of Blake's eye, eternity in a grain of sand. (That is a meaningful misquote.) To lie somewhere, with a merciless sun whose edge is only stropped by the wind, and read Donne is something all freshmen do, and some dons. I missed it, however. When the poetry eddies into my head and mists the vision, I turn to Dostoyevsky, The Idiot, which after three readings is sheer exhilarating relaxation. You can guess, from the above, the kick I am on Trying to keep myself righted in the seas*

of mysticism, a beckoning, a symmetrical flood it is too, is a job one approaches with relish and fails at without grace or dignity.[23]

The letter continued with a few sentences telling Ginsberg that Holmes had no news of Kerouac. "One supposes he broods in the mountains of his grey and golden Karma, or searches out the good bad (of Life) in Denver."[24] Then, in an abrupt change of tone, Holmes suddenly requested detailed answers from Ginsberg to a series of questions about his visions—without telling him specifically why he was asking him.

Also, and now the caprice is over, I would like any and all information (new data) on your poetry and your visions. A tall order? Yes, because my interest, though anything but cursory, will probably net you little. However, I should be grateful for whatever bits you would care to pen.

Do I dare presume? Yes, because I have always suspected that you would overcome modesty if approached in the right light. Firstly: what are the experiences, ideas, fantasies of your life up to the time of your visions which you feel bear some relevance to them? Secondly: what is the connection, actual, symbolical, psychological and social between your poetry (before and after) and your visions, in light of the first question? You say somewhere "the language of the vision shall be flesh"; document this further if you care to. Thirdly: what associations do you make between your Reichian analyst, your visions, your father, and perhaps later the police? Answer that one (provided that you care to at all) quickly and entirely without thought. Fourthly: (and this one might be in some detail if you are of a mind), did the symbolisms in your poetry become, after the visions, less symbological and more actual to you? In other words, did the symbol cease to be a denotative arrow referring to something below the surface, and become, in terms of your poetry and your thinking, an object, almost unto itself?[25]

As he closed the letter, Holmes made it clear that he was aware of what he was asking. "This is presumptuous, isn't it? If I received such a letter I would be stunned by the matchless audacity of the correspondent. But you know me, and my interest is sincere. I am not trying to prove anything at your expense, and anything you say will evaporate here."[26]

Whatever Ginsberg thought of the request, he responded generously with a nine-and-a-half-page letter describing his visionary experience, and Holmes wrote in considerable excitement to his mother and sister on June 21, "It is a moving and confusing letter, whole chunks of which I can use in my novel."[27]

Holmes' exchange of letters with Kerouac was even more crucial for him, since he felt much closer to Kerouac. On June 16, Holmes had written a long, ebullient letter to Kerouac in Denver, among other news telling him, "I have not been able to get to work as yet, but my projected novel on a Ginsberg-type of person stews in my brain."[28] Kerouac immediately responded that Ginsberg was always posing with everyone, never giving away what he actually thought about anything, and that the only way to get to know him was to drill a hole in his brain, crawl inside, and catch him asleep. Kerouac's advice was that instead of relying on information from Ginsberg, Holmes should invent the details he needed for his novel.[29]

On July 3, 1949, Holmes responded to Kerouac's long letter with six single-spaced typed pages of his own. He'd found Kerouac's letter of June 24 waiting for him in General Delivery at the post office and began reading it immediately in a bar in Provincetown while sipping a cheap beer and listening to Billy Eckstine records on the juke box. He finished the letter "filled with a melancholy joy and nostalgia for just a pinch of Sixth Avenue and one lost chorus of Tristano."[30] Holmes was so moved by the letter that he left Marian, Stringham, and Susan Lyndon in the bar with Cannastra and headed back to the cottage by himself. Alone in the gentle swell of the sand dunes, he read some of Kerouac's letter again and felt himself inspired to run up the next hill, shouting "'Everything's going to work out!' Like a dervish driven mad by the sun, I made for the sea and the distance."[31]

Holmes tried to explain to Kerouac what he found so moving in the letter:

Let me explain: the weeks have made me dry with thirst for anything creative, questioning, real. Up here one is obliterated by the immensity of nature, the intense cruelty of the sun, the vegetative life that it demands of one. It has been breeding a vast irkishness in me, a short temper responsible for inaction work-wise. Try as one will, one cannot keep out of the water, the heat, get down to work. Also we have been leading an indolent life intellectually. We talk some, read at night aloud and discuss, but other than this, I rot with a calculated collaboration. The one bright ray of light came when we read Tolstoy collectively and I swooned at the simple architecture of the man, the great childlike love of him! For the rest it is tedious poetry, the rich, lush Frenchism of Stringham's tastes that are discriminating, but susceptible to decay in a warm temperature. I wanted something hardy, a call to duty, a return to concern and that infinite, strong, worried love out of which work is born. Your letter was that to me. What the hell did this lazy, futile life mean to me? Let the sea dry up, the sun burn out, let nature screw herself! I wanted something of

*the old confusions, a little of that disorder out of which grows wonder and
the desire to know.*[32]

As he considered again what had gone wrong with his first novel, Holmes
told Kerouac that his approach to his protagonist Frankel had been too ab-
stract, too intellectual, as if Holmes had been posing as a social worker.

> *I had written all my feelings out of him, I had understood him in the best
> symbolic, intellectual way, but I had not felt for him. The pathos, as you
> so sharply pointed out, was always off-stage. My own agony and wonder
> at him had been dispensed with before I sat down to write the book. It
> was more a work of "new criticism" of Frankel than it was a great, bleed-
> ing novel about him.*[33]

In his next novel, Holmes promised not to "kill my work with a creeping, atrophying caution" or "maim it with my very gentleness."[34] He would
take Kerouac's advice and try to describe the entire New York scene in what
Kerouac had called "great canvases," though his main concern was "to know
why our craziness, where does it go?"[35] He told Kerouac,

> *It is a large canvas and right now it all seems to center itself around Al-
> len and his madnesses and wonderings, his deep sincerity about lots of
> things, his mad desire for ridiculousness when it comes to others. I would
> have to refer the story to myself of course, the hesitant, overly intellectual
> skeptic, intrigued by the madnesses subjectively as well as mass-observor-
> like, the young married reservist, described by another character as "that
> well-known modern phenomena, a minor poet who does not believe in
> himself". . . Suffice it to say, I plan to use huge portions of my journals,
> parties at Ginsberg's and other things, the whole pattern of last year laid
> down, from fourth of July last (when I met you and Allen) to past his
> arrest and your novel being taken and mine being turned down. I think
> there is a kind of form to that, what you might call "deep form." The form
> I feel is thoroughly emotional and that is what I want.*[36]

Marian had resigned herself to their life continuing in its old pattern,
and she reluctantly encouraged Holmes' idea for his new novel. She had
repeatedly said that he "tended to over-identify" himself with Dostoevsky.[37]
She welcomed the idea of him writing "about what you know first-hand—
all the discoveries, all the hysterics and crap you've just lived through—
Jack, Neal, Allen, all of it. It could make a startling story. It's obviously

excited you so."[38] She was considerably more down-to-earth than Kerouac. "You know it first-hand, not some third-hand booky idea. Anyway, Johnny, I know you can do it."[39]

In Provincetown John and Marian ran out of money sooner than they expected, and instead of staying for the entire summer as they planned, they had to leave the cottage and return to the city late in July. Before they left there were still more parties, still more swimming in the ocean, still more nights of Benzedrine-fueled conversations with their friends, but Holmes was filled now with a hunger to begin work on his new book. The weeks in their cottage had given him a new intensity and direction. He also crowed in his letters that it had been an idyllic few weeks with Marian. In letter after letter he described her dark suntan, her new vivacity. He wrote to friends about their long walks together across the dunes for the mail or for Provincetown parties, their days in the cottage without bothering to dress, and their nights skinny dipping in the surf. For once, in his accounts of the endless conversations, he sometimes included her voice.

Chapter 10

IN THE TEMPLE OF THE GODS

I will only know my place in this Dostoyevskian New York when I hurl myself fully into it, without an escape, without a chance, making an irrevocable leap. It may absorb me, I feel I might drown in it. . . . I have had a gray vision of my life in this fathomless Petersburg of my imagination, in which everyone that I have ever known lived. They are scattered in endless, tottering, labyrinthine tenements quartered all over this thronging city. There is no rest for me but to rush from one to the other—without time for pause or reconsideration—rushing pell-mell (for my life depends on it, it seems) in search of some message. . . . There is no time in this vision; the day, the never-ending day of my life, goes on and on, and there is always time for another frantic dash across town to see so-and-so, because he, after all, may have the urgent news.
—JOHN CLELLON HOLMES, journal, February 3, 1949

The first night after his return to 681 Lexington Holmes began his new novel. He and Marian came back from their weeks in Provincetown without even enough money for food, so she went to stay with her family in Chappaqua, leaving him alone. New York was in another of its summer heat waves—oppressive, lifeless, stale, and sweaty. This was before most New York apartments had air conditioning, when bedside fans only pushed stifling air listlessly around the room. Photographers created a vogue of night pictures of New York families crammed onto fire escapes, trying to find enough relief from the heat to sleep. Holmes worked at night, beginning at midnight, breaking off about two for coffee and a doughnut at Riker's Cafeteria and then walking slowly over to the East River in search of a cool breeze. After the walk he went back to the typewriter and worked until he collapsed at five in the morning.

As the months passed, Holmes spent most of his time at the typewriter, with occasional late nights engrossed in the nervous, frenetic, cigarette-and-alcohol-fueled conversations he fell into with anyone who'd happened to drop by the apartment. In the mornings he awoke with a hangover and his mouth burning from the endless cigarettes, but from all he'd read, he was convinced that this was the way serious writers were supposed to work. Despite the hours he spent arguing with friends or getting off on the new bop or eating dinner with Marian—often the two of them together with his mother and his sister upstairs—through the next year he steadily, doggedly wrote and rewrote, fretted, despaired, and persisted.

His photograph from this time shows him painfully thin, awkwardly tense in his pose. His eyes were large and probing, with an anxious intentness that was at once lost and driven. He stayed at his typewriter filling hundreds of pages and throwing away almost as many, but at the end he finished his book. It was in those grudging months that he became a writer.

Immersed in his novel, Holmes' life was mostly centered in his work. For the others in their crowd, however, the year was even more chaotic than it had been in their disheveled past. Holmes tried to keep in touch with everyone as they reeled off on sudden trips, drifted in and out of relationships, unexpectedly changed their lives and just as unexpectedly changed them back again. On October 9, 1949, both he and Kerouac enrolled in classes at the New School for Social Research at the northern edge of the Village, where Marian was working.

During the summer, after Kerouac had made an effort to move his family—his mother, his sister, her husband, and their baby—to Denver to begin a new life in a small house he rented on the city's outskirts, he had discovered that it was another of his mistaken attempts to set his life on a new path. They arrived on June 2, but his mother missed her job at the factory, quickly decided there was nothing in Denver she wanted, and on July 4 she rode the train back to Brooklyn. Kerouac's brother-in-law missed his favorite fishing places, but more importantly he didn't like being so far away from his elderly parents in North Carolina, so he took his wife, Nin, and their son back a few days later.

Kerouac lingered another few weeks, then in an abrupt decision made a confused trip to California to join Cassady, who at that moment was living again with his pregnant wife, Carolyn, and their young baby—the newborn that Cassady had left behind for his frantic trip back to New York with LuAnne and Al Hinkle in the new Hudson sedan at the end of the previous December. In San Francisco, however, Carolyn quickly tired of Jack and

Neal's continual prowling for drugs and for whatever kicks San Francisco had to offer, and three days after Kerouac had shown up from Denver she demanded that they leave. By the end of August 1949 Kerouac was back in New York City. He settled in his mother's new apartment in at 94-21 134th Street, in Richmond Hill in Queens, not far from her old address in Ozone Park—and with him was Cassady.

In the first weeks after his return Kerouac went into the Harcourt offices—the publisher that had accepted *The Town and the City*—to work on the final revisions before the book went into production. Although he was certain that the novel would establish him as an important young writer, he understood that his education had been interrupted when he left Columbia, and he encouraged Holmes to begin the fall term at the New School with him. Neither of them intended to give more than cursory attention to their courses, but as veterans they were entitled to the GI Bill, which didn't pay them much, but it supplemented the small salary Marian was earning and the weekly checks Kerouac's mother was paid at the factory.

Holmes enrolled in two courses, medieval literature and the philosophy of religion.[1] Kerouac took classes in American literature on Thursdays and Fridays taught by Alfred Kazin and Elmore Lenrow, and he probably showed up more than Holmes. Kerouac even managed to write papers on Walt Whitman for Kazin and on Thomas Wolfe for Lenrow. Kerouac had a flare-up of his old problem with phlebitis, however, and in the late fall he was forced to spend days in bed at home.

For Holmes the classes at the New School were an upsetting interruption to the writing. He stormed into lectures and found his exams a "great aggravation,"[2] but he and Marian had such a problem with money that he couldn't drop out. He preferred to linger in the cafeteria over cups of coffee and cigarettes, talking to other students about the future of American literature, among them the aspiring novelist William Styron, enrolled in Hiram Hayden's class on the novel. When Kerouac cut his classes, Holmes signed his name to the attendance forms so his checks would continue to be sent to Richmond Hill.

As if there hadn't been enough distractions, Holmes also found himself swept up again in the literary tumult around *Neurotica* and its editor Jay Landesman. They had been exchanging letters after Landesman returned to St. Louis, even though Gershon Legman had assumed the role of New York editor that Landesman had considered offering to Holmes. The decision had finally been to let Legman take over the magazine for a few issues, in which Holmes concurred, since he was husbanding his time and his writing energy for the novel. Landesman wrote in his memoir,

The conference with Legman before leaving settled the future of Neurotica. *He would be supervising the production and arranging for the editing
of it in New York. His manuscript,* Love and Death, *would be serialized
in four installments beginning with "The Psychopathology of the Comics," and when all four installments were published, the same type would
be used to bring it out as a book published by the Neurotica Publishing
Company. Legman would get a small amount of money for overseeing the
production.*

*"No more poetry," he said with a shit-eating grin, "unless it makes a
point. I'm going to get you writers who clearly see that American is on the
brink of a nervous breakdown." I didn't have the nerve to ask if they would
save America or push it over the edge.*[3]

"The Psychopathology of the Comics" had appeared in the third issue of
Neurotica in the autumn of 1948, and it aroused the predicted controversy,
as much over Legman's bombastic style as over the incisive ideas condensed
into the article's eighteen pages. The feature of the spring 1949 issue was
another eighteen pages from Legman's book, "Institutionalized Lynch—The
Anatomy of the Murder-Mystery." Although in St. Louis Landesman was
working in the family's antique business and helping his partners run their
Bohemian bar, he was continually distracted, concentrating more on the
magazine and its day-to-day problems, along with his more or less open
affairs.

Landesman's personal life was also strained. His wife, Pat, was still depressed over her miscarriage, and their marriage continued to deteriorate.
Finally they agreed to divorce, and with the divorce behind him, Landesman realized that he also had to separate himself from St. Louis. He moved
to his sister's apartment in Stamford, Connecticut, and slept on her couch.
He was only a short commuter train ride from Manhattan, and for some
months he came in and out of the city before he finally found himself an
apartment on West 53rd Street. Holmes welcomed him back, and soon
Landesman was joining the crowd at the perpetual parties. Legman was
less welcoming, suspecting that Landesman had returned to take active
control of the magazine. He walked Landesman up and down the New York
streets, insisting that everywhere around them were sexual symbols, "a cen-
totaph to man's sexual demise." He warned him, "One slip, Landesman, and
you'll be sucked in with the rest of the victims."[4]

Cassady stayed in New York City for several months, longer than he had
the previous winter when he'd driven from San Francisco with LuAnne and
Al Hinkle. For a few days Mémêre put him up in her apartment in Queens,

but at a Manhattan party in early September 1949 Cassady met another of the beautiful women whom he usually managed to attract wherever he went. Soon his life spiraled into a level of confusion that was confounding even for him.

The woman's name was Diana Hansen, and she had an apartment at 319 East 75th Street, on the Upper East Side not far from Holmes' apartment on Lexington Avenue. She is usually described as a fashion model, but the only thing that seems certain is that she was beautiful enough to have been a model. She had graduated from Barnard College, married one of her professors, and divorced him before she drifted into the crowd. At one of the parties Kerouac and Holmes watched as Cassady sent her one of his patented longing smiles from across the room. Within a few days he had moved into her apartment, and, for once, he helped support the arrangement by working at a parking lot. He soon was climbing the stairs to Holmes' apartment on Lexington Avenue, impatient to discuss literature and to learn about writing from another serious author. Along with virtually all of the men and several of the women in their crowd, he had decided to become a novelist.

Despite the distractions, Holmes wrestled with the new book. In a letter on October 14, 1949, to Alan Harrington, still in Arizona, he complained about his New School classes and described his struggles with the writing. As the letter makes clear, over these months Kerouac was Holmes' steadiest support for his writing—even if it was a support that was sustained by continual disagreements and redefinitions. At this point Kerouac's work had come to a standstill on his own novel-in-progress, still titled *On the Road*, while he continued to revise *The Town and the City* as he waited for its publication in the spring. Kerouac's notebooks from this period were filled with his complicated rationalizations and his bewilderment at finding he could get nowhere with the new book. His afternoons talking with Holmes were edged with his own frustration, but at that point in Holmes' work on his new novel, this kind of persistent challenge was probably the best thing Kerouac could have offered him. In the letter to Harrington on October 14 Holmes wrote,

> *Things totter on. I sit angrily through my classes at the New School, and all are agreed that I am a difficult student, begrudging every moment I must give to it. A cold and then more wisdom tooth trouble (my particular cross!) have bogged me down as far as my own work goes, but I am about ready to begin again. I show every new batch to Kerouac and we*

have arguments and consolings over them. I defend myself, he attacks; I humiliate the work, he supplies the needed crutch. I never knew what a precarious person I actually am. Minute by minute I die in such a situation. But the discussion, the disputation is good for me. Everything is called in question. Never for a moment can I get too entranced in my own dream. This constant reference to "the outside" keeps me on my toes, bobbing and weaving with a wary agility. Jack likes it, then he doesn't. "This is the best you've done," he'll say. Then, "Why the hell are you a writer anyway? You really hate people! You're writing a savage book!" I am hurt, angry; I rail and rave; I try to pin him down, to destroy him. He broods for a moment and, seeing that I mean it, replies: "Hell, man, why do you think I know what I'm talking about?"[5]

By December 1949 Holmes' manuscript had grown to forty thousand words. Harrington read what Holmes considered as a rough draft on December 4 and liked the book. In the initial version the first nine chapters of *Go* were written with the actual names of the novel's characters, so at that stage it was like reading from Holmes' journals. Rae Everitt, still acting as his agent, continued to submit "The Transgressors" to a long list of New York publishers, but at the same time Holmes was showing a large section of his next book to his friends. When she finally told him at the end of 1949 that she gotten another refusal and wouldn't continue to circulate the manuscript, Holmes simply put away the first novel he'd labored on for so long.

Kerouac stopped by the apartment whenever he came into town from Queens, and as Holmes later wrote to Harrington, they had "long, bleak early morning talks over coffee, in which we get very close. We walk down Sixth Avenue watching everybody and waiting for something to happen."[6] Kerouac was still cajoling and prodding Holmes over his writing, but Jack had become more encouraging.

He reads each new chapter I complete and gives me his strange, creative hints here and there. He liked my last chapter so much, he wants to show it to Giroux. I haven't decided on this as yet. "You're doing Ginsberg better than I ever did," he says, much to my surprise. "He's really an unbelievable character the way you've done him!" All of which is soul-balm to me, although I know most of it is his momentary enthusiasm.[7]

Allen Ginsberg was still spending his week days in the New York State Psychiatric Institute uptown, but since his father was providing him with a room in New Jersey, he was allowed to leave on the weekends. The patient he'd met on his first day in the hospital, Carl Solomon, had been released, and Ginsberg suggested that he rent an apartment in time to give a New Year's party to usher in 1950. Landesman went to the party with Holmes, and it was at this party that Landesman, dressed in a tuxedo, first met both Ginsberg and Solomon. He wrote about the encounter in his memoir.

> We followed the sound of bop to the top floor of the house, and were met by two strange-looking young men dressed in bathrobes, which didn't surprise me as much as it did them, when Holmes introduced me as the editor of Neurotica. The skinny, toothy kid with the big horned rimmed glasses fell to his knees in a kind of mock-Japanese ceremony.
>
> "I'm Myshkin," he said.
>
> "I'm Rogozhin," the other guy said. When they got up off their knees they told how much they loved Neurotica and what a pleasure it was to meet its editor. I would have felt like a celebrity if only they hadn't been wearing their bathrobes over their street clothes.
>
> . . . Talking to them later during the party, the skinny kid said he was a poet, and the other guy, slightly hysterical, identified himself as a certified ex-patient just out of Rockland State mental hospital. He immediately told us that he had sustained a series of insulin shock treatments administered by doctors who didn't know what they were doing while they were performing the operation.
>
> "They constantly checked in the manual on shock therapy while connecting me up." His laugh was even more hysterical than mine; we both saw the humor of the situation.[8]

Landesman realized that this could be something for the magazine, "straight out of the victim's mouth," and asked him to send something about his experience. He asked the man's name again. "'Solomon, Carl Solomon. I'm a friend of Allen Ginsberg—you know, Myshkin.' He added, as if he were passing on an atomic secret. 'You ought to get something from him—he's a great poet.'" As the evening passed, Landesman was approached by each of the party's resident writers. "Before I left, Kerouac came over to tell me what a great poet Ginsberg was, and Ginsberg told me how great Kerouac was, right after Solomon had told me how great the two of them were."[9]

Ginsberg later insisted with some resentment that Landesman had made him get down on his knees before he'd accept one of his poems for publication in *Neurotica*. The poem—Ginsberg's first in something other than a school magazine—was a collaboration with Kerouac. Despite Ginsberg's pleas, however, Landesman only used four verses of the poem in the spring

1950 issue of *Neurotica 6*. When Legman saw the new contribution to the issue, his disgusted comment was, "Did it take two of them to write that piece of shit?"[10]

Ginsberg's poem, four verses of the collaboration with Kerouac titled "Song: Fie My Fum," was printed with only Ginsberg's name in two short double columns on the bottom of page 44. Its playful innocence—it opens "Pull my daisy, / Tip my cup"—almost seemed like an afterthought, a space-filler, but for Ginsberg it was possibly a way of making the kind of connections that would help his hopeful career as a poet.

On March 2, 1950, Ginsberg attended a reading given by the older poet William Carlos Williams at the Guggenheim Museum in New York, and soon afterwards, perhaps emboldened by the publication of *The Town and the City* on that date, he wrote Williams a letter introducing himself, "in spite of the grey secrecy of time and my own self-shuttering doubts in these youthful rainy days."[11] Williams was so pleased with the letter that he included it and a subsequent one from Ginsberg in part four of *Paterson*, Williams' personal epic. The older poet was more critical of the nine rhymed poems that Ginsberg included with his letter. He told Ginsberg, "In this mode, perfection is basic,"[12] and he advised the younger poet to make a radical change in his writing style. Ginsberg should abandon traditional rhyme and adopt Williams' own open form poetry based on syllable count. He proposed that Ginsberg should begin using a variable breath-stop length for verse measurement and look back at his own experiences for the material of his writing.

Working in this new style, Ginsberg went back to diaries and journals and rewrote passages using Williams' characteristic poetic form. In the fall of 1950, Ginsberg gave a group of both new poems and old poems that he'd revised to Holmes, who had offered to send them with a covering letter to poetry editor Delmore Schwartz as a submission to the *Partisan Review*. On November 6, 1950, Holmes wrote Schwartz:

> *You once asked if there was anything you could do for me. There is: You might give the enclosed poems special attention. I suppose it's unusual for a poet to submit another man's work (and to write a letter concerning it), but I feel that a word of explanation for anyone approaching these poems cold was need [sic], and Ginsberg was disinclined or unable to give it. . . .*
>
> *They are fragments (in more than the usual sense) of a larger continuity of work. I think the development of the metaphysical imagination is illustrated interestingly in them. . . . The poems are arranged*

chronologically. . . . . [T]hey do possess, I think, the flashes of an intense
and original imagination, working overtime. . . . I do feel that Ginsberg
has something exciting to give the diligent reader who can pierce below
the surface, and will consent to fish for his pleasure.[13]

A month later Schwartz returned Ginsberg's poems, suggesting that
Holmes send them to Jay Laughlin at *New Directions*, "for he has more
space for poetry than we do."[14] At this time Holmes' own career as a poet
was becoming more solidly established, since he had just sold a new poem,
"Night Music," to *Harper's* magazine. He later remembered that it was his
"most formally elaborate poem," written in two hours and sent off to *Harper's* immediately.[15] Ginsberg was impressed when he saw it in the issue of
May 1951, though probably as much because it was in an important magazine as it was for his response to Holmes' poetic style.

With *Neurotica 6* in the spring of 1950 Landesman had taken back the editing of the magazine from Legman so he could make it a literary issue, the
so-called Beat issue. Besides Ginsberg's and Solomon's work, the magazine
contained a short sketch "Mambo" by Anatole Broyard, a young New York
author who was contributing to *Partisan Review* and *Commentary*, as well
as the aspiring novelist Chandler Brossard's story "Parties—Pathological
and Otherwise." The issue also featured psychoanalyst Theodor Reik's essay "The Fear of Touch" and Pulitzer prize–winner Peter Viereck's poem
"Hotel Universe."

Neurotica 6 also included a collaboration between Landesman and Holmes using the pseudonym "Alfred Towne," titled "Sexual Gentlemen's Agreement." Much of the article's language seems to be Landesman's, but both
of them were friends with the many homosexuals in their crowd, among
them Bill Cannastra, Edward Stringham, Alan Ansen, and Herbert Huncke,
at a time when homosexuality was generally treated as a kind of disease.
Even Kerouac, despite his own occasional drunken same-sex experiences,
insisted that Ginsberg wasn't really a homosexual. After Ginsberg's release
from the hospital he began to date young women, and Holmes noted in his
journal on February 1, 1950, "Jack takes me aside and says, 'See, what did I
tell you! I never really thought he was queer!"[16] To today's reader, however,
"Sexual Gentlemen's Agreement" veers close to homophobia in its analysis
of what Holmes and Landesman label "the he's-more-to-be-pitied-than-
censured approach to the homosexual problem."[17]

The point they were attempting to make was that there was a homosexual presence in American culture, but, as Legman would have said, there was

a conspiracy to keep it hidden. They felt that homosexuality was already part of American life, but it was never openly acknowledged. They noted the actor Clifton Webb's success in the films *Sitting Pretty* and *Mr. Belvedere Goes to College*, and pointed out that "Truman Capote, Gore Vidal, Speed Lamkin, and a dozen more homosexual writers were establishing their literary reputations" without critics mentioning that they were homosexuals. This amounted to what Landesman considered "a conspiracy of silence."[18]

In their article Holmes and Landesman argued that not acknowledging openly that these writers were homosexual when they often presented a view of women as "shrews, whores, idiots, and man-traps"[19] had led to "a new kind of Gentlemen's Agreement, by which the minority (homosexuals) seeks to impose its views of life and love upon the majority (heterosexuals)."[20] The article's conclusion was that "by not coming out of the closet, we are stuck with the effeminization of artistic and sexual values."[21] Landesman might have felt he was revealing a dire conspiracy, but it was easy for readers to miss the article's point.

Their discussion of the contradiction in American social attitudes continued in their second collaboration as "Alfred Towne" that appeared in *Neurotica 7* in the autumn of 1950. Their new subject was "The Myth of the Western Hero." In this article Landesman and Holmes adopted Legman's Freudian approach to popular culture, insisting that in the Hollywood western, "the psychological frontier defined by headlines, wars, economic insecurity, etc. is turned into an actual physical frontier abounding in just as many menacing elements, with the one saving grace: you are given a gun and allowed to defend yourself."[22] Ironically underscoring their exposure of the gun as potency symbol in the movies, the authors placed Bret Harte's deadly short poem "What the Bullet Sang" at the conclusion of their article.

Holmes' apartment was functioning now as a casual crash pad for his friends, despite Marian's exasperated protests. Even Landesman began to find the confusion a little daunting. He remembered that "Holmes' pad was like Grand Central Station with characters dropping in at all hours of the day and night. On one of my visits I found Kerouac sleeping on the floor and Holmes and his wife wondering what to do with the body." Landesman suggested, "Let's go out and get a drink," and he recalled that "at the mention of the word 'drink,' Kerouac came to life."[23]

At one of the parties Landesman sat down next to a pretty twenty-three-year-old blonde in a large felt skirt with appliqué flowers whom he thought looked "expensively square."[24] She snubbed him for wearing a suit and tie, thinking he'd just come from an office job. A week later he saw her again at the fountain in Washington Square, where he had gone with the new *Neurotica* contributor Anatole Broyard to take in "the scene of Morris dancers, throbbing bongos, and 12-string guitars entertaining the assorted audience in an impromptu amateur night variety."[25] Broyard knew the young woman well enough to call her "Peaches" as a complement to her flawless complexion. He introduced her to Landesman as Frances Deitsch and mentioned that she was usually called Fran. Always conscious of clothes, Landesman noted that this time she was wearing a "peasant blouse, a wide belt around another flaired skirt, and a pair of Capezio flats," and for a moment he considered putting her down for dressing in "the uniform of the day."[26]

To Landesman's surprise he heard himself politely say hello. This time "she flashed a smile that told me that she might have been waiting to meet me all her adolescent life."[27] Landesman returned her smile, and they walked off together without bothering to say good-bye to Broyard. They never stopped talking, and later that evening Fran brought him uptown to her parents' deserted apartment at the Kenilworth on Central Park West and 75th Street, where Landesman mixed them a pitcher of martinis in "a very large living room that looked like a small wing of the Metropolitan museum."[28] Fran's father, a very successful Seventh Avenue dress manufacturer, was actually one of the museum's trustees. Later she led Landesman into the family bedroom where "we slept together that night as if we'd been doing it for years."[29]

Soon afterwards Fran moved into Landesman's apartment. Holmes met her there and immediately approved of Landesman's choice. Holmes learned that among other things she was puttering with several artistic projects and was addicted to diet pills. On May 29, 1950, Holmes wrote Kerouac that Landesman was so entranced with her "that he bruised the martinis he was making. She consoled him by goosing him playfully."[30]

On July 15, 1950, Jay and Fran were married at her parents' Connecticut estate in a lavishly drunken ceremony with John and Marian in the crowd of guests. It was an afternoon wedding that ended with the bride showing off her figure by slipping into a bikini and leading all the younger guests into the private lake for a dip. In his memoir Landesman remembered that "it was quite a sight to see Holmes and his wife running across the lawn with bottles of champagne in their arms and big smiles on their faces."[31] Even Legman got into spirit of the event. The day before the wedding, he came to Landesman's apartment to offer advice about the best method of birth control: "'Take her temperature every day, Landesman,' he warned me. 'In the rectum,' he added."[32]

By the summer of 1950, *Neurotica* had begun to run into trouble with the postal authorities, who had been alerted to the sexual content in Legman's articles. When bulk mailing privileges were denied, Landesman was forced to carry individual copies of the magazine to the post office disguised in a plain wrapper for their subscribers. He made an emergency phone call to Holmes, who spent the next few afternoons standing in line with Landesman at the main post office in Manhattan behind Pennsylvania Station, his arms filled with bundles of the magazine. Legman was triumphant he had caused a stir, but Landesman wasn't so certain this was what he thought of as success. Drinking coffee on the morning of his wedding in the kitchen of the Connecticut estate owned by Fran's parents, he mused:

> *I looked around at the perfectly designed room with all its major appliances mixing so well with the shelves of early American pewter and glass. I had a twinge of guilt that I could be so happy among that display of good taste and materialism. I thought of poor Legman, sitting in his miserable kitchen, wondering where his next meal was coming from and realized that Legman and I were the most mismatched pair of conspirators in the world. Fighting the good fight with Legman didn't seem as rewarding as living the good life with Fran.[33]*

There was no contest—Jay chose Fran. A short time later he made the decision to turn *Neurotica* back over to Legman, who somehow managed to publish the magazine's ninth and final issue.

Adding to the perpetual drift of friends through Holmes' apartment on Lexington Avenue, Alan Harrington showed up from Tucson in March 1950 and Holmes let him take over one of the couches. Harrington had left his wife and child behind in Arizona, and he proposed to stay with Holmes while he finished his novel *The Revelations of Dr. Modesto*. As the months passed, he and Holmes continually argued about almost any subject that arose. Their friendship cooled, but Holmes was unwilling to ask him to leave. In November, Harrington's wife, near death from what was later diagnosed as tuberculosis, also arrived in New York with their young son. Harrington finally felt obliged to rent a vacant apartment on the fifth floor of 681 Lexington, just down the hall from where Betty and Liz Holmes were living.

Holmes, with the rest of the crowd, had watched Neal Cassady's slick moves on Diana Hansen, and later he described the beginning of their affair in a freely poetic profile of Cassady, "The Gandy Dancer," that appeared in

Ken Kesey's magazine *Spit in the Ocean* in 1981. It was written in a dizzying rush of language that caught Cassady's rush of energy.

> *Who, that night in Cannastra's Caligari-loft, amid smashed records, empty bottles, twenty-five watt shadows, where sullen, end-of-the-world whoopees were hopelessly raised against the inevitability of hangover-dawn, cottoned to a girl, Diana, somebody's ex-wife, sojourning among the lost that year, who melted out of her midtown hauteur under his acetylene concentration, his laughing cajolery, wickedly raised brows, and roving hands through which the shoulder's electricity pulsed with strange grace till she drowned in such attention, knees spread around him on a stained ticking, feeling a pierce of Western sun warm New York's barren womb—this Pied Piper of brief, Miraculous Conversions, this connector of the broken circuit between star and rocket, this assuageless spurter-of-energy hinting that all else was sham and drag—could anyone fail to light up? pushed by the weed, the rod, toward new orbits.[34]*

During the winter of 1950 Holmes, with some amusement, witnessed Cassady's hapless slide into what Neal considered a prison of domesticity with Diana. Cassady had

> *settled into her pin-neat upper Eastside apartment, bearing red paper shades for her bulbs, a bounteous stash, the screaming cream of Sixth Avenue record bins, a jockstrap and a shortie kimono, precipitated by desire and convenience into yet another equivocal relationship with a bedmate, groaning (eyes to ceiling) at the snares of domestication his imperious need (for wherewithal and kicks) so often set them to lay for him.[35]*

In his desperation the by-now stir-crazy Cassady tried to persuade Holmes to "breakout" of his marriage with Marian and run off to Mexico: In his sketch, Holmes described Cassady's self-pitying mood:

> *Slumped by her [Diana's] window, staring down at broken bricks, over-turned ashcans, and blown newspapers in the backlot blear, depthless eyes quietly fierce with mad and wearying purpose, trying one more time to stoke up cooling embers, saying "—just run down to Mexico—see Jack and Bill—why not?—got me a red spavined junker, but'll make it—four-five days maybe if we get the breaks—always get the breaks though—then all that evil weed and crazy talk, and all jalapeno cunt!—and*

you—absolutely, no excuse—have to make it with me, man!—Figure early Friday, got some bennies, gas no problem, straight through—John, you need a breakout, yes, yes—I don't mean Maid Marian—I mean—well, you dig what I mean."[36]

In February 1950, when Cassady celebrated his twenty-fourth birthday, Diana committed the cardinal sin in his world—she became pregnant. After Cassady had moved in with Diana after leaving his wife, Carolyn, in San Francisco pregnant with their second child, he had found himself in one of his familiar dilemmas of attempting to balance his life between more than one woman. This time, however, it was more complicated because each of them was about to have his baby. Diana persuaded him to divorce Carolyn so their baby would be born in a legitimate marriage, but Cassady couldn't bring himself to make the phone call.

When Carolyn picked up the telephone at their apartment in San Francisco, she heard another woman telling her that she was pregnant by Cassady, and that he was asking for a divorce so they could be married. Stunned, Carolyn insisted that Neal had to agree to it, so he and Diana wrote a letter which he signed and sent to San Francisco. With confused emotions Carolyn accepted what seemed to be inevitable and agreed to begin divorce proceedings. Their second daughter, Jamie, born on January 26, 1950, was—by rough count—Cassady's sixth child, and the one Diana was carrying would be his seventh.

If the situation had been settled at that point, it would still have been confused, but Cassady learned that a California divorce required a year's waiting period, which meant he couldn't marry Diana until after the birth of their child. He decided that he would take an old Ford jalopy, drive down to Mexico to get a quick divorce, and then rush back to New York so he and Diane could be married. Cassady never seemed to be able to drive anywhere alone, since he always needed help with gas money.

First he asked Holmes to come with him, and Holmes was eager to go. Then realizing that Holmes had no money and couldn't drive a car, Cassady precipitously roared off by himself, headed to Mexico by way of Denver, where he picked up Kerouac and a new friend named Frank Jeffries. That spring Kerouac had been devastated to learn that *The Town and the City* was having such poor sales that the only money he would make from the book was the thousand dollars he had received as an advance. In late May 1950 he persuaded his editor Robert Giroux to pay him $120 for the plane fare to Denver so he could sign copies of the novel at a book-signing party at Daniels and Fisher. Kerouac was so broke that he rode a bus from New York to Denver instead, pocketing the difference between the bus ticket and the plane fare.

After Cassady drove Kerouac down to Mexico City in early June, they spent a week there in a numb blur of whorehouse sex, alcohol, and drugs. It seems obvious that part of the motivation behind the trip was to pick up a load of marijuana along with the divorce, which Cassady could sell when he needed money, always provided he had enough of a stash for himself. His biographers Dave Sandison and Graham Vickers summed up the adventure:

> *The divorce document Neal eventually brought back (after a week of hot nights full of high jinks, drink, drugs, sex, and at least one casualty in the shape of a fever bound Kerouac, whom he abandoned at William Burrough's home in Mexico City), was described by John Clellon Holmes as "twenty sheets of foolscap studded with red seals." These papers, which looked impressive, were in fact invalid.*[37]

In San Francisco Carolyn had dutifully filed the papers for her divorce, and in June 1950 she came into court to formally petition for a disolution of her marriage. Al Hinkle, who had trailed along to New York with Cassady the year before, appeared as her witness. His wife, Helen, had been staying with Carolyn in her San Francisco apartment, both of them with young babies, consoling each other over their mutual predicaments, since Hinkle had spent part of the year in Maine with one of his friends to avoid being jailed for bigamy. Cassady certainly felt justified in thinking that after two different divorce proceedings he could go ahead and marry Diana, and the ceremony was performed in Newark on July 10, 1950. Their son Neal Junior, rechristened Curtis Neal, was born on November 7, 1950. The witnesses at the wedding were Holmes, Ginsberg, and Harrington.

Then—almost as though he felt the entire farce needed some kind of finale—Cassady rushed back to San Francisco two hours after the ceremony, using railroad passes, with the vague pretext that he had to renew his employment status for the railroad job he'd begun the year before. With no outward sign that he knew what he'd put everyone through, on July 14 Cassady turned up at Carolyn's apartment four days after his wedding to Diana Hansen. In her memoir Carolyn wrote, "He walked slowly and softly around the house, gazing reverently at everything like a man returning from the dead. Barely audibly he said, 'Oh darling . . . you don't know how great it is to be home.'"[38]

The summer before, as Cassady's personal farce was scattering his friends and his wives and his children, John and Marian had stolen a few weeks away in the windswept dune cottage in Provincetown, where John had seen more of Bill Cannastra, who had also come to the Cape for the summer and was working on a scallop boat. In his letters and journals Holmes often winced at the price that Cannastra was paying for the alcohol consumption that was wasting his friend's body and his mind. In a letter to Kerouac on July 3, 1949, Holmes wrote from Provincetown, "Great, dark circles are forming under his eyes, he is the ruin of a man, his lips quiver involuntarily, he forms words haltingly and goes after a glass of beer with the manic-thirst of the desperate."[39]

Holmes went on to portray Cannastra's new girlfriend in Provincetown as typical of the many naïve young women who drifted in and out of the crowd.

With him and Bruce [Cannastra's roommate for the summer] in the house, is a non-descript girl by the name of Yvonne, one of those typical young girls that Cannastra finds somewhere, fresh, seemingly innocent, impressed by every[thing] in a wide-eyed, freshman manner, on the road to an unbreakable neurosis, indistinquishable from the one who proceed and the one who will, in a month or two, follow. . . . Cannastra tells everyone that he has brought her here to kill her, and she simpers again.[40]

By the next year, although Holmes seemed unwilling to face what was happening to them, nearly everyone in the crowd was drinking as heavily as Cannastra had been the summer before in Provincetown. In his journals Holmes noted without comment that Lucien Carr had collapsed on the street in a drunken stupor the night before and that Ginsberg passed out in a bedroom at a party and that Kerouac—or almost any of his friends—had stumbled to the end of a party too drunk and too sick to be moved. For Holmes and Kerouac, who didn't have jobs they had to get to, the day often began with quart bottles of beer at Holmes' apartment and continued there until two or three other people showed up and they took the party around the corner to their favorite neighborhood bar. John and Marian themselves often drank to the point of oblivion and stumbled through their mornings fighting relentless hangovers. When Holmes began to complain in his journals that their sex life was not as satisfactory as what they had experienced when they were first married, he never considered that his alcohol consumption could be part of the problem. Also, as with any crowd of drunks, the only people they seemed to know were the friends they drank with.

In his gnawing need to be always the wildest of the group, Cannastra's fits of drunken craziness became more edgy and more dangerous. As an ex-lover of Tennessee Williams, he threw wild parties at his Manhattan loft that were legendary, attracting a literary crowd that included W. H. Auden, Chester Kallman, *New York Times* dance critic Edwin Denby, *New Yorker* poetry editor Howard Moss, and Random House editor William Frankel.[41]

One morning at 3:00 a.m. Cannastra decided that he and Kerouac should run around the block naked, and although Kerouac, who would never appear in front of his friends without wearing clothes, made the run in his underwear, Cannastra ran blissfully naked. At some parties he would stumble up to the roof and threaten to throw himself off, at other times bottles were smashed and the floor was covered with broken glass so he could walk barefoot in the rubble. Holmes kept some distance from the shifting crowds clustering around Cannastra, but he was conscious of his magnetism. In a journal entry on July 2, 1950, he wrote,

> *When you talk to people here in New York who have pretensions toward sophistication and you mention Cannastra an eager, naïve glow creeps into their eyes. One fancies that they estimate you higher because you can call him Bill. One starts to feel that there are hundreds of lonely, selfless young people who are slavishly preparing gigantic campaigns the result of which will be entrance into Cannastra's coterie. They are trying to trap him into recognition of them. In madder moments of thought about this, I sometimes feel that most everyone I know is becoming a writer, a mathematician, a dancer or whathaveyou, [sic] not for itself, but only to win introduction into Cannastra's. When you inform them that the door is always open, and that you can just walk in, they are stunned and somehow refuse to believe you. It cannot be that simple. One does not merely amble into the temple of the gods. There must be some price of admission.[42]*

It was Cannastra who would be the first of the crowd to pay the price of their wildly indulgent lifestyle. On the night of October 12, 1950, he was part of a drunken group out on the town. When they ran out of money in the Village they decided to borrow a few dollars from Lucien Carr to continue their party. There are several accounts of what happened, all differing in their details, but Barry Miles' description of the tragedy has a sense of authenticity.

> *Around midnight Cannastra decided they should take the subway to go and borrow some [money] from Lucien. As they reached the Bleecker*

Street station, someone mentioned the Bleecker Tavern. The train began
to pull out of the station, and Bill, as a joke, leapt up and lunged at the
open window, as if he were going to the bar. He misjudged his leap and
found himself hanging too far out of the window. The others rushed to pull
him back as he struggled to regain his balance, but his coat ripped away
in their hands. The train gathered speed, and he began to scream for help.
As the train entered the tunnel, he ducked his head to avoid the pillars.
There was a thud and he was torn from their hands, out of the window,
and onto the roadbed, where he was dragged for fifty-five feet before the
train stopped. He was rushed to the Columbus [sic] Hospital but died on
the way.[43]

After a dismal funeral ceremony his friends couldn't think of anything to
do except get drunk again, but as a kind of memorial gesture they eventually moved the party to Hoboken, across the Hudson River in New Jersey,
so they could eat steamed clams while they drank. Holmes described Cannastra's death and the emotions in the last hours of their drinking party
in a despairing chapter in the last pages of *Go*. In the book Cannastra was
named "Agatson," Kerouac was named "Pasternak," Ginsberg was "Stofsky,"
Stringham was "Ketcham," Lyndon was "Trimble," Holmes' own name was
"Hobbes," and Marian became "Kathryn."

He looked at the others, at the semicircle of intent faces around the bar,
and he seemed to see the gnaw of isolation devouring each one. Trim-
ble's exaggerated laughter was actually a mask behind which was hid an
emotion of which he was inordinately proud or ashamed. Janet, making
a harassed tea party face, was foolish and brave as she wearied in her
contest with fear, but would not relent in the greater struggle to keep this
secret. Ketcham's cool poise was suddenly the emblem of deep distrust
of all confidences, perhaps anger at himself for those he had exchanged
to no purpose with Bianca. Pasternak, gloomy and irritated, seemed to
be wondering how to fit the joy of his book's acceptance into the dreary
facts about Stofsky and Agatson. Hobbes peered into them and knew these
things. But it was Kathryn's expression that hurt him most. He seemed to
see inside her where even she could never see. . . . And then he felt sick.[44]

Cannastra's death turned into a sudden and completely unexpected
opportunity for Kerouac. He was back again in Mémère's apartment after returning from Mexico City, where Cassady had abandoned him when
Kerouac had collapsed during a bout of dysentery. Late one chilly night,

wandering in Manhattan the last week of October, Kerouac passed the building at 125 West 21st Street where Cannastra had lived, saw lights in the window of the loft apartment and called out, hoping there was a party going on. Cannastra had preferred sex with men, but there always seemed to be a young woman staying with him at the loft, and there was one living in the apartment now. She looked out of the window, saw Kerouac in the street, and told him to come up. She was a pretty twenty-year-old named Joan Haverty, the last in the stream who had passed through Cannastra's life. Haverty offered Kerouac a cup of hot chocolate, and they sat and talked.

Kerouac was emotionally and financially dependent on his mother, whom he would never leave, but during these years he was endlessly frustrated, living in her back bedroom without an opportunity for sex. He was to profess himself in love again and again with any young woman he met who lived in her own apartment, worked a job to pay the rent, and had no steady boyfriend. Kerouac was even willing to put up with a husband or a steady boyfriend so long as he sometimes could share the bed, but he had been drifting for years, and suddenly there seemed to be a possibility for him to begin something more stable in his life.

Cassady was still considered part of the crowd, after his prolonged residence in Diane Hansen's apartment, and he had managed to settle only part of his life by his return to San Francisco and to Carolyn's apartment. In his letters to Diane he was continuing to assure her that after the birth of their son they would live together somewhere in California at the end of one of the railroad runs he traveled as part of his new job. Carolyn, he assumed, would continue to live as his wife at the other end of the run. On November 28, 1950, Holmes wrote him a long, wryly amused letter. His news was that Kerouac and Cannastra's roommate had gotten married, five weeks after Cannastra's death.

> *Firstly, let me give you some small account of the marriage of Our Boy. I tore up to Cannastra's flat (remember?) where Joan (the bride) lives, finding the happy couple (this on the day of nuptials) snoozing in bed. I routed them out, and after showers, coffee, hassles about preachers and final checks on license, Jack and I tore over to Lucien's (just down the street) for a few last, bachelor-type sentiments. Lucien and Liz (a small spaniel of a blonde with petulant lip and eatable smile) were curled up in an arm-chair listening to Brahms.*[45]

The day of the wedding the only thing Lucien Carr could find to drink in his apartment was some "lousy" French wine, but as they were finishing the bottle, it became clear that Kerouac had done nothing about arrangements for someone to perform the ceremony, and it was already after five in the afternoon. They rushed back to Joan's and found Ginsberg sitting with Roger Lyndon discussing the English social philosopher Bertrand Russell. Ginsberg was immediately sent out to make a canvas of the neighborhood churches, "hoping to locate one of God's men who would join the quaking couple."[46] So many people were expected to turn up at the wedding party that Holmes decided he should go out and order a keg of beer. With that crucial arrangement taken care of, he hurried back to Joan's apartment.

> *No one was dressed. Joan was pressing Jack's suit, putting the finishing touches on a coat she had made to be married in, and Ginsberg had been able to dig up no one. Jack had, however, made emergency arrangements with his sister who said she would attempt to get in touch with a certain Judge Lupiano, a local Italian ward-heeler who had made the bench in the last election. It seems a friend of her husband's was related to the Judge's wife's cousin . . . or something.*[47]

By this time the afternoon had turned into another frantic party, complete with Kerouac's precipitous interludes on the bongos.

> *Everyone was in a furor, the phone was ringing continually. Jack would rush from shaving to the bongos (Cannastra's old bongos) to accompany some wild Mambo that poured out of the radio. Joan, like a Violetta in La Boheme, was working diligently along on her sewing machine, still three seams from the finish. Roger was smiling happily in a corner, tipping a bottle. Ginsberg was lost in his own dark thoughts. Then Jack's sister called, saying she had got Lupiano and that he would perform the ceremony at 6 o'clock. It was close to that now. Lucien and Liz arrived, and the women got off in corners, doing womanly things.*[48]

When they got out of their taxis, Lupiano was waiting for them in his apartment below Sheriden Square, and they learned that he had never performed a wedding ceremony before and he was even more nervous about it than they were. There was a final noisy altercation with his three children who were gathered in front of a sixteen-inch television set in the living room.

> *The kids were loath to leave the TV, because Rocketgun Harry, Space Cadet was just coming on. But the wife, rosy with before-dinner shots of*

whiskey and (perhaps) remembrances of her wedding day and what came after, insisted. The Judge brought out a printed card with the ceremony on it, and holding the license in one hand and this sheet in the other, we grouped around. The whole thing was over in forty-five seconds and the kids only missed the commercial on Space-Cadet.[49]

The party that assembled at the loft on West 21st Street, now the temporary home of Kerouac and his newly wed bride, was up to the crowd's usual strenuous standard, and it continued long into the night. Holmes' account to Cassady assumed some of the tone of a society-page news article.

Revelry reigned that night. Fantastic hordes of people arrived from everywhere! Jay and Fran, Tom Livornese, Harrington, Roger and Susan Lyndon, George and Eleanor Bowman, Ol' El Lenrow (remember?), the Stringhams (Edward and George), and uncountable others. I insisted on drinking the gigantic head off the keg and got cloudy and lighter-than-air immediately. I was once more available for dancing in the streets. Also vodka, whiskey, gin and champagne arrived. I don't remember much of the night, except at the end I had to be torn away from all the women. I recall dancing with numbers of them, kissing them all meloncholically [sic] as I went out the door. At one point I saw Roger Lyndon lying on his back in the hall, then I saw Marian throwing beer happily at Lucien. El Lenrow was stunned by all this, but drank his share of the keg. At dawn Winifred, a large 220 pound Negro girl arrived with Ansen and other cronies. Further madness occurred that I was too drunk to recall later.

In any case, the boy is married and no one has heard from him for a week.[50]

After the letter to Cassady on November 28, 1950, describing the wedding the previous week with a giddy sense of its moments of hilarious confusion, Holmes also wrote an affectionate letter to Jack and Joan on the same day, still in the emotional afterglow of the new marriage. In the letter was his wedding present to them. It was a marriage poem, a finely wrought epithalamium, in a wry, often unexpected blend of classic diction and abrupt borrowings from everyday speech that recalled the tone of W. H. Auden. Almost as a challenge to himself, Holmes had chosen to write it in a complex traditional meter and rhyme, as befitting a wedding poem, and in one stanza he asked "William" Cannastra, whose death had made this day possible, to forgive their joy. Holmes ended the letter with his poem, introducing it diffidently:

Here, by the way, is the poem which I wrote for you both on your marriage-day. It is a poor gift, and needs still to be polished, but it is for you both.

EPITHALAMIUM *(made for the marriage of Jack Kerouac and Joan Haverty, brought together by the death of a mutual friend, November, 1950)*

Death is now in season
And sense and purity
Are headless on the knife.
At last, in lieu of reason,
There's more surety
In human love than life.

The world of violence
Where no one can be chaste
Is aboriginal
Beside the innocence
In which a nuptial haste
Is deeply virginal.

William, pardon these
Death has brought together
On the stone you're under.
All the mysteries
Living creatures weather
Love can pull asunder.

Friends, in toast and praise
Pretend you understand.
Joy so very grave
Is young enough to raise
Castles in this sand:
To love at all is brave.

World, give them a night
Where no anxiety
Can roll its noisy carts.
And keep tomorrow's blight,
Today's propriety,
From their courageous hearts.

O night, abandon sleep
To tender images.
The body's hour of light
Be dreamless and be deep.
Is gilt and full of night.

Nourish, love, this pair;
Preserve the creature's breath
In Husband and in Wife.
For in the midst of death,
In love they are in life.[51]

The poem was never published. It was perhaps destroyed by Mémêre or lost in the confusion of Kerouac's move from his mother's apartment into Cannastra's loft for the first weeks of his new married life, before he and Joan moved back in with Mémêre when the rent came due. Kerouac never referred to Holmes' affectionate poem or to his letter, which ended, "Harrington, Virginia, Steve, Marian and I all send you love, and whenever you come in town call us up, for Pete's sake . . . and come in soon. Best to your mother, Jack. A kiss to your sweet bride."[52]

The group's chaotic saga had played out another one of its turbulent scenes. Next would come the chronicles that told their story.

Chapter 11

A TORRENT OF WORDS

And now, about your predicament, which I hope I am not wrong in mentioning. In The Town and the City *the form was implicit in the material. Perhaps you did not worry overmuch about it. Perhaps you let the great flood of material take you and find a form itself. You told me, one of the first times I met you, "You know, John, I haven't got any form really. But I think my book has deep form." . . . I think it is true of you, and true of many American writers. . . . But now, in* On the Road, *you are struggling with the difficulties of form and mould. Where to put all this vast heap of material? How shape the mountain to a hill the eye can contain? How domesticate the wild and majestic elephant?*
—JOHN CLELLON HOLMES, letter to Jack Kerouac, December 27, 1950

Even though it was a long subway ride into midtown Manhattan from his mother's apartment in Queens, Kerouac still climbed the stairs to Holmes' apartment at 681 Lexington Avenue almost every day through the winter of 1950–1951. Usually they started with whatever beer was in the refrigerator and listened to some of Holmes' new bop singles. Whatever they began talking about they inevitably picked up their old quarrel over what they felt the other should be writing, and they continued their dispute on long afternoon walks through Manhattan. They tried to make it back to the apartment to clean up the mess before Marian got home from her job, since they knew she'd be angry with them if she came back to empty coffee cups and the stale smells of beer and cigarettes. Untidy debris made it clear that Holmes had spent most of the day in a rush of talking and drinking with Kerouac and hadn't done any writing. They knew the storm of accusations would always blow over, since Marian liked Jack, and despite her resentment at her situation she'd finally come to accept John's need for Kerouac's friendship.

As Holmes explained to Alan Harrington on December 2, 1949, his relationship with Kerouac "has always been alternately close and wary, a hectic course from the very beginning."[1] As insecure, aspiring young novelists they circled each other in unacknowledged competition, yet Holmes believed that in ways he considered important they were also basically sympathetic. He continued in the letter,

> We are younger, somewhat, than the rest of you; city- educated boys, who got a haphazard urban schooling, and whose first rebellions were not necessarily rational. We are both given to excesses. I usually bottle them like the old surgeon collecting foetuses in alcohol. Jack spews them out over everyone in sight, and so they pass away. I castrated myself at an early age by an essential distrust of my abilities and my ideas. This made me more intellectual and constantly given to accept rational, brittle systems to explain everything at one shot and give me a rest. . . . With Jack, I explode. I assume my proper level once in awhile. I open myself up. We argue, rant, giggle and run riot, and I'm learning that honesty is the only safety. It's showing in my book, because there's an enthusiasm I would have been ashamed of once, an eloquence, faulty, rhetorical, verbose, that would have turned my stomach before, and a wonder that I mocked at one time. . . . I'm trying to write down what I did feel, realizing that some of it was stupid and self-centered and lots of it wrong and indiscrete [sic]: but what else do I have to go on.[2]

Although their stubborn arguments and fretful discussions never settled their differences, each of them was continually forced to defend their own decisions about how they wanted to write and how they conceived the form of the novel. The artistic path each of them would ultimately follow was hacked out in their disputes.

In May 1948, after Kerouac finished the first draft of *The Town and the City*, he had made his first start on his road novel, but for nearly three years he fumbled ineffectually with his manuscript. He had difficulty even finding a title that satisfied him. In his gnawing efforts to find some structure for the book, he was alternatively titling it, among scores of other choices, "Souls on the Road," "Love on the Road," "Home and the Road," "Hit the Road," "In the Night on the Road," and "Along the Wild Road."[3] An early version he showed Holmes, as Holmes later told an interviewer, "started in New York City with a rich family, a poor family, all kinds of crazy things. The opening scene was in a penthouse. The mother was based on my mother, whom Jack knew quite well by then."[4]

The problem was that Kerouac couldn't break way from the stylistic influence of Thomas Wolfe. Still thinking in terms of a family saga that would continue the story of *The Town and the City*, he was unable to find a way to begin his road narrative that held his interest for more than a few pages. In his notebooks he complained about his growing sense of futility, and his frustration helped fuel his arguments with John. After six months of struggle with his novel Kerouac wrote in his notebook on November 17 that Holmes' response to his ideas gave him more of a vision than he was able to conceive for himself.[5]

The main area of their contention was their almost total disagreement over the nature of the novel as an art form. Holmes repeatedly maintained in his journals that a novel should dramatize ideas—that the novel functioned as one voice in a continuing intellectual debate that he could trace back to the Greek playwrights. It was Dostoevsky and Camus whose names he cited when he expanded on what kind of a novel he wanted to write. Kerouac returned as stubbornly in *his* notebooks to his position that a novel should not be a vehicle of ideas—it should be a free expression of personal experiences, and in his notes to himself it was the name Thomas Wolfe that occurred repeatedly. At that point Kerouac's word for what he wanted to achieve in the form of his novel was "moods."

Neither of them made more than a passing reference in their writing to the disturbing events of the last half of 1950, while the nation drifted further into the Cold War. The newspapers were absorbed with the threats to American civil liberties as Senator Joseph McCarthy made his charges of Communist infiltration of the State Department and professors at the University of California campuses were dismissed for refusing to sign a non-Communist oath. As North Korean Communist troops prepared to capture the South Korean capital in Seoul, the Atomic Energy Commission published its recommendations for civilian defense against an atomic bomb attack. A month later, as the North Korean army poured into South Korea in September 1950, the United States found itself involved in a major war.

Holmes had been the most politically engaged of their crowd, but he was so absorbed in the problems of his novel that his only mention of the situation in Korea came in the middle of a letter on June 26, 1950, to Kerouac, who was at that time still recuperating in Mexico City from his bout of amoebic dysentery. There Holmes wrote, "The heat has settled down on this town like a hand. It is broken only by news reports from Korea and a fairly steady Ganges of beer." Later, in his description of his road adventures with Cassady, Kerouac included only a single paragraph describing a military parade they had witnessed blearily when they passed through Washington in January 1949 just before Truman's second inaugural ceremony.

Whatever Kerouac's ambitions, his ideas about the aesthetic form of the novel were severely tested during the spring and summer of 1950 when his newly published *Town and the City* met with unenthusiastic, polite reviews and poor sales. He was already reading and criticizing sections of Holmes' new novel in October 1949, only a few weeks after Holmes had written the first pages, at a point where he was still unsure himself of what he was attempting in his own book. Apparently Kerouac read nearly every chapter of the novel that would be published as *Go* as soon as Holmes completed it and, as Holmes told Harrington, Jack continued to offer "his strange, creative hints here and there."[6]

Dostoevsky was still Holmes' model, primarily his novel *The Idiot*, with its numerous characters all linked by a common plot. In what he called his "Dostoyevskian framework," Holmes conceived his narrative in philosophical terms as "a dialectical situation, everyone working on everyone else."[7] Although Holmes had given himself an almost unworkable set of conditions for his book, he was piling up so many pages beside his typewriter that it was obvious he'd created a usable plot to dramatize his story, while Kerouac's work on his own novel had come to a standstill.

Through all of their disagreements Kerouac was distracted from his struggles with his road novel by his almost daily reading of Holmes' new pages. Also something that Holmes had overheard at one of the endless stream of parties could have been another reason for Kerouac's uncertainties with his stalled manuscript. In a letter to the Lyndons on January 29, 1951, when Holmes was working in the final chapters of *Go*, he described an argument with Ginsberg at a drunken party, after he'd overheard Ginsberg and Harrington talking about him. Harrington had responded to something that Ginsberg had said by suggesting that he should ask Holmes for his opinion. Ginsberg's reply, "smiling crookedly," was that Holmes had "no opinions." Holmes' letter continued,

> "I just listen," I [Holmes] said.
> "That's what Jack was saying the other night," Ginsberg said eagerly. "He was berating you for over an hour. He said you had no right to write a book about everyone's private lives, and he thought you were savage and hated people anyway."[8]

If Kerouac was insisting in their long arguments that Holmes had no right to use the lives of his friends as material for his novel, even though Kerouac had done this himself at the end of *The Town and the City*, how could Kerouac continue to use the same people, the same settings, and the same incidents for his road novel? Did he have any more right to invade their privacy than Holmes did? Kerouac, however, never seemed to be conscious of the contradictions in his arguments with Holmes, and later Holmes referred only casually to their use of autobiographical material:

> *Certainly we shared a similarity of attitude based on the same experiences, and we were both trying to write directly from our own lives in those days. These lives were occupied with things like drugs, madness, visions, booze, jazz, and unconventional sexual mores, and these things surfaced in both our books in the natural course of writing.*[9]

Kerouac's dilemma was that he had found no other way to write that he could sustain for long. After completing *The Town and the City*, he gradually discovered that he wasn't, in any ordinary sense of the term, a novelist. In the two years he had already spent attempting to write his road novel, he found he was unable to develop a plot with imaginary characters. He was conscious that there was no place in his prose for the larger generalizations that shaped the historical form of the novel or for any central narrator except himself. Every effort he made to invent a plot or characters inevitably ground to a confused halt in his lack of belief in the forms and the functions of the traditional novel. In his perpetual arguments with Holmes, he had managed to paint himself into a corner.

Kerouac's struggles with his road book were also compounded by his efforts to earn some kind of living. After his marriage to Joan Haverty he decided to go back to his old job of writing plot synopses of motion picture scripts, this time for 20th Century Fox, which had an office in midtown Manhattan. Kerouac hadn't altered his conviction that it was his wife's role to support her writer husband while he sat at his typewriter, but he was conscious that of the three people in his mother's apartment, where he and Joan had moved when they couldn't pay the rent on Cannastra's loft, he was the only one who didn't go off to work, and he didn't like to be left alone. It was at this point that a giddy, Benzedrine-fueled letter from Cassady in San Francisco, written on December 17, 1950, arrived on his mother's doorstep.

Later called the "Joan Anderson" letter, the original was subsequently lost, but Kerouac estimated on December 27 that it was 13,000 words long. Though Kerouac later claimed that the original letter was 40,000 words long, the postage on the surviving original envelope in the Allen Ginsberg archives at Columbia University indicates that the size of the letter was between twelve and twenty pages, which would mean 10,000 to 16,000 words.

In a 1966 interview in the *Paris Review*, it was the "Joan Anderson" letter that Kerouac was referring to when he called it "the greatest piece of writing I ever saw."[10] What is apparent, however, from the dates of the letters crossing back and forth between San Francisco and New York, is that the model for Cassady's bragging letter was another swaggering letter giving an account of teenage sexual conquest that Holmes had sent Cassady three weeks earlier.

Kerouac seemed to be unaware that Holmes and Cassady had been corresponding frequently over the past weeks. On November 20 Holmes had received an animated letter from Cassady that opened with a long passage laboriously copied from Oswald Spengler's *Decline of the West* that Ginsberg had presented to Cassady in a two-volume edition. Then, breaking off from Spengler, Cassady continued with a description for Holmes of his first job as a bicycle messenger with the Dime Delivery Company in Denver, including a high-spirited, visual account of another messenger named Ben Gowan, whom Cassady joined in thieving expeditions when they got off work.

A week later, on November 28, 1950, Holmes replied to Cassady's account of his bicycle messenger days with a ten-page single-spaced letter that opened "Dear, pure Neal." Holmes assured him, "I'll never, for the rest of my born days, forget Ben Gowen, nor you in that 'hard hard cold winter of 1949.'" In a rush of topics Holmes continued with an account of Kerouac's wedding before he drifted into a reminiscence about a Ben Gowen–like character he'd known named Robert Troska and then went on to free associate about some of his own on-the-road adventures as a teenager.

Finally Holmes began a long story about his favorite sixteen-year-old sex queen, Fay Kenney, a "soft, cuddly little Irish girl" he said he'd known in New Jersey. In his "Fay Kenney letter" Holmes described in wildly improbable sexual detail nights when he would go out on double dates with Fay and her parents. They would start off on a drive, then her father would park off the road.

These parents fancied themselves progressive or something. Fay and I would sit in the back seat, wrestling and whispering, while the mother and father would disappear down in the front seat. . . . Anyway, about ten o'clock, after an hour or so of this heavy feeling—up, they would get so hot they'd either get out of the car, walk up the road a little, stretch out and tear off a piece, or they'd tell us it was getting late, and tear back home, with us in tow, she feeling his cock for him while he drove, and he trying to restrain himself from blowing off in her hand. They would rush upstairs,

leaving us alone down in the kitchen, and we'd listen to the heavings and
creaking of their big double bed. I would always try to get Fay. She'd never
let me go all the way.[11]

After Holmes finished his heavy-breathing description of his efforts to
win over Fay Kenney, he segued into a three-page rhapsody for Cassady
about their mutual friends in New York. As Holmes paused to catch his
breath, somewhere about page 10, he looked back at what he'd written and
concluded,

In any case, in reading over this letter I see that it is not a unity at all,
but in turns a gossip column, a wild ritual in the celebration of America,
a strange elegy and eulogy of people, a lament, an epic, a piece of misty
doggeral, a snatch of far-off blues, a little pinch of bop, a mite of mambo;
in fine, a stew.[12]

Eight days later Cassady responded to Holmes' "Fay Kenney" letter. Cassady's letter to Holmes on December 7, 1950 began "Wooooooooooooooooo
oooooooooooooooooooooooo—EEEE! A real whiz of a letter" before Cassady ripped into another account of his boyhood, this time about living in a
tenement with a "poverty-ridden couple on Denver's lower eastside" whose
"fine life before the depression rankled their memory, but they knew it was
gone forever."[13] Soon tired of all the typing, which Cassady did very clumsily, he ended his short letter, promising to return to New York City within
the month "to continue this verbally soon."[14] Cassady's subsequent letter
to Kerouac was written ten days later. The account of the "Joan Anderson"
hospital visit and the sexual exploits that followed read like a continuation
of the letter Cassady had begun writing to Holmes.

The tone and rush of Cassady's letter only aggravated Kerouac's own
writing problems. Holmes was conscious that for some time after receiving the "Joan Anderson" letter his friend was despondent, and when he
slumped on the couch at 681 Lexington he admitted he was at a "creative
loss."[15] In his initial excitement, however, Kerouac rushed to show the letter to Holmes and Harrington, certain that Cassady's letter was a literary
masterpiece comparable to Dostoevsky's *Notes from the Underground*.

They agreeably praised the letter for its rush of enthusiasm, but they
failed to see any connection between Cassady's frenetic rhapsodizing about
his teenage sexual experiences and Dostoevsky's relentlessly somber narrative. For Holmes, Cassady's letter to Kerouac was an echo of the sexual
boasting Holmes had done in his own "Fay Kenney" letter to Cassady three

weeks earlier, and if he failed to show much excitement over the letter Kerouac showed them it was partly because it was old news.

Kerouac was so furious at their lack of enthusiasm that in his fervent reply to Cassady on December 27 he assured Cassady that his writing ability was superior to any of the authors in the American literary canon, as well to the writing of everybody they knew. In a blustering boast Kerouac insisted that within twenty years he was certain he and Neal would dominate the American literary scene. In his outburst Kerouac went on to tell Cassady that he was convincing his new wife to write her own life story, and that they would flee New York together to live in Mexico City or in California to be closer to Cassady, his only true friend.

During these months it is almost impossible to sort out all the letters going back and forth between Cassady, Holmes, and Kerouac, though their tireless writing left an imprint on the manuscripts Holmes and Kerouac were struggling with. Holmes wrote to Kerouac on November 28 telling him about exchanging letters with Cassady, but Holmes' letter also included his "Epithalamium" for Kerouac's wedding, which Kerouac never acknowledged and perhaps never received.

On December 27, 1950, Holmes wrote one of his most emotional letters to Kerouac. In part it was an elaborate apology for having disappointed Jack and Joan by not showing up at Gabrielle's apartment to celebrate Christmas Eve. Holmes lamely explained that Marian had been indisposed with the flu, but it was evident that they had been too hung over from other holiday parties to make the long subway ride out to Queens for the dinner that Kerouac's mother had cooked for them.

Once past his apology Holmes made another effort to help his friend through his writing crisis with *On the Road*, encouraging Kerouac to begin his book again. "Now I say that you must take heart as well. Fill [it] with that sure compassion and sadness out of which your best work has come." Finally, in a torrential outburst, he challenged Kerouac to go back to his book with the kind of fervor that would give life to the "daily heap."

Remember all the madness, the Fellaheen people on the dark roads, those strange, apocalyptic moments with Neal, and all the other crazy things you know better than anyone else. Go back to the moment (if this can be done) when "On the Road" came to you out of nowhere. Go back to that instant, and remember it in all the naked excitement it possessed then. . . . Think only of your own feelings and believe in them. Turn neither to right nor to left! Start writing some night, in this reverent mood, and go on.

Fill your head (and page) with everything you can think of, in its natural order, in the beauty of its happening, and then worry later about the rest. You have so much that must come out. . . .

Do not cogitate the effect of your work, do not plumb the undecipherable and incalculable mysteries of the world which will choose or reject you. . . . There is some truth in the statement that we cannot know its ways. We can only do our best, amaze and astound ourselves. Keep simple and lonely faith with yourself, Jack. In no one's eyes but your own inner, secret eyes, seek to shine. I know your genius. Often I tend to flatter myself that I know it better than most others. . . . I know that there is much inside you, and I worry, fret, and feel a strange, personal misery when you have trouble with it. Make your book as defiant, pure, dastardly, sweet or crazy as you will. If the tone is right, man will weep when you tell me. . . . Fill your book with everyone who lives in your head, make them live and readers will commend you and buy. I seem to know these things, as I have said. Forgive my strange advice, concern and love brings it forth.[16]

The new style of the book Holmes was demanding when he urged his friend to tell his story "in its natural order"—"do not cogitate the effect of your work, do not plumb"—was the book that Kerouac wrote three months later.

On December 31, 1950, at a drunken party in Lucien Carr's loft, Holmes and Kerouac patched up their quarrel about missing Mémêre's dinner on Christmas Eve. At five o'clock on New Year's morning they placed a thick wreath on Ginsberg's head and huddled together with Marian circling them as they composed "a kind of Handelian oratorio around the words (for some forgotten reason): 'Fuck Allen Ginsberg.'"[17] A week later Kerouac finally stirred out of his apathy long enough to begin a series of letters to Cassady that flowed into a looser style of directly personal narrative that was a prefiguring of how he would write *On the Road.* On January 8, 9, and 10, 1951, at his typewriter in his mother's apartment, Kerouac wrote what became a linked story of his childhood, continuing it from letter to letter. The final letter on January 10, an exuberantly lewd account of his adolescent sexual adventures in Lowell, fills fourteen pages in his *Selected Letters.*[18]

In a second letter on the same day Kerouac wrote Cassady again, this time answering a letter he'd just opened from Cassady announcing that he would soon arrive in New York. In his usual impatient effort to organize his friends' lives, Cassady demanded that Kerouac must save money so they could buy the truck they needed to drive back to San Francisco together.

Cassady's letter was in his most hyperbolic mode. He insisted, "Immediately, immediately, immediately, not tomorrow, you hear, you lazy lout, but right now, YOU GET A JOB!"[19]

Cassady was rushing back to New York on his railroad brakeman's pass for the christening of the son he'd conceived with Diana Hansen, now Diana Cassady. On January 18, 1951, Holmes wrote in his journal that Kerouac had come by the apartment "all abrood about California"[20] and proud that he was earning fifty dollars a week writing script synopses for 20th Century Fox. By coincidence, ten minutes after Jack left to go back to his mother's apartment, Cassady phoned Holmes from Pennsylvania Station. Soon afterwards when Cassady arrived at 681 Lexington, he informed Holmes that he had "to be back in Frisco by the seventh of February, which is a tight squeeze, because Jack has, at this writing, no money and they need to buy that truck."[21]

Holmes told Cassady that his Joan Anderson letter the previous month had really thrown Kerouac "for such a creative loss" that Kerouac had "given up everything to write him [Neal] a long series of answers detailing the entire history of his life (The True Version)."[22] These were the linked series of letter from January 8 to 10. In his journal Holmes recorded Cassady's immediate response: "Gee, man, that's fine, but you don't make no dough that way!"[23] Holmes noted that this was "an intelligent comment, and one which I hope he passes on to Jack."[24] Holmes then went on to give his own thoughts on Kerouac's situation:

> Poor Jack! Things never do go right for him. But still I must register that I think it ooky [sic] to be taking off at this point (not because California is any den of thieves) but because he seems to be making this move in the light of some insane depression about his writing, and, I feel sure, because he has had such difficulties getting really started on ON THE ROAD. He says they'll get some acres eventually and be "self-sufficient." Hot dorg! [sic] Grow your own beans, kind of stuff. I know that he's had this idea for quite sometime. "Since I was a kid, I've thought of holing up in a cabin somewhere!" He's still got to come to terms with the creative problem of presenting his material so people will be interested. I believe that he can nevertheless tell the truth while doing this.[25]

A month later, on February 23, 1951, Holmes finished the first draft of Go, a year and a half after he'd started writing his novel. He was particularly satisfied with the final chapter, the New York crowd's response to Cannastra's death in the subway accident, which Holmes thought the finest writing in the book. He couldn't give way to too much jubilation, however, for he was conscious that Kerouac was still defeated in his struggles with *On the Road*. Too wired for sleep, Holmes picked up his journal to describe a trip downtown he'd made in mid-February to see Jack and Joan's new place at 454 West 20th Street, a room Joan rented when she could no longer stand sharing Jack with his mother.

> *Jack and Joan are living in a nice large room in a private-type brownstone down on West 20th, across from a Protestant seminary. It looks just like Cambridge out their windows. I went down and saw them a week ago. Jack zipped off his synopsis for 20th Century, and Joan was sick in bed with flu or whathaveyou. Pleasant hour spent. Walked all the way uptown with Jack, along river, good close talk on deserted wharf, digging the streets, and talking contemplatively of life, his mother, marriage, books, our work.*[26]

One of the first people to see Holmes' completed novel was his teenage sister, Liz, still living upstairs with her mother while attending high school. Liz wrote movingly of her response to the manuscript of *Go* in her memoir about these chaotic years at 681 Lexington.

> *Some time in 1951 John came upstairs and gave me the manuscript of* Go *(then called something else). "Here's the book, Liz," he said with a spare humility, laying himself in little sister's hands. "You know a lot of all this, so here it is." And left.*
>
> *I tore into it the moment he left and finished it in two days. With each page I was breathless and amazed. Here they all were—Jack, Ginsberg, Huncke, Neal, LuAnne, Stringham, Cannastra—all the people I'd seen, all the parties I'd heard about as a high schooler in John's fervid and exhaustive monologues until they became mighty legends in the telling— Cannastra's demonics, Allen's visions, Neal's dashing across the continent that he had made into his neighborhood. And here was John—no longer a myth-maker—now a confused and earnest young man writing abstract love letters to a girl from Columbia—the Mira Kent that he has talked of long ago to us who was his intellectual comrade. Here finally were John and Marian battling through their marriage—quarreling and jealous, always pulling at each other, so grave and serious and working at it. It was astounding to watch monologue, lecture and declaration become fiction. Alchemy—turning of the base metal of talk into the gold of literature. Because to me then it was literature in the same class as the Wolfes and*

Hemingways I had read. I found it beautiful and oddly modest and ter-
ribly sad. The long agitated verbal afternoons would never have led me
to expect this—these humble, hoping pages that brought together a whole
world of unique people trying to forge new and strange ways of living in
this dark and rainy city.[27]

Two weeks later, on March 7, 1951, Holmes wrote in his journal that
Kerouac had dropped by the day before to leave the first chapter of "his new
ON THE ROAD," conceived this time as another family drama in which
Kerouac cast his editor Robert Giroux as his father.[28] Kerouac was still writ-
ing third-person narrative, as he'd done in *The Town and the City*. While
Kerouac was in the apartment, Holmes let his friend read the final chapter
of *Go*. Kerouac's response puzzled Holmes:

He got up and went to the window after he finished and stood there with-
out a word for a moment. I couldn't figure it. "It's very moving," he finally
said. . . . But I don't know whether he actually liked it or not. I am full of
guilt about not having gotten to work on the re-writes as yet; full of trepi-
dation about the book itself. Has it form? Has it structure? Is it clear? Is
it interesting only to me? I am so tired of these age-old questions.[29]

Later that same day Kerouac wrote Holmes an admiring letter saying,
"In the last pages 'Paul' [John's pseudonym in the novel] is so fine and so
humble and such a gentle defense counsel in the big court that I hesitate to
call anyone else in the book a greater character."[30] Kerouac could see that
Holmes' stubborn work over the last months had resulted in a much better
book than Holmes' unpublished first novel, even though Holmes' rational
view of what it meant to be "beat" was in complete contrast to Kerouac's
emotional one. *Go* reflected a dark, Dostoevskian vision of "the deeper drift
in all the madness"[31] of what Holmes considered the "spiritually lawless"
behavior of his friends.[32] Earlier Kerouac had insisted that Holmes was the
one who could write "great canvases," the large-sized portrait of the group
Kerouac had named the Beat Generation, and Holmes appeared to have
done it.

In his criticisms of the novel, Kerouac noted that the first chapters
weren't as strong as the second half of the book, but he felt this was something Holmes would remedy in his next draft. As an afterthought, he advised Holmes to add a scene at the end with Cassady's return to New York,
since that always happened.[33] What Kerouac wasn't telling his friend was
that despite his praise, he was appalled at what he considered the cheerless-
ness and "horror" that the novel described.

A few days later, on March 12, 1951, Holmes turned twenty-five years old, a bitter day for him because he'd just found out that Joan and Jack—who turned twenty-nine on that same day—had given a birthday party without inviting him and Marian. He also had learned that despite Kerouac's letter, he was "still all pissed off about Pasternack."[34] It is obvious that Kerouac was upset that Holmes had managed to describe their tumultuous New York scene before he did, since he felt that he owned the material, but there were also more serious problems. Not only did Kerouac hate the dark mood of Holmes' book, but he was also dismayed to discover that Holmes had woven him into the novel with such fidelity to the actual events he described that other people, his mother among them, would also read the book and realize that he was "Pasternak."

What concerned Kerouac were any possible repercussions over the sexual details that Holmes disclosed about him in *Go*. In the novel Pasternak has oral sex with a girl he brings home from a party, he seduces and abandons a married woman after getting her pregnant, and he has a one-night stand with his best friend's wife. In Kerouac's description of his relationships and travels in his own writing up to that time, he had always been careful not to include any sex scenes that might offend his mother. If she were to read Holmes' manuscript it would be immediately obvious that "Gene Pasternak" was her son, and she would be very upset at his callous promiscuity. There was even the possibility that his sister, Caroline, and her husband might be so disturbed at what Holmes had described of his sordid lifestyle that they would move Mémêre in with them and force Kerouac to fend for himself, the everyday reality he was never able to face.

Go was to cause considerable resentment from several of the people Holmes described, but of all the novels, poems, and memoirs written by the other members of the group, it gives the clearest picture of the undeniable realities of their self-absorbed, self-destructive lives. As Holmes had said about his journals, his accounts were written the morning after, and to create his novel, all he had to do was go back to his journals' pages.

Go, however, was more than a extended series of diary entries. The richness and the authenticity of the book's text grew out of Holmes' complex vision of their scene and his absorption in the lives of the people in it. Long passages in the book were drawn from his journals, diaries, and letters, but reworked and reshaped as he told the story through the eyes of the character Paul Hobbes, whose marriage to Kathryn was obviously similar to the life John and Marian lived together in Manhattan. Initially he had conceived the novel around the character of Allen Ginsberg, presented as the young poet "David Stofsky," whose personal crises take up the majority of pages in the book. However, as Holmes continued writing, the strained relationship between Paul and Kathryn Hobbes became its primary focus.

Holmes' novel differed from reality in one important respect: he invented the incident in *Go* when Kathryn has sex with Gene Pasternak after a drunken party and returns home to her husband, Paul, to confess her infidelity. Holmes told Harrington that he described Kathryn as unfaithful in order to stress Paul's immaturity, his "misuse of his influence" on his wife by giving her to Pasternak, "whose friendship he seeks to hold and test."[35] Holmes' implication that Marian had been unfaithful in this fictitious plot device troubled his conscience, and he continued to justify it twenty-five years later in an introduction to a new edition of the novel.

> *The only completely invented incident in the book is when Pasternak sleeps with Kathryn, and this, again, was put in because it seemed thematically correct—though I am not unaware that I might have been trying to shift responsibility for my own peccadillos.*[36]

It was perhaps the same failure of understanding that led Holmes to think that friends he portrayed in the book such as Kerouac, Ginsberg, and Cassady would somehow be pleased that for the most part he always told the "truth" in what he wrote. Early in the novel, Pasternak brings a new girl named Estelle back to Hobbes' apartment after one of David Stofsky's parties. Holmes wrote about the incident in his journal entry of November 8, 1948, where he said that the girl told him that "Jack's mad at me" because she wouldn't agree to intercourse with him and gave him oral sex instead. Holmes said that he was "amused by the whole mess. Jack later told me that they had argued, danced some more, she in only a garter belt this time (a nice pornographic touch)." In *Go*, Pasternak tells Hobbes,

> *"You know what that dame did to me? She was a virgin all along. A virgin! I argued with her for half an hour, but she wouldn't give in. What do you think of that? . . . Then she got up and danced in just a garter-belt and told me about all the guys she's been 'giving satisfaction to' lately. And she's a virgin! She wouldn't even let me kiss her for an hour! I almost batted her at one point!"*[37]

A few paragraphs later, Pasternak tells Hobbes, "Hell, I think she's a Lesbian anyway. . . . You know, I bet I'm the only guy that's ever been turned down by a whore. Yah, that happened to me once when I was young. A whore! I've got no luck with women at all."[38] Holmes had noted Kerouac's comment that "I'm the only guy who's ever been turned down by a whore" in his journal on October 30, 1948. In another journal entry less than two weeks later, on November 10, Holmes recorded Kerouac saying "Everyone's just an apple to be eaten," a comment that turned up again in the novel when Pasternak complained about "one of these 'emancipated' women who's really cold as a snake. . . . No, but think of apples! Everyone's really just an apple after all. The rest is only mental, psychological."[39]

Although Kerouac blustered over Holmes' use of him as a character in the novel, he was also uncomfortably aware that he made the same kind of fictionalized use of his notebooks in his own writing. In his biography of Kerouac, Barry Miles wrote,

In reading Holmes's manuscript, Jack was also concerned to find great chunks of his conversations with John reproduced verbatim in the book. Holmes had recorded the conversations in his journals and used them whenever appropriate. Jack later accused Holmes of plagiarism, despite the fact that Jack's own books use the same method and appropriate not only dialogue but entire life stories from other people.[40]

Holmes may have confused the issue by insisting he was only telling the truth in *Go*, but comparing Holmes' journals and letters with the final text of his novel makes it clear that Holmes always used his material in a creative way. If he took a passage from a journal or a carbon copy of a letter, he modified it to set it into the flow of his narrative. On May 4, 1949, for example, he wrote a description of Allen Ginsberg in a letter to Howard Friedman that began by quoting Ginsberg:

"Everyone has a monster, the thing they could not bear to be faced with. I want to confront them with there [sic] monster. For instance, Jack's mother feels that I am physically dirty and scabic. One morning I shall rub myself with mud and paint great festering sores on my skin and ring her doorbell."

In *Go*, David Stofsky (Ginsberg) elaborated on the concept of a personal monster, and Holmes created a vivid metaphor for him when he explained to Pasternak,

"Of course everyone has his monster, the personification of everything he really fears. A sort of Dracula in daylight! . . . for instance, your mother thinks I'm unclean. Oh, I've known it a long time. She's nervously polite

when I'm in your house as though she thought I would soil everything. Well, for her I'd get all made up in filthy rags and paint huge running sores and pimples on my face, and then knock on the door and groan pitifully when she opened it!"

Although he said nothing, this did not amuse Pasternak at all, for he was sensitive about his mother, who was still working in the shoe factory she had entered so that he might write his novel.[41]

Holmes' description of Cassady in *Go* fell very short of Kerouac's and Ginsberg's idealized view of their Denver friend. Holmes' account of his first sight of Neal Cassady, renamed "Hart Kennedy" in the novel, was taken from his journal entry of December 29, 1948, after Cassady and Al Hinkle first came to party at 681 Lexington. In *Go* after introducing Hart Kennedy by describing him as "the small, wiry Hart, who moved with itchy calculation and whose reddish hair and broken nose gave him an expression of shrewd, masculine ugliness,"[42] Holmes developed his fictional portrait:

Hobbes put on a bop record, hoping it would relax everyone, and after only a few seconds of the honking, complex tenor sax, Hart broke into a wild eyed, broad grin and exclaimed:

"Well, yes, man, yes! Say, that's great stuff!"

He stood by the phonograph in a stoop, moving back and forth on the spot in an odd little shuffle. His hands clapped before him, his head bobbed up and down, propelled, as the music got louder, in ever greater arcs, while his mouth came grotesquely agape as he mumbled: "Go! Go!"

Hobbes wandered about nervously, feeling he should not stare at Hart, but when he saw Stofsky looking at the agitated figure with an adoring solemnity, he stared frankly with him. . . .

"Really, he's tremendous," Pasternak said with dark belligerency. "Really. . . . You know, at these bop clubs, Hart sits around and yells 'go, go!' at the musicians, But all the people around him are yelling 'go!' at Hart!"[43]

Holmes might have been unconscious of the problems his friends would have with the book, because he was as unflinching in his depiction of himself as the character "Paul Hobbes." He gave unattractive personal details, such as the fact that after a party Hobbes made himself go into the bathroom and vomit "as was his habit whenever he was too drunk or sick to sleep."[44] Holmes also included an account of his failure when he tried to make love with his agent Rae Everitt that was based on his frank journal entry for January 22, 1949.

I was overwhelmed by the opulence of her body and the intensity of her passion. Her last defenses fell and I was given a wealth of wonderful sensations that stunned me. I was quivering with desire, as though incapable of believing it all, and yet I could not get an erection. I could feel all the desire well up just behind my penis, surging to get out, but it was just out of reach.

In *Go* Holmes fictionalized the incident by turning it into a sexual encounter between Hobbes and another character named Estelle, an older woman working as a secretary in a midtown export firm. As they begin to make love, Holmes included his own line "I can help you only so much, but then I've got to help myself" without any sense of irony, weighing the tone of his narrative with a ponderous seriousness. As he developed the scene in *Go*, he used an awkward metaphor to suggest Hobbes' feeling of dismay at his impotence:

Then it suddenly occurred to Hobbes that his erection was gone. It was like waking up, getting to your feet and finding that one of them is still asleep. You stamp it on the floor, you walk about, you know the foot is touching the floor and that you are walking on it, but you cannot feel it. It hit him with tremendous surprise and embarrassment, but he was sure, at first, that simple consciousness of it would correct it.[45]

Kerouac objected to what he considered the horrors of some of the New York scenes in Holmes' book, but often Holmes' journal notes were written right after he and Kerouac had taken one of their long walks together, when his impressions were still particularly vivid. One night in late March 1951, after "thousands of beers," Kerouac looked up at the dark midtown sky above the Third Avenue El and confided to Holmes that he wanted to call his own novel "The Bebop Night."[46] A few days later in the same journal entry Holmes described another walk together, what he called "a pilgrimage down the Hudson River waterfront." There he and Kerouac witnessed "sailors, chippies, drunks, tottering old men, sour faced youngsters, hoods and whores" walking in the "lonely, empty streets" in the meat-packing district of the city. "Blood on the streets, faint voices and at one withering corner of the night a terrible, black vision for us all: a bundle of rags scraping along across the street," an old man dressed in rags pulling himself toward the Hudson River with "a withered old cane."[47] Holmes' description of this walk on April 2, 1951, concluded with the note, "I just know that it was a great, frightening period, there was no end to what we discovered or how mad we were, or what damage it has done."

Later on April 2, 1951, the same day Jack and John had prowled Manhattan's "dark waterfront night," Kerouac finally went back upstairs to his typewriter and this time the torrent of words burst through his old barriers. As a form of discipline, so that he wouldn't have the excuse of breaking off his work at the bottom of each page to insert a new piece of paper into his typewriter, he took a roll of architectural tracing paper he'd found in Cannastra's loft and cut it up into ten-foot sheets (later Kerouac taped the twelve sheets he'd cut back together to make one long roll). He trimmed enough off the side of each sheet so that it would fit between the rollers of his typewriter.

The crazy notion of creating a book on ten-foot-long pieces of paper suggests Kerouac's poverty, and it also suggests his will power to write the book trapped behind the log jam. Cassady's "Joan Anderson" letter may have fuelled Kerouac's determination to find a way to write about his trips with Cassady, but it had been three months since that letter had arrived. When Kerouac finally began his weeks of typing after his waterfront walk with Holmes, it had been only three weeks since he had read the last chapter of *Go*.

It could also have been an anxious suggestion from his wife that pushed Kerouac toward the form that his narrative finally took. Joan was working as a waitress at a Stouffer's restaurant to earn the money to pay the rent on their apartment. Later in *Nobody's Wife*, her memoir of their life together, she related that Kerouac was becoming increasingly frustrated over his difficulties saving up enough money to buy a truck for their trip back to San Francisco with Cassady, and endlessly fretting that he was unable to find the form that would allow him to do what he wanted with his book. Joan told him that he should try to write it straight off as a letter to her about his trips with Neal. One night after coming back from her job, she recalled:

> I sat down across from Jack and looked tiredly back at him. "What was it like, Jack?" I finally asked, after a long silence.
> "To be on the road with Neal?"
> "Yes, what happened, what really happened?"
> I started asking questions. Questions about Neal, about travelling, cities, trains, New York, Mexico, cars, roads, friends, Neal, Neal, Neal, and Neal.

"Jack," I asked him again, "what really happened? What did you and Neal really do?"

The questions, after a time, seemed to ignite some spark in Jack. He went back to his typewriter, and now he typed with accelerating speed, pounding keys, late into the night.[48]

Whatever the reasons that finally enabled Kerouac to break free of the suffocating "literary" style of his previous attempts to write *On the Road*, he had made the most important artistic decision of his life. It could have been Joan's suggestion that Jack write his story as a letter to her that helped him to make a fresh start on his book. Later Kerouac's poet friend Philip Whalen said after reading the book, "It feels funny, reading about you & Neal & everybody, so far away. Sometimes it reads like a letter from you."[49]

Sitting at his typewriter, Kerouac returned intuitively to the "this-happened-and-then-that-happened" first-person narrative style of his letters. Even more important, in this version of his road book he created the persona of himself as the innocent, open-hearted "Sal Paradise," almost as if he were refuting Holmes' portrait of him as the selfish womanizer Gene Pasternak in *Go*. Narrating his story as the idealistic, naïve Sal Paradise, Kerouac finally discovered the way to write his road novel. His use of the pronoun "I" would enable generations of young readers who found their way to the book to fantasize that they were traveling on that road themselves.

Before feeding the first ten-foot sheet of paper between the rollers of his typewriter, Kerouac cut off a small piece to prepare what he called a "Self-Instructions List" for composing his book that he kept on his desk as a "chapter guide."[50] It began with the phrase "shining mind—dark mind." The list wasn't a conventional plot outline, but rather a reminder of the topics he wanted to cover in his narrative, including "Talk about Neal with Hal," "Describe Allen monkey dance," "Allen's whither goest thou America in thy shiny car at night," and "Joan paper—wants to know what's happening." The list ended with the words, "New poem for end—'What will come of Neal?'"[51]

In Kerouac's opening sentences he was clearly referring to Holmes' dark view of their situation when he wrote that "everything was dead," and he ended his first chapter by explaining that all his New York friends were intellectuals "in the negative, nightmare position of putting down society," another clear reference to Holmes' existential despair. The genesis of the so-called scroll version of *On the Road* has been endlessly discussed, but certainly Kerouac's uncomfortable awareness that Holmes' book had been completed while his had stumbled to a halt was one of the emotional goals that spurred him. It was as though the new manuscript was his final word in the long, acrimonious debate that he'd been having for months with Holmes about the art of the novel. *On the Road* was the mirror image of *Go*. The "shining mind" had answered the "dark mind." It was Kerouac's yea-saying to Holmes' nay-saying. Kerouac was insisting that "the mad ones" such as Neal Cassady could renew what the critic Rick Ardinger has called "the spontaneous impulses of America."[52]

Three weeks after Kerouac began typing, the first draft of his novel was finished. Much is made of the speed at which he wrote his book, but many pages of it were actually rewritten from his notebooks and journals and Cassady's letters and earlier drafts of the road novel he'd been obsessed with during the past two years. Kerouac's novel was not a book shaped by any central idea, but its prose rushed on with such speed and energy that its sympathetic readers considered this was its strength. For the publishers whom Ginsberg persuaded to read the manuscript in its various retyped versions and who continued to turn it down for the next five years, this was its weakness.

Since the manuscript was so loosely structured and incorporated so much earlier material, Kerouac could break away from the rapidly growing torrent of words on the scroll jammed between the rollers of his typewriter to join his friends at their usual parties. Holmes dropped by the West 20th Street apartment when Kerouac was a few days into the typing marathon and insisted that he take a break. Even though Kerouac had finally found a way to write his book, he was still doing script synopses for 20th Century Fox to earn a little money. On April 9, 1951, Holmes recorded his morning visit with Kerouac in his journal:

> *Got tipsy in the morning, feeling the old urge to be off and away, and decided to go visit Jack. Bleery, bleak ride downtown, frosty, strange light in the sky. Got Jack up, he had gone to sleep sometime that early morning. He has been writing madly. Score that morning (as of): 34,000 words done. He showed me the manuscript. It is a series of sixteen [sic] foot rolls of thin tracing paper, which he is putting through his machine without stopping for paragraphs or chapter breaks, and he is full of it. We had coffee and I inveigled him out into the day. He had to go up to 20th Century anyway, and we walked, pausing in bars. He was full of good fellowship and I, eager for drink and escapade. We did a few White Roses, some bar on Sixth Avenue, others here and there. We told all the news and talked, talked, talked, walking all the way. I sat drunkenly in the office of 20th and looked down my nose. We walked across to town to Third and had*

beers in a series of bars, ending in Glennon's, where I got off on New York
and the future. . . . It was like old times. At the apartment, we brought in
more beer and played records and talked and got high. He wondered if
there mightn't be a party for the weekend, and I said I'd get in touch with
Lucien, who now has a phone.[53]

It is the usual perception that Kerouac spent the first three weeks of
April 1951 in an absorbed concentration on his new manuscript as he fueled his obsessive writing with endless cups of coffee and bowls of pea
soup. In May while he was retyping the book, Joan remembered his T-
shirts soaked with sweat from the Benzedrine he extracted from drug store
inhalers. But during the composition of the scroll version of *On the Road*
many of the days seemed to have passed like the other days when Kerouac
was piling up long word counts. One Thursday when Holmes went over to
Kerouac's apartment, they spent the rest of the day drinking together. Then
the next night, according to Holmes' journal, Kerouac was out again, this
time drinking with his friends Seymour Krim and Jerry Newman. On one
of the weekends Jack and Joan went to a party at Lucien Carr's, where they
met John and Marian. The rooms were so crowded that Ginsberg got only
as far as the door of the apartment with the young woman he'd brought
with him before she became so nervous about what she could see of the
chaotic scene that she refused to enter. Holmes wrote in his journal,

We started to dance, to drink, Jack and I going off for beer (after a col-
lection) and meeting Ginsberg coming back down Sixth Avenue, having
dumped the girl and hung up about it. She said something about Sunday
School to me earlier. Whew! Jack dumped twenty cans of cheap beer on
the floor and there was a scramble.[54]

Holmes' comment at the end of an additional single-spaced page describing the rest of the night was a wry, "We were hung over the next morning . . . what the hell."[55]

Of all the criticisms of the work Kerouac did over those weeks, one
has tagged after *On the Road* like a bedraggled tail, the novelist Truman
Capote's later dismissive comment that the book wasn't writing, it was
typing. To a considerable extent what Kerouac was doing in his book *was*
typing, or retyping from a variety of sources. Despite the distractions of
the weekend parties and his trips up to the office of 20th Century Fox,
however, Kerouac's concentration on his scroll was to bring a lyric flow
and a focus to his narrative. Although the book has never been presented

as a model of a novelistic plot, he had achieved his own goal, and there is no book in American literature like it. The ultimately exhausting physical demands he made on himself had enabled him to sustain an unforgettable "mood" through the long length of his scroll. The theme of his road book also tapped into what later academic critics such as Blake Nevius regarded as "perhaps the most durable and pervasive theme in American fiction, the theme of dispossession and flight, on both the physical and spiritual levels, that has preoccupied every major novelist from Cooper's day to our own."[56]

In late April Holmes was the first to read the scroll manuscript. Kerouac gave it to him even before he took the time to read it himself through to the end. Holmes read it in a single eight-hour stretch, sitting in his apartment on a rainy day while the Lexington Avenue traffic sputtered and roared outside his window. At 5:30 p.m. he met Marian after work at the RKO Fifty-Eighth Street Theater to see a movie, but he remembered later that "*On the Road* blurred the picture for me. I couldn't concentrate on it; I wanted to enthuse, and I felt both troubled and elated."[57] Holmes kept the scroll manuscript for a few more days to give himself time to think about what he'd read. He finally turned to his journal to sort through his impressions on April 27, 1951.

> *I read Jack's book a few days ago. He wrote it in 20 days, and it is one long strip of tracing paper, one hundred and twenty feet long, it seems. It has much wonderful material in it. And, surprisingly enough, the style is straight-forward, genuine, simple, still as lyric, but not as curlycue as it once was. If anything this book is, in most important aspects, more mature than T&C. It needs work. The transitions are weak. There is, perhaps, too much of it. The character of Neal around which it gradually centers itself needs to be focused a little more clearly. Those sections where he does not appear might be thinned, pointed in his direction. It comes close to being a developed study of Neal, with his gradual changes from energetic juvenile delinquent to the kind of W. C. Fieldsian wanderer that Jack feels he is. This part of it is very good I think. Jack's knowledge of this subject bespeaks itself from every line. I think that, with the necessary work it will make a very exciting and important book indeed. All the material is there, it only needs to be sharpened, brought out, smoothed a bit. The writing, with only occasional, minor exceptions, doesn't need any alteration. At least that is my impression. The descriptions are fine, clean things, filled with Jack's old power, without the plethora of wordage*

he sometimes used to dull the glass. He has made a decided improvement here, I believe, and now has his own style. There will certainly be no comparisons to Thomas Wolfe this time.[58]

When Holmes went back to West 20th Street to return the manuscript, he found Jack at home with Joan.

I went down to visit he [sic] and Joan a night ago to take the ms. back to him and tell him my impressions. We had a nice evening, with beer, a spell at a water-front bar, and even fifteen dark, cool minutes out on a cluster of pilings at the end of a pier watching a huge, lovely liner, all crusted with warm lights, steam slowly out of the harbor, her pinkish smoke-stacks lit up. A beautiful, silent giant, dwarfing even the Jersey coast beyond. I told Jack that I could not entirely be objective about the book (which is very true, even now that I have had several days to think about it); told him this because I know all the people, and have lived so close to the conception and the execution of all the drafts through which On the Road *has passed. But I did, I think, communicate to him my enthusiasm about it, and my feeling that it will make exciting and stimulating reading when the few minor faults are wrestled out, and the line of it honed just a bit. The book had cleaned me out, exhausted me, because I had read it straight through without stopping for anything but cups of coffee, It took me a little over eight hours.*[59]

After countless unsuccessful starts on his novel, abandoned beginnings of other books, lists of books he planned to write but never did, and months when he couldn't write at all, Kerouac had at last completed *On the Road*. Holmes' final note was that when they separated that night after their long, close talk, Kerouac was thoughtful for a moment. For over two years he and Holmes had encouraged each other in their struggles to complete their novels, each helping to shape the other's book in their long, unresolved arguments about writing and the art of the novel itself.

Jack said: "You know, kid, your book and mine constitute a new trend in American literature."
I said "amen" to that.[60]

Chapter 12

THE LIVEITUP KID

> *They stood on the front deck where it was chilly, and a fresh salt wind drove cleanly over the wide blackness of the river. Looking down into the current that swept just below him, Hobbes wondered for the only time in his life if giving up to death was really ignoble, foolish, mad. But then Kathryn, huddled against him, her hair blown softly up into his face, said drowsily:*
>
> *"You won't let me fall off the boat, will you?"*
>
> *And he held her closer, and gazed out across the dark, rushing water at New York, a fabulous tiara of lights toward which they were moving. For a moment he stood there in the keen gusts that came up in the middle of the river, and searched the uptown towers of that immense, sparkling pile for the Chrysler Building, so that he might look just north of it and imagine that he saw lights in their apartment.*
>
> *"Where is our home?" he asked himself gravely, for he could not see it yet.*
>
> —JOHN CLELLON HOLMES, *Go*[1]

The final paragraphs of *Go* were the book's emotional culmination. Its story ended in an anguished shudder of despair at the meaninglessness of their lives as Hobbes and Kathryn huddled drunkenly on the night ferry taking them back to Manhattan after the shambles of the crowd's attempt to mourn their friend's senseless death. If only for a moment, Hobbes had contemplated suicide as he stared into the darkness, searching in the lights ahead for some sign of a place that he could call home. Although there was no way Holmes could foresee what would happen, before another year had passed he would take the first steps toward finding a home at last. The irony was that it wouldn't be Marian who would find it with him.

Although Holmes seemed to be unaware of what he had created, even this first rough draft of his novel presented fully dimensioned portraits of the people around him that were so bare, so vivid, and so unflinching in their details that everyone in the crowd who read some of the manuscript pages was dismayed at his insistence on concealing nothing, however personal or embarrassing. What had seemed an obvious necessity to them in Dostoevsky's raw descriptions of the characters in *Notes from the Underground* became disturbing when Holmes turned the same clear gaze on their lives.

After *Go's* publication, Ginsberg (with the mistaken idea that the book's editor was poet John Hall Wheelock) wrote Cassady, "But I say Wheelock is a fool, and Holmes, because he talks nice and treats self badly in book, as badly as me or you, is not so much of a fool."[2] When Ginsberg complained to Holmes about the description of his Blake visions, however, he also softened his disappointment with a comment that at least Holmes had gotten some of it right. "You haven't really caught the way it felt, but you've caught something else. You've caught the solemn funny little kid I guess I must have been in those days."[3]

During the spring of 1951, Holmes found himself adrift once more in the sea of rewriting. The first draft of his novel had left him optimistic that he was on his way to creating something that could satisfy his complicated ambitions, but now that he'd come this close, he momentarily lost the focus he needed to finish it. He could see that he had to revise this rough draft, but as the weeks passed he became increasingly uncertain about how to begin. After reading Kerouac's scroll manuscript of *On the Road*, Holmes was no longer confident that he knew what to do next. Completely adrift, on March 7 he wrote in his journal that he wondered if he should add "lots of wild, small chapters to my book. Get in mothers and other characters. . . . I am getting those fears that the material is too special, too personal to me. Will anyone else be interested?"[4]

In May, Holmes struggled to find some way to return to his manuscript. When one of his most consciously elaborate and skillful poems, "Night Music," was published in *Harper's*, he was too obsessed with his novel for the poem's publication to lighten his mood. Even the new music that had been one of his wells of inspiration as he was writing had lost its ability to revive his energies. He and Marian, with Kerouac coming along, went out for one of their nights listening to jazz, but Holmes couldn't stop thinking about his manuscript and his obsessive need to finish it. It was a wasted evening for all of them. Marian, as usual, didn't like the music, but this time it also seemed to the two men that the exaggerated showmanship and the insistent frenzies of the bop that had excited them only a few months before had lost their edge.

The hopeless contradiction in Holmes' literary ambitions was that while he was recognized as a promising new poet and as a talented journalist writing on popular culture, he only wanted a career as a novelist. All of his literary models were novelists, and he was determined to join them. But with his manuscript at a standstill, and still needing to scrape up some income as he procrastinated over the revisions of his novel, he turned to articles commissioned by mainstream magazines that had become aware of his writing through the essays he'd written for *Neurotica.*

With Landesman's contacts Holmes was able to get the kind of hack work he had continually resisted doing. The tensions that hung in the air when he tried to talk to Marian made it impossible for him to turn the assignments down this time. He went back to his typewriter in the late spring and his article on homosexuality in American culture was published in the *American Mercury* in August 1951. A second article, "The New Taste in Humor," followed in the magazine's September issue. With this work behind him he could begin to think about his book again.

By now Holmes was drinking even more heavily, and he fell back into the restless round of parties he'd avoided while he worked on the final chapters of *Go.* He wasn't conscious of any change in himself, and he was continually surprised when in the midst of a new party's confusions women came up to him with curious smiles and said they'd been told that he was wildest of all the people in the crowd. He noted in his journal, "To many people I am the liveitup kid [*sic*], one of the dissolute. What will they say to my book . . . that should be something odd."[5] A physical collapse after a two-day binge at the end of May finally frightened him enough about the amount he was drinking to lead to a half-hearted effort to pull himself back from the edge.

Finally, his mood lifted. In a short journal entry on July 6, he wrote that he was optimistic he'd finally found some way to begin the revisions that had to be done on his manuscript. "I bought two notebooks today, and plan to do the re-writes in pen this summer, or die trying. This will be harder than the typewriter, of course, but something in me has frozen over in this apartment and in the city. The sharp change, the sun and sea, may break me out of it. Here's prayers."[6]

Kerouac, despite his initial elation over finally completing a first version of his book, was experiencing many of the same frustrations that Holmes was struggling with. Kerouac had enough experience with publishing to understand that the scroll couldn't be published as he'd written it, even if he'd grandly unrolled it on his editor Robert Giroux's desk. Clearly bewildered by the scroll, Giroux became practical, pointing out to Kerouac that there was no place on the scroll for him to do any editing. His suggestion was that Kerouac should go back to his typewriter and retype it as a conventional manuscript on 8½ by 11 inch paper. Sitting at his typewriter again and revising his book at Benzedrine-driven speed, Kerouac completed the new manuscript by the beginning of June 1951, a little more than a month after he had finished the scroll version. Since Giroux had been unsympathetic to his exuberance over the scroll, Kerouac refused to let him read the revised manuscript and instead gave it to Rae Everitt to find a publisher.

The long, exhausting bouts of re-typing *On the Road*, and the large quantities of Benzedrine that had kept Kerouac going, had worn him down and he had a severe attack of phlebitis. There were also signs of other troubles. On June 8 Holmes noted in his journal that he had seen a disturbed Kerouac the week before.

> *Jack was here several nights ago, and everything seems to be going wrong in bunches. He talks of "cutting out", and says he is telling me only so I won't think he's deserting Joan when he goes: but he can't bear to live with her at this point. We talked and drank, drank and talked, and finally went to Glennon's.*
>
> *"Nobody could be more sympathetic than you are, John," he said, and I wondered why. He hasn't even been eating at home. He looked in terrible shape and yet was not ranting and roaring as he might have been in such a situation.*[7]

When they separated after watching a savage fight at the bar, Holmes went back to his apartment and found Joan Kerouac sleeping on the couch. "She had been, the story goes, unable to get into their apartment and intended to sleep here, but in the morning she was gone. Lackaday!"[8]

Holmes was to learn a few weeks later that Kerouac had made a fumbling misstep that was to have serious consequences. One late night in May, after hours of incessant typing, high on the Benzedrine and the coffee he was using, he became aroused sexually by the story of his affair with the Mexican girl in Southern California that he was copying from the scroll. He woke Joan up and insisted on having sex with her. She was only half awake, and he wouldn't let her leave the bed to go to the bathroom for her contraceptive supplies. She became pregnant, and Kerouac was even less capable of handling the emotional maturity that fatherhood demanded than Cassady, who was younger but who had been through the experience several times.

Holmes noted in his journal on July 2, 1951, that Joan had also had a complicated emotional response when she understood how little support she could expect from her husband. Holmes described her as "mother-hungup, and going to get drunk in Harlem upon learning that she is seven weeks pregnant by Jack. What to do?"[9] Kerouac tried to convince his wife to have an abortion, and when she refused he became increasingly desperate.

With their husbands seeing so much of each other, Joan and Marian had become friends, and on July 13, 1951, with Kerouac away, Joan scrawled a twelve-page letter to Marian telling her she was pregnant. She was due in about six months, and she was "wonderously happy about it. It's the most glorious thing that ever happened to me." She also said, with rueful hindsight, that she realized with the marriage she and Jack had done each other a "great wrong." She had been "hi [sic] on despair and loneliness, and you know what he was hi on." She was aware that Kerouac didn't love her. "He got all mixed up in the picture of himself as the head of a household—for a change—with a dutiful wife who washed sox and underwear and scrubbed floors with a pleasant smile."[10]

Once Joan had opened a window on her impossible situation, her unhappiness poured out.

> *This gal in Jack's picture was different things at different times. Around the house while he was working, she was always happy, perhaps wearing a little calico frock and a ruffled apron and humming a French can-can ditty. She cleaned the house in three minutes flat and when he was ready to go out and on a binge with his friends, there she was, miraculously slickly attired—a hip chick if ever you saw one, and her conversation—so witty—so clever—so very amusing—she was never tired and she blasted like a fiend. She stayed up till 6:00 am and was off to work at 9:00 am sharp, always affectionate, protective, and yet submissive. . . . [S]he needs no affection, no sweet words, no consideration—never—nothing goes wrong in her world. Loving him is all she needs. If she's going to have a baby, the solution is simple—an abortion. . . . It's not his "responsibility." Don't "blame him." He is cursed with a talent and must therefore spend the rest of his life doing exactly what he wants to do—writing.*[11]

Fleeing his situation with his wife, Kerouac rode a bus to North Carolina with his mother to stay with his sister Nin while he tried to heal his phlebitis. He wrote Holmes from their house on July 14, with a leg propped up on a chair because of the pain. In a mood of blustering self-justification he acknowledged that no one who had seen the new version of his manuscript liked it. Ginsberg and Lucien Carr had found problems with the book's shapelessness and its length, and Rae Everitt felt there was no chance it could be sold without complete revision. Even a friend from their jazz excursions around the New York clubs, Seymour Wyse, wrote from England agreeing that Kerouac would have trouble selling the new book. Writing to Holmes, Kerouac, upset but still confident, optimistically outlined his ideas for revisions that amounted to an entirely new novel. He confided to Holmes that he had written to Cassady to ask if he could move to San Francisco and stay in his attic, but no one should be told of his plans so Joan couldn't find him. He wouldn't come to San Francisco as the senior, veteran writer he had once seen himself, but as a beginner who would learn the craft of writing from Cassady.

Holmes answered Kerouac on July 18. The heady mood of a year before, when everyone in the group was certain that they were all geniuses, had soured. Holmes was the only one in the crowd who still supported Kerouac and the new ground he'd opened up in *On the Road*. However he also suggested carefully to Kerouac that he felt some of the criticisms might be justified.

> *Know something of what you mean about ROAD; think you should consider Rae's suggestions, but follow only those you believe in. Some cutting would not injure the book. Certainly, as I think I told you upon reading the first draft, you should sharpen the book toward Neal wherever possible. I still believe that much of the first trip is artistically (not to mention spiritually) necessary. Perhaps it could be pruned, but not overmuch: and don't touch the little Mexican girl; simply aim that section toward the next trip.*[12]

Holmes repeated his belief in the book, and in Kerouac's creative ability. "Mainly I think this book should reach the world with its essential soul intact; compromises not involving that soul can be made without true damage." Holmes also was convinced that his agent, Carr, and Ginsberg were "more frightened by the material than the readers for whom you have labored. The main thing is to reach them and to go on. Don't be downcast." He assured Jack that Rae Everitt would give the manuscript her best effort and repeated his encouragement. "I know this book will reach your audience. Let me do anything I can to help." John's response to Jack's proposal to live in San Francisco was equally positive: "Your plan sounds good. Pursue your truth. The lack of jingle in the jeans is always a hangup, but Frisco may be easier to make it thru than here. You know the geography of your wish. The ship will come in too; that I know."[13]

With Kerouac hiding from his wife and the troubling problem of her pregnancy, Holmes turned to Ginsberg for the long nights of drinking he was used to with Kerouac. Holmes' journals for the early summer were filled with accounts of shambling trips through barrooms and lesbian bars, but now Ginsberg was leading. Often Lucien Carr came along, pushing their recklessness to its limits. He chauffered them on lurching car rides through the night city in an open convertible, with Ginsberg sitting up on the back of the seat shouting lines of poetry to anyone they saw on the streets. It wasn't until Carr and Ginsberg disappeared in August on one of the crowd's impulsive trips that Holmes finally had to face his novel again. Carr had been invited to a wedding in Texas, and it seemed natural to keep on driving to see Burroughs in Mexico, driving an old undependable car which broke down in Texas on their homeward journey. Kerouac had been planning to drive with him, but at the last moment he was hospitalized for the problems with his legs, and it was an excited Ginsberg who joined Carr instead.

Holmes had also been seeing more of Jay and Fran, along with the new writers Landesman had brought to *Neurotica* who usually turned up at the seemingly continual parties. Landesman was becoming disenchanted with New York. He was unwilling to find a job to pay the cost of their apartment and liquor, but he was also losing interest in his magazine, worried that his new marriage was disintegrating. As he watched the collapse of Kerouac's marriage and sensed the increasing strain between John and Marian, he told Holmes he'd decided a normal marriage wasn't possible in New York. He was trying to convince Fran that she should move back with him to St. Louis, an idea that to someone as committed to New York as Fran was incomprehensible, and their parties took on a hectic edge of desperation.

Anatole Broyard and Chandler Brossard were new to the crowd after they had published pieces in *Neurotica*. Holmes barely knew them, and he was irritated by their assumption that they also had an inner knowledge of the New York hip/beat world. Holmes had heard that Brossard had written a novel about the downtown hipster scene that was to be published early the next year, and despite his dismissal of the idea that someone else could know as much about it as he did, he wanted to meet him. Brossard was four years older than Holmes—the same age as Kerouac—but he'd been working as a staff writer for the *New Yorker* since he was nineteen, and to Holmes and the others in their crowd Brossard was uncomfortably regarded as as an interloper, a vague threat to their sense of their own uniqueness. When Holmes, already drunk, noticed both Broyard and Brossard at one of Landesman's parties in August, Holmes tried to provoke an argument.

At one point I was buttonholing Brossard and saying, very thickly I am sure, that hipsters and the "beatness" of our country now is the subject matter for the next ten years. He didn't bat an eyelash. . . . Brossard has a novel coming out about Anatole (Broyard), or an Anatoleish character. Why? Little to say. He doesn't know the uptown (and thus real) hipsters, I don't think. I think he will hate my book, which is something for it anyway.[14]

Brossard's novel, *To Walk in Darkness*, was published early the next year, and with its scenes of drunken parties and its evocations of the ennui of the postwar generation in Greenwich Village it is sometimes called the first Beat novel. Brossard himself kept a disdainful distance from Holmes' uptown crowd. He told later interviewers that he agreed with the French critics, who were excited about his novel in its French translation and considered it instead one of the first "New Wave" works of fiction.[15]

Jay and Fran finally left for St. Louis, despite Fran's misgivings. She had never been west of New Jersey and she was suspicious of the idea that there even could be someplace like St. Louis. The couple swirled out of New York at the end of the summer with a flash of Landesman's imperturbable style, riding in a 1936 yellow and black Ford convertible.

Despite all the stumbling confusions and distractions of the summer, the unending parties, the trips to Connecticut and Massachusetts to stay with the Landesmans and the Wood-Thomases, Holmes found at last, to his relief, that his plan to begin the revisions on his novel in the notebooks he'd bought in July had led him out of the dead end he'd written himself into. He wrote Kerouac on September 6, 1951, telling him that he'd seen Rae Everitt, who was on her way to Mexico for a short vacation. She had reported that Pat Covici at Viking was "pestering her about your book, and wants dearly to take a peek at it."[16] She had told Covici that Kerouac was re-writing *On the Road* and that other publishers had first chance at the manuscript. Then Holmes went on to say that he intended to have his own book ready for her when she got back on September 24. The next day, however, September 7, while he was reading in the apartment at noon, Harrington knocked on his door and handed him a brief news item from the *New York Post*. The article read:

> *"William Tell" Misses*
> *Mexico City, Sept. 7 (UP)—An American tourist trying to imitate William Tell killed his wife while attempting to shoot a glass of champagne from her head with a pistol, police said today.*

> *Police arrested William Seward Burroughs, 37, of St. Louis, last night*
> *after his wife Joan, 27, died in a hospital of a bullet wound in her forehead*
> *received an hour earlier.*

Holmes had never met Burroughs, but he had heard long stories about him from Kerouac and Ginsberg, and he was concerned that Carr and Ginsberg had been in Mexico City, staying in Burroughs' apartment, only a week or two before. What he didn't know was that they had found Burroughs away in the countryside, and they spent their brief visit with Joan and the two children. The tragedy only added to the foreboding sense of disintegration that Holmes felt about the group. One night earlier, when he was sitting in a bar and the people around him were talking about Cannastra's death, Ginsberg had wondered "who was going to be next."[17] Carr had called Holmes the night before, trying to get in touch with Kerouac, and after John read the news item he called Marian, wondering what he should do about Carr.

> *In any case I phoned Marian, told her, and she was abashed, and said:*
> *"That crazy fool!" just as with Cannastra. She, too, thought I should*
> *phone Lucien, who I thought would be asleep. He answered gruffly and*
> *said he had not been. I asked him if he had seen the item on Burroughs.*
> *"No, what's happened," he said laconically, but also guardedly. I started*
> *to read the clip, but he stopped me in the middle, saying he had seen it,*
> *and I guessed that he simply wanted to know how much the papers had.*
> *"I killed it for the morning editions," he said coldly.*[18]

As the United Press night man, Carr edited the stream of news items that came across his desk, and he had thought he might hold off the news at least until he could reach Kerouac.

Ten days later, on September 17, Holmes wrote in his journal that he was finally ready to begin retyping his manuscript. Remembering Kerouac's frantic pace of the previous spring, he gave himself even less time to finish his revisions, though he'd added twenty-five thousand words of new material in his notebooks. On October 3, 1951, there was an exhausted but triumphant short entry in his journal. Holmes had beaten Kerouac's speed record by a week, but what was more important, his novel was finished. "The typing was a huge chore: thirteen actual days of heavy typing straight through. Yesterday to correct, today the epilogue, one page back in the ms. that had to be fixed, and then the numbering."[19]

On an even more emotional level, what was important about the book was that Holmes believed in what he'd done.

I believe in it, I think it has great scenes: about the hanging together I don't know, but that may be blindness. I wrote the epilogue last night and this morning, typed it in the final, and delivered it at four o'clock. Now I am home, drinking beer and listening to bop. I have hopes . . . hopes but the book will always live for me, no matter what happens.[20]

The next day, once more attempting to deal with his life's realities, Holmes had to write a letter to his mother, asking help to pay that month's rent. Holmes' financial situation was still precarious, but by this time his marriage was in serious trouble. His sister Liz, living upstairs and often alone herself when she came back from high school since her mother worked an office job, couldn't help noticing the tensions between Marian and her brother. In her memoir she was painfully honest in her description of the situation that Marian was facing, and of Marian's efforts to keep her out of it.

Marian was protective of me in this period—using my innocence as a cover for her own distaste for much of the wild life of dope, criminals, unsavory visionaries (Ginsberg never reached her with his mystical probing into everyone's dark corners and his nude Blakean antics) and unruly roustabouts—Neal bursting in with contraband to stash in her domicile. "He's just a con man, Johnny, and you make him out to be some kind of prophet of the new life. He cozies up to every girl in town, bangs them, marries and moves on to the next. Goddamn prick! . . ." Marian was a tough little bird with a beautiful brown face and hair, a thin mouth that broke into a sideways smile against her will - brown hurt eyes that were defenseless even when she was angry. And she was angry a lot during these years—working at two-bit jobs that barely kept them in beer and cigarettes and a few private dinners at the Ritz Food Shop up on Lexington in the sixties. The rest of the time she had to get by on the largesse of our mother who staked us to the family dining room—Joe's Italian Restaurant—and whose help was needed on the rent most months. Here, on her $40 a week secretarial job, coming home to loud bebop and a husband and assorted marginal guys banging on her pots, drunk on beer, glasses littering her rented kitchen table and her big glass ashtrays running over with butts and her rented couch draped with a dirty sheet where Jack had passed out the morning before just before she had to get up with her own cigarette and coffee cup and grab her shoulder bag and swing her wide hips in the plaid

skirt out the door—banging it in one defiant noise to her passed-out men,
"Goddam crash pad for every drunk in New York! My home!"[21]

What was impossible for John to comprehend was that Marian considered her home was "demeaned" by their drunken crowd of friends. As Liz
expressed Marian's feelings, she was helplessly trying to defend "the little
line of home against the tide of chaos that was sweeping over their lives."
Often Liz was upstairs with her mother when Marian knocked on their
door looking for some solace, so she also recognized that Marian—despite
everything she had to deal with—also had a sense of what Holmes and his
friends were trying to do.

She was also a naturally brainy girl who perceived much of what was
going on with these "nuts"—in a small believing corner of her heart, she
thought they were on to something, disruptive and unsavory as they were.
Like so many of us she was soft on Jack—sweet as he was in his soul, retro
as she was about the old family—Italian, Canuck—nostalgic and simple
of spirit. Outrageous as he was she couldn't turn him out.[22]

Kerouac was still hanging on in New York, but he climbed the four flights
of stairs to Holmes' apartment less frequently. His legs were so painful he
had trouble walking. Gabrielle wanted to move permanently to North Carolina to live with her daughter, and Joan had given up her apartment to be
with her mother during her pregnancy. On June 10, 1951, Kerouac began a
blustering, optimistic letter to Cassady. His news was that he was sleeping in
either Ginsberg's room or Carr's loft, holding himself together until he sold
the newest version of *On the Road*. If he heard from Giroux in two weeks
that he would take the book, the thousand-dollar advance would solve all
his problems. The letter broke off when he admitted he was too drunk to
write any more, then picked up at Carr's the next afternoon with new feverish excitements about traveling to Mexico City to stay with Burroughs. He
was already thinking about his next book—a jazz book about tenor saxophonist Lester Young which would be titled *Hold Your Horn High*.

Cassady, who had been working steadily as a railroad brakeman, replied
by inviting him to come stay in the attic of the house with him and Carolyn,
who was now pregnant with their third child. But when Kerouac wrote Cassady again on June 24, he was devastated. *On the Road* had been rejected by
Robert Giroux, and he was bewildered by his friends' negative responses.
Holmes was the only one who still believed in it.

Kerouac's plan now, he wrote Cassady, was that since he had no money
to get to San Francisco, and he was too crippled to go to work, he would get

out of his predicament by taking the bus to stay with his mother in North Carolina. She'd cook sausages and eggs for him and he could have a little peace and quiet so his legs could heal. After borrowing enough money for the bus trip, Kerouac found that there was no room for him with his sister and her family with Mémêre already living there, and that his legs were in worse shape than he had realized. He spent a month with his legs propped up, impatient and sullen at the dullness of the small town life and his situation as an unwanted guest in the house. It became apparent that he needed extensive medical treatment for his phlebitis. Early in August Kerouac rode the bus north again and on August 11, the day when he had thought he would be riding in Carr's car to Mexico City to visit Burroughs, he checked himself into the Knightsbridge Veteran's Administration Hospital in the Bronx.

On August 31 he wrote to Cassady describing the anguishing scenes he witnessed when he was pushed in his wheelchair from one hospital section to another. In a sentence close to end of the letter, he also casually noted that Joan had gotten a court order against him, demanding financial support for her medical expenses while she went through her pregnancy. His response was to complain to Cassady that as a wife she never had given him the love she knew he had to have.

Responding to Kerouac's distress, his mother had kept her apartment in Richmond Hill so he would have some place to live after he left the hospital. A month later, on October 1, 1951, Kerouac wrote to Cassady again— congratulating Neal and Carolyn on the birth of their third child, a son they named John Allen after Kerouac and Ginsberg—and he also outlined his immediate plans to leave the city. The letter was brief and hurried, since he was fleeing from Joan and the responsibility of the pregnancy. He insisted he had made a private agreement with her to pay five dollars a week out of the money he made reading film scripts, but she had gone to court and had the bargain made binding. When Kerouac didn't make the payments, she had him arrested. Two police cars roared up to his mother's address in Richmond Hill and hauled him off to jail. He was left in a crowded cell while the police sorted out the circumstances of the complaint against him. Even with serious legal difficulties hanging over him after he returned home, he delayed in his mother's apartment until he received the royalty check from *The Town and the City* he was expecting on October 25.

Kerouac began to spend hours on what he considered a fresh start on his road book using a new way of writing prose that he called "sketching," spontaneous attempts to capture his impressions and memories in a formless, ecstatic prose rhapsody finally published as *Visions of Cody*. He wrote Cassady that this was at last the "deep form" he had been looking for, and he sent three pages of the new version about the visionary character whom he was now calling "Dean Pomery," the name he gave Cassady in this latest version of *On the Road*.

Holmes saw Kerouac briefly during this time, but he had no idea that his friend had found what he later called "his writing soul at last." Preoccupied with a new direction his own life was taking, Holmes caught only a glimpse of Kerouac on October 26, 1951. He noted in his journal that Kerouac looked very down and out in "his terrible no-overcoat poverty. He goes about the city in these grey autumn days shivering, looking for a few dollars from 20th Century Fox, and reading the labels on delicacies in the windows of delicatessens."[23]

Despite all of the ragged ends of their disordered lives, Holmes and Kerouac were still young men. John was twenty-five. Jack was twenty-nine. In the photographs taken of them at the time the effects of their continual dissipation hadn't left signs on their faces. Both of them had always been good looking, Kerouac with his strong face, dark hair, and the eyes, still with their appealing sensitivity. Holmes was his physical opposite, blond, his hair in a kind of upswept pompadour that was then a popular style. Behind his glasses his eyes had the same insistent search that people immediately noticed in Kerouac. They also had all the physical hungers and insistent emotional needs of men whose lives had become unmoored, and in most of the photos taken at parties or gatherings the women surrounding them were as young, and as physically radiant.

With the revision of *Go* finally an accomplished fact, Holmes' writing in his journals became less concerned with the philosophical struggles over concepts of tragedy and morality that had obsessed him for the last two years. At the end of October, he began a different series of journal entries. The first of them was presented as an idea he had for the next novel he was planning to write. He headed the entry on October 31, 1951, with a casual introduction:

I think of this kind of beginning for the Verger novel:

Verger walked to meet her on Thursday. He had had lunch with her on Monday too, and after it had resolved not to see her again, and not to answer his phone if she called. He had even gone into a church on Park Avenue, and kneeling with embarrassment in the stuffy chapel, prayed that it would all work out and no one be hurt. He, an unhappy disbeliever, had prayed for help; then at ten on Tuesday morning, he had answered the phone, and it had been her, and he had agreed to lunch again. He was afraid of hysteria most of all, afraid she really loved him, afraid she wanted him as much as he wanted her.

"I was sick after yesterday," she said when she arrived at the restaurant to find him over a beer. "I was stunned. I never knew I could be just honest with anyone and have them be like you were." And his heart rose, and sank at the same time. As for the past month, he had been praying that she would love him, now he prayed inside his frightened heart that she would not. He looked into her open, enigmatic face, into her somewhat dreamy smile, her bright, quick eyes, and saw there all the agony that lay ahead. He wanted to hold her, to kiss her with manful gentleness, to see that she was never unhappy or lonely again. And to keep her from being hurt in this terrible darkness that was the future, he had to hurt her at this moment.[24]

Although for the past five years Holmes had used the journals as a record of literally everything he was experiencing, a record that as far as he was concerned was open and accessible to anyone who was interested, there had obviously been evasions. The entry on October 31, however, was something different. He was conscious that someone else might pick up the journal and read its pages, perhaps Marian herself, and for this entry he made a clumsy effort to disguise what he needed to write as a "scene" from a projected novel.

If he had written it as a journal entry, without any effort to disguise the identity of the people in the scene, it would have been immediately obvious, despite the literary license of his prose, that something was changing in his life. As a journal entry, the same pages would have begun, "I walked to meet Shirley on Thursday. I had had lunch with her on Monday too, and after it resolved not to see her again and not to answer my phone if she called."

Despite the difficulties in his marriage, he and Marian might have continued trying to piece something together out of the shambles, but abruptly the marriage ended, and the final step that brought it to an end was one of the most commonplace. Holmes had fallen deeply in love with another woman. If the woman Holmes had met had been part of their usual New York crowd he probably would have noticed Shirley Radulovich as simply another of the pretty, eager, brightly interested young women he glimpsed casually through the haze of cigarette smoke at their parties. She entered the crowd, however, as an outsider, and she was unlike the other women Holmes was used to meeting. It was Jay Landesman who eventually introduced them.

One of Landesman's partners in his bohemian bar in St. Louis had been a muscular, tough ex-paratrooper named Stanley Radulovich who had dreams of turning himself into an artist. When he came to his first meeting with the other partners in the bar's office he was wearing a suit with his veteran's discharge button in his lapel. The third partner in their enterprise, Richard Rubinstein, noticed it and jeered, "Take that corny medal off, soldier. You'll never get laid with that on." Radulovich's first impulse, through the laughter of the people around them, was to take a swing at Rubinstein, but he realized that as an ambitious young painter this was not the right response. Landesman waited for some outburst, but as he wrote in his memoir, "To Radulovich's credit, he took the button and flushed it down the toilet to tumultuous applause."[25]

While still in St. Louis, Radulovich met a young art student at Washington University named Shirley Anise Allen. She was from Louisiana, and she had spent some of her adolescence as a student in a convent after her parents' acrimonious divorce. Partly to escape her domineering mother, she married Radulovich in the fall of 1949, when she was only nineteen. When Landesman moved to New York in the spring of 1950, Radulovich decided to follow him to take studio courses in painting at a New York art school. His young wife moved with him, and in the familiar pattern of a wife working to support her husband's artistic ambitions, Shirley Radulovich took a series of office jobs to support her husband's dreams of the artist's life. Stanley noisily attempted to bull his way into the New York art world, without much success. At the same time, in the also by-now familiar pattern of the Landesman's crowd, Radulovich quickly became involved with another woman. He was having an affair with a young woman painter Holmes knew only as "Gladys." Perhaps because John was seeing Shirley through Jay's eyes as Radulvich's wife, at first he took little notice of her.

The first time John mentioned Shirley in his journal was on June 8, 1951, when he noted that Radulovich "also has problems with his wife." A page later in the journal he recorded that "Stanley is having a 'puppy love' affair with Gladys. . . . [S]he is rich but her husband insists on boating all the time and she is eager to get back to Woodstock to paint. Who knows? In any case, Stanley laid her, Jay tells me, and this is the root of his problem with the wife, who remains a mystery to me."[26]

By July 2, when Holmes was invited to an afternoon party held by the Raduloviches, John knew Shirley's name. He noticed that she was also someone who drank. His comment was, "Shirley getting drunk like a southern girl should, all enigmatic smiles and dark remarks, leading and following and turning her back." Later in the afternoon he found himself "being fed inordinate amounts of potato salad and endless dill pickles in the kitchen by Shirley, who said, . . . 'Let's get real degenerate before we join the others,' not knowing what she was saying, and drunker than I had any idea of, and finally creeping away without anyone seeing her to pass out in the bedroom."[27]

The next day Holmes noted in his journal,

New Orleans is where to rot to death [sic], and Shirley Radulovich has something of this sweet rot inside her, and with polite evasion keeps it to herself. Stanley is only a rough intense shouting mountain goat. . . . But he gets drunk and steals worthless statues from the civic parks of St. Louis and makes it into a cause celebre for modern art.[28]

It was obvious that John was attracted to Shirley. She was very pretty, small and trim, with short blond hair, and she shared his social background. Like Holmes she was struggling in an early marriage that had obviously been a mistake, but despite her unhappiness he caught glimpses of her warmth and intelligence.

By the middle of August Holmes had become so entangled in the situation between the Raduloviches that one night when he and Jay and Marian went out to eat and Stanley refused to get Shirley to eat with them, Holmes tried to persuade him to change his mind. "I go down on my knees in the saw-dust and pray for his soul. He stares at me like I am John the Baptist, creating a nuisance. I don't mind."[29] He slowly realized that he was falling in love with Shirley. It could have been for many of the ordinary reasons: she was pretty and she was young—eight years younger than Marian—she was obviously unhappy, and his own marriage had reached a stale plateau of dissatisfaction. But there was another reason that he only partly understood himself.

What drew him to Shirley was need, her need for someone to help her undo the mistake she'd made by marrying so young. In all of his other relationships, even his marriage, he was always conscious he was taking something from the woman he was involved with. This time, however, with Shirley he could give something to someone, and with all the contradictions that make love so unpredictable he could tell himself that by allowing himself to fall in love with her he was for once doing something that was right. As the autumn passed, John and Shirley stumbled toward each other in stolen meetings for lunch, or hurried moments talking in a corner over the noise of one of the parties. By November their inhibitions and their fear crumbled and they became lovers.

In the tensions of his new love affair, the sale of his novel to a major publisher was almost an anti-climax. First the manuscript was quickly passed over by Carl Solomon at Ace Books, probably because Solomon knew everybody in the book and he'd been to many of the parties and he didn't appreciate Holmes' dark portrait of their lives. Next Rae Everitt tried Macmillan, since they had shown the most enthusiasm for Holmes' earlier novel, but their editor's final conclusion was that while the story itself held up, none of the characters could be considered sympathetic enough to justify publishing the book. Then a few days after Christmas, Rae phoned Holmes to tell him triumphantly that Scribner's had accepted his novel. There would be an initial advance of one thousand dollars, and publication was tentatively scheduled for the next winter.

Although the confusion over his new relationship with Shirley dominated John's moods, he also was going through the process of becoming a published novelist. For much of what happened over the next months with his book, however, he found himself often a hapless bystander. The wandering path to the publication of the book took so many turnings that it was almost as though as a neophyte novelist Holmes was being given a condensed introduction to all the hurdles that can be strewn in a young writer's path. Part of the difficulty, though Holmes didn't seem conscious of it, was that his publisher's attentions were riveted elsewhere. At the same time *Go* was making its way through the press, Scribner's was publishing Ernest Hemingway's *The Old Man and the Sea*, which was clearly destined to be one of the most successful books of the decade. It would win Hemingway the Nobel Prize for Literature.

In his introduction to a later edition of *Go*, Holmes wrote that the first of the problems he faced was the still sensitive issue of censorship:

> *Scribner's itself got nervous about possible censorship as publication approached, and submitted the book to a lawyer, who finally cleared it on the proviso that I make a few changes, which mostly involved a slight toning down of the sex scenes. With considerable reluctance, I agreed to do this, but balked when I was asked to cut to* three *Agatson's* six *desperate "Fuck Yous" in the latter part of the book. "What's the difference between three and six?" I wondered. "He's not talking about sex, he's cursing the world." I stood my ground, and refused. As a result, Scribner's seriously thought of not publishing, and then suggested that if I would agree to withhold the book from paperback publication (where most censorship suits arose in those days) they would go ahead.*[30]

As a way out of the dilemma, Burroughs Mitchell, Holmes' editor at Scribner's, suggested a complicated solution that would soon give Holmes the chance to change his life, though at the moment it had the appearance of being just one more step in his disillusion with a novelist's career.

That good man, Burroughs Mitchell, realizing that my only hope of mak-
ing any money lay in a paperback sale, solved the problem by getting
Scribner's to relinquish all the reprint rights to me on the proviso that
nowhere in any paperback edition would there be any mention of the fact
that they had published the book originally.[31]

A publisher generally takes a 50 percent share of any reprint sales of a
book by a new author, so by giving up the possible income from a reprint
sale the publisher was saying, in effect, that they didn't expect anyone to
be interested in reprinting the book. As Holmes concluded, "This didn't
inspire confidence in an unblooded young author, who wanted to believe
that his publisher believed in him."[32]

To add to the already confused situation, there was a problem with the
novel's title. Holmes' first choice of *The Daybreak Boys* was too similar to
a recent Scribner's novel about the public relations world titled *The Build-*
Up Boys. After much fruitless searching it was finally Burroughs Mitchell's
wife who suggested the title *Go* just as the book was about to go to press.
As confusing as it all had become, there was still another knot to untangle.
The English publisher had problems with *Go* because there was a popular
British travel magazine with the same name. The book was finally published
in England as *The Beat Boys*, and Holmes' wry comment was that "the circle
(not to mention the confusion) was complete—in that some Englishmen
still think that *The Beat Boys* is a wholly different novel than the unobtain-
able *Go*."[33]

Unfortunately Burroughs Mitchell was also not the editor the manuscript needed. Holmes was a new and still inexperienced writer, and the
manuscript ideally needed to be tightly edited to eliminate its stretches of
awkward prose and to mute some of its hyperbole. As an in-house editor,
Mitchell was probably assigned the Holmes novel as part of his normal
work schedule. During this period he was editing the very successful novels
of James Jones, and though his support for Holmes was genuine, he gave
the manuscript only minimal attention. He suggested that Holmes cut the
first four pages of the text and drop the epilog, and at that point Scribner's
walked away from the book. Holmes wrote a pleased letter to Mitchell after
a long lunch where they discussed the book and its editing, but perhaps
because he sensed that his editor had been a little distant when he was discussing his manuscript, Holmes began his letter, "Dear Mr. Mitchell."

In January 1952 Rae Everitt moved to one of the largest and most successful of the New York literary agencies, MCA, and she was now in a

position to obtain higher advances for her authors. Scribner's advanced $1,000 to Holmes for the hardcover rights to his novel, but he kept only $250 of it for himself. The rest went to Marian to pay their bills. With the first glimmerings of some economic stability, and with his involvement with Shirley now turning into a serious commitment, he left Marian and moved into a seventh-floor walk-up furnished room at 135 East 35th Street. Ginsberg helped him find a temporary job doing market research for the Gallup poll so he could pay his rent, $9 a week for a roach-infested filthy tenement room.

A dozen years after he and Marian were divorced, Holmes wrote about their final months together with a self-lacerating tenderness and apology. For much of their marriage he had taken a bitter satisfaction in his ability to deceive her with his continual infidelities, but the guilt he continued to feel finally became a corrosive element effecting them both. As he wrote, the deterioration of their relationship had continued until Marian

> *felt more whole at the office than at home, until that look came up in her eyes, that grieving, irritable, baffled look of women who have not captured their men, and for the first time realize that marriage is an armistice in the personal war, but not a lasting peace; until she beered and disbelieved as intensely as I in Glennon's bar, at Cannastra's in the soggy dawns. In the San Remo, Minetta's, Louis', in our dusty apartment with faceless crowds and label-less bottles. Until everything had been said, except the dreary litanies—"Well I love you too," "But do you really have to go out tonight?" "You never read the things that are changing my life." "Why should I have to apologize for being tired?"*
>
> *Those words were said (plus the taunts, the tears, the accusations) the words from which there can never be any going back, the glimpses (given out of despair rather than trust) into the chaotic center of one person, from which the other recoils, having seen himself as the author of all the wreckage there, all of it eroding the other's face until that morning when we no longer see ourselves mirrored in that face, or in our own, and realize with a start that, though yesterday may be regretted, it is beyond change. . . . My lies and her restraints, guilt and hostility—around, around until the wheel broke down. Until our voices were hoarse and murky; our eyes tireless and tired; our nerves perpetually strung up tight as bailing wire, and we had mercy on ourselves, and on each other, and gave it up.*[34]

Over the next months Holmes' situation became less endurable. At least his living situation improved in April 1952 when Rae Everitt found him an apartment for twenty-five dollars a month at 302 West 48th Street. The rent was cheap because the building was scheduled for demolition to clear the area around the new United Nations building. Holmes paid the fifty-dollar deposit on the apartment with a check that Landesman sent him from St. Louis after John had written that he was completely broke after leaving Marian. He was continuing to write short segments of his "Frankel novel" in his journal in an attempt to keep some record of his love affair with Shirley. Otherwise her name disappeared from his journal pages. He could find no solution to their situation. They were both married, Shirley to someone who had been a friend of Holmes' but who was also an unpredictable stew of angers and resentments. As Holmes later wrote in an fictionalized account of these months, he was overwhelmed with anguish both by their moral situation and his fear that if Radulovich found out about their affair, Shirley could be in physical danger.

Marian had forced herself to accept John's earlier attachments as a painful part of their marriage, but when she became aware that her husband had fallen in love with Shirley, she immediately sensed that this affair was different. It was a relationship that could end their marriage, just at the moment when her years of thankless jobs had finally born fruit with the publication of *Go*. Her own situation had also improved. She had at last found decently paid work she enjoyed in the Film and Drama Department of the City College of New York in northern Manhattan, but it did little to quiet her emotional storms. She was enraged and humiliated, and on April 23, 1952, she sued Holmes for divorce, citing adultery as grounds and naming Shirley and her husband as co-respondents. She also demanded financial compensation from Holmes that would have made it virtually impossible for him to marry Shirley. Shirley had also taken a decisive step. She had left Radulovich and moved into a small apartment, though still without telling her husband about her relationship with Holmes. Until the divorce proceedings were settled, she and John made the painful decision not to live together, though they continued to meet almost daily.

The next months were to be one of the most difficult periods of Holmes' life, and Kerouac's situation was by now almost as chaotic. The title of the unpublished novel that Holmes would write later of his struggles during this period—"Perfect Fools"—was a painfully accurate estimate of the situation that each of them was facing.

Chapter 13

PERFECT FOOLS

All the people in Go *("Go" is the chic word to yell at a musician, prefer-ably a tenor saxophonist, clarinettist or trumpeter when he takes off on some private dream of his own) are teaheads, or marijuana smokers, either out of curiosity or some intellectual conviction too infantile or regressive to be tacked down anywhere but on an analyst's couch. A couple of them are "mainliners" or addicts who take heroin directly into the bloodstream and are sometimes portrayed as trying to "kick" or get rid of the nasty habit.*

A number of others are forever getting themselves tangled up in fragments from Blake, Dostoevsky and the Bible, usually winding up either drunk, incoherent or both. Now and then, someone beats up his girl, or gloomily seduces someone else's wife. They circulate endlessly and uneasily from apartments in the Village to lofts on the West Side, sleazy flats in midtown on the East Side and Harlem, talking all the time. Some of the talk isn't bad at that.

—GILBERT MILSTEIN, review of *Go, New York Times*, November 9, 1952

Those uneasy weeks before a first book appears are one of the most dif-ficult ordeals any writer can face. It seems that whatever happens will alter forever their own perception of themselves. After so many years of strain-ing and dreaming to become that other person—a *published* author—it's difficult not to think that for a moment at least the earth will stop turning. For most writers, however, the only change they find when they come out from under their cloud of anticipation is that their friends regard them differently. The people close to them who were involved in the months or years of struggle were certain that the long-awaited book would be a new literary masterpiece, but when they skim through the pages what they al-most always find is that it's only another book, not much different from the hundreds like it that they've read before. For the writer hungry for any kind of praise or excitement, the politeness of wives or husbands, lovers or friends only intensifies their disappointment.

For Holmes the mornings as he waited for some response to *Go*'s publication were sharpened by his worries about his use of the people he knew as characters in the novel. What would they think of what he'd done? On September 24, 1952, he railed in his journal:

> *No reviews, the silence I expected thus far. From all friends, silence also. Interesting. Stringham has not called me at all, and he has had the book for two weeks. Ansen did not like it but at least discussed it with me. Lucien sneered and insulted me at a recent party. Harrington has been good, stuck by me, but I do not think he has read the book, or if he has said nothing to me about it. The Lyndons are silent. Jack, it seems, is back in Frisco. Interesting all of it. I sit here alone all day, knowing I must work and not care. . . . I sit and wonder. I have outcast myself from all men by this book. I sometimes peek into it and read a few lines. I cannot think it is so terrible. Lucien's grinning, mocking face that night will remain with me, and I was terribly hurt by that. He insulted Shirley too, about Marian I suppose. It is so terrible, that part of it. Everyone's infidelity but mine passes muster. But that is the way.*

Holmes only found one faint breath of consolation in his bleak morning: "Marian called and was kind, as she is being these days."[1]

Once Holmes had become a published novelist, he realized that he was still facing his old demons. He had no idea how long he could continue to live in the condemned apartment on East 48th Street, and he was, as always, facing an uncertain future. For a few days he was elated when his agent negotiated a $20,000 advance from Bantam in an auction for the rights to a paperback edition of his novel. The publisher was under the illusion that *Go* was a sensational account of the "dope menace" like Nelson Algren's *The Man with the Golden Arm*, a best-selling mass-market paperback in 1951. But even receiving a check for the first half of the advance money did little to lift Holmes' spirits.

His mother's life would soon change, however, and unexpectedly his own would be totally changed with it. The death of Betty's wealthy Aunt Julia in Newport had left her with a substantial inheritance. It was enough, as Betty said wryly, to get her furniture out of storage. Although her teenage daughter, Liz, had found a life for herself, Betty had become disenchanted with Manhattan. She found a large Victorian house in the small

Connecticut coastal village of Old Saybrook, sixty miles from New York City, which she bought with the plan of remodeling it as a bed-and-breakfast country inn named "The Victorian." Holmes gave half of his paperback advance to Marian as a financial settlement to facilitate their divorce, and with the remaining money he helped his mother buy the property in Old Saybrook. It was a return for the financial help she had tirelessly doled out to him. Holmes thought that he and Shirley could vacation in Connecticut to get away from New York.

What the old crowd knew about Holmes' house in Connecticut was to be still another irritant for many years, but they didn't understand his situation. His mother's house was substantial and imposing, and his talking about it exaggerated its possibilties, but it wasn't a Victorian "mansion," as the rumors went. Betty had bought a large, once elegant eighteenth-century frame house originally built as a minister's home on Old Saybrook's main street. It had been neglected for years and it was now in need of serious repairs. There was a much smaller wooden frame school building behind it without electricity, water, or heat. This was the building that Holmes eventually took over. After years of back-breaking labor he and Shirley eventually made it livable, and it became the home he had been seeking all his life.

Another seismic shift in Holmes' life occurred after *Go*'s publication. On October 21, 1952, he received a letter from a lawyer in Chappaqua informing him that his divorce had been entered in the court docket. Two days later he wrote to Shirley's mother in Louisiana, telling her that he loved Shirley and wanted to marry her. Betty moved to Old Saybrook, and with the money from Holmes' advance she also bought a car, so it was possible for John and Shirley to stay with her for extended visits while they worked together painting and carpentering to help turn the old house into a New England inn. On October 1 Holmes had already signed one of the first copies of *Go* for Liz, but his novel wasn't getting the attention he had expected. The purchase of his mother's house in Connecticut helped dull the edge of disappointment that had followed the first few days of the book's publication, and then he began the salvage work of picking up whatever small consolations drifted his way.

On October 12, 1952, the New York *Herald Tribune* gave Holmes his first long review, concluding that "Mr. Holmes' style is almost appropriately slack and erratic. Occasionally it bulges out into cramped lyricism—only to retreat, fatigued into a bare transcription of happenings. 'A beat generation,' philosophizes Paul Hobbes toward the end. We hope he is not right. But that adjective seems useful."

The most significant review of *Go* appeared on November 9, 1952. It was written by a young reviewer for the *New York Times* named Gilbert Milstein, who five years later would help to make Kerouac's *On the Road* a best-seller with a glowing review in the newspaper. Milstein's short, generally negative review of *Go* in the *Times*, titled "The 'Kick' That Failed," was a forerunner of the hostile media storm that awaited the Beat writers, though it couldn't have been anticipated when Milstein first turned to Holmes' book. What the critic reviewed was not the novel itself, but the scenes of drunkenness, drug abuse, and drab sexual encounters that *Go* described. What Milstein was reviewing was the Beat lifestyle, and this refusal by reviewers or critics to see anything beyond the surface of the writing to the larger issues in the books was to be the continual response to Beat poetry and fiction during the next decades.

Milstein gave a backhanded compliment to Holmes' novel when he grudgingly admitted that "some of the talk [in the book] isn't bad at that." He told Holmes that originally his review had been longer and more favourable. In the last of the three paragraphs which appeared in the *Times*, his editors had pruned his summary of *Go*'s plot so rigorously that his review ended with his casual dismissal of the "beat generation" that the book was purportedly about:

> *About the least hopeless of all these amateur Rimbauds are Paul Hobbes and his wife, Kathryn. Kathryn works for a public relations outfit while Paul stays home and writes a bad novel. Revolving around them are a burly individual called Pasternak, who writes a presumably good novel, or at least one that gets sold; Stofsky, a homosexual and literary whirling dervish; Hart, a frantic character from out of town; Verger, a tubercular intellectual, and a number of others who tend to merge into each other. Ultimately, after Kathryn is seduced by Pasternak and Paul fails to seduce another girl, the two decide that they're through with what the author calls the "beat generation."*[2]

Despite Millstein's obvious discomfort with the disordered lifestyle described in *Go*, a few days after his review appeared he contacted Holmes and asked if he would write an article for the *New York Times* on the new term he'd used in the novel, "the Beat Generation." He offered to pay two hundred dollars. Holmes' article, the ground-breaking essay "This Is the Beat Generation," appeared on November 16, 1952. The article became more widely read and discussed than *Go*, and it established Holmes' role as the earliest spokesman for his friends and their ideas.

What was unexpected about the article was its poised professionalism. Holmes could be tentative in his prose in the novels, but in this piece of cultural journalism he set the piece in motion without a moment's hesitation. In his opening sentence he gave the same indefinable, certain sense of being sure of his ground that characterized his writing in his journals and his poetry. He chose a visual image for the first paragraph that in a few sentences summed up the essence of his belief that rebellious young people throughout the United States comprised the Beat Generation, and they have no consciousness that what they are doing is anything more serious than personally rejecting what they can't accept about American society.

> *Several months ago, a national magazine ran a story under the headline "Youth" and the subhead "Mother Is Bugged At Me." It concerned an eighteen-year-old California girl who had been picked up for smoking marijuana and wanted to talk about it. While the reporter took down her ideas in the uptempo language of "tea," someone snapped a picture. In view of her contention that she was part of a whole new culture where one out of every five people you meet is a user, it is an arresting photograph. In the pale, attentive face, with its soft eyes and intelligent mouth, there was no hint of corruption. It was a face which could only be deemed criminal through an enormous effort of righteousness. It only complaint seemed to be: "Why don't people leave us alone?" It was the face of the beat generation.[3]*

In the article Holmes parried possible criticism of his definition of "beat" by saying, "Any attempt to label an entire generation is unrewarding," but he continued to trace the ties between the word itself and the emotional situation of the immediate postwar generation, "the generation that went through the last war, or at least could get a drink easily after it was over." His explanation of "beat" was a description of a mood more than a definition. His prose suggests the strong feelings he and Kerouac shared when they first began to give the word its new context, suggesting the intensity of their convictions during their long nights of excited talk over countless quarts of beer at 681 Lexington, with Symphony Sid broadcasting a counterpoint of bop in the background.

> *More than mere weariness, it implies the feeling of being used, of being raw. It involves a sort of nakedness of mind, and ultimately, of soul: a feeling of being reduced to the bedrock of consciousness. In short, it means being undramatically pushed up against the wall of oneself. A man is beat whenever*

he goes for broke and wagers the sum of his resources on a single number: and the young generation has done that continually from early youth.[4]

The article was written quickly—Holmes remembered that it took him only four days—although to write it he found he had to decide for himself what the word "beat" actually meant, since he had never hammered out anything specific in his talks with Kerouac.

There was an immediate response from readers of the *Times*. Holmes might have been disappointed at the lack of response to his first published novel, but after his article appeared he was inundated with personal letters from its readers, most of whom agreed with him. The newspaper published responses for the next two weeks, such as the one from Michael Theil (Cornell '54), who found little in the article "that can be refuted."[5] At the time when Steinbeck's *East of Eden*, Edna Ferber's *Giant*, Herman Wouk's *The Caine Mutiny*, and Micky Spillane's *Kiss Me Deadly* dominated the best-seller list along with *The Old Man and the Sea*, Holmes' article even prompted a satiric rebuttal by G. B. Palmer (born 1907), a writer for *Time* magazine. Titled "Lament for the Normal Generation," it began, "A man doesn't seem to rate these days unless he can mournfully identify himself with some regrettable generation. If he isn't Lost, or Forgotten, or Defeated, or Mislaid, or Tragic, or (right now) Beat, he finds it hard to get into a conversation, write a book, or run up a tab in a saloon."[6]

Many readers felt threatened by the challenge to the status quo in the idea of a young, emerging, rebellious Beat Generation. Previous social misfits and rebels had been anarchists or Communists, or bohemian expats living in Europe. Holmes' article left the disquieting sense that the dissidents now harboured at home appeared to be the children of ordinary Americans.

Holmes' article also stirred the flurry of interest from editors and publishers that he had hoped might come with his novel. In a letter written on November 25, only a week after the appearance of the *Times* article, the fiction editor of *Harper's Bazaar*, a popular magazine with intellectual interests, praised the intelligence and liveliness of the article, and noting that Holmes was the author of the recent novel *Go*, asked him if he would submit short stories. Phyllis Jackson contacted him to say that *Glamour* magazine was running a piece on new and young personalities in the March issue and they wanted to photograph him. The editor-in-chief at Houghton Mifflin approached Holmes and asked if he would do a book on the Beat Generation. On December 19, 1952, Holmes did his first television interview on CBS as part of a program on the new media attention. Of all the responses the one that probably gave him the most satisfaction was a letter from Landesman in St. Louis on December 3, telling Holmes that now he was recognized as their spokesman.[7] Some months later even Kerouac responded respectfully to the article with a note in a letter, "I see you have considerable journalistic talent, like Lucien—something Allen and I don't have from secret wildness."[8]

Another of the momentary glints of light in the darkness Holmes felt after the publication of *Go* was a letter from an instructor at Portland State College named Alex Scharback. He enthusiastically praised the novel and asked Holmes questions about the book for an article he was preparing for the *College English Journal.* He sent the piece to Holmes early in December, saying he was also going to write to the critic Mark Shorer at the University of California at Berkeley about the novel. He expressed the hope that Holmes was working on his new novel full-time, adding as an afterthought a sentence that John must have read with a thin smile: "Surely you don't have to work for a living?"[9]

The weeks in December were quiet. Shirley had gone to Louisiana to be with her family over the holidays and Holmes spent most of his time with his mother in Old Saybrook. He wrote for hours at a stretch, breaking off to bring firewood into the house or do some of the cooking. It was what he termed a hermit life and though he missed Shirley intensely he found the days passed easily. In his answer to Scharback he discussed the writing he was doing and compared what he was planning to do with what he had already presented in *Go.* "The people in *Go* had little or no choices; they were damned by their lacks. In the world of my new book, all the characters live continually in the 'day of choices.'" He went on to say that he couldn't go into more of a description of what he was doing, "for I truly discover my work only as I fashion it." As to his financial situation he felt there was a chance for someone like him, since the market opening up for pocket books would make it possible for him to hold out.[10]

Kerouac, during these months, was also dealing with his old demons, but he hadn't even the solace of the small nibble of success that *Go* had brought his friend. Almost as if he were fleeing himself he journeyed incessantly, living for weeks, sometimes months, wherever he was certain he would be taken in. The only fixed point through his swings of euphoria and despair was his emotional dependency on his mother, and as each Christmas came closer he found it impossible to be away from her. Somehow Kerouac usually found his way back.

By the spring of 1952 he had worn out his welcome with the Cassadys in California, and he wrote to Burroughs in Mexico City asking if he could stay there. Burroughs answered with a friendly letter that showed some interest in Kerouac's writing, and for the next few months he found a refuge in Burrough's apartment on Orizaba Avenue in Mexico City. Everything about the relationship in the crowded Cassady household, now with a new baby, had been edgy, especially after Jack had begun an affair with Carolyn while Neal was away working on the railroad. It became obvious that it was time for him to move on. Neal and Carolyn drove him as far as the Mexican border at Nogales, with the back seat of the car pulled out to make a bed for their three children and a place for Carolyn to sleep. Kerouac's work on the railroad had given him enough of a stake to make the journey, but to husband his savings he bought a second-class bus ticket to Mexico City for six dollars and careened south, joining up with a young Mexican he met on the bus as they came to the small fishing port of Guaymas, on the coast of Sonora.

Kerouac related his rhapsodic adventures in a long letter to Ginsberg on May 10, 1952, after he had reached Burroughs' apartment. Drinking mescal in the back of the bus, Kerouac sang bop for the assorted passengers, who responded with songs of their own. In Culiacan, a bigger town that Kerouac described as the opium capital of this part of the world, he left the bus and stumbled into the poverty-marked Indian neighborhoods where the journey dissolved into a drug-fueled series of mystic encounters during which Kerouac insisted that with his Canadian French he understood everything that was said to him. Sometime during the night he even saw himself as an illuminated Jesus Christ.[11]

He wrote Ginsberg again on May 17, 1952, an ebullient note telling him that he had just mailed the new "sketching" version of *On the Road*, now titled *Visions of Cody*, to their friend Carl Solomon, who was still editor at his uncle A. A. Wynn's Ace Books, which had accepted Burroughs' *Junky* for publication as a mass-market paperback. Solomon had given Kerouac a three-book contract, and his interest in the novel was based on a sample about Cassady playing in a football game as a teenager in Denver. Kerouac seemed to feel that with his most recent version he would finally break through, despite the misgivings most of his friends had expressed about the inchoate "deep form" he'd discovered. In a long letter the next day he was certain that Ginsberg and Solomon would share his excitement over this new version of his book, and he devoted a long enthusiastic paragraph outlining the series of books he was ready to write in the same style.

As he waited for Ginsberg's answer, Kerouac spent his days sitting on the toilet in the hall, since Burroughs had forbidden him to smoke marijuana in his apartment. Kerouac filled his notebooks with the handwritten version of *Doctor Sax*, the fantasy novel of his childhood in Lowell that he had begun writing along with his endless versions of the opening chapters of *On the Road*. Burroughs' situation was tense. He was out of jail on bond while he awaited trial for the accidental shooting of his wife, and he was paying a lawyer for his defense, which was taking most of his money. He grew impatient at Kerouac's unwillingness to help pay for his share of their food, and he was apprehensive that the smell of the marijuana Kerouac smoked steadily would drift out under the toilet door and bring the police up the stairs. Kerouac was hoarding his money to buy drugs, and he told Burroughs he was thinking of buying a large amount of marijuana and peyotl that he'd store in the apartment. Burroughs realized that if the police were to make routine check on him as he awaited trial and they found a large supply of drugs, he would be immediately sent to one of the notorious prisons for drug offenders. Burroughs insisted that Kerouac had to get out.

On June 3, 1952, Kerouac wrote to Holmes from Mexico City. The letter opened with a peremptory response to a friendly letter from Holmes describing a jazz novel he planned to write, titling it *Afternoon of a Tenor Man*. It would be Holmes' take on their old mutual love, saxophonist Lester Young. Kerouac's letter began as a stern protest, and the idea of Holmes' jazz novel was to be an irritant between them for years. Kerouac had already written to Ginsberg about his idea to go on to a jazz novel about Lester Young when *On the Road* was revised. He even had a title for it, *Hold Your Horn High*, riffing on Lester's distinct style of holding his saxophone out in a line almost parallel with the stage. The chapter on Billie Holiday was to be called "Heroine of the Hip Generation." In their unending conversations in the apartment on Lexington Avenue he and Holmes had sketched out the jazz novels they each planned to write, and as Holmes' journals confirm, the title that finally he chose, *The Horn*, was one of the titles Kerouac had proposed for his own novel.

Writing on the drift of a peyotl high in Mexico City, Kerouac impatiently reminded Holmes that he had been the one who was going to write the novel about Lester Young and Billie Holiday, and he reminded his friend that he'd left some things out of *On The Road*—a New Year's party in 1949—because Holmes was already describing it in *Go*. When Kerouac wrote again only two days later, however, the dispute over the jazz novel was forgotten in a rushing account of a visit by young American hipsters who had brought their own supply of peyotl. What he wanted to tell Holmes about was that sometime during their high, a friend, a San Francisco bass player named "Wig," had shown up, and asked them if they wanted to hear some music. Wig's name was Wig Walter, and he turned up later in New York. He would be named "Cash" in *Junky*. Piling into Wig's car, the crowd drove to his apartment and picked up his new LP turntable and speakers and a carton of new bop records. It was the music that Kerouac was impatient to tell Holmes about—his love of bop suddenly returning in a rush with the baritone sax playing of the "marvelous" Swedish musician Lars Gullin.

Kerouac's mood, soaring with the easy availability of drugs in Mexico City, was too optimistic about the chances of his manuscript in New York for him to continue being angry with his old friend. In his letter to Holmes he rushed on to describe his dreams of writing books in his new "wild form," which was in its essence freedom from all form, and he signed off in a soaring outburst of joy and love.

When Kerouac finally received the letter he was expecting from Ginsberg in response to the new manuscript he had sent, what he found in the envelope was one of the most exasperated letters his friend ever wrote him. Ginsberg was particularly upset that Kerouac had paid no attention to his protests each time that he'd been sent the revised pages of *On the Road*. Ginsberg had complained again and again that the new writing didn't work, that it wasn't readable, and worst of all, that it wasn't saleable. By now the new pages later titled *Visions of Cody* had only the character of Neal Cassady, called here Cody Pomeray, to connect it to the novel *On the Road* that would be published five years later. Kerouac had disdainfully abandoned his style in the scroll version of *On the Road* as simple story telling, and what he had moved on to was what he termed his free-blowing mode. The new manuscript included pages of transcriptions of the conversations he recorded with Cassady, both of them noisily stoned, riffing into the microphone of a tape recorder in Cassady's apartment.

Ginsberg made no effort to hide his impatience. "I don't see how it will ever be published, it's so personal, it's so full of sex language, so full of our local mythological references, I don't know if it would make sense to any publisher."[12] Ginsberg tried to soften his dismissal by adding, "The language is great, the blowing is mostly great, the inventions have fullblown ecstatic style," but he insisted that he wasn't going to praise Kerouac. The manuscript called *Visions of Cody* worried him because "it's crazy (not merely inspired crazy) but unrelated crazy."[13]

Holmes' response was equally baffled. Later he recalled,

When he sent me Visions of Cody, *and even* Doctor Sax—Doctor Sax
*came first—I thought, man, no one's going to publish this. It's brilliant.
It's youth. It's something absolutely new and unique and important, but
no one's going to publish it. I'll never forget the afternoon. . . . I was living
on 48th Street on the fifth floor of an old tenement, and I read the whole
damned book* Visions of Cody *in one day. And I was depressed, not by
the book, but by the fact that I knew he wasn't going to make it with this
book. He wasn't going to get through. Nobody but me and Allen and a
few people would ever read it, it seemed to me. I thought, "Oh God, Jack!
Why can't you write something that can get published so somebody can
understand what you have?"*[14]

But when Holmes read *Doctor Sax*, a book about Kerouac's childhood in
Lowell, he loved it. Struck by the correspondences with his New England
boyhood, Holmes wrote to Kerouac that it was a "tender book," a "wondrous thing."[15] He marvelled at "the perfection" of Kerouac's memory and
was happy that "the defiance" in the tone of *On the Road* was "fortunately
absent here." In his letter Holmes ended his praise by recognizing, "You
have touched, finally, the roots of your past. This is your myth; these are
your sources; oddly, all of them together."[16] He was also happy to see that
after what he considered the shapeless flood of "sketching" or what Kerouac
later called "spontaneous prose" in *Visions of Cody*, Kerouac had returned
to loosely chronological storytelling in *Doctor Sax*.

Months earlier Kerouac had discovered "sketching" when he followed a
suggestion that his Denver friend Ed White made to him while they were
eating dinner in a Chinese restaurant north of the Columbia campus on
October 25, 1951. Kerouac had complained to White that he was dissatisfied with his revisions of the scroll version of *On the Road* because he felt
he couldn't expresses the full spiritual dimensions of Cassady's character
by using a conventional English prose style. White proposed that Kerouac
should try to stop thinking so hard about what he was doing as a writer and
try his hand at sketching his subject freely like an artist, using words instead of paints, just writing down the words his mind formed as he looked
at a physical object or reflected upon an image in his imagination.

Kerouac rode the subway back to his mother's apartment, mulling over
what his friend had suggested, and before he went upstairs he took out his
pocket notebook and started "sketching" what he saw through the window
of a nearby bakery. He got so excited by what he was doing that it kept him
up all night. Using a small notebook that he could slip into his shirt pocket,
he printed his freely rhapsodic verbal responses in wavering pencil lines
across the cramped pages. The following day he went back to Manhattan to

re-visit a place he associated with his first meeting with Cassady, Hector's Cafeteria in Times Square, where Neal had taken LuAnne to eat when they first got off the Greyhound bus in Manhattan in 1946.

After Kerouac "sketched" the lavish display of food in the cafeteria that had impressed Cassady, he rushed over to 681 Lexington Avenue and climbed the stairs to Holmes' apartment to show his friend the sketching exercises. Kerouac tried to explain that with his new writing he was trying to capture Cassady's hunger for life, but Holmes didn't understand what Kerouac was trying to tell him, perhaps because Holmes was preoccupied with finding a new direction for his own life after falling in love with Shirley. Instead Holmes felt that Kerouac had reached "rock bottom."[17]

It wasn't until nearly a year later, after reading *Doctor Sax*, that Holmes understood what Kerouac had meant. With this book, Holmes realized that Kerouac had reached a major turning point in his development as a writer. He'd found a writing style that enabled him to achieve what he called "deep" form, and he had found his true subject, telling the story of his own life. After Holmes' letter praising *Doctor Sax*, Kerouac, now in an expansive mood, confessed that he had changed his mind about *Go*: he had decided that it wasn't so bad when you saw it printed as a book, since Holmes' sincerity was everywhere on its pages.[18]

In the fall of 1952 Kerouac returned to San Francisco to take a railroad brakeman job that Cassady set up for him in California. While living in a skid row hotel, Kerouac wrote one of his most lyric prose sketches in his new, freer style, "October in the Railroad Earth," looking out of his window at the skid row bums leaning against the wall across the street. When he had his seasonal layoff from the job, he had saved enough money to return to Mexico to continue the writing he had begun. Cassady again drove him as far as the border so he could pick up a supply of marijuana. This time Kerouac rented his own small room on the roof of Burroughs' apartment building, staying on his own with a friend of Burroughs in the building, Bill Garver, as someone to talk to when he wasn't writing. Still hiding from Joan and his baby daughter, he used his mother's name as a cover for his mail, "Senor John Levesque." Burroughs' situation had become almost Kafkaesque, since his lawyer had been involved in a shooting of his own and the authorities were demanding that Burroughs post additional bond money. Still fearing that he would be arrested, he skipped bond on December 8 and fled to Colombia.

From his rooftop Kerouac wrote a tender letter to Carolyn, telling her that he was cooking his own breakfasts and had gathered a sufficient supply of drugs, uppers and downers, for him to begin writing. His hope was that she would come down to visit him, and he was certain for some time that she might join him. Carolyn realized that though Neal had seemed unconcerned at first at the affair that had begun between her and Jack, he was angry at the thought of her leaving him to stay for some time with Kerouac. Even if the trip had been something she seriously considered—though with their three children it is difficult to imagine that Kerouac's encouragement was more than a wishful dream—she didn't join him.

There still had been no notice that Holmes would have to leave his condemned apartment on East 48th Street, so he clung to his room, writing and rewriting the first chapters of his sequel to *Go*. He titled it *Perfect Fools*, a sardonic reference to the situation he had forced on both Shirley and himself. He was often in Old Saybrook, helping Betty with the renovations on her house, but he was writing steadily and by February 1953 had completed seven chapters. Kerouac had returned to New York City at Christmas and stayed on with Gabrielle in her new apartment in Richmond Hill. Before Mémère had found the apartment, Kerouac had used Holmes' room as a forwarding address. Kerouac complained to Cassady that Holmes was away too much in Connecticut, and Kerouac didn't like having to wait for his mail.

Sitting at his typewriter in his mother's kitchen—Mémère was renting a smaller apartment without a separate bedroom for her son—Kerouac began a new project, continuing with his plan to go on telling the story of his life that he had begun with *Doctor Sax*. In January and February 1953 he wrote a short book about his first high school love affair with an Irish girl named Mary Carney. It was titled *Maggie Cassidy*. If Kerouac had been furious over Ginsberg's continual complaints that his spontaneous prose produced shapeless, self-indulgent manuscripts without any potential for sales, he had nevertheless internalized the criticism. With the new novel he had gone back to the simpler style of "story-telling" he had derided after he'd used it in the scroll manuscript of *On the Road*.

The new novel was the story of his adolescent crush on an Irish girl he'd known in high school. It was one of his most immediately accessible books, and what carried the story was the emotional texture of the prose, the energy of his reminiscences, and the physicality of his descriptions. For better or worse, a wash of sentimentality colored every page. Kerouac had taken a step back from his experiments with the visionary chance-taking of his attempts to capture the essence of Cassady in *Visions of Cody* and the fantasy of his boyhood recollections in *Doctor Sax*. Ironically, both he and Holmes were still continuing along the different paths to creating the books they had described to each other in their unending arguments years before.

For both Holmes and Kerouac, as well as for Burroughs and the others in their crowd of would-be novelists, there was the continual problem of finishing books and getting them published. For long periods Ginsberg attempted to be helpful. He was now living on the Lower East Side, acting as a self-styled literary agent for Kerouac and Burroughs. Kerouac, however, became upset at the kind of interest that Ginsberg was stirring up with his continual proselytizing for the group and with his characterization of their ideas. On February 21, 1953, he sent Ginsberg a stiff letter denying the permission to use his name in an article that was being prepared for the *New York Times* literary notes column to advertise the publication of *Junky* as an Ace Book.

Kerouac was irritated that the article named him in connection with a book promoting drug use while Burroughs was allowed to shield himself from prosecution by publishing the book under the name "William Lee." Kerouac insisted that his book *The Town and the City* not be named in conjunction with *Go*, which he felt implied some sharing of artistic aims, and he demanded that he not be quoted by saying that " William Lee" was one of the important members of the early Beat group. The return address he used was his current agent, Phyllis Jackson at MCA, who had taken over from Rae Everitt. He signed the letter "John Kerouac."

Despite the quarrel, when Kerouac found himself feeling stifled in his mother's small apartment he went into Manhattan to visit Ginsberg on the Lower East Side. After days of heavy drinking and shoddy sex he would go home groggily to recuperate with a period of relative sobriety, sitting at his typewriter hammering out his pages of *Maggie Cassidy*. But now the New York scene had a different character. Everyone was older. Lucien Carr had married and his wife was expecting a baby. The giddy intellectual atmosphere of Joan and Edie's apartment near Columbia a decade earlier was long gone. The old recklessness of the days when Holmes and his friends drank at Glennon's bar and everyone was certain they had the world at their feet had lost its edge. There was still as much alcohol, as much sex, and now more drugs, but each of them was more focused on his work.

Ginsberg had begun to assume the role of representative for the subculture that was emerging from the beat bars, the garbage strewn streets, and the run-down tenement apartments of the neighborhood known as "Alphabet City," the avenues east of New York's numbered north-south avenues, which east of First Avenue became Avenue A, Avenue B, and Avenue C. Since 1950 he had also become close to a young poet named Gregory Corso whom he'd met in a bar shortly after Corso had been released from a New York state prison after serving a three-year sentence for robbery. Kerouac regarded Corso as a rival because he was already picking up admirers for his first poems, and he was only twenty-three. He was very good looking, with dark curly hair, an open boyish face, a quick smile, and an infectious enthusiasm. He also had a compulsion to be noticed that drew him to Ginsberg, another poet driven by a need for fame.

Holmes was so distracted by his own situation that he made no effort to be part of the new directions his friends' lives were taking. He was without money, and though he was certain he and Shirley would stay together, he was playing out the hopeless purgatory scenario of a separation he'd set up for himself. Kerouac's situation was even more desperate. In the long days in his mother's apartment he wallowed in the sloughs of his disappointments—still hiding from his wife, living off his mother or his friends, losing himself in days of drunkenness. For once the torrents of typing didn't help him shake off his demons. Kerouac brooded over his jealous impression that since Holmes had sold his novel for a large advance and he was able to go away from the city and spend time in a large old house in Connecticut, he was obviously riding a tide of success. Kerouac made no effort to hide his feeling of being mistreated.

Though Holmes' own finances were always precarious, five months earlier in September 1952—after a particularly anguished letter from Kerouac—Holmes had felt he should make some gesture to help his friend. Holmes explained to Kerouac that once when he'd been desperate and described his difficulties in a letter to Jay, he received a note back enclosing a check for fifty dollars. Thinking that it would be a kind of "passing on" of a gift from one writer to a writer brother, Holmes sent Kerouac a check for fifty dollars in a friendly letter on September 12, 1952, explaining his impulsive gesture.

Let me explain about the check. It's got to do with me not you. When I was at my lowest point early last spring, money running out, condemned to that rooming house like a devil's island of loneliness, Jay Landesman (out of the blue and without my saying a word) up and sent me fifty dollars. It saved me from having to humiliate myself before my father, and, when a week later I found this apartment, it was that fifty which secured it for me. Now I've sold my book to reprint. MCA got out and managed to create a lot of interest somehow, the offers came in: and finally I took Bantam's offer because it was the best. I've made a good sale, and should be all right financially for a while. I'm sending the fifty back to Jay, but I'm a superstitious son of a bitch. I think there should be a fifty out somewhere, so. . . . For God's sake, don't get angry or pissed off or anything. It's for

me, not you. I'm not trying meddle and it's not a loan. It's a sort of tithe,
because of my good fortune. Maybe you can have a few beers or one good
night out somewhere. Please don't be offended, because (no matter what
you say or may think) I believe in you, and that's that. For God's sake, let
me do this little thing.[19]

Initially Kerouac responded gratefully to the check, saying in a letter to
Holmes on October 12 that he accepted it with gratitude, but five months
later it became his justification for a long attack on Holmes for a number
of imagined grievances. Now Kerouac turned on Holmes, as he had on
Ginsberg, convinced that Holmes had been consciously trying to humiliate
him. Mémère involved herself in their exchange after Kerouac told her that
Holmes had been stealing ideas for books from him for years. It seemed to
them as if Holmes had sent the token check as a shame-faced acknowledge-
ment of his guilt.

On March 11, 1953, Holmes came closer to ending his friendship with
Kerouac than he would at any time in the long years that they knew each
other. He was angry enough to include Gabrielle in his dismissal of Jack's
accusations.

About the fifty dollars. What you've written doesn't deserve or require
any answer from me. I believe that I begged you when I sent it not to get
hungup about it. I asked you not to interpret it in any way. That sort of
paranoia contained in your letter is just what I meant. When I got my
reprint money, if you remember, I had just received a letter from you
full of misery: you had been forced out of Carolina, no one loved you
anymore, you were down and out in Frisco, you were afraid you were go-
ing mad. I sent you the fifty because "money is life to me" too, and at the
time I presumed that it might mean life to you as well. But now, off the
road, with three squares a day, it seems to be nothing more than "toying
with grandeurs of pride." . . . Tell you mother she needn't be suspicious
about the money either. Tell her that I thought I was friends with her son,
and that on that assumption I concluded that he wouldn't take offense
at a small check which he had led me to believe (unconsciously) that he
needed desperately. Tell her I seem to have been wrong.[20]

By helping Betty move to Old Saybrook and spending weekends working
with Shirley and his mother on the renovations of the old house, Holmes
had alienated most of his old drinking crowd, who considered that he had
become a deserter from their cause. Holmes might have been born to a

distinguished ancestry, but the family life he remembered had been a series of dead ends and displacements, and he never understood what the consciousness of his background could mean to someone from an immigrant family like Kerouac's. Burroughs *was* gentry, and during the years they all knew each other in New York he received a monthly check from his family, but he was enough of an obvious social outsider that even his moves to Mexico and Tangiers failed to put him outside their own circle. Holmes was so upset by Kerouac's letter that he went on to respond to everything else that Jack had flung at him.

> *Somewhere you seem to have gotten the idea that I'm landed gentry. This is amusing when you consider that very probably your father made more money during his life than mine. But whenever you have a beef against me, I suddenly am transformed into "a man of inherited wealth." I resent this. Frankly I'm fed up being the butt of your ingrained resentment. I have not once pre-judged you as a member of the "working class," and I don't really think (the self-righteous tone of your letter to the contrary) that you'd have tolerated it if I had.*
>
> *I'm sick of wrangling with you. I'm fed up with your tacit, and handy, assumption that no one but you is serious, no one but you is healthy, no one but you is clean, no one but you knows about life, no one but you has ever suffered, no pain but yours is real. It is often true that no one bleats and complains and bemoans about it as much as you do, but nevertheless it isn't true you know. . . .*
>
> *Right now, I frankly think you're a goddamn son of a bitch. I'm afraid I'll be suspicious of your goodwill for a long time. But I wish you well. You must know what I think of your work and of your heart. I hope that everyone leaves you alone, as you seem to wish, and doesn't force "their councils" upon you. . . . Excuse the bad temper, but I've just had one too many disputes with you, been called too many names by you, been pre-judged and "dragged to death" one too many times. If it was only a specious N.Y. connection that brought us together, it's better off ended. If you ever want to talk, or anything else, give me a ring. Let's not talk about this shit though. And don't ram me with letters like this one again, Jack. They can only be written by friends, and frankly you don't sound like one.*
>
> *I wish us both a happy birthday.*[21]

The letter was sent unsigned. The two hostile friends whose days were spent writing books they weren't sure would ever be published, without any place they could consider home, and who desperately were attempting to retreat from their hopeless situation with alcohol and continual emotional evasions, were still the "Perfect Fools" that Holmes had chosen as the title of his new novel.

The quarrel with Kerouac was only one of the storms that had blown over Holmes during these harrowing weeks. In March he had run out of the small amount of money left from his advance, and the eviction notice he had been dreading turned up in his mailbox. He began building a desk for himself in Shirley's small apartment at 28th Street and Lexington Avenue, so he could move in with her. To earn some kind of money he turned to one of the contacts that he had made in the months after *Go*'s publication. He signed a contract with *Holiday* magazine to write a profile of the folk singer Burl Ives, who was having a run of success with a New York stage show. Then on March 23, 1953, Holmes received the first royalty statement for *Go*. The book had sold 1,211 copies and earned only $418.43 of his $1,000 dollar advance. He would earn as little from the copies of his first novel as Kerouac had earned from his.

To compound Holmes' problems, like many other inexperienced writers, he hadn't understood that he would have to pay income tax on the large Bantam advance, perhaps because it had been spent so quickly. Early in April he was contacted by the I.R.S., demanding payment. He estimated that his new novel was 60 percent completed, but he was so discouraged with its progress he decided to begin again, and reluctantly he turned to the article on Burl Ives he was contracted to write. To add to his difficulties, Ives, then at the height of his popularity, was perpetually called away to do something else more important. Holmes wasted days trying to find an hour when he could interview the singer for the biographical material he needed to finish the piece.

Perhaps one of the differences between the way their friends perceived Kerouac's problems and Holmes' even more perilous situation was that in his letters Holmes usually didn't give way to the pages of self-pitying despair that fueled many of Kerouac's letters. Holmes had been clinging to expectations of a trip to St. Louis to visit the Landesmans, but he was forced to write them that the person he had planning to ride with had disappeared and he had no money for a train or airplane ticket. Holmes attempted to pass over his disappointment in a jaunty, newsy letter he wrote April 23, 1953, but his agony at what he was enduring finally broke down his attempts to keep a smile in place. "Guess you know I got a last minute cancellation on my booking in St. Louis; my transportation crapped out on me. Was all set; had packed my trick suit and my yellow shoes; had worked up a terrible thirst for friends and bourbon; had filled an unfilled slot in my schedule. Nothing."²²

"My trick suit and my yellow shoes" was a joking reference to the stage shows at Landesman's new enterprise, the Crystal Palace, a very successful bar and cabaret theater that was the center of Landesman's life in St. Louis. In the early 1950s, with its young singers and stand-up comedians, it played an important role in the spread of the new alternative American culture. Then Holmes acknowledged that his new novel was going badly.

> *I've been contending with work-problems; my book has shown a bitchy nature. I went back a week or so ago and found great wastelands in it; the red-pencil has been at work, leaving a depressing shambles behind it. I'm in the dumps without a can-opener. I've been lushing up here and there, which is bad for the intestine and doesn't help the soul much either, but can think of nothing else to do. New York seems to have buckled down to some serious task of which I'm not aware.²³*

Holmes also noted that their friend Alan Harrington had finished his novel and that MCA would be trying to place it. He glossed over his recent quarrel with Kerouac, and he was as diffident about his relationship with Shirley, referred to by her maiden name "Allen."

> *Kerouac came bounding into town with half a dozen new epic novels, had a flirt with Viking, got bitched-up, and left again for the Canadian Pacific. He and I even had a tiff, things were that bad. But everything ends, even love and war, so don't worry. . . . Speaking of Sugar-face Allen. I'm squiring her about when I have the dough, and seeing her steadily, and it's nice. We dig the world and its ways fairly much the same; I'm not hot for tons of company and particularly not the effort of selling myself too hard to newcomers, so it works out.²⁴*

The letter ended on a sad tone of rueful reminiscence.

> *Sometimes I think about everything that has happened. We've all lived a few years. Particularly I wonder why we have done what we have done: in my own case, all the wasted time, all the abused strength, all the fabulous dissipations, the hollow idols after which I sniffed. I regret nothing, except that time is not transferable. I remember fond afternoons with you and a shaker of martinis; all the huge and immense fun that was being anywhere near Neurotica in the old days; Village nights; drunken*

*afternoons around Times Square, and whatever happened to the neat
and well-dressed young matron whom we encountered on 46th Street to
whom you said: "This is Sin Street, Madam. Get off it!" . . . Memories,
memories.*

*This is at least a two-hankie letter. Will gross large in Hobokus, but
will do nothing business on the Main Stem. Maybe somebody will get a
few yuks over the martinis at the Shiny Chandeliere. Why don't you and
I get up an act to work the spot: snappy songs and shitty patter. I can see
us in straws, dirty sport-shoes and strong ties. Perhaps some false mous-
taches. I can do an off-to-buffalo and follow it with a back-flip. It should
be good. In any case, we can tell 'em all a few stories, man.*

*Don't quit now is what I have to say to anyone who's listening. This boy
is betting on life, everyone's.*[25]

Holmes signed his letter with the name of a well-known comedian
whose stock-in-trade was his sorrowing face, Ben Blue.

Chapter 14

THE RISING TIDE OF FAME

I think of you and wonder where you are, and all the others. . . . I see no one. I begin this week to write a new novel, one that I want to write quicker, purer, even though the world has turned around. I thought of you in Shreveport where the oil men stand around in the noon sun with their hats tipped over their eyes, smoking without touching their cigarettes and shifting from foot to foot. And again in the red clay, piney hills, where the paintless cabins stand in the middle of worn out cotton fields where the cypress trees come black and ugly and weird out of the creeks and bayous; and once more when we came back through Vicksburg in heavy midnight, and pressed our noses against the window to see the little red lights on the bluffs, hanging in the huge dark. And other places, and other times. I know, Jack, about the rough words, and the wild prides, and all that. We are the same. It doesn't matter. We are all older now, and I've been crazy several times this year, or I know very close.

And, more and more, I feel there is something awesome and natural to the fact that so many things and people are dispersed. I used to believe in my time, as you may remember. I was a young Werther about it, I am sure. But so was everyone once.

—JOHN CLELLON HOLMES, letter to Jack Kerouac, August 11, 1955

During the next four years, Holmes struggled against a steady erosion of his emotional reserves as he realized that he couldn't live on what he was earning as a writer. The shadow of financial catastrophe continually hung over him. Yet the first few times Kerouac saw him after the publication of *Go*, he managed to give the impression that he was doing well.

In late September 1953 they met unexpectedly when John and Shirley visited Ginsberg in his new apartment on the Lower East Side. It was the first time Holmes met Burroughs. Burroughs' first book, *Junky*, had been published in April 1953 by Ace Books. He was staying with Ginsberg while he assembled his notes for another drug book for A. A. Wynn, *The Yage Letters*, about his travels in South America in search of yage, a hallucinogenic plant. Holmes hadn't seen any of the old crowd in over a year, and it was the first time he had brought Shirley, who had just become his wife. They had been married for only two weeks, but it was six months later before Holmes managed to separate himself from his unfinished novel long enough to write a letter to Landesman describing the simple ceremony.

The evening in Ginsberg's dim, red-bulb-lit living room was strained and confused. Kerouac was tormented over his suspicions that Gregory Corso was moving in on the young woman Alene Lee, with whom Kerouac was having an affair that summer. She typed up the first collaged manuscript of *The Yage Letters*. A month later, in October 1953, after breaking off with Lee, Kerouac sat in his mother's kitchen in Richmond Hill and wrote a chaotic account of the affair, titled *The Subterraneans*, in three Benzedrine-driven nights. His portrayal of Holmes in the book was both unforgettable and unflattering. Unlike the brief glimpses Kerouac presented of most of the "subterraneans" in his crowd, he spent an entire page on Holmes.

The negative depiction of Holmes stemmed from Kerouac's conflicted feelings about Holmes' success, veering between his uneasy resentment of Holmes as a literary rival and his lasting memory of their old friendship. Holmes' pseudonym in the book—always a clue to Kerouac's intentions— was "Balliol MacJones," a sly dig at Holmes' distinguished family name. In the opening pages Kerouac hovered between descriptions of Holmes that were usually negative, but often still admiring. He credited Holmes with having been one of their crowd who shared not only a literary response to their new attitudes in naming Whitman, Thoreau, and Melville as their predecessors, but also a consciousness of the deeper meanings of their experience. In the book he wrote that Holmes understood

> the mystery, the silence of the subterraneans, "urban Thoreaus" Mac[Jones] called them, as from Alfred Kazin in New York New School lectures back East commenting on all students being interested in Whitman from a sexual revolution standpoint and in Thoreau from a contemplative mystic and anti-materialistic as if existentialist or whatever standpoint, the Pierre-of-Melville goof and wonder of it.[1]

In the early pages of the novel Holmes was called a distinguished visitor to the apartment, yet only sentences later he was Kerouac's worst literary enemy before Jack went on to recall that in the early years of their friend-ship "we used to slop beer on each other's knees in leaning over talk ex-citement."[2] Unfortunately Holmes' large advance for the paperback sale of *Go* had come between them. The only real sales success of anyone in their group was Burroughs, whose *Junky* sold 113,170 copies as a mass-market paperback in its first year,[3] but Kerouac was still resentful that Holmes had gotten a twenty-thousand-dollar advance for telling their story, a staggering sum when Kerouac couldn't even find a publisher for his own portrayal of the group.

The evening began badly when Jack and Alene walked into Ginsberg's apartment and found John and Shirley sitting on the living-room couch, talking to Burroughs. Kerouac forced himself to shake hands firmly with Holmes, but then he sat brooding while the others continued to talk, so ill at ease that he got up abruptly and went to sulk by himself in the bedroom. Finally Ginsberg broke the tension by commissioning Kerouac to go out and buy quart bottles of beer for the party. When he returned, everyone but Lee had moved into the kitchen, where Burroughs was showing the notebook drawings he'd made in South America. After Holmes encouraged Kerouac to show his drawings too, the mood lightened and they finally became friends again.[4]

More relaxed after a few beers, Kerouac now noticed Holmes' expensive new clothes and wristwatch with approval, while Shirley—a good cook—concocted an impromptu supper for the crowd out of the cans she found on Ginsberg's kitchen shelves. Then when everyone trooped out into the street to find a bar where they could continue drinking, Kerouac swept Lee off her feet and carried her along the sidewalk, grandstanding in front of Holmes and the others. Kerouac might have been frustrated over his stalled career, but at least by that action he felt he'd just proven that he still was ahead of Holmes, "never getting older, always in there, always with the young, the new generations."[5]

Five years later, in 1958 when *The Subterraneans* was published, Holmes assured Kerouac that he didn't mind being presented as the crowd's suc-cessful square, though it was a portrait that would forever define Holmes for readers of Kerouac's books. Like Gary Snyder, who never could shake the portrayal of himself as the West Coast collegiate rebel "Japhy Ryder" in *The Dharma Bums*, Holmes' portrait was preserved for all time, like an insect trapped in amber.

In March the next year Holmes finally broke off from his obsession with his novel-in-progress to tell Jay and Fran about his marriage to Shirley. They were married in a simple ceremony in Haddam, Connecticut, on September 9, 1953. Holmes opened his letter with a lame excuse: "I haven't written a letter in over six months, so pardon my dust. I mean to anyone. But I've done my words for today, and I've been thinking of you."[6] His account of his marriage to Shirley was pleased, if consciously laconic.

> *We ran off up the Connecticut River one day to a little town which time and the railroad have bypassed, got ourselves a license from an old biddy with high-piled hair and a pencil over her ear, went to a justice of the peace who mumbled a few words, which ended "hope youse'll be very happy," and cooled out in the local hotel with scotch and water. The local hotel is a great mansard-roofed affair, with twenty foot ceilings, verandas all around, hanging over the lip of the river. It was all very nice.*[7]

Later John remembered sweeping Shirley into his arms after the ceremony: "our hearts married a long time before—but feeling idiotically, that now we were safe, and we just held on, and laughed against one another's ears, and it was the best joy I've ever known."[8]

Holmes' financial situation was as desperate as always, but he allowed himself a few scraps of optimism. He told Landesman he was nearly two-thirds done with *Perfect Fools*, and he'd finally turned in the article about Burl Ives to *Holiday* magazine. The only possessions he managed to salvage from his marriage to Marian were his books, which over the past several months he'd carried over from East 48th Street to Shirley's apartment at 123 Lexington Avenue. He felt a quiet pride that he made her place soundproof "against the rough clamor of the world by walls—full of my books."[9] Shirley was working an office job, just as Marian had done, to support them as he worked doggedly on his novel. Hounded by the I.R.S. for back taxes on his advance for *Go*, they were so broke that Shirley had gone to her family begging for money, since this time Betty couldn't help. With Shirley's salary and the low rent on her tiny apartment, Holmes somehow convinced himself that they could hold out until he received an advance for his new novel. *Go* was scheduled for reprint in April, when he expected to be paid the second half of his advance from the paperback sale.

Landesman had begun his own book about their scene, joining Kerouac, Harrington, and Stringham, who were all writing about what they had been through together. Holmes encouraged Landesman with a positive response to what he had read of the manuscript in another disjointed letter in June 1954. Then almost as an aside, he mentioned that Kerouac had dropped in a month earlier.

Jack Kerouac turned up at my door one night after almost a year. We spent the evening together, and the next day. I had forgotten how much I can drink in twenty-four hours without passing out on the street. It went on and on, like the old days. One sleazy bar to the next, a stream of nickels in the juke boxes, hundreds of soapy beers; and odd moment in the sunny Second Avenue afternoon, throwing pennies to Puerto Rican children. The floor of the apartment was covered with gin bottles the following night, and I finally did pass out. The next morning I realized that I'm too old for this stuff anymore; you can't get lost again. . . . Jack was in good shape; no paranoia, no angers, acceptance. He had been to California and the railroad since I saw him. He had taken up Buddhism and spent hours under an almond tree near the railroad tracks.[10]

Kerouac described the same visit in a letter to Ginsberg in May 1954, wryly commenting that the scene in John and Shirley's apartment felt very familiar. Kerouac had brought a "junky" girlfriend with him, and as in the old days, they listened to records of Billie Holiday and Lester Young and talked incessantly. This time since Holmes had made so much money with *Go*, as Kerouac still insisted, Holmes was deputized to buy the liquor. He came back with two paper bags full of gin bottles, enough to drink until they all passed out.

The next morning, after Shirley left for work, the other three nursed their hangovers in seedy Second Avenue bars, where Kerouac wrote Ginsberg that he drunkenly told Holmes they were "Brothers Forever, and mean it." That evening, back in the apartment, waiting for Shirley to return tired from her job, Kerouac felt a rush of sympathy for her when she opened the door and saw the three drunken bums and lushes in the room. She sighed, leaned against the door "just like Marian, and it's the same thing again as Marian."[11] After 1954 nearly every one of Kerouac's visits to Holmes would turn into drunken shambles. While Kerouac never tried to rein in the havoc he caused around him, Holmes was beginning to realize, as he told Landesman, that at twenty-eight he was "too old for this stuff."[12]

Kerouac's life had also slipped back into a familiar pattern. After finishing *The Subterraneans* he traveled again to California in late December 1953 to take a job parking cars, which Cassady had set up for him. Kerouac resumed his affair with Carolyn in the Cassadys' home in San Jose, after Neal had recuperated from a serious accident and returned to work on the railroad. In April Cassady had broken most of the bones in his foot and ankle when he fell off a boxcar that hit a bumper while he was setting the brake. The Southern Pacific offered only a small sum in compensation for the accident, so the Cassadys hired a lawyer and sued the railroad. Eleven months after the accident, as Carolyn later wrote in her memoir *Off the Road*, they "ended up with $16,000. . . . But even that amount made us feel rich—and it was tax free."[13]

While he was living in San Jose with the Cassadys, Kerouac began a spiritual journey which for the next several years was to be the most sustaining force in his life. Browsing in the San Jose Public Library, he found volume ten of *The Sacred Books and Early Literature of the East* on the shelves. The book accidentally opened to a page in the chapter titled "India and Buddhism in Translation," where Kerouac found the passage "O worldly men! How fatally deluded! Beholding everywhere the body brought to dust, yet everywhere the more carelessly living; the heart is neither lifeless wood nor stone, and yet it thinks not 'All is vanishing.'"[14]

The words spoke directly to Kerouac's fear of death and need for spiritual comfort, particularly following a vision of what he called "the anxieties of Heaven" during a bad Benzedrine experience in Mexico City the previous year.[15] Deciding that "Buddha goes beyond Christ,"[16] Kerouac began to devour Buddhist scripture in Dwight Goddard's anthology *The Buddhist Bible*, and from December 1953 to March 1956 he kept a journal of his Buddhist studies in an idiosyncratic attempt to integrate the Christian idea of a personal God into his own interpretation of Buddhism.[17] His studies intensified during his nearly four months with the Cassadys in San Jose, as he argued with both of them over their conversion to the ideas of Edgar Cayce, a controversial "channeler" whose teachings espoused a theory of reincarnation.

At the end of 1953, Ginsberg left New York City for Mexico and California. In May 1954 he also stayed with the Cassadys in San Jose after Kerouac had left. Ginsberg was still desperately in love with Cassady, but when Carolyn surprised them having sex in her bedroom she angrily told Ginsberg he had to leave immediately. She drove him to Berkeley, gave him twenty dollars, and said that he was on his own. In San Francisco Ginsberg looked up one of Kerouac's friends, a seaman named Al Sublette, who rented a room in the Hotel Marconi. Ginsberg also got a room there, and within a few days he met a woman named Sheila Williams Boucher in Vesuvio's Bar in North Beach. She had been a jazz singer, smoked marijuana, and knew bop musicians such as Dave Brubeck.

Ginsberg moved into her apartment and found himself trying to act like a father to her four-year-old son. He found an office job as a market researcher, dressed in a suit and tie, and for several months succeeded in his new attempt at heterosexuality. Even Cassady accepted the change and came by Boucher's apartment to sort out the marijuana he was dealing and to read Proust to them as he'd done in the old days in New York. Increasingly dissatisfied with his new life, however, Ginsberg began to see a psychiatrist, and as part of his therapy he told Boucher about his involvement with Cassady. At first she demanded that Ginsberg leave her apartment, but they managed to patch up the quarrel.

In December 1954 Ginsberg went into a Foster's Cafeteria in San Francisco where he met a painter named Robert LaVigne, who asked Ginsberg if he wanted to come back to his nearby studio on Gough Street and see some of his paintings. At that time there was a talented group of musicians, writers, and artists gathered in San Francisco, and they often met in loose, informal session of talk in brightly lit, wanly decorated all-night cafeterias like Foster's close to Market Street. The cafeterias let them congregate at a table away from the usual grifters and street drunks and argue through the night. The poets would later be described as the "San Francisco Poetry Renaissance" and for a few crucial years they allied themselves with the Beats.

In LaVigne's studio Ginsberg found himself irresistibly drawn to a large portrait of a beautiful, blonde young man. A moment later the young man himself came into the room. His name was Peter Orlovsky, he was only nineteen, and though he felt that he was basically heterosexual, he was also painfully shy. He had been a virgin when LaVigne seduced him. LaVigne passed Orlovsky on to Ginsberg, saying, "All Peter needed was sweet companionship."[18] Ginsberg and Orlovsky were to be together for the rest of Ginsberg's life, though Orlovsky would also form lasting partnerships with women.

During the months that Ginsberg was in California, John and Shirley began the work of renovating the old school building behind Betty's house in Old Saybrook that would finally become their home. Shirley quit her office job and subleased their Manhattan apartment, and they spent the summer of 1954 living with Betty while they worked on their own house. They tore out walls, opening out a thirty-by-forty-five-foot living room. Originally the building had been divided into twelve rooms, but John and Shirley redesigned the two-story interior into nine rooms. Holmes taught himself plumbing and wiring, as well as stone masonry to build a massive fireplace in the living room. He also worked as his own carpenter in order to build bookshelves from floor to ceiling up both walls of the stairway to the bedroom floor. Shirley landscaped and planted a garden, and they worked together to paint the exterior of the house a sensible gray. They often finished their day's chores with a drive to the nearby beach and a twilight swim.

It was a sustained productive period, and by the end of the summer they felt they had earned a break. They vacationed for a week as guests of their old friends the Lyndons, who were renting a house on Nantucket Island. The island attracted a more fashionable crowd than Holmes was accustomed to in Old Saybrook, and it left him with a noisy blend of impressions of "crooked, cobbled streets; huge, lovely old houses; piers that haven't changed since Melville; and the whole island swarming with the Madison Avenue set. I felt quite forlorn without my Bermuda shorts."[19]

Roger Lyndon had become a professor of mathematics at the University of Michigan at Ann Arbor, and he and his wife, Susan, planned to drive back home by way of New York City. The Lyndons offered John and Shirley a lift to Manhattan as if to emphasize the new life they felt was beginning for all of them. They came in time for the opening of a chic new Upper East Side supper club called the Renaissance owned by Shirley's ex-husband Stanley Radulovich, who had also remarried. The fears and apprehensions that had driven Holmes to isolate himself in his apartment for months after he left Marian were resolved in the three days of non-stop partying to celebrate Radulovich's new club. When John and Shirley returned to their house in Old Saybrook, it was to dig in for the fall. Holmes planned to have *Perfect Fools* finished by November.

The optimistic mood of the summer quickly dissipated. At the beginning of October 1954 Shirley received word that her father, Vance Allen, was critically ill in Louisiana. The initial diagnosis was cancer, and Shirley immediately flew down to Shreveport to be with her family. Holmes stayed in Old Saybrook, working "monkishly" on the book until Shirley called to say that her father was more seriously ill than she had thought. Holmes had never met her family, so they decided he should join her in Shreveport. Holmes remained in Louisiana for a month, spending time with Shirley's step-mother and meeting Shirley's relatives, who were scattered throughout the state. Then, with her father's condition still uncertain, they decided to return to Connecticut. They traveled by train to St. Louis and spent a week with the Landesmans. The round of partying gave them a breathing space from the emotional scene in Shreveport.

Once back in Old Saybrook, facing the winter, Holmes closeted himself in his work room and picked up the manuscript of *Perfect Fools*. He had grown more optimistic about the book. As he developed the theme of his period of separation from Shirley during their long wait for her divorce to become final, the novel had become, as he'd hoped, the study of a man undergoing a self- inflicted moral crisis. Nearing the end, he anticipated beginning the third novel that would conclude the ambitious trilogy he believed he'd started with *Go*. After *Perfect Fools* was completed on January

19, 1955, he sent the manuscript to his agent Rae Everitt, still working as his agent.

Over the next few weeks his feelings of relief at finishing his novel slowly eroded. Vance Allen's condition became more critical, so Shirley hurried back to Louisiana on the train, traveling again through St. Louis. She was in the station long enough to have a drink with Landesman, who met her there before she made the last leg of the journey to Shreveport. In Old Saybrook Holmes received word that her father had died, he guessed, just about the time Shirley and Jay were sitting in the bar in the station.

Anxious to offer Shirley whatever support he could, Holmes flew down to Shreveport two days later. He stayed in Louisiana for two weeks before he became concerned about his manuscript, since it had been almost a month since he delivered it. He wired Rae Everitt, who replied with a brief note saying that Scribner's had rejected the book. She had forwarded a copy of the letter from his editor Burroughs Mitchell on to Old Saybrook. Upset at the news, Holmes immediately phoned her, and with some reluctance she finally read the letter to him. Despite Mitchell's effort to soften the effect he knew the letter would have on Holmes, he held out no hope that Scribner's would ever take the new book.

It was a rejection that would have been difficult for any writer to hear, but for Holmes it was devastating. The problems, Mitchell felt, were in the plotting and in the development of the two central characters, "Danno" (the name Holmes had given to himself) and "Laura" (the name he'd given to Shirley). Mitchell wrote,

> You are grappling with moral issues—rendering them with the utmost seriousness, with passion. But you do not have here the structure to support your gravity of intention and your passion. I mean that the story is not big enough for its theme. The reader is not persuaded that Danno, the moralist must lie about his affair with Laura; that they must "sin to love." Toward the close, Danno wonders whether their "ordeal" could have been avoided. And that has been in the reader's mind for some time; he has not fully believed in the inevitability of the ordeal. And so the story has come to seem drawn out. The power of your book, the force of its meaning, has been vitiated.[20]

Mitchell's attempts to be reassuring were of little help in the circumstances. He wrote that sections of the writing in the book were "finer than *Go*; but for us, these merits remain secondary to the central defect." He concluded by saying that he and his colleague John Hall Wheelock at Scribner's believed in Holmes' "exceptional talent" and were certain of his writing career, "but we cannot believe this book to be a step forward in it."[21]

As a final twist in the knot Holmes felt tightening around him, his agent told him that Bantam books had decided they couldn't release their paperback edition of *Go*. They had just published Leon Uris's best-selling novel *Battle Cry* about the U.S. Marine Corps, an unheroic depiction which had aroused the hostility of veterans' groups everywhere in the country. Bantam feared that the drug-and-alcohol-fueled lifestyle described in Holmes' novel would only cause them more trouble. They were willing to negotiate a financial settlement with Holmes, since they had signed a contract to publish his book, but *Go* would not appear under the Bantam imprint. To fortify themselves for the two-day train journey from Louisiana back to Connecticut, he and Shirley bought a bottle of Ballantine's Scotch and a huge box lunch of fried chicken, stuffed eggs, and other Louisiana delicacies. They arrived in Old Saybrook hoping that the worst of their situation was behind them.

There were two breaks in the heavy clouds that Holmes could report to Landesman over the next months. One was that a publisher had seen a story in the August 1953 issue of *Discovery* that would later become the opening chapter of Holmes' jazz novel *The Horn* and offered him a contract to write a biography of Charlie Parker. The other was that he and Shirley had just heard the singer Anita Ellis perform a set of the songs that Fran had begun writing with Tommy Wolf, the resident pianist at the Crystal Palace, the theater club she and Landesman were running in St. Louis.

In *Rebel Without Applause*, Landesman wrote that one night at the Palace as Fran was talking about music with the pianist, he asked her half-seriously if there was some hip way to make a song out of the opening lines of T. S. Eliot's poem *The Wasteland*. The poem begins "April is the cruelest month / mingling memory with desire / breeding lilacs out of the dead land." Fran was thoughtful for a moment and suddenly joked, "How about, 'Spring can really hang you up the most.'" She expected Wolf to laugh. Instead he stopped playing the piano and asked, "Say that again?" He insisted that she should try to write some lyrics to go with her first line, and a few days later she nervously slipped a piece of paper into his pocket as he sat at the piano. She had written her first song.[22]

Fran's songs, in a wistful reminiscence of the older hipster style, were to become classics of the genre, blending the brittle mood of classic lyricists like Lorenz Hart and Cole Porter with her own wry, wide-eyed realism. Holmes wrote in his letter,

Last night we went to the Renaissance and listened to some fine, clean,
honest songs that were written by some sweet, perceptive St. Louis chick,
who has quit the racket to raise cherubic, hip children. Anita Ellis was
scotch-souring it and picked up the most. You'll probably be hearing. But
for real, Franny, they are class: sweet, straight things. And "How do you like
your love" is in a realm all its own. I know of nothing so wry, so perfect. And
"Listen, Little Girl" particularly flipped us, and Anita too. Wonderful.[23]

Fran had become the first of the old Glennon's drinking crowd to be
successful with the larger, and very un-hip, audience.

Although it wasn't a development he could have anticipated, during the
winter of 1955 Kerouac's quarrel with Joan Haverty over his failure to provide support for their three-year-old daughter Jan was at least temporarily
settled enough for him to be able to use his own name on his writing. In
January Kerouac was brought into court on charges of non-support, and he
asked Ginsberg's brother Eugene Brooks, an attorney, to defend him. When
Joan arrived in court, she found that Kerouac was demanding a paternity
test before the hearing could proceed. Brooks pleaded with the judge that
Kerouac's phlebitis was so severe that he was unable to work and assist his
wife with support of any kind. Jack and Joan talked for a moment, and she
showed him a photograph of their daughter. In a letter to Ginsberg written in his mother's apartment on January 18, 1955, Kerouac admitted that
Jan looked like him, "so she may be mine." Finally Joan gave up, saying that
she wouldn't insist upon child support if her ex-husband didn't have any
money, and the case was dismissed. For the moment Kerouac seemed in
the clear.

Kerouac's ultimately successful efforts to deny any responsibility for his
daughter were to have lasting effects. Gabrielle stubbornly believed his de-
nials that he was Jan's father. For her own reasons she was as determined
to keep her son close to her as he was set on avoiding any financial responsibility for Joan's child. Although Mémère had only one grandchild, her
daughter Caroline's son Paul, she accepted Kerouac's story that Jan was
the result of Joan's affair with a Puerto Rican waiter. Following the court's
decision, Joan withdrew her petition for support and raised Jan as best she
could. The one who paid the highest price was Jan, whose life became a
succession of stumbling efforts to win her father's approval until her health
was undermined by alcohol and drug abuse.

Kerouac spent most of the spring of 1955 in North Carolina at his sister's
house. Then with a small stipendium that Malcolm Cowley, an editor at

the Viking Press, had arranged for him, he traveled back to Mexico City. He rented a small apartment and began one of his most ambitious poetry projects, a serious of spontaneous improvisations written on a series of single notebook pages the way he felt a jazz musician improvised a chorus. The book was titled *Mexico City Blues*, Kerouac's memorial to Charlie Parker, who had died the previous spring. He was sending the new poems to Ginsberg, and their free-swinging "jazz" tone was to have an important influence on the poetry Ginsberg was writing in California. To help him break free of earlier poetic models, Ginsberg taped on the wall above his typewriter Kerouac's list of directions about how to write spontaneous prose. In a burst of creativity, Kerouac also began the first part of a short novel about a drug-addicted Mexican prostitute who had drifted into his life. The novel was *Tristessa*.

At the beginning of October 1955 Kerouac left Mexico City and reached Berkeley, where he stayed with Ginsberg in a small cottage Ginsberg was renting on Milvia Street. Kerouac arrived just in time for a reading that Ginsberg had arranged with a group of other young poets at the Six Gallery on Fillmore Avenue in San Francisco. Ginsberg had just finished the first section of a new poem titled "Howl for Carl Solomon," the patient he had befriended at the psychiatric hospital in Manhattan years earlier. It was dedicated to Kerouac and others in the group.

Ginsberg's poem was his depiction of the same postwar American scene that Holmes had chronicled in *Go*, Burroughs had described obliquely in *Junky*, and Kerouac had written about in *On the Road*. On the West Coast, however, Ginsberg's vision of the deepening social crisis he felt that the Beat scene represented—"I saw the best minds of my generation destroyed by madness"—and his intense reading of the first section of the poem before a noisily appreciative audience of about a hundred people at the Six Gallery caused a literary sensation. Ginsberg was eager for Kerouac to join the other poets on the program at the Six Gallery, but Kerouac was too shy. Instead he collected money from the audience and rushed out to buy gallon bottles of California wine before coming back to sit at the edge of the stage encouraging Ginsberg. Kerouac's shouts of "Go! Go!" punctuating the rhythms of the poetry encouraged the audience at the Six Gallery to join in the clamor.

It was with Ginsberg's reading of his new poetry, along with readings of their unpublished work by Gary Snyder, Michael McClure, Philip Whalen, and Philip Lamentia, that the stirrings of the "beat consciousness" that Kerouac and Holmes had defined that night at 681 Lexington eight years before would break through to the larger audience. There were many others now who shared their sense of alienation from mainstream American politics and culture. The Bay area's busy community of small press publishers showed immediate interest in "Howl." The prestigious avant-garde publisher Berne Porter offered to do a limited edition of the poem in an expensive letter press edition. At the same time Ginsberg received a Western Union telegram from one of the owners of a small Columbus Avenue bookshop, Lawrence Ferlinghetti. The telegram was Ferlinghetti's now famous message, which began by quoting Emerson's greeting to Whitman after receiving a copy of *Leaves of Grass*: "I greet you at the beginning of a great career. When do I get the manuscript?" Ferlinghetti proposed publishing Ginsberg's poem in an inexpensive paperback edition that would be the third in his series of City Lights Pocket Books.

Kerouac's intense explorations of his new way of writing and the spiritual solace of his new-found Buddhism fueled a sustained period of writing. As he outlined in a letter to Malcolm Cowley in the autumn of 1955, he had already written seven volumes of what he called "The Duluoz Legend," an epic chronicle of his life begun after he'd discovered spontaneous prose. He listed the books for Philip Whalen in a letter on March 6, 1956, including *On the Road, Visions of Neal, Visions of Gerard, Visions of Mary, Visions of Doctor Sax, Visions of the Subterraneans, Visions of the Railroad*, as well as his *Book of Dreams, Book of Dharma*, and *Books of Blues*, the poetry he had begun writing in San Francisco and Mexico City. It was millions of words, all unpublished. Cowley was pushing for Kerouac to achieve some kind of recognition, and Jack began revising *On the Road* in response to some of Cowley's criticisms. Finally in March 1956, Kerouac borrowed fifty dollars from his mother and hitchhiked from North Carolina to California, hoping to talk to Cowley in Palo Alto, where the editor had been teaching a course in creative writing at Stanford University. Kerouac hadn't understood that Stanford, unlike eastern universities, was on a trimester schedule. Cowley was already back in New York by the time Kerouac reached California hoping to meet him.

On March 18, 1956, Ginsberg and the poets who had read at the Six Gallery staged a repeat of their performance in a small theater on Stuart Street in Berkeley, close to Shattuck Avenue. Although Orlovsky was now living off and on with Ginsberg at the Milvia cottage, he attended the reading on a blind date with Ann Danberg, a student at the University of California at Berkeley whose family lived in Los Angeles. Orlovsky felt an immediate affinity with her after they spent hours walking and talking together in Berkeley. He wrote his mother, Kate, on March 21, 1956, "I've been feeling extremely good, so good that living doesn't seem like a big negative problem as it did before. There's a big blue-eyed mystical looking 19-year-old girl here who likes me and I her, so the world's a little bit like heaven now. She goes to Cal University English major, studying Thomas Hardy right now."[24]

Since Orlovsky didn't have a car and the young woman lived in a co-op above the campus, by the time he walked there to pick her up for the reading, and they walked together back to the cottage on Milvia Street, they arrived too late for the spaghetti dinner Orlovsky had prepared for a pre-reading party for the poets and their friends. Although Orlovsky described her as a big girl, she was about the same height as Orlovsky, and she was as slim as he was. She admired his blonde good looks and was surprised by his old-fashioned good manners. After they stood around with glasses of cheap red California wine poured from a gallon bottle in the crowded single room of the cottage, lit mostly by candles, Orlovsky made a place for her on his lap in the backseat of a car and they drove off with the others.

Later at the small theater in Berkeley, while the poets arranged mismatched chairs with battered upholstery from the last theater production out on the stage for their reading, Orlovsky showed her the drawings in the lobby. It was hung with sketches LaVigne had done of Ginsberg making love with a young man who Orlovsky told her was himself. She could understand that Ginsberg and Orlovsky were living together, but she was startled that they had made an art show out of their lovemaking. Afterwards in the theater lobby in the intermission she saw a married student named Sam Charters, whom she had met in her music classes a year earlier. They had also taken long walks in the Berkeley hills, talking about their shared interests in music and literature.

That night at the poetry reading in Berkeley, Ginsberg for the first time read all of "Howl" and the effect was electrifying. He was wearing a ragged sweater and he leaned over the podium, tense and overpowering in his conviction. The audience found itself swept into his cadences and with a few lines they began to respond with shouts and laughter. There was none of the solemn atmosphere of the usual reading of poetry; instead it was the kind of exchange that went with the high dramatics of an inspired jazz performance. When Ginsberg finished with the last shouts of "Moloch, Moloch" someone backstage began turning the overhead stage lighting on and off, bathing the stage in shades of yellow, red, and blue. The other poets, who were sitting on the stage behind him, stood up and solemnly shook his hand. It was clear, as it had been at the first reading from "Howl," that a line had been crossed, and there was no returning to the world that had been left behind.

Kerouac had been corresponding from North Carolina with Gary Snyder, another of the poets who took part in the Six Gallery reading, and in April 1956 Kerouac moved into a cabin Snyder invited him to share across the bay from Berkeley in Mill Valley. When Snyder left for Japan later in the spring, Kerouac stayed on in the cottage. Then he spent the summer working Snyder's old job as a fire watcher in an isolated lookout in a forest in the Cascade Mountains. During his weeks on his mountaintop he wrote the first part of his next book, *Desolation Angels*.

As if Holmes sensed the excitement in the Bay Area, he noted in his journal on March 28, 1956, that he had abandoned his planned trilogy. The publisher had never sent a contract for a Charlie Parker biography, so he turned to the jazz novel he and Kerouac had argued about over the years. A version of its first chapter, titled "The Horn," had already been published as a short story. In March and April 1956 he and Kerouac exchanged letters before Kerouac left Mill Valley. Holmes told him that the winter had been hard, though he glossed over the finality of his editor's rejection of *Perfect Fools*. He also didn't mention that Shirley had been forced to find a job as a secretary for a local businessman to pay their household expenses. Instead Holmes confessed that he felt exiled in Old Saybrook and was beginning to obsess about the past.

> We have had a bad year. My poor second novel has not found a home. Everybody likes it, but they want me to castrate it, and as yet I haven't been able to do it. I don't know, I feel stubborn and outlandish, but I just can't take out the knife and slice it up. The new one is even farther out, and I feel even more that I can't help it. That is the way my mind turns right now, so what are you going to do?
>
> We freeze to death up here. We have no heat in our house and I build dismal fires all day long. Now, of course, the worst is over; you can feel some-thing stirring everywhere, though every morning is still icy and bleak. I am alone during the day, and putter, putter, and think. It has been a strange exile, and for some reason I have not minded it as much as I thought I would. New York is a grim dream in some one else's head. I fret and think of giving up smoking and will be thirty next week or so. I remember and remember, and try to fashion all this into strange, almost Chekhovian little sketches. It is what I feel now. . . . I have been beset by paralyzing periods of indolence in which the oil in my mind seemed to freeze. It is passing now. . . . Mainly I write to say, hello and happy birthday, because this will get to you somewhere before the 12th [of March].[25]

On April 14, 1956, Kerouac answered with a postcard from Mill Valley, saying that his own situation was as precarious as his friend's. He was living in a shack with a woodstove and he had no money, no publishers, nothing. He asked if Holmes remembered the sexual revolution they had anticipated in 1948. It was happening in the Bay Area all around him now, but without him, since he had given up sex since his conversion to Buddhism. He even disparaged his new religious beliefs, calling himself not really Buddhist, just a sad drifter without any expectations.

Holmes' response on May 25 picked up their old friendship.

It sounds a monastic life. I too read and think about the leathery serenity of Tibetan faces, and the terrifying purity of the silence in new mountains. I think of them there, and I too have gone some distance along the way. Though I'm no Buddhist for some reason.

The fate of On the Road *infuriates me, but it's an old, tired infuriation and I won't bother you with it. I slump along under flowering fruit trees in Connecticut, glad that spring did come back from wherever she has been hiding these last months. . . . I watch the Great Birth, and love New England because it comes with such a pang up here.*[26]

Although neither Ginsberg, Kerouac, nor Holmes had any idea that anything had happened, their situation was about to change. The Bay area poetry readings and the raw power of Ginsberg's "Howl" had attracted so much local attention that when Kerouac, Ginsberg, Orlovsky, and Orlovsky's younger brother Lafcadio decided to go back to New York at the end of October 1956, they were already celebrities. The *Village Voice*, Greenwich Village's new newspaper, announced their return with the headline "Witless Madcaps Come Home to Roost." Whatever their new notoriety, however, their immediate problem was to find a place to stay. Ginsberg had given up his apartment when he'd moved to San Francisco, and Kerouac's mother had moved to Florida to be close to her daughter. The Orlovsky brothers went home to Long Island to stay with their mother, and Ginsberg called a friend, the poet Richard Howard, asking if he and Kerouac could spend a few nights on the floor.

Howard introduced them to a young woman named Helen Weaver, who was sharing an apartment with a friend in Greenwich Village while working as a secretary in a publishing house. Filled with romance of living as a single girl in the Village, Weaver invited Kerouac to her apartment, and he immediately moved in. The relationship lasted only a few weeks. She found that with Kerouac sharing her bed so many people dropped by that there was a perpetual round of parties, and she quickly felt herself losing control of her own life. She asked her father to pay for psychiatric counseling, and her doctor suggested that Kerouac was part of her problem.

Weaver brought Kerouac home to Scarsdale to have dinner with her very proper parents, and Kerouac surprised her by finding things to talk about with her father. A few days later, however, a second dinner in Greenwich Village with Henri Cru, Kerouac's classmate from Horace Mann, didn't go as well. Cru was a gourmet cook and served excellent wine, but to Weaver's dismay Kerouac retreated into one of the dark moods that overcame him when he felt one of his friends had a better grip on their lives than he did. He refused to eat, he kept singing the same song over and over, and he got drunker and drunker. Weaver remembered that as she looked at him across the table, she realized, "My handsome lover had disappeared and in his place I saw an old wino with haunted eyes."[27]

Kerouac disappeared over Christmas, when he went to Orlando to spend the holidays with his mother. He was away for twelve days, and during that time at another party in Manhattan Ginsberg introduced Weaver to Gregory Corso. In a mood of impatience with Kerouac, she went to bed with Corso, unaware that three years before Corso had been Kerouac's rival when he had sex with Alene Lee. In Weaver's letter to Kerouac after a New Year's party, she told him, "He [Gregory] tugged at my heart because he seemed so much like you."[28] Whatever had happened between Weaver and Corso, when Kerouac returned to New York, he went back to her apartment since he had nowhere else to go.

Kerouac wrote to Holmes from Weaver's apartment on January 10, 1957, with the exultant news that he was at last about to sign the contract with Cowley at Viking for *On the Road*. His long struggle to get the novel published was over. Viking Press, which had earlier rejected all of the revised versions of the manuscript, finally resolved the final obstacles to publication that the legal department had raised. Lawyers prepared waivers of objection for Neal and Carolyn Cassady, Lucien Carr, and Allen Ginsberg, and finally the way was cleared.

Weaver was clinging to her talks with the psychiatrist and trying to get enough sleep to function at her job despite Kerouac's nightly drunken celebrations of his book's acceptance. Late one night Kerouac and Lucien Carr reeled into her apartment after she'd gone to bed. Kerouac turned on the phonograph and began playing her album of *My Fair Lady*, singing along with Carr. Furious at the disturbance, she rushed out of her bedroom and began hitting them, pushing them into the bedroom of her roommate, who was away. The next morning they were gone. Finally, on January 14, Weaver told Kerouac he couldn't come back any more.

Now Kerouac had no place to stay. He packed his clothes in his rucksack and put his pile of unpublished manuscripts in a cheap cardboard suitcase. As always it was Ginsberg who again found a place for him to stay. Ginsberg phoned another young woman, one who had her own apartment uptown on the West Side and also worked in a publishing house. She was an aspiring novelist named Joyce Glassman. On a freezing winter night Glassman rode the subway downtown to meet Kerouac at a Howard Johnson's restaurant in the Village. There she paid for his supper and took him home.

Earlier that fall Ginsberg had sent a copy of *Howl and Other Poems* to Holmes, who responded with an enthusiastic letter of praise on September 26, 1956. Despite the differences between *Howl* and the poetry he had been writing ten years before, Holmes felt the poem's power and sensed the effect it would have. He wrote to Ginsberg on September 26:

> *I've just read it through once, and had to say, "Yes'm" and couldn't wait. Rumblings had reached here, of course. . . . And Jack, in letters here and there, had described the evenings to me, and wakened a nostalgia for it all that almost led to bus tickets. But now the small, black-bordered, quite respectable-looking sheaf has exploded in me, and I want to say to you, "Yes, my friend! Yes!"*
>
> *The beautiful tenderness of it is with me now, beneath everything else, the real tenderness (so really rare!), the sweet humors, the wise giggles. You have a fat tone, you blow clean. You make me very sad to think of time. I wish I could tell you of the sweet lumps I got in reading "America"—such a beautiful, straight honest thing it is! You make me love a world whose punished children still can love it so. I hope it listens to you, old friend.*[29]

The next month a second chapter of Holmes' jazz novel, now titled *The Horn*, was published in *Nugget*, one of the new men's magazines that were reaching a masculine audience that responded to the idea of itself as "hip." He found that the book wrote itself easily, with a flow that had eluded him in his struggles to achieve the density and moral obsessions of the European writers he admired. Holmes knew nothing about the turmoil of Kerouac's break-up with Weaver or his new relationship with Glassman, but to his pleased surprise, after many invitations Kerouac, Ginsberg, and Orlovsky took the train to Old Saybrook for a weekend visit. Betty Holmes was spending the winter in California, and after the visit John wrote her on

January 22, 1957, to tell her the surprising news that Kerouac had become a Buddhist.

> *[He] lives entirely like an itinerant poet, or even monk. With him on the train he bought everything he possesses: a few hardy, easily-kept-clean clothes on his back; an army knapsack with sleeping bag, cooking utensils, sewing kit, etc., and also a satchel of manuscripts which are still in progress. Last summer he spent all alone on the top of Desolation Mountain in the Great Cascades of Washington and Oregon, earning a little money as a government firewatcher. He has written part of a book about his two and a half months of absolute solitude. He will go to Africa with Allen (and a few others) and spend a few weeks there, and then go to Spain (somewhere in the south, a small village), get a rooftop (something he has been doing in Mexico), and think and work. We had fond, close hours over the weekend, and it was very good to see him again.*[30]

In Holmes' journal entry, he jotted down that during the weekend "the music was never off, the glasses were rarely empty, we played football in the snow, and Peter did perfect figure-eights on the ice-covered North Cove." Indoors in front of the fireplace, Holmes took out his tape recorder so everyone could read into it: "Allen did part of 'Howl,' Peter described his sexual initiation as a teenager, Jack read boozily from Shakespeare, and I read a section of Whitman's *Specimen Days* and a late doomy poem of Robinson Jeffers." It was Kerouac's best visit to Old Saybrook. Later Holmes recalled, "It was a fine time of friendship and fun, during which I snatched moments to read the first part of *Desolation Angels* and *Tristessa*, both still in manuscript. We all parted quenched and affectionate."[31]

With money for the first time Kerouac was determined to travel outside the United States. Burroughs, after his flight from Mexico, had finally settled in Tangier. It was a place where his interest in drugs and boys didn't arouse problems with the authorities. Kerouac decided to make Tangier his first stop on his journey, and Ginsberg and Orlovsky would meet him there. He sailed on February 15, and on March 8 the other two followed him. They photographed each other on the beach, swimming in their underwear while Burroughs, fully clothed, lay on the sand regarding them sardonically. Kerouac, however, was too restless to settle in Tangier. He soon left for Paris and London, and he was back in New York City by late April 1957.

From New York he traveled to Florida, where he persuaded Mémère, who had just begun receiving her social security checks so she could quit her factory jobs, to start another new life with him, this time in Berkeley.

It was like the disastrous trip he had undertaken years before when he had moved his mother, sister, brother-in-law, and their young son to Colorado to begin the simple life he had imagined in the West. The California trip was another effort to make a home close to the places where he had his friends. In May 1957 Kerouac and his mother made the tiring journey on Greyhound buses from Orlando, Florida, to Berkeley, California, fortified by aspirins and frequent nips of cheap bourbon. With the help of Philip Whalen, they settled into a shabby apartment on Dwight Way, near the Berkeley campus of the University of California. Since Gabrielle was afraid that her son would get involved in a drunken accident, she never allowed him to own a car, and Kerouac would soon feel marooned in the East Bay.[32]

On May 21, 1957, two weeks after they arrived in Berkeley, the police entered the City Lights book store in San Francisco, purchased a copy of *Howl and Other Poems*, and arrested the person behind the counter, Shig Murao, along with Ferlinghetti, for selling obscene literature. The trial went on through the summer, attracting national media attention as a series of literary figures defended the poem's importance. The mainstream publishers on the East Coast may have had their own reservations about Ginsberg's poem, but they noticed the attention aroused by the trial and the subsequent sales of the City Lights volume, as well as the dedication of the book mentioning Kerouac and listing his unpublished manuscripts, "eleven books written in half the number of years."[33] In a few months the publishers' scramble for Kerouac's books would begin, and his years of neglect were over.

On June 23, 1957, Kerouac wrote to Holmes about the new interest in his writing. "My very best 'wild' prose appearing at last." His lyric rhapsody of his life in a San Francisco skid-row hotel, "October in the Railroad Earth," would be appearing in *Evergreen Review*, "Neal & the Three Stooges" in *New Editions*, and his poetry would be published in *Measure*. Already bored in Berkeley, he complained that he was lonely and begged Holmes to write him. Holmes responded with a four-page letter filling in all the news of their friends in New York. Ginsberg and Orlovsky were still in Paris, but Kerouac's and Ginsberg's activity had become part of the general gossip that gathers quickly around new celebrities. Holmes' letter opened,

Heard news of your return from Europe via Alan H[arrington], via Edward S[tringham], via someone else. . . . Have read about you in Variety *of all places, who did a story on the Tangier scene, in which you, Bill and Allen were all mentioned as being found each day eating sumptuous 39¢*

meals in some sidewalk café or other . . . so have not been without news
exactly.[34]

Holmes could also report that the excitement was casting some light on
him as well.

How's this for weird? Ace Books has taken Go *for reprint, the only house*
that dared to do it, after Bantam paid me off (somewhat) and said they
wouldn't do it. . . . They had to cut it, not for sex or anything, but for length,
but I figure I can't kick, it keeps us alive, and who's to argue. . . . Also my
*queer little article "The Beat Generation" (*New York Times *years ago) is,*
for reasons I can't understand, going to be in an anthology to be used in
college English courses. How do you love that? And on and on. Even my
whorish Burl Ives has been reprinted, little or no dough, but who cares?[35]

When *On the Road* was published on September 5, 1957, Kerouac was living
again with Joyce Glassman on the Upper West Side. *The New York Times*
appeared on the newsstands the night before its morning editions, and he
and Joyce got out of bed to buy a paper because they'd heard it would include a review of his novel. It was by the same Gilbert Millstein who had
written the generally negative review of *Go* five years earlier. This was the
critic who had also commissioned Holmes to write an article on the term
"the Beat Generation" for the *New York Times* in 1952. Now more sympathetic to their lifestyle, Millstein heralded Kerouac's novel as a "historic
occasion," a "major novel," an "authentic work of art." In a paragraph of
Millstein's review of *On the Road*, he quoted Holmes' article approvingly:

He [Holmes] said, among many other pertinent things, that to his kind
"the absence of personal and social values . . . is not a revelation shaking
the ground beneath them, but a problem demanding a day-to-day solu-
tion." How to live seems to them much more crucial than why. He added
that the difference between the "Lost" and the "Beat" may lie in the latter's
"will to believe even in the face of an inability to do so in conventional
terms": that they exhibited "on every side and in a bewildering number of
facets a perfect craving to believe."[36]

Five years earlier, Millstein had criticized *Go* for what he considered
Holmes' romantic depiction of wasted lives, but Holmes' subsequent article
on the Beat Generation had taught the critic how to read *On the Road*. The
Times review was so complimentary that Glassman saw Kerouac looking

confused, as though he didn't really understand what it meant. The next morning, as she later wrote in her memoir *Minor Characters*, the phone began ringing and Jack was famous.[37]

Although other reviews of the novel were less enthusiastic—even the review in the daily edition of the *New York Times* was sourly critical—the book appeared on the paper's influential best-seller list, finally reaching ninth place. Less than a month later, on October 3, 1957, Judge Clayton W. Horn, presiding over the obscenity trial against *Howl and Other Poems* in San Francisco, announced his decision. He had taken considerable care reviewing the charges, even consulting the trial on the same charges against James Joyce's *Ulysses* thirty years earlier. Judge Horn's conclusion was that the issue was not a simple judgment about obscenity itself, but about a larger issue of social importance. Within the society there were things that could in themselves be obscene, and the issue was whether or not those things considered obscene in a work of literature that described these scenes or acts could be judged to have a value to the society it reflected.

Judge Horn ruled,

I do not believe that "Howl" is without redeeming social importance. The first part of "Howl" presents a picture of a nightmare world; the second part is an indictment of those elements in modern society destructive of the best qualities of human nature; such elements are identified as materialism, conformity, and mechanization leading to war. . . . "Footnote to Howl" seems to be a declamation that everything in the world is holy, including parts of the body by name. It ends with a plea for holy living.[38]

Judge Horn's conclusion that "Howl" was not obscene because the poem had "redeeming social value" was a landmark decision. It set a precedent that cleared the path for other banned books such as D. H. Lawrence's *Lady Chatterley's Lover*, Vladimir Nabokov's *Lolita*, and William Burroughs' *Naked Lunch*. As biographer Bill Morgan noted, "The *Howl* case was hailed as an important judicial decision upholding the constitutional amendments protecting the freedoms of speech and a free press. It was one of the first rays of hope for the country after the repressive McCarthy era."[39]

In the fall of 1957, what no one could have foreseen was that with the *Howl* trial and the success of *On the Road*, the crowd who had argued and partied in New York bars and spent nights talking about writing and listening to bop would *all* become famous. Kerouac quickly collapsed under the barrage of newspaper reporters and television interviewers eager to talk to the writer they considered the new Marlon Brando of literature.[40] As

Glassman recalled, he couldn't even bring himself to leave her apartment to attend a party Millstein gave to celebrate the publication of his novel. "He lay in bed shaking, and I had to phone and say he couldn't make it, he wasn't feeling too well."[41] When Millstein told her that Holmes had come to the party to see Kerouac, Jack asked his old friend "if he could leave the party for awhile. Holmes came uptown and sat with Jack, and he calmed down a little. He spoke to Holmes of not knowing who he was anymore."[42] Kerouac's inability to deal with his notoriety and its consequences was another continual torment that led to even more alcohol and even less control over his life.

It wasn't only Kerouac who felt the pressure, though as a spokesman, however unwilling, he could never evade the spotlight. Just as a tidal flood of water lifts all boats, the people in Kerouac's books and in his life suddenly found themselves famous. Neal Cassady's sexual exploits would become the subject of books and films, and Cassady himself, in part because of the notoriety of his role in *On the Road*, would find himself in prison on a drug charge. Herbert Huncke's fugitive writings would become published, reprinted, and studied in college classrooms, and the Times Square hustler would take on the mantle of literary respectability. Bill Cannastra's name would take on a new dimension as his death in the subway accident made its way into books and articles. Mary Carney, the girl from Kerouac's adolescence in Lowell whom he had fictionalized as "Maggie Cassidy," was brought into a light so blinding that for a time she intimated that a daughter she had born out of wedlock many years before was Kerouac's. Gary Snyder would try for years to distance himself from Kerouac's romantic portrait of him as "Japhy Ryder" in *The Dharma Bums*.

Holmes had been part of the Beat story from the beginning, and his role as their chronicler also gave him an immediate, and for a time a marketable, fame. He quickly became known as someone who had been there and who had had the prescience to write it all down.

The Holmes children: Liz, age 2, John, age 9, Lila, age 11, Englewood, New Jersey, 1935. Photo courtesy Lila Dizefalo.

On the beach at Peconic, Long Island, with assorted cousins: Lila at left, John in the middle wearing black trunks, their mother holding Liz in her arms, mid-1930s. Photo courtesy Elizabeth Van Vogt.

Liz and John, Chappaqua,
New York, spring 1943. Photo
courtesy Elizabeth Van Vogt.

Marian Milliambro, John's first wife, 1940s.
Photo courtesy Elizabeth Van Vogt.

John, Provincetown, Massachusetts, 1949. Photo courtesy John Clellon Holmes.

Neal Cassady, New York City bus terminal, 1946. Dodd Archive.

Bill Canastra, 1940s. Dodd Archive.

Jack Kerouac and Lucien Carr at Columbia University, summer 1944. Dodd Archive.

Go, 1952.

On the Road, 1957.

Go, Ace Books paperback reprint, 1957.

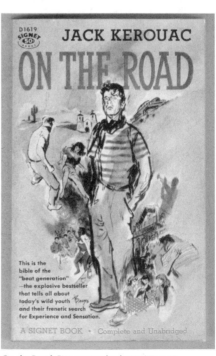

On the Road, Signet paperback reprint, 1930.

William Burroughs, Lucien Carr, Allen Ginsberg, New York City, 1953. Dodd Archive.

John Clellon Holmes and Shirley Allen on the day of their marriage, September 9, 1953, East Haddam, Connecticut. Photo courtesy Elizabeth Van Vogt.

The Horn, 1958.

From left to right: Jack Kerouac, Gregory
Corso, Allen Ginsberg, Julius Orlovsky,
Peter Orlovsky, in the Zocalo, Mexico City,
summer 1956. Dodd Archive.

Herbert Huncke and Allen Ginsberg, Lower East Side, New York City, 1966. Photo Ann Charters.

Allen Ginsberg and Ann Charters, 1966.
Photo Herbert Huncke.

Jack Kerouac, Hyannis, Massachusetts, 1967. Photo Ann Charters.

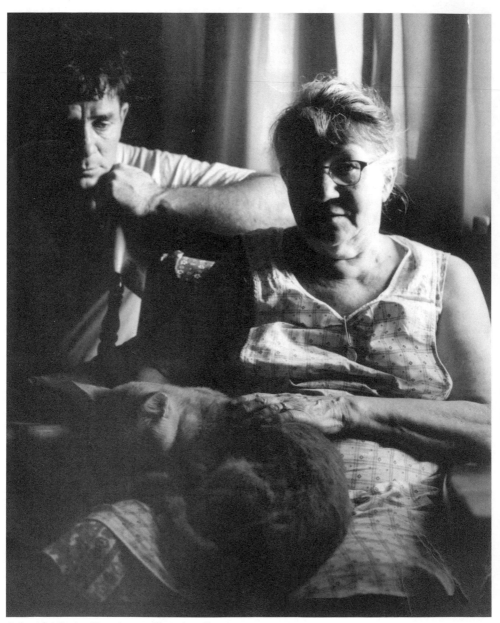

Jack with Mémère, Hyannis, 1967. Photo Ann Charters.

Jay Landesman's memoir, *Rebel
Without Applause*, 1987.

Jack with Shirley Holmes, Old Saybrook, Connecticut, 1967. Photo John Clellon Holmes.

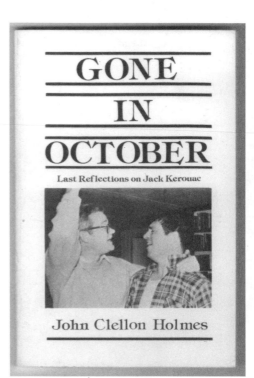

John Clellon Holmes

Gone in October, 1985. Photo of John and Jack in Old Saybrook by Shirley Holmes (1967).

At Kerouac's graveside, Lowell, Massachusetts: John Clellon Holmes, Allen Ginsberg, Gregory Corso, October 24, 1969. Photo Ann Charters.

John on the back steps, Old Saybrook, 1981. Photo Ann Charters.

John Clellon Holmes and Ann Charters on the back steps, Old Saybrook, 1981. Photo Samuel Charters.

From left to right: Carl Solomon, Samuel Charters, John Clellon Holmes, on the porch at Naropa, Boulder, Colorado, 1982. Photo Ann Charters.

John and Shirley at home in Old Saybrook, 1985. Photo Ann Charters.

John in **his** study reading a proof copy of *Visions of Cody*, Old Saybrook, 1985. Photo Ann Charters.

Chapter 15

WHAT AM I DOING HERE?

The hipster is victim of the most hopeless condition of slavery—the slave who does not know that he is a slave and is proud of his slavery, calling it "freedom." Incurable? Nearly. The posture of negation and passivity thinks it is religion and rebellion; instead it is a mob phenomenon. These Nihilists sail dreamy down the Nile of throughway America, spending many a sleepless day figuring out something real cool to do at night, and end up trying to convince themselves, as Jack Kerouac does, that Charlie Parker is God. Kerouac's birdmen in his novel On the Road, *search for coolness within their beatness, hipness within their jeans-and-dirty-hair dream of quickies with marvelous girls (who also wear dirty hair and jeans). Occasionally, as in the Kerouac variety of super frantic sub-hipster, sex takes the place of dope. This is a kind of sex which also takes the place of sex. The way some men gloat over possessions, he keeps score of his hero´s erotic blitzes, forgetting that—if you are the trooper who uses sex as a weapon—every notch in a weapon weakens the weapon.*

The hipster is a street-corner, bar, and partying phenomenon, a creature of mobs. One Rimbaud may be a genius; a crowd of them is a fad.
—HERBERT GOLD, "The Beat Mystique"[1]

In San Francisco Judge Horn may have found in his judicial opinion that *Howl* had "redeeming social value," but in hindsight he seems almost as detached from the mood of American society as Ginsberg and his friends were. The emergence of the Beat phenomenon in 1957 caused a furor that continued with unabated force through the next decades. At first, oblivious to the coming storm, Holmes and Kerouac were carried on a tide of their own satisfaction. They had always reassured each other that this moment might come, with recognition and some kind of financial reward—but the long years when success always hung just out of reach had dampened their optimism.

Less than a month after *On the Road*'s publication, Holmes finished his new jazz novel which he titled *The Horn*. He had written the first two chapters in 1952 and 1953, and he completed the rest of the book between the spring of 1956 and the fall of 1957. On October 10, 1957, he told Kerouac that he was waiting to hear from his agent about his manuscript's fate, but before he passed on the news of his own book he was lyric about Kerouac's book, the novel Holmes had championed for over six years. For him *On the Road* was a triumph.

> *Kudos pile up: Liz read your book and promptly wrote you a letter to Viking, which you may or may not have received. I don't know what she said, but she was flipped. Shirley (one of the deepest Kerouac-fans) seconds everything, and tells me to tell you how sorry she was to have missed you when you were in town. As for me . . . Of course, I have read it again, and is as I remember it. You are right: this book is really the book over which Viking haggled for all these years. The additions only amplify, the cuts do not detract. It is great, Jack, the heart always there, you always there. Far, far better than* The Town and the City, *albeit different. But freer, looser, a fat tone, a good ride to it.*[2]

Holmes felt that the portrayal of Neal Cassady as the character "Dean Moriarty" was one of the novel's strengths:

> *And Neal. . . . You have him, and more. You have created (or life has!) one of the first spiritual heroes in an American novel. He grows and grows! He is unaccountable, fascinating, profound, moving. Indeed, there are things here in the book which strike me as final, and I'm surprised that anyone understands them. The deep sense, particularly of the conversations (which one reviewer at least called incoherent), has grown on me every day since I finished it. It is good, and you must know it.*[3]

Holmes' summation was his realization that as the journeys took Kerouac back and forth across the United States, the setting of the novel expanded to include all of the country. "Your stage is an entire continent." His enthusiastic response to the book ended with his own evaluation: "I love it, Jack."[4]

Continuing his letter, Holmes was casual but satisfied about his own recently completed manuscript.

As for me, no word as yet. Too soon to expect it. MCA and I agreed to try Random House first. I once had an understanding with Hiram Hayden up there, and he might just dig it. . . . I think it has something about jazz, and jazzmen . . . and perhaps even human life, that hasn't been done. I love it anyway. It is full of prose, and for me at least daring, and it came out as I meant.[5]

He added, "By the way, months ago I dedicated it to Shirley and to you. If that is alright . . . any jazz book of mine has to be dedicated to you, because . . . you opened the door."[6]

Holmes concluded with a reverie of his mood of the recent days. For the first time he could feel himself part of a New England autumn without the anxieties and worries that had tormented him in his struggles to break past the deadlock in his writing since he'd moved to Connecticut. He and Shirley had taken a picnic to the beach to celebrate the finish of the book.

Two days ago, one of those warm, clear, fresh, apple-tart days when the trees are all fantastic splashes of wild colors, up to a promontory (an old cemetery) over water, with French bread, and good white, sharp cheese in hunks, and good fine clean red wine, and had our lunch like peasants, and then I smoked a pipe (wanting that taste), and dreamed and drifted and gabbled on the grass as Shirley sketched and communed with herself, until I finally napped wineilly [sic] there, addled by the sun, and had long, isolated, sweet thoughts, and we came home. A beautiful day it was, my first since the book . . . to just goof. But then you know what fall and October here can do; it fills one with rare, brief, smoky thoughts, and old imaginings.[7]

The surge of media interest that would flood over both Kerouac and Holmes had already begun to offer them its more obvious rewards. Holmes was approached by *Esquire* and offered a much higher sum than he was used to for another essay explaining the Beat Generation to the magazine's upscale readers. He felt some concern that Kerouac would be upset because once again he was taking on himself the role of a spokesman for something that he thought of as more Kerouac's than his own, but Kerouac was already talking to interviewers in his own attempts to answer the same questions. Holmes commented, in a presentiment of what Kerouac was to face for the rest of his life, "You have no idea how interested people are in any detail from your life, any detail about you. Or maybe you do." Holmes assured his friend that the article wouldn't be anything he wouldn't want to read. It would be "pro-beat, pro-Kerouac. I hope on God's side."[8]

By early October 1957 Kerouac had already left New York City and was living again with his mother, who had moved to a small apartment in Florida to be close to her daughter Caroline and her family. Kerouac spent his most of his days in the sun. He responded to Holmes' letter with a long ecstatic rap of his own, reverting to the limitless energies of the letters they had written each other nearly ten years before, again using alcohol as a prop. He crowed that his garden had grapefruit, oranges, and tangerines, and that one especially blessed tangerine had fallen on his head as he was reading a Buddhist text, the *Diamond Vow of God's Wisdom*. He insisted that Holmes should feel free to write anything he wanted for *Esquire*. His response to Holmes' rhapsodizing about the picnic was a wondering "How beautifully you write."[9] Then he followed with his plans for future books and an almost bewildered account of the media attention he was receiving. He added a note saying that he was going to write Hiram Hayden and tell him he should take Holmes' book.

On November 11, Kerouac followed up on his promise and wrote a note to Hayden praising Holmes' writing and adding that he hoped Hayden would take the manuscript.[10] Whether or not Hayden was responding to Kerouac's enthusiasm, he immediately purchased *The Horn* for Random House. The letter that Holmes sent Kerouac a month later was one of the most enthusiastic he ever wrote.

> *Great, good letter; good news throughout! Somebody is smiling, I guess, for all of us, because Random up and grabbed my book in just two and a half weeks after I (groggy and reeling and wore out) put down the last breathless and ecstatic words. MCA did a fast reading, and shot it off, and a little over two weeks later—they love it! Just back from New York where I spent much of a rainy afternoon with Hayden in his large office, looking out on 51st Street, and listening to some very flattering things. Little English secretaries scurrying in and out like country mice, bringing coffee, and looking at me shyly. . . . Hayden is nice, clear-headed, no bullshit, and only suggested that I do a little thinning in the first quarter of the book—a job he has left in specifics to me, and which will not take me more than a week at most, if that. "Don't cut too much now!" he said, and he wants to know just what I take out, for fear of losing (and this floored me) some of my "songs" (prose-poems on America, etc.).[11]*

The advance was small, only a thousand dollars, but John and Shirley had already decided to use it to make their long-delayed trip to Europe.

They had just met Alan Harrington, who had flown over to London to be there for the British publication of his novel *The Revelations of Dr. Modesto.* Harrington had steered clear of Holmes' close friendships with Kerouac, Ginsberg, and Cassady, though he shared their sense of alienation from the American mainstream and found them sympathetic company in small doses. As a satiric novelist in the tradition of Nathaniel West, he was an elegant prose stylist, and he was enjoying the success of his first novel after the years that had gone into writing it. Alan talked expansively of evenings of drinks with the new British novelist John Braine, and of night journeys and endless London parties. Everything that he described was what John and Shirley also hoped was waiting for them.

In a letter to George and Francesca Beaumont, married friends in London who had offered to put them up, Holmes wrote they planned to sail from New York on December 12, after he had completed some "thinning" of the first half of *The Horn.* By staying with the Beaumonts, they would save enough money to go on to the continent and visit some of the places Holmes had only dreamed about. Shirley had already spent a year in Italy, living in Rome, visiting Florence, and surviving a bad summer in Venice, but this would be John's first trip. Their ship would reach England on December 20, and in his letter to the Beaumonts he described the Christmas he hoped to experience with them.

> *At this moment, I can't see beyond the utter delight of Christmas in London, which has always been to me, due to an early, fatal exposure to Dickens, the one, great, single Christmas city in the Western world. And to spend it among the music, liquor, charm, conviviality which I will always associate with the Beaumonts is caviar to a very battle-weary general indeed.*[12]

In his optimistic rush of excitement Holmes instructed them to mail him a list of things they'd like him to bring over: "Books, clothes, cigarettes, Elvis Presley records, or something by the Modern Jazz Quartet, those four decorous, bearded wise men who have become so chic."[13]

The same day he wrote to the Beaumonts, he also wrote to his agent Phyllis Jackson at MCA, telling her that he had decided to use his full name for his writing. He had been asked to drop "John" Holmes by a literary magazine when he'd first begun to publish poetry in 1948, since at that time the poet John Holmes, who taught at Tufts University, was well known. Holmes wrote that though he usually felt that three names were one too many, he wanted his own name John back, but at the same time he had been Clellon Holmes on everything that had appeared in print for the past decade, so he felt he shouldn't drop it. In the future he would be John Clellon Holmes.

Shirley and John sailed from Newark on December 12, 1957, and after a six-day crossing they arrived at the Beaumont's flat in London. London, however, was not the experience Holmes had expected. He hadn't realized that the war had left such a pall over England. Few people outside of Britain understood that the effort of rebuilding the bomb-damaged cities and the battered transportation system, and dealing with the crippling foreign debt, while at the same time struggling to create a new, more democratic society under socialism, had drained the country's resources—physically, financially, and emotionally. Holmes wrote later that London was *gray*. "Gray faces pinched with austerity. Gray clothes making everyone look as anonymous as refugees. Miserly fires in the pubs. Roast beef and roast potatoes drowned in glutinous gravy. Green Park gray with coal smoke. Whitehall befogged with gray purpose."[14] The days were "perpetually murky, yellow, leprous, and the dim streets stank like so many pissoirs, dizzy with disinfectant."[15]

He was right about the acrid sting of smoke. In those years before England had begun to heat the houses and apartment flats and to cleanse the effects of the industrial emissions, the smell of coal smoke hung in the air over every English village and city. Like most Americans Holmes hadn't understood what the country had endured. He and Shirley did some of the usual tourist things: they looked at the Elgin marbles, but Holmes was more excited by Karl Marx's manuscript of *Das Kapital* on display in a glass case at the British Library. Shirley was moved by the Turner paintings in the Tate Gallery, though there were fewer to see than they had expected. Holmes was dismayed by the pessimism of the new writers. His response to Lawrence Olivier's brilliant portrayal of the seedy music-hall artist Archie Rice in John Osborne's *The Entertainer* was a complaint that Osborne "had portrayed Britannia as no better than a *Follies*-girl pretending to be Valerie Hobson."[16] Their first days in England were so depressing he compared them to having to eat Christmas dinner in one of London's cheap chain restaurants.

He had even higher expectations for their journey to France in the Beaumont's car, but it was winter, and Paris in the winter has little of the charm of the popular songs. Holmes found "a clammy touch of the morgue to Parisian streets in winter."[17] To add to his discomfort he wasn't well. "I had gotten trivially sick, and slumped around the bitter quays, telling myself that I didn't feel rotten, and feeling rotten anyway."[18] They held out for four days, then abandoned Paris for the south, driving down to the Riviera at St. Tropez. Their days there were pleasanter.

On their return to England, John and Shirley elected to leave London, and they stayed alone for a week in a small village on the coast of Dorset. In the country they could leave London's gray streets behind them, and they fell into a comfortable mood of muddy walks to look at the sea and warm nights in a local pub. One night John held Shirley in his arms as she wept with pleasure at the kindness they'd been shown by the pub's regulars. They took the good memory of Dorset back with them when they returned to New York at the beginning of February, and in letters to his friends Holmes insisted that the trip had done everything he had hoped it would do for him. At least it had cleared his mind of the deadening effects of the long struggle to revive his long-stalled writing career.

Holmes' absence from the United States, even for only two months, also gave him some perspective on the new commercial exploitation of the idea of "the Beat Generation." On February 20, 1958, he turned to his journal and clarified his reaction to the new media attention in an extended, and pre-scient, entry. After reading articles that had appeared in the national press confidently explaining the new Beat Generation to their curious readers, he wrote:

> I got the strange feeling as I read about the antics of these "beat" people at these supposedly "beat parties" that Jack, Allen G., and I had created something out of our heads quite casually to fit a need we felt, that it had validity, and that it still does as a perception (particularly the ideas and attitudes ends of it), but that it had suddenly become fashionable and everyone was copying the most exterior forms of it, not understanding, falsifying it, weirding it up terribly. It's rather like hearing a casual saying of yours suddenly repeated on every chic lip all over the country. I tried to imagine Jack or myself at one of these parties: we would strike all these people as terribly un-cool, un-hip, and un-beat, as they understand it. All things fester and get out of hand.[19]

As Holmes considered how he could make use of his new insights in the writing he was planning over the next months, he broadened his perspective:

> I would never had suspected how little the pundits of the world seem to realize about the state of the world today—in the big picture. Why

is it only the young people know it is rotten? Not just any jazz about capitalism, conformity, the cold war, and all that; but indeed the entire content of rationalist, scientific-oriented western civilization which has been steadily and without halt atrophying the souls of men. . . . But then I suppose that is a big bite for most of them to swallow.[20]

A few days later he went back to his journal, measuring the response of the critics against what he felt was the creative accomplishment of himself and his friends. Holmes understood that what they were attempting was an unprecedented challenge to the literary assumptions of virtually everyone else who considered themselves writers. Even today, with the Beat Generation conventionally categorized under the general heading of "Nostalgia," the ideas behind Beat writing are as threatening as they were several decades ago.

Out of fear, as the night the day, hatred inevitably comes. I see that in the . . . reactions to Kerouac, Ginsberg, et cetera. . . . They fear these people; it is more than disagreeing with them. They feel an undisciplined, anarchic power in them; and more, perhaps, a kind of creative certainty that (far more than the distaste over the material and the disapproval of the mindlessness) affronts them. Kerouac and Ginsberg, to all the reviewers, are perfectly "outrageous" to believe these things, to come out and say them, to be able to get them published, to have people taking them (even facetiously) seriously. It is best summed up this way: "If they're right, I'm wrong."[21]

Holmes' conclusion was more an expression of his disappointment than the anger and the disillusion that he felt.

How difficult it is for people to understand something for which they are not emotionally or intellectually prepared. How sad this is. . . . It speaks highly for education, for the continuing efforts of the mind to conquer new realities, strange attitudes, new approaches. How sad it is to consider how few intelligent and creative people are capable of this effort.[22]

The "Beat frenzy" sweeping over Holmes and Kerouac had surfaced at the poetry reading in San Francisco at the Six Gallery on October 7, 1955, when Ginsberg read the first part of *Howl*, but it had gained momentum with the publication of *On the Road* and the *Howl* obscenity trial, which was covered by *Life* magazine. On the West Coast poetry readings to jazz accompaniment mushroomed in Bay Area clubs and art galleries, where Lawrence Ferlinghetti announced "the *resocialization* of poetry" as writers took poetry off the printed page and conceived it as "oral messages."[23] The second issue of the new magazine *Evergreen Review*, published by Grove Press in New York City, devoted its entire issue to the "San Francisco scene," featuring poetry and prose by Henry Miller, Ginsberg, and Kerouac—who weren't part of the scene—as well as Kenneth Rexroth, Robert Duncan, Ferlinghetti, Michael McClure, Philip Whalen, and several others who were.

The word "Beat" suggested breaking established literary and social rules, but it was so vague that people could interpret it to mean whatever they wanted it to mean. As Joyce Johnson understood, "It began as a code word among friends, and then it got widely dissimilated after the publication of *On the Road*."[24] Soon the word's connotations – whether cultural, political, social, musical, or literary—depended on the person using it. For example, in number eleven of the widely circulated paperback anthology *New World Writing*, Rexroth wrote an essay analyzing "Disengagement: The Art of the Beat Generation," in which he noted with approval that the adjective "Beat" referred to a "younger generation culture pattern characterized by total rejection of the official high-brow culture."[25] A short time later Henry Miller wrote a sympathetic preface to Kerouac's *The Subterraneans*, which followed *On the Road* early in 1958, in which Miller concluded, "Let the poets speak. They may be 'beat,' but they're not riding the atom-powered Juggernaut. Believe me, there's nothing clean, nothing healthy, nothing promising about this age of wonders—except the telling. And the Kerouacs will probably have the last word."

Commercial interests were quick to hype the latest fad as early as November 1957, only two months after the publication of *On the Road*, when Atlantic Records linked their jazz musicians Charlie Mingus, Milt Jackson, and the Modern Jazz Quartet to what the record company called "the jazz-cum-poetry movement out in San Francisco."[26] The ad boasted that "Atlantic is the label in tune with the BEAT generation. We produce the music with the BEAT for you."[27] Publishers also rushed in to announce the latest literary sensation. Dell, a New York mass-market paperback publisher, brought out a fifty-cent anthology, *The Beat Generation and the Angry Young Men*, that sold all the copies of its first printing in a month. It featured the writing of Holmes, Kerouac, and Ginsberg, along with those whom the editors considered their English counterparts—novelists and playwrights such as Colin Wilson, Kingsley Amis, John Wain, and John Osborne. In the anthology they were all presented as "Rebels Without a Cause."

A product of the Age of Anxiety, this is today's writer: the HIPSTER, a man without a country—who digs everything and is shocked by nothing—whose greatest demand upon society is that it permits him to indulge in his own "kicks" unmolested. . . . [T]hese Beat and Angry young men are the logical spokesmen for our confused and confusing atomic age. Out of its chaos they have fashioned some of the most brilliantly dynamic literature of our time.[28]

After the lively spate of gunshots fired to announce the lineup of the new Beat poetry and fiction, the sound of the heavy canons leveled by influential mainstream critics against what they considered the latest—and unmistakably threatening—literary fad was deafening. In the spring of 1958 the cultural commentator Norman Podhoretz was one of the first to attack the new writers whom he labeled "The Know-Nothing Bohemians" in the leading American intellectual journal *Partisan Review.*[29] In September 1958 Robert Brustein went after Kerouac and Ginsberg and the other so-called poets of the San Francisco renaissance, attacking "the adolescent quality" of their rebellion in his article "The Cult of Unthink" in *Horizon* magazine.[30] Gilbert Highet, a professor of classics at Columbia University, gave a radio talk explaining that Beat meant "frantic and exhausted" and assuring his listeners that the members of the group weren't Communists. Instead Highet considered them anarchists who were a "disparate minority, eccentric, and to many normal eyes perfectly invisible."[31] His talk was printed and distributed to tens of thousands of readers throughout the United States who were members of the Book-of-the-Month Club.

Even Holmes' friend, the journalist Herbert Gold, took a swing at the Beats in a *Playboy* article in February 1958, only a few months after the publication of Kerouac's novel. Gold was forced to use the unsatisfactory word "hipster" to define the phenomenon since the appearance of the more useful term "beatnik" was still a few months away.

The hipster teases himself toward the black battiness of oblivion, and all the vital refreshment which religion has given the mystics of the past is a distraction from the lovely stupor he craves. Unlike Onan, who spilled his seed on the ground, the hipster spills his brains and calls it piety. He also wears music, art, and religion as a kind of badge for identification. Instead of the secret handshake which got him into Uncle Don's Boys' Club or the Orphan Annie Secret Society, he now says, "You dig Bird? Proust? Zen?"[32]

Although the puritanical tone of most of Gold's polemic suggests a young writer's envy at someone else's success, his long attack felt like a betrayal, since Holmes had talked to Gold and felt that they understood each other. On February 20, 1958, Holmes wrote in his journal,

> *Gold says pretty much what Highet said. He says it more intelligently, with much more savvy and inside dope, but it amounts to the same thing: escapism, unmotivated laziness, stupidity. He emphasizes the drug-thing out of proportion, but then that's his kick. Basically he says: "These punks, unlike Rimbaud, Van Gogh, Villon, etc. haven't earned their right to be the way they are. They haven't suffered poverty, prejudice, and class-hatred." Which, of course, so wildly misses the point that there's no discussing it.*[33]

One of Gold's points was that the classic authors of rebellion had "picked themselves up by the seat of their pants" as an act of rejection against their own society, something he felt the Beats hadn't done themselves. Holmes disagreed with him:

> *The beat-kids are self-exiled, alright; they have, precisely and exactly, picked themselves up by the seat of their jeans and thrown themselves out of society, in exactly the same way that Rimbaud, Villon, Van Gogh, and the others did—none of whom were forced out, excluded, etc. Kerouac would love to have the world love and understand his work, just as Van Gogh and Rimbaud would have loved it, but in exactly the same way the world does not really understand, much less love or accept his work. If the beat-kids were exiled and angry because of poverty, callous hatred, and the rest they wouldn't be interesting or symptomatic at all. They'd just be more victims. Their personal, unmotivated (from Gold's sociologist-psychologist way of thinking) rejection of society is profound, interesting, and symptomatic, for the precise reason that its reason is very, very much deeper than economics or ego emotions.*[34]

By far the most successful effort to belittle the Beats occurred on April 2, 1958, when journalist Herb Caen coined the world "Beatnik" in his *San Francisco Chronicle* column to describe the bohemians hanging around the North Beach bars and coffee houses who refused to take a job. Caen had been inspired by the nickname of the Russian satellite "Sputnik" that had succeeded in being the first launch in space, an embarrassing defeat for the United States during the Cold War. The derogatory nickname "Beatnik" quickly became popular, softening the outlines of the vaguely threatening word "Beat" with its troubling social connotations of poverty, unemployment, drugs, and crime.

With the usual speed with which a new trend can be commercially exploited, suddenly the rush was on to ridicule the new bohemianism. Novelty stores sold black berets, long plastic cigarette holders, and fake goatees associated in the popular mind with 1920s "Lost Generation" bohemianism so people could supposedly dress like Beatniks and throw Beatnik parties with gallons of cheap wine, jazz records on the turntable, and mattresses on the floor in case any of the girls were willing. One of the endless stream of popular Elvis Presley movies presented a "Beatnik chick" who wore the obligatory black toreador pants and read poetry. Suburban couples who had moved out of the city could "rent a Beatnik" for their parties, if they wanted to be part of the latest fad.

After "Beat" became "Beatnik," it was definitely time for Holmes and Kerouac to move on. In Kerouac's journal on February 11, 1960, he wrote that he was convinced that the "Beatnik" movement had been taken over by Leftists and it was no longer possible to experience the original idea of beatific joy which he felt had been exemplified by Sal Paradise in *On the Road*, Ginsberg in *Howl*, Cassady in his letters, and Hart Kennedy in *Go*.[35]

In a painful memoir written several years later, Holmes caught the tempo of the storm that had engulfed Kerouac. He saw the insistence of some of Kerouac's readers to drag him into their fantasy of his life, and he understood that Kerouac was helpless to defend himself against them.

They tended to drive their cars more recklessly when he was with them, as if he was "Dean Moriarty," and not the Kerouac who hated to drive and whom I had once seen crouching on the floor of a car, in a panic, during a drunken, six-hour dash from New York to Provincetown. They plied him with drinks, they created parties around him, they doubled the disorder in the hope of catching his eye, and so never glimpsed the Kerouac who once confessed to me: "You know what I'm thinking when I'm in the midst of all that—the uproar, the boozing, the wildness? I'm always thinking: What am I doing here? Is this the way I'm supposed to feel?" They pecked at him as if he was some Petronius Arbiter of cool, detached hipness, and saw, to their confusion, a man who always turned the volume up, who tapped his feet and exulted, and loathed the hostility for which coolness was a mask. They saw the seeker after continuity who, no matter how rootless his life may seem, has always known that our anguish is uprootedness. Wherever he went he was confronted by that other man. Once in

L.A., alone in a coffee house, he tried to strike up a conversation with the guy behind the counter, saying "Hey, I'm Jack Kerouac. Let's have a talk or something," to which the guy replied with hip disdain, "Sure you are. They all say that."[36]

Cassady had already paid the price for the glare of attention that was cast on him by the sentimentality that filled the pages of *On the Road.* On April 8, 1958, he was arrested for possession of narcotics, held in prison for a week, and released for insufficient evidence. Although there are suggestions that he might have been set up by narcotics police following the attention he received in the novel, the truth was that Cassady had been selling marijuana more or less openly for years. He was arrested again the next morning on new charges, and after a complete mishandling of the case by the public defender he used instead of hiring a lawyer, he was sentenced to five years in the federal penitentiary in San Quentin. The charges this time were intent to sell, and the judge described Cassady as San Francisco's major supplier. On July 20, 1958, his wife, Carolyn, wrote a sad letter to Ginsberg, attempting to explain what she felt was her part in what had happened when she refused Neal's plea to mortgage their house to put up the money for his bail.

The first time he got a great PD [public defender], but the second and last time got a bum. His bail was set at $28,000. He had this reduced and tried to get me to put up the house to get him out. I must have lost my mind maybe, but I didn't. I didn't because he was so wild. The first time he had been real calm about it and had been a savior in the jail. The second time he got violent and kept yelling about some mysterious 100,000 dollars he had to get out and get. If he hadn't said that I'd not have been so worried about him and done it. He sounded so unlike himself, I was a sissy and feared he'd do something worse and we would have lost the house, the only thing the kids had left. I was probably wrong, and I don't blame him for being mad; since which time I have seen some of the things that maddened him, and I'm even madder. Anyway, he has forgiven me and understands my stupidity.[37]

Cassady was released on appeal on June 3, 1960, after serving two years in the penitentiary. He was placed on parole, under supervision for the remaining three years of his sentence. Gary Snyder, another of the friends who had found himself in an unwelcome spotlight after his appearance of one of Kerouac's books, also spent years untangling himself from the

character of "Japhy Ryder," the name Kerouac gave him in his idealized portrait in *The Dharma Bums*. Unlike Cassady, Snyder had already dealt with
the situation by moving to Japan. He spent years with his studies in a Zen
monastery, where no one banged on his window begging him to go camp-
ing in the mountains.

In the summer of 1958, at the height of the media attention, Allen Ginsberg
and Peter Orlovsky had returned from Europe and were living in an apartment they rented at 170 East Second Street in New York's old tenement
neighborhood on the Lower East Side. Ginsberg was also drawn into the
frenzy that had swirled up around the idea of the Beat Generation, but
Ginsberg, who had always felt a need for attention, realized that the situation was an unexpected opportunity. It became the platform from which
he could present his own views on American society, and he could also
lobby for social changes, such as the legalization of drugs and the lifting of
criminal penalties for homosexual acts.

People came and went in the apartment. Ginsberg visited publishers;
got offers to read at Columbia, Harvard, Yale, and Princeton; advocated
the legalization of marijuana on radio talk shows; and gave copies of *Howl*
to musicians he idolized, like Thelonius Monk, whose response was, "It
makes sense."[38] On February 14, 1959, after his Columbia reading, Ginsberg
wrote approvingly to Burroughs that "the Beatnik-poetry reading thing has
swelled to monstrous proportions."[39]

At the same time, Ginsberg was uneasy at the exploitation of their ideas
by Kerouac's new book, *The Dharma Bums*, published in the summer of
1958, though there were things he approved about it. Six months earlier
Kerouac had written it at the insistence of his editor at Viking Press and his
new agent Sterling Lord, who seemed to have in mind a series of sequels
to *On the Road* something like the Tarzan books. Ginsberg sent a letter to
Kerouac after he read an advance copy of the new novel on August 20. He
had immediately noticed that *The Dharma Bums* had been written in the
linear prose style Kerouac had tried to leave behind him in the revisions
of *On the Road* after its initial rejection in 1951. Ginsberg asked his friend,
"You settling down in simpler prose, or just tired like you said?" He thought
the characters based on their Berkeley friends John Montgomery and Gary
Snyder were well done, but he was less satisfied with the persona Kerouac
had created for Ginsberg himself: "I don't dig myself (too inconsistent mentally) (in the arguments)." Ginsberg asked Kerouac,

> *I say, perhaps Viking and Lord are neglecting your good books and try-
> ing to get you to write "potboilers" according to their idea of what your*

*writing career should develop like. . . . My opinion—don't let Madison
Avenue try [to] water you down and make you palatable to reviewers
Mentality by waiting on Wildbooks and putting out commercial travel-
ogues (however good)—Sax is logical next book and you're in a position
to do what you want.*[40]

At the same time that the concepts of Beat and Beatitude were being attacked, a question lurked in the background behind all of the media attention. It is still a question that is raised today. Why did *On the Road* become
a kind of road map for an abrupt swing in American attitudes and mores?
In part the question had already been answered by the success of an earlier
novel of youthful alienation and despair that became one of the best-selling
books of its time, *Catcher in the Rye.*

One of the saddest moments in modern American literature comes on
the last pages of J. D. Salinger's novel, which in many ways prefigured the
themes of Kerouac's novel. It was published in book form in 1951, a year
before *Go* and seven years before *On the Road* appeared—however briefly—on the *New York Times'* best-seller list.[41] Salinger's protagonist, sixteen-
year-old Holden Caulfield, is one of the first disaffected postwar teenagers
seeking an alternate path through the maze of American life. At the start
of the novel Caulfield has been thrown out of his latest school, and he's
decided he won't go back home. After a futile, frustrating weekend in New
York City, he's gotten up from a sick bed and he's leaving town. His plan is
to take a bus through the Holland Tunnel to New Jersey, where he'll start
bumming rides and hitchhike out to the west where he'll build a cabin close
to a forest and live alone. It was the dream that later Kerouac described in
his own book.

Before Caulfield leaves to begin hitchhiking rides, he decides he has
to say good-bye to his little sister, Phoebe. He leaves a note at her school,
asking her to meet him at the Metropolitan Museum. Phoebe idolizes her
older brother. When they meet he sees that she has packed all her things
into a huge suitcase and is straining under its weight as she walks along
Fifth Avenue. She is determined to leave with him. As the afternoon passes
they argue and he checks her suitcase and takes her to the Central Park
Zoo, then sits in a driving rainstorm watching her go around and around
on the merry-go-round. At the end of the afternoon he's too sick to go off
on his planned journey, and in the final paragraphs he tiredly goes home
and realizes that he'll probably return to school in September.

If Holden Caulfield had suffered from the same turmoil and confusion
only seven years later, he would have known what to do. The pages of *On
the Road* would have given him an idea of what happens when you leave

Manhattan, go through the Holland Tunnel to New Jersey, and try to bum rides out to the mythic American west. Holden Caulfield's dreams of hitch-hiking out west and building a cabin to live the life of a quiet recluse was the dream Kerouac had proposed for himself since his own teenage years. Until he wrote his novel most rebellious American teenagers had no idea how to begin the journey themselves.

Today the publication of On *the Road* seems to signal a breakthrough, a turning point, but it wasn't the Beats who first defined the malaise that seemed to many others to effect American society at mid-century, what Holmes had described as the "rationalist, scientific-oriented western civi-lization which has been steadily and without halt atrophying the souls of men."[42] There had already been a stream of books by American intellectu-als heaving with frustration and disappointment at the 1950s, when the arms race with the Soviets during the Cold War became the official excuse to justify the development of a military industrial complex in the United States. Gradually red-baiting became a national pastime, and conformity the official rule. The title of Sloan Wilson's best-selling novel *The Man in the Gray Flannel Suit*, published in 1955, became an epigraph for the postwar conformist American way of life.

The outcry from the people who didn't choose to be part of the Beat rebellion—the social majority—was loud and cynical. As a result of the years of unrelenting, invidious attacks on the Beats and the commercial ex-ploitation of what was taken to be their lifestyle, it was as though Thoreau, in many ways their model, had walked outside his cabin at Walden Pond one morning and found a paved parking lot alongside his pond and a new motel on the road to Concord putting his mother's boardinghouse out of business.

In the spring of 1958, Holmes became concerned that a problem had arisen between Kerouac and himself over the media attention that On the Road had stirred up. He wrote Kerouac a long note on June 19, quietly insisting that he was going his own way as a writer, and that there was nothing for the two of them to quarrel about. Holmes was worried that in the glare of attention directed toward them, he and Kerouac were being considered as spokespersons who could be used interchangeably for the interviews and comments that made their way into the press and magazine coverage. His note was in one sense his statement of aesthetic independence from Ker-ouac, but it also was his clarification for himself of the different ways each of them would go over the next years without losing the sense of the spiri-tual closeness that had always characterized their relationship. Perhaps it was significant that after Holmes wrote the note and signed it, he scrawled on top, "Not sent." He had written it as much for himself as he'd written it for his friend.

The note opened with his wry comment that the publication of *The Horn*, promised for June, had been delayed again. In the interim Hiram Hayden, his editor at Random House, had asked Kerouac for a statement for the book jacket.

> *So June too dies, and I am informed by phone that Hiram sent you proofs, asking for a comment, and I really didn't want that, and was not told of it until it was too late, and heard your comment too—for which, in any case, I thank you. But our skeins are awfully tangled, Jack, and I can sense your irritation, and believe me I don't want a hitch-hike to anyone else's Valhalla—that's for sure, and also don't want this BG [Beat Generation] left with me; I am, as you must know, just as chagrined to be paid attention to now simply because of your success and the accidents of time, but who can help that? And I have never fostered it. I don't mind being Bailliol MacJones in your books, because I know you, Jack, and how you think, and how tangled it becomes; but I don't want a ride on any star, and whatever I have to say is my own things, as I hope you know.*[43]

It was important for Holmes to emphasize that although they had traded manuscripts and read each other's writing years before, there was no way his writing could be influenced by Kerouac's at this point. "I haven't seen enough of you to any longer, even unconsciously, be influenced by you, or steal your stuff, or anything else; and from now on what I will do, and what you will do, probably will have no more relation than that we write of the same world."[44] Holmes was also conscious that the articles he'd been asked to write could be a sensitive point with Kerouac, since they had talked out so many of the ideas in those tireless nights at 681 Lexington when they got so excited at what they were saying that, as Kerouac put it, they "used to slop beer on each other's knees."[45]

Holmes made it clear that it was annoying for him to be left with the feeling after some of the requests for interviews that he was only being approached as a substitute for Kerouac, who was more difficult to locate.

> *I don't like to be called to substitute for Kerouac on radio and TV, and have turned all this down (quite a lot of it since that damned anthology came out) [The Beat Generation and the Angry Young Men] for that reason, wanting The Horn to appear before I spoke to anyone about*

*anything, believing it would make me clear; and not really wanting to
talk anyway.*[46]

The article that had caused Holmes to write to Kerouac appeared in the
February 1958 issue of *Esquire* and brought him a much wider audience
than he'd had for his first essay on the Beat Generation six years earlier in
the *New York Times*. Holmes' new article, titled "The Philosophy of the Beat
Generation," was longer and more diffuse, though it emphasized some of
the same points. This time Holmes began by quoting from Millstein's review
of *On the Road*, repeating his assertion that Kerouac's novel was "likely to
represent the present generation" just as Hemingway's *The Sun Also Rises*
represented the 1920s. Then Holmes offered a succinct definition of "Beat"
that often would be quoted by subsequent commentators: "To be beat is
to be at the bottom of your personality, looking up, to be existential in the
Kierkegaard, rather than the Jean-Paul Sartre, sense."[47] Holmes insisted that
to compensate for their sense of feeling "emptied out," the Beats' response
to the hypocrisies and tensions of postwar life in the United States was to
make an inner spiritual journey. Members of the Beat Generation were on
a quest, and "if they seemed to trespass most boundaries, legal and moral,
it was only in the hope of finding a belief on the other side."[48]

The next month, in its March 1958 issue, *Esquire* ran Kerouac's expansive explanation of the meaning of the Beat Generation, "Aftermath: The
Philosophy of the Beat Generation," written the previous summer for Pa-
tricia MacManus, the publicist at Viking Press. Presented as a historical
overview, Kerouac offered a much more romantic view of his subject. He
objected to what he felt was Holmes' unnecessary emphasis on delinquency
and criminality in the Beat Generation as epitomized by the inarticulate
high school dropout and the leather-jacketed motorcyclist portrayed by
actors James Dean and Marlon Brando in the popular films *Rebel Without
a Cause* and *The Wild Ones*. Kerouac began by crediting Holmes and Ginsberg for sharing his initial vision of a generation of wild hipsters flinging
themselves across American, "beautiful in an ugly graceful new way" that
had never been seen before.[49] The word itself he insisted was now heard
everywhere.

In the article Kerouac explained that in the late 1940s the Beat Generation had few members and was short lived, disappearing only a few
years after its emergence. Ginsberg had chronicled their wasted lives in the
first part of his poem "Howl for Carl Solomon." Then "by some miracle of
metamorphosis, suddenly, the Korean post-war youth emerged cool and
beat, had picked up the gestures and the style, soon it was everywhere."[50]

Bop became popular, then rock and roll; hipster slang like "go" and "crazy" drifted into common usage; and "drugs were available everywhere (including tranquilizers such as Valium."[51] Kerouac concluded his article by leaving the reader with a casual question that needed no answer: in the "sunset of our culture," the effect of the Beat Generation has "taken root," but he asked with a final shrug, "What difference does it make?"[52]

Holmes finally received his first copies of *The Horn* in July 1958, probably the least promising month of the year in the publishing calendar. The reviewers are away, the potential readers are distracted by vacations, and the fall season is waiting, when all the excitement begins. Publishing a novel like *The Horn* in July is like opening a window and dropping the book on to the sidewalk in the hopes that someone will pick it up. The publisher had obviously decided that its audience would be the jazz world, though they overestimated the size of this world and printed eight thousand copies.

Probably to keep his mind off the delayed publication of his second novel, Holmes spent time making notes for his next book, the final part of the trilogy he felt he had begun with *Go* and continued in his still unpublished novel *Perfect Fools*. This last part was to correspond to Dante's *Paradiso*. Holmes' working title for the manuscript was *Calk*. When he dropped a note to Kerouac on July 16, 1958, and wrote a longer letter to a friend Gene Baro on July 23, he was able to deal with the tepid responses of the first reviewers of *The Horn* by talking about his next book. Baro had been asked to review the novel for one of the New York newspapers. In Holmes' letter to Kerouac he noted that he wasn't experiencing the same emotional storm he had gone through with the publication of *Go* six years earlier, and he thanked Kerouac for the endorsement he had sent to Hiram Hayden.

> *Thanks for the puff. Don't know whether they'll use it or not, but the thought was good. The book comes out in a day or so; the two reviews I've seen have been anything but raves, though they seem to take it seriously enough; but I'm not concerned, being deep in new things, and finding the second time around isn't half as bad as the first.[53]*

When Holmes wrote Baro a week later, *The Horn* had finally been published, and there had been additional reviews that John felt positive about:

> *The book is out now, and enough reviews in for me to get some idea of the way it will probably go critically: (1) There hasn't been a pan yet; those that are not restrained raves, at least take it seriously; most have pointed*

out that it is authentic, and the "best" [jazz novel] since The Young Man
with a Horn. *(2) The Beat Generation tag has been either ignored (it having nothing to do with the book), or mentioned only in passing, for which
I am grateful.*[54]

Holmes also jokingly thanked Baro for his review in the *Herald Tribune*.
"The very best review so far has been in the *Tribune* for last Sunday, written by Gene Baro (do you know him? I don't), the lead fiction review, and
an outright direct hit. I was awestruck and humbled to read how deeply he
had dug 'the little lower levels' of the book." Holmes' final comment was a
laconic, "All in all, I'm pleased—and that's that."[55]

Jay Landesman was so enthusiastic about *The Horn* that he spent a half
hour reading from it on St. Louis radio, and he sent Holmes an excited letter, a "rave" as Holmes described it to Baro, and there were "lots of calls" to
the station after the reading. Holmes also mentioned to Baro that he had
seen Landesman during a quick trip to New York, though he was so rushed
that they had time only for a day of their old partying. In the course of
their celebrating Jay somehow procured a pith helmet, which he wore on a
somewhat unsteady walk up Fifth Avenue.

Though Holmes was able to deal with the tempered response to *The
Horn* in the weeks after the reviews had begun to accumulate, it was to
have an effect on the writing he was planning over the next months. He had
written the book in what for him was a short period of time—a little over
a year—and on the surface it was a story about the last day in a troubled
jazz musician's life. The novel, however, was more complex than most of its
reviewers—or its readers—realized. On a structural level it has the distinction of being the only "novel" that he or Kerouac was to write. With *The
Horn* Holmes had tried for something more complicated than the autobiographical "picaresque romances," which is perhaps the most helpful description of Kerouac's fiction. Holmes had attempted a book that was more
layered emotionally and structurally, and the pitch of the language and the
shape of the characters were drawn with this larger dimension in his mind.
Kerouac immediately understood that it was "more cerebral" than any book
Holmes had written earlier.[56] Whatever Holmes wrote his friends, he had
to be affected by the critical reading that praised it only as a "jazz novel."
Sketched on a larger canvas, it was much more ambitious than that, and it
was to be the last book he would attempt to write like it.

Chapter 16

THE HORN

Edgar Pool blew methodically, eyes beady and open, and he held his tenor saxophone almost horizontally extended from his mouth. This unusual posture gave it the look of some metallic albatross caught insecurely in his two hands, struggling to resume flight. In those early days he never brought it down to earth, but followed after its isolated passage over all manner of American cities, snaring it nightly, fastening his drooping, stony lips to its cruel beak, and tapping the song. It had a singularly human sound—deep, throaty, often brutal with a power that skill could not cage, an almost lazy twirl on the phrase ends: strange, deformed melody. When he swung with moody nonchalance, shuffling his feet instead of beating, even playing down to the crowd with scornful eyes averted, they would hear a wild goose honk beneath the tone—the noise, somehow, of the human body; superbly, naturally vulgar; right for the tempo. And then out of the smearing notes, a sudden shy trill would slip, infinitely wistful and tentative.
—JOHN CLELLON HOLMES, *The Horn*[1]

Often with ambitious novels it is difficult to trace the structure that lies beneath the events of the narrative or the descriptions of each character's idiosyncrasies. With his brilliant, troubling testament to jazz, *The Horn*, however, Holmes wrote detailed notes on what he was attempting to do. Any reading of the novel has to be done with an awareness of what he considered its creative intentions as well as his book's ultimate achievement. Holmes wrote at length about the conception of the novel in a letter on July 25, 1977, to Richard K. Ardinger, who had become interested in the Beats as a student and was compiling Holmes' bibliography.

The real origin of the book . . . lay in my feeling that the jazz artist was the quintessential American artist—that is, that his work-hang-ups, his personal neglect by his country, his continual struggle for money, the debasement of his vision by the mean streets, his ofttimes descent into drugs, liquor, and self destructiveness—all this seemed to me to typify the experience of our great 19th Century American writers: Poe's loneliness, drunkenness and obscurity; Melville's half-of-life anonymity; Hawthorne's hermit years; Emily Dickinson's spinster-bedroom full of immortal poems; Mark Twain's wastage of so much of his talent on get-rich-quick schemes; Whitman's decision to stay with the trolley drivers and whores and good old boys from whom his work took so much sustenance. The novel as it evolved, then, was to be about the American-as-artist.[2]

A month earlier Holmes had also discussed his specific aims in the book with the young academic Tim Hunt.

I was working on three levels at the same time. I wanted each of these characters to represent an American writer, which is the only reason why I put those little epigraphs in front of each chapter. But I also wanted him to represent a particular kind of jazz musician, and I had to create a fictional character doing these things, so that Edgar Pool, for instance, is Edgar Allan Poe.[3]

It was an ambitious concept, and realizing that few of his readers would understand what he was attempting, Holmes structured *The Horn* as a kind of dual narrative, each of the narrative streams illustrating and complementing the other. Each of the major characters was introduced in chapters titled "Chorus," and the choruses alternated with chapters titled "Riff," which told the novel's story. To make his intentions clearer, Holmes preceded each Chorus with a quotation from one of the nineteenth-century American writers who had given him the novel's theme. With the quotations he was suggesting an identification in each chapter between the jazz musician and the individual writer, and he tied the substance of the quotation as closely as he could to the chapter itself.

Although the framework he constructed of Choruses and Riffs could have been difficult to follow, Holmes was very precise in his identification of the subject of each Chorus. *The Horn* is a very tightly written work. The quotation for the first Chorus is from Thoreau, and the name of the musician is Walden Blue. "Walden" is an obvious allusion to Thoreau's *Walden* and "Blue" as clearly identifies him as a musician. He is a young

tenor saxophonist who plays in the style of Lester Young, the novel's prin-
ciple figure. The quotation from Thoreau could have been an image from
the scene that begins the novel as Blue sits up on his rumpled bed to face
another bleary day.

*"Men will lie on their backs, talking about the fall of man, and never
make an effort to get up."*[4]

The novel's opening paragraph is a modern rephrasing of Thoreau's laconic sentence.

*Consider that it was four o'clock of a Monday afternoon and under the
dishwater-gray window shade—just the sort of shade one sees pulled
down over the windows of cheap hotels fronting the sooty elevateds of
American cities where the baffled and the derelict loiter and shift their
feet—under this one shade, in the window of a building off Fifty-third
Street on Eighth Avenue in New York, the wizened October sun stretched
its old finger to touch the dark, flutterless lids of Walden Blue, causing
him to stir among the sheets a week of dawn time lying down and twilight
getting up had rumpled.*[5]

The second Chorus introduces an alto saxophonist named Eddie Wing-
field "Wing" Redburn. The quotation is taken from Melville, whose fourth
novel was titled *Redburn*. It is Melville's most overtly autobiographical
book, and it relates the events of his voyage to Liverpool as an inexperienced twenty-year-old cabin boy aboard the merchant ship *St. Lawrence* in
1839. Its theme is an innocent young man's initiation into a corrupt world, a
subject that Melville was to turn to again in his later books. The quotation
reads,

"Let me look into a human eye. . . . [T]his is the magic glass, man."[6]

This Chorus was one of the first sections that Holmes wrote for the novel
in 1952, when he was most closely adhering to his metaphoric program. In
The Horn, "Wing" Redburn, who is like Melville young and inexperienced,
leaves a touring swing band for a short romantic interlude with a young
woman he meets in a southern small town. Holmes' comment to Hunt was
that "Melville's too big, and he threatened to take over the whole book. . . .
So I had to limit it. But I did have him have his little 'Typee experience' with
the girl down in New Orleans and stuff like that."[7]

Commenting twenty-five years after he'd written the chapter, Holmes has mis-remembered. In *The Horn*, Redburn stops in a small Mississippi town on his way to New Orleans, meets the woman there, but does not go on to New Orleans after their brief interlude. In *Typee*, Melville's first novel, the seaman who is the character representing himself jumps ship on an island in the Marquesas chain in the South Seas and finds an uneasy refuge in an isolated native village. He falls in love with one of the maidens of the tribe, the legendary "Fayaway," who in one popular passage is described swimming naked with other young women in a mountain pool. As the novel's exotic theme found an enthusiastic response in nineteenth-century England, "Fayaway" became the object of romantic searches through the South Seas by parties of Melville's readers.

A quotation from Hawthorne introduces the Chorus presenting the pianist Junius Priest:

"The deep, warm secret—the life within the life."[8]

Holmes' description of Junius in the novel is one of those "crank Americans . . . who nod to their neighbors and are still thought of by the old ladies downstairs as 'nice, quiet boys' but who are, all the time, writing an immense, standard-topping poem, or conducting outlandish chemical experiments in the transmutation of metals, in their stuffy back bedrooms."[9] For Holmes a man like Junius exemplifies—as he made clear with the quotation—"the great American inner life that flowers here and there behind drawn shades on the most uneventful blocks."[10] Holmes told Hunt that the musician who was the model for Junius was the avant-garde jazz pianist Thelonious Monk.

The central woman figure in the novel is a singer named "Geordie Dickson," who is locked in a despairing, unending relationship with the novel's main protagonist, the tenor saxophonist Edgar Pool. The Chorus introducing her is one of the longest and most richly achieved sections of the novel, and its essence is her painful consciousness of the tormented interdependence that has characterized their years together. At the same time, the Chorus stresses her awareness that finally her own career is continuing without him. She has at last become free of him. The quotation that presents her Chorus is taken from Emily Dickinson, and it functions as a cryptic summary of the section's theme.

"Captivity is consciousness,
So's Liberty."[11]

The name Holmes has given his singer, "Dickson," is obviously derived from the American poet's name. Holmes conceived his character as a combination of singer Billie Holiday and Emily Dickinson, though there is only a tenuous connection between Dickinson's spinster life and Geordie's long, tormented relationship with Pool, as well as her obvious sexual awareness. Holmes had spent many hours in New York clubs listening to Holiday sing, and he describes her physicality in a way that no one would have thought of describing Dickinson. Pool has just left Geordie's rundown hotel room after attempting unsuccessfully to borrow money from her.

> *She walked to the ponderous varnished and revarnished bureau to get a cigarette, and caught a curiously objective glimpse of herself in the mirror.*
>
> *"Just look at you," she said aloud almost dispassionately. "You thirty-five if you a day."*
>
> *What she saw was her own flesh (for she had on nothing but a slip); what she saw was the faint beginnings of wrinkles in her neck, and the skin's sheen across her wide shoulders imperceptibly duller, and the breasts softer and heavier than she remembered. This is what he had seen just now, and not the supple, firm-fleshed girl he had taken out of a Charleston gin-mill years ago; and she was suddenly shocked to realize that she had not been that girl for a long time.*[12]

The name of the trumpeter Curny Finnley is derived from the archetypal figure "Huckleberry Finn," and the Chorus introducing him opens with a quotation from Finn's creator, Mark Twain.

> *"Goodness sakes! Would a nigger run south?"*[13]

Holmes probably intended the quotation to refer to the relative isolation of New York's Harlem, which is centered in the northern third of Manhattan. During Holmes' New York years Harlem residents often spoke ironically of never going south into the rest of Manhattan where they felt uncomfortable. In his interview with Hunt, Holmes also elaborated on the creation of his characters in general and in particular on Curny Finnley, who was in part modeled on trumpeter Dizzy Gillespie.

> *I did it this way not because I thought I could say anything profound about all this, but it gave me a control mechanism and a way to think about it and a way to create a character out of whole cloth, which is*

really what I was doing. Curny Finnley is both Dizzy Gillespie and Mark Twain—you know, wordy, funny, weird, and also tremendously interested in commercial success as Dizzy is and Twain was but always failing at it as both Dizzy and Twain did.[14]

The Chorus introducing the tenor saxophonist Metro Myland opens with a quotation from Walt Whitman,

> *"By God, you shall not go down!*
> *Hang your whole weight on me."*[15]

Metro Myland is introduced as another musician whom Wingy Redburn and Walden Blue are looking for to help them in their search for Edgar Pool. They believe that Metro might know where Edgar would be and they are discussing which of Metro's favorite Harlem bars might be his refuge for the afternoon. The quotation probably is referring to the unlikelihood of their finding Metro anywhere south of 110th Street, Harlem's informal boundary. "Myland" is an allusion to Whitman's personal sense of his Americanism, of the nation as "My land," as Whitman expressed it. Metro, for Holmes, was "just any great big yawping tenor sax player, but he's also Walt Whitman."[16]

> *Walden nodded, knowing that Edgar had more secrets about him than most, but when Wing added, "So I guess we'd better try uptown, we'd better go find Metro," he frowned, as if to say, "What, Metro? Yawper in wild Harlem bars? Metro who never comes downtown, and blows a sax as crude as a climbing stud?"*[17]

Whitman with some pride considered the American literary expression a "barbaric yawp," and Metro is intended as a stand-in for Whitman himself, a "yawper."

The final two Choruses portray Pool's last hours. The citations for both of the Choruses, depicting the trauma of Pool's final appearance in the story, are from doomed, desperate, Edgar Allan Poe. Holmes' comment on the character of Pool was that his novelistic character was, of course, Lester Young, but also Poe. The first Chorus reads:

> *"Endure—no—no—defy!"*[18]

And the second one reads:

"Ah, broken is the golden bowl!
The Spirit flown forever!"[19]

The Horn closes with a coda focusing on the reactions of a younger musician who had tagged after Pool through most of his shambling day, an eighteen-year-old pianist named only as "Cleo," who hoped somehow to persuade Pool to make an appearance at a club where he was supposed to perform. The coda has no opening quotation. It is possible that Holmes derived the name from the figure of mythology "Clio," the Muse of History. He did not discuss the book's overall structure in his letter to Ardinger, but its plot utilizes so many elements of classic tragedy that the presence of Clio as a participant would be entirely justified.

Tragic drama, as Holmes probably was using its narrative structure as a model for the novel, is defined by the Aristotelian rules of unity of action. The events of the play should take place within a single day, and the action is set ideally in the same scene. The protagonist's fate must be ordained from the play's beginning, and nothing that happens in the course of the action can alter this fate. Another rule, that the play should take no longer than an hour, was as much determined by the physical nature of the Greek stage and the presence of the audience, and as a novelist Holmes allowed himself some liberty with the classic rules.

Although the action of the novel drifts between a number of musicians' apartments and Harlem bars, it is essentially set within the same scene, as Aristotle proposed. Already by the seventeenth century dramatists had begun modifying the rules so that the place could be a series of locations that could easily be reached within the proper time frame of twenty-four hours, and Holmes' characters moved only from one bar to another or to apartments close to Times Square. Holmes' novel takes place within a single day, as the rules propose, but he employed reminiscences by the main characters to intensify the emotional drama of the situation by filling in the background of their stories. There was no intent to escape the rule of the inevitability of the tragic fate of the protagonist. The tragedy of Pool's death is ordained from the novel's first pages. As an aid to himself in clarifying the book's structure, Holmes wrote the Choruses first, which described his principal figures. He then wrote the Riffs sections, creating the narrative around his fictitious characters.

The language of *The Horn* is often extravagant. There are rhapsodic generalizations about America and American life that some reviewers as well as some later commentators found overblown, just as many of the same commentators considered much of Kerouac's later prose to be loosely extravagant. If *The Horn* had only been what it seemed to be on the surface, a novel about the jazz scene of the 1950s, their reservations could perhaps be justified, but no one who wrote about the book seemed conscious of its complex structure. What is clear from Holmes' interviews, however, is that he already conceived the idea for the book in its larger metaphoric outline before he was even certain of the novel's final structure. Responding to the criticisms of his writing style in his letter to Ardinger, he wrote:

> *The prose, though sometimes over-lush & romantic, seemed proper for what was a mythic tale, and I let the stops pull themselves out. To find a metaphor, as an example, for Parker's lightning flights of sheer song, I had only to think of the wild, agile, fleet base-running of a ball player. There was the same absolute self-belief, the incredible coordination between body and spirit, the haughtily-accepted loneliness of a man pitting his vision against his weaknesses, the inevitable defeat of the man through triumph of the vision.*[20]

Holmes was also conscious of the negative response that greeted Herman Melville's attempt to create a similarly over-reaching metaphor in his epic narrative, *Moby Dick*. *The Horn* is a novel about jazz and jazz musicians only on its surface of narrative and physical detail, just as *Moby Dick* is only on its surface a story about the adventures of the crew of a whaling ship. Melville's prose, like Holmes', often lifted the narrative with the same "over-lush & romantic" flood of language, but the passages that so offended Melville's critics at the time of *Moby Dick*'s publication are now regarded as significant achievements of American prose. In his interview with Hunt, Holmes specifically cited Melville as the source of the novel's prose rhythms, which he likened to iambic pentameter. "I was tremendously influenced by Melville in those days, and Melville, of course, was working with Shakespearian rhythm."[21]

It is obvious from Holmes' immersion in the milieu he describes that jazz was something with which he was very familiar, and one of the first rules drilled into neophyte writers is that they should write about something they know. In *The Horn*, the scenes of rehearsals and idle talk in musicians' bars ring so true to the reality of these informal gatherings that it is almost impossible to believe that Holmes hadn't been part of that life as well. Although he set the novel in the world of Harlem's jazz clubs, he intended the theme of the book to have a much wider scope. He included the names of a number of white musicians, among them Frankie Trumbauer, Bix Beiderbecke, Pee Wee Russell, Woody Herman, Bunny Berigan, Peggy

Lee, Mildred Bailey, and Lenny Tristano, when he listed the names of jazz artists who had suffered from the neglect and misunderstanding that he considered to be the predestined fate of any creative artist in the United States.

An important element in the novel's effectiveness is, as many jazz writers emphasized, its authenticity. To make his presence in the scene clear, Holmes took an unexpected step and included both himself and Kerouac in the narrative. On one level, it is obvious that all novelists are protagonists of their own fiction, even if their presence is only intimated by an attitude or an idea, or even by the pose of a character on the page. In *The Horn*, however, Holmes has included Kerouac and himself as characters in two scenes in the book. Although he tried to maintain a casual attitude about the novel and its reception, it was a book that he had conceived with such serious ambitions that it is not unexpected that he would make an appearance in its pages himself. In their two scenes Holmes and Kerouac are representative figures, standing in for the countless young jazz fans who filled the clubs in those years.

Holmes and Kerouac make their appearance early in the evening, as Cleo is attempting to maneuver Edgar toward the club where he was expected to appear, and where he could pick up a little change to make a bus trip back to "Kay-Cee." It is the long dreamed-of bus trip that has been Pool's ostensible purpose in his day of compulsive drinking, as he placed pleading phone calls from barroom phone booths and unsteadily made a series of futile visits to anyone who might lend him money. As he and Cleo drift along the street they encounter Holmes and Kerouac shouting drunkenly to each other in front of one of the New York City record shops that played music out on the sidewalk. Although Jack as "the dark-haired one" is not named, John presents himself as "Paul," the name he adopted as the character "Paul Hobbes" in *Go*. Edgar is in the middle of an obsessive, interminable monolog when he suddenly breaks off,

> *"But, hey, look!" he interrupted himself in a different voice, actually pointing. "Man alive, dig them!"*
>
> *For there, in front of a record store that had an outside speaker through which a husky tenor sax poured its poignant wail out upon the dead, thronged sidewalks, were two young white men, muffled to the chin in flapping raincoats, transfixed upon the curb by the very sound, heads bobbing, snapping as they sang along all unaware that they were singing, catching hold of one another as they teetered toward the gutter, their laughing exultant faces astream with rain and sweat, riffing and entranced, oblivious of everything but that wild, hot horn.*

Edgar stopped dead in the middle of the sidewalk, a few feet from them,
letting people jostle past him, staring at them, a curious, warm half-smile
unconsciously starting to touch his lips, utterly outward for an instant,
just as the dark-haired one seized the shoulder of his friend in the glasses,
and exclaimed, "Listen to it, listen! That's the new tenor, Paul, that's the
one, that's him! . . . Oh man, this crazy country! . . . And I'll bet he's going
to blow his first, vast, really great solo tonight, just imagine—I'll bet you,
and everyone'll be destroyed by it, and amazed they could have gotten
through their lives not knowing it, not realizing!" He shook his friend by
the shoulder, his face full of goofy, excited laughter. "Where the hell is he,
Paul! Where is he![22]

In the book's closing pages the two friends are portrayed a second time
sitting at a front table in the crowded club when Edgar finally stumbles
through the door. Again, it is Kerouac who is the more extroverted in his
excitement, while Holmes describes himself as remaining painfully stiff and
silent, though he shares Jack's burst of excitement with the music. Edgar
notices them at the moment that he begins to feel the pulse of the rhythm,
not remembering that he'd already glimpsed them on the street a few hours
earlier.

Edgar felt that quick lift in his heart that occurs only when everyone, inex-
plicably, miraculously, has found the same pure groove; the good, hopeful
life of jazz (which is always on God's side, after all); the lift forward and
up. And just as he felt it his eyes lit on two young white men transfixed at
a table right before him, their faces full of ecstasy and music, and all at
once, staring and shivering, he seemed to know them, their very souls: the
dark one, probably the sort given to muttering with drunken frustration
at four in the morning, "Jus' give me a piano and a drum. Man. I'll make
the bass, doom, doom, doom. But, oh, let's jump"; the one with glasses,
listening a little too intently, as if he did not quite trust his ears or heart—
one of those sad, somehow crippled young Americans whom jazz alone
had reconciled to his country.[23]

The jazz sessions and the club scene Holmes described were written
from quick notes he wrote the night before he went to the typewriter. As he
explained to Ardinger, "I had a large record collection, and after each day's
work, over a drink or two, I'd listen to examples of the kind of jazz I'd be
writing about the next day, free-associate images and ideas, jot them down
in a note book and be ready."[24]

Although the characters in *The Horn* were based on the lives and the careers of the jazz musicians Holmes admired, they were, as he admitted, "loosely based, because I knew little or nothing personal about any of them."[25] He wrote that besides the model of Edgar Allan Poe, the protagonist, Edgar Pool, was a combination of the lives of two musicians, Lester Young and Charlie Parker. It was Parker's death that had suggested the ending of the novel to him, not the events of Parker's life and career. Holmes told the interviewer Michael Schumacher that Pool

> *was based on Edgar Allan Poe and Lester Young, and on my awareness of how territory-explorers are by-passed by settlers of that territory. I invented the details out of that awareness and out of thin air. By late-1955, the book already a quarter-written, Charlie Parker, who died that year, entered the character, mostly by providing me with the finish for the book. I happened to be in Birdland the last night Parker played there—his last public appearance anywhere, I believe. The scene as depicted in the book is a literal rendering of that final session. I was there with Don Allen, then an editor for, I think, Criterion Books, who had suggested that I write a biography of Bird, and I was there to meet him and arrange a schedule of sessions with him. I did meet him briefly between those two disastrous sets. We sized one another up, liked each other, and were to get together when he got back from a date in Boston. Two or three days later, he was dead. Don, Shirley, and I—and somebody from Time—went to the midnight memorial concert at Carnegie Hall, and later to an after-hours place; we stayed up until 9:00 in the morning, drinking and talking and going silent as a pianist played Bird-tunes to a mostly quiet crowd.*[26]

Although at its publication *The Horn* received mostly moderate reviews from the mainstream press, it was rapturously received by knowledgeable critics with a close connection with jazz, among them Studs Terkel in Chicago and Ralph Gleason in San Francisco. Terkel began his review in the *Sun-Times,* "At last, an authentic novel about jazz."[27] In the *Nation* Gleason wrote that he believed Holmes had written "the first novel of the jazz life that is not entirely a 'fan's' mirage."[28] The sales were modest, but Holmes could satisfy himself with a second printing, translations in five European countries, and paperback publication in both Great Britain and the United States. The book had such a positive reception that it was only if he compared it to the stunning success of *On the Road* that he might continue to think of himself as a failure as a novelist.

As more time passes between the book's original publication and its newer readers, it seems certain that there will be a reevaluation of Holmes' achievement. The mythic elements in the novel will stand out even more sharply, and its troubling, pain-ridden metaphor of the uncertain place of the artist in American society will become recognized as a definition of the aesthetic consciousness at mid-century. It is not too much to assume that Holmes' novel will finally be accepted, like Kerouac's *On the Road*, as a modern American classic. Holmes himself was satisfied with his workmanship.

> *When I finished the last page, I had a moment of satisfaction that was as near to complete happiness as I have known. I felt I had accomplished very near what I had had in mind when the book came to me years before.*[29]

Chapter 17

TOO-LATE WORDS

Camden nights dire with honeysuckle,
back of hospital streets,
stoops murmurous with baseball—
Sucking peppermints in an alien town,
I carried plastic tubes of sleeping pills,
aspirin, iodine, and oil of camphor—
prepared against myself but ill-prepared for vigils
in South Jersey shipyard Whitman night,
    or the irony of turnpike smashup
        that brought you here,
            my urbane father.

Scotches in Bruno's across the street at nine,
watching, as I do, the drinkers at the bar,
the television-starers, the pinball athletes,
the beehived waitresses—mothers mostly—
who like to serve hot food to men.

Wore the same suit a week, my only suit,
and watched till midnight in your room
    the waning flickers
       of mortality.

—JOHN CLELLON HOLMES, "Too-Late Words to My Father"[1]

With the attention being paid to their books—Kerouac's work causing major controversy and Holmes' second novel a success in their world of jazz writing—each of them at this point in his life could expect some kind of stability, but instead over the next few years each found himself spinning out of control.

For once Kerouac's problems didn't revolve around money. He had a steady stream of income from his articles and appearances, as well as from the sale of new manuscripts and the expected royalties from *On the Road*. Though he continued to use Joyce Glassman's apartment as a place to stay over when he was in New York, with his new economic stability his immediate plan was to buy a house for himself and his mother. Whatever he might have told or written to a succession of women, earnestly rhapsodizing about settling down with one of them in a state of married bliss, when he finally was able to foresee a more stable future it was with Mémère.

In a letter to Holmes on April 13, 1958, Kerouac described what he called his "nice home"[2] in the small community of Northport, on Long Island's north shore. He had clearly been influenced by Holmes' decision to leave New York and try to make a more settled life in a house of his own. Holmes and Kerouac could now have been neighbors across the waters of the Sound. It was an ironic footnote to the media tumult over the Beat Generation that two of its defining members were both living a quiet life in the kind of commuter suburb that their followers held in such contempt.

Kerouac tried to manage the money that he was now earning, but he was an inexperienced home owner. The house in Northport had cost only fourteen thousand dollars, which he paid half in cash, and he insisted on paying off most of the mortgage within a year. He was daily expecting an influx of cash from the movie sale of *On the Road*, but he had received only modest sums from the publishers, and his attempts to pay off the mortgage and his taxes left him continually without money in his pocket. As far as his friends could see he was still as shabby and as tapped out as ever. The only difference Holmes noticed was that now Kerouac was drinking brandy, instead of cheap wine, which was even harder on his body.

The publication of *The Subterraneans* only six months after *On the Road* had heightened his visibility. Now when Kerouac attempted to go back to his old habit of drinking himself into a stupor in a favorite bar, he was an obvious target for everyone who wanted something from him. He was also a noisy, bellicose drunk. In one of his favorite Village bars three men, one of them a professional boxer who was homosexual, followed him out to the street and beat him savagely. The boxer insisted that some slurring remark about homosexuality he thought he'd heard from Kerouac was directed at him. Kerouac stumbled back to Glassman's apartment, his nose and his arm broken.

When Kerouac wrote another card to Holmes a few weeks later, he had moved into his Northport house, and he was delighted with the ordinary garden work and the household chores. He was still certain that money was waiting for him with his movie contracts, but his agent was unsuccessful in his negotiations. Either he insisted on a larger sum than the film companies were ready to offer, as in the case with *On the Road*, or he accepted an unsatisfactory offer, like the fifteen-thousand-dollar flat fee he was paid for *The Subterraneans*. Kerouac was now convinced that *The Dharma Bums*, soon to be published, would take care of his financial worries.

In October 1958 Holmes faced another crisis, this one confronting him with an unexpected emotional situation. His father suffered a heart attack, and even though they hadn't been close for years, John traveled to Washington to be with him. His father's condition was less critical than the doctors had thought, however, and he was able to report with some relief to his sister Liz in a letter on October 23 that their older sister Lila had been in Washington to help, and that his father seemed to be out of danger. During their bedside talks he and his father finally became reconciled. In a letter to Kerouac early in November he described what he was feeling.

> Last week I had to go to Washington to see my father, who had a severe heart attack awhile ago and is convalescing. Poor man, he has never been in bed so long in his life, or been alone so long or had to think so deep, and it is giving him trouble—though he's going to pull through all right, I'm sure. We had good, long, somewhat final talks together—and how beautiful are human reconciliations, after all! You know what I mean.[3]

Though both Kerouac and Holmes were attempting to distance themselves from the hectic exploitation of the Beat concept, they still were continuously asked to talk about it. Their lives were so filled with demands for interviews and appearances that they wrote each other only sporadically, and their letters had little of the torrential outpouring that had marked their earlier correspondence. In his letters Holmes gave only glimpses of the domestic difficulties that dogged his life as the months passed after the publication of *The Horn*. He and Shirley found themselves facing the winter in Old Saybrook without any income. Betty Holmes had realized that it was too costly to heat her large house in the winter, when her inn was without guests. For those months she rented the house and moved to California, leaving John and Shirley to keep an eye on her property in their unheated wooden building behind hers.

Although they anticipated a difficult winter, for a moment they had some slack in their financial tangle. With another inheritance Betty was able to give them money to pay off the remaining mortgage of $4,730 on their old schoolhouse. They were, at least, free of the threat of foreclosure. Shirley couldn't face the dark, dreary kitchen in the house, so John found used lumber and redid the walls with new cabinets and painted them white. For decoration he hung maps of France on the walls. After his weeks of carpentry he spent most of his time cutting wood to feed their fireplaces and stoves as the weather turned colder. There was little writing, and their situation was so discouraging that it would have been difficult for him to do anything more than magazine articles and occasional journal entries. He completed an ambitious piece on jazz, which appeared as the lead article about the current jazz scene in *Esquire*, but the other projects he proposed were turned down.

By mid-January 1959, John and Shirley were running out of firewood, just as the winter was in its coldest period. With obvious relief he wrote to Allen Ginsberg on January 14 saying that they would be able to get away from the house for some of the time. Friends who lived further north on a bend of the Connecticut River were going to spend a month in Yucatan to take part in an archeological dig, and they had asked John and Shirley to stay in their house to keep it warm and take care of their dog. Holmes was looking forward to nothing "more distracting than the ice breaking up, which is certainly bound to happen sometime."[4] In his letter he also wrote that he had just had a visit from a journalist, Al Aronowitz, who had asked him many of the same questions about the beginnings of the Beat Generation that Holmes was heartily tired of. "He wanted to know what you and Jack thought about my damn 1952 article, and shit I didn't know, and don't, and it seems so long ago, and who cares?"[5]

What had been more interesting to Holmes was that Aronowitz had talked about new writing by Ginsberg and Corso, assuming that Holmes also knew what was happening with his friends. Among the new poems Aronowitz mentioned was something of Ginsberg's about his mother, the recently completed long poem "Kaddish," and Holmes was impatient to see it. Aronowitz had made him uncomfortably conscious that his isolation in Old Saybrook had put him outside of the literary scene that had developed around the others in New York City. Ginsberg hadn't included him in the dedication of *Howl and Other Poems* in 1956, and a recent magazine article by Seymour Krim had described the group and its ideas without mentioning Holmes.

In his journal early in February Holmes wondered why he wasn't becoming as widely known as Kerouac and Ginsberg. In his discouraged mood he wondered if it was because of his questioning of the whole Beat ethos in the wake of the media exploitation. He wrote plaintively, "Why don't I simply *believe*?"[6] With so many more pressing problems hanging over him, however, the tired questions about what they all might have been thinking about a decade before seemed—at least for the moment—irrelevant. Aronowitz's articles in the *New York Post* were some of the few sympathetic, in-depth accounts of the Beats in popular newspapers, and Holmes was appreciative that Ginsberg had sent the journalist to Old Saybrook to interview him.

Through all of the winter's uncertainties, however, Holmes was still in touch with Jay Landesman in St. Louis. Landesman had written Holmes an immediate, breathless response to *The Horn*, which came as a welcome antidote to the caution of some of the reviewers. On February 3, 1959, Landesman wrote that he had heard something about Holmes' problems. "Word comes that you're not up to snuff . . . plagued by all sorts of things, most of them connected to the business of writing."[7] Two days later he sent Holmes a check for one hundred dollars as a "loan" so he could finish installing the heating in the house. With the money John and Shirley finally were able to deal with the winter and they moved a television set upstairs into their bedroom.

Jay and Fran at this point were in the midst of their most expansive period in St. Louis. Landesman's own view was that so much had happened in the fourteen months since they'd left New York that it might have been fourteen years instead. The Crystal Palace Cabaret Theater had become more successful than he could have dreamed, and he was continuing to work with his brothers in the family's antique business. Fran had given birth to a son and, despite her problems with miscarriages, she would soon have a second son. However complicated Landesman's life might have become, he somehow managed to present an image of himself as a business man, which was picked up by the national media. A cover article in *Pageant* magazine was headlined "RICH FULL LIFE IN ST. LOUIS, MO." The article began, "Three of the luckiest and most amazing people in the world are the Landesman brothers, who have discovered it is possible to do what they like and make it pay."[8] After six gushing pages the article concluded,

> *Well-liked and respected by their fellow St. Louisians, the Landesmans are, despite the unconventionality of their lives, by no means bohemians. They are devoted family men who are not so rich that they don't have to work—and fairly hard—to make a living. Their secret, and the moral of this story, is that it takes talent plus a measure of wisdom to make money doing the things you would like to do to make money.*[9]

What the magazine article didn't mention was that Jay was having a series of affairs with the waitresses and the customers in his establishment, appearing as a stand-up comedian if one of the acts failed to turn up, drinking too much, and enjoying whatever drugs he came across as he rushed through the days. Fran was spending more time at home with their family, and she was also having an affair with Tommy Wolf, the house pianist who was collaborating with her songs.

Landesman found that he had a flair for running a small theater, as long as his audience could sit and drink while they were watching. His first production was the Midwest's initial production of Beckett's *Waiting for Godot*, which became St. Louis's hot ticket for an extended run; then he'd found an improvisation company in Chicago that he felt was as exciting as anything he'd seen anywhere. He imported some of their performers to his theater in time to catch the widespread wave of popularity for improvised theater. Two of the members of the troupe, Elaine May and Mike Nichols, went on to major careers in theater and television. With his cabaret theater enlarged to three hundred seats, Landesman introduced, among many others, neophyte artists like Lenny Bruce, Woody Allen, and Barbra Streisand, nursing them through their beginner's nerves and neuroses. Despite misgivings he generously brought Lenny Bruce back for an extended run after he'd become the victim of his own drug excesses and the official censorship of the time. His audiences now came largely to incite Bruce into saying something that would cause him to be arrested again.

After a series of three overly ambitious flops in his theater, one of them a surrealistic play by the *Neurotica* contributor Chandler Brossard, Landesman now could report to Holmes that the seats were filled again. He was presenting St. Louis with a unique theatrical experience—the first and still the only musical comedy with the old New York Beat crowd as its subject, *The Nervous Set*. In the wake of their trio of disasters Landesman and his director, Ted Flicker, had set out to find something that might break the trend. With the furor over *On the Road* there was still a lot of interest in the Beats in St. Louis, and Flicker wondered if they could find some kind of story to serve as a setting for Fran's songs.

Landesman remembered his previous attempt to capture the early Beat scene in the novel he'd written about all of them when everyone in the crowd seemed to be writing their personal account of the scene. Holmes had been encouraging, but he'd felt there was still much work needed with the manuscript. When Landesman looked at it again, he was pleasantly surprised to find that it wasn't as hopeless as he'd thought. He realized he had been painfully prescient about Kerouac's problems, later describing him in his 1987 memoir *Rebel Without Applause* as a symbol of the archetypal Beat character who becomes famous and then sets about destroying himself.

The word spread about the musical's success, and after a few weeks of sold-out performances there were offers to bring the production to New York. In Landesman's letter he told Holmes with considerable excitement that *The Nervous Set* would open on Broadway later in the spring. He was expecting to see John and Shirley at the opening, and he also had hopes of cajoling Kerouac into joining them in the audience. The one hundred dollars he'd sent Holmes was an expression of the affection he still felt for all of them.

The opening of Jay and Fran's musical on May 18 was an excuse for John and Shirley to get into New York again and lose themselves in the usual round of alcoholic parties and equally alcoholic gatherings of old friends. The New York critics were generally dismissive, but Holmes was pleased with the songs and with the story Landesman had put around them, though he was uneasy about the dialogue in Landesman's glib, throw-away manner. For Holmes what was most important was that there was an original cast recording of the songs which broadened the audience for the wry bitter-sweet lyrics Fran had created. Landesman managed to convince Kerouac to come for a performance, but he showed up drunk and once in his seat immediately fell asleep. Landesman noticed that the only time Kerouac woke up during the first act was when his name was mentioned, then he fell asleep again and after mumbling that it was fine, disappeared during the intermission.

It had already been a strained year for John and Shirley, but a few weeks after the round of partying with Jay and Fran he found himself facing a new emotional dead-end. Early in July his father was seriously injured in an automobile accident. Holmes wrote to Kerouac on July 31, 1959:

My life has become, again, a shambles; not a real word done in over a month; reason: my father had a foolish, tragic, ironic smash-up on the Jersey turnpike at five o'clock on Monday afternoon, seems like ages now, and was taken to a grimy, old fashioned hospital in Whitman's Camden, had a hand taken off, and then a few days later was struck down with a stroke, cerebral thrombosis type, and has been paralyzed down the "good" side ever since. I rushed down one stormy midnight, and stayed there a grubby, hopeless week, as the doctors gave him up, one by one, and we couldn't get nurses because of the 4th of July, so I sat up with him hours and hours; he couldn't speak, he was delirious with 105 fever, fighting for life, and I watched and watched, and learned about life. Nothing in his past, in his own life, kept him going; that I know at last; the doctors were non-plussed; they repeatedly consigned him to coma, and I started making laying-away arrangements; but he would not quit; HE WOULD NOT CLOSE HIS EYES AND GO; one nightmarish wild day I kept a light sheer naked bulb on where he could see it, and he seemed to understand, and stared at it all day, and when it got too much, lifted up his stump to peer at it curiously and turn it round and round; and would not rest and go.[10]

The trauma of the days and nights at his father's bedside would haunt Holmes for years. In his confusion he began writing a poem about the weeks at the hospital—though it had been years since he'd thought of himself as a poet. The poem, "Too-Late Words for My Father," was not completed until 1973, fourteen years later. As he wrote in the poem, he was staying at the outskirts of Camden in a cheap motel, and searching every night when he left the hospital for a bar still open so he could down three scotches to help him sleep. His father's fever broke, and it seemed that he would live, though one of his feet was paralyzed and he would always be bedridden. Holmes tried to find some way to stimulate the paralyzed foot by using the techniques he had learned in the navy hospital in San Diego. Most of the next weeks went to finding his father a place in a Veteran's Hospital in Brooklyn, where he could be close to his wife, who had also been injured in the accident and was being taken care of by her daughter in a private hospital in Brooklyn. Alan Harrington had been staying with John and Shirley on alternate weekends so he could spend time with his son, who was with Alan's ex-wife in Old Saybrook. Harrington loaned Holmes enough money to cover the mounting expenses of his father's hospitalization.

By the end of the summer Holmes was close to exhaustion. With his sister Liz in Europe and his older sister, Lila, also not on the scene, most of the responsibility for his father fell to him, "there being no one else."[11] At the end of August, only a few weeks after Holmes' father had entered the Veteran's Hospital, he died in his hospital bed. It was October before Holmes wrote Kerouac to describe what had happened.

Poor man's spirit finally broke, he just quit on us, looked around the hospital and somehow realized (no one really knew extent of brain damage) that he would be flat on his back for whatever remained of conscious life, and, as I knew, this broke something in him. Turned face to the wall . . . and simply went away. This consumed weeks and weeks of time, left no

will, affairs in tremendous maze, wanted cremation. I had to arrange that
and where to bury, the rest of the family didn't come thru, my job thus.
. . . Horrible funeral service, wife wanted it that way, so went through it,
pious emptiness by well-scrubbed young cleric who had never known him,
and read properly harmless selections from Bible, all the truth taken even
out of this, the last thing, death itself.[12]

The only consolation Holmes could salvage from the funeral was the appearance of his paternal grandmother, Frieda Holmes, with whom he had
felt close since the Long Island summer days of his boyhood.

My wonderful Long Island grandmother, whose face is full of a soft, old,
pink certainty of faith, wouldn't listen to him, or look in the open coffin
(ghoulish note!) but stayed among the flowers in grim impersonality of
Jerico Turnpike Funeral Home, chatting and feeling petals, bless her![13]

The long autumn and winter, and the turgid weeks of the next spring,
were one of Holmes' most unproductive periods. He was unable to throw
off his grief at his father's death so soon after their reconciliation, and this
deepened his crisis. He wrote little besides the long entries in his journals.
A short essay, "Existentialism and the Novel: Notes and Questions," was
published in the *Chicago Review* while he was with his father in the hospital, but it would be a year before he sold two additional magazine pieces.
The first was a review of one of the earliest books about the Beat scene,
Lawrence Lipton's description of the alternative lifestyle in Venice, California, *The Holy Barbarians*, that was published in *Venture* in the spring/
summer issue of 1960. The other was one of Holmes' handful of published
short stories, a western titled "A Length of Chain" that appeared in the
men's magazine *Nugget* in August.

Holmes had tried earlier to rewrite his stalled novel as a first-person
narrative, but he quickly realized that although this approach was successful for Kerouac it wouldn't work for him. He now began a novella-length
story portraying an unrepentant town drunk who seemed to Holmes to
epitomize the determination of the individual to stand up against the stale
prohibitions of his society. The title was "Old Man Molineaux," and although the setting was Connecticut and it was an unpitying description of
alcohol abuse, both subjects he knew well, he found it almost impossible
to complete the narrative. Later Holmes compared what he was trying to
achieve with Kerouac's writing in *Doctor Sax*:

But it was New England that spoke in Doctor Sax, *where all the coagulat-ed evil in the world gathers like a cosmic boil, and then bursts into a husk of doves. Equally it was New England that drove my Old Man Molineaux (in* Get Home Free*) to struggle against his kedge anchor, hungering after wild places, only to collapse at the end, capitulant and secretly relieved, having experienced them all in his imagination anyway. In New England, speculation is no farther away than the woodpile; spiritual bliss comes to the swinger-of-birches.*[14]

Determined to work his way through his writer's block, Holmes filled the pages of his journals in a desperate effort to find his direction. As Shir-ley watched in despair, their relationship deteriorated, and their nightly drinking ended in sodden quarrels and recriminations. With both of them drinking heavily, the money from Shirley's job went to liquor and the ex-penses of their car. She was working for a deodorant company in the nearby town of Old Lyme, and they had to keep the car running so she could get there. They knew more people in Old Saybrook now, and there were oc-casional trips to New York City, but when Holmes was approached by his old editor Hiram Hayden for something new for Hayden's new publishing imprint, Holmes had to say reluctantly that he had nothing to send him.

Through all of the turmoil Holmes was still in contact with Kerouac, whose plan of living outside of New York to rid himself of the crowds that fol-lowed him had collapsed. In June 1959 he sold his Northport house and sent his mother back to Florida. His plan now was to build two neighboring houses in Sanlando Springs, one for his sister and her family, the other for Gabrielle and himself. As he waited for the building project to get started in Florida, he stayed by himself in the empty house on Gilbert Avenue. When the Florida plan fell through, he bought a smaller house in Northport, again telling his friends that the address should never be given to anyone. By Oc-tober his mother was settled back with him on Long Island. Kerouac would never again face the kind of economic difficulties that had dogged him for so many years, but his alcohol and drug addictions were so serious that he was never free from the torments within himself.

In November, Kerouac was asked to appear on a national television show with the comedian and pianist Steve Allen in Hollywood, and per-haps because there was no crowd waiting for him inside the studio it was one of his most touching and sensitive appearances. He read passages from *On the Road* and the still unpublished *Visions of Cody*, standing beside the piano as Allen played a soft accompaniment. Despite his nervousness it was one of the few moments in this period when Kerouac seemed at peace with himself.

Pleased with his performance, Kerouac journeyed north to San Francisco where the old chaos engulfed him. He planned a visit to San Quentin to appear at one of the prison classes Cassady was attending, as Ginsberg and Snyder had done, but characteristically he overslept and didn't see his old friend. Finally two new friends, a young poet, Lew Welch, and a student of Zen Buddhism, Albert Saijo, offered to drive him back to New York in Welch's jeep station wagon. They delivered him back to Northport early in December. In a few weeks he was writing to Snyder that he realized was drinking too much, while to his editor at Grove Press, Don Allen, he confided that he couldn't get Benzedrine in Northport and was unable to write without it. He asked Ginsberg to help supply him.

Lawrence Ferlinghetti at his City Lights Press was publishing Kerouac's *Book of Dreams*, and in response to Kerouac's anguished complaints about the impossibility of writing in the swirl of visitors that descended on him, Ferlinghetti offered his isolated cabin in a coastal canyon outside of Big Sur for a summer of meditation. The summer visit, which lasted only three agonized weeks, turned into a long, interminable drunk, with crowds of people coming down the path to the cabin for continual parties. Cassady had been released from San Quentin on June 3, 1960, and although Carolyn felt he had been changed by his years in prison, he was soon racing up and down the highway between Big Sur and San Francisco, his car filled with friends and new girls.

After drinking blindly for days, Kerouac fell into a stupor and suffered what he described in letter to Phil Whalen a few weeks later as "a serious nervous or mental breakdown."[15] When he returned to his mother in Northport he spent weeks trying to recover, but the experience had left him as marked as Cassady's years in San Quentin. Kerouac later described his alcoholic collapse at Ferlinghetti's cabin during the summer of 1960 in his novel *Big Sur*. It was his most harrowing and most honest book, though it virtually destroyed what remained of his literary reputation.

With Kerouac's life in shambles, Holmes' crisis in Old Saybrook was daily becoming more serious. His attempts to sell the novella *Old Man Molineaux* had been unsuccessful, and during the interminable hours, unable to write, Holmes filled the pages of his journal while he continued to drink and smoke, waiting to quarrel with Shirley when she returned from her job. Even with the financial situation they faced he was unable to think of himself as anything but a novelist, however it might effect their lives.

By September 1961 he was forced to hide upstairs from the electric company when they attempted to get into the house to turn off their electricity for an unpaid eight-dollar bill. The climax came a month later, with his arrest by the Old Saybrook police for shoplifting. For some time Holmes had been stealing food from a local market, justifying the thefts in his journal entries with the self-righteous questioning of the rights of the individual and the rights of property soon to be embedded in the hippie culture only a few years away. With the same attention to detail that he used for his literary notes, he wrote in his journal on October 4:

> *Yesterday ended my career as a petty thief. I was caught in Universal with a can of deviled ham, a can of tuna fish, and a ½ pound of cheese. The butcher said to the cashier, "I know I was going to catch him one of these days," and called the police—Officer Herb Welles, a short, inarticulate, nice enough fellow, who took me to the station, and wrote a statement for me to sign. In a bone-head move, I admitted to having lifted items from Universal before. In a further bonehead move, so chagrined and embarrassed was I, and what little mathematical ability I have failing me completely, I said that in total what I had taken might come to ten dollars. He went back to get a statement from the store and they intend to prosecute me. "They feel there's more to it than you say, and they want it to come out in court," the policeman said. I was booked, fingerprinted, and released on $50 bail.*[16]

As a relatively new arrival in a small town who had made no particular effort to become part of the community, Holmes was devastated by the effect of his arrest on many of the people he encountered over the next few days. He might have been able to escape some awkwardness, but the local newspaper picked up the news item and made a joke out of the fact that Holmes had been so broke that he'd stolen sandwich makings but hadn't taken anything to put them on. The jeering headline over the short piece in the *Courant* read, "What, no bread?" He also had to face the incredulity and embarrassment of the few people they had become friendly with. Shirley advised him just to talk, to treat it lightly, and try to hurry past what had happened, but in his journal entries Holmes felt anguished by the public humiliation. On October 6, he wrote, "I feel a nausea of a guilt far out of proportion to what I have done; it swims up out of me at a moment's notice unless I keep a tight hold & a clear mind."[17]

At least his court appearance was over quickly. He was released after a brief lecture by the judge and fined twenty-five dollars. His only part in the trial was to say "Guilty" and stand silently while his lawyer followed with "reason why." It led him, however, to consider his situation with a self-accusing objectivity.

> *Time, time that passes everything by. All the disciplines are in disrepair, and I must start to rebuild them now. High, dark sky, sullen with cold heaped clouds overhead, and the deep chill in the air, leaves coming down in yellow flight, some trees entirely bare now. The lost sun sinking with all the sad cold reds of late autumn. . . . All truths coming out now. I need a month of deep creative absorption. I've been drinking too much again, wasting days & visions.*[18]

By the fall of 1961 the tone of Holmes' journals and his letters had become even more strained and bewildered. At the same time the first serious academic anthology/textbook appeared with the Beat Generation as its subject, *A Casebook on the Beat*, by Thomas Parkinson, a professor at the University of California in Berkeley. Parkinson had attended many of the early Bay Area readings and been friendly with the writers of the San Francisco poetry renaissance. In a section titled "Some Writers of the Beat Generation" he included writing from Ginsberg, Kerouac, Corso, Burroughs, Ferlinghetti, Snyder, Whalen, and McClure. In the anthology's "Criticism and Commentary" section he included excerpts from essays and criticism by, among others, Kenneth Rexroth, Norman Podhoretz, Warren Tallman, Henry Miller, Herbert Gold, and John Ciardi.

To Holmes' acute disappointment, he was not included in the anthology. He was already being written out of the story of the literary movement he had helped to define only a decade earlier.

Chapter 18

A SWEET ATTENTION

What can a beat do when he is too old to go on the road? He can go on the sauce. . . . In the end he settles for a howling emotional crisis—which on a grown-up would look very much like the DTs.

A child's first touch of cold maturity—even when it occurs in a man of 41—may seem ridiculous, and is certainly pathetic. In Kerouac's case, though, there may be compensations. Think of the books, man, a whole new series: The Dharma Bums Grow Up, The Dharma Bums on Wall Street. *Who knows, maybe even* The Dharma Bums in the White House?

—*Time* magazine review of Jack Kerouac's *Big Sur*[1]

In the weeks after Holmes' humiliating day in court for shoplifting, whatever had been blocking his writing shook loose, and he found he could write again. When he was presented with an opportunity to get away from the isolation of Old Saybrook and the frustrations of his stalled career as a novelist, he was too buoyed up by the work on his new novella "Old Man Molineaux" to consider breaking off. He was certain that his writing was moving in a new direction, even if he was uncomfortably aware that the novella's length would make it difficult to place with any of the magazines which took his work. Although the immediate rejections for his piece were no more pleasant than rejections ever can be, their language at least encouraged him to continue working. There was generally enthusiasm for the writing itself, although the problem was not only the length, but also the character of the unregenerate, whining village drunk he had chosen to portray. His editor at *Harper's Magazine* wrote that the novella was "an extraordinary piece of writing and I have read it with much admiration. We are sorry indeed that the subject matter isn't right for a Harper Supplement."[2]

Most of the other rejections echoed the first letters. The *New Yorker* returned it with an ironic comment, considering the success of Hemingway's much longer novella *The Old Man and the Sea*, which had first appeared in a single number of *Life* magazine. Although the editor at the *New Yorker* admired the prose, "we do not feel we wish to run anything nearly this long about an old man."[3] *Esquire* also rejected it because of its length, just as they rejected the short novel *Mrs. Bridge* by Evan S. Connell, which would go on to become a modern classic. Otherwise the editors were positive in their response, asking if Holmes could "do some short stories for us, this good?"[4] His nonfiction autobiographical piece, "The Booze and I," originally titled "Through a Glass Darkly," was accepted by *Nugget*.[5]

Nugget was a new magazine, and although it had first been stereotyped as another of the fashionable "men's" magazines that were making a run for the audience that *Playboy* had discovered, it was beginning to attract a more attentive readership. Its readers were young male professionals with university backgrounds and solid entry-level jobs who were concerned with new ideas and trends, along with the ubiquitous pinups, cartoons, and the stream of articles helping them negotiate the unsettling changes in sexual attitudes. *Nugget*'s current editorial director was Seymour Krim, the essayist and social critic, who had been familiar with the Beat scene since its earliest days. When he looked at the proofs of the piece on alcoholism, he wrote Holmes and offered him a job as a senior editor, telling him, "We would very much like you to be a steady easy-does-it contributor to *Nugget*."[6] The job would have meant an income of twenty thousand dollars a year, and an end to their interminable problems with money. It was the first offer Holmes had received from anyone, but it would have left him no time for the writing he was doing. He turned Krim's offer down without serious consideration.

During this period Kerouac was restlessly attempting to deal with the demons haunting him as he spent the winter of 1962 in Orlando with his mother. They had left Northport in late April 1961, embarrassed by the gossip in town after his ex-wife Joan Haverty Aly sold her story about Kerouac's refusal to pay child support to the newspapers.[7] Joan insisted that Jack, with his success, should acknowledge his daughter Jan, and a claim of non-support was her only recourse. She had remarried and given birth to twins, but she had separated from her husband and she was struggling to support three children on a meager salary as a waitress. Now ten years old, Jan's legal name was Janet Kerouac. In letters to both Ginsberg and Holmes,

Kerouac had admitted she could be his daughter, but he hadn't the courage to tell his mother that he'd lied to her about Joan's supposed adultery.

Ginsberg's brother Eugene Brooks represented Kerouac again when the case was heard before a judge. This time there was an agreement they would take a blood test. Kerouac flew up from Florida in the middle of February 1962 and met Joan and Jan in a bar in Brooklyn, where they had lunch. In her memoir *Baby Driver* (1981) Jan wrote that she understood why her mother had been attracted to him. "He was so handsome with his deep blue eyes and dark hair hanging in a few fine wisps on his forehead."[8] She remembered, "I couldn't take my eyes off my father, he looked so much like me."[9]

After their lunch they went to Manhattan, where Joan and Jack took the blood tests. In this pre-DNA era blood tests were much less accurate and were only successful in showing that someone could *not* have been the father of a child. The result in their case was the conclusion that Kerouac could have been the father, and the judge awarded Joan child support of fifty-two dollars a month. When Kerouac wrote Holmes a few weeks later, he blustered that he was again being made out to be a liar.[10]

Although Holmes still swam in the sea of his anxieties, the spring continued to bring him signs of interest from editors in his writing. On April 1 he wrote in his journal that he wanted to attempt a "first person autopsy of the Dead Fifties sort of a relieved farewell to a Bad Decade."[11] His agent at MCA sent the essay "Farewell to a Bad Decade" to *Esquire*, since the magazine had published his long essay on jazz in 1959, and it still paid among the highest fees to its writers. When the article was rejected, MCA sent it on to Krim, who accepted it immediately. As Krim wrote to Holmes later in the summer, he felt it was nonfiction that could best deal with the times they were living through. "How much more pertinent to our answer-searching time is nonfiction than fiction *right now*."[12] Krim was apparently referring to the emergence of a new art of personal reportage that would later be called "the New Journalism," articles by literary journalists such as Truman Capote, Joan Didion, Norman Mailer, and Tom Wolfe, who wrote for many of the magazines that also published Holmes.

Holmes had been out of the fast-changing Manhattan scene for nearly a decade and couldn't identify with any group except the Beats, but he was determined to break out of his self-imposed isolation. In Chicago, his sister Liz had become friendly with the novelist Nelson Algren, who had had a major breakthrough with his challenging novels *The Man with the Golden Arm* and *A Walk on the Wild Side*, which had some affinities to the scene

Holmes had described in *Go*. Algren was a complex man who had worked his way through the Leftist movements in Chicago in the 1930s and, for some turbulent years, been the lover of the French novelist and social critic Simone De Beauvoir. Whatever Holmes thought of his own situation, for another rebel writer like Algren, who was seeing Holmes' name in the best of the new magazines and knew he had two novels behind him, one of them the well-received jazz novel *The Horn*, Holmes was someone to meet. When Algren came to New York in the late spring, Holmes took the train to the city to meet him. They immediately became friends. Algren later was a visitor in Old Saybrook, and their friendship was a useful balance to Holmes' obsessive broodings about the early New York scene.

Holmes wrote Kerouac on July 29, 1962, that MCA Talent, the literary agency which had been representing him for several years, had closed, and he had taken Kerouac's advice and contacted Sterling Lord. Lord had written Holmes in February at Kerouac's suggestion, saying that he understood Holmes was interested in changing agencies and felt they might have a successful relationship. Lord had been acting as Kerouac's agent since the success of *On the Road* had made his name marketable to a variety of popular magazines. Holmes went into Manhattan to meet Lord, and when he left the office he took an advance copy of *Big Sur*, scheduled for publication in the fall.

Back in Old Saybrook, Holmes read the book in one sitting, and though he had his usual visceral response to Kerouac's prose, he was immediately aware that the book would become yet another easy target for Kerouac's growing chorus of critics. In a letter to Kerouac on July 29 he offered sympathy: "Holy Shit man, is there no end to your hells? It's a harrowing, beautiful book, and you're going to get pasted on all sides."[13] Holmes found much in the book's raw honesty that he knew from his own painful experiences.

I've never had the hallucinatory meemies [sic] steam up off the page in quite this way. I've done a bit of drinking of the sort you're describing, and I've had that special spiritual anguish that descends like psychic death after a four day binge, but I've never encountered it in words before; and let me tell you that you've grabbed it, and wrestled it, and flung it down on the floor, the very red meat of everything it costs to survive these days, for everyone to see. But, believe me, they ain't going to like it.[14]

Holmes was aware that, whatever the difficulties readers might have with the book, Kerouac had come closer to the realities of his life than he had allowed himself before. Kerouac had always censured his writing, minimizing scenes of his sexual experiences to keep from offending his mother. With this novel Kerouac seemed to have decided that she wouldn't read it anyway, and if she did, nothing would change between them. Despite his misgivings Holmes praised the style of the book, and, like many of Kerouac's readers, he was impressed by the sound poem "Sea" at the end of *Big Sur*, written as Kerouac sat on the beach and attempted to capture the sound of the surf of the Pacific Ocean in a conscious homage to the writing of James Joyce.

> *If anything, this book is harder, truer, more deadend than most you've done. So I think. . . . I'd say that writing it must have cost you almost as much as surviving it, except that I know that isn't true. Also, by the way, the poem at the end may be the best poem I've ever seen of yours. . . . You know, you make the big Pound-sounds better than anyone, and SEA is astonishing.*[15]

Kerouac disagreed with Holmes' prediction that *Big Sur* would be met by a bad reception. His logic was that since the critics had been attacking him for his rosy-hued descriptions of the Beat Generation, they should be pleased that he had exposed everything that was destructive about it. His final comment was a shrug that good writers were always attacked, Holmes among them, and that he wasn't going to think about it.

Most of Kerouac's letters were filled with desperate complaints about his life in Florida and his equal desperation with his drunken visits to New York. The new Florida house turned out to be close to the space center, in a newly built subdivision called Kingswood Manor, and there had been an explosion of building around them. Kerouac felt that they were living in what was only a newly built slum. One afternoon he looked out the window and saw thirty-two small children playing noisily in the street. It was also eight miles outside of Orlando, and he and his mother were twelve miles from the liquor store and the post office. They had no car, and they were dependent on his sister to drive them wherever they needed to go. Kerouac resorted to a bicycle if he had to get to the liquor store, but the heat was stifling and he and his mother felt themselves closed into the jerry-built walls of the house by the perpetual sun. His drinking had to be done in the house, since there were no bars close enough for him to get to.

With some understanding of his situation, Gabrielle allowed his current girlfriend, Lois Sorrells, to come down from New York and stay with them for a week. In his nervousness and anxiety at having her in the house with his mother, Kerouac stayed drunk and he was impotent in his attempts to have sex with her. Kerouac wrote Holmes that he'd told his mother he was thinking of marrying Lois so she could help them to settle in New England again. Mémère suggested that instead he should ask Holmes to help him, since Holmes was a decent New Englander and the only one of Kerouac's friends whom she liked. Kerouac's response was that as soon as his mother said it, he knew she was right.

Kerouac's letter was the warmest and most affectionate that he'd sent Holmes in many years. With an uncharacteristic concern for Holmes' writing schedule, he asked if he could come to Connecticut in September so his friend could drive him around to look at houses he might buy in Old Saybrook. They would become neighbors, close enough for Holmes to drop in whenever he was in the mood. In his earlier letter, Holmes had also mentioned that he'd been asked to do a prose volume about the beginnings of the Beat Generation. Kerouac's response was a shrewd insight into his friend's strengths as a writer. He thought it would be Holmes' best book. Kerouac's feeling was that there was much more Emerson the essayist in him than there was Hawthorne the novelist.

A few weeks earlier, Holmes had gathered up a loose selection of his nonfiction dealing with the 1950s and his agent had sent it to Bobbs-Merrill. John conceived it as "a wrap-up of the new attitude of the generation, the whole business, the painting, the theatre of the Absurd, Kerouac's balls, the meaning of Kennedy, what Jackie has under her pill-box hat, everything! Everything!"[16] When the concept proved to be too much for Bobbs-Merrill, the material was offered to a select group of publishers in a closed auction. The rights were won by Viking. Holmes' plan was to use the advance to rescue Shirley from "her cornflake job"[17] and get them back to Europe. He signed the contract with Viking a week before Kerouac was planning to arrive, taking an immediate advance. Shirley could leave her job after four unpleasant and poorly paid years. She wrote to her friends Fran and George Beaumont, "I'll be home where I belong and we can live like people again."[18]

A letter came from Kerouac two days later saying that he would be arriving on September 9, and that this time it would be a calm visit. They would drink only beer. He had just come off a weekend drinking binge, more than a quart of whiskey every day to help with his mood after the fiasco of Lois's visit. Holmes hadn't understood that in Orlando Kerouac was facing the same isolation that Holmes found so harrowing in Old Saybrook. Kerouac wrote that he was certain none of this would happen when he and Holmes were neighbors, since they could cooperate in confusing unwelcome visitors by sending them on to a small town somewhere in Texas. He also repeated his perception of Holmes as Emerson by announcing he would be the Thoreau of their friendship.

Kerouac stayed with John and Shirley in Old Saybrook September 9–15, 1962, but despite his resolve in his letter, within a few hours of his arrival he was as bleary with alcohol as he'd been at any time Holmes had seen him. With more money Kerouac was drinking large amounts of brandy, which was more damaging to him than the beer or wine they had drunk together when they were younger and poorer. They didn't seem to have looked at any houses as the days went by in drunken stupor. There was also a sexual edge to Shirley's response to Kerouac, though both were too drunk to attempt anything more than fumbling kisses when Holmes went upstairs to sleep off some of the alcohol. Kerouac finally decided that he wanted to see his friends in Lowell, so Shirley obligingly mixed him a quart of brandy and water in a Mason jar, and Kerouac insisted that they call a cab for the sixty-mile drive. After Lowell, he spent another ten days in New York before he returned to Orlando.

Back in Florida Kerouac wrote an apologetic card to Holmes, repentant at the memory of behaving so badly in Old Saybrook. He had yelled drunkenly that Holmes shouldn't write books about things he didn't know anything about. Holmes' letter in response was sympathetic and affectionate.

Mad? About what, old son? Your card hinted at sweet penitence for un-committed slights, when, after all, it was I who yelled and ranted, and who have been wondering if perhaps you were miffed. So goes the sleazy Marseilles circus of the mind in the rain of back streets. Christ, Jack, there can be no real war between us ever again, you know that. . . . The week was great for Shirl and me, though I haven't got your amazing strength for late hours anymore, and figured you'd understand when I had to go upstairs to refuel with a little sleep. But such talk! It's been years and years, and it was good. By the by, as you know, Shirley loves you too, the week only sealed the glimpses and intuits she's had before. So no more bleak thoughts of lorn, m'boy, nothing undoes what drink and time have stitched, only next time let me buy the brandy, because after you'd gone the terrific amount of dough you'd spent came rocksliding home to me, and I thought, shit, did old Jack get any fun, food, ecstasy, surcease out of it? Hope so. Anyway, you know our house is your house whenever, for however long, wherever it may be.[19]

In Holmes' letter he also asked Kerouac about his reception in Lowell, referring to names and places he only knew from Kerouac's books. "How did Lowell find you? G. J.? [Apostolos] Did you slunk [*sic*] down Moody Street, eye cocked for Doctor Sax? Did it all end with tears at four in the morning, alone by the Merrimack? Anyway you got home safe, home free."[20]

When Kerouac answered on October 9, he was still struggling with his mood of remorseful self-flagellation. The cognac depressed him more than anything he'd tried except Irish whiskey, and he was certain he had said things that had offended John and Shirley. He went on to apologize for the wasted time. His mood lightened when he answered Holmes' questions about his reception in Lowell. Kerouac spent a week with his old friends there, crowing to Holmes that he had "stood poor Lowell on its head,"[21] performing a Cossack dance in a rock-and-roll club when he was introduced to the audience. He was told he recited poetry on Moody Street one night as he was carrying a bottle in his hand, and when he turned up the night before he left at his old favorite bar, he walked into a roaring farewell party. He saw G. J. Apostolos and Mary Carney again, his high school girlfriend who had become "Maggie Cassidy" in his book. The Sampas family was just as welcoming, putting him up to stay in a small house owned by one of the brothers of his high school friend Sebastian Sampas. His final word on the Lowell trip was "had ball."[22]

In a flush of enthusiasm Kerouac decided again that he and his mother should move to Old Saybrook so they could have John and Shirley as neighbors. To show her support for his decision Gabrielle made the surprising gesture of sending Shirley a present with a letter saying she also felt that it would be good for her son to live closer to Holmes, who was a much better influence on him than others in the old crowd. Shirley answered her warmly on October 10, 1962, assuring her that it would good for the two friends to be closer, and sympathizing with Mémère's complaints about Florida's heat and insects.

> *Dear Mémère,*
>
> *It was so nice to meet you in your letter . . . which was so warm and sweet, like you must be, that I feel I know you well. And thank you so much for the lovely bag you sent me; it's so pretty and practical, and I certainly can use it.*
>
> *It was wonderful to see Jack, and of course it meant a great deal to John for them to have some time together after all those years. They sure did talk! And talk and talk and talk! And even then I don't think they got everything said that they wanted to. Obviously the only solution is for you to move up here; then they can talk and we can cook . . . and I'll bet we'll*

outlast them. I wish Jack had found a house. I hope he will in the spring, like he thought he might. . . .

Believe me, I know what you mean about the bugs and the heat down there, being an old Louisiana bayou girl myself. I went home in Novem-ber *last year and nearly died; I honestly don't think I could take a summer in the south again. The Connecticut climate has spoiled me rotten I'm afraid.*[23]

Back in Florida, Kerouac put their house on the market, but in another of his unpredictable changes of mood he decided that he wanted to return to Northport, where he had some drinking friends and familiar bars again instead of Old Saybrook, which seemed to be much more staid. On Christmas Eve 1962, he and his mother arrived at the Long Island Railroad Station in Northport with their three cats in carrier cages, and they moved into a new home on Judyanne Court.

After the stormy, exhilarating interruption of Kerouac's visit, Holmes began to feel a guarded optimism. At the end of October, he finished a new short novel titled "Hobbes and Little Orkie," which he paired with "Old Man Molineaux" under the title *Allee Allee Out In Free.* The title was taken from an old children's game called Kick the Can played in alleys everywhere in the Northeast. The person who was "it" shut his eyes to give the others time to hide, then he left the "base," usually a tin can, searching as far as he dared go for the ones who were hiding. The object of the game was to race past him, or sneak up behind him as his back was turned, and kick the can. With that wild burst of action the game was over. The one who had been "it" would call out "Allee allee out in free" to let the others who were still hiding know that someone had kicked the can, and they could come "home" now. The cry meant everyone still hiding was free to come back home. For Holmes, the novel was emblematic of the tension-filled world situation during the Cold War. He wrote to Algren on December 4, 1962, that he felt "our human dilemma these days resembles nothing so much as a global game of Kick-the Can."[24] He mailed the new book to Sterling Lord on December 19.

The new manuscript was difficult for his publishers to grasp, and the dismissive, lecturing tone of their rejections lent a somber note to the long winter. Holmes' editor at Viking, Tom Guinzberg, returned it to Lord with the dismissive note, "This is not nearly as good a book as John ought to be writing or can write and I say this candidly but with real regret."[25] The rejection from McGraw-Hill was brusque: "a bad book by a very good writer."[26]

For the present the income from Holmes' magazine pieces, along with the advance from the nonfiction manuscript, had made it possible for Shirley to leave her job. Though they were beginning to run out of money, she enjoyed being a housewife full-time again so much that nothing else seemed nearly as important. She insisted that Holmes also take a break and he went into New York for ten days, meeting a few old friends, sitting in his old bars, and slowly pulling himself into some sort of shape to go on with his struggle over the new book. As he wrote Kerouac on March 15, 1963, he tried to "let the streets, and the anonymous hurrying thousands, and the cold blank light of Village Sunday afternoons work their magic on me."[27]

The healing effect of the trip to New York lasted only a couple of months. Back in Old Saybrook, Holmes came as near to a complete breakdown as he had ever come. When he wrote to Kerouac at the end of his dark agonies on June 6, he could be as open as he could be to anyone, since Kerouac had known that same moment of physical and emotional collapse at the end of his three weeks in Big Sur. What Holmes didn't tell Kerouac was that in these lost months he had also filled pages of his journals with sexual fantasies and tormented questioning of his sexual relationship with Shirley. In the letter he only confessed to his own alcohol abuse, since that was what Kerouac was upset about, then he moved on to a new subject. His hope was that the nonfiction book he'd contracted to write could help him out of his emotional torment, and he had already begun to work his way into the project.

Along with his letter he sent Kerouac the long, detailed set of questions that he had prepared for his chapter on his friend in the collection of essays he would title *Nothing More to Declare*. He had re-read all of Kerouac's books published to date because in his essay he primarily wanted to focus on Kerouac's writing, hoping to clarify what he called "the moody history" of Kerouac's prose style.[28] Holmes began his questions, however, by trying to ascertain that his view of Kerouac's life was accurate. Holmes considered Kerouac first and foremost an important American author, in a class with Melville and Faulkner, though this was an idea that contradicted most contemporary critics' narrow view of Kerouac as a Beat writer with connections to Ginsberg and a few noisy California poets. In Holmes' view, Kerouac's development as a writer began at the time that they had become friends:

I see pivots in your life: uprooting from Lowell and entrance into World City [New York City] with its fevers, interests, ambitions, involvements, but you are basically still the youth after first weaning. Then in 1949, the choice between Fame & Cocktail parties and all that, and the "trucks on the road." Which, however, led to end-of-the-road Mexicos where everything became clear and blank: the last pivot turning you back, your brood has been on consciousness ever since, because the road ended after all, and the outer world has only distracted and momentarily interested you since; when you went down into yourself in SAX you came back forever different; no major pivot really since then; only losses & exasperations & Melville's unfolding of the onion day after day, but the onion is yourself at last. What of these pivots?²⁹

Holmes went on to ask specific questions about the novels, particularly *Doctor Sax*, his favorite among Kerouac's books. Not only literary queries such as "I must ask about [James] Joyce's shadow on this book," and "What about spontaneous prose, the book-movie, etc." and "Why is the color BROWN the color of your boyhood?" but also "Hateful query now: SAX *can* be read as masturbatory guilt fantasy (World Snake: penis) . . . rather as if you fought through fear and guilt of Catholicism to acceptance of the befuddled, complex loneliness of pro-adult life. Is this all errant, PR crap on my part?"³⁰

In particular, Holmes asked his friend to clarify his intentions in creating the various books of the Duluoz Legend individually as a "piece of the whole," comparing Kerouac's creative impulse to the way that Faulkner

once described the germination of SOUND AND FURY as the single image of a girl, shimmied up a tree, peeking in an upstairs window, her muddy drawers being observed by her little brother lower on the tree. He went on to discover what led up to, and away from, this single image. Comment on that in terms of your arbitrary cutting of the Legend into suitable lengths.³¹

Warming to the questions, Holmes then reverted to his interest in how Kerouac had found a different style after he'd written the scroll version of *On the Road.*

I remember the anal, Giroux, one-sentence-an-hour, Melville of the Pierres, FIRST attempt at On the Road, *that so boggled you (nights in Glennon's reading enormous, complex, exfoliating sentences of pot-perception), and that finally led to your sitting down (in Chelsea with roll of paper) to just BLOW the book; it seems the breakthru happens (as it does in Zen). . . . Until finally a what-the-hell, not-for-me exasperation pushed you over the top into satori-prose, and simply putting-down-what-was-there in continual, unbroken onrush. Is true?*[32]

Finally Holmes turned to questions about his friend's often criticized attitude toward African Americans ("They accuse you of being Crow-Jim romantic, adolescent") and his interest in Buddhism ("What moulting of the consciousness has carried us all beyond the either\or of the Faustian intelligence?") before closing with questions about the influence of Cassady ("Neal is the secret after which you ran so long, or he embodied it. What was it?") as well as Ginsberg ("Now you run in separate grooves, but ominously side by side, though a world away. . . . Or am I again oversimplifying?"). Holmes ended his letter with a confession that previously "what prevented me from ever really *understanding* you was the very lust to understand which proved to be nothing but MY image of you, and not you at all."[33] He assured his friend,

> *I'm sincere, Jack, I'm serious too. I can't enlarge myself beyond my limits, or lay all ghosts that skulk my ramparts, but I've no interest in bending your work to my whim, and would give it what you once called "a sweet attention." Also, these days, I'm somewhat wacky, and impatient myself, but I've only one last word to say in the Big Court, and for once I want to say it all.*[34]

Less than two weeks later, on June 23, 1963, Kerouac answered from Northport, saying that he'd worked for three nights on his responses and they had to be quoted in their entirety, since he had consciously framed his words for publication. Reluctant at first to answer Holmes' questions, Kerouac was so conscientious that he numbered his answers, twenty-six in all, to make them easier to follow. Though he refused to answer Holmes' final questions, which concerned his attitude toward women and his suicidal drinking to the point of physical collapse, Holmes had courteously provided him with an escape by asking him to "pardon the intimacies."[35]

By the time Kerouac responded to the questionnaire, he had been so frequently flailed by hostile critics who misunderstood and undervalued his books that he was understandably raw and bitter toward the literary world, and his early optimism about his career was lost in the past. He made light of Holmes' query about the "pivots" in his life, and he insisted that he was more indebted to Proust than to Joyce as a literary model. But Holmes' question about the color brown caught Kerouac's fancy, and he went into detail about the beloved objects in his boyhood—chairs, river, radio, his mother's bathrobe—that were all brown. The query about "book-movies" took two pages to discuss, though Kerouac made short work of Holmes' idea of *Doctor Sax* as "masturbatory guilt fantasy."

Most memorably, Kerouac was taken with Holmes' question about the organization of the books in the Legend of Duluoz, revealing that, like Faulkner, he germinated *Doctor Sax* out of a dream image and thought of the individual books in his Legend, like Mozart, as various musical forms— some as long as symphonies and others as short as sonatas. He gave quick answers to Holmes' questions about his views toward African Americans (unlike the author James Baldwin, Kerouac had no time for politics) and Buddhism (no short response was possible for such a vast subject). Finally, Kerouac's responses to Holmes' questions about his relationships with Cassady and Ginsberg were fond, gracious, and succinct. He considered himself Cassady's biographer for life, and he had learned from Ginsberg—along with Burroughs and Huncke—what Kerouac termed the less positive or homosexual side of life and literature, though he was never of their camp, always only someone observing from the side.

Kerouac had done justice to Holmes' questions, but when Holmes wrote his essay he had to put aside Kerouac's letter. He took Kerouac at his word and didn't use any of his responses in the essay, since each of Kerouac's careful answers to the questions was too long to quote in full. Instead Holmes relied on his memories of his close friend, creating a dense, personal texture of insightful commentary on Kerouac's books by recounting memories of their shared experiences and quoting extensively from his own journals and Kerouac's early letters. When he wrote about the books, Holmes described his excitement reading the manuscripts as Kerouac sent them, even admitting candidly,

> *I did not always have the courage of my own tastes. I remember, for instance, reading* Visions of Cody *one muggy afternoon, and then going out to walk by the East River, cursing Kerouac in my head for writing so well in a book which, I was firmly convinced, would never be published. To this day, whenever I grow complacent about my own good sense, I recall that river walk.*[36]

Holmes' essay about Kerouac as "The Great Rememberer" in *Nothing More to Declare* is one of his best, a fitting tribute to the man he regarded as his "brother-soul."

As Holmes began to scramble back from his physical collapse at the beginning of the summer his situation suddenly brightened. On June 14 he heard from his agent that Dutton was taking his novel *Allee Allee Out in Free*. There was an advance of fifteen hundred dollars, and their only proviso was that his editor wanted him to strengthen the central character. The title, which had been more confusing than illuminating, was changed to *Get Home Free*. Holmes could suddenly lift his head and look around him with some confidence. He had contracts for two books, the nonfiction book about the 1950s he had contracted for in the fall, and now the novel, as well as acceptance of new ideas for articles by some of his magazine contacts. Shirley invited guests to stay with them every weekend, including Algren, who visited for two days in June. Holmes wrote an account of the visit in his journal which he used later in an insightful essay on Algren's writing:

> *Algren here these past two days. Hours of funny talk; he seems in goodish shape; reserved,* hooded, *somehow, the light going out of his face sometimes, as it does when he loses interest. He sleeps in odd little hour-long cat naps right around the clock. Blue-back cotton shirt, blue slacks, blue pin striped jacket, moccasins for the house, riding boots for outside, his strange, vaguely pop-y blue-brown eyes, like a spaniel's eyes in their depth, his protruding jaw thrust out to make a point with pursing lips, his scraggle of thin & thinning sandy-gray hair, his habit of ruffling it, of rubbing his eyes, of looking away; the odd flatness of the back of his head. Quick judgments arrived at after some time; the slowness of speech in a musing, mock-black drawl; his "oh, yeses, oh sure," after making a comic point. There is something special about him, severed, cut-off—sometimes you'll look up & he has simply vanished—literally. He is as quiet as a lean cat, padding softly up & down stairs, locking himself in the bathroom, asking for nothing, rarely speaking, with his odd little chortle, and his sudden rises off the couch in the middle of a tale, to walk to the back window, falling into silence, or standing staring at a book case, and then continues his monolog. He is slightly more assertive in public. . . . A curious, secretive, somehow* abashed *man, more itinerant than ever, more uprooted, hard to triangulate, with strong opinions on people that seem based on how they were to him, economical (as all good writers are) with his energies & attentions.*[37]

Shortly after Algren's visit, another writer friend Vance Bourjaily made Holmes an offer that he finally couldn't refuse. After his own promising literary career as a novelist had flattened out, Bourjaily had taken a teaching position in the highly regarded Writers' Workshop at the University of Iowa, directed by Paul Engles. It was considered one of the most advanced and successful writing programs in the United States, largely because of

Engles' commitment to bringing new writers to Iowa City to take over the classes. Bourjaily's letter to Holmes on June 21, 1963, asked if he'd like to join the faculty for the coming year. Though he couldn't have known of the cauldron of self-flagellation from which Holmes only recently emerged, it was probably the most auspicious moment Bourjaily could have chosen to offer him a break from Old Saybrook. Holmes was uncertain about what he should do and hesitated for a few days, then he made a quick decision and accepted. On July 22, 1963, he wrote to Kerouac,

> *Into the middle of this labor came an offer to be a kind of visiting lecturer at the U. of Iowa this coming year—Engle's Writers' Workshop, Iowa City, seven months, two afternoons a week of two hours each, rest of the time to myself, about a thousand a month. I hate the idea, Academe is epicene, all that, but then I thought, shit, it'll get us out of here, it'll give me a year without any financial worries in which to finish up this work, it's as good as a license to steal, and I'll get clear of it with dough ahead and two books coming out, and a chance to start wandering the face of the earth at last. In short, I've said "yes", and barring disasters or miracles we'll leave here, in car, in early September, renting this house, and hoping that "Ioway is sweet like its name."[38]*

In his letter to Bourjaily accepting the offer, Holmes asked some practical questions: how much teaching would be involved in the two hours he met with students? "Do you talk for two hours? How soon do you have to plan out the course, make up reading lists, etc."[39] Bourjaily's response on June 30 was relaxed and friendly: "Let me start by saying that if there's anxiety in our situation here it's because it's too undemanding."[40]

Before John and Shirley left for Iowa two months later, however, there was to be another purgatory that would indelibly stain the summer. It would lead them onto new sexual pathways and leave them both with agonies of self-revelation that would undermine their marriage for years to come.

Chapter 19

TO THE EDGE OF EROS

I seriously think of raising a couple of thousand dollars to publish, on my own, in cheap paper and paper-covers, a 1,000 page limited edition of my journals of these past three years, an amazing document it would be, not writing, not a book, but evidence, a huge lunar landscape that has resisted all my efforts to mine it, or transpose it, into other, saner works, but which (to me at least) comes closer to what I am, and mean, than anything I've written, or perhaps will ever write, and which I would publish in an edition of a hundred copies or so, and send out free to friends, critics, and whomsoever else, and then rest, because it could never be published legally, openly, because of wildest erotic writing of last forty years, all very serious in intent, but still absolutely no holds barred, and also the document is so self-damming in its intimacy and revelation that no publisher would believe I don't care who knows it, so it would have to be mailed out all in one batch, so the P.O. wouldn't get wind of it until too late—but I am secretly thinking of doing this some day soon, off-set press, cheapest paper, no apologies, no editing for prudery or protection (except to witless innocents), and then really sit back, and go on with what I'm doing, secure in the knowledge that I won't vanish without leaving some trace.

—JOHN CLELLON HOLMES, letter to Jack Kerouac, June 6, 1963

In the early 1960s Holmes began to describe his sexual experiences in his journals, which resulted, as he wrote Kerouac, in a "document so self-damming in its intimacy and revelation that no publisher would believe I don't care who knows it."[1] There is no question that Holmes intended to publish what he'd written, since near the end of his life he worked for months with his bibliographer Richard Ardinger preparing all of his sixties journals for publication. If Holmes had the financial resources, as he wrote Kerouac, he would have published the journals himself.

The graphic content of the material has to be given a place in Holmes' story since it was an expression of a conviction that had been emotionally decisive for him since he and Kerouac had shared their ideas of sexual freedom as young men in their ebullient conversations at 681 Lexington. Fifteen years later, Holmes didn't realize that the corrosive effect of his sexual fantasies involving Shirley would become a long, oppressive shadow that cast its darkness over their marriage.

In the early 1960s Holmes' experimentation was his attempt to become "whole again" by breaking through the sexual inhibitions he believed were at the core of all human violence, a New Age idea he clung to without an understanding of the possibly disastrous consequences it could have on Shirley and himself. He expressed his deep dissatisfaction with conventional sexual attitudes and his desire for a "New Consciousness" in the essay "Revolution Below the Belt," which won *Playboy*'s Best Non-Fiction award for 1964. In the essay Holmes equated the global violence that had erupted in the twentieth century with the suppression of sexual feelings.

> *More and more, something whispers to us that we are doomed to this nightmare of insanity and murder if we do not become whole again. More and more, something whispers that one source of wholeness lies in the mysterious sexual energy through which we can still experience our uniqueness, even when anxiety has most obscured it. And more and more are we willing to assume with Lawrence "that people would [not] be villains, thieves, murderers and sexual criminals if they were freed from legal restraint," rather than assuming the opposite, as totalitarians of all persuasions have always done. For the essence of the New Consciousness, in sex as in everything else, is the simple insistence that man is more creative than destructive. And a more revolutionary creed, given our world, would be hard to imagine.*[2]

Among John and Shirley's friends in Connecticut was a woman they had known as a neighbor who was five years older than John. Whatever her convictions were about the New Consciousness, she had begun to test her freedom in her marriage to enlarge her own sexual horizons. After a long drunken evening of frenetic talk and dancing when Allen Ginsberg and Philip Whalen stayed over in Old Saybrook, the woman had sex with Whalen in the living room as John and Shirley slept off the night's drinking upstairs. Harrington was staying with them every other weekend to see his young son, and Alan and the woman began an affair which continued for several months, even though Harrington assured Holmes it wasn't anything he took very seriously.

There had been some of this casualness in the couplings in the crowd at Glennon's Bar in the late forties, but now in the early sixties the sex had become more open, and the expectation was that it would be less guilt-ridden. The pages of Holmes' journals at this time move uneasily between his desperate sense of loneliness and his obsessive physical desire, what he termed his "despair-become-lust." His frustration became stronger as the months slipped past, turning his quarrels with Shirley into despairing verbal brawls. He wrote in his journal on July 31, 1962:

> *Yesterday the bottom fell out of my soul—after a foolish, despairing fight the night before; so I drank most of the day, feeling utterly lost & dejected, wanting a voice, a word, a look, anything. . . . [I]n the late afternoon, TV'd, read; overcome by sheer maddened loneliness I was toppled by a desperate sexual craving,(as if my consciousness would slip away from me, my very self, if I couldn't feel even the spurious momentary warmth of any simple, crude contact), but Shirley was asleep, and even my despair-become-lust couldn't wipe out the sight of her weary lidded eyes, her willingness, her intention to keep us both alive till the demons withdrew. I couldn't transform that true world out of a desire that was not a real, fleshy desire but only the enflamed proddings of my impotent ego, so I let it go, and the evening was pleasant & minimal, & I wrote (after a restless night) oddly hangover less. But did no work.³*

Over the summer of 1962 Holmes' writing took on some of its fluency again, and by the fall, when Harrington ended the affair, the woman appeared to have managed some kind of reconciliation with her husband. Whatever Holmes might have been feeling about his neighbor, though, a drunken evening when he and the woman kissed caused a furious outburst on Shirley's part.

> *Drink & propinquity etc. led to the foolish and aimless kisses with her before S. erupted, and I thought we had gotten it clear by the next morning when S. explained her outburst had been only a return to old insecurities & fears of "betrayal," but that she realized that a few drunken sexual forays didn't constitute betrayal. The other woman was drunk, as I was, and (I suppose) also aroused by the ease of being able to talk about masturbation & her encounter with Alan—which she had done, by the way, with both of us. And then S. went off to bed, leaving me pleasantly stewed, and the woman in her shortie-nightgown & shortie kimono. Actually she wanted to talk about Alan, which we did, and, frankly I was too tipsy & exhausted to notice when this subject became more of a pretense*

than anything else. She lay on the mattress, 1st on back, then on stomach, her sex right there for me, though in thinking back on it I believe most of it was unconscious, and then somehow (like a muddle-headed dolt) I realized she was saying something oblique about desiring me, and I kissed her out of confusion and obedience, the kiss leading to absolutely nothing further. She fled to the bathroom when S. burst in to fix herself coffee, and I went off to bed immediately. But, of course, the real volcano erupted the next night, after a day in which I clearly sensed that S. was disturbed, and trying to deny it to herself. Brandy & weariness caused the worst knock-down, drag-out, despair & dissipation scene we've ever had. She was going to get out of there no matter what, having had half-a-pint of brandy in less than an hour. Nothing—no blows, not acceding to her wild idea (tho I got the car stuck), not even threatening to destroy my mss.—deviate her; only the promise that I'd get her away first thing in the morning. Which, of course, I did, driving the 200 miles to Deerfield [to visit friends] in the toils of a second-day hangover & utter blank despair & indifference. We went on to Provincetown and in the two days there we managed to salvage a few things. The repercussions that lay ahead, here in Saybrook, were simply more of the same—though the real sting had gone out of them.[4]

Holmes attempted to shift some of the responsibility for what had happened on to Shirley and lamely justified himself with something that she had told him about a late evening when Kerouac had stayed with them the previous month.

Sexual-jealousy in women seems to be beyond the reach of sense and reason, and really, I suppose, has very little to do with sex per se. S. and Jack had a little scene while he was here—"we necked & tried to decide whether to fuck or not, but we were too drunk," is the way they described it to me the next morning—and, of course, S. knows how harmless and foolish this was, as do I, and so, of course, I said nothing, and felt nothing about it. If she had slept with Jack, my reaction would have been the same, knowing it would have been the result of drink & propinquity, rather than any overwhelming passion. In any case, I don't think my relationship with her can be threatened, or even much affected by such a pointless, even though perhaps pleasurable, sexual foray.[5]

In his uncertainty, unable to reach Shirley or even to understand the tensions between them, Holmes turned again to the old knotted argument of differences between men and women and their experience of sex. After settling into Old Saybrook, they had made the decision not to have children for many reasons. Both had been traumatized by their parents' divorce, and Shirley still had a strained relationship with her overbearing mother. Holmes, like Kerouac, never felt secure enough as a writer to take on the financial responsibility of children. Nearing forty, Holmes continued to obsess about sex like an adolescent. He wrote in his journal,

> *Do women essentially* lack *the fleshly despair out of which libertinism all too often comes? Do they have a less damaged sense of themselves than men, and thus do not need to go for the prodigious sexual exacerbations, which are perhaps the distinctive hallmark of the sexual life of this mid-century. . . . The experience itself is what men want—as if it might hold out a goading strangeness, or newness, that would in itself stir up the deepest dormant emotions—as if one might experience a further, more irrevocable anxiety, from which, at least, one might healthily recoil. This is why, for instance, I am not remotely interested in merely sleeping with another woman—for what would that be? Bodies are only bodies, after all. But ménage a trois, or S. conspiring with me in the act, and finally I suppose the touch of imminent lesbianism, which would sweeten the situation—these things do of course darkly interest me. For all that can be gained from sexual gymnastics, is further knowledge—and this is what one is after—perhaps only because one darkly suspects one can't fall back into life until one has the knowledge, some ultimate knowledge, of how fruitless the pursuit is in the first place. This, after all, is the reason for all pornography, all pretending, all picture-taking in the sex act—to open up the deepest drawers, to get it all as conscious as possible. You realize that all of this is a profanation in a way, but in this time you have to accept the inner-logic of Genet's contention that only via degradation can we be ennobled—a very old, very black idea that has run thru the Western consciousness for centuries, surfacing more & more in the last 150 years or so. Everyone feels it now: an ultimate sign of how desperate is our plight.*[6]

Holmes found himself thinking obsessively of a sexual experience with both women, Shirley and their neighbor, though he continued to insist to himself that he wasn't drawn physically to their friend. She was older, her body fleshier than Shirley's, and he told himself she was not attractive to him. But as the months passed he found himself continually imagining images of the three of them together. On December 23, 1962, he noted in his journal, "The mystery & reality of the flesh (in which the other person lives) is about all that goads my musings any longer. Sexual explicitness has taken on a new aura to me. I may be seriously misled, seeing no problems where problems there actually are. I think, like some idiot of God, that we should all fuck with one another, if only to tear down something, to experience the otherness."[7] He realized that Shirley didn't share his sexual obsessions, since in self-protection she had responded by withdrawing from him, drinking too much brandy, and going early to her bed. As Holmes continued in his journal he envisioned a kind of sexual epiphany which would return Shirley to him.

The sex urge taken beyond objectification; beyond its aura of personified desire; into the unknown country of the simple flesh itself. Is this possible? The naked bodies of women—their breasts, bellies, hips, thighs, buttocks— something of the quick is grasped in the very nakedness. Or is this only more exacerbation? Shirley's mind is temporarily lulled, as happens with women, because her flesh is asleep. A few wild days would bring her back, but I still feel a shiver of sexual-jealousy in her, as if she was afraid of my mind, and my direction. Normal enough, of course, but I believe she is, or could be, a venturer with me, a pioneer into the new & dangerous territories, if I could only get her keyed enough towards it. She has been on some occasions; fearless & curious & wanton & willing; keyed as I say to the possibility that lies at the zenith of desire. But now she is lulled, asleep, she falls back—as I do, as is natural. And, of course, the book done, that inhuman tension of the mind over—I snap right back into heightened sexual awareness, with no "steps" in between, and women are not really capable of this. Also, S. is uncertain now, somewhat closed over in self-protection, and fears (as I have, God knows!) the danger implicit in the naked, sudden sexual contact—the dangers of opening, of being defenseless with someone not completely trusted to handle this exposed quiver of self with tact & delicacy. How to overcome this strange formality which comes down between people, who have touched every square inch of each other with tongues & eyes & words? An odd formality, an infinitesimal drawing-back, a kind of cautious recoil from the dangerous source of heat & light—until we become cocooned, enwrapt, withdrawn, as if our arms were clasped across our chests in the proverbial attitude of protection & relinquishment which has always seemed proper to the dead about to meet their Maker. The beautiful, mysterious perfection of the aroused genitals, the warm aura of genitality itself, remains like a fretful, reminding stir in the air around me.[8]

On February 26, 1963, Holmes' obsessive thoughts of a *ménage a trois* seemed closer to reality.

Our friend on Sat. Alcohol, music, dancing, straight talk etc. She stayed over and the three of us had breakfast, wine & TV in our bed on Sun. The possibility of a "trois"? S. seemed unlovely willing enough—in her mind anyway. Our friend? Who can really tell? I would think she would react against it, but women keep fooling me on these levels. I was too hung [over] to be able to carry the ball very far anyway. Certainly, however, the idea of it, and the proximity of the three of us (half dressed) stirred Shirley, or so I felt. . . . The talk between the three of us grows very open, very frank—and certainly it tends in one direction. How do I feel? She attracts me sufficiently—that is, under the right circumstances, I could make love to her. I think it is more her mind, venturing outward these days, than her body, which is nice, but not the sort of body I usually go for. The idea of the three of us intrigues me most of all. In a curious way, it seems the simplest solution—no complications, no misunderstandings, a sally into the unusual, and that's all. But, in any case, the moment (if it was a moment) was missed. . . . Anyway, beyond a point all is unknown territory (which is what stimulates us, after all) and no outright schemes can be made. Certainly our friend, and perhaps even Shirley, might be surprised to see (nakedly) the degree of verbal intimacy that exists right now between the three of us. In effect, we have talked about everything but ménage a trois, *and, when, after all, two women lie next to one another, in nothing but loose kimonos, and a man lies with them in his shorts, and they talk about the most intimate details of sex, more than mere good fellowship, propinquity, and the spirit of candor is involved. Or am I being incredibly conventional?*[9]

On June 17 Holmes wrote in his journal that he finally had spoken openly to Shirley and their friend about the three of them having sex after they had sat for hours drinking and having another of their sex-filled conversations. Their neighbor had recently separated from her husband, and Holmes had become impatient with their continued circling of the possibility of a threesome. In the muddle of drunkenness both women seemed to respond to the suggestion. There was still too much hesitancy and nervousness between them for something to happen quickly, but now it hung in the air. Holmes was as uncertain himself, uncomfortably concluding, "Who knows what the reality would arouse in any of us."[10]

Although Holmes had insisted to Kerouac that he would publish everything he had written in his journals about his sexual experimentation, when he came to edit the material he omitted the pages from the next two months, when his sexual journey with the two women began. Holmes might have hesitated because he was aware of the real possibility of libel, which had hung over the writing both he and Kerouac had done from the beginning of their careers. It had been necessary for Kerouac to obtain releases for his first novel, *The Town and the City*, from Ginsberg and Burroughs, who were described so specifically in the final chapters that they were immediately identifiable. The publication of *On the Road* was delayed for months while the publisher's lawyers dealt with the libel issue. The efforts to avoid any pretext for a libel action led both Holmes and Kerouac to invent occasionally absurd pseudonyms for their characters. *The Subterraneans*, with its swirl of sexual hungers and its lyric and very explicit descriptions of Kerouac's efforts to bring his girl to orgasm, caused the most difficulty for his publishers. Beside changing the names of all the characters, the entire novel had to be rewritten to change its setting to San Francisco, instead of New York where the relationship had taken place.

Whatever Holmes' reason for omitting the material, he kept a later journal entry where he returned to his memory of his first sexual experience with the two women. Their first attempt to find a sexual release with each other was less of an epiphany than he'd expected—perhaps they had drunk too much; perhaps there was too much mutual embarrassment. The second night was more successful, and he was surprised at Shirley's "sheer cold sexual lust" for the other woman. She was curious about the neighbor's vagina, "spreading her cunt, opening it—'Isn't it strange?—is that what I look like?'—and then wanting to put her mouth there. For them (they were drunk) I didn't exist."[11]

Although Holmes had been obsessed for months with the possibility of three-way sex, at first he was disconcerted at being reduced to a spectator.

They embraced one another's naked bodies with sexual desire. Shirley licked her open pussy, head between the full flung-back thighs; they mouth kissed, mashing each other's breasts. Shirley got the other woman to reciprocate, to go down & part S's black wiry bush and thrill her clitoris with her tongue. Their clear, strong, perverted lust was real enough to make me jealous after I had come into my hands watching them. Shirley's mouth tasted of the other woman's sex; they convulsively rubbed their wet pussies together. Shirley couldn't come, though she had dressed, & made up sexily for her, & got drunk, wanting specifically to experience a real, fleshly perversion.[12]

As he became part of their embrace he also had an intimation of the half-acknowledged edge of violence that was an almost inevitable dimension of their sexual encounter.

> *Shirley watched me screwing the other woman, watching my cock plunging in & and pulling out of her sex-spread cunt. She saw the woman's flattened buttocks, the dark slit where her ass was, she talked "dirty" to us so I could ejaculate into the woman, who kept turning her head away so I couldn't get my tongue down between her lips. Cruelty, of a sexual sort, awakened in Shirley. She wanted me to take her, force her, denude her, say obscene things to her. She massaged the woman's breasts as I sweated down on her. Later, she took my prick, tasting of the woman's wet vagina, in her mouth. And just that once, that second night, I know she felt a perverted desire—not for the woman—but to have cunt-sex, to commit an absolutely new, dangerous act. The woman, I'm convinced, desired to have intercourse with Shirley more than me. They lay on the bed (I went down & got drinks) tongue kissing, the woman on top of Shirley. I studied her heavy buttocks, Shirley's thighs spread around her, their erect stiffened nipples, their fingers playing rough with each other's clitorises. I wanted to mount her, and while she embraced Shirley, their wet opened cunts pressed together, I slipped my cock up her twat from behind.*[13]

Whatever Holmes might have felt about the inevitability of what the three of them had experienced, it's surprising that he used the word "perverted" to describe Shirley's desires when he was so eager to push the limits of conventional sex. He never urged Shirley to explore three-way sex with a second male partner, which would have involved Holmes in homosexual acts that might have revealed another side of his own sexual nature. The excitement he had felt watching his wife having sex with his neighbor was enough; it had clearly shaken all of his earlier preconceptions.

When Holmes returned to his journal the next day, the description he had written became the occasion for a technical question—how could he transfer writing that was so sexually explicit into a fictional narrative or the script of a play? In his attempt to define the problem he came up against the difficult subject of pornography and censorship, which he felt was in itself almost as complex a matter to deal with as his emotions after participating in a sexual triangle. If Kerouac had any misgivings about including his descriptions of sex with his black lover in *The Subterraneans*, he never felt the need to discuss them in his journal or in any of his letters to his friends, but Holmes asked himself,

How to handle the sex? The above [what he had written in his journal the day before] is, of course, far too heated, too pornographic. How much do I need? . . . I wanted to write a dense, dark, mercilessly honest treatment of exacerbated sexuality, & the sexual descriptions were going to go all the way, so that they might embody my idea that our deepest psychic shifts & alterations often occur directly in relationship to the expanding or controlling of our sexual energy; sex become more than sex; sex as communication, ritual, game, testing, escape, fantasy, acting out, etc. to accomplish this tale, then, I conceived that I would have to write more candidly, more graphically, & with less reserve, abstraction, & analytical window dressing than had been done before in serious fiction. I am aware how easily this could slip over into outright pornography, and I don't want that—that is, I don't want the fantasy, the wishfully obsessive gymnastics, the Johnnie-One-Note quality of pornography.[14]

Just as Holmes had set for himself the impossible task of recreating the moral world of Dostoevsky in his first attempts to write about his scene in New York, he seemed again to have created a scenario for a novel that would be as difficult to write as his first books. In each of his projects his intention was always to create a work of fiction that would express his complex moral concepts through his characters. He was conscious that he had already come close to describing a lesbian relationship in *Get Home Free*, but he had decided that there would be a structural problem if he introduced a new element in his already heavily burdened plot.

The brief lesbian moment in Get Home Free *was, of course, short circuited (so as not to introduce an extraneous theme)—though [it] probably would have done further. . . . I will, of course, have constant reference to our experience with the other woman, but I still have to find the* proportion *which will be proper to the problem. . . . Can it be done? and can the last, terrible, blasphemous explosion be made coherent to the reader who will be, of course, shocked, and should be, as well, even disgusted, but must be, finally, saddened by the starved natures turning so convulsively in their empty longings. I will cut out anything that is merely repetitious, but everything that marked a turn, a pivot, an intensification, a revelation, must be included. There's no point in writing it if the sex isn't clear, if the reader doesn't see it, feel it, experience it (the only way to understand it).[15]*

Despite his determination to create a successful novel with an erotic center, Holmes was never able to finish the project. It never even got so far as a working title. He also couldn't bring himself to acknowledge that his adventuring to the edge of eros had devastated his relationship with Shirley. It took years before their sexual relationship recovered. It seems obvious that the entanglements of the summer had only brought to a head years of resentment and dissatisfaction. Shirley had paid a much higher price for supporting Holmes' obsession with his writing than either of them was willing to acknowledge, even in their incessant drunken quarreling. Neither of them would admit that they were now living their life through alcohol, and it was as deadening and defeating as any of the drugs that had been part of the scene they'd left behind in New York. Holmes' insistence that Shirley take this final step over what he considered their sexual boundaries continued to torment them as a wound that was long to heal.

Perhaps because the sexual experiments of the summer had such long-reaching consequences, Holmes turned again and again in his journals to D. H. Lawrence, the literary source of his quest. He had taken as his "working-rule D. H. Lawrence's statement: 'Man is a great venture in consciousness.'" believing that "this venture into new areas of awareness is the underlying theme of most important 20th Century fiction."[16] In his novels Holmes had taken "the rebel, the outcast, the artist" as his subjects because they were "all those whose extremes of consciousness match their extremes of experience."[17] They reflected his own dedication as a writer to the idea of a "search for new continuities to replace those of the family, religious faith, and social idealism—continuities in comradeship, passional love, and artistic creation."[18] Reading Lawrence's novels to "illuminate" his own life had reassured Holmes "that others live as intensely as ourselves."[19]

Reading The Rainbow *for the 1st time in years, and struck . . . by the revelation of what Lawrence's "prophetic" quality really was: the new sensibility, the new consciousness that he announces & describes is almost precisely the sort of opened, translucent consciousness everyone is seeking to unlock these days—via mixed media happenings, hallucinogenic drugs, and, even, McLuhanism to some extent. Lawrence's people "receive" one another, and their own experiences, in precisely this nonverbal, non-logical, instantly intuitive sense. Some of his best moments have an uncanny Zen-like flash to them that one either digs or doesn't. Of this wide consciousness, Lawrence is the single, great prophet among all writers in English in this century. Forty years ago, he saw its necessary-coming, described most of its central elements, was preoccupied himself with everything that it could be preoccupied with (sex, religion, passional contact between all living things, the oneness of creation, the hell of the intellect, the death of mind & its false structures, etc. etc. etc.). He is the great prophet whose heirs are N. O. Brown, Bataille (in some ways), and certainly Ginsberg, Mailer, myself and most everyone else who is seeking to shake loose the old, stunted, rigid consciousness so man can enter into a valid relationship with the new & rather scary world our times have created. I find him, too, very existential in some ways, if you read him correctly. Indeed, Lawrence's characters may be the "freest" characters in all literature. They vibrate intensity down into their natures at everything they encounter. A study of "freedom," in the existential sense, as it is a theme in Lawrence needs to be done.*

He is, without a doubt, the single most important creative writer in the 20th Century to me. His work was for the future, and nothing that he says (no matter how incomprehensible) should be ignored. His work is a never-ending source of creative fulfillment for me, a spring of continually uprushing perceptions. And now, these days, I can at last feel his movements, it is all coherent to me, clear, inevitable, a shower of richness.[20]

Holmes had intuited in Lawrence the struggle to break free of the restriction of sexual conventions that in the first years of his long friendship with Kerouac and Ginsberg had been one of their continual themes. However they may have considered that their beginnings lay in the Existentialists or Dostoevsky, it was the larger sexual freedoms Lawrence proposed that excited them.

Although Holmes didn't include another name, he had also been fascinated by this resistance to conventional limits of experience in the writings of Gershon Legman when they had met in 1948. Legman's obsession with freedom of sexual expression had been a revelation for Holmes, even though Legman had finally been driven out of the country and had taken refuge in a half-ruined country chateau in France. Legman's obsessions had been fired by what he insisted was the need for a *literary* expression of sexuality, but what John found in Lawrence was the insistence on the physical *experience* of sexuality. Holmes continued in his journal,

Strange that I should have felt this about him [Lawrence] from the age of 16, even though it was not until recent years that I ever, truly dug what he was saying. Kinships are the most mysterious conjunctions in human life; the like that speaks to like speaks on a level below our understanding. Time, & striving, & experience, gradually peel the onion till the inmost core is revealed. I've still not gotten near the bottom of the man, but I understand him, at his deepest level, at last.[21]

At the end of the summer of 1963, Holmes was conscious of the deep confusions that neither he nor Shirley could have anticipated when they stretched out on the bed with their neighbor in their underwear and began their half serious, half shy, drunken bantering about the possibility of a sexual adventure. As Holmes began packing books and clothes into the car for the trip to Iowa, he also couldn't know that the conflicting swirl of emotions he had aroused in his wife were still unresolved. Their perilous journey into the far distances of eros was by no means ended.

Chapter 20

GYPSYING

*Life here has become a pleasant routine. Of course I am having to work
harder than was advertised, but I find it stimulating, and as I get more
efficient it is becoming less demanding as well. I have one very capable
Salinger, an awesomely earnest and absolutely devout Catholic Wolfe,
a winsome Samantha Rama Rau, an Updike or two, the inevitable
Roth and Malamud, a bitter, bearded Beat who is unfashionable, and
a clot of others who will probably give up the illusion of wanting to
scribble by next year. . . . In my seminar, I have been talking a great
deal about "the world." It gradually dawned on me that, in speaking
of Dostoyevsky, Camus, Miller, Kafka, etc., they [the students] were
exclusively concerned about these men as representatives of a personal
point of view that had nothing to do with a given moment in history.
We have had to spend a lot of time establishing the connection between, say, [Dostoevsky's] The Man From Underground and 19th century scientific rationalism; between Camus' The Fall and the collapse
of Humanism, etc. Their eyes gradually open.*
—JOHN CLELLON HOLMES, letter to Alan Harrington, November 7, 1963

In the middle of September 1963, John and Shirley left Old Saybrook for a
year at the Iowa Writers' Workshop. They brought nothing with them except the books that filled the car and the clothes they'd need for the winter
there. After some initial indecision they decided to rent someplace away
from the campus. Iowa City, the former state capital where the University of Iowa was situated, was a quiet city, with enough contact with the
cultural world through the Workshop to sidestep some of the daunting
provincialism that pervades university campuses situated out of the social
mainstream. Although Holmes later commented on the disparity between
the city's comforts and the Workshop's "tin shacks beside the river,"[1] its site

on the hillside beside the Iowa River and its broad tree-lined streets left many students with a pleasant memory of its beauties and its calm.

Initially John and Shirley found it difficult to rent a place to live that he felt had the isolation he needed for his writing. They finally found an old farmhouse far enough outside of the city for them to feel that they were only tangentially committed to the unfamiliar situation of an academic life. For the first time Holmes used the term "gypsy" as a verb in his journal describing his emotions. They would be gypsies in the Iowa fields, perched in a lonely farmhouse on the curve of a road on an Iowa hilltop. Eight days after they'd left Old Saybrook he wrote that they'd driven twelve hundred miles, they'd moved twice before settling on their hilltop, they'd spent two or three days collecting enough salvageable pieces of furniture to make the house livable, and they'd even managed to get through an evening at a dance hall in a neighboring town. When he turned to his journal in the middle of September he was too tired to think of anything beyond the first impressions of the fields outside the door and the emptiness of the curve of their lonely road.

> *Minute yellow butterflies in the soft autumn cornfields of Iowa. An unhappy cow lows somewhere in the dusk, the peculiar bovine [low] not of complaint. We gypsy here among our clump of trees, a quarter of a mile from the nearest light, free of excess baggage, and me, for sure, dedicated to making the new experience give up all it has. Iowa is gentle; the full grandeur & terror of the continent is still West of here; though we have hints of it here in the ever-flattening pastures and fields the moment you venture a little West. . . . The tireless, lonely, rusting headlights of America's continual nightmare hurry [?] veer around the curve on which our house sits. The heat of September here is dense, rich loamy, there is no freshening breeze that has passed over water. One is aware of an immensity of land on all sides; the Unknown is subtler, somehow less graspable. Eventually, everywhere, there is a town.*[2]

A few days later Holmes' meeting with the other faculty revived his old self-consciousness at his lack of any kind of university background beyond a few postwar classes at Columbia, where he'd wangled places by pretending that his high school transcripts were on their way. The Iowa Writers' Workshop was recognized as America's premier graduate program in creative writing. Founded in 1936, it was directed from 1941 to 1966 by Paul Engle, a gifted poet and administrator who was himself an early graduate of the Workshop. For his M.A. in Creative Writing, Engle had written a collection of poems, *Worn Earth*, that had won him the Yale Younger Poets prize. In 1963–1964, the academic year in which Holmes was invited to teach classes in fiction writing in Iowa, the program had over a hundred students and a distinguished faculty of published novelists such as Vance Bourjaily, Kurt Vonnegut, and V. S. Cassill.

When Holmes was introduced to the assembled Liberal Arts faculty, he felt as though he was some kind of "hairy-breast"[3] among the men and women with advanced degrees. To add a little heft to his slim credentials, John Gerber, head of the English Department, added that he'd heard that others "of the so-called Beat Generation thought of him as their philosopher & elder statesman,"[4] which brought some laughter, probably at the incongruity of someone being an "elder statesman" of a literary movement that at that point—as far as the general public was concerned—was only a few years old. The meeting went on for an hour and a half, but Holmes found the only real difficulty was that he had to get through the ordeal without a cigarette.

Since he and Shirley had arrived at the school only a few days before classes started, he had no time to request writing samples from the students in his fiction workshop, so he decided to present them with a short story by D. H. Lawrence, without revealing the name of the author: "an obscure one if I can find it—and see how they respond to a pseudonymous *good* piece of writing."[5]

Holmes found that his friend Vance Bourjaily, whom he'd first met when Bourjaily was an editor of the literary anthology *Discovery* and publishing Holmes' writing, was comfortable in Iowa City. Holmes still enjoyed Bourjaily's company as much as when they'd first met ten years earlier. After the success of his first books Bourjaily's career had settled onto the kind of plateau that often stretches before middle-level novelists. He was established enough so that he didn't have Holmes' problem of finding publishers, and his reviews were generally positive. Like Holmes, however, he had found that it was difficult to make any kind of steady income as a writer, but he was willing to make compromises with his dreams of artistic success. The most significant difference between their situations was that Bourjaily had children, and he was conscious of his responsibilities. For John and Shirley, their only responsibility was to themselves.

In his journal Holmes described Vance as "older, wearier, fatter, settling into himself—and that's all to the good."[6] Somewhat to his surprise he also found that Bourjaily had "a rather admirable, rather naive, belief in the worthiness of the Workshop."[7] During these years the Iowa Writers' Workshop had assumed a near-legendary status among young American writers because it offered one of the earliest and best university programs in writing fiction and poetry. Part of the program's effectiveness was the commitment of gifted instructors like Bourjaily.

Holmes also noticed that—in his practiced judgment—Bourjaily was showing signs of aging, since he didn't take as long to get drunk, and that he was more lethargic in his drunkenness. "His eyelids flutter shut; his pauses become almost embarrassingly prolonged; but he is not as bitchy, there is nothing mean in him."[8] At forty-one Bourjaily was only four years older than Holmes, but he was settled into a quiet family life in a spacious red farmhouse, with ponies and pony carts for his children. The house had a music room and a trailer was parked in the backyard for their vacation trips. To Holmes, he was "almost the country squire now."[9] He was conscious that Bourjaily had found a life that not only satisfied him, but also supported his career ambitions.

Both John and Shirley were immediately drawn into the casual social life that was part of the Workshop's ambience. The weeks passed quickly, and he found that there was less stress in his classes than he had anticipated. Holmes had returned the edited proofs of *Get Home Free* to Dutton shortly after his arrival, and he was in that emotional holding pattern of optimism and apprehension that every writer experiences waiting for a new book's appearance.

While Holmes' academic year was settling into what would be a relatively quiet period with his students and his casual contacts with the other writers at Iowa, Kerouac was finding his writing continued to meet a determined rejection from the literary establishment. In September, as John and Shirley were moving into their farmhouse, Kerouac's *Visions of Gerard*, a fictionalized memoir of the death of his older brother when Kerouac was four, was published. It was illustrated with sensitive drawings by James Spanfeller that complemented the book's tender response to the story of childhood loss. Kerouac himself was so pleased with the book's illustrations that he and his mother had one of them framed for their living room.

Kerouac intended the book to be a gentle evocation of his love for his brother Gerard. He wrote it in a dozen night sessions in his sister's kitchen in North Carolina after the rest of the family were asleep, and he'd fueled the writing with his by now customary reliance on coffee and Benzedrine. The reverent mood of *Visions of Gerard* was very distant from the torments of *Big Sur*, but the reviewers again were negative, many of them critical of his method of composition. On October 5, 1963, Kerouac wrote Holmes that he was physically sick at the attacks on him. The review in *Newsweek* magazine had offended him by referring to his French Canadian background, while *Time* magazine dismissed "the self-indulgent gush of his prose." The *New York Times* insisted that the book was a debasement of the sorrow at his brother's death with its "garrulous hipster yawping." For many of the reviewers *Visions of Gerard* gave them a chance to renew their attacks on Kerouac's literary methods.[10] The review in the *New York Herald Tribune* echoed what had now become the general response to Kerouac's work.

> *A text very much like everything else [Kerouac] has published in the past five years: slapdash, grossly sentimental, often so pridefully "sincere" that you can't help question the value of sincerity itself—and most distressing of all, disclosing here and there that the author is a man with a subtle sense of human nature and gift of language every bit its equal.*[11]

The reviewer emphasized that there was something about the book that could have redeemed it, but he concluded with an impatient dismissal.

> *Set against dramatic New England seasons and in the bosom of a warm French-Canadian family, it is a tender, compassionate story of innocent suffering and harsh effacement, and in someone else's hands it could have been moving. Even in Kerouac's own hands, it could have been good, if only he had made writerly demands on himself. As it stands, though, it just amounts to 152 more pages of self-indulgence.*[12]

The only positive review Kerouac noted was from another French Canadian, writing for a newspaper in Albany, who was touched by the book's "compassion."[13] For Kerouac's editor, Robert Giroux, who had paid him an advance of ten thousand dollars for *Big Sur* and *Visions of Gerard*, the reviews were catastrophic. In what seemed to be a matter of only a few weeks following the stream of negative reviews, *Visions of Gerard* was dumped as a publisher's remainder. Stacks of copies turned up in New York's Eighth Street Bookshop at a give-away price of sixty-five cents, where they were shelved beside the unsold remainder copies of *Big Sur*.

Kerouac was also upset over a lawsuit brought in Italy against *The Subterraneans* for pornography, and he admitted to Holmes that he feared a break in his flood of creativity. Unless he could convince Giroux to publish a new long manuscript titled *Desolation Angels*, he would have no book waiting for publication for the first time in six years. The manuscript was a memoir/novel of his travels on the West Coast and in Mexico, beginning with the weeks in the summer of 1956 when he took over Gary Snyder's job as a fire spotter overlooking the forests around Desolation Peak in Washington State. The manuscript had been written in two sessions—"Part One" in 1956 and "Part Two" in 1961. The book began by incorporating the actual journal Kerouac kept on the mountaintop, an honest, painstaking record of his inability to enjoy the several weeks of isolation where he had the opportunity to write and meditate in self-imposed solitude, very different from his enthusiastic, fictionalized account of the same experience at the end of *The Dharma Bums*.

Kerouac continued to complain to Holmes that he only wanted a life of quiet contemplation, and Northport had once again turned out to be too close to the bars in New York City. Long Island was also too accessible to the steadily increasing crowd of hangers-on and drinking companions who found their way to his house. At forty-one Kerouac had already left most of his youthful glamour and high spirits behind him, but since he had become a celebrity none of his new friends seemed to notice that anything had changed. After staying for less than two years on Judyann Court, Gabrielle persuaded him to move back to Florida once again so she could live closer to her daughter.

Iowa, in contrast, was to give Holmes a few months that were at least free of the financial crises and the creative torments that had muddied his recent years in Old Saybrook. There was a muting of his creative doubts and hesitations as he gave most of his attention to teaching his classes. After John and Shirley had been in the house only a few weeks, however, the sexual tensions between them rose up again as a divisive issue. None of Shirley's confusions had been resolved. She was still so disturbed by the emotional effects of the sexual explorations Holmes had initiated with their Connecticut neighbor that she continued to deny him any sex, and they sank into an emotional, and increasingly drunken, lethargy in their lonely Iowa farmhouse. In his journals he tried to reassure himself that they could find some way out of the dead end they'd reached. "I think idly of sex. The blank reality of the shared genital. It's there, our thin interest is there too . . . something *might* happen. An awareness, the shuddering passage of an unprepared for emotion over wastelands."[14]

Holmes was also worried that the woman who had been the third part of their sexual triangle was possibly coming to Iowa the next month, and he was unsure what the effect of a return of their sexual explorations would be on Shirley.

[She] may be visiting here for a week in November, and Shirley has some trepidation about the sex-scene with her. I, too—though I keep thinking that if the proper lust could be introduced we could unsettle something far enuf [sic] to make it an experience. Is anything so calculated capable

of being an experience? The lust of the others is the price we put on our own lust.[15]

At the end of November 1963, everything was swept away by what happened in a brief afternoon moment in Dallas. On November 25, Holmes wrote,

The death of the President, and everything that followed it, has made the weekend a nightmare. I was at the oculist's, unarmed, when the initial announcement of the shooting came over a TV set there—just the flat announcement in the middle of a soap opera. Of course, I couldn't believe it, and felt that somehow he couldn't be mortally wounded. I instantly thought, as did so many others, that he had been shot by a right-wing fanatic. A cold bitterness against the Dallas extremists, so active recently, filled me before I could think twice. And then, coming downtown, in a dreary rain, to drop Shirley for some shopping, it came thru [sic] that he was dead. We went to the Workshop where I had a conference with Don [Lehman?], whom we took to the Union for coffee. I called off the conference, and we sat, stunned, unable to get our minds to grasp the fact itself. Students sat in shock & confusion, others merely sat listening to the reports coming in.[16]

As for many others, the assassination of John F. Kennedy was to cause wrenching reconsiderations in Holmes' convictions. The shock of the assassination and its effects on the government's course were intensified as the new president, Lyndon Johnson, supported the passage of far–reaching social programs that had been proposed by Kennedy during his brief period in office. Johnson also chose to continue the U.S. intervention in Vietnam, and the war was to be the specter that harried the country for the next decade. The trauma of the assassination was further prolonged by the investigation into the murder by the Warren Commission, and their conclusion that the assassin Lee Harvey Oswald had acted alone. The report's conclusions prompted a wave of disbelief at the commission's conclusions that something of such momentous consequences could have been committed by a single individual of such numbing ordinariness. There was an abrupt birth of a culture of conspiracy theories that would continue to haunt the country nearly half a century later.

Holmes was not drawn to any of the passionately offered and defended conspiracy theories. He was, instead, obsessed by the physical act of the murder, and he was continually drawn to the incongruity of the accused assassin himself. The figure of Oswald presented him with someone who was beyond his comprehension. In Holmes' first journal entry he was already struck by the incongruities of the events when he added in a note, "The assassin dies across the hall in the hospital from the room where his victim died; he dies never having admitted his crime; he leaves nagging doubt behind him; his killer is a night-club owner, without ascertainable politics."[17] The next year Holmes was to write one of his most probing and insightful essays into the enigma of Lee Harvey Oswald.

Despite the troubled confusions of his relationship with Shirley, Holmes continued to correspond with Kerouac, although nothing in his letters intimated at their personal crisis. Some of the old antagonisms between them flared up again when Kerouac responded to the publisher's request for a promotional blurb for *Get Home Free* with a few sentences which Kerouac had been pleased with but that Holmes interpreted as condescending. By January 1964, social engagements with his friends on the faculty took whatever energy Holmes had left after the hours he gave to his classes and the individual conferences with his students. The pressures of the work had affected his heart and he'd visited his doctor to deal with the symptoms. Holmes noted in his journal that he had decided not to stay on at the Workshop, even though the job had given him the first financial security he'd experienced since he left the navy. He continued to be obsessed with his ambitions for his novels.

Never seem to have time these days—work—another heart-panic after a 21 hour day of teaching, making up MFA exams, desires & what have you—the Mitchells tonite, the Halls last night—a day spent reading "for myself"—Gins's [Ginsberg's] new one, REALITY SANDWICHES, Connelly's "Enemies of Promise," and a night or so ago, those fine Isaac Babel stories RED CAVALRY. My heart was, I suppose, only shredded nerves & weariness, and (perhaps) a pleural adhesion—or so the Dr. said. The wind howls in true Wuthering Heights fashion outside my window, 40 or 50 miles an hour. I've been formally asked back next year, and privately decided I won't come. We both like it, but I don't get enuf work done & do, of course, miss the East somewhat. But basically it's that I've still fish to fry out there in the world, and don't fancy a backwater just yet.[18]

The entry continued with a troubled description of a night he and Shirley spent in Chicago over the semester break, when the sexual rupture between them was exacerbated in a drunken episode with a couple who were old friends from New York. The emotional consequences hung over them for the rest of their time in Iowa. It was the kind of corrosive encounter that would become more common as other couples attempted to find some balance in the unsettling sexual turmoil of the 1960s. For Shirley, already struggling with her difficulties of the summer before, the effect brought her close to a breakdown. Over the next months Holmes groped for some understanding of what had happened, unable to offer her any kind of help through the crisis.

> I have yet to write of Chicago—[their friend] so desperate & drunk & besieged, suddenly acting out the cornered, plaguing nightmares of so many men of my generation: "Tell me why we just don't all of us take off our clothes & show each other our 'things'?" He did, and I did & finally Shirl did, and then even his wife. He standing with a sad half-hard-on in the doorway; Shirley in my shirt, his wife cowering on the couch because she wasn't wearing any undies. Shirl & [their friend] into the bedroom to make it; his wife stripped and I tried to get excited by her little-girl, sullen face turned away, her smallish breasts with the brick red nipples. I tried to go down on her to imagine something sufficient enuf to arouse me, but she was skittish, and I was very drunk, and (more's the pity) she's never stirred me the least bit somehow. She went down on me, and other things, but I called it off. He passed out, and we were all hung over and up the next day in our separate ways. And all this happening over two bottles of Johnnie Walker in a suite in the Ambassador Hotel! It took a day or two to recover from the boozing, and the aftermath of nerves and despair. Shirley said I raved on & on all night while sound asleep. But somehow it was necessary that it happen this time, for [him] certainly, and for me too in a sense—and even Shirley perceived this & went along & had a good enuf time, all things considered.[19]

The events of that night added another level of recriminations to the already formidable wall between himself and Shirley. In a journal entry a month later Holmes tried to analyze his wife's physical rejection, and for once he seemed to feel some anguish at the explicit nature of his journals. He was also close to despair at the injury he had done to their marriage.

> Candor, or what use are these pages to me? To fail to write less than the truth, because these entries are available to Shirley, or to write something here so that she will know it, are alike silly. And I have nothing to hide. Fears of my sexual impotence assailed me last night, as they do sometimes when I can't sleep. I try to fantasize them away: images of all manner of

girls, all sorts of situations, bringing no stiffening of desire. Our sexual life is nil right now, due to Shirley's difficulties. I sympathize with her, I would help but it is very hard for me right now—the longest period of solitary desire I have been thru in 20 years. We are like strangers in flesh. The idea of intimacy actually contorts her features. She loathes herself, and the notion of me touching her. She is having mysterious vaginal discharges that she believes to be her bad ovary, but they have been occurring for almost 2 months now, and she will not go to a doctor. I must wait, though it is against my desire, my better judgement in terms of us, and my premonition. I simply don't know how to reach her on "our" level.[20]

By the spring of 1964 Holmes found their situation even more incomprehensible. They took a short trip into the countryside around Cedar Rapids as the winter faded, but his journal entry describing the journey quickly segued into his attempt, again, to understand what was happening.

I do not think I have felt so helpless in any relationship before. We are more out of contact than total strangers because even civility, even the most shallow talk, is potentially a source of a further misunderstanding— which both of us want to avoid at all costs. We don't argue anymore— neither of us could bear that. The house has become horrible to me: centerless, dark, uncomfortable, no place to sit in it (but the breakfast room) that does not tempt me to booze or cigs or the "wrong sort" of talk. Shirley stays in her room, sewing, ironing, or what have you most of the day. Due to this, & my work, I don't imagine we say more than 100 words to one another all day. SHE IS TERRIFIED OF ME. What good would it possibly do to ask why? I know most of the reasons, and she would deny the condition if I mentioned it to her.

A terrible, dismaying alternative: she is crazy, or I am. Does it come down to that?[21]

Shirley's despair clearly had many of the symptoms of a breakdown, and Holmes was as affected himself by his emotional and sexual impotence as his wife became more troubled. She hadn't shown any revulsion after he had taken photographs of their costumed sexual play some years before. It was the three-way-sex with their neighbor in Connecticut that she flung at him as the cause for her trauma. "Shirley says: 'You have wounded me in the one thing I could be certain of—my sexual nature.'"[22] Confronted with the accusation Holmes could only equivocate. "I am appalled, I never meant to, I think it is not *just* me who has done this, but she won't talk about it except in terms of recriminations: the only specifics seeming to be my 'acceding to [the woman in Connecticut]' all those months ago."[23] Holmes still was unable to accept the reality that the conviction which had obsessed him for several years—his belief that a freely expressed sexuality was the last frontier of truth and understanding between human beings— had a dangerous underside.

Holmes was correct in sensing that there were other factors behind Shirley's breakdown. The loneliness of her situation, marooned through the Iowa winter in an isolated farmhouse, would have been an emotional trial without any additional complications. At least Holmes had his students and the other members of the faculty to distract him, as well as the campus itself as a place for him to get away from the farmhouse. He was making a sustained effort to give up smoking in Iowa, and he had done without cigarettes for three months, which he blamed for some of his own tensions. For some days he filled his journal pages with pornography, as an attempt to revive some of his own sexuality, but finally by mid-March Shirley once again permitted him to have sex with her again, though it had to be careful and restrained, without the pleasures of exploration and discovery he had always experienced between them.

In this bewildering confusion he received the first copies of his new novel *Get Home Free* from Dutton. The reviews were uneven, but generally less enthusiastic than they had been for *The Horn*, and it was immediately and painfully clear to everyone that sales again would be modest. Once again a book that he'd spent years writing with struggles and misgivings would pay him almost nothing for the effort that had gone into its composition. One after another the critics lined up to attack his work. In the *New York Times* Charles Poore considered it "a kind of elegy to the Beat Generation's approach to middle age." He described Holmes as "an industrious part-time existentialist" whose vision was limited to "a mournful highway cobblestoned with four-letter words, fringed with the wrecked-car dumps of outmoded vehicles for expression."[24] In the *New Leader* Stanley Edgar Hyman concluded that "Holmes does not write well enough to bring off this complex and ambitious novel."[25]

In the Sunday *New York Times*, Haskel Frankel was slightly more positive, if still reproving. He found the novel was "a neatly wrapped package of futility that is both depressing and impressive" because of Holmes' "gift of creating character and incident which hurls fireworks into the gloom. *Get Home Free* might prove too depressing for consumption. After all, it's an unthinking person indeed who has not gotten past the age of twenty-five without discovering that life is difficult, that all our years, no matter how fierce the struggle, must end in death."[26] As the weeks passed Holmes finally understood that he would have to come to terms with his inability to reach any kind of large audience for his novels, even if he was reaching his readers in the nonfiction he was contributing to national magazines.

Though later readers sometimes came to the conclusion that *Get Home Free* was his best novel, and he often agreed with them, when he re-read the book after its publication, he could understand the consistent responses of most reviewers. The book's structural form in itself was a problem. The two novellas that made up most of the book, "Old Man Molineaux" and "Hobbes and Little Orkie" were not related thematically, and they had originally been conceived as free-standing prose pieces. He had been unsuccessful in his efforts to interest any of the magazines that published his nonfiction essays in taking them. His decision was to place them as sections within a novel, since the main objection to the pieces from the editors who rejected them was their awkward length. To provide a linking narrative he returned to two characters from *Go*, "Verger" and "May," and wrote three sketches of their deteriorating relationship and its final tentative reconciliation, without relating them to the two novellas. "May" was the name for the character of Joan Haverty, Cannastra's companion at the time of his death and Kerouac's second wife. The time of the book opened a year after the events described in *Go*. The three sketches were placed through the book, one at the beginning, the second separating the longer pieces, with the third ending their story.

To compound the difficulties for the reader, the novellas were each written in the first person, but the persona of the writer telling the story changed from one of the pieces to the other. The narrator of the second was also a woman—a challenge for any male writer, and one that Holmes' skills were not entirely equal to handling. The character of Hobbes, which had been Holmes' pseudonym in *Go*, appeared again, this time as a burnt-out junkie who had somehow ended up in the southern barrooms where the novella was laid. The three New York sections were in the third person and were closer in style to his writing in the unpublished second novel in his projected *Go* trilogy, *Perfect Fools*, and projected some of the same uncertainties without coming to any clearer conclusions.

Holmes later sometimes described *Get Home Free* as the third novel of the *Go* trilogy, with related themes and attitudes, as well as some principal characters, to give the three novels some coherence as a creative unity. In the nearly fifteen years that had passed as he labored on the three books, however, the moral questions he had intended to raise in the books had become blurred. Although he continued to think of himself as a novelist, *Get Home Free* was the last long piece of fiction he was to publish.

John and Shirley returned to Old Saybrook in June 1964, and again, as had happened when they drove to Iowa the autumn before, their sexual turmoil was part of the baggage they loaded in the car for the trip back. In their hours of drinking in the familiar rooms of their home, the renewed accusations of mutual infidelities took on a maudlin tone of recrimination. For some time he even questioned whether he was drinking beyond his body's capacity to absorb the alcohol he was putting into it. Holmes' hapless decision was that his effort to break with his lifelong smoking habit was contributing to the drinking, and in July, after seven months without a cigarette, he started to smoke again. Even though he could immediately feel its negative effect on his body, he also was certain that smoking helped him to begin writing again. He had been filling his journals with pornographic fantasies, since Shirley was unwilling to have sex with him, but in August his thoughts returned to Kennedy's assassination after he read the Warren Report. Holmes wrote his article on Lee Harvey Oswald quickly. He had "just resumed smoking after a seven month layoff, and could write effortlessly. Turned it into an article in a morning."[27] *Playboy* paid him two thousand dollars for the essay, which surprised and pleased him, and it was published in the November issue.

With the possibility that he could make a living from the magazines, Holmes quickly turned out two more pieces for publication. In December an essay about his lifelong enthusiasm, the movies, was published in *Harper's*, "15¢ before 6 PM: Those Wonderful Movies of the Thirties," and he responded to a question from *Books* with a comment on a new enthusiasm, "Bob Dylan—That's Where It's At." What was more important for him was that he had also begun work on the new nonfiction book he had sold to Viking. Since Holmes had always thought of himself as a novelist, this was the first time he had considered writing a book that he described to friends as a "semi-memoir."[28] The essays he published over the next months were to be some of his most sustained and successful writing. On October 30, 1964, he typed up a page of instructions to himself for the new project, as though he had become his own student.

> *Spend a day locating & typing up relevant, key quotes to define the scope: several single-spaced pages of them: [Tate's?] "touchstones"—even if they do not seem directly, logically applicable. . . . Do the same for your*

journals: single lines, images, ideas. Start gathering materials, so some
notion of the scope of the book, of the ground *will form in you. The book*
has been dogging you because you can't glimpse its shape, direction, its
modesty, if you will. Set up limits, & then transcend them. The "new
consciousness" idea is too all-inconclusive just in itself: the frame should
be smaller—yourself and your times—and then perhaps the larger in-
timations will emerge & be even more provocative. You don't want to
write a hortatory book, an argument, a thesis. That gets you into an
elaborate skein of proofs—all so mind and patience-wearing. Start mod-
estly, more narratively . . . & let the rest seep out *of this ground. But get*
started. Try this new approach. Give it several days to establish itself,
so that you can discover its possibilities & its limitations. This is the
immediate task.[29]

For the first time Holmes took a contemporary writer as his model. He
had come out from under the long mantle of Dostoyevsky, Kafka, and Lawrence and their themes of guilt and sexual redemption that had obsessed
him and caused him to stumble awkwardly as a novelist. Instead he followed the direct, precise voice of William Carlos Williams, in particular the
multi-leveled structuring of poetry and prose that Williams had achieved
in his complex self-portrait *Paterson*, which also, ironically, included letters
that Ginsberg had written to Williams a dozen years before. Ginsberg's letters were his response to the moment that Williams' influence had shown
him the way to break with the classical models that had hobbled his poetry,
just as Holmes' Olympian models had heaped too much weight on the burden of his fictional narratives.

On November 7 Holmes continued in his journal,

Read the entire "Paterson" today, the second run-thru [sic] of it this year.
Ostensibly searching "touchstones," I discovered it was word-quality, tone,
image, & rhythm I was noticing more & more, and that Williams' use of
language, his ear, is what I want for the prose-tone of the book, & par-
ticularly the section I've been struggling with this week. I isolated three
sections, and will type them up, just as he writes them, but as prose,
and study the yoking of the words, the short cuts, quick dissolves, leaps,
changes of point of view etc. . . . Williams touchstone "Say it, no ideas but
in things!" is precisely what I have been getting at.[30]

It was obvious from Holmes' new stylistic freedom that his year of teaching had given him the insights that a gifted teacher can pass on to an eager

student. What was unique in his situation was that both the teacher and the student were himself.

On February 8, 1965, Holmes wrote in his journal that once again he'd had the opportunity to play the role of a voyeur in the sex games that unexpectedly resumed between him and Shirley and their Old Saybrook neighbor.

> *Hours of obsessive fucking after midnight on Sunday morning. Too drunk to remember it all. But S. and the woman screwed wildly, all our mouths tasted of sex. . . . S. almost came as the woman blew her. She blew the woman passionately, making orgasm. If we go on, I want to introduce pornography, obscenity, ass-fucking. Most of all, the woman & S. going all the way -- S's first real & thorough lesbian experience. The usual ruins yesterday & today. Booze, cigs, too long at the [fair ?]. Better now, but the horrors of withdrawl [?] last night, sleep on & off today (Monday). Better now.*[31]

Holmes might have thought he was "better now," but Shirley definitely wasn't. Two days later, recovered from her hangover, she lashed out at him, blaming him for what he described as "having 'forced' her into these unnatural roles."[32] In his journal he wrote that he felt "awfully responsible" for her anger, assuring himself that he "wasn't *forcing* her into anything."[33] He wondered if Shirley was fighting "not only aging, but the idea of aging."[34] He rationalized her anger toward him by indulging himself with some psychological babble: Shirley's "central pshchic [sic] pattern" was "the loyalty-snydrome, the betrayal-complex, a kind of elephant-fixation—once an idea or a suspicion is planted in her head, nothing will get it out."[35] In his journal he fretted that Shirley

> *cannot seem to get over the notion that I have betrayed her, that I am violent, vicious, & "unfaithful," that I mean to destroy her. . . . And here we are: 39 and 37. I have no money in the bank, and it all began five or six years ago. . . . Suddenly, arbitrarily, she will resume with [the woman] again (all fine with me; simply a surprise; I believe, however, that doing it suddenly & arbitrarily that way is the way to do it); but what if I had resumed it that way? The jealousies & suspicions in her would have instantly boiled to the surface.*[36]

In Holmes' letters he concealed the fact his relationship with Shirley was deeply troubled. On February 4, 1965, he wrote his sister Liz, "We are well, and happy. . . . We have fires every night, and most of our bills are up to date, and we don't stay up till all hours, and generally have no complaints."

From Shirley's point of view, her resentment of what she considered Holmes' constant bullying finally overflowed in a seven-page, single-spaced, typed statement she wrote on October 31, 1965, trying to explain to herself the underlying causes of what her domineering husband called her "sickness." Shirley complained, "I can't think in this stifling bag of John's mind. I'm *not* him and I get at things differently than he does. And he's wrong to try to force me into his mold. I'm not a student who needs to be pushed and shaped and who wants to be pushed and shaped in the first place."[37]

Shirley had decided that during the twelve years of their marriage John had undermined her self-confidence because he didn't allow her any intellectual freedom:

> It's terrible to be so afraid of my own opinions. I want so much to always feel just like John does, it's so much easier when I do, that I've come to try not to feel anything strongly if it's not in agreement with him. He makes no allowance anymore, these years, for a contrary feeling. If I'm not in total agreement, I'm then "against" him, I'm "attacking" him, I'm "not taking [him] seriously," I'm not treating him like a "serious person." It's awful for me and awful for him.[38]

In Shirley's list of grievances, John's casual assumption that she would do all the housework, even while she worked a full-time office job to earn the money to pay their expenses, was another painful issue between them.

> He does nothing in terms of sharing responsibility for the daily details of human living. His meals are bought, cooked, cleaned up after, his clothes washed and pressed, along with my own, the bills are paid, the phone handled, the cats fed, the house cleaned, his mother placated with time spent with her. I work some of the time and worry all of the time and am worn out the rest of the time.[39]

As in most troubled marriages, the most painful issue of all, even more than their disagreements about sex, was money. There was so little of it that John apparently blamed Shirley for spending what he called "his" money. These were funds from his advance for his next book, *Nothing More to Declare*, that he'd hoped to save for their second trip to Europe, but that he accused Shirley of having "pissed away."[40] She was so furious with him for being so selfish that she wrote she felt she'd been living in a "dream world" since their marriage.

> *That he's capable of feeling such a thing has thrown our whole relation-ship into a horrible light for me, it makes it all look different, all the past, everything that's happened. It implies such an objective point of view of us, everything we've done and felt together, I feel that I have been living in a dream world, that John really isn't the man I feel I know, that all this time it's not only looked and felt different to him but it's been* separate *to him, us I mean. That he's* always *looked at me as if I were a stranger.*[41]

Shirley's only recourse, since she didn't think she could walk away from her marriage, was to withdraw emotionally for long periods during the next decade. She told herself, "If you don't like it and you can't stand it and you feel it's killing you, just get out."[42] But the ties between them and their mutual dependence on each other were too strong to break. Without writing about it in their journals, they apparently agreed to stay together to ride out the storm.

In their letters to friends and family, they glossed over the difficulties between them and assumed a tone of determined cheerfulness. On September 9, 1965, for example, Holmes wrote Kerouac that he and Shirley planned to get away for a week. "I'm going to put Shirley in the car, and we're going over to lonely North Fork of far-out Long Island to a beach full of Celtic stones where I spent summers in the 30's. There, we'll do nothing but sun (if there is any) and screw (if there isn't), and generally mend up, and vacuum out our heads." On December 2, Holmes wrote to Ginsberg, enclosing the chapter on him included in *Nothing More to Declare*. "Here's a chapter on you from my new non-fiction, semi-memoir book which I guess you ought to see before it's published. . . . Shirley sends love, as do I. And regards to anyone who knows me." On February 16, 1966, Shirley wrote to John's sister Lila, her husband, Ray, and their son, Chris, who were looking after the cats she and John left behind when he took a four-month teaching job at the University of Arkansas. In the letter Shirley mentioned that "neither of us yet feels quite up to par," but she dutifully ended by sending "our love" to her Old Saybrook neighbors, including the name of the woman who'd participated in their drunken sex games. Two days later Holmes wrote to Landesman that "Fayetteville makes Iowa City look like Paris," and that he had "classes-full of pert, pretty, empty-headed coeds."[43]

As Holmes was finding his way into his manuscript of *Nothing More to Declare*, Kerouac was still struggling to find a publisher for *Desolation Angels* and his financial situation was as desperate as ever. He wrote Holmes on October 16, 1965, that his sister, Caroline, had died unexpectedly soon after he moved his mother to a new house he bought in St. Petersburg. Two months later he reported ruefully that he'd been arrested and jailed for urinating in the street. It was obvious from Kerouac's letters that his alcoholism had moved to a more damaging level, but Holmes was the last person to lecture to him about the problems of alcohol.

There was no further word from Kerouac, but on November 6 there was a quick visit from Jay and Fran Landesman, who had moved to London. Holmes found them content and comfortably Anglicized. Landesman had already made himself the center of London's Beat scene, and the heady days of their creative partnership with *Neurotica* and his own years in St. Louis running his experimental cabaret theater in the Crystal Palace were now nostalgic memories. What pleased Holmes most about the visit was that Landesman spent some time with the manuscript of *Nothing More to Declare* and "seemed to like whatever he saw there."[44] What he read was the sympathetic profile Holmes had written about him, "The Pop Imagination."

The next Thursday afternoon Kerouac abruptly showed up in Old Saybrook with two friends. He'd sent a scribbled note saying he'd arrive "by Friday," and they arrived a day early. Although they had been corresponding steadily, Holmes hadn't seen Kerouac since his visit to Old Saybrook three years before. It was another unending drunk, though Kerouac's drinking habits had changed. He didn't have the money for the brandy that had fueled his rants three years before. The 1965 visit quickly resumed the atmosphere of their old sessions of shouting arguments, screaming insults, deafening music, and—despite the tumult—the experience again of the spiritual affinities that had kept them close as friends for almost twenty years. The days with Kerouac were also to be a step back for Shirley from the abyss where her revulsion had left her after the sexual adventuring Holmes had initiated. After Kerouac left, Holmes tried to sort out his memories of their four days of drinking together. On November 15, 1965, he wrote in his journal:

> *I had a fairly bad hangover by Saturday and wasn't much good for the sort of frenetic, mind-storming attention that Jack demands these years. . . . He drinks a lot of white wine (ten or 12 bottles of it passed through the house), & beer & vodka. Physically, he is at last showing the signs of*

these years of prodigious boozing: he looks (as Shirley said) rather like Balzac in the body, his torso is enormous, a more or less unbroken belly & huge chest & arms. I was reminded that his father was immensely fat, & I could see that Jack would become so too. His legs seemed shorter, stumpier; he has a huge jowl now, a bad scar on the bridge of his nose, and his features have blurred—just as Dylan Thomas's did. But he was in good spirits, rarely morose, and only going into furies over Jews, Negroes, intellectuals, & most of the other racial & class shibboleths which these years in the South, & off the road, have made seem menaces to him. At several points, he became positively demented on the subject of the Jews—venomous, irrational, sneering, parodying, ugly as a street corner tough. Then the fury would go down (everyone disagreed with him vehemently), and he would be warm, wacky & fun again.[45]

After years of feeling an attraction for each other, Jack and Shirley spent the second night of Kerouac's visit together. Holmes considered the sex as simply something natural that happened between them. It was almost a replaying of the scene between Jack and Neal and Neal's wife Carolyn fifteen years before, when Cassady—leaving them alone as he went off for a few nights on his brakeman's job—smiled at them and said, "My best pal and my best gal."[46] In their complicated relationships, both Holmes and Cassady were so close to Kerouac that each of them was willing to let their gifts to him include their wives. Holmes continued in his journal,

He and Shirley made it on Friday night: he was lonely and insistent & winsome, and she has always been both fond of him & attracted to him. An [illegible] of trying to combat the impending drink in him, culminating in one straight fuck; followed by further hours of a second attempt, which ended in a successful blow-job.[47]

The next day they each approached Holmes, since he had been too drunk to be aware of what was happening the night before. What was of most concern to him was that neither of them should feel any guilt about what they'd done.

Seemingly no bad after effects for either of them. Shirley told me about it 1st thing on Saturday morning. I was so hungover I didn't think I'd be able to properly reassure her, but managed, I guess. Jack, also, was candid about it when we talked later, and was impressed with Shirley. "She said, 'I'm going to teach you lust!'" he said with astonishment. "And then she

told me to jerk off, and 'come in my mouth'. . . . I should have a girl like
that, you bastard. I'll have to get rid of you somehow.'"

But there was none of the expected Kerouac guilt-reversion, which in
the old days always made him blame the friend whose girl he had laid—
though, of course, this may come with Florida & sobriety.

For myself, I fucked Shirley twice that day just to nail down seignoral
rights, and also spurred to it by my usual hangover-horniness. And things
seem okay after a talk about it all today. Ironically, it may have unclogged
Shirley a little, and she stoutly maintains that it was good for her. Which
is hopefully the case. I'm just as content about it, for that matter, if it can
all be kept clear, and the true emotions flood in their proper direction—
without any unneeded reversions or shiftings. So far I feel none in the
offing.[48]

Neither John nor Shirley, however, were certain where they had come in
their hesitant attempts to find a way back to each other.

Chapter 21

A TURN OF THE CIRCLE

Why the continuing interest [in the Beats]? The Beats constitute the single most important literary movement in America in the last fifty years. It isn't the drugs, the sex, the jazz, the tone of feverish apocalypse that accounts for this. It's the urgency with which they view the artist's aesthetic and social function. It's not their supposed irresponsibility which compels the critics to go on re-assessing their work (even in superficial terms); it's precisely the opposite. It's the fact that they were so responsible to the big questions, the big facts. Their almost-maniacal efforts to find new modes, new forms, new styles to go with their material, their new vision, has kept their work not only relevant, but consequential. Oddly enough, the Beats are the direct heirs of the solidest tradition in American literature, what Matthiessen called "the American Renaissance" of the mid-19th Century. History will sort it out. Perspective is the last turn of the wheel.
—JOHN CLELLON HOLMES, *Interior Geographies*[1]

In the late autumn of 1965 Holmes began to worry about the manuscript of *Nothing More to Declare*. It had been weeks since he'd delivered it to Viking, and there had been no response, even though Viking had signed a contract for the book and paid him half of the advance. His years of disappointments had already prepared him for small sales and little change in his reputation, but like all writers who have labored long on a manuscript and felt they had said something they believed in, he wanted the book to come out. As the weeks passed and he heard nothing, he already had begun to accept the worst, but when he heard from Viking after four months that they were turning the book down, he was even more shaken. The only buffer for his disappointment was that for once he hadn't been anticipating the rest of the advance to get them through the next few months. He was again gypsying, a semester of what he termed "gypsy-teaching," at the University of Arkansas at Fayetteville. He and Shirley were planning to drive there on January 22, 1966, two days after the Viking rejection arrived at his mailbox.

Holmes had been hired for the spring semester in Arkansas as a Writer-In-Residence in a trial Master of the Arts program in creative writing. In Iowa he had been one of the Workshop's many instructors; this time as a writer-in-residence he was on a small, and perhaps indefinable, level above his situation in Iowa, though the job itself, in an academic department without the status of the Iowa Workshop, had none of the gleam of his previous job. Fayetteville was a small city in the northwest corner of Arkansas, in the South that Holmes never had known. It had many social affinities to Alexandria, Louisiana, where Shirley had grown up, and she felt at home there. The university was hoping that the results of this trial program in the spring would make it possible for the English Department to introduce a full MFA writing program in the next academic year. In his journal, Holmes allowed himself a final, angry protest at Viking's decision before he and Shirley went back to packing the car.

> *Reactions: I'm a little colder than I was. A little more sick of having to put off my modest little millennium yet one more time. I feel ill-used, and I ponder the believing heart. . . . The bastards! The unfeeling, impolite bastards balancing their wheels of commerce on their noses. I can survive these blows to the self-esteem these years. I'm in no tailspin. But each one cost me a little more of the only fuel I've got: the belief that honesty, and cleaving to the truth, will at the last suffice.*[2]

Holmes had wanted to know Viking's response to his manuscript before they began the trip to Fayetteville. He concluded with a shrug, "I'd hoped to have the book settled, and I suppose something about it is."[3]

As John and Shirley drove south, they were more relaxed about the prospect of once again participating in academic life since they had the successful experience at Iowa behind them. The spring of 1966 in Fayetteville was a respite, the time they each needed to breathe more easily. A month after they had made the drive from Connecticut and settled into an apartment close enough to the campus for Shirley to take a morning course in Italian, Holmes summed up their situation in a more satisfied journal entry on February 27, 1966.

All in all, this will probably be a pleasant sojourn: we are in good spir-
its, we must of necessity keep busy & thereby out of trouble. I honestly
begrudge days lost to hangover, and thus don't want revelry with others.
. . . I commune with my classes, organizing my thoughts to get some com-
plicated things said once & for all, and doing (thereby) a lot more work
than I need to, but choosing it. I know I am good at this sort of job, and
loosen a little even from the comparative relaxation of Iowa. And I learn
too. I press a button here, a suppressed discouragement there, and see
light & surprise flood an ingathered face. . . . I disagree with colleagues
. . . without leaving a bad taste. I am certain of some things and speak my
mind without emotion. Beyond that, perhaps Europe is reachable now,
and I can go down into myself to wrest out the next accomplishments
. . . the actual coming-into of whatever gift or vision I possess. It seems at
least possible this time.

And I am curiously calm where I have been dangerously agitated these
past years.[4]

When the semester was over, John and Shirley returned to Old Saybrook, and in July he had unexpected encouragement. The publisher who
had brought out *Get Home Free* two years before, E. P. Dutton & Company,
agreed to publish *Nothing More to Declare*, Holmes' collection of essays.
Their decision had perhaps been influenced by a paperback edition of the
novel that had been released in the spring in an edition of thirty thousand
copies, with an English edition planned for the coming November. Holmes
was now realistic enough to realize that the hardcover release of his new
nonfiction book probably wouldn't have large sales, but this was no longer
an issue. He spent some weeks revising the manuscript, changing the order
of the pieces and cutting out repetitive passages, and he recovered some of
his satisfaction with the quality of the writing in the book.

Holmes still believed he could salvage something from the years he'd put
into his old manuscript of *Perfect Fools*, and his journal pages filled again
with the by-now familiar questionings and uncertainties as he turned to it
after sending off *Nothing More to Declare*. He had returned to the name of
the novel's protagonist in his journals, referring to it as "Frankel," the same
name he had used in his abortive first novel twenty years earlier.

At this time Kerouac was also beset with troubles, but they were different from the emotional turmoil that hovered over John and Shirley's marriage. Whatever the critics thought of Kerouac's literary style, or lack of it,
his publishers could at least be sure of some attention, and they were also
aware that a steady stream of European publishers were ready to buy the

reprint rights to Kerouac's books. There was always some income from his books but it was steadily decreasing, so Kerouac was continually in need of money for himself and his mother. His months in St. Petersburg had been a series of drunken, hostile encounters in barrooms, sometimes leading to fights in which he was badly beaten and once again ending in another arrest for urinating in the street.

After her daughter's untimely death from a heart attack, Mémère was ready to leave Florida. Again Kerouac sold a house he'd bought only a short time before, and in April 1966 they moved north again, this time to the small town of Hyannis, Massachusetts, on Cape Cod. Their new home was in a development of modest ranch and Cape Cod houses built close to the center of town with a food market, a liquor store, and a post office within easy walking distance. He was able to buy it for less than he'd made with the sale of the Florida house, but he wrote Holmes that the cost of moving had eaten up half of his profit. Kerouac still had some hope for a new book due to come out in the fall, a manuscript he had completed after his brief trip to Europe a few months before, *Satori in Paris*. It appeared in three issues of Grove Press's *Evergreen Review* in February, April, and June, for which he was paid contributor's fees, and it was scheduled for hardcover book publication in November.

To both Kerouac and Holmes, it seemed that nothing had essentially changed in the situation they had been facing for several years. They each were struggling to earn an adequate income, and although Kerouac was being published regularly, the reviews were dismissive, the publishers were less enthusiastic about new manuscripts, and most of his hardcover books were remaindered so that his royalties only trickled in. What none of the publishers realized, however, was that by the mid-1960s the readers of Kerouac's books had changed, so that the market for his books was changing as well. Ferlinghetti was right in the 1950s to believe in the importance of the paperback book, though mainstream publishers had resisted the new trend. In July 1967 Kerouac had to beg his editor Arabelle Porter at the New American Library to re-issue *On the Road* and *The Dharma Bums* as new trade paperbacks with covers targeting the growing market of "hippie" and "Love" generation readers. Once that happened at the end of the 1960s, his books began to sell in the tens of thousands in paperback editions both in the United States and abroad, and the sales boom has never stopped.

The cultural changes in America during the decade after the publication of *Go*, *Howl*, and *On the Road*, including the growing importance of paperbacks, were in part brought about by a flood of small press books by poets and novelists associated with the Beat literary movement on both the East and West coasts and cities in middle America. It was almost as though Ginsberg's and Kerouac's writing had cleared the ground for an unprecedented flowering of new work. This decade saw the flourishing of small presses such as City Lights, White Rabbit, Oyez, Black Sparrow, and Semina in California, and a raft of others throughout the United States, as well as the little magazines produced on mimeograph machines by such dedicated poets as d. a. levy and Tom Kryss in Cleveland, and Diane di Prima and LeRoi Jones in their *Floating Bear* in the Lower East Side.

1958 and 1959 signaled the appearance of the first books by the young poets associated with the 1955 Six Gallery reading in San Francisco: Michael McClure's *Peyote Poem* and *Hymns to St. Geryon*, Gary Snyder's *Riprap*, and Philip Whalen's *Self-Portrait from Another Direction*; as well as Lawrence Ferlinghetti's best-selling volume *Coney Island of the Mind* and Gregory Corso's *Gasoline* and *Bomb*. In 1960 Donald M. Allen's widely discussed anthology *The New American Poetry*, published by Grove Press, gathered together a representative sample of a new generation of poets in the tradition of Williams and Pound, some aligned with Black Mountain College, such as Charles Olson, Robert Creeley, and Denise Levertov, and others such as John Ashbery and Frank O'Hara grouped in New York City. Allen's choice of the Beat poets in the volume included Kerouac, Ginsberg, Corso, Orlovsky, Whalen, Snyder, McClure, Ray Bremser, LeRoi Jones, John Wieners, and David Meltzer.

In 1961 William S. Burroughs was championed as an important American author by Mary McCarthy at the Edinburgh literary festival in Scotland. The customary put-down of the Beat writers as lightweights was no longer a self-evident proposition. With *Naked Lunch* (1959), *The Soft Machine* (1961), *The Ticket That Exploded* (1962), and *The Yage Letters* (with Allen Ginsberg, 1963), it was clear by the early 1960s that Burroughs was an international presence on the contemporary literary scene. In the theater, McClure's two-character play, *The Beard*, caused a sensation in 1965 when the characters Billy the Kid and Jean Harlow simulated oral sex onstage.

During this tumultuous cultural ferment at mid-century, women Beat writers such as Diane di Prima also played an important role. Her books *Dinners and Nightmares* (1961) and *Memoirs of a Beatnik* (1969) heralded the work of a steadily growing number of small press books by women writers, among them Joanne Kyger's *The Tapestry and the Web* (1965), Bonnie Bremser's *Troia: Mexican Memoirs* (1969), and Lenore Kandel's *The Love Book* (1965), the only book of poetry by a Beat writer after Ginsberg's *Howl* to be brought into a San Francisco court to be tried for obscenity.

After 1965 Beat writing became even more specifically political when the American military presence in Vietnam escalated to a full-sized war against the Communist Vietcong. That year in California Ferlinghetti's poems *Where Is Vietnam?* and *Tyrannus Nix?* appeared, followed the next year in New York City by Tuli Kupferberg's *1001 Ways to Beat the Draft*, only three of many so-called underground works that helped to fan the embers of fervent resistance to the war. Earlier, the existence of a small but vocal peace movement had been nourished by the second-generation Beat poet Ed Sanders, a Ginsberg protégé, whose *Poem from Jail* (1963) was written after Sanders was arrested and jailed for protesting against the American military build-up of nuclear submarines in New London, Connecticut.

Seemingly overnight books of poetry and prose by Beat authors were translated into every major language in the world and sold in the thousands of copies. Though Kerouac loathed his status as a media star, he had been taken hostage as a representative of the new culture, and he and Ginsberg appeared on television panels and were interviewed by respectable literary magazines such as the *Paris Review*. The society around Kerouac and Holmes had gone through far-reaching changes through the widespread availability of two new chemical substances: the birth control pill and LSD. The new rock culture that had crowded jazz off the center of the stage loudly advocated the primacy of sex and drugs to every excited listener in the land.

In what seemed only a moment in time the Beats metamorphosed into Beatniks and then into hippies. Ginsberg and Snyder played seminal roles as political and spiritual writer-activists. They became father figures to the hippie movement[5] when they took on a new presence after reading from their poetry on the big outdoor public stage at Golden Gate Park in San Francisco, celebrating the "Human Be-In" on January 14, 1967. The new society or "counter-culture" adopted many of the aspects of the lifestyle described in the widely distributed Beat books: Cassady's sexual freedom and casual use of marijuana; Kerouac's romantic view of the open road; Ginsberg's advocacy of mind-expanding drugs, free speech, homosexuality, and radical politics; and Snyder's "rucksack revolution" return to nature and Zen Buddhism.

Perhaps the most prescient comment by any of the young group of writers was the response of the young poet Diane di Prima in *Memoirs of a Beatnik* (1969), who recognized after reading *Howl and Other Poems* in 1957 that "if there was one Allen there must be more, other people besides my few buddies writing what they spoke."[6] She was not alone in her positive response to Ginsberg's poems. In the next quarter century the City Lights volume would go through twenty-nine printings with 375,000 copies in print. "Howl" galvanized many of its readers and made them feel part of a larger, disaffected community for the first time. Di Prima was quick to sense that Ginsberg was in "the vanguard of a much larger thing" because "even those friends claiming it 'couldn't be published'—waiting with only a slight bitterness for the thing to end, for man's era to draw to a close in a blaze of radiation—all these would now step forward and say their piece . . . . I was about to meet my brothers and sisters."[7]

By the mid-1960s there was even a patina of nostalgia beginning to appear over the first Beat books such as *Go* and *On the Road*. After the assassinations of John and Robert Kennedy and Martin Luther King, the increasing tensions of the Vietnam War made those years seem like the last vestiges of a lost childhood. A half century later, authors like the Peruvian novelist Mario Vargas Llosa recalled that when he was a student in the late 1950s and early 1960's, he still

> *firmly believed in the notion that the writer's commitment was to his own times and to the society in which he lived, that "words were actions," and that through their writing a man or woman could influence history. . . . The notion that the world could be changed for the better, and that literature should contribute to this, struck many of us as both persuasive and exciting.*[8]

For most Americans, however, despite Kerouac's efforts to redefine "Beat" as "Beatitude" and his and Holmes' insistence that a quest for spirituality was at the heart of the Beat Generation, the general attitude was still negative toward "those crazies," especially after the debacle of the 1968 Democratic Convention in Chicago, when violence flared over police attacks on anti-war demonstrators. Within a decade after the publication of *Howl and Other Poems*, the mood of the country had darkened. By 1969, dismayed by the escalating social chaos after King's assassination, Kerouac had retreated into a surly conservatism. In his last published article he proclaimed with resentment that he was a "Bippie in the Middle." While Holmes accepted the cultural changes, he sought with *Nothing More to Declare* to bring the "Beat" chapter of his life to a close and begin anew. As he told the interviewer Michael Schumacher in 1985, he believed that the early Beats

> *were all non-violent in spirit. We wanted to change the world, I suppose, but we had long since recognized this could not be done in violent*

terms—that *the violence, was part of the problem, and clearly not the solution. . . . When "flower power" turned ugly and merely disruptive, it turned us off. Insofar as that happened, the generation that felt we were progenitors completely misunderstood us. It was a revolution in the soul that we were speaking for.*[9]

In the mid-1960s another group of people had begun to take an interest in preserving and bringing some order to the flood of publications generated by the new literary movement. University libraries began to collect the books, pamphlets, broadsides, and other small press publications where the new writing appeared, which is always the first sign of a long-term involvement. Adventurous book dealers such as Andreas Brown at the Gotham Book Mart in Manhattan and Peter Howard at Serendipity Books in Berkeley acted as agents, selling Ginsberg and Kerouac letters and manuscripts to library archives and affluent collectors. Poetry lovers had begun to fill their shelves with the numbered volumes of the small City Lights pocket poet series distinctively designed with uniform covers. On their walls they hung the new poetry broadsides by Ginsberg, Corso, Snyder, and McClure as well as many other poets from Oyez, White Rabbitt, and scores of other dedicated small presses. At stores such as the Eighth Street Book Store in New York City, at least as many of the remaindered copies of new Kerouac novels were purchased by book collectors as they were by ordinary readers.

On Greenwich Avenue a few blocks away, the venerable Phoenix Bookshop, still with its pot-bellied stove at the back of the shop for the winter cold, had been recently purchased by a young book dealer named Robert Wilson. He knew a wide circle of people who were collecting Beat literature, and he began asking especially passionate collectors to compile bibliographies of their favorite writers. He showed Ann Charters, who was a steady customer, the Gregory Corso bibliography compiled by his friend Marshall Clements and asked if she could add to his series with one for Jack Kerouac. Wilson knew that she had been collecting Kerouac's work since 1961 and had a sizeable number of his books, as well as the mainstream and avant-garde magazines that published his fiction and poetry. Wilson thought that Kerouac's mother probably had the best collection of his work, since fans had stolen most of Kerouac's copies of his own books. It was public knowledge that he was an unpredictable alcoholic recluse who often spurned people turning up unannounced at his door. Wilson advised sending a copy of the Corso bibliography with a covering letter to Kerouac's mother, care of the Sterling Lord Agency, explaining that the Phoenix Bookshop wanted to publish a similar one for Kerouac. "Jack will probably be so jealous of Gregory that he'll agree to help you," Wilson explained.

His strategy worked. On August 5, 1966, Kerouac wrote me from Hyannis saying that he was willing to help if nobody else learned of his address. In a second letter he sent the directions to his brown-shingled Cape Cod home for a visit on August 16 and 17. During these two days he promised to cooperate fully, helping to compile the most complete bibliography possible at the time.

When Kerouac opened the front door of his small ranch-style house in Hyannis I was shocked to see his physical deterioration from the decades of hard drinking. I thought for a moment in bewilderment that the stocky, middle-aged man who stood before me in the door frame, a dumpy figure with a tired, blurred face dressed in a clean if rumpled white T-shirt and chinos, entirely devoid of physical attractiveness or sex appeal, was his father. At forty-four years old he looked totally different from the radiant young man with the movie star's chiseled face, searching wild eyes, and muscular athlete's body in the photographs taken only a decade earlier for the dust wrappers of his books. He hadn't tried to hide the changes. He'd lamely described the shambles his life had become as an alcoholic in *Satori in Paris*, which I'd read recently in installments in *Evergreen Review*. I'd been so caught up in the earlier image of the young heroic Kerouac that his later words hadn't really registered with me. The young hero was the man I'd been imagining I was going to meet during my long drive from St. Mark's Place in New York City to Cape Cod.

In the four months that Kerouac had lived in Hyannis, he'd been arrested twice for public drunkenness, and during the two days of work with his archive in mid-August I saw him empty nearly two bottles of Johnny Walker Red Label Scotch and toss down the contents of dozens of cans of Schlitz malt liquor. Nevertheless he stayed lucid enough to answer questions about how he wrote each of his books, giving extremely useful comments for the bibliography. Later he and his mother even posed together for photographs.

I was also completely unprepared for the conventional home Gabrielle Kerouac had made for him. Nothing about the way he was living now had anything to do with the bohemian "pads" he'd described more than a decade earlier in *The Subterraneans* and *The Dharma Bums*. Mémère wore a limp, flowered cotton bib apron with a religious medal pinned to it over her much-washed housedress, and she had conventionally furnished her living room with new "Colonial-style" maple furniture upholstered in patterned chinz fabrics, and a large television set beside the upright piano. She had tacked a Hyannis pennant onto the wall of the small bedroom at the back of the house that Kerouac used as a study, as if her son were still in high school. Only the collection of classic French novels arranged neatly on Kerouac's desk and on the shelves of his small bookcase suggested his immersion in literature and his dedication to his own writing, as well as the sharpened pencil attached to a worn piece of string tied to the post of his single twin bed. Kerouac explained that the pencil had to be available on his bedside table if he awoke in the night and wanted to write down his dreams.

Jack and Gabrielle began speaking their joual French to each other, but I understood one of his mother's first questions. She asked Kerouac if I was a Jew. I answered that I was a Jew and Kerouac asked uncomfortably, "You speak French?" They spoke English for the rest of the time. At the end of the first day Mémère prepared a chicken potpie dinner to celebrate Kerouac's bibliography, and she and I finished a bottle of champagne. Kerouac sat down with us at the table, reminiscing about his family's good times in Lowell, drinking scotch steadily but eating nothing. Once he left the kitchen to return with a much-thumbed black-and-white snapshot of his mother as a young factory worker, saying proudly, "That's the girl I want to marry." She told him to shut up and put the picture away.

The next day I continued to sit at Kerouac's desk in his bedroom study, where he had laid out careful piles of the different periodical publications in which his writing had appeared so that I could make a list of them for the bibliography. Kerouac also opened his bureau drawers to show me a few of the manuscripts of his books, meticulously gathered in groups of small notebooks and tied together with string and rubber bands. He had kept a surprisingly complete literary archive. As the hours went on and he got steadily drunker, he plaintively asked me to have sex with him, insisting that I didn't really love my husband. He wasn't aggressive about it, and his mother kept coming down the hall and into the room to offer me coffee and sandwiches, so he always kept a respectful distance until the last moment when I sat down on his twin bed to pack up my notebooks and papers. Then he leaned over to plant one shy kiss on my bare right arm.

Less than a month later Gabrielle suffered a severe stroke that left her bedridden, and Kerouac's life changed again. To help him care for his mother, he married Stella Sampas, the sister of his high school friend Sebastian Sampas, who had continued to correspond with Kerouac during his long absences from Lowell. He and Stella returned to Lowell with Mémère so that Stella could live closer to her family there.

In the spring of 1966, Holmes caught a glimpse of how famous the Beats had become when he received two new books by old friends. The first was a copy of *The Fake Revolt* by Gershon Legman, whose controversial earlier book, *Love and Death: A Study in Censorship* (1949), had won him acclaim for his ability to expose the underside of mass culture. *The Fake Revolt* was a pamphlet viciously lambasting what Legman considered the hypocrisy of the Beats and the hippies. The second book was Alan Harrington's new novel *The Secret Swinger*, which he'd dedicated to John and Shirley Holmes. Like Legman, Harrington had never shared Holmes' belief in the idea of a Beat Generation, and his novel contained a satirical portrait of Allen Ginsberg as a self-inflated, degenerate homosexual poet preying on his young admirers. Harrington assured Holmes that Ginsberg had forgiven the unfavorable characterization of him, saying that "fiction is always acceptable,"[10] but John and Shirley were uncomfortable with the savage attack on one of their old friends in a novel dedicated to them.

In September Holmes spent a weekend in New York City in order to go over the copyedited *Nothing More to Declare*. After finishing the job, he and Shirley took a cab down to East Tenth Street on the Lower East Side for a reunion with Ginsberg, who was settled into a large apartment in an old tenement building. The streets and the building itself were the same squalid scene Holmes remembered from twenty years before, but now Ginsberg and his partner Peter Orlovsky were at the heart of it. Holmes wrote in his journal on September 16, 1966:

Up the dim stairwells, the dirty white tiles, the varnished, or painted-over-again-and-again woodwork, to the fourth floor flat so like old apartments of mine on 89th Street and 48th Street of long ago, a couple of pudgy building-girls standing in the open doorway, Peter in jeans and shirt, looking like an Apache brave with his coccyx-length brown hair drawn straight back & held in a sort of pony-tail by a barrette, features become somewhat hawk like, hostile, cagy, the air of a harassed and canny wife on whom too much has descended, who gives the impression of having barely put aside the recent fight-over-the-visitors which just preceded their arrival. . . .

And Allen: in an old ratty bathrobe, carelessly tied, with that huge, almost ringletted mass of black hair framing his face—the hair & beard of the same enveloping density & thickness, the now well balded skull shining through the few dark hairs left above the forehead, the lips (glimpsed through the heavy mustache) somehow pink and sensual as Whitman's lips are described; the eyes were Allen's old eyes still—though no longer feverish, simply bright and inquisitive, almost shy, too, with me at the first, gauging me without psychology, *aware of the NOW—a sign of his maturity that I noticed all night.*[11]

As Orlovsky tended to his two mentally ill and very needy younger brothers, who slept in bunk beds in one of the other bedrooms, Ginsberg led John and Shirley into the living room where they sat on mattresses placed on the floor against the wall under the uncurtained, filthy tenement windows. Ginsberg began to sing Sutras, holy songs, gently tapping the rhythm with his finger cymbals while Holmes pumped the bellows of the harmonium. For Holmes the slow rhythms of the Sutras shifted the mood of the room into one of an open, calm receptivity. Then Ginsberg began to read from his recent poetry. One of the new poems was *Kral Majales*, the ebullient account of his trip to Prague, where he had been crowned King of the May by students, only to be escorted out of the country by the Communist authorities. Then he read from *Wichita Vortex Sutra*, the long poem which he'd written on a car journey through the American Midwest. Holmes' judgment was that it was "a work that stands with *Howl* and *Kaddish* as a gigantic pier on which his ultimate accomplishment will rest."[12] As much as he was impressed with the achievement of the poetry, Holmes was as moved by Ginsberg's *presence.*

He read quietly, with absolute assurance that no emotion, no radical modulations, were necessary, with very little of the giggling, incantation, or theatricality of days when he felt less in charge of his own vision. I looked at him through the unfolding of the poem, and somewhere during it decided that he has now, of course and at last, become what we can only call in these faithless times "a saint"—that is, a man utterly without any life separate from the life of his spirit, a man speaking directly to the broken soul of his age because he speaks directly about his own.[13]

The Vietnam War hung heavily in Holmes' thoughts as he listened to Ginsberg's reading, and his conclusion about *Wichita Vortex Sutra* was that it was the "finest work of the Vietnam War, a vast diastole of sanity and clarity which (I thought in my slightly-intoxicated state of revelation) might actually bring the world to its senses, if anything still could."[14]

When I visited Kerouac in Hyannis, Kerouac had told me that Holmes knew more about his writing than anyone else, so I wrote to Holmes, asking if I could visit. On a bitterly cold day in mid-February 1967, bundled into a sheepskin coat over a short skirt, a pair of black woolen tights, and a bulky sweater that I hoped would disguise my early pregnancy, I took the 10 a.m. train from New York City to Old Saybrook to interview Holmes about some home-recordings he'd made of Kerouac reading his work.

Holmes was waiting at the train station. At forty years old he was indistinguishable from the other suburban commuters standing on the snowy platform, a tall, somewhat faded but still good-looking man in an old tweed overcoat. He wore heavy glasses with horn rims that he pushed back on his nose. His blonde hair was tinged with gray, his manner polite, his voice low and solicitous. His first words were that he hoped the four-hour journey from New York had been "not-unbearable." We drove in his old Chrysler sedan a short distance through the center of Old Saybrook to his home on Shepard Street, while he explained that his house had originally been built as a nineteenth-century schoolhouse.

Once inside the front hall, Shirley welcomed me, dressed casually in slacks, a sweater, and loafers, and after we hung up our coats I saw that John was wearing a navy blue V-neck sweater over his dress shirt and slacks, protection against the chill of what they told me was a very drafty and poorly insulated old house. In the living room they introduced me to their two cats, Dodger and Orkney, and I sat on one of the two battered Victorian sofas while John went off to the kitchen to help Shirley bring in our lunch. The sofa faced a massive rough stone fireplace that he told me he'd built entirely by himself.

In rebuilding the old schoolhouse, Holmes had left the ceiling beams exposed and lined the walls with bookshelves. More sagging wooden shelves lined both sides of the narrow stairway that led to what he called the "cold floors," a cubby hole office crammed with papers and four small bedrooms. Holmes guessed he had about five thousand books in the house. We had lunch in their formal Victorian dining room at an old mahogany table: pastrami sandwiches, coleslaw and pickles that they'd bought at the local delicatessen, and beer and coffee. Holmes talked steadily while we ate. He'd been invited to the National Book Award ceremony at Lincoln Center in a couple of weeks with a crowd from his publisher, when he and Shirley would go down to Manhattan for a few days. He'd received an offer to teach a seminar in June at the Western Writers Conference at West Illinois University in Macomb with the novelists Richard Yates and Kurt Vonnegut.

I noticed that Holmes chain-smoked throughout lunch and that his nails were bitten down to the quick. Shirley addressed him with affection as "Johnny." Their manners were so impeccable I had no idea until later when I read Holmes' journals that they often barely spoke to each other for long periods and that most of their lonely nights ended with drunken quarrels. Later I also learned that they put away more than a gallon of J. W. Dent bourbon a week and had so little money that they mostly lived on what he described to his sister Liz as "peanuts and stews."[15]

It was clear that they had very little money—in the kitchen the refrigerator was so old that its door had to be propped shut with a chair, the furniture throughout the house was shabby and second-hand, and the "wonderfully baroque"[16] bathroom plumbing was undependable. They'd chosen to decorate the house in the Victorian style because they could find cheap furniture in local antique stores, and Holmes also wanted the house to have what he called an "ancestral" atmosphere.

Once settled back in the living room, Holmes lit a fire in the fireplace, promising that he would write a full description for the Kerouac bibliography of the four acetate discs of the primitive home-recordings he had made nearly ten years earlier at 681 Lexington. Holmes played the discs for me, Kerouac reading brief selections from *The Town and the City* and drunkenly riffing over recorded jazz solos. For the rest of the afternoon we talked about Kerouac's books. As Kerouac had told me, Holmes knew more about them than anyone except Kerouac himself.

Holmes was most eager to talk about his idea for a "Kerouac Reader" that he had proposed to Sterling Lord in July 1965, an anthology he would edit of Kerouac's writing to clarify the chronology of the books in the Duluoz Legend. The novels had been published out of their chronological order in Kerouac's life story, so his readers failed to understand that his separate narratives fit together as a thinly disguised autobiography, the story of a life "lived on the run." Holmes felt that this anthology of Kerouac's work could possibly make critics understand his place as an important American writer in the same way that Faulkner had become important after Malcolm Cowley's edition of a Faulkner reader in the Viking Portable series. So far the idea of a Kerouac reader hadn't interested any publishers.

What I told Holmes about my visit to Hyannis with Kerouac and his mother only confirmed Holmes' impression of Kerouac's life now. Holmes didn't confide in me, but later I learned from his journals that for several months he'd been refusing to take Kerouac's late night drunken, abusive phone calls when he was "more or less smashed out of his skull,"[17] so he felt slightly out of touch with his old friend. Being Kerouac's "brother-soul" could be a burden.

In the early evening Holmes drove me back to the railroad station, and on March 6, 1967, he dropped Kerouac a note about my visit: "I saw Ann Charters up here for a whole afternoon: played her the records and tipped her off to a few Kerouac items she didn't seem to know about. I kind of dug her mini-skirt. And I learned from her that you've moved to Lowell. . . . I seem to be way out of touch."[18]

Three years later the *Village Voice* journalist Vivian Gornick visited John and Shirley in Old Saybrook and wrote an article describing a similar afternoon of pastrami sandwiches and intelligent conversation. Gornick wanted to know what had become of the earliest Beat writers, whom she described as "those fine weary spirits of twenty years ago."[19] She was impressed with Holmes' Old Saybrook house—"beautiful floors, windows, plants, sunlight, old furniture, early American cozy look everywhere"—though she sensed an oddly discordant atmosphere behind the make-shift "cozy" appearance, what she described as a "strange, romantic quiet that seems to perch on the house rather than soak through it."[20]

Much as Huncke had lectured him twenty years earlier, Holmes talked to Gornick about the Beats, she thought, "almost as though he were addressing a grad student on a piece of distant history."[21] Explaining that Kerouac had been to him what Neal Cassady had been to Kerouac, Holmes spoke passionately about his friendship with Jack. Gornick quoted Holmes as saying, "It was as though we were on a spiritual journey, in search of our very souls, during those [early] conversations."[22] She left Old Saybrook feeling disappointed, sensing that Holmes hadn't revealed much of himself to her. "I might just as well have spent the afternoon talking to an ex-Republican lawyer who had seen the light and retired from it all."[23] Later Holmes was hurt when he read her characterization of him as an ex-Republican lawyer in the *Village Voice*.

Early in 1967 Holmes had another moment of disillusionment in his long friendship with Kerouac. Holmes had sent him a copy of the newly published collection of essays about the Beat Generation, *Nothing More to Declare*, inscribed "For Jack—Duc D'Kerouac, good ol' Zagg, Chief Konkapot, Jean Louis, brother on the road."[24] Holmes wanted Kerouac's reaction to the essay on him titled "The Great Rememberer," but Kerouac's response was in the dismissive manner he adopted when he felt uncomfortable with a compliment. Holmes noted coolly in his next letter that with the book of essays "my Boswell-days, my apprentice-years, are over."[25]

"The Great Rememberer" was the most perceptive and sympathetic response to Kerouac's writing that had ever appeared, and it had been difficult for Holmes to write. He confided to the novelist V. S. Cassill, whom he met in Iowa, that the tone of the book had been "the hardest thing for me to modulate to the right pitch, much less control thereafter."[26] He also told his friend Carol Munn, the wife of one of his students in his Iowa writing workshop,

> *It's so much easier to write about someone you know only slightly and have a firm and single opinion of. Jack eludes one at every step of the way, and I'm having to settle for a kind of quick sketch, which, hopefully, will suggest some of his astonishing personal charisma, but certainly will not be able to explain the sources of his vision. People, of course, think of him mostly as a sort of hip Jack London, and I'm trying to dispel some of that malarky. But whether I'll be up to catching the world-and-mind weariness, and the continual molting of consciousness, which is both his gift and his fate, I have no idea. Anyway, I can pay off a few old scores.*[27]

The reviews of *Nothing More to Declare* were the best Holmes had received since *The Horn*, though nobody reviewing *The Horn* had seemed to understand the novel's larger symbolic dimensions. In March 1967 *Life* magazine gave *Nothing More to Declare* two columns under the sly heading, "Nothing Like Age to Beat a Beatnik." On March 9, 1961, in the *New York Times*, reviewer Thomas Lask found the book "admirable" enough to make him take the Beats seriously as "a generation that came between the socially conscious theoreticians of the nineteen-thirties and the New Left activists of the nineteen-sixties." Lask understood that Holmes had found that "the conventional solutions in politics, morality, and religion were unsuitable, and like the others in his group, was forced inward for the answers to the questions that plagued him." Lask concluded by saying, "I don't see how anyone who makes the nineteen-fifties his subject will be able to ignore" the book.

Reviewers also found much to praise in Holmes as a literary stylist. On April 1, 1967, the *Chicago Daily News* critic E. W. Johnson found that Holmes wrote "with the images of a poet." Johnson understood that

> *Though the book is non-fiction, its structure is closer related to the novel (Holmes has three to his credit) than the essay: constant overlapping, shifting focus, foreshadowing, a compliment of characters, etc. . . . the section "The Forties" (an impressionistic autobiographical sketch) containing the best and most poetic writing in the book.*[28]

Nothing More to Declare brought Holmes more praise than any other writing he published. On August 2, 1967, the *International Herald-Tribune* considered the book "a key document in the history of the Beats." A year later, after the book was published in England, Julian Moynahan in the *Listener* praised Holmes' "real gift for discrimination and definition." *Newsweek* even asked for photos of Kerouac and Landesman to run with their review. His publisher was hopeful, but orders for the hardcover book were slow, only twenty-two hundred copies, and there were many returns. By the end of the year it had been remaindered, just like Kerouac's books.

In his discouragement that there had been no paperback sale, Holmes wrote his editor at Dutton, saying, "I know there's interest in the colleges, among the hippies, with a whole new generation that, believe me, *is* involved with this, but there seems no way to present the book in this light."[29] He also asked his agent to look into why *Go* and *The Horn* were out of print. After some months, Sterling Lord wrote back that he'd offered the two novels to Avon Books, the cheap mass-market paperback house, but they'd shown no interest at all.

Back in Lowell, Jack and Stella bought a large house with the financial help of her brothers. While his new wife cared for his mother, Kerouac tried to earn money for medical expenses by writing *Vanity of Duluoz*, a book about the missing period 1939–1946 in his Duluoz chronology. Living in his hometown for the first time in decades, Kerouac relaxed a little, though he worried constantly about his mother and continued drinking heavily. In a film of him shooting pool in a social club with his old buddies, speaking his joual French, he seemed to be at ease in a way he was nowhere else he'd journeyed.

In November 1967, Kerouac faced the usual critical disappointment with his new book, *Satori in Paris*, and it is difficult to disagree with his reviewers' responses. Whatever Kerouac had planned to do on his journey to France—a search for his ancestral roots in Brittany—the trip had drowned in a flood of alcohol, missed appointments, and botched interviews. By January 1968 he was thinking of moving his bedridden mother back to Florida, where she could escape the cold Massachusetts winters, and by the end of the year he was settled in a new tract home in St. Petersburg with Stella and Mémère.

Increasingly disturbed by the Vietnam War, John and Shirley shared a dream of making a second trip to Europe. With a contract signed to earn nine thousand dollars for a twelve-week spring semester of teaching at Bowling Green University in 1968 (three times his entire income in 1966), he gingerly approached his local bank for a loan to pay for a four-month trip to Europe in early September 1967. He planned to write a book titled *Walking Away from the War* about their travels to give them some financial justification.

On Labor Day John and Shirley flew to Shannon, Ireland, the first destination of their European trip. Feeling that "the very air in America had become poisonous"[30] after the war escalated in Vietnam, he and Shirley rented a car at the airport and drove straight to Kinvara on the west coast of Ireland, looking for signs of Yeats in his tower in Thoor Ballylee. There Holmes marveled at the words the Irish poet had inscribed in stone near his tower—"may these characters remain \ when all is ruin again." Holmes was so worn down by his worries, and so in need of a vacation, he felt that Yeats' words "smacked of a stubborn certitude on which not even the least existential scribbler of my era would have bet his ego. My own house in Connecticut did not even have my name on the mailbox."[31]

In London, he and Shirley stayed a month with the Landesmans, who encouraged their friends to settle into the basement of the large house they'd bought in Islington. Holmes found "Dowdy old London" had changed in the years since their first visit—it "had gone bonkers with chic."[32] They partied with the Landesman's wide circle of celebrity friends, everyone from party girl Christine Keeler to William S. Burroughs to Yoko Ono to singer Cass Elliott of the rock group the Mamas and the Papas. John and Shirley attended a cocktail party at the Playboy Club on Park Lane where "Jay sported a four-inch-wide psychedelic tie; Fran looked ever-more like Zelda in a fur-trimmed 1920s coat of her mother's; Shirley's paisley-print shift did justice to her classy knees," and John felt himself "invisible in my only suit."[33]

By the time John and Shirley left London, their mood had lifted. His essays described the rest of their trip to Paris, Munich, Venice, Florence, Rome, and Naples. His collection *Walking Away from the War* never found a publisher, but over the next five years several of the chapters appeared in magazines and the book was included in its entirety in *Displaced Person: The Travel Essays.*

Back in Old Saybrook, when Holmes received the unexpected news of Neal Cassady's death on February 4, 1968, he was thrown into confusion. In his journal he wrote about Cassady's death from exposure:

Lying by the side of railroad tracks (bitter irony) in San Miguel, Mexico— a combination of booze and barbiturates, it seems, stoned him, and (I guess) a chilly night did the rest. The end of that furious, stubborn, driven life: no one so selflessly, fiercely pursued "kicks" in the special way young Americans did (and do) these years—that is, he wasn't a decadent, a hedonist; there was always a human aim at which he loosed his energetic rocket. I've missed him intensely, now and again, in the fifteen years since I saw him last: there were moments when no one but Neal would do, and

I knew him before he became a legend by which other people proved their "in-ness." At least, I remember his young, bony, Paul Newman face, haggard sometimes from the road, the hassles, the humiliations. . . . Terrible that a man should be thought of as an archetype—it was Neal's secret contempt for us literary types, including Jack, that we too often tended to respond to his unique but not-mythic energy and point of view in these terms—but he was a con man; that is, he conned for the best in life, he was not above conning joy, continuance, surcease, and I never saw anything contemptible in that. He gave as much as he took.[34]

In 1981, in response to an invitation from Ken Kesey to contribute a piece on Cassady for the magazine *Spit in the Ocean*, Holmes wrote an eloquent response to Cassady's incandescent spirit. He began by brilliantly summarizing his various impressions of Cassady throughout the years, but he ended by chastising himself for failing his old friend.

Sorry! Sorry that his perpetual hunger for some Dickensian more had been apostrophized as vision, sorry that his natural rumble-seat sexiness had been mythologized as Dionysiac, sorry that his kinetic flux of energy had been so encrusted in legend that he himself had been prematurely entombed in it. For a moment, the vampirism of the writer's lust appalled me.

What business did Capote, Mailer, Kerouac, or myself have messing up the lives and fates of the Perry Smiths, the Gary Gilmores, or the Neal Cassadys of the West with our inky and romantic abstractions. They were victims of thirsts that couldn't be slaked, hungers that couldn't be fed by glum America. They lived at variance with its progress, its uniformity, its wealth, and its power. And their "delinquence," their "criminality," their "a-socialization" were signs of a pathetic failure of the dreams by which Americans have always lived. What right had anyone to make a celebration, or even a lament, out of their wretchedness?

For Neal was alone. The man died, as he had lived, excluded, exploited, exiled from those lasting satisfactions that lead a man to bed of nights, not out of exhaustion but because he is replete. Neal's Larimer Street ran all the way down across the border to San Miguel Allende, and his final admonition to us remained unheard. What we missed was something I'd seen in his face as he stared out that New York window, as if staring down into the iron rail yard of his whole life. What I saw was the sad, bewildered aftertaste that comes over all the surfeited Californias of our long tradition of hedonism—in the gloaming, in the end.[35]

Chapter 22

GONE IN OCTOBER

I pushed my way through the crowd alone, fearful that I might be re-vulsed and then it would all come down on me if anything of Jack were actually there, and over the dark silhouette of a shoulder, I saw him— laid out in flowers, in the prescribed funereal attitude of tranquil slumber, hands folded with a rosary entwined in a pale shirt, a natty bow tie, and a sport jacket. No need to say that no one had ever seen him that way since he was Harcourt Brace's soulful young Thomas Wolfe twenty years before. And the face? It had been made to look as peaceful as a babe, the brows slightly knotted but with perplex rather than pain, all the fevers gone, the mouth not his mouth at all, the color of the flesh a rather pale pink in the lights, Jack's sweaty, grin-ning, changeable expression nowhere to be seen. He looked thin, calm, waxen, almost choir-boyish—and Jack had once been choir-boyish all right—but this was a faintly prissy, I'm-all-right-Jack Jack, and no Jack I'd ever known. Later, Allen would say: "I stood there, and sud-denly I expected him to wink. That is, the Jack that was watching all of us watching him would have made that eyelid wink to tell us that everything was all just so much vapor circling upwards in the void."
—JOHN CLELLON HOLMES, "Gone in October"[1]

Holmes had often confided to friends that he didn't think Kerouac would live much beyond forty, but he was stunned at the radio announcement on October 21, 1969, that his friend had died that morning in St. Petersburg, Florida. Kerouac was forty-seven. At the time of his death he'd been work-ing on *The Beat Spotlight*, another book in his Duluoz Legend. Around noon on October 20 Stella heard him vomiting blood in the bathroom and she called an ambulance to take him to the hospital, where he underwent extensive abdominal surgery for hemorrhaging esophageal varices. After hearing the news, Holmes sat down and wrote his immediate response in his journal:

Jack is dead. I was reading about him in an old journal when Shirley called out from downstairs, having heard it on the radio. There were the bad, pointless moments waiting for a repeat of the newscast, there were the waves of awareness—coming up and then receding—death is only a word, it is an abrupt absence *that has reality, and you have to think a minute to realize that.*

The horror of his conscious life, with which I have lived for years, came first. I realized how stubbornly, even bitterly, I had wanted him to be happy, acknowledging nevertheless that there was nothing you could do with such a gifted, such a driven man.

Then, all of a sudden, I found myself weeping, because I have always addressed my sentences to him, to his disapproving, canny eye, and it would be different to write from now on. Allen Ginsberg called (how thoughtful, knowing I would be heartbroke). By happenstance he will be in New Haven tomorrow & we will go down. "He didn't live much beyond Neal," he said as a matter of interest. "Only a year and a half." There was that attempt to be cheerful, that warm insinuative tone in the voice, that feeling of an old camaraderie that should be acknowledged despite time and disputes. I spoke to Gregory too—they were all at the Cherry Valley farm. I phoned Sterling who had been wakened at 5:30. "He drank himself to death," and I felt that now, between Sterling and I, it could be said, and neither of us had said it baldly-out before because of protectiveness for Jack, and both have known it (perhaps better than some of Jack's old friends) for years. We wired Mémère & Stella—hopeless, useless words. If the funeral's in Lowell (as seems likely), I'll go, of course, because—Well, if love is total involvement, deep emotional clairvoyance about the oth-er's soul, fury, and hunger all intermixed, he was the only man I've ever loved. He changed my life irrevocably. Portents of his death, somewhere, sometime, have plagued me for 8–10 years—as recently as last Thursday I thought of him dying in St. Louis or Chicago on some Kerouac-crazy trip.

I haven't dared think about his mind in its last hours. What can we say? He's gone. It's over for him.

I don't know what to do.

Words, words, words, words, words, words, words—[2]

Kerouac's body was sent from St. Petersburg to Lowell, where the fu-neral was being arranged by the Sampas family. In the tumultuous months after Jack and Stella had returned to Lowell with bed-ridden Mémêre to be closer to friends and family, the Sampases had struggled as much as they could with Kerouac's alcoholism. They had tried to keep him sober enough to function and out of jail, humoring him in his unpredictable barroom harangues and giving him money so that his mother and his new wife could pay the mortgage on their house and have something to eat. His attitude toward them was as unpredictable as his drinking binges, turning in a moment from fumbling gratitude to petulant insults.

Holmes was in touch with Ginsberg and learned that he would be reading at Yale the night before the funeral, with Orlovsky accompanying his songs on his banjo. Corso was also coming along with them to film Kerouac's burial in Lowell. Holmes immediately suggested that the three of them stay overnight at his house, rather than the usual university lodgings. He and Shirley drove to New Haven, only thirty minutes from Old Saybrook, to bring them back to the house. The next morning they would drive on together to Lowell for the funeral. On the trip to New Haven through the autumn darkness Holmes found himself thinking of Kerouac, with the usual despairing regrets that follow any unexpected death.

> No more Jack, *I repeated to myself as I drove, his death a fact too inexplicable, too final, to go down. I'd known him for half my life. Whatever sort of man and writer I'd become was due in no small measure to our friendship. As young men we had shared those important, exuberant years that sometimes shape the rest of the life.* Damn him! *I caught myself thinking.* Why does he do things like this? *I'd talked to him on the phone not ten days ago, and we had bickered as we often did when he was drunk, and he had challenged me to call him back in an hour, and I hadn't done it, exasperated by his boozy monologues. And now the phone was permanently dead.*[3]

The phone did ring again, a call from the *New York Times* asking Holmes for help with Kerouac's obituary. They needed someone who could give them what John called "a sober, critical assessment" of Kerouac's writing, and Holmes had to turn them down. "I had to say that I didn't know of a single one, and that (aside from his friends) I had never met anyone who had read the entire, vast cycle of the books. He remained an essentially unknown element in our literature."[4]

In Lowell the next day, the mood in the Archambault Funeral Home was subdued. Although Kerouac's final years in Lowell had been harrowing, the family honored his friends at his funeral.

In Brooklyn I learned the news of Kerouac's death from an upstairs neighbor who knocked on my door after hearing the first news announcement on the radio. The next morning Sam and I flew from New York to Boston and rented a car at the airport for the drive to Lowell. When we came to the address we'd been given, we found that when I had visited Kerouac's Lowell neighborhood three years before, I had prophetically photographed the entrance to the funeral home. The name Archambault was set into the pavement in an elaborate mosaic tile lettering. Inside we joined Ginsberg, Orlovsky, Corso, and the others beside the casket. We stood silently, trying to absorb the fact that this bulky figure reclining on a bed of satin, surrounded by flowers, dressed in a bow tie and a brand-new sports jacket, his hands clutching a rosary, was the wild-spirited Kerouac of his books. Later, when we stood quietly talking with John and Shirley, Ginsberg insisted that I follow him back to the coffin. He had touched the body's arm and face and found that they were stiff. He wanted me to touch Kerouac's face as well. With Ginsberg watching, I placed my right index finger on the forehead of the waxwork body in the coffin and assured Allen that Jack was gone.

The customary Greek family wake had an unexpected mood of celebration which helped to lighten the dark mood of the funeral home. The wake was held in the home of Stella's mother, an old-fashioned house where thirty years earlier Kerouac had often visited Stella's brother, his close friend Sammy Sampas, while they were still at Lowell High School. There were pleased murmurs from some of the younger family members when they learned that Ginsberg, a personality they knew from the newspapers and television, had come into the house. I talked to Stella as she sat among the older Greek women, family and friends, many of them also widows. Perhaps the Sampases' respect for Kerouac was most thoughtfully expressed by the oldest brother, Charles, who was news editor of the local paper the *Lowell Sun*. When Sam asked him what the opinion in Lowell was about Kerouac's writing, he nodded, looked away for a moment, and answered seriously, "He wrote the great Lowell novel."

The next morning at the graveside I photographed Holmes, Ginsberg, and Corso side by side, looking on solemnly as the coffin was lowered. My camera caught the moment when Holmes took a handful of earth and stones and leaned over to drop them into the grave. Later that afternoon we gave Ginsberg a ride back to Logan Airport for the flight we took together to LaGuardia. We watched as he patiently answered the questions of several people on the plane who came up to kneel by his aisle seat and ask him about Kerouac's funeral.

dream you will have forgotten by twilight smelled deliciously of coffee and eucalyptus and money."[10]

A moment talking with one of the people living in a hillside house in Beverly Glenn turned into a pungent portrait: "He was wearing a pair of portable stereo-earphones, with ten-inch antennae, that made him look like a large nut-brown insect, tuned into the inaudible static of interstellar space."[11]

Parking the car on a hillside gave him a desolate view of the city's pestilent smog: "I turned onto Mulholland Drive, and pulled over, and got out for a cigarette. Down there, the smog, which at street level lent a faintly leprous cast to everything (exactly as if the eye had been rinsed in linseed oil), hung in a dirty zone of grease smeared above the Civic Center complex that rose like a group of headstones almost ten miles away."[12]

His days of aimless driving through Los Angeles also took him back in poignant memory to the months he had lived with his mother and sister in Altadena, only a few miles from the center of the city, when he was five, and this other California was always present in what he saw out of the car window so many years later:

> As it happened, my personal version of the Great American Daydream of innocent, bucolic boyhood was centered around Los Angeles, and over the years since I had been here last, a certain kind of winter's-end morning had always aroused in me a powerful longing for California. The fugitive smells of orange grove and just-cut lawn would tease my nostrils, a taste of guava and avocado would come up into my mouth, and I would suddenly recall the five-year-old boy, who had once stood barefoot in the hot, dusty sunlight of Pasadena in 1931, watching the rain inexplicably falling just down the block, and experiencing the first amazed discovery of a world of which he was not the absolute, dreaming center.[13]

What the emotions of the essay made clear was that among the things that had drawn Holmes and Kerouac together was their shared nostalgia for their childhood, for the streets and noises and smells and voices that had shaped them and that were a continuing presence in everything they wrote.

There never was a moment in Holmes' life when he would consider himself as anything other than a novelist, but for the next fifteen years he spent more time in the classroom than he did in his Old Saybrook cubbyhole study at his typewriter. He always diffidently justified his series of teaching positions as only a strategy to buy himself writing time, but he was a gifted teacher. He devoted hours responding with insight to student writing, and he prepared outlines and examples of what he would say when he taught classes in the modern novel. It was also significant that although he was known to most of his colleagues and students as a representative of "the Beats," however they defined the term, Holmes' lectures were consistently in the literary mainstream.

In August 1970 he was invited back to a small college in northwestern Ohio, Bowling Green State University. Their offer was to teach for a term in the fall, or spend a week on campus as a visiting writer. He had already spent two months at the campus as a visiting writer, so he chose to come only for a week the following January to meet with students and discuss their work. The next fall, in September 1971, he accepted a contract for the academic year at Brown University in Providence, Rhode Island, which had the advantage of being close enough to Old Saybrook so that he could commute, though he rented an apartment close to the campus.

When Holmes prepared his reading list on September 12, 1971, for his course at Brown, "British and America Fiction, 1900–1945," the writers he chose were Faulkner, Conrad, Forster, Lawrence, Sherwood Anderson, Hemingway, Nathaniel West, Ford Madox Ford, Fitzgerald, Henry Roth, Christina Stead, Liam O'Flaherty, Graham Greene, Joyce Cary, and Henry Miller. It is a list that would have satisfied any university English Department at the time. It reflected the academic view of literary fiction in the 1970s, and as well as excluding the Beats, himself among them, he also excluded almost all women and African American writers. In a broader overview for a course he had taught before at the University of Arkansas in the spring of 1966, "Form and Theory of Fiction—Contemporary Literature," Holmes had included Richard Wright's *Native Son*, but of the work of his close circle he included only Nelson Algren's *A Walk on the Wild Side*. The West Coast Beat writers were represented by Ken Kesey's *One Flew over the Cuckoo's Nest*. Holmes didn't teach a course that included Kerouac until 1985 at the University of Arkansas.

Although Holmes' collection of essays about his trip to Europe in the fall of 1967 failed to find any interest from a publisher, he had considerable success selling individual essays to the magazines. He continually had to fight off the copy pencils of editors who were uninterested in anything beyond the standard "travel piece," and he was inevitably impatient and disappointed with their insistence on rewriting his work. Despite his exasperation at his agent's failure to get a book contract for the articles, Holmes certainly was better paid for their various magazine appearances than he would have been for a hardcover collection. It was, however, a consolation he would gladly have been spared. In April 1970 *Venture* magazine published "An American Requiem in Paris"; in June "See Naples and Live" appeared in *Playboy* and won one of the magazine's literary awards for the year.

The next year, in November 1971, *Playboy* published "Thanksgiving in Florence," which was, with the Venice essay, one of the most vivid and insightful of the travel pieces. It won the magazine's "Best Non-Fiction Award," including a cash bonus, for the year. Holmes was considerably more satisfied with its appearance in the magazine than he had been with the heavily edited appearance of the Venice essay. As he wrote Ardinger, the key to the piece was the unlikely juxtaposition of Michelangelo's statue *David* and Florence's whine of traffic as they jostled together in the same narrow street, and he also drew comparisons between their wanderings and Shirley's memories of Florence from when she was there as a young student. Another of the travel essays from his European journey, "Encounter in Munich," appeared in *Playboy* a few months later, in March 1972, and again won a *Playboy* nonfiction award. In February 1973 his moving essay on Kerouac's death, titled "Gone in October," appeared in *Playboy.* He described its genesis to Richard Ardinger:

> *After returning from Jack's funeral in 1969, I wrote a journal-entry on the typewriter, simply recording the simple facts of those days, an entry that was almost twice as long as this piece. I sent it to a few friends. I hadn't thought to turn it into a piece, but as the years went on the myths about Jack and his death accumulated, and finally in 1972, in the spring, teaching at Brown, I took that journal-entry and turned it into the piece as published. It was painful. I had loved the man and love doesn't die with its object. I cut a lot of details, and added some perspective. I tried to trim it to its bone and yet preserve the emotional flow.* Playboy *took it immediately. We were in Maine, dead-broke, and it was a fine night, that night when we heard—mostly because I thought the piece had personal truth, its own quiet dignity.*[14]

The most ironically sympathetic response Holmes had to his piece on Kerouac's death was a letter from Betty Sampas, the wife of Charles Sampas. She wrote on March 8, 1973, that the article had caused several of their religious friends to buy the issue of the magazine, something they wouldn't have otherwise considered: "several people at our church bought their first copy of *Playboy* in order to read your article."[15]

It also was another sign of the effect that Kerouac's death had on Holmes that his obsession with a career as novelist had lost some of its impetus. His meeting Kerouac on the fateful Fourth of July weekend in 1948 and reading the manuscript of *The Town and the City* had reinforced his early dreams of becoming a novelist, despite the immediate interest in his poetry from the literary journals. Holmes would never completely give up his infatuation with the novel, but returning to the arduous labor demanded by his long fictional narratives became less crucial.

By the early 1970s he was turning to poetry again, even though for some time he didn't consider it for publication. In a letter to a friend, Don Lehman, on March 17, 1973, he half-seriously talked about his new writing plan. "I'm planning, secretively, to put together a book of poems. . . . I've stopped thinking of the Nobel Prize. . . . It's like you give up the possibility of certain golden girls as you get busier and older. It's not as painful or as hard as it seems."[16]

Holmes' response to Kerouac's death had initially been his long, deeply affecting memoir-essay, but now it was to poetry that he turned when he faced his emotional need to express his grief at the abrupt death of his father so soon after their reconciliation a decade earlier. In 1959 he had written a tentative draft of what became his poem "Too-Late Words to My Father," after he had attempted to pour his feelings into his letters to Kerouac and Ginsberg. He soon realized that "the feelings demanded a heightened expression."[17] It was not until several years had passed, however, and he had begun to work with poetry again, that he returned to the poem about his father. As he later told his bibliographer, he had found in his initial drafts that the syntactic elements of his earlier style inhibited the flow of his emotions.

It didn't go well, my head still jammed with the pentameter I had hammered into it years before. I did another draft a year or so later, cutting and adding, and trying to find the proper "measure" as Williams called it. It got better, tighter, with a more laconic tone, but I wasn't satisfied with it. During these years of the 60's, I began to write poetry again—more or less in earnest. Reams & reams, trying to uncoil my spring. I got a little more at ease, as a result of extensive readings and mullings in Snyder, Williams, Pound, Roethke, and particularly the Tang poets of China and certain of the Japanese. . . . I spent at least two weeks, between other chores, reworking "Too Late Words" to shape it into uneven stanza patterns. I chopped away at the rhetoric, trying to build the emotions as deep into the lines as I could. The little tags at the end of each stanza gave me

a direction to move towards, and they also reminded me of the gradual
shortening of lines toward the bottom of New England headstones. The
poem was finished in its present form by the late spring of 1974.[18]

In a comment Ardinger wrote that the poem "sprawls across the page, each line poignantly tense with grief, apology, and regret that the two men had not grown closer until the last few years."[19] This is from "Two-Late Words to My Father (1899–1959)."

> *All that I know is useless—*
> *fathers doomed to bafflement at sight*
> *of their myopic sons with time to burn;*
> *sons orphaned in the heart before the fact—*
> *Missed chances as sour in the mouth*
> *   as mornings of remembered*
> *   pettiness. . . .*
>
> *You didn't seem afraid of the conclusive night ahead,*
> *stared quizzically at your bandaged stump,*
> *keeping in life that way, and sometimes*
> *looked at me out of your oxygen-dark*
> *wondering who it was sat up so long with you-*
> *I talked on with awful pointlessness,*
> *embarrassed by my breaking voice.*
> *But I spoke out of time and its ego -*
> *the shame of something-more-to-lose -*
>
> *And end this now,*
> *   become your son*
> *   At last.*[20]

When Holmes was asked back to teach for the spring semester of 1975 at Bowling Green State University, where he had spent a week as a visiting writer four years earlier, his financial situation was again so difficult that he didn't feel he could say no to the offer. Shirley had been suffering from problems with her right eye, and the diagnosis was glaucoma. She could no longer work, and they were completely dependent on John for their income. This time she stayed behind in Old Saybrook. When Holmes arrived in Ohio he enjoyed his students, they were "obstreperous & brilliant,"[21] but his isolation in the small Ohio town became nearly unbearable. He seized every opportunity to return to the East Coast, and we met again on one of his trips.

In the autumn of 1974 I had begun teaching at the University of Connecticut after the publication of my biography of Kerouac. Sam and I met Holmes at a conference on Beat writing at Mount Holyoke College in Western Massachusetts in March 1975, where John and I were panelists for a discussion of Beat poetry with Michael McClure. Winter still lingered, and the campus was gray and cold. Holmes didn't know most of the other participants, so we spent much of the time together. He was as polite and pleasant as he always was—the "well-mannered boy" who had been popular among mothers at his high school parties—but we also sensed his depression. His face was tired and pensive, and he had little to say.

Of the two days we spent together on the campus I only remember Holmes responding to one of the events with something of his usual dry humor. We had been to a student performance of McClure's play *The Blossom*, which McClure had written in his experimental "beast" language. For long passages the characters shouted "Grahh!" at each other, in a spirited simulation of a lion's roar. As we walked back across the dark campus Holmes, who had said nothing since we left the theater, suddenly turned to us and shouted "Grahh!" rattling the silences of the shadowy buildings. Then finally his mood lightened and he began to laugh.

During the months Holmes was teaching in Ohio, he and Shirley exchanged a stream of letters, and finally, encouraged by the tone of her messages and desperate to see her, he agreed to present a lecture at another symposium, The Beat Movement in Painting and Literature, at the Atheneum in Hartford, only a short drive from Old Saybrook. Unexpectedly, their weekend together became a reaffirmation of their sexual relationship that he had feared had been permanently lost, and he celebrated the moment with the poem "Weekend Away."

> *And if there can be love again*
> *between such wearied people*
> *there can be oysters*
> *smiling in their shells,*
>
> *Franz Kline, cold marts, bouzouki music—*
> *There can be night's laughter on Atheneum Square*
> *and dawns with an end in sight—*

return of the old sensual fevers
resting the expended parts of us.
So life's got savor now—
There's grace in it.

For if there can be flesh-love again
between bodies so self-haunted—
hand-colloquies in hotel beds,
words become tongues—
in time there could be all the rest,
memory proven tougher than despair,
an end of soldiering-through. . . .[22]

In mid-August 1975 we had a hurried letter from Holmes. The University of Arkansas needed someone to teach creative writing in the fall semester, and as he put it, made him an offer that he couldn't refuse because the money could support him for more than a year while he worked on his current novel. "We leave in a few days (they start early down there), and we'll be back in Saybrook just after Christmas. If you're having visiting speakers this year, and you think your class might profit from my head, keep me in mind for the second semester."[23]

In the spring of 1976, when Holmes was back in Old Saybrook, he took a short break from his writing to drive up to the University of Connecticut to lecture on *On the Road* in my Beat literature class. Holmes asked if I could help him get a permanent job teaching in Storrs, close enough to Old Saybrook so that he could continue to live at home. Now an experienced instructor of creative writing, Holmes was the author of three novels, many poems published in prestigious literary journals, a much-praised book of essays, and several prize-winning articles in major magazines. When I asked the chairman of the English Department at the University of Connecticut to consider Holmes for a tenured faculty position in creative writing, he responded with a thin smile: "We already have one Beatnik here, why would we want another?" With hindsight it was clear to both Holmes and myself that instead of taking *On the Road* as his subject, if he had wanted to impress my colleagues in Storrs, he should have lectured on the poetry of Wallace Stevens. So in the fall of 1977, he and Shirley packed up their car again and returned to the University of Arkansas, where he taught in their new writing program as a tenured member of the faculty. The pattern of his life, as well as a much welcome financial security, was settled for the next nine years.

The mood of the decade Holmes lived through after Kerouac's death was in his thoughts when he looked back in a later essay and reviewed what he had accomplished. It seemed that he had settled into a kind of holding pattern that had given him time to sort out his thoughts and consider directions he might go.

As you get older, you husband your attentions, they seem to concentrate themselves more, you are more fluent about less. You use your energies and, with any luck, they burn with an intenser light. . . . One can't get on if paralyzed by the grinding knowledge of the brevity of life, and the ephemerality of works. And getting on is our most imperious duty, a vow we make in the worthiness of the baffling endeavor of remaining human. One part of being human is sometimes failing to keep the faith. For a writer, who spends his time so many fathoms down in the murk and complexity of the human personality, periods of "savourlessness" are inevitable. As I say, they usually presage an on-coming change, and the only way to initiate that change is to pass through (not around) the temporary melancholia. You can't reach dawn without enduring the night. Wishing won't make it so.[24]

Chapter 23

ON A PORCH IN BOULDER

Part of me had never been part of the Beat Phenomenon. I had always stood a little aside from it, my back to the wall and my eye on the door. By nature I was an outsider (even among outsiders), a marginal man who went off by himself to think out the meaning of things, and yet I felt an unaccountable sense of kinship with the men and women with whom I had spent the last days. It demanded no expression, it required no recognition. Simply, they were my crowd. I knew the things they knew. We had been shaped by the same weather in the same world. We had the same certainties and the same hopes. And suddenly I recalled having felt that same sense of fraternity years before, after my first awareness of what seemed like a new vision, and saying to Kerouac, "Something may come of this, after all."
—JOHN CLELLON HOLMES, "Envoi in Boulder"[1]

The mornings were quiet on the wide porch of the old wooden house above Boulder. There was a dining room inside where anyone who got up early could have breakfast. After a cup of coffee a casual crowd slowly gathered to sit on the porch. In later years there would be other gatherings in other cities of some of the same people who sat talking on the Boulder porch, but this would be the last time so many of us would come together at the same moment. It was the summer of 1982, and Allen Ginsberg had gathered everyone who could come to Colorado to celebrate the twenty-fifth anniversary of the publication of *On the Road*. It was a celebration of Kerouac and his major book, but it was also a celebration of the Beats and of everything they had achieved. So many of us had come, and so much was happening that there was no one place large enough for us to stay. Ginsberg had scattered us through this small city in apartments and in spaces of the Naropa Institute where the celebration was centered. The largest group of us were together in this old building, the Columbine Lodge, that had been part of the city's Chatauqua Center, a near-forgotten cultural movement of nearly a century before. It was in Boulder that Ginsberg and Anne Waldman had established their center for Beat studies at Naropa, an institution they named the Jack Kerouac School of Disembodied Poetics.

Ginsberg sometimes hurried over to greet new arrivals. Carolyn Cassady, new to many of the people here, found herself the center of respectful groups who pulled up chairs to sit close to her. Ginsberg had arranged for filmmaker and friend Robert Frank to document whatever he chose of the gatherings on the porch, since it was obvious that it wasn't an occasion that would be repeated. During the ten days of the conference, the Columbine Lodge was home to Gregory Corso, Lawrence Ferlinghetti, Robert Creeley, Herbert Huncke, Diane di Prima, Carl Solomon, Robert Frank, Michael McClure, David Amram, Ted Berrigan, Jack Micheline, Ray Bremser, Carolyn Cassady, Abbie Hoffman, the Charters, and John Tytell and his wife, Mellon. Other writers like Anne Waldman, William Burroughs, and Ken Kesey had been given rooms closer to the conference center. Occasionally one of the participants, his appearance over, would leave for the airport a day or two early. Others showed up on the porch steps in the darkness after a late-night flight had brought them to Boulder for the next morning's panel.

Ginsberg had put Holmes and the Charters together in Columbine Lodge. Ann and I were on the second floor and Holmes was only a few doors away on the same corridor. He'd come without Shirley, and because of the years he'd spent at his typewriter in Old Saybrook or in the classroom at Arkansas he'd never met some of the people who had been given rooms in the somewhat worn, but respectably clean house. Herbert Huncke was in a room downstairs, and he and Holmes had picked up their old friendship as if so many years hadn't intervened since Holmes had first met him in Ginsberg's apartment in 1949.

Holmes often was busy with one of the media events, workshops, or readings that Ginsberg had scheduled, but at the any of the large gatherings he found his way through the crowds to his friends from the *Neurotica* years Jay and Fran Landesman. They had flown over from their Islington row house in London to take part in the conference. John and Jay fell into their old laughing, half-ironic conversations, with Fran's pleased voice joining in above theirs. Neither Ann nor I had ever met Landesman, but he lived up to his advance billing. He was tall, still slender, and colorfully flamboyant. Among a crowd of counter-culture figures dressed in blue jeans and T-shirts he presented himself in flowing jackets, dark shirts, and dress trousers, usually with a colorful light scarf draped around his neck, a broad-brimmed fedora and dark glasses. Since Landesman had left the group in the early 1950s, and lived first in St. Louis and then in London, only the friends from their old Glennon's barroom days such as Ginsberg and Holmes, remembered him, but Landesman, as ebullient and as expansive as ever, immediately picked a new crowd of young admirers.

Fran, beautiful with a dark-haired, almost elfin look of shyness, soon gathered her own crowd, many of them young women happy to have someone they felt they could talk to. Ginsberg hadn't included her in any of the programs, but suddenly at an open microphone session following one of the big auditorium gatherings, there was Fran at the mike—slight and brightly smiling, wearing a dark dress that sagged below her knees and looked as if she'd borrowed it from someone considerably taller. She nodded to us with a satisfied smile and began singing her songs without accompaniment, beginning with her classic "Spring Can Really Hang You Up the Most." Her own place in the early story of the Beats had never seemed so self-evident.

For Holmes the conference was a homecoming, even if it was coming home to a crowd including writers such as Ferlinghetti and di Prima whom he'd never known. He had arrived at the Denver airport to be picked up by one of the volunteer drivers who moved everyone around to the scattered events of the celebration, and he reached the Columbine Lodge after an exhausting eleven-hour journey from Old Saybrook. He had no anticipation of what he'd find, but he was immediately relieved that the kind of jostling of egos that usually was part of any literary gathering was absent.

When he described the conference in his essay "Envoi in Boulder," it was this unexpected sense of familial respect that stayed with him. The conference, as he had hoped, was to be a celebration of Kerouac, and Kerouac and his writing would be the center of the days in Boulder. Holmes wrote,

We were there to remember him, his flaws as well as his accomplishments, his follies and his genius, his influence on us as individuals, and his contribution to our national literature. We didn't talk very much about Kerouac on the porch of the Columbine Lodge; there was very little outright reminiscing and no mawkish nostalgia. Jack was very dead to us, but—exhausted beyond belief by the third day, tied to an overscheduled schedule, pestered by the gnats of the media, phoning our absent families every few days—we discovered we were very much alive to each other. We never spoke or thought of ourselves as a hard-bitten rag-tag of lucky survivors to be listened to because of our longevity (as many

*who attended the conference seemed prone to do) or as a group of ag-
ing rebels who had finally matured out of their outrageousness (as the
lead-ins to most of the media stories described us). There was little or
none of the self-aggrandizing talk of careers and forthcoming books and
internecine feuds that make most conferences of writers so wasteful of
time and spirit, and inevitably leave the taste of an irrelevant debauch
in the mouth as you wait in the dead deodorized air conditioning of the
airport for the flight out.*[2]

Ann spent hours with her camera, trying to capture as much of the
moment as she could crowd into her lens. Many of the people there, like
Herbert Huncke and Diane di Prima, willingly posed for portraits in their
rooms, and there were continual new faces on the porch whose appearance
would be documented. The days, as Holmes noted, were overscheduled,
and most of us spent hours waiting on the porch for our drivers to appear
to take us somewhere else, since the main buildings where everything was
taking place were down the sloping hill at the University of Colorado more
than a mile away. Ann was giving a panel with Holmes on Kerouac's texts,
and I would do an auditorium presentation titled "Jack and Jazz."

Holmes was also teaching a writer's workshop for two days, where he
planned to talk as much about Kerouac's writing as his own. Ann's schedule left her time for Holmes' workshops, and she sat in the back of the
room with about a dozen students dressed in jeans and T-shirts who had
gathered in one of the smaller classrooms on the University of Colorado
campus to listen to him. Holmes had told her that he didn't mind if she took
notes. He was in a short-sleeved shirt and chinos, wearing blue sneakers
and smoking cigarettes steadily throughout his workshop. His talk was recorded by a Naropa technician, and when Ann listened later to the hours of
tape the sounds of his cigarette lighter flicking on and off and his frequent
dry swallows punctuated his words throughout the sessions. She felt immediately comfortable with the mood in the room. "I realized that Holmes
had thought carefully about what he wanted to say. I had the feeling that
he was taking advantage of the moment to explain his writing methods and
compare them to Kerouac's."

Holmes began by talking about his own approach to writing novels, explaining that unlike Kerouac, he didn't feel comfortable creating autobiographical fiction.

*You can write in the first person if you understand that the first person is
not you. A first person narrative has to be as characterizing of the narrator as a third person narrative would be. You need control. Take the first*

person narrator in Dostoevsky's Notes from the Underground. *He may resemble Dostoevsky, I don't know, but you can start to tell what that man is like from the first sentence by what he says. He is characterizing himself for us. If you write about yourself in the first person, you're going to get into trouble unless you know an awful lot about yourself. . . . Building anything is a laborious, boring, time-consuming thing to do. All the details. Unless you're Jack Kerouac, you probably can't write a book in twenty days. I'm a much slower writer than Jack. It takes me an average of two years from vision to completion.*[3]

At another moment, when Holmes referred to Melville's *Moby-Dick* to make a point, it was apparent that he was a very experienced classroom teacher.

Creatures other than man rarely act out of malevolence—they act out of impulses of hunger or fear. But in Melville's novel Ahab projects his own human malevolence onto the white whale. It's Ahab's obsession, not Melville's. So Melville is in control. He puts layers of meaning into his story to create a myth. His imagination is on fire, it opens fully, he's not just thinking rationally. That's the job later for critics—they can't do anything else. They can only use one side of their minds.[4]

Always courteous, Holmes suddenly remembered who was sitting in the classroom behind the other students. Anxious not to offend by comparing literary critics unfavorably to great novelists, he broke off, saying, "Excuse me, Annie. I forgot you were hiding back there."[5]

At the first session, the students wanted him to talk about how he read Kerouac's books, especially *Visions of Cody*. Holmes' reminiscences about reading Kerouac's manuscripts took most of the workshop. During the second session, Holmes was asked practical questions about his habits as a writer, especially why and how he kept journals, and his answers were always clear, never hurried. When the conversation shifted to substance use and abuse among writers. Holmes became very serious. "We were lucky. We never used mind-altering drugs for kicks."[6] The students insisted that alcohol was the worst offender: "It's the writer's disease."[7] Holmes agreed: "Habits established in your twenties become problems as you get older. For example, cigarettes are probably the most dangerous. You just keep on smoking until sleep comes."[8] He described his own reliance on alcohol: "At the end of a writing session, you want oblivion—it's so stressful. You're intellectually worn out, and alcohol promises a brief return to your previous self. It gives you a little more energy, and then it promises oblivion."[9]

Then he asked them why they thought alcohol was the writer's "drug of choice? Why did Kerouac stop smoking pot and return to alcohol?" Holmes answered his own question:

> *I can't understand the profundity of things I've written on pot unless I get high. Kerouac drank from stress—he was terrified of public appearances. He told me, my life is glum without the booze. His soul was in pain, not just his body. He knew I would understand, since I was also into the booze, though not an alcoholic like Jack. He suffered the agonies of hell with the DT's. I went through it once and said I'd never go there again. There was nothing you could do to stop his drinking without treating him like a child, and he wasn't a child.[10]*

Holmes insisted that the only thing he considered important was Kerouac's writing, and not the price he paid to do it.

> *But you've got to remember, Jack was a writer. At the end of his life his body was wasted, and eventually his mind. But his life was not a waste. He wrote twenty-two books before he died, leaving a record of his presence in the world. People don't want to hear the truth that's in his books—love one another or die. . . .*
>
> *People took one look at me and they knew I wasn't a beatnik. I was too cautious, too careful. I didn't make wild statements. Once before I went on the Mike Wallace show on live television, I met Ginsberg unexpectedly in front of the New York Public Library. He told me, "Great, you've got a terrific opportunity here. Answer two questions, and then look directly into the camera and announce the second coming of Christ." It was live TV, they couldn't edit anything out, and Allen was quite serious. But I'm too cautious, I suppose. For almost thirty years I've been talking to people who don't understand. I can talk their lingo. I'm not happy in that role, but . . . I wanted to help people understand what it was all about, not drown them or make them disappear. If you read Kerouac carefully, you'll see that the happy moments in his books are poignant. Jack's perspective was that the present is important because the future is going to come. He was an Existentialist, telling us to live fully in the moment. This anniversary conference is to urge Americans to take Kerouac seriously, because his message is important. Jack's gone—I'll never see him again. It's not personal. His life is all in his books. They are a connection, like all literature. You are connected to Kerouac through his books. As a great writer, he's achieved a post-human voice.[11]*

After the workshops, Ann had a short meeting with Holmes upstairs in the Columbine Lodge before they gave a joint presentation of Kerouac's writing, going over ideas about his literary methods in the Duluoz Legend. In Holmes' own note of the conference, "Envoi in Boulder" he wrote, "Enjoying my few moments in Annie Charters' room, a scant hour or so before we were to give a panel on Jack's texts, two friends working in quick tandem, our minds running easily in the same groove."[12]

Later in my presentation of "Jack and Jazz" in the main auditorium, I treated Holmes' and Kerouac's descriptions of the music as a jazz performance by reading their different prose renditions of two tenor sax solos—Holmes' in *Go* and Kerouac's in *On the Road*—as a late night jazz club cutting contest. During one of the choruses, as I beat out the rhythm in time to the prose, I saw Holmes sitting in a front seat, his feet enthusiastically tapping along with the beat, his face smiling at the pleasure of old memories.

Often on the porch, however, Holmes seemed to be withdrawn, involved with something inside himself, answering if someone spoke to him, but often looking away into the trees during quiet conversations with friends. He generally settled in one of the wooden chairs to talk to the Los Angeles writer Lewis MacAdams. In the photos of him from those mornings there was a guarded sense of withdrawal. He said nothing about it, but a "sore on his gums" as he described it in letters, had not responded to the first treatments. The medical diagnosis was that the years of heavy smoking had left him with a cancerous condition in his mouth. He finally explained quietly that he had been able to attend the celebration only by postponing the surgery the doctors were insisting on. His operation was scheduled for the day after he returned to Connecticut, and whatever happened in the operation, he faced months of rehabilitation. Despite what he faced, however, he looked back on the gathering on the porch at Naropa with a pleased sense that he had been part of the celebration.

The last three decades, like massive cliffs of glacier-ice, broke off from the main and slipped slowly backwards into the past. I was glad I'd been a part of it. I was glad it was over. Pride in my crowd, and affection for my friends, settled my stomach with the coffee.
  I'd go home and get on.[13]

To Holmes' relief the first operation, though causing considerable pain and an uncomfortable stretch of recuperation, seemed to have successfully removed the cancerous tissue and he could return to Arkansas and the classroom. Although he had again begun another novel, the unfinished *The*

Quincy Girls, which dealt with the situation of working women in the New England mills in the early decades of the century, he returned to a heavy teaching schedule and there was little time for writing. He had also been asked to teach a film course, and he found in his courses an opportunity and a challenge to turn to filmmaking himself. With a small Guggenheim Grant he was able to fulfill a dream of his adolescence. In an interview with Arthur and Kit Knight in 1981 he had spoken of his interest in film, which had been fired by his obsessive movie going in the years before the war. He purchased his first camera as a fifteen-year-old in 1941. "The camera cost me eight dollars, and soon broke down. Besides, I couldn't afford the film, and knew nothing about movies technically, only aesthetically."[14]

Once he'd begun his film course, Holmes quickly discovered that his youthful enthusiasm for filmmaking had returned.

> *When I accepted the permanent job in Arkansas it was understood that I would be able to teach in the film program down there, as well as in Creative Writing. I was on a Guggenheim that year, and decided that if I was to teach film I ought to know how a movie is made. I spent part of the Guggenheim money on a $60 GAF Super Eight, and a projector to match.*[15]

He also learned, to his relief, that making films wasn't as demanding as his struggles to complete his books. In his first year as an amateur filmmaker he completed three short films, then spent the next two years working on and off on a feature-length film loosely based on the life of actress Paulette Goddard, who had been married to three "extraordinary" men, Charlie Chaplin, Burgess Meredith, and Erich Maria Remarque. To play the role of "Godard," Holmes cast a young poet in the creative writing program in Arkansas, Charlotte Mears. Much of the film was improvised, and he shaped it as he went along. When he spoke to the Knights there were more than one hundred minutes of edited footage, and he would continue with the filming over the following months.

As stimulated as Holmes was by the opportunity to explore the possibilities of film, during the next few years it was poetry that became his most significant creative expression. He had begun working on poems again in the late 1950s, but at first he considered them as something he was writing only for himself. In the 1970s, however, editors of fugitive publications of the burgeoning alternative culture took an interest in his work, and his new poems quickly began to appear. The sequence of poems he had written in Ohio during his difficult estrangement from Shirley were published as a chapbook, *The Bowling Green Poems*, in 1977 by Arthur and Kit Knight, who were editing a little magazine of Beat writing titled *the unspeakable visions of the individual*. Holmes had sometimes written to friends that he dreamed someday of having a small collection of his poems, and when the Knight's small book appeared it was his first book to be published in ten years. There had been nothing since his valedictory *Nothing More to Declare* in the spring of 1967.

The interest continued in Holmes' poetry, and he was also encouraged by Richard Ardinger, who had interviewed him for the bibliography Ardinger was compiling of Holmes' work. Ardinger was now teaching at the University of Idaho at Pocatello, where he had established a small press, the Limberlost Press. Working closely with Holmes, Ardinger published two important collections of his poetry, the first of which, *Death Drag*, in 1979, also included some poems from the 1940s and 1950s.

In his new work Holmes finally realized the promise of his apprentice years, when he was considered one of the bright hopefuls of the poetic scene of the 1950s. He wrote now without the misgivings and equivocations that had dogged him when he was a young poet. In his return to his roots in Williams, Pound, and Lawrence he had come back to something he understood deep within himself. Now as he worked with his poems he also was free of the old apprehensions of failure. As he wrote in the revised version of his introduction to the collection *Death Drag*, "Falling short, as in hurling a discus at the moon, is as worthy as all attempts to leap beyond the usual prose through which we make our hazardous way."

Part of his assurance was his consciousness of new possibilities in poetry itself. In an earlier letter to us Holmes had written that it was now his understanding that "breath" was the new measure of the poetic line, rather than the metrics he had labored to learn as a beginner.[16] He had also begun reading his poems into a tape recorder, later telling Michael Schumacher that "you can hear a bad, bumpy line faster than your eye or mind can glimpse it. Befuddled meanings also come clear when you listen."[17] He was striving to "understand and conquer breath-length as the source of the evolving form of a poem."[18] He had learned that "to get the rhythm right in breath-length poems is far more difficult and subtle a process than relying on iambics or trochees and the like. More like jazz. In neither will the simple metronome suffice. It's a question of tuning your ear. And that implies your full consciousness as well."[19]

In his last years Holmes' poetry achieved the suppleness of the new line, but he had also lost none of his earlier skill with words and phrases themselves. The poems glint with unassuming assonance, and he used alliteration subtly but effectively. As he revised successive versions of a long elegy he wrote over many years for his father, he began to return instinctively to his sense of the poetic stanza, determinedly searching for an interior form in the new breath of the poems. His new work was in the idiom and the clearly defined line of the work of recent poets like Robert Lowell, Elizabeth Bishop, and John Berryman, but his years of honing his language for the commercial editors he faced, and his long and close association with poets like Snyder and Ginsberg, whom he admired, had given him his own voice. As the years passed Holmes' voice deepened and burned clear of its last redundancies, and he achieved a final mastery.

Holmes also drew material for his poetry from the pain and apprehensions of his illness. It was now clear that the initial optimism after his first operation had been premature. Included in the collection *Dire Coasts* was a poem titled "Sickbed Blues for Billie," dedicated to the jazz vocalist Billie Holiday, who had been the model for "Geordie" in *The Horn*. The poem's final words, "Miss Brown," are an allusion to the defiant assertion of one of her best-known recordings, "Miss Brown to You."

Sickbed Blues for Billie

Hush now don't explain
Not the gardenia yellowing over the ear
alive yet dying like things died
suddenly in 1943 on 52nd Street,
nor breasts as over-ripe as evening fruit,
nor sense of belly, thighs, of flesh
*   victorious over despair.*
Nor we white boys, late sixteen, pathetic
in our need of what you knew,
loving a music more than an idea—
Anyway, certain we would fail
in the trial of war ahead.

Hush now, your remonstrance to our awe,
expecting the worst of life, of us
but eyes saying, Don't explain—
*   Get on without lies,*
get back from girl, binge, war or grief
(the honied voice a slur of sex)
but, baby, don't explain.

And last night, seeing you on a TV doc
I cried remembering my love
(art makes you love, even what's hurt it into life),
     remembering "Easy Living"
carried as sole possession by Huncke
through the crash pads of the world
played talismanically on crank machines—

"—living for you / is easy living—"
remembering too my horror at the Bird Memorial
     you spitted like a sparrow
     on the fires of junk,
the specter of how life eats us up
"—it's easy to do / when you're in love—"
Whatever man I became had one source
in your lifted eyebrow as you blew.

Hush now don't explain
not even making a Lilith of you in a book—
Dark Lady of the War—
but making you save yourself in the end,
making you survive the dead gardenias—
     sadly false to fate—
because, just over thirty then,
I still needed flowers in my world.
Most of the man who's left of me now
is the part I heard possible in you:
     courage the refusal to explain
     or die for a cheap love

or believe less in love for that—

(Broken-jawed
     HUSH
bitter, HUSH NOW
 butchered
     DON'T EXPLAIN)

Honest, I understood you
same way you dug Pres—
We make it by such crazy certainties,
They busted you on your deathbed—

Now I'm flat in hospital too
pestered by unimportant pain,
the TV on, and impotent with rage at my luck,
    till all of a sudden
I see your shadow move in 1956,
Head off-bobbing double-time,
Lester playing with pure tenderness
(never apologize, never explain)
as you listen, as you answer,
wild honey slurred against the beat,
all the courageous love come back.
Maybe the kid was brave enough,
    Miss Brown.

Yale-New Haven Hospital, August 1986[20]

Despite the aggressive surgery for the cancer in Holmes' mouth and jaw, and the radiation treatments he endured, there were still years when his letters were busy and optimistic, and our times together were filled with talk and laughter. On John and Shirley's overnight visit to our new house in Storrs in the fall of 1984, we celebrated their arrival with the music all four of us loved as we sorted through piles of LPs. For a few hours we renewed our enthusiasm for the old styles of classic jazz Holmes had championed before he was swept away by his new infatuation with bop. Shirley sat smiling with closed eyes as John leaned toward the phonograph, his feet thumping out the beat. The next morning we talked about the introduction he had agreed to write for Ann's forthcoming book of photographs of the Beat writers, *Beats & Company.* In 1985 Ann followed up the photo session on the steps of their house four years earlier with a series of photos of John and Shirley in their living room. Holmes' face showed some of the trauma he had survived, but he and Shirley seemed poised and relieved, with his cancer for a moment in remission.

A year later, on July 15, 1986, in a letter to Ann about the projected Jack Kerouac reader, Holmes revealed that his cancer had returned.

I don't think I can do the Kerouac Viking Reader. You are the one to do it. Use my name, and I'll help in any way I can. I know I suggested it to Jack 20 years ago in a letter, and he liked the idea. . . . Certainly time to introduce the idea again. Yes, the Dulouz Legend as basis is the way to go. Do for Jack what Cowley's Portable Faulkner did for him. Go forward with it, and I'll help. I don't want any money. My situation: cancer of the lower jaw. Some of it removed the first operation. I go into the hospital again next week for more. Prognosis for getting it all: 50–60%. I'll have no jaw and need yet a 3rd operation to reconstruction. Quite a blow, quite an irony. You can see why I can't make any long range plans, demanding any expenditure of energy. Wanted you to know.[21]

A few weeks later Shirley wrote to let us know that John had come through the operation, though the recovery would be slow.

John's doing fantastically well under the miserable and painful and exhausting circumstances. It seems like we spend most of the time in the car—going to Norwich every morning for radiation, going to New Haven for the surgeons to cluck approvingly over him, going nuts trying to get used to this routine for the next 4–5 weeks. Sure shoots the shit out of the day.[22]

Back in Old Saybrook, recuperating at home, Holmes labored to pull together a record of his tortured struggles in the 1960s from his journals, a chronicle of his sexual confusions and creative roadblocks. Working with Ardinger, he selected hundreds of pages from the hundreds more he'd written. His intention was to create a portrait of his mind as he had stumbled through those years. Ardinger labored to make out blurred words and names, typing page after page. The sexual record was left complete and without any attempt at concealment, but since Holmes used the original names in his accounts there would have been a legal problem with publication. The final manuscript, nearly six hundred pages long, was sent to one or two possible publishers, but without any clarification from Holmes himself or editorial oversight of the material, the manuscript was never given any serious consideration.

The three collections of Holmes' essays for the University of Arkansas Press were to be the work that defined his writing in these years of his terminal illness, though he never completely turned away from his poetry. Through the months of traumatic recuperation and the roller coaster of emotions as he wavered between defiance and acceptance of his condition, Holmes continued with the only thing he had ever told himself he wanted to do. He wrote. There was a stream of poems, and the essays were reconsidered and reshaped in his typewriter. In a letter to us on January 29, 1987, he summed up the months of work with considerable satisfaction. Emotionally he had gone beyond the usual protestations of diffident modesty with which writers generally—Kerouac always the exception—present their new work to each other. As Holmes explained in his letter,

> *The second volume [*Passionate Opinions: The Cultural Essays*] is done now, the last part, the preface, goes to the typist day after tomorrow. It's an interesting book, I think, far less cobbled-together than the first volume,* Displaced Person: The Travel Essays, *which will be out sometime in the Fall. I'll have the Univ. of Arkansas Press send you a copy of it. It's got some gorgeous writing in it, particularly in the section "Walking Away from the War," about our 1967 jaunt to Europe. But the new one, to be called* Representative Men: The Biographical Essays, *collects everything I've written about Legman, Landesman, Ginsberg, Kerouac, Algren, Cassady, W. C. Fields, Lawrence, Henry Miller, Lee Harvey Oswald, and others. Lots of stuff that few people have ever seen, because it appeared in fugitive little mags or in Europe. Anyway, I'm enamored of it at the moment, and a little jaunty with the realization that, despite all my god damn medical problems—radiation, operations, long recuperations, etc.—I've managed to prepare 700 pages for the printer in the last seven months, about 130 pages of it brand new. That's a prodigy of work for me. Don't know how to account for it—perhaps being free of teaching, perhaps the sound of time's winged chariot, perhaps being unable to talk. In any case, I'm free now to do some poetry (Arkansas Press talks about doing a collected poetry eventually), and hopefully a longish piece of fiction when I get out of the hospital this time, ole!*[23]

The three volumes of essays for the University of Arkansas Press did, as Holmes wrote with some satisfaction, contain extended passages of "gorgeous writing," and the volumes also were cohesive and cross-referential in a manner that he could only have achieved by the sustained concentration he had given them. His doctor's insistence that he virtually stop drinking was certainly another factor.

Unlike most collections of essays by authors who confine themselves to reprinting earlier work, Holmes reconsidered and shaped his prose, carefully weighing the place of each essay in its connection to the others in the volume. The reminiscences about his friends in the biographical volume are direct and perceptive, and his sympathetic considerations of the Beat consciousness could only have been written by someone whose heart and whose attention had been fully engaged at that moment in time. His essays are in many ways the most important aid we have left to us in our efforts to understand the meaning and the dream of that historical moment. They are also the most vividly written portraits we are certain to have of the colorful figures around him who created this literary movement.

Despite the emotional trauma of his situation, Holmes continued to write as much as he could. He turned down an invitation to lecture at the University of Connecticut in Storrs, not only because of the uncertainties of his recovery, but also because of his unwillingness to think of breaking away from the work he was doing. He knew now that it was the only time he would have to do it.

> *I rise each day and get to work and don't think, and am happily tired and ready to risk sleep at the end of light. I am superstitiously afraid that if I pause, if I change hats, if I take on any task that's even the least bit stressful, the gloomy speculations about futurity may come. I have a horror of becoming a gelded, introspective semi-invalid, of wasting anymore of my life in needless ruminations, when work alone is what I was born for, and work alone will justify the life I've led. Sounds awfully somber, don't it? It's not really. I've had, miraculous to report, days of absolutely blissful happiness of spirit in these last months—A kind of isolated, private, incommunicable purity of mood that has redeemed years of angst, worry, fret, and waste. I fill my time now. I'm painting again—splashing about as happily and as sloppily as a child, painting trees and faces and self-portraits, having no other models. I plan wildly, happily, crazily— an addition to the house, stories, poems, memoirs. I'm eager. It's what a brush with mortality does for you, I guess. And my brush goes on, and probably will for whatever time I've left. Chances of recurrence, in other words, are to be expected. Don't really care, if you can believe, I feel free, and it's joy.*[24]

Chapter 24

FINAL CHORUS

Together, we restored the house, our sweat
and fantasy bequeathed us ownership—
the right to put off chores and loaf,
letting whatever fictive rest remains
affirm the final act of homelessness:
    A home is where you have the chance
    of dying where you chose to live.

—JOHN CLELLON HOLMES, from "The Old Saybrook House"[1]

The letters from Holmes became more infrequent, but they continued to express his concern about the collected volume of Kerouac's writing that he still hoped he and Ann could edit together for the Viking Portable Library series. His letter on March 10, 1987, contained news that he would return to the hospital on April 3, and the letter continued with the disturbing news that Shirley would also go to the hospital the next week, "for what will be hopefully a minor exploratory operation on her lung." Shirley's years of smoking had finally taken its toll on her body, as it had done on his. She found out that she was also afflicted with the cancer threatening to overwhelm his life.

Holmes was still in touch with Richard and Rosemary Ardinger, who continued to work on the new collection of his poetry for their Limberlost Press, which they were setting by hand. From his hospital bed Holmes sent them new poems and revisions of poems he'd sent before, assuring the patient Ardinger, as writers do in the throes of a book that means much to them, "These are the only changes I've made, hopefully the last, but do let me know when you begin setting type."[2] The new collection, *Dire Coasts*, was planned for publication the next year. The periodicals where some of the new poems had first appeared make it clear that Holmes had become part of a new literary world, rambunctious small presses instead of the stolid New York slicks. Among the journals were *Staten Island Review*, *Poetry Northwest*, *Poetry NOW*, *The Kerouac Connection*, *Exquisite Corpse*, *Friction*, and the Ardinger's own *Limberlost Review*.

The work with the poems took most of the space in his letters to Ardinger, but another letter on June 19, 1987, including changes of lines in two poems, began with a brief glance at his situation:

> *OUT OF HOSPITAL almost a month, I guess, after a baddish time. Twenty days in the slammer after a 10 hr. surgery. It's left me voiceless in Gaza. That is, I make sounds—vaguely visceral grunts that occasionally, to the initiated, form themselves into primitive simple words. Mostly I scribble on pads. Also, I now feed myself directly into belly through tube, thus saving myself the burden of tasting food. It's nothing but raw fuel to me now. But, wonder of wonders, I work on, somewhat weakened now because of aftermath-pain for which I take small doses of morphine, having to rest more often, but still the mind is clear, and I get a few hours in every day at the desk.*[3]

A few days later, on June 23, 1987, Holmes used his hours at his desk to write a letter to us answering three literary questions: the first about the form of *Go*, the second about the ideas from the literary American Renaissance the Beats had inherited, and the third about the source of the yearnings of his own character fictionalized as "Paul Hobbes" in *Go*. Holmes' answer took two single-spaced pages, in which his clarity and his sympathies were still strongly in evidence, though we knew from telephone calls that the last hospital stay had been a grim ordeal and the pain now was a steady presence. In his answer to the second question on the sources of the Beat Generation in the American tradition, he affirmed, as he had said before, that it was Emerson, and through his influence on the writers of the time, from Melville to Thoreau to Whitman, who had been a wellspring. The final question, about the character of Hobbes, he answered for himself.

> *I was hungry to know everything then. New York is, after all, the richest kitchen midden the world has ever known. It was a thrill to be young, energetic, imaginative, curious, and selfless in the New York of those days. One could entertain the notion that a long, rich, varied shelf of books lay ahead that might do for one's New York what Balzac had done so profligately for his Paris. And we were unafraid in those days—alike of such*

audacious dreams and *the chancy areas of experience into which we were venturing.*[4]

He signed it with a concerned question: "Any help? John."

The hours that were relatively pain free continued to be given to the work. On July 9, 1987, he sent us a long letter following up on a question about Rimbaud and contemporary writers who had influenced both him and Kerouac. On September 24, he introduced his younger sister, Liz, who would follow Shirley as his literary executor in a "worst-case scenario."

> *My will states that in the event of my death Shirley becomes my literary executor, and in the event of hers, my younger sister Elizabeth, becomes the executor of my estate. When the will was drawn up, years ago, it all seemed silly and remote, but now it's taken on some hard-edged meaning. My sister, seven years younger, with whom I've always been close, was educated at NYU, Bloomington, and of all places Storrs. I think she got her MA there. Anyway, she went on to teach in the Midwest, and ended up teaching in Chicago, the city-wide university system there. She married a marvelous guy, a couple of years older than me, who had five children, and whose first wife was in a mental hospital. Liz took over everything, becoming a wife & mother all in a flash and proving to be a success. . . . Carl, who'd been teaching in the same system as Liz since right after the war, retired early, and they have been living in Maine, surrounded by books and music and winters of blessed hibernation, followed by summers full of children and grand-children—all in all, a wonderful life for two intelligent, hard-working, probing, sensitive people. Liz writes too.*[5]

In his next letter on October 10, 1987, Holmes wrote that he hoped we could visit soon. Before mailing it Shirley appended a note saying that John was too tired, still, to see anyone, but she would let us know when we might drive down to visit them. The next month Holmes wrote to ask if the University of Arkansas Press might use the photographs of him from our session on his porch steps in 1981, a different one for each of the volumes. Jokingly he said he appointed Ann his "official photographer."[6] A letter on January 5, 1988, repeated that we must drive down for a visit, but with it, the letters ceased. We continued to talk on the telephone with Shirley, who was struggling against the spread of her cancer but still concealed her condition from everyone.

Two months later Holmes left a short poem in the notebook beside his hospital bed, responding to an image he'd seen of a tribal sculpture from the island of Samoa.

Samoan Head

Once, very sick,
late one night,
I saw the icon of a man
trying to breathe like me, his mouth
puckered for the sweet air—
to take it into his body
there in the South Pacific
five hundred years ago—
"A-h-h-h" I breathed for him.

The last poem written in the night March 27, 1988[7]

Holmes died in the Yale–New Haven Hospital of cancer of the jaw on March 30, 1988, at the age of sixty-two. After his death Shirley chose to go to a near-by hospice rather than the hospital, where she died of lung cancer on April 12, less than two weeks later. She was fifty-nine. Holmes had been the younger "brother" in his long relationship with Kerouac, but he had outlived Kerouac by fifteen years. They had also died at different moments in their spiritual pilgrimage. At Kerouac's death his writing was still being intentionally misunderstood or dismissed or—the most difficult to accept—ignored. Much of what he had written had already been dropped from his publishers' lists. His last letter, written the night before he collapsed, to his nephew Paul, Nin's son, was angry and resentful, flailing out at the world he felt had abused him. Holmes' life had continued long enough for the frustrations and the turmoil that had disfigured those same years—his mid-thirties and mid-forties—to have been smoothed by the years of relative economic security after he accepted a tenured teaching job. His final questionings and creative self-doubts were resolved by the last months of his illness.

In his letter to Kerouac in June 1963, when Holmes was thirty-seven, he had written of his fears that he might "vanish without leaving some trace."[8] In his letter to us on September 24, 1987, twenty-four years later, he could write,

Irony of ironies, this spring Thunder Mouth Press in New York (they publish Richard Wright and Algren and others in quality paperback) is bringing out The Horn *and* Get Home Free, *which together with the NAL [New American Library]* Go, *plus all the non-fiction from Arkansas will mean that most of my work will be in print again.*[9]

Of the dreams and ambitions that had crowded Holmes' early years, one had outweighed all others, his dream of writing, of being a *writer*. In those final months he understood that his work would live at least for a little longer. For anyone whose life has been filled with a dream of writing, that is a glow of light that helps win an acceptance of the coming of darkness.

In one of his final poems, "Sweet Charity," included in his collection *Night Music*, published a year after his death, Holmes looked back at that moment when he had first begun to be the writer he became. This poem celebrates a morning in New York City when his dream began, and it foretells the joys that finally would come to him with the fulfillment of those dreams.

Sweet Charity

Walking down 3rd Avenue
in the 50s on a June morning,
a morning so good no one is
talking to themselves,
my shirt collar is as fresh as lettuce,
I have a good session
of words behind me;
there are twenty dollars in my wallet
to buy whatever midday taste I favor,
and my hangover is a not unpleasant large ache.
I am due to meet a friend
in Clarke's in twenty minutes.
I will be early
and will order a small martini,
then on to Annette's
where the fines herbes omelettes
are validated like passports
to Provence.
The thought
completes and crystallizes
my mood:
I am beyond happiness.
I wish for everything for everybody.[10]

NOTES

The John Clellon Holmes Archive in the Howard Gotlieb Archival Research Center in the Mugar Library at Boston University contains Holmes' boyhood diaries, journals, notebooks, manuscripts, and carbon copies of his correspondence including letters from his family and friends, among other materials, as well as Shirley Holmes' correspondence. The unpublished material cited here is from this archive unless otherwise noted.

John Clellon Holmes will be cited as JCH. Works frequently cited have been identified by the following abbreviations:

BIBLIO.	Richard Ardinger, *An Annotated Bibliography of Works by John Clellon Holmes*
DP	John Clellon Holmes, *Displaced Person*
NM	John Clellon Holmes, *Night Music Selected Poems*
NMTD	John Clellon Holmes, *Nothing More to Declare*
PO	John Clellon Holmes, *Passionate Opinions*
RM	John Clellon Holmes, *Representative Men*
IG	Arthur and Kit Knight, *Interior Geographies: An Interview with John Clellon Holmes*

CHAPTER 1: A USABLE PAST

1. *DP*, 4.
2. *PO*, 5.
3. Schumacher, *Break the Black Heart*, 16.
4. See footnote 57, chapter 11.
5. *PO*, 20.
6. Letter to JCH from E. A. Murkham of Brookside, Florida, on January 2, 1966, tracing the descendants of George Holmes of Roxbury, MA.
7. Family history of Doctor Edwin Holmes and S. F. Emmons supplied by Lila Dizefalo and Elizabeth Von Vogt.
8. *IG*, 6.
9. Ibid., 27.
10. Ibid., 1.
11. Ibid.
12. Maher, 3–9. In an "Author's Note" to *Lonesome Traveler* (1960), Kerouac listed his nationality as "Franco-American." There he stated that his "people" originated in Cornwall, Brittany; that his first North American ancestor was Baron Alexandre Louis Lebris de Kerouac, "1730 or so"; and that his first U.S. ancestor was his grandfather Jean-Baptiste Kerouac, a carpenter. *Satori in Paris* (1966) is an account of Kerouac's journey to France to trace his surname. It contains what Grove Press described as his "surrealistic conversation" with his Bretan namesake, Ulysse Lebris, in which Kerouac first drunkenly asked himself, "Is he Jewish? Pretending to be a

French aristocrat?" (96), before he concluded that Lebris was "an old noble Breton" (97).

13. Kerouac, *Visions of Gerard*, 95.
14. *NM*, 61.

CHAPTER 2: THE MAGIC OF WORDS

1. *DP*, 8.
2. *PO*, 21.
3. *IG*, 2.
4. Ibid., 5.
5. Lila Dizefalo to Ann and Sam Charters, Feb. 2, 2006 (letter and tape).
6. *IG*, 6.
7. *PO*, 21.
8. *IG*, 2.
9. Ibid.
10. *PO*, 21.
11. Ibid., 22.
12. Ibid.
13. *IG*, 3.
14. *PO*, 50.
15. Ibid.
16. Miles, *Jack Kerouac*, 24.
17. Ibid., 14.
18. Jack Kerouac, *Visions of Gerard*, 129–131.
19. JCH diary, Sept. 6, 1939.
20. Ibid., March 2, 1939.
21. Ibid., July 29, 1940.
22. Ibid.
23. *IG*, 5.
24. *DP*, 5.
25. Ibid., 3.

CHAPTER 3: WHATEVER WORLD THERE WOULD BE

1. *PO*, 7. "Clearing the Field" was first published in *Contact* (1962) as "A Few Loves, A Few Deaths."
2. Gewirtz, Notes.
3. Kerouac-Parker, 65.
4. Ibid., 71.
5. Ibid., 106.
6. Ibid., 71.
7. Ibid., 73.
8. Miles, *Jack Kerouac*, 55.
9. Jack Kerouac, *Orpheus Emerged*, 50.
10. Robert Creeley's introduction to *Orpheus Emerged*, 13.
11. Not only Kerouac's books. Some version of the story of the Carr-Kammerer homicide appears in memoirs and novels written by Chandler Brossard, William Gaddis, Alan Harrington, John Clellon Holmes, Anatole Broyard, Howard Mitchem, and

James Baldwin. Kerouac wrote a version of the story in *The Town and the City*, with his characters "Kenneth Wood" and "Waldo Meiser" based on Carr and Kammerer. Near the end of his life he also re-told the story in *Vanity of Duluoz*. See James Grauerholz's afterword to *And the Hippos Were Boiled in Their Tanks*, 194, 200.

12. Kerouac-Parker, 178.

13. Ibid., 245. During the winter of 1944–1945 on West 115th Street, when Kerouac and Burroughs collaborated on the *Hippos* novel based on the Carr-Kammerer story, they each wrote alternate chapters. According to Grauerholz, both Carr and Kammerer had a "number of sexual encounters" with Allen Ginsberg in 1944, but Carr "had never had any sexual contact" with Kammerer. *Hippos*, 188–189.

14. Kerouac-Parker, 245.

15. Conversation with Elizabeth Von Vogt, November 18, 2007.

16. JCH journal, Oct. 12, 1959.

17. Ibid.

18. *NMTD*, 206.

19. *Go*, 81.

20. JCH journal, Oct. 1, 1943.

21. JCH journal, Oct. 2, 1943.

22. Ibid.

23. *NMTD*, 214.

24. JCH to Marian Holmes, 1944 letter never sent in U.S. Naval Hospital Training Corps Manual.

25. JCH journal, April 3, 1951.

26. JCH letter to Rae Everitt, Feb. 4, 1949.

27. Ibid.

28. JCH spiral notebook from 1944.

29. *IG*, 3.

30. Ibid.

31. JCH journal, November 1951.

32. JCH letter to Nick Brownrigg, Aug. 26, 1960.

33. JCH ms. sketch about his friendship with James Macguire, April 29, 1945.

34. Elizabeth Von Vogt e-mail to Ann Charters, Feb. 17, 2009.

35. JCH journal, April 29, 1945.

36. Ibid.

37. *IG*, 3–4.

38. *PO*, 7–8.

CHAPTER 4: THE STALE BREAD OF DEDICATION

1. *PO*, 9.

2. Ibid.

3. Columbia University "Oral History" interview with JCH, 8.

4. *PO*, 11.

5. Ibid., 13.

6. JCH letter to Mira Kent, Dec. 27, 1946.

7. JCH journal, Jan. 9, 1946.

8–9. Ibid.

10. JCH journal, Aug. 8, 1946.

11. Ibid., June 10, 1947.

12. Ibid., Aug. 8, 1946.

13. Ibid.

14. *PO*, 15.

15. Llosa, 26.

16. *PO*, 15.

17. Camus, 3.

18. JCH letter to James Macguire, Sept. 13, 1947.

19. JCH letter to Torrey and Jean, Dec. 19, 1947.

20. *BIBLIO.*, 10.

21. *IG*, 5.

22. JCH letter to James Macguire, April 5, 1948.

23. *PO*, 26.

24. JCH letter to Howard Friedman, May 3, 1948.

25. *PO*, 22.

26. Ibid., 28.

27. JCH journal, Feb. 25, 1948.

28. Ibid.

29. JCH journal, March 22, 1948.

30. Ibid., June 25, 1948.

CHAPTER 5: A WEEKEND IN JULY

1. *RM*, 4.

2. *NMTD*, 17.

3. Ibid.

4. JCH journal, July 2, 1948.

5. *NMTD*, 17.

6. JCH journal, July 2, 1948.

7. *NMTD*, 17.

8. JCH journal, July 2, 1948.

9–13. Ibid.

14. J. Landesman, *Rebel*, 55.

15. Ibid., 56.

16. Ibid., 65.

17. Ibid., 118.

18. *Neurotica 1*, 3.

19. Ibid, 5.

20. J. Landesman, *Rebel*, 55.

21. Ibid., 56.

22–23. Ibid., 57.

24. JCH journal, July 2, 1948.

25–30. Ibid.

31. J. Landesman, *Rebel*, 60.

32. Ibid., 106.

33. JCH journal, July 2, 1948.

34. *NMTD*, 24.

35. J. Landesman, *Rebel*, 61.

36. *RM*, 8.
37. J. Landesman, *Rebel*, 61.
38. *RM*, 75.
39. Ibid.
40–42. Ibid., 76.
43–44. Ibid., 77.
45. *NMTD*, 48.
46. Kerouac, *Windblown World*, 101.
47. *RM*, 77.
48. Ibid.
49. Ibid., 78.
50. Ibid., 79.
51. Ibid., 81.

CHAPTER 6: A KIND OF BEATNESS

1. JCH journal, July 12, 1948.
2. Ibid.
3. JCH journal, Aug. 31, 1948.
4. Ibid.
5. Maher, 171.
6. JCH journal, Sept. 13, 1948.
7–9. Ibid.
10. JCH letter to Lila and Jack Sanders, May 14, 1948.
11. Ibid.
12. JCH letter to Mira Kent, July 25, 1948.
13. JCH letter to Howard Friedman, Aug. 23, 1948.
14. Von Vogt, 34.
15. JCH journal, Oct. 10, 1948.
16. Ibid.
17. JCH letter to Mira Kent, Oct. 18, 1948.
18. *Neurotica 3*, 32.
19. *Neurotica 4*, 35.
20. JCH journal, Oct. 8, 1948.
21. JCH letter to Alan Harrington, Nov. 4, 1948.
22. JCH journal, Oct. 30, 1948.
23. Ibid.
24. JCH journal, Nov. 10, 1948.
25–26. Ibid.
27. *Windblown World*, 163.
28. JCH journal, Nov. 10, 1948.
29–31. Ibid.
32. *PO*, 54.
33. Kerouac, "The Origins of the Beat Generation," in *The Portable Jack Kerouac*, 566. In Kerouac's journal entry on Nov. 3, 1948, he described his talks with Holmes, describing John as an "amazing guy" because he shared Kerouac's enthusiasm for the "One Prophecy that's arising in the world now—another great friend for me, the taker" (*Windblown World*, 162). In 1957 Jack developed this idea of "the One Prophecy,"

which originated in talks with Burroughs about Oswald Spengler's *Decline of the West*, in the essay "About the Beat Generation." Kerouac's essay begins, "The Beat Generation, that was a vision that we had, John Clellon Holmes and I, and Allen Ginsberg in an even wilder way, in the late Forties, of a generation of crazy, illuminated hipsters suddenly rising and roaming America, serious, crazy, bumming and hitchhiking everywhere, ragged beatific, beautiful in an ugly graceful new way." This idea that Beat was a religious movement was later published as "Aftermath: The Philosophy of the Beat Generation" in *Esquire*, March 1958. See *Portable Jack Kerouac*, 551–552, 559. In *681 Lexington Avenue*, xx, Elizabeth Von Vogt cites an Italian doctoral thesis by Daniela Platania titled "Holmes and Kerouac: Revelation Is Revolution," arguing that "Jack was the revolution but he needed a revealer: John was that—he delivered the revelation of that revolution" (Universita Degli Studi Di Catania, 2003–2004).

34. Kerouac quoted in JCH journal, Oct. 10, 1948.

35. Dempsey, 176. In the fall of 1948, when Kerouac and Holmes coined the term "Beat Generation," Existentialism was so popular among young intellectuals in New York City that had Kerouac shared Holmes' passion for philosophy, he might have said, "We're an Existentialist generation," and the word "Beat" might not have come up at all. For an analysis of Holmes' progression during 1945–1959 from Sartre and Camus to Kierkegaardian Existentialism, see Charters, "John Clellon Holmes and Existentialism" in Sharin Elkholy, ed., *The Beats and Philosophy*. On the other hand, Kerouac began defining himself and his friends as a generation years before he met Holmes. For example, in a letter of March 14, 1945, to his sister Caroline, telling her that the novel he'd just completed with Burroughs (*Hippos*) had been sent to the publishers Simon and Schuster, Kerouac wrote, "For the kind of book it is—a portrait of the 'lost' segment of our generation, hardboiled, honest, and sensationally real—it is good, but we don't know if those kinds of books are much in demand now, although after the war there will no doubt be a veritable rash of 'lost generation' books." Quoted in *Hippos*, 199.

36. Gornick, 11. On December 13, 1948, Kerouac wrote his friend Allan Temko that a new "beat" generation was "rising" in the United States, a revolutionary change in human consciousness. It was not a "Communistic" or a "New School liberal anemic revolution"; instead it arose from "spiritual & sexual energy" (unpublished letter in the Berg Collection, New York Public Library [NYPL]).

37. JCH letter to Nick Brownrigg, Aug. 26, 1960.

38. Ibid.

CHAPTER 7: NEAL & CO.

1. JCH journal, Dec. 29, 1948.

2–5. Ibid.

6. JCH letter to Alan Harrington, Jan. 4, 1949.

7. Ibid.

8. JCH letter to Alan Harrington, Dec. 15, 1948.

9. JCH letter to Howard Friedman, Nov. 8, 1948.

10. JCH journal, Nov. 22, 1948.

11. JCH letter to Jack Kerouac, Nov. 23, 1948.

12. Ibid.

13. JCH journal, Jan. 8, 1949.

14–17. Ibid.

18. JCH journal, Jan. 19, 1949.

19–23. Ibid.

24. JCH letter to Alan Harrington, Jan. 20, 1949.

25–28 Ibid.

CHAPTER 8: THIS PARTICULAR KIND OF MADNESS

1. JCH letter to Alan Harrington, Jan. 20, 1949.

2. JCH journal, Jan. 22, 1949.

3–7. Ibid.

8. Alan Harrington letter to JCH, Jan. 29, 1949.

9–13. Ibid.

14. JCH letter to Alan Harrington, Jan. 31, 1949.

15. Ibid.

16. JCH journal, Feb. 16, 1949.

17–20. Ibid.

21. Kerouac, *Visions of Cody*, 14.

22. JCH journal, February 16, 1949.

23. Ibid.

24. JCH letter to Alan Harrington, Jan. 31, 1949.

25. JCH journal, Feb. 16, 1949.

26. Amburn, 41–42.

27. JCH journal, Feb. 24, 1949.

28–29. Ibid.

30. JCH letter to Alan Harrington, Mar. 30, 1949.

31–38. Ibid.

39. JCH letter to Alan Harrington, April 28, 1949.

40–44. Ibid.

CHAPTER 9: ANGELIC VISIONS

1. *RM*, 85.

2. JCH journal, Feb. 24, 1949.

3–4. Ibid.

5. JCH letter to Howard Friedman, May 4, 1949.

6. Ibid.

7. Miles, *Ginsberg*, 99.

8. Ibid., 100.

9. Ibid., 101.

10. JCH letter to Howard Friedman, May 4, 1949.

11. JCH letter to Jack Kerouac, May 10, 1949.

12. Charters, *The Portable Beat Reader*, 167.

13. Miles, *Ginsberg*, 121.

14. JCH letter to Jack Kerouac, May 10, 1949.

15. JCH letter to Alan Harrington, May 31, 1949.

16. JCH letter to Jack Kerouac, June 21, 1959.

17. JCH letter to Alan Harrington, June 11, 1949.

18. JCH letter to Nick Brownrigg, Aug. 26, 1960.

19. JCH letter to Elizabeth and Betty Holmes, June 21, 1949.

20–22. Ibid.

23. JCH letter to Allen Ginsberg, June 14, 1949.

24–26. Ibid.

27. JCH letter to Elizabeth and Betty Holmes, June 21, 1949.

28 JCH letter to Jack Kerouac, June 16, 1949.

29. Jack Kerouac letter to JCH, June 24, 1949, in Kerouac, *Selected Letters, 1940–1956*, 195–200.

30. JCH letter to Jack Kerouac, July 3, 1949.

31–36. Ibid.

37. JCH letter to Russell Lyndon, May 31, 1950.

38. Von Vogt, 69.

39. Ibid.

CHAPTER 10: IN THE TEMPLE OF THE GODS

1. JCH letter to Alan Harrington, Sept. 7, 1949.

2. JCH letter to Alan Harrington, Jan. 12, 1950.

3. J. Landesman, *Rebel*, 67.

4. Ibid., 77.

5. JCH letter to Alan Harrington, Oct. 14, 1949.

6. JCH letter to Alan Harrington, Feb. 1, 1950.

7. Ibid.

8. J. Landesman, *Rebel*, 63.

9. Ibid., 64.

10. Ibid., 102.

11. Miles, *Ginsberg*, 126.

12. Ibid.

13. JCH letter to Delmore Schwartz, Nov. 6, 1950, Boston University, Mugar Library, *Partisan Review* archive.

14. JCH letter to Allen Ginsberg, Dec. 12, 1950.

15. *BIBLIO.*, 12.

16. JCH journal, Feb. 1, 1950.

17. *Neurotica 6*, 24.

18. J. Landesman, *Rebel*, 105. At this time the real "conspiracy of silence" was the fact that no major American newspaper would review novels by openly homosexual writers. In early January 1948, G. P. Dutton published Gore Vidal's novel *The City and the Pillar*, described by critic Bernard Levin in the London *Times* as "the first serious American homosexual novel." Later Vidal wrote that in 1948 the *New York Times* would not advertise it, and the newspaper would not review any of his other books for the next six years. Vidal, *The City and the Pillar*, 5.

19–21. *Neurotica 6*, 28.

22. *Neurotica 7*, 3–7.

23. J. Landesman, *Rebel*, 79.

24–29. Ibid., 107–115.

30. JCH letter to Jack Kerouac, May 29, 1950.

31. J. Landesman, *Rebel*, 136.

32. Ibid., 132.

33. Ibid., 135.

34. JCH, "And Here Comes Neal," in *Spit in the Ocean 6* (1981), 10.

35. Ibid.

36. *RM*, 204.

37. Sandison and Vickers, 183.

38. C. Cassady, 118.

39. JCH letter to Jack Kerouac, July 3, 1949.

40. Ibid.

41. Amburn, 151–152.

42. JCH journal, July 2, 1950.

43. Miles, *Jack Kerouac*, 131–132.

44. JCH, *Go*, 309.

45. JCH letter to Neal Cassady, Nov. 28, 1950.

46–50. Ibid.

51. JCH letter to Jack and Joan Haverty Kerouac, Nov. 28, 1950.

52. Ibid.

CHAPTER 11: A TORRENT OF WORDS

1.   JCH letter to Alan Harrington, Dec. 2, 1950.

2.   Ibid.

3.   Gewirtz, Notes.

4.   JCH interview in Gifford and Lee, 76.

5.   Kerouac, *Windblown World*, 169.

6.   JCH letter to Alan Harrington, Feb. 1, 1950.

7.   JCH letter to Alan Harrington, Dec. 21, 1949.

8.   JCH letter to Roger Lyndon, Jan. 19, 1951.

9.   JCH, *Go*, xx.

10. *Paris Review* 43 (Summer 1968), 60–105.

11. JCH letter to Neal Cassady, Nov. 28, 1950.

12. Ibid.

13. N. Cassady, *Collected Letters*, 232–233.

14. Ibid., 234.

15. JCH journal, Jan. 18, 1951.

16. JCH letter to Jack Kerouac, Dec. 27, 1950.

17. JCH journal, Jan. 18, 1951.

18. Jack Kerouac, *Selected Letters, 1940–1956*, 293–310.

19. N. Cassady, *Collected Letters*, 262.

20. JCH journal, January 18, 1951.

21–25. Ibid.

26. JCH journal, February 23, 1951.

27. Van Vogt, 83.

28. JCH journal, March 7, 1951.

29. Ibid.

30. JCH, *Go*, xxiii.

31. JCH letter to Jack Kerouac, April 26, 1950.

32. JCH journal, April 28, 1950.

33. Jack Kerouac letter to JCH, March 7, 1951.

34. JCH journal, March 12, 1951.

35. JCH letter to Alan Harrington, December 21, 1949.

36. Most of the women at the parties in 1948 through 1950 whom Holmes described in *Go* were girlfriends and wives, but a number of women in his New York crowd were actually dedicated artists, dancers, and writers, such as Nell Blaine, Jane Freilicher, Alice Neel, and Barbara Epstein, whose sense of self-preservation and belief in their own careers steered them clear of the self-destructive behavior of many of their male counterparts. In *Go* Holmes described only one woman artist when he created the minor character Bianca. She devoted herself to her painting in her loft studio, but she could not break free from her masochistic emotional attachment to Bill Agatson.

37. JCH, *Go*, 27.

38. Ibid.

39. Ibid., 57.

40. Miles, *Jack Kerouac*, 174.

41. JCH, *Go*, 10–11.

42. Ibid., 114.

43. Ibid., 114–116.

44. Ibid., 153.

45. Ibid., 213–214.

46. JCH journal, April 2, 1951.

47. Ibid.

48. Kerouac-Haverty, 201–202. In 1967, newly married and living in Lowell, Kerouac wrote *Vanity of Duluoz* (1968) as a letter to his third wife, Stella Sampas.

49. Philip Whalen letter to Jack Kerouac, Fall 1957.

50. "Beatific Soul" exhibition, New York Public Library, 2007.

51. Ibid.

52. Conversation with Rick Ardinger.

53. JCH journal, April 9, 1951.

54. Ibid., May 9, 1951.

55. Ibid.

56. Nevius, xii.

57. Schumacher, *Dharma Lion*, 135. Holmes would have read this description of himself in the scroll version of *On the Road*: "At John Holmes' the party went on. John Holmes is a wonderful sweet fellow who wears glasses and peers out of them with delight. He began to learn 'Yes!' to everything just like Neal at this time, and hasn't stopped since" (227–228). The same description is repeated in the edited *On the Road*, where Holmes is called "Ian MacArthur." Edward Stringham is "Tom Saybrook" and described as "a sad, handsome fellow, sweet, generous, and amenable; only once in a while he suddenly has fits of depression and rushes off without saying a word to anyone" (125–126).

58. JCH journal, April 27, 1951.

59–60. Ibid.

CHAPTER 12: THE LIVEITUP KID

1. JCH, *Go*, 311.

2. Miles, *Ginsberg*, 143.

3. Ibid.

4. JCH journal, March 7, 1951.

5. Ibid., July 2, 1951.

6. Ibid., July 6, 1951.

7. Ibid., July 8, 1951.

8. Ibid.

9. Ibid., July 2, 1951.

10. Joan Haverty-Kerouac letter to Marian Holmes, July 13, 1951.

11. Ibid.

12. JCH letter to Jack Kerouac, July 18, 1951.

13. Ibid.

14. JCH journal, Aug. 20, 1951.

15. S. Charters, "Chandler Brossard," entry in A. Charters, ed., *The Beats*, 1:43. For more on Brossard and others in the early New York Beat scene, including Anatole Broyard, Seymour Krim, and Milton Klonsky, see Jim Burns, "Behind the Scenes," in *Beat Scene* 48 (Summer 2005): 39–41; also *The Scene Before You*, ed. Chandler Brossard; *The Beats*, ed. Seymour Krim; and Anatole Broyard, *Kafka Was the Rage*.

16. JCH letter to Jack Kerouac, Sept. 6, 1951.

17. JCH journal, Sept. 7, 1951.

18. Ibid.

19. JCH journal, Oct. 3, 1951.

20. Ibid.

21. Von Vogt, 66.

22. Ibid., 66–67.

23. JCH journal, Oct. 26, 1951.

24. JCH journal, Oct. 31, 1951.

25. J. Landesman, *Rebel*, 39.

26. JCH journal, June 8, 1951.

27. JCH journal, July 2, 1951.

28. JCH journal, July 3, 1951.

29. JCH journal, Aug. 16, 1951.

30. JCH, *Go*, xx–xxi.

31. Ibid., xxi.

32. Ibid.

33. Ibid., xxi–xxii.

34. *PO*, 42–43.

CHAPTER 13: PERFECT FOOLS

1. JCH journal, Sept. 24, 1952. Gilbert Milstein was prescient in asking Holmes to write an article for the *New York Times* on the Beat Generation. By the summer of 1952, there had been what William Burroughs called in a letter to Allen Ginsberg on June 15, 1952, a "deluge" of books about hipsters and drug use in the United States, including Leonard Bishop's *Down All Your Streets* (Dial Press); David Hulburd's *H is for Heroin* ("A Teen-Age Narcotic Tells Her Story"), published as a Popular Library paperback; and Chandler Brossard's *Who Walk in Darkness* (New Directions). The subject was, as Burroughs said, so "Hot Now" that it is not surprising that an early *Publisher's Review* comment about *Go* put Holmes' novel in their company. See

Oliver Harris's introduction to Burroughs' *Junky*, xix. Harris also speculates about Kerouac's "on-off literary rivalry with Holmes" on page xxxii.

2. Gilbert Milstein, Review of *Go* in the *New York Times*, Nov. 9, 1952. Six years later, the San Francisco critic and poet Kenneth Rexroth condescendingly praised *Go* in the opening paragraph of his generally negative review of Holmes' second novel, *The Horn*, in the *Saturday Review*. There Rexroth wrote, "John Clellon Holmes is famous as the inventor of the Beat Generation. But if he is himself a Beatnik, he is a Beatnik with insight, a coherent Beatnik. His novel *Go* was not so ambitious as a work of art as Jack Kerouac's *On the Road*, let alone *The Subterraneans*. But it is far more comprehending. I know the point of beat literature is precisely its lack of comprehension—oh, I dig—but if you want to understand the little group of Greenwich Villagers Allen Ginsberg so pathetically called 'the best minds of my generation,' *Go* is the book."

3. JCH, "This is the Beat Generation," in Charters, *Beat Down to Your Soul*, 222–223.

4. Ibid., 223.

5. *New York Times Book Review*, Nov. 23, 1952, 15.

6. *New York Times Magazine*, Dec. 7, 1952, 15.

7. Jay Landesman letter to JCH, Dec. 3, 1952.

8. Jack Kerouac to JCH, Dec. 9, 1952, in Kerouac, *Selected Letters, 1940–1956*, 388.

9. Alex Scharbach letter to JCH, Dec. 11, 1952.

10. JCH letter to Alex Scharbach, Dec. 22, 1952.

11. Jack Kerouac letter to Allen Ginsberg, May 10, 1952.

12. Allen Ginsberg letter to Jack Kerouac, June 11, 1952, quoted in Morgan, 150.

13. Ibid. Ginsberg needed another couple of years before he understood how he could use Kerouac's new writing style of spontaneous prose to create "Howl for Carl Solomon." Most other contemporary writers, such as Gore Vidal, remained critical. Later Vidal wrote, "For every Scott Fitzgerald concerned with the precise word and the selection of relevant incident, there are a hundred American writers, many well regarded, who appear to believe that one word is as good as another, and that anything which pops into the head is worth putting down. It is an attitude unique to us and deriving, I would suspect, from a corrupted idea of democracy: if everything and everyone is of equal value, than any word is as good as any other word to express a meaning, which in turn is no more valuable than any other meaning. Or to put it another way, if everyone is equally valuable, than anything the writer (who is valuable) writes must be of value, so why attempt selection? This sort of writing, which I call demotic, can be observed at its purest in the recent work of Jack Kerouac." Vidal, *United States*, 348. Vidal appears in *The Subterraneans* as the character Arial Lavalina.

14. JCH, quoted in Gifford and Lee, 158.

15. JCH letter to Jack Kerouac, Oct. 15, 1952.

16. Ibid.

17. JCH journal, Oct. 26, 1951.

18. Jack Kerouac to JCH, Oct. 12, 1952, in Kerouac, *Selected Letters, 1940–1956*, 382.

19. JCH letter to Jack Kerouac, Sept. 12, 1952.

20. JCH letter to Jack Kerouac, March 11, 1953.

21. Ibid.

22. JCH letter to Jay Landesman, April 23, 1953.

23–25. Ibid.

CHAPTER 14: THE RISING TIDE OF FAME

1. Jack Kerouac, *The Subterraneans*, in the Library of America, 477.
2. Ibid., 547.
3. Gertz, 9.
4. Jack Kerouac, *The Subterraneans*, in the Library of America, 548
5. Ibid., 549. Kerouac's wish to appeal to the new generations would be fulfilled after his death by the worldwide popularity of his books among young readers.
6. JCH letter to Jay Landesman, March 18, 1954.
7. Ibid.
8. JCH letter to Nick Brownrigg, Aug. 26, 1960.
9. JCH letter to Jay Landesman, March 18, 1954.
10. JCH letter to Jay Landesman, June 21, 1954.
11. Jack Kerouac letter to Allen Ginsberg, early May 1954, in Kerouac, *Selected Letters, 1940–1956*, 413.
12. JCH letter to Jay Landesman, June 21, 1954.
13. C. Cassady, 230.
14. Gewirtz, *Beatific Soul*, 154.
15. Ibid., 155.
16. Ibid.
17. Ibid. 165.
18. Morgan, 189.
19. JCH letter to Alex and Radka Scharback, Jan. 19,1955.
20. Burroughs Mitchell letter to JCH, Feb. 15, 1955.
21. Ibid.
22. J. Landesman, *Rebel*, 191.
23. JCH letter to Jay and Fran Landesman, March 18, 1955.
24. Morgan, 215.
25. JCH letter to Jack Kerouac, March 8, 1956.
26. JCH letter to Jack Kerouac, May 25, 1956.
27. Weaver, 67.
28. Ibid.
29. JCH letter to Allen Ginsberg, Sept. 26, 1956.
30. JCH letter to Betty Holmes, Jan. 22, 1957.
31. JCH journal, Jan. 22, 1957.
32. In Kerouac's journal from spring 1962, he considered going to driving school in Florida, but he knew that he couldn't stay sober long enough to get his license. He wanted to buy a car, but he reminded himself that he didn't need a license to walk (Berg Collection, NYPL).
33. Ginsberg, dedication page of *Howl*.
34. JCH letter to Jack Kerouac, June 27, 1957.
35. Ibid.
36. Millstein review in Charters, *Beat Down to Your Soul*, 411.
37. Johnson, 185.
38. Ehrlich, 119.
39. Morgan, 250.
40. Gifford and Lee, 240.

41. Johnson, 191.
42. Ibid.

CHAPTER 15: WHAT AM I DOING HERE?

1. Gold, quoted in Parkinson, 255. Originally in *Playboy* magazine, February 1958.
2. JCH letter to Jack Kerouac, Oct. 10, 1957.
3–8. Ibid.
9. Jack Kerouac letter to JCH, Nov. 8, 1957, in Kerouac, *Selected Letters, 1957–1969*, 78.
10. Jack Kerouac letter to Hiram Haydn, Nov. 11, 1957, in Kerouac, *Selected Letters, 1957–1960*, 84.
11. JCH letter to Jack Kerouac, Nov. 18, 1957.
12. JCH letter to George and Francesca Beaumont, Nov. 21, 1957.
13. Ibid.
14. *DP*, 63.
15. Ibid., 74.
16. Ibid., 63.
17. Ibid., 99.
18. Ibid.
19. JCH journal, Feb. 20, 1958.
20. Ibid.
21. JCH journal, Feb. 23, 1958.
22. Ibid.
23. Lawrence Ferlinghetti, "Note on Poetry in San Francisco," in Charters, *Beat Down to Your Soul*, 169.
24. Joyce Johnson, participating in a "Panel Discussion with Women Writers of the Beat Generation" in San Francisco in 1996. See *Beat Down to Your Soul*, 620.
25. Kenneth Rexroth, "Disengagement: The Art of the Beat Generation," in Charters, *Beat Down to Your Soul*, 507.
26. Atlantic Records advertisement, quoted in Charters, *Beat Down to Your Soul*, xx–xxi. The commercial hype about the San Francisco jazz and poetry scene offended many older poets, even William Carlos Williams, who had contributed an introduction to the City Lights volume of *Howl.* On March 28, 1958, Williams wrote to the aspiring poet Joseph Renard, "Do you know any of the San Francisco gang who are making a name for themselves in the papers now-a-days? Your own poems are not an offshoot from that impetus—which is really illiterate though I should be strung up [if] it were known." Letter in A. and S. Charters' collection.
27. Ibid.
28. Feldman and Gartenberg, advertisement on first page.
29. Norman Podhoretz, "The Know-Nothing Bohemians," in Charters, *Beat Down to Your Soul*, 479–493.
30. Robert Brustein, "The Cult of Unthink," in Charters, *Beat Down to Your Soul*, 49–58.
31. Gilbert Highet, "The Beat Generation," radio talk printed by Oxford University Press for Book-of-the-Month Club, 1958.
32. Gold, quoted in Parkinson, 255.
33. JCH journal, Feb. 20, 1958.
34. Ibid.
35. Jack Kerouac journal, Feb. 11, 1960 (Berg Collection, NYPL). By the end of the 1950s,

as San Francisco poet Michael McClure later understood, the Beat writers had been "identified by the media as a dangerous revolution" (McClure interview in Colin Still DVD). Steeped in Cold War politics, Holmes gave a talk on the Beat Generation at Yale University on April 1959, and in his notes he stated that to many people the word "Beatnik" implied a "Russian secret weapon." In his lecture he went on to explain that "nihilism seeks to introduce chaos, anarchy, disorder. It seeks to destroy. The Beat attitude says 'no' in order that it may say 'yes.' As Albert Camus has said in *The Rebel*, in our time it seems that you can't be positive without first being negative." Holmes' philosophical explanation had little force against the media's commercial exploitation of—and swift attempt to put down—the idea of a rebellious generation of Americans. For example, the 1959 film "The Beatniks" introduced its rowdy group of young white thugs with a trailer advertising, "Now—here it comes! The screen's first story of a Mutinous Generation! Demanding! Defiant! Explosive! 'The Beatniks.'"

36. *NMTD*, 83.
37. Carolyn Cassady, letter to Allen Ginsberg, July 20, 1958.
38. Thelonious Monk quoted in Morgan, 278.
39. Included in NYPL exhibition "Beatific Soul."
40. Allen Ginsberg letter to Jack Kerouac, Aug. 20, 1958.
41. On July 18, 1951, Holmes wrote Kerouac that Salinger's *Catcher in the Rye* had just been published and noted, "His hero might be the young Lucien [Carr], and wouldn't critics be scared if they knew how it all turned out in the end." By 1962, after the 21st printing of the book, hostile critics such as the academic John Aldridge viewed Holden Caulfield as "a beatnik Peter Pan." See Grunwald, xv.
42. JCH journal, Feb. 20, 1958.
43. JCH letter to Jack Kerouac, June 19, 1958 (not sent).
44. Ibid.
45. *The Subterraneans*, the Library of America, 547.
46. JCH letter to Jack Kerouac, June 19, 1958 (not sent).
47. JCH, "The Philosophy of the Beat Generation," in Charters, *Beat Down To Your Soul*, 229.
48. Ibid.
49. Jack Kerouac, "About the Beat Generation," in his *The Portable Jack Kerouac*, 559.
50–52. Ibid.
53. JCH letter to Jack Kerouac, July 16, 1958.
54. JCH letter to Gene Baro, July 23, 1958.
55. Ibid.
56. Jack Kerouac letter to JCH, June 3, 1952 in Kerouac, *Selected Letters, 1940–1956*, 367.

CHAPTER 16: *THE HORN*

1. JCH, *The Horn*, 8.
2. JCH letter to Richard Ardinger, July 25, 1977.
3. Tim Hunt, interview with JCH (1977), in Zott, *The Beat Generation*, vol. 2, *Authors A–H*, 467.
4. JCH, *The Horn*, 3.
5. Ibid., 5.
6. Ibid., 31.
7. Hunt, 468.

8. JCH, *The Horn*, 55.

9–10. Ibid., 60.

11. Ibid., 78.

12. Ibid., 54

13. Ibid., 123.

14. Hunt, 468.

15. JCH, *The Horn*,152.

16. Hunt, 468.

17. JCH, *The Horn*, 152.

18. Ibid., 196.

19. Ibid., 217.

20. JCH letter to Richard Ardinger, July 25, 1977.

21. Hunt, 468.

22. JCH, *The Horn*, 150–151.

23. Ibid., 153.

24. JCH letter to Richard Ardinger, July 25, 1977.

25. Ibid.

26. Schumacher, *Break*, 15.

27. Studs Terkel, *Chicago Sun-Times*, July 20, 1958.

28. Ralph Gleason, the *Nation*, Nov. 14, 1958.

29. *BIBLIO.*, 5. In 1985 *The Horn* was read sympathetically in the context of classic American literature by Theo D'Haen in his essay "John Clellon Holmes's Intertextual Beat."

CHAPTER 17: TOO-LATE WORDS

1. *NM*, 25.

2. Jack Kerouac, *Selected Letters, 1957–1969*, 120.

3. JCH letter to Jack Kerouac, Nov. 4, 1958.

4. JCH letter to Allen Ginsberg, Jan. 14, 1959.

5. Ibid. Ironically, early in 1959 JCH's isolation in Old Saybrook couldn't have been more different from Ginsberg's experience of basking in the Beat spotlight and using it skillfully to promote his own agenda. On February 14, 1959, Ginsberg wrote a three-page letter to Burroughs in Tangier saying that "the Beatnik-poetry-reading thing has swelled to monstrous proportions" after Ginsberg, Orlovsky, and Corso had done a benefit reading in Chicago that drew 800 people. At their reading the previous week at Columbia, 1,400 people came to hear them and the police were called in to surround the Macmillan Theater on upper Broadway in order to control the crowd "like it was Nixon." Ginsberg told Burroughs that at Columbia he "read huge mad poems, queer poems, dope poems, Kaddish to my mother, my father and relatives in audience all amazed, it was pretty triumphant." Ginsberg believed that "the whole social psychic fabric of the States [was] so paper mache that the three of us coming on raw and natural talking about cocks & tea & God seem to penetrate instantly—in fact it's scary. . . . [T]he whole country, you could take it over like Hitler, that's what McCarthy did, I suppose" (Gewirtz, Notes). Ginsberg's description of the reading at Columbia is in contrast to Diana Trilling's petty, belittling account of the same event in her essay "The Other Night at Columbia: A Report from the Academy" in *Partisan Review* (spring 1959). Ginsberg's crusade against the literary establish-

ment was always social and political. As he told his biographer Barry Miles, "The reason I was so eager to ally with Rexroth and Duncan and the old San Francisco Renaissance was because we basically had the same politics—which was like philosophical anarchism. I thought it was urgent for the poets to make a united phalanx: Black Mountain, Northwest, San Francisco, Renaissance, Beat, and New York School, to try and correlate our efforts and publishing. Because to me, Williams' 'open form' meant 'open mind'. . . . I wasn't just plugging and promoting my friends, I had a much larger agenda" (Miles, *Ginsberg*, 212).

6. JCH journal, early Feb. 1959.
7. Jay Landesman letter to JCH, Feb. 3, 1959.
8. *Pageant* magazine article quoted in J. Landesman, *Rebel*, 208.
9. Ibid., 211.
10. JCH letter to Jack Kerouac, July 31, 1959.
11. JCH letter to Jack Kerouac, Oct. 15, 1959.
12–13. Ibid.
14. *DP*, 7.
15. Jack Kerouac to Philip Whalen, Sept. 1960, in Kerouac, *Selected Letters, 1957–1969*, 302.
16. JCH journal, Oct. 4, 1961.
17. JCH journal, Oct. 6, 1961.
18. Ibid.

CHAPTER 18: A SWEET ATTENTION

1. *Time* magazine, Sept. 14, 1962.
2. Letter from editor at *Harper's* to JCH, Nov. 3, 1961.
3. Letter from editor at the *New Yorker* to JCH, Jan. 19, 1962.
4. Letter from editor at *Esquire* to JCH, March 7, 1962.
5. "The Booze and I" was published in *Nugget* 7 (4) (August 1962): 62–63.
6. Seymour Krim letter to JCH, March 19, 1962.
7. Jack Kerouac, *Selected Letters, 1957–1969*, 324.
8. Ibid.
9 Jan Kerouac, 63.
10. Jack Kerouac, *Selected Letters, 1957–1969*, 385.
11. JCH journal, April 1, 1962.
12. Seymour Krim letter to JCH, Aug. 10, 1962.
13. JCH letter to Jack Kerouac, July 29, 1962.
14–15. Ibid.
16. JCH journal, early July 1962.
17. Ibid.
18. Shirley Holmes letter to Fran and George Beaumont, Sept. 2, 1962.
19. JCH letter to Jack Kerouac, Oct. 5, 1962.
20. Ibid.
21. Jack Kerouac letter to JCH, Oct. 9, 1962, in Kerouac, *Selected Letters, 1957–1969*, 348.
22. Ibid., 349.
23. Shirley Holmes letter to Fran and George Beaumont, Sept. 2, 1962.
24. JCH letter to Nelson Algren, Dec. 4, 1962.
25. Tom Guinzberg letter to JCH, Jan. 28, 1963.
26. Letter from editor at McGraw-Hill to JCH, March 21, 1963.

27. JCH letter to Jack Kerouac, March 15, 1963.
28. JCH letter to Jack Kerouac, June 6, 1963.
29. JCH letter to Jack Kerouac, June 10, 1963.
30–35. Ibid.
36. *NMTD*, 82.
37. JCH journal, June 7, 1963.
38. JCH letter to Jack Kerouac, July 22, 1963.
39. JCH letter to Vance Bourjaily, June 1963.
40. Vance Bourjaily letter to JCH, June 30, 1963.

CHAPTER 19: TO THE EDGE OF EROS

1. JCH to Jack Kerouac, June 6, 1963.
2. *PO*, 134. Holmes had the full text of Lawrence's *Lady Chatterley's Lover* (written in 1928) available in the spring of 1959 after its publication in the United States by Grove Press. Immediately banned for obscenity, in July of that year it was cleared in a landmark case when Judge Frederick Van Pelt Bryan in the U.S. District Court of New York declared it to be a work of art. In *Lady Chatterley's Lover*, Lawrence dramatized through what critic Harry T. Moore termed the author's technique of "heightened erotic realism" his concern that in an industrial society the intellectual or "mind knowledge" of men and women had subjugated their instinctual power or "blood knowledge" (Lawrence, 289). In the modern age, "the world of smoke and iron," Lawrence "found no balance, no harmony which would restore our 'vivid and nourishing relation to the cosmos and the universe'" (291). Holmes admired Lawrence because the English author believed that the novel was a powerful medium that could change the consciousness of its readers. As Lawrence wrote in *Lady Chatterley's Lover*, "After all, one may hear the most private affairs of other people, but only in a spirit of respect for the struggling, battered thing which any human soul is, and in a spirit of fine, discriminative sympathy. . . . It is the way our sympathy flows and recoils that really determines our lives. And here lies the vast importance of the novel, properly handled. It can inform and lead into new places the flow of our sympathetic consciousness, and it can lead our sympathy away in recoil from things gone dead. Therefore, the novel, properly handled, can reveal the most secret places of life: for it is in the *passional* [sic] secret places of life, above all, that the tide of sensitive awareness needs to ebb and flow, cleansing and freshening" (94). Later in the novel, the gamekeeper Mellors tells Lady Chatterly, "I do believe in something. I believe in being warmhearted. I believe especially in being warm-hearted in love, in fucking with a warm heart. I believe if men could fuck with warm hearts, and the women take it warm-heartedly, everything would come all right. It's all this cold-hearted fucking that is death and idiocy" (193). To Mellors, who expressed many of Lawrence's ideals, "the root of sanity is in the balls" (203). This view was endorsed by both Kerouac and Holmes.
3. JCH journal, July 31, 1962.
4. JCH journal, Oct. 22, 1962.
5–6. Ibid.
7. JCH journal, Dec. 23, 1962.
8. Ibid.
9. JCH journal, Feb. 26, 1963.
10. JCH journal, June 17, 1963.

11. JCH journal, Aug. 9, 1964.

12–13. Ibid.

14. JCH journal, Aug. 10, 1964.

15. Ibid.

16. Holmes' statement on his work for *Contemporary Novelists of the English Language*, Dec. 29, 1970 (typescript in Holmes' archive).

17–19. Ibid.

20. JCH journal, Oct. 11, 1966. Like Holmes, Norman Mailer was a cultural radical who had dedicated himself to bringing about "a revolution in the consciousness of our time." See Mailer, *Advertisements for Myself*, 17. Also like Holmes, Mailer believed that social problems had sexual roots, insisting that "the orgasm is an anathema to the liberal mind because it is the inescapable existential moment." See Mailer, *Presidential Papers*, 198.

21. JCH journal, Oct. 11, 1966.

CHAPTER 20: GYPSYING

1. Until 1966, the Workshop classes were held in prefabricated Quonset huts set up along the Iowa River (McGurl, 176). In 1963 Paul Engle, the director of the Workshop from 1941 to 1966, was completing a textbook-anthology entitled *On Creative Writing* (1964). Later he and his wife, Hualing Nieh Engle, developed and co-directed the International Writing Program at Iowa. As the network of Iowa Workshop graduates and faculty fanned out to develop creative writing programs at other American universities, Holmes was offered more teaching jobs, such as the offer from V. S. Cassill, who went on from his job at the University of Iowa to a tenured position at Brown University.

2–9. JCH journal, Sept. 16, 1963.

10. Jack Kerouac letter to JCH, Oct. 5, 1963, in Kerouac, *Selected Letters, 1957–1969*, 371.

11. Ibid., 370.

12. Ibid.

13. Ibid., 371.

14. JCH journal, Oct. 19, 1963.

15. Ibid.

16. JCH journal, Nov. 25, 1963.

17. Ibid.

18. JCH journal, Jan. 11, 1964. Holmes recommended Nelson Algren to replace him in Iowa.

19. Ibid.

20. JCH journal, Feb. 25, 1964.

21. JCH journal, March 1, 1964

22–23. Ibid.

24. Charles Poore, the *New York Times*, April 9, 1964.

25. Stanley Edgar Hyman, the *New Leader*, April 27, 1964.

26. Haskel Frankel, the *New York Times Book Magazine*, May 3, 1964.

27. *BIBLIO.*, 14.

28. JCH letter to Allen Ginsberg, Dec. 21, 1965.

29. JCH journal, Nov. 1, 1964.

30. JCH journal, Nov. 7, 1964.

31. JCH journal, Feb. 8, 1965.

32–36. JCH journal, Feb. 10, 1965.

37. Shirley Holmes letter, Oct. 31, 1965.
38–42. Ibid.
43. JCH letter to Jay Landesman, March 18, 1966.
44. JCH journal, Nov. 6, 1965.
45. JCH journal, Nov. 15, 1965.
46. C. Cassady, 159.
47–48. JCH journal, Nov. 15, 1965.

CHAPTER 21: A TURN OF THE CIRCLE

1. *IG*, 11.
2. JCH journal, Jan. 20, 1966.
3. Ibid.
4. JCH journal, Feb. 27, 1966.
5. Morgan, 432. In Holmes' "Foreword" to *NMTD*, he wrote, "Whether we like it or not, a new vision is abroad in the land now, a vision that was fathered by my generation's attitudes and antics, a vision that perhaps can best be understood by understanding us" (12). Holmes was prescient when he recognized the significance of the "new vision" held by ideologically engaged young people, though he was dismayed by many of the "alienated youth torn between idealism and violence" (13).
6. Di Prima, 127.
7. Ibid.
8. Llosa, 26.
9. Schumacher, *Break the Black Heart*, 7.
10. Alan Harrington letter to JCH, May 1, 1966.
11. JCH journal, Sept. 16, 1966.
12–14. Ibid.
15. JCH letter to Elizabeth Von Vogt, March 28, 1961.
16. Nick Brownrigg to JCH, March 1, 1962.
17. JCH letter to Alan Harrington, July 23, 1966.
18. JCH letter to Jack Kerouac, March 6, 1967.
19. Quotations from Gornick's article in the *Village Voice*, Nov. 19, 1970, 11–12.
20.–23. Ibid.
24. JCH journal, Jan. 27, 1967.
25. JCH to Jack Kerouac, April 4, 1967.
26. JCH to V. S. Cassill, Dec. 8, 1966.
27. JCH to Carol Munn, May 11, 1965.
28. *New York Times*, March 9, 1967; *Newsweek*, March 13, 1967; the *Christian Science Monitor*, March 16, 1967; the *Chicago Tribune*, March 26, 1967; the *Chicago Daily News*, April 1, 1967; *The Listener*, June 27, 1968.
29. JCH letter to E. P. Dutton, May 12, 1967.
30. *DP*, 17.
31. Ibid., 26.
32. Ibid., 64.
33. Ibid., 83.
34. JCH journal, March 1, 1968.
35. *RM*, 209–210.

CHAPTER 22: GONE IN OCTOBER

1. *RM*, 177–178.
2. JCH journal, Oct. 21, 1969, 12:45 p.m.
3. *RM*, 157–158.
4. Ibid., 196.
5–8. Ibid., 179–180.
9. JCH letter to Ann and Samuel Charters, Jan. 23, 1970.
10. *DP*, 215.
11. Ibid., 216.
12. Ibid., 218.
13. Ibid., 211.
14. *BIBLIO.*, 16.
15. Betty Sampas letter to JCH, March 8, 1973.
16. JCH letter to Don Lehman, March 17, 1973.
17–18. *BIBLIO.*, 17.
19. Richard Ardinger, "John Clellon Holmes," entry in Charters, *The Beats*, 1:260.
20. JCH, *Dire Coast*, n.p.
21. JCH letter to Richard Ardinger, June 21, 1978.
22. JCH, *Bowling Green Poems*, n.p.
23. JCH letter to Ann and Samuel Charters, Aug. 13, 1975.
24. *IG*, 8.

CHAPTER 23: ON A PORCH IN BOULDER

1. *RM*, 276.
2. Ibid., 267–268.
3–11. Quotations from Holmes' talk in his two-day writing workshop at the 1982 Naropa Conference celebrating the 25th anniversary of *On the Road* are taken from Ann Charters' notes and the Naropa tapes of the workshop, courtesy of the University of Texas library in Austin, Texas.
12. *RM*, 271.
13. Ibid., 277.
14. *IG*, 17.
15. Ibid.
16. JCH letter to Ann and Samuel Charters, Jan. 23, 1970.
17. Schumacher, *Break the Black Heart*, 10.
18. Ibid.
19. JCH letter to Ann and Samuel Charters, July 15, 1986.
20. *Bowling Green Poems*, n.p.
21. JCH letter to Ann Charters, July 15, 1986.
22. Shirley Holmes letter to Ann and Samuel Charters, Aug. 28, 1986.
23. JCH letter to Ann Charters, Jan. 29, 1987.
24. JCH letter to Ann Charters, March 10, 1987.

CHAPTER 24: FINAL CHORUS

1. JCH, "The Old Saybrook House," in *NM*, 68–69.
2. JCH letter to Richard Ardinger, June 19, 1987.
3. Ibid.

4. JCH letter to Ann Charters, June 23, 1987.
5. JCH letter to Ann Charters, Sept. 24, 1987.
6. Ibid.
7. *NM*, 72.
8. See epigraph to chapter 19, JCH letter to Jack Kerouac, June 6, 1963.
9. JCH letter to Ann Charters, Sept. 24, 1987.
10. *NM*, 71.

BIBLIOGRAPHY

Algren, Nelson. *The Man with the Golden Arm*. Fiftieth anniversary critical edition, edited by William J. Savage Jr. and Daniel Simon. New York: Seven Stories Press, 1999.

Amburn, Ellis. *Subterranean Kerouac: The Hidden Life of Jack Kerouac*. New York: St. Martin's Press, 1998.

Ardinger, Richard. *An Annotated Bibliography of Works by John Clellon Holmes*. Pocatello: Idaho State University Press, 1979.

Bartlett, Lee. *The Beats: Essays in Criticism*. Jefferson, NC: McFarland, 1981.

Brossard, Chandler, ed. *The Scene before You: A New Approach to American Culture*. New York: Rinehart and Co., 1955.

———. *Who Walk in Darkness*. New York: New Directions, 1952.

Broyard, Anatole. *Kafka Was the Rage: A Greenwich Village Memoir*. New York: Carol Southern Books, 1993.

Burroughs, William. *Junky*. Edited by Oliver Harris. New York: Penquin Books, 2003.

Burroughs, William, and Allen Ginsberg. *The Yage Letters*. Edited by Oliver Harris. San Francisco: City Lights Books, 2006.

Camus, Albert. *The Rebel*. New York: Vintage Books, 1956.

Cassady, Carolyn. *Off the Road: Twenty Years with Cassady, Kerouac, and Ginsberg*. London: Black Spring Press, 2007.

Cassady, Neal. *Collected Letters, 1944–1967*. Edited by Dave Moore. New York: Penguin Books, 2004.

———. *The First Third: A Partial Autobiography & Other Writings*. San Francisco: City Lights Books, 1971, 1981.

Castronovo, David. *Beyond the Gray Flannel Suit*. New York: Continuum Publishing Group, 2004.

Charters, Ann. *Beat Down to Your Soul: What Was the Beat Generation?* New York: Penguin Books, 2001.

———. *Beats & Company: Portait of a Literary Generation*. New York: Doubleday, 1986. Foreword by John Clellon Holmes.

———. *A Bibliography of Works by Jack Kerouac, 1939–1967*. New York: Phoenix Book Shop, 1967. Second edition, 1968.

———. "John Clellon Holmes and Existentialism." In Sharin Elkholy, ed., *The Beats and Philosophy*. Lexington: University Press of Kentucky, 2011.

———. *Kerouac: A Biography*. San Francisco: Straight Arrow Books, 1973.

———, ed. *The Beats: Literary Bohemians in Postwar America*. Parts I and II. Detroit: Gale Research Company, 1983.

———, ed. *The Portable Beat Reader*. New York: Penguin Books, 1992.

————, ed. *Scenes along the Road: Photographs of the Desolation Angels, 1944–1960.* New York: Portents/Gotham Book Mart, 1970.

Christy, Jim. *The Long Slow Death of Jack Kerouac.* Toronto: ECW Press, 1998.

Cook, Ralph T. *The City Lights Pocket Poets Series: A Descriptive Bibliography.* La Jolla, CA: Atticus Books, 1982.

Coolidge, Clark. *Now It's Jazz: Writings on Kerouac & The Sounds.* Albuquerque: Living Batch Press, 1999.

Dempsey, Amy. *Styles, Schools and Movements.* London: Thames & Hudson, 2002.

D'Haen, Theo. "John Clellon Holmes's Intertextual Beat." In *Beat INDEED!* ed. Rudi Horemans. Antwerp (Belgium): EXA, 1985.

Di Prima, Diane. *Memoirs of a Beatnik.* San Francisco: Last Gasp, 1988.

Dostoevsky, Fyodor. *Notes from Underground.* New York: Signet Classic, 1961.

Ehrlich, J. W., ed. *Howl of the Censor.* San Carlos, CA: Nourse Publishing Co., 1961.

Feldman, Gene, and Max Gartenberg, eds. *The Beat Generation and the Angry Young Men.* New York: Dell, 1959.

George-Warren, Holly, ed. *The Rolling Stone Book of the Beats.* New York: Hyperion, 1999.

Gertz, Stephen J. *Dope Menace: The Sensational World of Drug Paperbacks, 1900–1975.* Port Townsend, WA: Feral House, 2008.

Gewirtz, Isaac. *Beatific Soul: Jack Kerouac On the Road.* New York: New York Public Library, 2007.

————. Notes for the exhibition "Beatific Soul," New York Public Library, 2007.

Gifford, Barry, and Lawrence Lee. *Jack's Book: An Oral Biography of Jack Kerouac.* New York: St. Martin's Press, 1978.

Ginsberg, Allen. *Howl and Other Poems.* San Francisco: City Lights Pocket Poets, 1956.

Gornick, Vivian. "The Discomfort of Mattie Ambersole: Being Beat Ten Years Later." *Village Voice*, November 19, 1970.

Grunwald, Henry Anatole. *Salinger.* New York: Harper & Row, 1962.

Harrington, Alan. *The Revelations of Dr. Modesto.* New York: Knopf, 1955.

————. *The Secret Swinger.* New York: Knopf, 1966.

Hemmer, Kurt, ed. *Encyclopedia of Beat Literature: The Essential Guide to the Lives and Works of the Beat Writers.* New York: Facts on File, 2007.

Hickey, Morgen. *The Bohemian Register: An Annotated Bibliography of the Beat Literary Movement.* Metuchen, NJ: The Scarecrow Press, 1990.

Holmes, John Clellon. *Bowling Green Poems.* California, PA: A. and K. Knight, 1977.

————. *Dire Coasts.* Boise, ID: Limberlost Press, 1988.

————. *Displaced Person.* Fayetteville: University of Arkansas Press, 1987.

————. *Get Home Free.* New York: E. P. Dutton, 1964.

————. *Go.* New York: Scribner's, 1952. Thunder's Mouth Press, 1997.

————. *Gone in October: Last Reflections on Jack Kerouac.* Hailey, ID: Limberlost Press, 1985.

————. *The Horn.* New York: Random House, 1958.

————. *Night Music Selected Poems.* Fayetteville: University of Arkansas Press, 1989.

————. *Nothing More to Declare.* New York: E. P. Dutton, 1967.

————. *Passionate Opinions.* Fayetteville: University of Arkansas Press, 1988.

————. *Representative Men.* Fayetteville: University of Arkansas Press, 1988.

————. *Visitor: Jack Kerouac in Old Saybrook.* California, PA: A. and K. Knight, 1981.

Horemans, Rudi, ed. *Beat Indeed!* Antwerp, Belgium: EXA, 1985.

Hunt, Tim. *Kerouac's Crooked Road: Development of a Fiction.* Berkeley: University of California Press, 1996.

Johnson, Joyce. *Minor Characters.* Boston: Houghton Mifflin, 1983.

Jones, Hettie. *How I Became Hettie Jones.* New York: Penguin Books, 1984.

Jones, James T. *Jack Kerouac's Duluoz Legend: The Mythic Form of an Autobiographical Fiction.* Carbondale: Southern Illinois University Press, 1999.

Kerouac, Jack. *And the Hippos Were Boiled in Their Tanks.* New York: Grove Press, 2008.

———. *Book of Blues.* New York: Penguin Poets, 1995.

———. *Book of Dreams.* San Francisco: City Lights Books, 1961.

———. *Doctor Sax Faust Part Three.* New York: Grove Press, 1959.

———. *Jack Kerouac Selected Letters, 1940–1956.* Edited by Ann Charters. New York: Viking, 1995.

———. *Jack Kerouac Selected Letters, 1957–1969.* Edited by Ann Charters. New York: Viking, 1999.

———. *Maggie Cassidy.* New York: Avon Books, 1959.

———. *Mexico City Blues.* New York: Grove Press, 1959.

———. *On the Road: The Original Scroll.* New York: Viking, 2007.

———.*Orpheus Emerged.* New York: ibooks, 2002.

———. *The Portable Jack Kerouac.* Edited by Ann Charters. New York: Penguin, 1995.

———. *Road Novels, 1957–1960* [*On the Road, The Dharma Bums, The Subterraneans, Tristessa, Lonesome Traveler, Journal Selections*]. New York: The Library of America, 2007.

———. *Satori in Paris.* New York: Grove Press, 1966.

———. *Some of the Dharma.* New York: Viking, 1997.

———. *Visions of Cody.* New York: St. Martin's Press, 1972.

———. *Visions of Gerard.* New York: Farrar, Straus, 1963.

———. *Windblown World: The Journals of Jack Kerouac, 1947–1954.* Edited by Douglas Brinkley. New York: Viking, 2004.

Kerouac, Jan. *Baby Driver.* New York: Thunder's Mouth Press, 1998.

Kerouac, John. *The Town and the City.* New York: Harcourt, Brace, 1950.

Kerouac-Haverty, Joan. *Nobody's Wife: The Smart Aleck and the King of the Beats.* Berkeley: Creative Arts Book Company, 1995.

Kerouac-Parker, Edie. *You'll Be Okay: My Life with Jack Kerouac.* San Francisco: City Lights Books, 2007.

Knight, Arthur, and Kit Knight. *Interior Geographies: An Interview with John Clellon Holmes.* Warren, OH: The Literary Denim, 1981.

Krim, Seymour, ed. *The Beats.* Greenwich, CT: Gold Medal Books, 1960.

Landesman, Cosmo. *Starstruck: Fame, Failure, My Family and Me.* London: Macmillan, 2008.

Landesman, Jay. *Jaywalking.* London: Weidenfeld and Nicolson, 1992.

———. *Rebel Without Applause.* Sag Harbor, NY: The Permanent Press, 1987.

Lardas, John. *The Bop Apocalypse.* Urbana: University of Illinois Press, 1996.

Lawrence, D. H. *Lady Chatterley's Lover.* Afterward by Harry T. Moore. New York: Signet Classic, 1959.

Lee, Robert A., ed. *The Beat Generation Writers.* London: Pluto Press, 1996.

Llosa, Mario Vargas. *Wellsprings.* Cambridge, MA: Harvard University Press, 2008.

MacAdams, Lewis. *Birth of the Cool: Beat, Bebop, and the American Avant-Garde.* New York: The Free Press, 2001.

Maher, Paul Jr. *Kerouac: The Definitive Biography.* New York: Taylor Trade Publishing, 2004.

Mailer, Norman. *Advertisements for Myself.* New York: G. P. Putnam's Sons, 1959.

———. *The Presidential Papers.* New York: G. P. Putnam's Sons, 1963.

Martica, Sawin. *Nell Blaine.* New York: Hudson Hills Press, 1998.

McGurl, Mark. *The Program Era: Postwar Fiction and the Rise of Creative Writing.* Cambridge: Harvard University Press, 2009.

Miles, Barry. *Ginsberg: A Biography.* New York: Harper-Collins, 1990.

———. *Jack Kerouac King of the Beats.* London: Virgin Books Ltd. 1999, 2002.

Morgan, Bill. *I Celebrate Myself: The Somewhat Private Life of Allen Ginsberg.* New York: Viking, 2006.

Morgan, Bill, and Nancy J. Peters, eds. *Howl On Trial.* San Francisco: City Lights Books, 2006.

Neurotica, 1948–1951. London: Jay Landesman Ltd., 1981.

Nevius, Blake. Introduction to James Fenimore Cooper's *The Prairie.* New York: Penguin Books, 1987.

Nicosia, Gerald. *Memory Babe: A Critical Biography of Jack Kerouac.* New York: Grove Press, 1983.

Palmer, Donald D. *Sartre for Beginners.* Danbury, CT: For Beginners LLC, 1997.

Parkinson, Thomas, ed. *A Casebook on the Beat.* New York: Thomas Y. Crowell, 1961.

Phillips, Rod. *"Forest Beatniks" and "Urban Thoreaus."* New York: Peter Lang, 2000.

Plimpton, George, ed. *Beat Writers at Work.* New York: The Modern Library, 1999.

Salinger, J.D. *The Catcher in the Rye.* New York: Little, Brown, 1951.

Sandison, Dave and Graham Vickers. *Neal Cassady: The Fast Life of a Beat Hero.* Chicago: Chicago Review Press, 2006.

Schafer, Benjamin G., ed. *The Herbert Huncke Reader.* New York: William Morrow, 1997.

Schumacher, Michael. *Break the Black Heart: An Interview with John Clellon Holmes.* Still Night Press, 1985.

———. *Dharma Lion: A Biography of Allen Ginsberg.* New York: St. Martin's Press, 1992.

Skerl, Jennie, ed. *Reconstructing the Beats.* New York: Palgrave Macmillan,2004.

Stephenson, Gregory. *The Daybreak Boys: Essays on the Literature of the Beat Generation.* Carbondale: Southern Illinois University Press, 1990.

Still, Colin. *No More to Say and Nothing to Weep For: An Elegy for Allen Ginsberg.* 1995. DVD-D4141. See www.kultur.com.

Swartz, Omar. *The View from On the Road: The Rhetorical Vision of Jack Kerouac.* Carbondale: Southern Illinois University Press, 1999.

Theado, Matt, ed. *The Beats: A Literary Reference.* New York: Carroll & Graf, 2001.

Tolson, Annette. *Letters Home: Hitch-hiking and Fruit-picking in America, 1949–51.* Sussex, UK: William Horder, 2008.

Treveno, Philip. *Landesmania! A Biography.* London: Tiger of the Stripe, 2005.

Tytell, John. *Naked Angels: The Lives & Literature of the Beat Generation.* New York: McGraw-Hill, 1976.

Vidal, Gore. *The City and the Pillar.* New York: E. P. Dutton, 1948.

———. *United States: Essays, 1952–1992.* New York: Random House, 1993.

Von Vogt, Elizabeth. *681 Lexington Avenue: A Beat Education in New York City, 1947–1960.* Wooster, OH: Ten O'Clock Press, 2008.

Watson, Steve. *The Birth of the Beat Generation: Visionaries, Rebels, and Hipsters, 1944–1960*. New York: Pantheon Books, 1995.

Weaver, Helen. *The Awakener: A Memoir of Jack Kerouac and the Fifties*. San Francisco, City Lights, 2010.

Weingarten, Marc. *The Gang That Wouldn't Write Straight: Wolfe, Thompson, Didion, Capote & The New Journalism Revolution*. New York: Three Rivers Press, 2005.

Weinreich, Regina. *The Spontaneous Poetics of Jack Kerouac*. New York: Paragon House, 1990.

Widmer, Kingsley. *The Literary Rebel*. Carbondale: Southern Illinois University Press, 1965.

Wilson, Elizabeth. *Bohemians: The Glamorous Outcasts*. New Brunswick, NJ: Rutgers University Press, 2000.

Wolfe, Tom. *The Electric-Kool-Aid-Acid Test*. New York: Bantam Books, 1968.

Zott, Lynn M., ed. *The Beat Generation: A Gale Critical Companion*. Detroit: Thomson/Gale, 2003.

INDEX